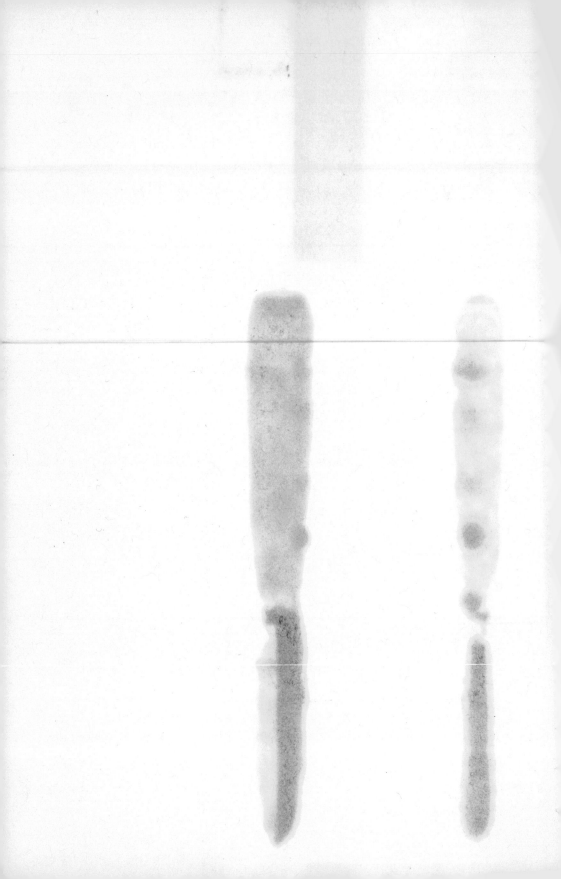

Seven Continents
and Forty Years

Books by C. L. Sulzberger

Seven Continents and Forty Years

A Concentration of Memoirs

C. L. SULZBERGER

Quadrangle / The New York Times Book Co.

SEVEN CONTINENTS AND FORTY YEARS: A Concentration of Memoirs
is a condensation of the following volumes
published by The Macmillan Company, New York, New York.
A Long Row of Candles (1969)
The Last of the Giants (1970)
An Age of Mediocrity (1973)
Postscript with a Chinese Accent (1974)

Designed by Ardashes Hamparian

Library of Congress Cataloging in Publication Data

Sulzberger, Cyrus Leo, 1912–
    Seven continents and forty years.

    Autobiographical.
    Includes index.
    1. Sulzberger, Cyrus Leo, 1912–   2. Journalists
—United States—Biography.   3. World politics—
1945–   I. Title.
PN4874.S786A37   070'.92'4 [B]   76-9705
ISBN 0-8129-0655-1

For my dearest wife, Marina, who shared thirty-four years of my life and travels with loving help and boundless gaiety, until her sudden, tragic death in 1976.

Acknowledgments

I am deeply indebted to André Malraux for his kindness in writing a generous preface.

I wish to express my gratitude to Roger Salloch for his patient, diligent assistance in preparing this text and to Linda Lamarche for her invaluable help.

I also acknowledge with thanks permission from Macmillan Publishing Company, Inc., to use extensive excerpts from four of my books which they published: *A Long Row of Candles* (1969); *The Last of the Giants* (1970); *An Age of Mediocrity* (1973) and *Postscript with a Chinese Accent* (1974).

Foreword

Here is the book of the last dinosaur—a species which the author says has become useless. Dinosaurs, rather, are on the way to extinction, for the press isn't yet dead. But when it no longer instigates books like this, people will dream of them.

This one required a combination of talent and good luck. First of all, the author was a privileged correspondent of a prestigious newspaper. That enabled him while still young to visit Turkey just after the death of Asia's first liberator, Kemal Ataturk, as he recently, so many years later, talked with Chou En-lai. When Sulzberger went to Ankara the Ottoman empire was still remembered by most people as one of the world powers; the British empire remained so, while China had not yet rediscovered its vitality.

As for the book's content: First, I am astonished by the resemblance I find between his portraits of people I know and of others I have never met. Can this be attributed to the nature of his talent? Or to peculiarities of focus?

Next, all these chiefs of state alike say "what should be said to the American public." Their likeness to both the transcriber (Sulzberger) and the invisible listener (the public) will give cause for reflection in fifty years time.

One exception: Ben Gurion. Sulzberger's portrait is masterful but so is the model. He was no longer in power. All the same, think of Churchill, the wild boar, of whom no better portrait than Sulzberger's exists.

He and I publish tomes, and our friends read them as though they were books. Of course they are only chapters. There is but one book, the entire work. Sulzberger has succeeded in his task since his work is irreplaceable. He is offstage in a corner, half visible, half hidden, like the donors of old Flemish paintings.

Finally, the epoch; here is the soul of the book. After hearing the rattle of the last hansom cabs, the author, on television, watched astronauts from his country land on the moon. What other generation has witnessed so brutal a change? History has known no equivalent mutation—excluding disasters.

Perhaps some Romans saw the fall of Rome; Athenian contemporaries of Pericles who survived the Black Plague saw Athens die. But though the days of conquerors were brilliantly adventurous, it was relatively simple to change kings. Ramses II, encountering Napoleon in some Elysian field, could talk to him of armies, finances and maybe religion. Their profession was the same. This century humanity has altered many things, more than any other generation.

What distinguishes this generation from all those that preceded it—those agrarian and trading empires—is something for which we have not yet found a name: This is the altered fundamental relationship between man and life around him.

Historians have cast light on the profound analogies between cultures. Clans evolved into empires, then drifted into decadence following similar graphic curves. But even if the history of ancient Egypt parallels that of China, even if all those civilizations developed cosmopolitan cities, the analogy between Alexandria and Byzantium does not impose any similarity between Byzantium's destiny and that of New York. Because our civilization is not only the first to understand history, but also machines. Man's dialogue with the machine is equally strange under communism as under capitalism.

Our day has at least three characteristics whose conjuncture was never before witnessed by humanity: science, machinery, history—a history which seeks more and more as its object to make mankind's adventure understandable, to have science no more limited by the rationalism of the Enlightenment and the nineteenth century than by prerationalistic ideas.

For over four centuries, the planet's history was entangled with that of colonization. But in 1947, India became independent. In 1949 Mao Tse-tung entered Peking. The development of white power appeared to Westerners as a steady process, for they could look far back to their mastery of the high seas, when their gunboats toppled empires. Yet Marco Polo returned to Venice like an Afghan merchant came back to Kabul after making his fortune in America; in the age of the great kingdoms, military superiority of one over another was far from certain, and Louis XIV was careful not to declare war on the Turkish empire. But from the beginning of the era of square-rigged ships until World War II, Westerners kept thinking to themselves: "We discovered everyone else and nobody ever discovered us." If an Englishman in 1900 could have read the interviews in this book today, he would have been astonished to see how the twentieth century revived a pluralism of world societies.

Nietzsche prophesied that this would be the century of nations. Yet the national concept is a Western export, not something resurrected from the Han dynasty. Now that Asia and Africa are liberated at last, what world-wide values have been born outside Europe? Of course our 1900 English reader of Kipling would notice that Nobel Prizes are awarded to Indian chemists, Chinese nuclear physicists and Japanese cancer researchers. Nevertheless the world is still spinning with the momentum imparted by such Europeans as Einstein and Marx. I can hear Senegal's President Senghor bitterly reiterating what Nehru told me and what this book murmurs so often: The Third World will only vanquish poverty with Western technology. In twenty years, Negro sculpture will have burst out of its ghetto; but for the time being, the only non-Western contribution that has swept over the globe like an inferno or a religion is jazz—genius without a country and from the black world.

We teach how to cure illnesses and how to vote, maybe, but not how to live. Indeed, have we ever tried? Colonizing was not teaching people how to live. China's ideology came from Europe but not the Chinese way of life. In each of the cities whose metamorphosis is depicted by our author stand skyscrapers that we exported like empty shells. We seek ideologies in Asia. But while we vaguely await Indian metaphysics, what is happening to our own ideologies? We are powerful materially and powerless spiritually. I once wrote that our civilization is perhaps the first capable of conquering the moon to commit suicide on it. The author's talks with the masters of this world show us what they all sought; the book is likely to show clearly, but only to later generations of readers, what these same leaders all failed to search for in common.

We can regret the absence of such a book to bear witness to the period from the American war of independence to Britain's Indian empire. Yet we cannot imagine that seriously. For this book could not have been born before the telegraph, without which modern newspapers wouldn't exist; and airliners were essential to our author to a lesser extent. His book will have no successor either, because audiovisual media are radically modifying our relationship to our surroundings. Whoever is the intermediary between the twenty-first century and historical figures of that time, he will not be a great journalist. People wishing to read the dialogue between a century and its political leaders will have to delve into this book.

The author's talks with men so different from each other reveal an odd family likeness among them. Will this intrigue future readers as it intrigues us? When photos in an album resemble each other, people attribute it to the photographer's style. But it really is the style of an era that makes the photos appear similar. An interviewer is supposed to ask questions summarizing the questions suggested by his readers, ranging from picturesque subjects to matters of political beliefs. And what if the person interviewed is pressed hard with overinquisitive questions? This happens when H. G. Wells interrogates Lenin or Stalin; yet their answers do not vary. This does not result from a common evasiveness, so whence does the kinship between these discussions come? Whom is the interviewed leader answering? Not his questioner but the imaginary spectator the leader calls history. He tries to convince public opinion in order to convince history.

Of what?

Our author's experience with so many leading figures during so many years would enable him to imagine interviews with the great men of the past—Bismarck, Napoleon, Frederick II, Peter the Great or Catherine the Great, Cromwell or Jefferson. This would be easy with Napoleon, by summarizing what he affirmed in his "Memoirs from St. Helena," written more to guide his son, perhaps, than for posterity. But the imaginary interview game would end up like a monologue. Only a talk with Catherine II would sound plausible, for women of history then existed, journalists did not. When the Empress talked with Diderot, she stayed on her guard but not in the same way as with an interviewer.

Interviewing the dead could work if neither public nor its image of history changed. Yet Caesar spoke over the heads of his listeners and of posterity to a historical view particular to Rome. He justifiably subjected himself (as did other contemporary leaders) to the histrionics of those harangues in which the Emperor rent his toga while exhorting his soldiers. A modern head of state's conversations with a leading newspaperman resemble those harangues because our image of history watching us is symbolized by the press as the Roman image was symbolized by the army. An edition of a newspaper transforms a day into news and frames it in an imaginary world that is all the more gripping because it purports to be real. The press weaves things into a web of events and adds to the contemporary image of history guarded statements by those interviewed. That image will remain as transparent as air until made visible someday by whatever replaces the press, probably audiovisual media.

The intense feeling of time in our civilization results from news reports. We have to make an effort to understand that this feeling turns everything worth recounting into a big event. In former eras, news of a king's death or the loss of a battle reached people very much later; until the nineteenth century, humanity only learned of old events. In the Middle Ages, the sense of time was commemorative; Christmas in 1250 was closer to the day Christ was born than to December 24, 1250. Why should we attach more importance to this morning's daily paper than to any other issue of a paper that has been thrown away? Yet we all do, and the near future has irresistible force, because the daily paper is tomorrow more than today. That force is multiplied by television's ubiquity.

The talks with great men that compose this book refer to current events in the newspaper that published these interviews. So these articles implicitly refer to each other. Even if their order was not chronological, and even if undated, we cannot conceive of them in Caesar's time or the Middle Ages. Before the author wrote the first line of an article, he was magnetically oriented by the cross-references forming his time, meaning time in both senses of the word—era and duration.

Chou En-lai was oriented the same way before he started his first answer, for he was really talking to the elusive image secreted by the press—that of current events. All modern heads of state speak for the benefit of that image, whereas Napoleon spoke to his image of Roman grandeur. Our Dinosaur was an ear-witness to the concepts shared by the masters of the world throughout the span of his life; that is what makes this book irreplaceable.

We would expect imaginary interviews with past leaders to x-ray them, to reveal the supreme values referred to explicitly or implicitly by a Catherine the Great or a Charles V. Napoleon, for example, was a deist. In ancient Rome, the nation and the classes had transcendental value because the Lares (tutelary gods) presided over their destiny. But Rome lacked newspapers. The supreme value influencing our era is current news. Furthermore, we are no longer able to subordinate the questions posed by the news. Civilizations before us attached great importance to their roots; our century is the first whose Lares are the news.

In Russian history, periods of struggle for the Czar's throne were called "times of troubles." You are about to read a hubbub of giants' voices. Is this merely the chronicle of the Western will for power and its imitators in the Third World? Or is this rumble a warning for today's spiritual dinosaurs that heralds the first time of troubles on a world scale, following in the wake of the era of colonial conquest?

André Malraux

Seven Continents and Forty Years

I

LONDON WAS MY BASE UNTIL JUST BEFORE THE MUNICH AGREEMENT in October 1938, when Britain and France paved the dreary road to their own decline. I had heard so much about fascism without myself experiencing its ghastliness that I decided to inspect its morbid laboratory. I chose Austria. North American Newspaper Alliance gave me credentials, agreeing to accept articles, and Lord Beaverbrook's *London Evening Standard* hired me as a piece-rate correspondent.

I got visas and tickets to Vienna and Prague. Then I called on Jan Masaryk, son of the first Czech president, envoy in London and future foreign minister. He always gave me wise counsel. This fine man was the victim of a Communist *coup d'état* in 1948. The official story was that he jumped to death from his apartment in the Czernin Palace when visited by secret police. I have reason to believe it was not suicide.

Jan gave me letters, including one to President Beneš, and I took off for Vienna. That city had already been reduced to provincial status as capital of Nazi Germany's Ostmark. In Vienna I lodged at a hotel on Singerstrasse whose manager greeted me with "Heil Hitler" and the ridiculous salute the Nazis imagined was Roman. Posters bore the Führer's picture, and libraries were filled with works by him or extolling him. Most stores displayed signs saying "Aryan shop," or "This Jew is already in Dachau," or "This Jew ought to be in Dachau." I went to St. Stephen's cathedral and saw a uniformed man grab a young woman from the steps and march her along, followed by a jeering crowd. Inside many people silently prayed.

The atmosphere of this famous, ancient city combined the less pleasant features of menagerie and charnel house. I have since heard much about the charm and *gemütlichkeit* of Austrians and, indeed, often encountered it. But in those days it was absent. I felt enraged as a Jew and disgusted as a human.

Of the people I then knew perhaps the strangest was an American reporter named Robert Best, a tragic eccentric who turned traitor. After the war he was captured and sentenced to federal prison. He died there in 1952. But when I knew him he was helpful, ingenious and brave. Best was a familiar sight in Vienna. His two closest associates were a secretary and a mistress. The secretary, once tried for murdering her husband, had used her pretty legs to advantage in court and was acquitted by a sentimental jury. She later wrote her memoirs and became a journalist. The mistress was an Austrian aristocrat who probably introduced Best to dope. He loved her and decided not to return to the United States in the exchange of civilians after Pearl Harbor, becoming instead a Nazi propagandist.

Best helped me arrange the most distrained experience of my life. He found a corrupt official who handed on a bribe to the caretaker of the Jewish section in the city morgue so that I could be left alone there checking records. After dinner one night I took a streetcar to the Zentral Friedhof where, inside the gate, I was met by a small man in black coat and hat. He had two days growth of beard, and his breath stank of onions. He accepted an envelope containing money, led me through a building to a long room and nervously shut the door. I can still hear the sound of that clicking lock.

Having been warned against lights, I took a torch from my pocket and looked around. On a large desk I found two ledgers in which were hand-written entries listing the name, date and cause of death for each of the morgue's customers. Beyond, through an arch, was an oblong chamber where I could see the outline of many tables bearing flat objects covered with sheets. I checked five of these bodies by the numbers pinned to their coverings and compared my observations with the ledger listings. All five were recorded as suicides, and, in the case of three, it was difficult to judge if this diagnosis was, in fact, exact. On pulling back the sheets, it was obvious that the other two, at any rate, had been beaten to death. I have never known a man to kill himself by punching out his own eyes.

My torch disclosed shelves on three walls like those in a library. These contained rows of black pots resembling the noses of artillery shells except that the points were cut off flat so they could stand on end. They were remarkably light and seemed made of plastic. I examined several. Into the tin lids were stamped names and dates as, for example: "No. 1732. Städt Bestattungsamt München. Frank, Fritz. Hochschüler. *5.7.11 Wien 14.1.38 Dachau. F.B. 4.6.1938." This, being interpreted, meant that student Fritz Frank, born in Vienna July 5, 1911, had died twenty-seven years later at Dachau and was given a state burial, which meant cremation. With a faint, rustling sound, I put back the urn containing his ashes and was struck by how little a man's body weighed when the problem was scientifically reduced.

In this shriekingly silent atmosphere, I remained several hours, keeping as busy as possible in order not to yield to jangling nerves. I remembered Ambrose Bierce's story of a similar vigil, a corpse that moved, and a survivor who fled with sudden, snow-white hair. Before dawn there was a prearranged scratch on the door. The little man let me out, escorting me to the gate. I asked him about the urn collection: They were unclaimed bodies. Presumably all relatives were already dead.

Through the translucent night, I walked home. The city was strangely silent in the absence of those boot tramps that seem to give the Teuton special pleasure. Nevertheless, the smell of fear—a strange, intangible smell—pervaded everything. A needle-sharp cloud slid across the gibbous moon. That day I left by train for Prague, hiding papers and notebooks under my shirt and belt in case of prying customs guards.

❧

ONE bright summer afternoon I walked across the ornamented bridge above the placid, gleaming Vltava, filled with paddle boats, to the Hradčany Palace and paid a farewell call upon the president. Edvard Beneš was a simple, decent, thoughtful, upright man who, thanks to Masaryk's introduction, had been kind enough to receive me several times despite the onerous pressures of that moribund season. Had he been truly supported by his allies, instead of callously double-crossed, he might have been a doughty leader. Unfortunately, he was betrayed; and he lacked that flare, that nexus with invincible foolhardiness, which marks the difference between national hero and unhappy symbol of defeat. Had Beneš, for example, been reckless Serb instead of prudent Czech, had he pushed the disaster button with his own pudgy finger, disregarding his reluctant allies, history might have taken a different swerve.

I told Beneš I was planning to return to London and asked what he intended to do, now that Hitler had made it plain he would move into the Sudetenland, come what may, and Britain and France were confining themselves to weary words of advice. For an instant the president regarded me in silence. Then he rose to his diminutive height, walked to the right of his great desk, seized a pointer and, like a schoolteacher in a geography lesson, rolled down an enormous map of Central Europe. "Here," he said, "here" and "here," designating Czech and German cities.

"If Hitler bombs Prague," he said with cold precision, "I shall bomb Berlin. If Hitler bombs Pilsen, I shall bomb Nuremberg. If he bombs Bratislava, I shall bomb Vienna. We have an air force too and it is good." He then proceeded to recite military figures: the production of Skoda and other munitions factories, statistics on the serving army and reserve divisions, strategy and tactics. He claimed the fortifications facing Germany were impregnable, despite fifth column activities in Sudetenland, and that defense positions opposite Nazi Austria were rapidly assuming shape.

"We, too, have our own Maginot Line," he said, "and I remain confident in my allies. France is my ally and France has Europe's strongest army. England has an air force that must frighten Hitler. I am confident in my allies. But if by any chance they fail to move, I shall force the game. Do not mistake me. That means world war. France is our partner and France will come to our aid—whatever the English say or do. France knows its responsibilities and obligations. You know, we have entirely too many Sudeten Germans in our country, thanks only to French insistence at the Versailles Conference. However, the French are with us. We have this in common: we are democracies and we hate the Nazis. But even if they weren't, we are prepared to fight. We could hold off Hitler many weeks while the West makes up its mind. I repeat: I shall force the game."

"Supposing war does come," I inquired, "what would you suggest I do? You were once a journalist. I am twenty-five years old, without a reputation, and there are famous correspondents everywhere. Jan Masaryk told me to ask your counsel. What is it?"

"Go to the Balkans, Cyrus," Beneš said. "There is nobody in the Balkans. That will be the most interesting place. The other side of the Axis—the West knows little about it."

During February's last days the Germans began a formal entry. For me, one of the first results was a governmental order to depart. I was checked out across the frontier and never again saw Bulgaria under non-Communist rule.

When I got back to Belgrade, more and more foreigners were convinced that Jugoslavia would soon cave in. I believed that the tough, pepper-eating Serbs were ready to defend their country. On the premise that the government wouldn't cede or, if it did, that it would be thrown out by a people who preferred to fight, I made many large wagers. Alas, when it came time to collect, most of the losers had disappeared amid the hecatomb.

That spring, the Belgrade government finally knuckled under to Nazi pressure. Prince Paul, the elegant, art-loving regent, was forced, to his distaste, to grant Berlin permission for its armies to cross Jugoslavia. Lane, the American Minister, tried to prevent this concession, but Paul told him sadly, "You big nations are hard. You talk of our honor but you are far away." On March 25, in Vienna, the Jugoslavs adhered to the Axis pact.

The English had long been preparing for this possibility and acted with admirable promptness and efficiency. Leopold Amery, a cabinet member, urged the Serbs on the BBC, "Will you let your people become once more a subject race?" London's intelligence agents, including the two air attachés, Hugh MacDonald and Tom Mapplebeck, conspired feverishly with General Mirković of the Jugoslav air force and officers of the Royal Guard. They, in turn, contacted Colonel Mihailović, with whom Mac-Donald had been in touch for months. Meantime Hugh Dalton, head of London's Special Operations Executive (SOE), a cloak-and-dagger outfit, told his Belgrade representative, an oil man named Tom Masterson: "Use all means to raise a revolution." On March 27 the plotters struck, spreading violent slogans: "No war without the Serbs," "Better grave than slave," and "Better war than a pact."

The coup d'état worked with surprising success. It was made in the name of young King Peter (who had not yet attained his majority and was still subject to his uncle, the regent). Peter's signature was forged to a document making the air force commander, General Dušan Simović, prime minister. A voice resembling the King's broadcast over the radio that Peter had taken over power. Prince Paul and his wife, the beautiful Greek Princess Olga, were sent to Athens and later to South Africa. Simović dispatched a military mission to Moscow seeking aid. Early on April 6, a Soviet-Jugoslav treaty of friendship was signed. Stalin cynically canceled this and severed his new diplomatic relations when Jugoslavia was overrun. On the very day of the coup d'état the Führer issued Directive Twenty-five to smash Jugoslavia.

While a traumatic mobilization started, I rushed about Belgrade getting permission to accompany the army on what I so hopefully imagined would be an Albanian Dunkerque. Simović, the Prime Minister, gave me the only war correspondent's credentials I believe were granted for that brief campaign: a special visa authorizing me to join the attack in Albania but which required the stamp of each corps commander in the military districts en route.

Two days before the Axis onslaught Gastone Guidotti, the charming Italian chargé d'affaires (later Ambassador to London) invited me for lunch. He was a close friend, and his heart was firmly on the Allied side even though, in response to Ciano's orders, he had to wear in his lapel a Fascist emblem. Gastone had packed off his wife and daughters and sent most of the furniture with them. However, he gave me a superb meal, followed by excellent cognac in his barren sitting room. Then he said with some embarrassment: "Cy, it is no secret what is about to happen. And I must tell you as a friend that we and the Germans have been instructed to look for you as soon as we are able. Seiler of the German legation has already spoken to me of this. Won't you let me help? I don't want you to get caught. Will you permit me to drive you in my car to any frontier you choose?"

This was a remarkable offer. In order to save me Gastone was proposing to risk his own career and perhaps the safety of his family. I thanked him warmly but assured him I had made my own arrangements. (When next I saw Gastone in London, after Mussolini's fall, he told me the Gestapo had come to him shortly after their arrival in Belgrade and asked: "Where is your friend, the Jew Sulzberger?" Quite truthfully he replied he didn't know.)

Lou Fortier, American military attaché, had tipped me off that I had better start for Albania soon. Therefore, around 1:00 A.M. April 6 I paid my hotel bill, changing hundreds of dollars to cover immense telephone charges. (Before dawn the Srbski Kralj, with all that wealth inside, had burned to the ground.)

And now, like some delighted old Turk with his hubble-bubble pipe, reclining on a divan with sweet memories, I relax and reminisce about the Balkans. For that was a fine time and a fine place to be. The Balkans, which in Turkish means "mountains," run roughly from the Danube to the Dardanelles, from Istria to Istanbul and is a term for the little lands of Hungary, Rumania, Jugoslavia, Albania, Bulgaria, Greece and part of Turkey, although neither Hungarian nor Greek welcomes inclusion in the label. It is, or was, a gay peninsula filled with sprightly people who ate peppered foods, drank strong liquors, wore flamboyant clothes, loved and murdered easily and had a splendid talent for starting wars. Less imaginative westerners looked down on them with secret envy, sniffing at their royalty, scoffing at their pretensions, and fearing their savage terrorists. Karl Marx called them "ethnic trash." I, as a footloose youngster in my twenties, adored them.

In my day I came to know their kings and Communists, to argue with their priests and politicians, to love their princesses and their dancing girls. I learned to speak three of their languages—badly but fluently, accompanied four of their armies, was expelled from two countries and fled two others before advancing Nazi hordes. In the Balkans I was bombed, bullied, coddled, arrested and enticed. Once I took a letter from one group of revolutionists to another, suggesting a joint uprising in Bulgaria and Jugoslavia. Another time I bore a message from a Communist to a king, calling for alliance. In the Balkans I left part of my soul and found my wife.

The Jugo, or south, Slavs are vain (indeed megalomaniac), poets, brave, sly, generous, vital, intensely proud of their long and sanguinary roll of battles, most of which they lost. Theirs was a country of violence and long memories. When I reached their vibrant nation immediately after Munich, it was ruled by a regent, uncle of the boy-king whose father had been murdered and whose grandfather succeeded to the throne only after his adherents had chopped up the previous tenant and cast his body on a dung heap. The Prime Minister was an overconfident dictator, large, bland, mustachioed, then trying unsuccessfully to form his own Fascist party—green shirts, salute and all. He called himself *vodža*, or leader, until, to his astonishment, he was removed by Prince Paul.

The capital was a delightful peasant town. It smelled of fog, sweat and meat. Hundreds of wagons rattled through, drawn by horses adorned with jingling bells. In the early morning droves of oxen shuffled by. There was a constant squeak from the few automobiles, each of which carried two horns—one to scare people and animals and the other, a hand bulb, to be sounded once, twice or three times depending on which direction the driver intended to pursue. Country farmers, wearing slippers upturned at the toes, boat-shaped hats and homespun pants and jackets, greaved and gallooned with thick, gaily knitted woolen socks, strode silently along followed by their obedient womenfolk bearing bundles.

In the evenings I dined with friends at simple restaurants called *kafanas*, eating skewered mutton or spiced, skinless sausages and onions, and sweet oriental pastries, drinking enormous quantities of red wine and *šlivovica*, a colorless plum brandy. There was a pellucid white wine, made forty miles away at Smederovo, which we used to consume there, under the walls of an old Danubian castle, because it lost its savor if brought even the short distance to Belgrade.

In the *kafanas* febrile orchestras played and gypsy girls danced and sang wailing songs. As a token of appreciation it was the custom to stand up and hurl your glass at the wall. Each *kafana* had one or two employes whose only job was sweeping up the rain of glass. Wine was cheap. The ordinary bill amounted to more for glassware than its contents. On some evenings I saw thirsty students with no more money pass around eau de cologne.

In the Triglav, a dingy place with a renowned lambent fiddler, I often sat with a group of youngsters discussing their plans for raising insurrection. They showed me pictures of themselves doing secret military training in the wooded countryside. One of them, Slobodan Princip, was the nephew of Gavrilo Princip, who slew Archduke Franz Ferdinand in 1914 and started World War I.

I trained inland to Mostar, in Herzegovina, and Sarajevo, the Bosnian capital, center of Yugoslav Islam. There, in its *čaršija*, or bazaar, one saw masses of turbaned priests, tarbooshed men, women in shrouds and black gauze veils. The city was undergoing its annual visitation by special traveling Moslem priests who called themselves "beadles" and whose business was saving people's souls. I discussed this trade at length with one of them, an old Arab named Said Emir Akkad.

He came to Europe each winter to arrange to take the pilgrimage to Mecca on behalf of any rich pious men who had died before they, themselves, had had a chance to make the holy trip. Said Emir would contract with relatives or friends to substitute for the departed and make the necessary prayers. He received 100 pounds sterling for each client. He asked if I knew anyone in the United States who might need the services of a Mecca "beadle."

Shortly before Christmas I went to Split and boarded a boat headed southward to Albania. Had Shakespeare situated *Hamlet* instead of *Twelfth Night*, in Illyria, the following might seem more appropriate; for Albania is the ancient Illyria, and, when I arrived there at the end of 1938, the last act of a *Hamlet* in fancy dress was in its denouement.

Albania is a craggy, small land wedged between the Adriatic, Yugoslavia and Greece. Its people have been bastardized by centuries of war with Slavs, Greeks, Turks and Latins. Yet there are still two dominant tribal groupings, in the south, the Tosks, and in the north, the Ghegs. Among the latter are clans called Malissori, or mountain men, bird-featured and lean and known for their bravery, their cupidity, and the preference they accord to robbery over work. The Ghegs are, or then were, infinitely courteous, pursuing complex canons laid down in the thirteenth century by a sage named Lek. This, among other things, specified the laws of blood feud. If any man in the clan was killed, it became the duty of his nearest male relative to slay the murderer.

The Albanian language is known as Shqip, and the Albanians called themselves Shqipetars, which means "sons of the eagle," Eagle Men. When one saw a fierce, aquiline chieftain riding to market on a donkey, bearing his gun, while behind walked his women carrying bundles, one could understand the origins of the word. The men were blond, lean and hand-some, and many looked as if they could have stepped from the House of Lords. The women were lovely until they reached a mature age—around twenty-four. Work did not improve their beauty, and their lot was work, while the men protected them, hunting beasts or each other.

In 1938 Albania was an independent monarchy ruled by King Zog the First (and last). Zog's original name was Ahmed Bey Zogu. He had been chief of the Gheg clan of Mati and as such had been educated in both Constantinople and Vienna: a striking figure, tall, mustachioed and with the swinging gait of a mountaineer.

One of Zog's sisters, Nafije, had married another nobleman named Tsena Bey Kryeziu. Zog heard rumors that his brother-in-law, having learned the arts of conspiracy, was planning a coup himself, and he packed Tsena Bey off to Prague, more placid, less accustomed to gunmen and also further away. However, Zog heard further disturbing rumors and, at that point, a court official told me, the King started inquiries for a discreet unemployed expert marksman. A polylingual student named Agiadh Bebi was found.

Agiadh Bebi shot Tsena Bey dead as he was dining in Prague in 1927. Unfortunately, Agiadh Bebi was a better shot than plotter, and the Czech police easily captured him. Zog feared the young assassin might be indis-creet at his trial, so further inquiries were made for another marksman, more adept at evasive action. When Agiadh Bebi appeared in a Prague courtroom he was drilled by an assassin's assassin, who promptly disap-peared. The assassin's assassin surfaced in Jugoslavia, where he began to drink heavily and, when tipsy, talk too much. Word of this reached Tirana. Within a short time, an assassin's assassin's assassin was discovered. He killed the assassin's assassin and disappeared.

Since the King had only recently married, his heir was still Prince Tati, son of Tsena Bey, who had become sixteen, legally a man, shortly before my arrival in Albania. Zog was exceptionally fond of Tati and pampered him. Tati seemed to admire his affectionate uncle. Nevertheless, at sixteen, he was automatically subject to the blood feud obligations of any honorable Albanian gentleman, and friends of his father, the late Tsena Bey, began to whisper reminders to him. There was no legal proof that Zog had hired the assassin, but this was widely assumed to be the case. In Shakespeare the ghost of Hamlet's father appears on the palace battlements to instruct his son. No ghost appeared on the nonexistent battlements of Zog's modest pink villa. *Hamlet* played differently among the Eagle Men. Tati was only tormented by innuendo and by hints of what was to be expected in a land whose social ethic was the canon of Lek. This specified: "Blood vengeance, slaying a man according to the laws of honor, must not be confounded with murder. Murder starts a blood feud."

As a result of this background the poor little prince, who, like all Albanians, loved firearms, was deprived by royal order of his guns. A friend said to him: "Never shoot a woodcock; I'll give you a feather." Fortunately for Tati and for Zog there was not any final act to the drama. In the spring of 1939 Queen Geraldine produced a boy baby, and two days later the monarch and his family fled the country before Mussolini's troops.

Zog was an absolute ruler. He told one foreign diplomat: "Don't bother to talk with my ministers. They're only servants. If you want anything, come and see me about it." But behind him shadowy figures contested for influence. One man of major importance was called Abdurrahman Mati and came from the same clan as his sovereign. There was even gossip that he was Zog's real father. The King was openly devoted to him. When Zog's mother was alive she had insisted on supervising the cooking of his meals to prevent any poison plots. It was believed that Abdurrahman had assumed the role of food taster after her death. Abdurrahman was called by diplomats the "Rasputin of Albania" and by less-educated people the "Black Spot."

The bazaar claimed that whenever Zog received the chief of a rival clan, the Black Spot sat behind a curtain with two cocked revolvers. When he first arrived in Tirana, Abdurrahman had been poor, but his wealth grew substantially. He had a useful way of sending particularly tough carpenters to mend the fences around his estates, and somehow they always managed to move them several yards out in all directions as part of the repair process. Those who protested suffered.

Gold was still the established currency. The first time I dined at the home of Radoje Janković, Jugoslav Minister, whom I had known as consul general in New York, he asked me if I played poker. I soon found myself at a table with my host, Albania's Foreign Minister Libohova, and Fuat Togay, the Turkish Minister, while the ladies politely retired. As in many European countries the game was played with a stripped deck of thirty-two cards—minus everything below sevens—and only four sat at table. I was startled when the other three players pulled out chamois leather bags. There were no chips in sight. Janković noticed my surprise. He remarked politely, "Let me stake you. Tomorrow we can settle." And he opened his chamois bag, pouring a mass of gold coins on the table:

sovereigns, napoleons and louis d'or. These were the only chips used. I played with care.

One night Janković got rather drunk. "Come with me," he commanded, twitching his cicatrized face. Bearing a lantern, he stomped goutily down into the cellar of his residence where, beside an antiquated stove, stood a huge, old-fashioned safe. He opened this with several keys, then reached inside and pulled out a box of papers. "See what a swine that Zog is," said the Minister. He proceeded to show me receipts from the Albanian King for funds received from Yugoslavia. Some, dating back to his presidential days, were signed A. Zogu; the others merely Zog or Zog R. One was for $60,000; others for various amounts in gold coinage, listed generally as "Napoléons" or "Napoléons d'or." "The pig," said Janković. "We receive nothing in return. And he also takes money from the Italians, the British and the Greeks. What can you do with a man like that, a man who calls himself a king?"

Certainly the grandest experience of my Albanian visit was the last royal ball given by King Zog and Queen Geraldine, an occasion that took place New Year's Eve and showed off in full splendor the panoply of the Zogist court. I borrowed a tailcoat from a diplomat of such junior rank that he had not received an invitation and joined the procession of hired carriages forming before my hotel. It was raining. Trains of donkeys stumbled through the mud and, across the way, earnest little men in white fezzes were playing roulette beneath an umbrella, watching a rusty spinner wobble over a crudely ciphered piece of cardboard. Rain shone on the faces of the royal guards, lined up at the portico in plum-colored uniforms, mountain men from the King's own district of Mati. A squadron of ushers and officers swarmed around, and I sidled along with them, ending up in a reception room, rectangular, about 60 by 100 feet, with a high ceiling. Everyone stood in awkward groups: parliamentary deputies, cabinet ministers, a few foreigners' wives. There was a sprinkling of heavily decorated officers, including Zog's White Russian mercenaries wearing Czarist uniform with ribbons of St. George's cross.

❧

IN 1939, I left Albania by bus from Tirana to Elbasan, bumping hour after hour along the slushy track jammed against a peasant in sheepskin jacket and white cap who carried a blunderbuss that kept jabbing me in the ribs. I could not edge away from him, for next to me on the other side was an unhappy goat.

From Elbasan I caught another bus over the mountains to Pogradec on the Lake of Ochrid that divides Albania from Yugoslav Macedonia. Lacustrine Ochrid is fierce and lovely. It was once called Lychnis by the Greeks, who say Pan dwelled there with his shepherds. Pogradec itself had little to recommend it. But I could not get out, for the road to Yugoslavia was blocked by snow and a blizzard was raging. I persuaded two fishermen to take me across the lake in their rowboat so, on a glum morning, with wind whipping sharp flakes into our eyes, we set off into the gray distance. The fishermen were nervous and refused to deliver me at the town of Ochrid, on the Yugoslav side, because they said patrols would shoot at us.

Therefore they proposed to deposit me on the southeastern shore near the frontier. I paid them four gold sovereigns and clambered out with my baggage. As the boat withdrew into the blizzard, a Jugoslav frontier guard emerged, dressed in long greatcoat, his cap pulled over his eyes, pointed his rifle and demanded to know my business. I explained I was going to the monastery of Sveti Naum. It was too late to hope to get to Ochrid, and the Serbian monasteries were famous for their hospitality. The abbey of Sveti Naum was a renowned institution on a site that had first been endowed by Justinian and later named for one of the first three saints who preached Christianity to the Slavs. Its head, or *iguman*, relished the taste of my few American cigarettes. He puffed and puffed, exhaling with sweet pleasure, and we quickly destroyed one bottle of plum brandy; he called for another. As this bibulous pontifex drank, some of the liquor dribbled down his hirsute face. He would lean forward as I politely held a light for his Lucky Strike; but the constant flow of alcohol and conversation produced an aura of unsteadiness, and, time and again, small forest fires ran across the edges of his beard. Unconcerned, he patted these out with his massive hand as if it were the most natural gesture.

Eventually I reached Skoplje, capital of Jugoslav Macedonia, an attractive, dilapidated town with a clashing, jabbering row of bazaar stalls and many mosques whose minarets thrust eagerly toward the sky. From Skoplje I sent dispatches predicting that Italy would seize Albania. My London editor disbelieved me, and I earned little from my journalistic jeremiad.

◄§§►

FOR one dazed, brief instant the traveler who for the first time reaches Greece on a bright spring day is disappointed. There is neither the patterned geometry of fair France nor the green tidiness of England or forests of Germany; not even the grandeur of American ranges thrusting to eternity. Then, in one sudden flash it strikes. *Thauma!* This is pure beauty: land, sea and sky, each perfect in itself and perfectly composed. And once this truth encompasses, one is lost. I speak with the nostalgia of experience; for it is in Greece that I found my wife, in Greece that my son was born, and in Greece that I made the home where I shall spend my fading days.

Athens was in a frenzy. The Greeks held Italy in contempt but were forced to respect Mussolini's pompous boasts that he could muster 8 million bayonets. And they feared Hitler, leaning from Austria into the Balkans. Lincoln MacVeagh, the scholarly American Minister, said: "Now they are really between the devil and the deep blue sea. The Axis armies and their puppets are moving to the border. The English fleet is stretched along the coast. Saturday midnight, at the Easter service, everyone was nervous. The Fascists had finished taking Albania. After the service General Metaxas [the dictator] summoned the British Minister, Sir Sidney Waterlow. Metaxas was pale. Almost in tears, he warned Waterlow the Greeks would fight if an inch of their soil were violated."

In those days I first met Metaxas and King George II. The dictator was a pudgy, small man with pale, pasty face, spectacles, and not the slightest physical attribute one normally associates with a general or ruthless autocrat, both of which he was. Despite his unimpressive appearance and volatile Hellenic blood, he was cold-blooded, unemotional, and could be impassively brutal. He was hated by most Greeks. Yet, when he had the courage to say *oxi* (no) to an Italian ultimatum in October 1940, and when he showed his military genius by organizing an effective defense, he earned respect and admiration. As for King George, he was a fluent gossip and decidedly amusing although he had no talent for popularity among his ebullient compatriots.

During that agitated spring I saw much of A. C. (Shan) Sedgwick of *The New York Times* and met his nineteen-year-old Greek niece Marina, a slender girl with dark, iridescent hair and glowing eyes. She moved with secret grace, stood like a marigold and wafted the scent of lemon-fragrant verbena. To a jaded man of twenty-six Marina seemed but a sweet infant agreeably adorning her uncle's home when she came from her mother's country house to spend the night. Once, when I invited them to lunch, at the last instant Shan and his wife Roxane couldn't come, and I found myself tête-à-tête with Marina. Months later she confessed this was the first time she had been allowed to take a meal alone with a man. I offered her a dry martini, which she seemed to drink with pleasure. As we grew to know each other, this became a standard preliminary when we dined. Only long afterwards, the day of our wedding, did Marina confess she hated all alcohol, above all dry martinis; she had feared putting me off by seeming a teetotaler.

My uncle, proprietor of *The New York Times*, asked me to fly to London for a "business consultation." There I dined with him and his former magazine editor, Frederick Birchall, and they invited me to join the *Times*. I refused. They then proposed that I undertake a special survey of Balkan communications available in case of war. I agreed to this if it did not interfere with my *Standard* arrangements. Old Birch plied me with drink and, at what he judged the propitious moment, said: "Well, laddy, at least if you won't come with the *Times* now, will you give us first option if war comes?" At this point Uncle Arthur tactfully left. Birchall said: "If war comes I'll make you bureau manager for all the Balkans at $100 a week; and you can terminate the contract two weeks after an armistice, if you are fool enough." I had no desire to join a family enterprise but was ruefully forced to agree it happened to be a remarkable paper. Nevertheless, Birch's offer was financially unappealing, and I had learned to bargain in Tirana poker games and Sarajevo bazaars. Damning me as impertinent and avaricious, he finally met my salary terms. In little more than three months, when Hitler attacked Poland, the contract was applied. By the time World War II ended I headed the *Times'* entire foreign service, so I never exercised my two-week option to get out.

I decided to wait out the start of what was by then so apparently an inevitable war in Rumania. Because of the uncertainty of my stay I moved from a hotel to a small pension, where I was accorded two rooms in considerable comfort and where I completed my report for Birchall. The Rumania of those days was a striking testimonial to that old Balkan proverb: "The fish stinks from the head first." The government was lazy, crooked, unreliable and unbelievably avaricious. Graft was the great leaven. The very first official I met pulled open a drawer in his desk, exposing packets of foreign money, and sought to bribe me. When I declined he asked what black market rate I was receiving for my dollars, an odd question since it was illegal to change currency except at approved banks. I told him what the Athenée Palace porter gave me. "Why that man's a crook," he scoffed. "I'll give you 15 per cent more."

If ever a land deserved revolution it was Rumania. King Carol was later to assure me Rumanians were truly democratic because the peasants uncovered their heads and clutched their forelocks when he passed! He was an immoral, selfish man. When he finally fled his country in 1940, he managed to abscond with considerable personal wealth, and his mistress, the red-haired, violet-eyed Magda Lupescu.

September 1, 1939, I received an urgent telephone call from Berlin. It was Birchall. "Laddy," he shouted over the wire, "you're on. Set up a Balkan bureau and communicate with New York. Cheerio." Although war's spastic clutch did not reach out and seize me in my Balkan fastness for many months after I joined *The New York Times*, war dominated the thoughts of all I encountered for almost six full years, even before I was personally caught in its senseless grip and sought—seeing it, tasting it, watching it—to follow vainly in the footsteps of the first great journalistic pioneers of battle, Calisthenes and Xenophon.

During this period I acquired a car and a dog. I bought a Mercedes from a Polish count, who had loaded his possessions into a fleet of automobiles and driven southward. The dog, a three-month-old wire-haired fox terrier named Felix, was also Polish. He belonged to a diplomat named Czerwinski who, suddenly impoverished, was anxious to sell Felix. One day I was at a friendly craps game. The puppy showed intense interest in the dice and also stole champagne from all glasses on the floor beside the gamblers. These dual passions intrigued me, and I took the dog instead of cash. Thereafter Felix traveled all over with me, insisted on his drink each afternoon (either champagne or vermouth and soda), was wounded by bomb splinters in Greece, escaped to Turkey and finally died in Egypt.

That winter I often met my friends the young Jugoslav patriot-conspirators. Later on, all became high-ranking officers in Tito's Partisan army, and one of them, Lolo Ribar, was a member of the party Politburo. The organization to which these youngsters belonged called itself the "Youth Movement for the Defense of the Country" and was, I learned later, a subsidiary of the clandestine Communist Party. Its members carried little flags bearing the slogan: "We will defend our frontiers." All but one of these friends died during World War II. Poor Lolo was killed by a German bomb as he was about to take off on a liaison mission to Allied headquarters.

❧ ❦ ❧

I FLEW to Italy and the Middle East to survey Mussolini's famous North African army. In Tripoli and Benghazi I found strutting Fascist troop contingents led by bored officers who were just as friendly as they proved to be later in British prisoner-of-war camps. The only positive thing I acquired in Libya was a first-class case of malaria.

As soon as I was able to move, I went to Cairo: streets jammed with lorries in tawny desert camouflage, hordes of turbaned and befezzed peddlers, guides and idlers in long white gowns, snappily uniformed English guards officers and sloppy New Zealanders and Australians who refused to salute; a symbiosis of the martial and the miserable. I lunched with the British commander General Jumbo Wilson. He arranged interviews for me with the commanders in Jerusalem, Damascus and Beirut. General Weygand, the snippy little chief of France's Levant army, spoke with distaste of the British, contempt for the Americans and assured me France would smash Hitler that very spring. He also talked of a possible Allied attack through the Caucasus against the Russian oil fields near Baku and Grozny. However, he admitted that the Turks, with whom he had discussed that project, showed remarkable lack of enthusiasm. Weygand had six divisions of impressive-looking troops and boasted of their putative power. His own conceit and the *élan* of his staff were high. The latter seemed to congregate each night in an establishment known as the Kit-Kat Club, which featured a callipygian Finnish dancer wearing only three rhinestones.

The Levant army never launched the campaigns planned for it. Weygand went back to France, where he played a major role in engineering the surrender. The troops he left behind fought but one engagement—against the British and Free French in 1941. They were defeated.

From Aleppo, in North Syria, I boarded the Taurus express for Ankara, accompanied, as usual, by Felix. In Ankara I had the first of many meetings with Franz von Papen, former Chancellor of Germany who did so much to help Hitler into power and then Ambassador to Turkey. The last time I ever saw him was in the prisoners' dock at the Nuremberg War Crimes Trial. Papen was a smooth, well-mannered, erect gentleman, charming, interesting to talk to, with a strange chiliastic belief in his own political resurrection. He constantly referred to "when I was chancellor" and implied a hope that some day he might regain that post. The Ambassador had a large map of Russia on his desk. I asked him why he was so interested in a country which, to all intents and purposes, was then Germany's cobelligerent. He looked at me coldly and, without answering, inquired why the United States wanted to amend its Neutrality Act.

That spring of 1940, as the poppies came out under the fruit blossoms and the cruel winter winds, Bora and Kossova, subsided, Hitler invaded Norway and Denmark. The Balkan countries breathed more easily because they thought this reduced immediate German pressure. But when the Scandinavian campaign turned to total victory and then, on May 10, 1940, when the Nazis thundered through the Lowlands and past France's Maginot Line, a great gloom fell.

As an immediate result Jugoslavia developed a guerrilla syndrome embracing various factions. All the irregular conspiratorial societies that have featured South Slav history began to make preparations. Serbian Cetniks—veterans who hadn't done more than drink and gossip since 1918 —began to meet amid ineluctable clouds of café smoke. One hangout was Belgrade's seedy Hotel Balkan, where grizzled heroes of the Turkish wars sat tugging their hispid mustachios, fur hats jammed down over their ears, drinking numberless cups of thick, syrupy coffee. The word Cetnik, soon again to become renowned, literally means "bandit" but had a glorious legend attached to it in Jugoslavia.

While the Axis drums snored elsewhere, we became accustomed to fevered activity by German and Italian "tourists" and businessmen. The British intrusion was more subtle. One group of newcomers was charged with sabotaging Danube barge traffic. Sandy Glen, a bland, bespectacled stockbroker engaged in this endeavor, later was landed behind Axis lines in Albania and Norway and then sent to Rumania, establishing the first liaison with Marshal Tolbukhin's troops.

Another group was preoccupied with espionage and propaganda in Albania. Julian Amery, who subsequently became a cabinet minister but was still a slender youngster, not yet twenty, was involved in this intriguing task. Julian induced Parker, my Belgrade stringer, to quit journalism and accept the job of proconsul (*sic*) in Skoplje, capital of Jugoslav Macedonia and nearest city to Albania. Parker was later expelled as a result of Axis pressure, provoked by articles I had written after I took a trip along the Jugoslav-Albanian border and he showed me Italian maps including as Albanian great chunks of Jugoslavia and Greece.

In Sofia, my friend Grigor Vassilev, a politician with two pretty daughters, invited me to his house one night for dinner. The girls were agreeable and flirtatious, and we had that rare thing in Bulgaria, two bottles of burgundy. At the end Grigor and I retired with Turkish coffee and French brandy.

It was perfectly clear that something was up. Grigor, a tall, sallow man, was leader of the Agrarian Party but not always a serious political factor. When he detected in me a sufficiently expansive mood, he asked: "You are going to Belgrade tomorrow?" "Yes, to get my car and dog." "You will do me a small favor?" "Of course." "It is only a matter of taking a letter." "Think nothing of it."

Grigor poured another drink and seemed a trifle uneasy. "Maybe," he said, "I should tell you it is for Milan Grol [a Jugoslav Democratic politician]." "O.K. That's all right." "I want you to hand it personally to Grol." "Certainly." "However," and here his long Adam's apple gulped, "I must advise you that it would be better for the police not to see it."

Even my bemused senses caught an oddness in this affair. I told Grigor: "Damn you, now I've said I'll do it; the least you can do is show me the letter since there's something obviously fishy in it." He went to his high desk, unlocked a drawer, took out an unsealed envelope and read the document. It was an elaborate proposal for simultaneous revolutions in Jugoslavia and Bulgaria which would oust their royal rulers and proclaim a unified South Slav republic. I sobered rapidly, regarding the Cyrillic scrawl as if it were a lapidary inscription on my tomb.

Next day I rode nervously to Belgrade, the letter tucked in my underpants. I was positive the customs guards and militiamen who inspected our passports and compartments on each side of the border must surely have been tipped off and envisioned an immediate future filled with bastinadoes and firing squads. Nothing happened; but as soon as I reached the Jugoslav capital I called Grol and told him I must see him on a matter of extreme importance.

Somewhat quizzically he received me in the comfortable study of his house. I handed him the letter, he affixed his glasses and began slowly to read. As each second passed his already lemon-colored face grew more pale and his pendulous lower lip sagged. His hands began to tremble, and the more they trembled the greater his difficulty in reading the message. At last he finished, his hands absolutely palsied. He looked across at me with an expression of fear and horror, as if I were some ghastly afrit. "I am going to burn this right away," he said. "Grigor must be out of his mind. Now leave. Leave right away. And never tell anyone about this. Never tell anyone. If I am asked if I know you, I shall deny it."

In mid-summer 1940 Gino Tomajuoli, one of my closest Italian journalist friends, asked me to meet him in Budapest so he could tell me about an Axis conference in Salzburg and Vienna. He had spent a long evening with Count Ciano, Mussolini's son-in-law and Foreign Minister, and Ciano told him that Rumania was about to be carved up once again; also that the Duce was preparing to invade Greece from Albania. An English agent in Belgrade, later murdered on a mission to Tito, confirmed the latter. I predicted to my paper (August 3, 1940): "Further partition of Rumania under the auspices of her good friends, Germany and Italy, is at hand."

On September 5, 1940, the Hungarian army moved across the Rumanian border. I had toured Transylvania a few months earlier with a charming Rumanian princess who claimed the province contained only a handful of Hungarians. My less lovely military escort was determined to prove the contrary.

The occupation of Transylvania was a shambles. The Rumanians made no stand; they simply retreated, ripping up roadways and telephone lines, destroying the meager fortifications of the Carol Line, pulling down bridges. Rumanian nationals who didn't move eastward with their troops stayed furtively under cover so that, in truth, the population did assume a certain Hungarian air as we marched through, the sturdy little flat-faced soldiers, looking like leftovers from Attila, striding behind handsome, tall blond officers on horseback, dressed in London-tailored uniforms. This contrast stressed the feudal gap in Hungarian society.

Much of the occupying force was soon tipsy since villagers kept running out with buckets of wine. The infantry, largely garlanded with flowers, continually shouted: *"Eljen Magyar Honved! Eljen Magyar Honved!* Long live the Hungarian Army." This was usually followed by hoarse screams: "Forward to Bucharest!" Had the Rumanians tried to oppose this parade they could have caused much trouble because so many rifles were spiked with roses and artillery, limbered, was festooned in blossoms. Behind the army came trucks loaded with gendarmes wearing Beau Brummell hats crested with cock feathers. I accompanied this parade as far as Transylvania's capital, Cluj under the Rumanians, which promptly assumed its Hungarian name, Kolozsvar.

By then the Bulgarians were also preparing to devour their piece of Rumanian flesh. I reached Sofia in the third week of September. On September 21 the great operation began. An impressive cavalry charge across the old borderline had been scheduled. Several squadrons of horsemen formed up, and, as the old frontier post was knocked down, a scrawny Bulgar priest, his beard scented with garlic, started spraying holy water over the high command. This ceremony caused the steed of Colonel Antonov, commander of the vanguard, to bolt, and, as the distinguished officer lurched abruptly into the beloved province, seeking to keep his stirrups, the rest of the cavalry thundered behind.

Trumpets sounded; horses and a few armored vehicles wandered across the steppe amid high wheat and sunflowers. Men in lambskin kalpaks and women with heavily embroidered aprons and headdresses weighted with coins of the Russian, Austrian and Ottoman empires stood in the villages smiling.

❦

OCTOBER 4 Hitler met again with Mussolini and I wrote from Belgrade: "Many diplomats believe German occupation of Rumania is not excluded." Germany began Rumania's military occupation on October 11, among other things taking over two floors of the hotel where I stayed, ordering

the pro-French owner to hang the Nazi flag over the entrance or to hang
there himself.

The occupation was blatant, but reporters were ordered to say nothing
about it. We were warned all that would be passed was reference to the
presence of a German "military mission." I was able to write: "The German military mission here is, to say the least, ubiquitous. One air division
of the mission is arriving at Pioesti. Units of a Panzer division have been
seen [fifty-one words censored]. It was scarcely necessary to issue a communiqué to let the inhabitants of Bucharest know there was a mission
here."

Unit by unit I noted where the "mission" was being stationed and
added: "General Hansen arrived today. He also was present with the
German military mission to Rotterdam last spring." Rotterdam, of course,
had been destroyed.

During 1940–1941 the United States was represented in Bulgaria by an
unusual minister named George H. Earle, former Governor of Pennsylvania, a large, powerful man, rather handsome, with wavy hair and cold
blue eyes. He was extremely fond of feminine company. Before he had
been in Sofia long he was often seen with a beautiful Hungarian blonde.
This young lady, A., often dined with the Minister, me, and my own long-
legged friend, Madeleine, a former goosegirl from Kiskunfelegyhazar.
When Earle was subsequently sent as naval attaché to Istanbul, A. arrived
there on contract with Taksim's nightclub. A British officer was assigned
to investigate her. He found she was reporting to both the Abwehr and
Sicherheitsdienst, the principal Nazi intelligence branches.

The Danube Commission, which supervised the famous river's traffic,
admitted Russia as a member for the first time and was scheduled to meet
in Bucharest with a Soviet delegation on October 28. I purchased a ticket
to return there; but our Hungarian friends had told Earle the twenty-
seventh was my birthday, and he persuaded me to stay so he could give me
a party. The four of us had a rather uproarious night. Some time before
dawn on the twenty-eighth the telephone rang and the whispered voice of
our new stringer in Belgrade, Ray Brock, came indistinctly over the bad
long-distance connection, speaking softly like feathers in a wound: "Italy
has invaded Greece."

Madeleine packed my few belongings while I called in all directions.
Panayotis Pipinellis, the cool-headed, diminutive Greek envoy who was to
become his country's Foreign Minister and Premier, got dressed, went to
his legation and personally stamped a visa in my passport. Earle insisted I
should take his car, an enormous official Cadillac, and have his chauffeur
drive me as far as I wished to go inside embattled Greece. I accepted the
offer partially, explaining I would happily be driven to the frontier but that
I could not see the possibility of putting a charge on my expense account
for one destroyed Cadillac plus a dead Bulgarian. I paid my hotel bill,
Madeleine rode with me as far as the streetcar terminus at the city's end;

then Felix and I started down the long, long road to Greek Macedonia, behind an ashen, terrified driver. We finally got to the border, where, much to his relief, I dismissed the chauffeur and started off on foot carrying a suitcase in one hand and a typewriter in the other, Felix romping alongside.

Marina had become a lieutenant-nurse and worked immensely long hours at the military hospital in the capital, moving in to the Sedgwicks' from the country. She was given the nasty job of carrying out buckets of amputated hands and feet once wounds and frostbite had begun to do their dreadful work at the front. Tense, yet glowing with energy and patriotism, she still managed to come with me to *tavernas* on her evenings off.

Reporting was a nuisance. The censorship was rigid on both military and civilian affairs. Telephone calls abroad were carefully monitored. The official spokesman who gave daily military briefings was George Seferiadis, a delightful and cultivated poet. He subsequently became Greek Ambassador to London and won the Nobel Prize for literature under the name George Seferis.

The Greek army in Albania was based on the Epirote capital of Janina, where Ali Pasha had once drowned his wives in sugar-sweetened sacks. This pleasant town had become a base for the dilapidated but courageous forces that blunted Mussolini's initial armored thrust and were now shoving the Italian divisions northward and backward into the snows of the Acroceraunian range. The atmosphere was much that of an early twentieth-century Balkan war. Most guns and much transport were drawn by horses. Truck convoys of reinforcements arrived with flowers stuck in their rifles. The Italians had almost total control of the air, but the British gallantly sent up a squadron of Gladiator biplanes. These had to be helped on their muddy takeoffs by ground crews running along with the tails on their shoulders until they gathered speed.

The Italians had struck through the valleys and along the roads with their tinny tanks, but, once the Greeks stopped them, they counterattacked along the ridgecombs, taking along their dismantled mountain guns and pounding frightened enemy concentrations below. Often patrols, especially the tough evzones who parade in peacetime wearing pompom slippers and white kilts, would slip along the thorny brush at night, moving one blanket ahead of another to deaden the crackles and calcareous echoes, attacking outposts with knives and, when these got stuck, using their hands and teeth.

The durable Greeks, supported by pack howitzers, worked their way along the crests and deep into Albania, chasing the Italians out of southern and eastern towns and establishing themselves on the wild shores of Lake Ochrid where satyrs once tootled pipes. It was pathetic to see the little Italian corpses, looking especially small and cold, and batches of prisoners, not in the least bit martial, wanting only to get out of the Acroceraunian cold.

2

FOR ME 1941 WAS A STRANGE KIND OF ANNUS MIRABILIS. IT WAS CON-
sumed by a series of disasters, but during it I fell in love, and by the
time it ended the Germans had met their first massive defeat in
Russia, a blow from which they never recovered, and the United States
had entered the war, insuring Hitler's defeat.

I experienced various adventures. I tried, unsuccessfully, to save the life
of our string correspondent in Rumania, who had been sentenced to death.
I was expelled by the Germans from Bulgaria and driven by their armies
from Yugoslavia and Greece. I was forced by the Wehrmacht to evacuate
Moscow with the diplomatic corps and much of the Soviet government.
For my reports I was offered—and then had my name withdrawn by my
uncle—a Pulitzer Prize. But by January 1942 I was (and still am) happily
married, and the Allies had started to swim the tide of victory.

The New York Times had had a series of string correspondents in
Rumania since the regular incumbent, a Hungarian Jew, wisely decided to
leave for the United States. The job was handed to a Dutchman. I was
startled to learn that he had been arrested and was being held incommuni-
cado, charged with complicity in the murder of a Nazi major. I promptly
departed for Bucharest to save him.

Unfortunately, I could do nothing. Rumanian officials refused even to
receive me. The United States Minister, a conventional stuffed shirt, argued it was impossible to act since the man's legal position was too complicated. Although, indeed, he worked for an American newspaper it was
on a part-time basis; his country was occupied and therefore had an unusual diplomatic status; every inquiry he had tentatively attempted was
rebuffed.

The poor stringer was executed. I departed, feeling helpless, furious and
ashamed, over the Danube to Bulgaria.

In Sofia the process of Nazi colonization was proceeding fast. Hundreds
of Germans dressed in civilian clothes and carrying light baggage, with

smooth soapstone faces and cornflower blue eyes, had begun filtering into Bulgarian Dobruja. No uniformed Nazi troops had yet entered, but extensive preparations for military occupation were proceeding.

The English, knowing of my plans, had asked me if I would take one of their "diplomats" from Budapest as far as Bitolj (where the road forked southward to Greece and northwestward to Ochrid, springboard for the Albanian attack). Before meeting my passenger, I dropped by to say goodbye to Lane. He was playing a desolate game of poker with Fortier and two businessmen. They invited me to take a hand. I played for two hours, winning great quantities of dinars, none of which were to do me more good than the proceeds of my bet on Jugoslav politics or my payment to the Hotel Srbski Kralj. Finally, I said farewell and drove off. (It was weeks before I heard of Lane again. His house was bombed, but he and his staff, despite several narrow escapes, all behaved excellently. For his part, Lane had been informed of my death. He sent me a telegram in Turkey that May when he discovered the news was premature.)

Lines of cars were parked outside the British legation. I drew up and was introduced to Ben, the hulking young man who was hitchhiking in the direction of Greece. He proved to be a calm, resourceful, agreeable companion. He was later parachuted back into Jugoslavia on a mission.

We had a hard time threading our way out of town amid marching troops and their incredibly slow, lumbering, ox-drawn munitions carts. At a hill some miles out, where a World War I monument stands, there was a noise like the purring of distant cats and another noise like the far-off tearing of silk. At Kraljevo, a Serbian town, we learned that formal war had started with the dive-bombing of Belgrade, an operation that brought 17,000 deaths.

The drive was bumpy and increasingly fatiguing. Horse-drawn Jugoslav military transport had left so many additional shoe nails on the road that all told, before crossing the Greek border, I was forced to change tires fourteen times, removing the tubes and patching them, often while Nazi planes slid overhead. At night our headlights were covered with black cloth through which only the faintest slit of light was permitted.

Finally, worn out, I turned over the wheel to Ben, giving him what I thought were precise road directions. I dozed off, and Ben promptly took a wrong turning, heading toward a strip of the Bulgarian border where, unknown to us, an Axis thrust was in the process of being mounted. When the noise awakened me I found we were grinding along a dry creekbed and, before I had time to complain, a Jugoslav soldier popped out of the bushes, nervously pointing his rifle. He was bewildered to discover two strangely attired foreigners, one of whom pretended to speak no Serbian at all. The sentry summoned two companions, and, hands up, they ordered us out of the car. When my revolver and ammunition were discovered there was evident consternation. Hands still up, a rifle in Ben's back and a Schmeisser in mine, we were ordered to unit headquarters, having to balance nervously over a bridge that consisted of a barkless wet log stretched across a brook.

The lieutenant in charge of the outpost, already alarmed by the gathering Nazi attack, promptly concluded we were spies. With little waste of time, he told us we would have to be shot. I argued vigorously against this decision and gave emphasis to my logic by pointing out that there were two bottles of *šlivovica* under the rear seat of my Mercedes. A private was dispatched to confirm this report. First one, then the other bottle, was subsequently broached. Finally the lieutenant was persuaded to read my permit from General Simović (which he could barely do). As things happen among the Serbs, the atmosphere changed swiftly. Amid embraces and toasts we finished the *šlivovica* and were then escorted back to our car. Eventually we departed in the waning moonlight amid a jovial salvo, the only amiable shots discharged on that cruel border.

In Skoplje, capital of Jugoslav Macedonia, we were picked up by nervous security forces and taken to an old Roman dungeon. Everywhere there was chaos; tangles of telegraph wires; heaps of masonry; corpses of humans and animals; immense quantities of glass; a cacophony of noises —screams, thuds, shouts, blasts and the whine of bombers, bark of guns. At last I was conducted to military headquarters, where I had to get my papers stamped by the corps commander. He proved to be a small, resolute Serb with a boil on the back of his neck which made him open his high, old-fashioned uniform collar and protrude his neck like a chicken. As he examined my permit he calmly munched a piece of dry bread and onion and assured me that despite the bombings, all along his front the situation was excellent. Four hours later Skoplje was in German hands.

Instilled with putative confidence by the general, I gassed the car at his fuel depot and we headed for Veles, a sleepy town which we had to traverse in order to cross the boiling Vardar River and start the climb toward the Albanian ranges. I was horrified, on approaching Veles, to find that both its bridges had been bombed. The road bridge was absolutely out. Fortunately, the railway span was still standing, although part of it was on fire and the way was blocked by rubble and tangled wires. Ben and I cleared a passage and drove shakily through the embers. Veles was empty. The main street had been well shaken up, covered with glass and pocked with bomb holes. Many buildings were blazing brightly. At the outskirts we came upon a parade of refugees hurrying out along the high Pelargonian Plateau. Two hours later Veles was in German hands.

Still further on, lorries, loaded with troops, were heading in the direction of the Babuna Pass. This famous strategic feature blocked the twin entrances to Greece in the south, via the Monastir (Bitolj) Gap, and to Albania in the west, via the road around Lake Ochrid. The Babuna Pass was a vital military position that could easily be held a considerable time by determined defenders. None were in sight as we wound upward around its hairpin turns.

Not more than an hour after midnight the commanding general ordered the military evacuation of Bitolj. At 8:00 A.M. civil evacuation—including such bureaus as the National Bank—was ordered. The chief of police was told to remain in the Grand Hotel and surrender the town.

It was hard to believe that the Babuna Pass and Monastir Gap were being abandoned without any effort at resistance. Nevertheless, the chief of police personally confirmed to me his instructions to hand over when the Nazis reached Bitolj. Months later King Peter told me the area commander was a traitor.

Prevented by a craven command from carrying out my plan to join in an Albanian offensive which, as it turned out, never materialized, I decided to head for Greece. In the confused muddle near our hotel I spotted Ben by his huge height. I picked him up together with a Bosniak engineer and four other refugees and slowly, the car straining under its excessive load, we rumbled southward.

Collapse was immediate and total. Jugoslavia's martial repute was only later rehabilitated by Marshal Tito's famous guerrilla movement, which began organized resistance after Hitler's invasion of Russia. On the advice of the Serbian Orthodox Patriarch Gavrilo, King Peter and his entourage flew to Greece April 14. The next day he was followed by Generals Simović and Mirković plus several air force officers and some of the national gold reserve. Although Mirković spoke no English, he was subsequently given general's rank by the British in the Middle East. The Nazi Ambassador in Moscow demanded that Russia terminate its recognition of the Belgrade regime.

The British military in Athens were already making preparations to evacuate. I inquired about among caïque owners and located a redoubtable sponge-fishing captain named Mikhali Pantelis. I hired Pantelis at a fee of 2 gold sovereigns a day while waiting plus 100 sovereigns when needed for actual departure. I instructed him to secrete his boat in a cove near Raffina, northeast of Athens, to load it with fuel for his auxiliary engine, water and some food, and to report to me twice daily, ready to move with minimal notice.

For days I was so preoccupied by the onrush of doom and with professional affairs that I gave little thought to my own deep personal problems. The Sedgwicks prepared to leave on a British ship carrying diplomats to the Middle East and, one evening before their departure, Shan asked me with old-fashioned embarrassment just what my intentions were toward his adored niece.

After her uncle and aunt embarked I talked things over with Marina. I wasn't really certain I wished to marry at that time, nor did she, for her part, want to leave. Furthermore, Pantelis had told me I should merely carry a few clothes and be prepared to swim to Turkey from the coast because he doubted if he could actually land. He advised me not to take Marina because of what he described as the Turks' "Hostile attitude."

Marina said we should both reflect further on whether we wished to wed. Meanwhile she didn't want to leave her mother at that tragic moment. No one, at that time, could imagine the Germans, who had proclaimed such admiration for the Greeks, would behave with anything other than civility. There was not yet any hint of the merciless savagery Nazi occupation would bring. I therefore decided to leave Marina behind and she could join me abroad if we were still so resolved. Marina accepted this idiotic judgment with demure and courageous sympathy.

Because of the Luftwaffe, we sailed mostly in the dark. Our wake was phosphorescent, reflecting brilliant stars. Except for the occasional thunder of a plane, the atmosphere of peace and tranquility was almost oppressive.

We dropped off at Andros and other islands, finally reaching Chios, where Marina's family had dwelled in old Byzantine days. When we put in for water at a village on the southern shore, a fisherman came up and said: "We fought as bravely against the Germans as against the Italians. But we cannot go on forever. Tell America we fought well. She should know where our hearts are, still on the side of freedom. We will now suffer; but we have faith. Our struggle has not been useless." Mikhali added: "I know that in the end everything will be all right. We Greeks are little people but we have big hearts."

Pantelis had originally warned that he might have to drop us at the harbor town of Chios itself, some miles directly across from Turkey, but would arrange for a small boat to row us near the coast. However, he was astonished to find Chios near anarchy. Two cabinet ministers and a former mayor of Athens were already bidding competitively for any kind of transportation across the strait to Turkey. So, in the end, Mikhali seized his courage and took off, after a night of uncertainty, heading for the harbor of Tchesme. Hesitantly, he sailed along, mile after mile, and, when he found he was not greeted by gunfire, finally deposited us at the mole.

At that time *The New York Times* was having immense difficulty transmitting dispatches over the antiquated Turkish telegraphic system. Messages were delayed as much as forty-eight hours. Consequently, after some negotiation, I made a deal to hire the government radio for a modest sum every night, after 2:00 A.M., when it had ceased broadcasting. I arranged to have my articles precensored by a censorship that officially didn't exist, and I then began to dictate my articles to monitoring offices we had established both in New York and Berne, Switzerland.

When one dictates over the telephone and there is a difficult word one spells each letter with a familiar symbol to insure correct understanding. For example, if there is some strange name such as Erzurum (a Turkish city), one will dictate: "E-for-Edward, R-for-Robert, Z-for-Zebra," and so forth. I applied this system to the radio, but, whenever the letter *M* occurred I would never say the obvious "M-for-Mother." It was always "M-for-Marina." And it was "D-for-Dora" (her mother), "A-for-Athens," "G-for-Greece." At least, I was determined, Marina should have the chance to know I was thinking of her even if, as I had discovered, mail service with occupied Greece was completely interrupted.

May 1, 1941, her birthday, she and some friends, her mother and grandmother were sitting gloomily around the radio trying to gather crumbs of information from the distant outer world. Suddenly they heard a familiar voice pronouncing: "M-for-Marina." The phrase was repeated many times.

The next night, at precisely the same time, there were many more *M*s, *A*s, *G*s and *D*s, all carefully spelled out. It was evident I was trying to say something. Marina's neighbors were Eugene Vanderpool, an American archaeologist, and his wife, Joan, who remained in Greece throughout the occupation. Joan sat down with Marina and Dora to work out an elaborate code that would be fitted to my broadcast pleonasms.

This contained precise instructions covering various contingencies and was a highly practical device. If, for example, I said "M-for-Marina," it meant she should try and leave Athens as swiftly as possible and join me in Turkey. If, on the other hand, I said "M-for-Mother," it meant she should remain there for awhile until the situation had clarified. If I said "M-for-Moscow," it meant things were too nebulous and, for the nonce, she should not contemplate escape. And so forth.

This document was given to the kindly Turkish Minister on the eve of his departure from Athens, and he brought it with him to Ankara. Immediately the proportion of "M-for-Marinas" in my dispatches multiplied by geometric progression. But there was no way for Marina to communicate again. Only occasionally someone would elude the Nazi barriers, slip out of Greece and inform me that she still kept her nightly vigil by the radio.

At dawn on June 22, Hitler attacked Russia.

Immediately every newspaperman applied for a Soviet visa. The Russians accepted our applications with stony, uncommunicative expressions. But ultimately I (alone among the applicants) was approved.

I hastily made preparations to depart with Dragomir Bogić, a Jugoslav diplomat who was returning to Moscow after that capital had restored relations with his government. The opportunity presented itself when the Turks undertook, as neutrals, to exchange a trainload of Axis diplomats coming from the USSR against a trainload of Soviet diplomats coming from Germanized Europe. They permitted Bogić and myself to join the Russian party.

I left Felix with the McDermotts, who possessed his great friend, a Sealyham named Ian that closely resembled a sausage dipped in hair tonic. Geoffrey and Ruth promised to take care of Marina when she eventually showed up, and Ray Brock undertook to maintain the flow of code messages in nightly *New York Times* broadcasts.

The Soviet capital presented a quite extraordinary sight those vivid lengthy summer days. It had been extensively camouflaged by a corps of artists working with the Red Army command. The enormous Bolshoi

Theater was hung with a drapery that sought to give it the appearance of a Georgic village with little wooden houses peeking out from the penumbra of trees. Surfaces of the principal squares were carefully painted to look like rural communities and forests. It was forbidden to walk across these spaces for fear of disclosing their secrets to intruding reconnaissance planes.

Despite frustrations, I was forced to work seven days a week, eighteen hours a day. A batch of censors, including a pleasant young man named Kozhimyakho, conspired to hamper our journalistic efforts. When I received a cable from Marina in Ankara, shortly after my arrival, I began to wire her daily. Kozhimyakho, a handsome young man, was much intrigued. He pointed out that Marina was a Russian saint and that Lada (her maiden name) was a pre-Christian Russian goddess of spring. He begged me to bring her photograph to his office. When I did so, it elicited friendly admiration but no favored treatment for my dispatches.

Very few Russians were allowed to mix with the tiny foreign colony. I did manage to become acquainted with a handful. They included the famous Mikhail Borodin. Borodin had been sent to China as Stalin's representative with Chiang Kai-shek. Chiang finally expelled him, and he fell into disgrace. Having nothing to do and being deeply worried about his son, a soldier (who later was killed), he used to come by often and sit drinking vodka, a gloomy man with dark, hooded face, talking about America (where he was born) and China.

I came to know three writers well: a playwright named Afinogenev, a Ukrainian satirist named Evgeni Petrov and Ilya Ehrenburg, fulgurous in propaganda but a rather dismal novelist. I liked Afinogenev and Petrov immensely and actually drank *pyom na brüderschaft* with the latter, an old Slavic ritual that made us blood brothers. Evgeni, big, strong, swart, with sardonic expression and pointed satanic features, was an army colonel and did all he could, quite unsuccessfully, to try and help me to the front. He was killed at the Sevastopol Battle in 1942. Afinogenev was blown up by a Moscow bomb in December 1941.

Ehrenburg, whom I liked least, perhaps because he was a craven vis-à-vis authority and alternated in manner between unctuousness and arrogance, was nevertheless helpful. He was highly cultivated and spoke beautiful French. He invited me several times for meals in his small but (for Moscow) unusually comfortable apartment with its good French pictures and excellent food and wine. Ehrenburg had lived in Paris after the Russian Revolution writing thrillers in which the villain was always a Red Guardsman. Through Ehrenburg I also came to meet Alexis Tolstoy and Mikhail Sholokhov. Tolstoy, related to Russia's most famous author, was a talented writer himself. Large and flabby-looking, he hewed close to the Kremlin line, which involved him in acrobatic troubles. He had just finished a minatory novel about Peter the Great, lambasting him, and sent it to the Kremlin, when he learned that Stalin's line had changed and that the

Soviet dictator now admired Peter as a nationalist. So Alexis sat down and started a lauding biography of the old Czar. As for Sholokhov, who later was awarded the Nobel Prize for his wonderful series on the Don Cossacks, he stayed out of trouble by remaining drunk. Once I sat next to him at lunch. He was pickled to the ears. I remarked that he had been luckier than Tolstoy and less obscene than Ehrenburg in pursuing his literary career. "Yes," he chuckled, regarding me with a bleary stare, "because I drink like a shoemaker."

The diplomatic corps was almost as ill-informed and frustrated as the correspondents corps, although it dwelled in more comfort. Each ambassador and service attaché was ostentatiously followed by the secret police (NKVD). Their telephones were tapped, bugging devices were placed in their homes and offices, hardly any Russians save stooges and *agents provocateurs* visited them. Even the most important had difficulty in obtaining appointments with leading Soviet figures. When diplomats entertained they were forced to entertain each other.

The best known envoy was Sir Stafford Cripps, an ascetic, vegetarian British socialist, sent to Moscow on the assumption this bias might help him in a Marxist capital. Of course, it did the reverse; English lords and American millionaires were more popular. Isolated and often alone, Cripps spent much time communing with his excellent Airedale. He knew so little about what was going on that he was in London at the time of Hitler's attack. I saw Cripps occasionally, as he was a kind man, but I found his personality chilly, his intellectuality overrated. He looked like a rheumy American Pilgrim Father. Despite his loyal admiration for fruit juice and carrots, his sticky eyes and pendulous nose quite unfairly gave the impression of a reformed alcoholic.

In hotels it was a fixed rule that every tenant had to go to air raid shelters whether he wished or not. The chambermaid and a militiaman checked up from room to room, searching behind drapes, beneath beds and in closets for those who preferred sleep. Shelters became places of distinct social interest. There were special havens for superior personages: Stalin had his own in the Kremlin; and there was one for distinguished visitors, which was made available to Harry Hopkins.

The Metropole shelter had much local color. It was situated in a sprawling, barrel-vaulted cellar along the walls of which triple-decker wooden bunks had been erected. These generally were jam-full of temporary residents, including hundreds shepherded in from the crossroads above, many of them magnificently drunk. Three decades of Soviet dictatorship had in no way dampened their liking for talk and debate. They would sit in their upper bunks hollering, weeping, drinking, farting, and belching while watching chess games staged by fellow shelterers below. Whenever a chess kibbitzer became too assertive a debate would start concerning his right to speak freely.

In the Metropole I was much taken one day by a stocky man dressed in what was obviously a homemade French uniform. He strutted with a peculiar Gallic cockiness. His name was Pierre Billotte, and he was a French captain, son of a famous general, who had been taken prisoner of war by the Nazis. Pierre had escaped in spring, 1941, was interned by the Russians and released soon after Hitler's attack. A dynamic, formidably intelligent and most agreeable man, he was sent by convoy from Archangelsk to England. There he became de Gaulle's Chief of Staff, was promoted to general, and eventually became a Cabinet Minister in postwar France. He is still one of my closest French friends.

In September, after the Russians had staged a successful counterattack against the Germans, bringing in Siberian troops to punch a hole in Nazi positions around Smolensk, the authorities at last permitted some of us to visit the front. The trip was carefully supervised by functionaries and political commissars. They were obviously instructed to keep us out of danger, to overfeed us, and to inject us with alcohol beyond the normal call of journalistic duty.

From that front, I wrote:

> The Nazis are rushing up winter supplies and stores of skis from Norway. The cold already is descending and the winds are hustling huge rain-loaded clouds across the horizon. Soviet soldiers gazing across the slopes repeat the ancient proverb, "A Russian's meat is a German's poison."
>
> Lieutenant General Vassily Sokolovsky, forty-three years old, a husky, square-jawed, long-nosed man of grave demeanor, is chief of staff on the front. (Later he became a marshal and Red Army Chief of Staff.) He says: "The Blitzkrieg, in its essentials, has been transformed into blitz-destruction of German men and materials. This began at Smolensk. The Blitzkrieg has developed into a continuous grinding of the German war machine. The process resembles Verdun, but in terms of ten or one hundred times the destruction, because of the increased efficiency of new machines, such as tanks and airplanes. Our artillery is master of the field."

Late that summer, Moscow decided to use the surviving Polish officers and men scattered around prisons in the USSR after the 1940 roundup when Russia joined Germany in the partition of Poland. I say "surviving" because, as we were slowly to discover, an enormous number of Polish officers had been massacred by the Russians in the gloomy Katyn forest.

Soon after he was released from the Lubyanka prison, General Wladyslaw Anders, selected to command this new Polish force, received me at his country's reestablished embassy. In August, Anders had been moved to a more comfortable cell, barbered, saluted and treated with sudden courtesy. It was evident from his amplified diet that the NKVD was trying to fatten him up, preparatory to releasing him.

A stern-looking former cavalryman, he was still using a cane when I talked with him. His wounds from the 1940 campaign had not yet entirely healed. I noted: "Anders first knew of Germany's attack when he heard the thud of bombs not far from his cell. Shortly after that the jailer appeared and asked if there was anything he could do for his leg. Anders said he had been there more than a year and nobody had troubled about him; he saw no reason to change. The jailer persisted. Then Anders said: I know why you are so interested. Because Russia is at war now."

By mid-October it was evident a new crisis had begun. The German offensive took off from Smolensk and started down the main highway for Moscow. It broke through major defense systems, and only by mobilizing militiamen and police did Stalin manage to plug the gap. Women and school children were set to work digging trenches and earthworks on the capital's outskirts. The diplomatic corps was unofficially informed that it shortly would be moved farther east.

Finally, on October 15, we were ordered to get ready for swift departure. It was snowing heavily. We gathered that evening at the American Embassy residence. Each foreign colony met together for its own transportation. We assembled in the Spaso ballroom, dressed in winter clothing and carrying ill-assorted hand baggage. Leaving behind in charge of American property two diplomats, Llewellyn Thompson (later Ambassador to the USSR) and Fred Reinhardt (later Ambassador to Egypt and Italy), we loaded into official cars and took off through silent, snowy streets.

That night, every inch of the Kazan railway station was jammed with humanity: old women and children huddled around bundles; old men clustered in corners, waiting in the hope that ticket queues would eventually open again; limping wounded shepherded by nurses; expressionless reinforcements with knapsacks and rifles.

I doubt if history has ever seen an odder group of travelers. In one car were leading members of the world Communist apparatus, the Comintern, including Raymond Guyot and Dolores Ibaruri, better known as *La Pasionaria*. In another were prominent Soviet writers: Ehrenburg, Petrov, Afinogenov. In still others were the main apparatus of the Soviet government, except for key members ordered to stay in the Kremlin by Stalin's side. Two "soft" cars (each compartment including four berths) were reserved for diplomats and correspondents.

KUIBYSHEV, *October 28, 1941*

CONSTANTINE Oumansky. Soviet Ambassador in Washington now here, went to Moscow early this week to try to find a plane for the United States. He failed. He then wired Steinhardt to ask if Steinhardt could help arrange his (Oumansky's) transportation via train. This is incredible because Oumansky is being replaced as Ambassador by Maxim Litvinov. Apparently nobody has told him yet.

Kuibyshev was never designed to function as a national capital. The main church was hung with an enormous cloth poster championing the virtues of atheism. The main cinema displayed a film in which a nasty Jesuit priest seduced a peasant girl.

The Volga soon froze solid, and, after that, trains of double-humped Bactrian camels in their long winter wool padded solemnly across from the Asiatic side to unload sparse goods in the Kuibyshev bazaars. The wind started to form in distant Mongolia or the Altai Mountains on China's frontier, took off slowly and gathered force hurrying westward over the steppes. By the time it reached us it was formidable. Snow piled up soon and thick.

Considering the strain everyone was under, it seems astonishing on looking back how well the claustrophobic foreign colony seemed to get along: writers, generals, diplomats, air force officers, Communist agitators, Japanese, Americans; even Genya Petrov, who tried to shoot some RAF pilots simply because they were in British uniform, was happy to drink with English diplomats once he had finally sobered up.

One man I came to know well was George Andreichin. George was a Bulgarian peasant who had been adopted by King Ferdinand at a time the crown was seeking popularity by sponsoring poor lads. Andreichin became a Socialist, while still living in the palace. The King regretfully sent him off, giving him a good head start over his secret police. George went to the United States, became involved in the "Wobbly" movement (Industrial Workers of the World), was arrested during postwar "Red menace" days, and was furnished bail by William Bullitt, subsequently first United States Ambassador to the Soviet Union.

Andreichin jumped bail and headed off for Revolutionary Russia, the goal of every young revolutionist. He took a train in Western Europe and, sitting in a third-class compartment, rattled across the brand new country of Czechoslovakia when the door rolled open and in came a sturdy, bearded old gentleman in huntsman's costume, bearing a shotgun and game bag. "George," said the huntsman, throwing his arms around him. "Your Majesty," said George. He rode mile after mile recounting his adventures to the Bulgarian King.

Once he reached Russia, George ingratiated himself with Leon Trotsky. He became the first defense commissar's private secretary. Years later, during the great Stalinist purge, he was arrested and told by the NKVD: "Citizen Andreichin [it was always a mark of disfavor when a Communist was called "Citizen" instead of "Comrade"], you are going to be charged anyway but I will give you your choice. Do you wish to be arraigned as a Trotskyite or as an American agent?" George replied that it was well known he had been Trotsky's secretary and also that he had later been assigned to develop close relations with Americans. He opted for the latter accusation.

He was sent to a labor camp in the Far North whose arduous regime tested even his Bulgarian peasant's constitution. The prisoners learned about the Axis invasion from new inmates, including former and future allies. Andreichin was finally summoned to the commandant's office, told nothing, but placed in charge of a guard and sent to Moscow. He was released by the chief of the Lubyanka just in time to be evacuated to Kuibyshev. During the late 1940s, he disappeared again—into a Bulgarian Communist prison. This time he was older—and he died.

One felt desperately confined, picking up bits of information of that sort and filtering them through a muddle-headed censorship with maximum effort and minimum result while a massive new battle was starting up in Moscow. General Zhukov, who had begun to emerge as the most brilliant of the new generation, easing aside the old marshals—Budenny, Voroshilov, Timoshenko and Shapozhnikov—seemed to have seized the offensive around the capital. Only on December 13, after the Germans had already started to reel backward, were a few of us allowed to fly to Moscow.

Moscow had a gala atmosphere, now that it knew the Germans were being driven from the iron circle gripping its outskirts. On my first morning back, the sun rose propitiously, shining on placid white streets, filled with deep drifts because most of the usual women snow cleaners had been assigned to more urgent tasks. It was a Sunday, and numerous drawn-looking Muscovites, behaving with inordinate gaiety, bustled about on their shopping, jesting at the latest posters ridiculing the retreating Germans.

Along the broad avenues cavalrymen riding in pairs patrolled their beats, for the city still was under martial law. At each corner stood infantrymen—usually noncommissioned officers—still on the alert with bayoneted rifles. Readiness remained the watchword. Overhead was the constant drone of fighter patrols in the bright, clear sky, and occasional flights of bombers roared back from the west.

Many miles to the west, beaten German troops were retreating slowly, harried by the Russian cavalry and pounded by heavy artillery, which Stalin once called the god of war. Passing constantly through the streets of Moscow were Red Army trucks, staff cars and motorcycles on their way to the front.

I was fortunate enough to be taken to the army of a new star on the Soviet horizon, Lieutenant General A. A. Vlassov, who was at the peak of his career. He had become Zhukov's most successful field commander and was swinging a wide arc around and through the German sector north and northwest of Moscow, past Klin and Volokolamsk.

Little did anyone suspect that Vlassov would finish his dazzling career as World War II's highest-ranking traitor. He was captured in July, 1942, and, later, agreed to recruit an army for Hitler from among the hundreds of thousands of war prisoners the Nazis had taken. He ended up by briefly liberating Prague with his puppet troops, then retreating ahead of the onrushing Red Army and yielding himself to General George Patton's American forces. Patton turned him over to the Soviets, who hanged him.

Vlassov was then a national hero: a big man, about six foot three with his height further accentuated by his high, general's lambskin *kalpak*. He had a long upturned nose and thick glasses. When one stood talking to him outside, his nose rapidly acquired a small snowdrift of its own, and his glasses fogged.

The trip was fascinating but savagely cold. I carried a bottle of vodka in one pocket of my fur-lined coat and wore elbow-length tank driver's mittens, given to me by Genya Petrov, that were both lined and covered with sealskin. We only had time to eat once a day and were billeted where luck would have it. But it was an exhilarating experience. Hitler's first major defeat. I wrote:

> The ground is strewn with clusters of abandoned guns, tanks and trucks where rear-guard stands were made; litters of munition cases, used cartridges, machine guns and staff cars. This desolate landscape evinces the usual tragic scars of war—burned houses, ruined churches; and a ghastly touch is added by occasional corpses of men and horses, their blood instantly frozen bright red, dragged from the road and dumped in the fields, stretching stiff limbs starkly toward heaven. Here and there the mantle of new snow masks grim shapes that can only be suspected.
>
> One is struck by the resemblance of the snowy, littered Russian landscape to that depicted by Meissonier in his version of Napoleon's famous retreat. The difference in more than a century of inventions appears to be reduced before the bare enormity of nature.
>
> The gap is bridged by the Russians themselves, who are using everything from cavalry and horse-drawn sleighs to powerful new tractors from the Stalin factory to haul their attacking strength. I have noticed in the Soviet arsenal brand-new self-propelled guns and old Howitzers, stamped with the Czar's double eagle and the dates 1914, 1915. Ammunition and tank fuel are hauled up on horse-drawn sleighs.
>
> Frozen German bodies sprawl stiffly in the snow by crippled enemy tanks and trucks. Past a formation of intact, frozen Nazi tanks, a detachment of soldiers rides to the front in sleighs. Snow-spattered horses munch hay by an abandoned German antitank gun. A wounded horse stands shivering in a field; field guns thud across the hillside. A helmeted and hooded cavalry detachment with sabers swinging rides by a long train of wagons and trucks and marching men. Mechanics work on Russian tanks parked near trees.

In the snow Vlassov arrives. He is a giant and wears a high gray fur *kalpak* with a red top. He says he has just dispatched mobile and ski units to take Volokolamsk; the vanguard already is cutting off the last line of the Nazi retreat. Vlassov explains that another force is attacking Volokolamsk from the south, and because of the thick forests to the west the Nazis cannot escape. "They are trapped, I think," he says.

꠹꠹

By this time I felt I had done my job for *The New York Times* and had earned the right to leave Russia and get married. I obtained a seat on a plane bound for Teheran and handed over to Ralph Parker. The passengers included two British Ambassadors, Knatchbull-Hugessen from

Ankara and Sir Reader Bullard from Teheran, who had been in Moscow to confer when Anthony Eden saw Stalin. We bounded off the snowy Kuibyshev airport and took off at about the height of a tall man for Astrakhan, where we spent our first night.

I knew Astrakhan had been the world's caviar capital, so I rushed to the retail shop where there was a small queue. When my turn came I ordered two kilos (almost four and a half pounds) of the best gray-green esturgeon. By the time my tins had been filled and sealed, Hugessen and Bullard arrived. They were furious to find there was no more and insisted I share with them. "Gentlemen," I said. "Apart from the fact that both of you have access to all the caviar you want in Ankara and Teheran and apart from the fact that I believe in the American rule, first come, first served, I am getting married next week and this is for my wedding party. Sorry."

On a starry New Year's Eve, we landed at Teheran, the first lighted city I had seen for months, looking gay, friendly, warm and civilized. I summoned a carriage driver, who spoke Russian, and clip-clopped happily off to the modest Firdowsi Hotel, which looked to me like a combination of every Ritz in the world. Before greeting the New Year, I drank a whole bottle of champagne—alone.

On January 4 the young Shah received me: a quiet, courteous, solemn and rather timid youth. Mohammed Reza Pahlevi, then twenty-two years old, had suffered greatly. His father, a tough, self-made cavalry sergeant, had been forced to abdicate by the British and Russians. He himself had seen his country occupied by the two countries Persians most feared.

The Shah referred constantly to Iran as an "occupied" country. He seemed to resent more than anything that Iran was not accorded the right to defend itself with English and Russian aid but was only guaranteed protection. He said, there was no excuse for the Anglo-Soviet occupation, that the numbers of Germans and Italians could have been easily handled.

I took the famous southward bound Trans-Iranian Express that creeps through endless tunnels to the oil ports of the Persian Gulf. At Ahwaz I descended and was taken in charge by a British major who fed and lubricated me at the officers mess and gave me a hut with a latticed Indian charpoy bed on which to sleep. Most officers and men in the Iran-Iraq area were from the Indian army.

From Basra I rode a troop train up to Baghdad, a disappointing city, cold in winter, dusty and infernally hot in summer.

General Nuri as-Said, Prime Minister and dominant figure on the Iraqi scene, told me he would join the alliance against Germany in exchange for American economic aid. He said: "We are allies of Britain. We have already severed relations with Germany, Italy and Japan. We are helping Britain in all her needs and therefore believe we are entitled to have the United States lease-lend clauses apply to us. Iraq has ample grounds for a grudge against the Axis. Rashid Ali and other traitors wanted by the government are sheltered in Germany. There they are protected and paid. Axis broadcasters in the Arabic language are constantly attacking our government and the royal family in the most insulting terms. No nations can keep quiet before such insults."

After marrying Marina in Beirut, we went to Washington in mid-April, and I was persuaded both by friends in the Army and *The Times* that I would be more useful as a war correspondent than as a warrior. I have since questioned my own judgment and decision. The secretary of the Combined Chiefs of Staff asked me to talk about Russia to a group of War Department intelligence officers. They asked me to stick my neck out and predict what would happen that year (1942). I forecast the Germans would mount an offensive only on the southern front, would get to the high range of the Caucasus and as far as Stalingrad on the Volga, then would be forced to fall back.

I was asked to summarize all my impressions in a report which I dictated April 15. This said in part:

> Depending on Russia's strength after the war, it is my belief that she definitely intends to get back the Baltic states, Bessarabia, part of Poland, and the 1941 Finnish frontier. I believe she intends to try and gain a paramount diplomatic influence (greater than that of the Czar) in the Balkan slavic states and will encourage the Jugoslavs to demand a large piece of Albania and Trieste. She undoubtedly has also got her eye on a safe egress to the Atlantic, but her methods and ambitions will be dependent upon her position vis-à-vis the United Nations. I don't think for a minute she will agree to withdraw her troops from the southern Caspian seacoast and northern Iran.

Events proved I was wrong about northern Iran, although Moscow did manage to get a revision of the Caspian frontier. Events also proved I was wrong about Albania. For the rest, I believe the forecast was not inaccurate, even including the reach toward the Atlantic by establishing a common frontier with northern Norway.

I flew back to London, then North Africa, soon to be joined by Marina en route to Cairo.

At that time Montgomery's British army was hammering the Mareth Line, last Nazi defense to the east, and Patton's Second Corps was trying to break through from the west. I joined the latter in the neighborhood of a Tunisian hamlet called El Guettar.

I was with a small outfit on the Gafsa-Gabes highway when two army sergeants, a thin Devonshire boy named William Brown and a slight youngster named Joseph Randall, of State Center, Iowa, shook hands in midafternoon and slapped each other's backs. That was the way the British, coming from El Alamein, and the Americans, coming from the American east coast via Morocco and Algeria, met on the invious African continent. The scene was astonishingly tranquil, taking place on a road running through barley and wheat fields at the foothills of the Mannaou

Mountains. A yellow British armored scout car followed by two others saw some dull green vehicles approaching and when bowl-shaped helmets hove into view of their binoculars, Brown said: "Those are Jerries." Fortunately, an instant later someone shouted: "No, by God, they're Yanks."

In Cairo I established a combined home-and-*New York Times*-office in two large adjoining rooms of the Continental Hotel, overlooking a park filled with vermilion shrubs. I was glad to get back into the Arab-Balkan mixture of which the Egyptian capital was the focal point. By the spring of 1943 British Intelligence had spread out various tentacles including holding companies for guerrilla operations. Through our friends working under these umbrellas in Greece, Jugoslavia, Albania and even Rumania and Bulgaria, I was able to keep an eye on occupied East Europe. But as soon as I could manage to get away I returned to Russia.

Right after my return, I heard a story that gives me the creeps. When Stalin gave a dinner for Davies at the Kremlin, a movie was shown. Believe it or not, it was *Mission to Moscow*. Davies had brought a special reel with him. Apparently even the members of the Politburo snickered when they saw themselves represented in this ridiculous picture.

Working conditions for a reporter had not improved despite the perceptibly better military situation. It was the same old business of rewriting Soviet press dispatches, scrabbling about for tidbits from the diplomats, most of whom knew little, and arguing endlessly with the Soviet authorities, who neither allowed visits to the front nor permitted interesting interviews. One knew that the Red Army was better, that all the old officer traditions, even the shoulder-board *pogony* epaulets of the Czar, were back, and that, despite the end of the Comintern, the Red Army was directing highly efficient partisan movements in occupied Europe.

One night a Soviet architect named Alexandrov gave a tremendous party for diplomats and invited me. Poor Alexandrov lived in a squalid room far from the magnificent apartment where he was assigned to entertain on behalf of the government's propaganda and culture divisions. The apartment was filled with icons, handsome furniture, ecclesiastical monstrances, tapestries, drapes. There was an excellent orchestra and all the prettier young ballerinas of the Bolshoi chorus. We ate, drank and sang until morning, finally staggering out into the summer sunlight. When Alexandrov had seen us off with courtly gestures he slunk back to the sordid reality of his own furtive life.

Finally, after my last request to travel had been refused, either to Leningrad or to the front at Kursk, where it seemed there might soon be a big battle, I had an awful row with the press chief. He merely stared above his thick-lensed spectacles, saying nothing but glowing like a hot samovar. Soon the censorship of my dispatches was even tougher; I resolved to leave.

Eddy Rickenbacker, the World War I American flying ace, had come to Moscow in his own B-24 bomber on a liaison and propaganda mission, and Rick agreed to take me out with him to Cairo. On a July morning, before dawn, we stood on an airfield near Moscow. It was still so cold at that time of day that one's breath bellied forth as in winter. There was a full crew and no room in the plane, but I spread my fur-lined coat in the bomb bay, after extracting a promise from Rick that no one would absentmindedly open it. There I stretched out to sleep as we swayed gently through the summer air like a canoe. We flew nonstop to Habbaniyeh, in Iraq—then an unheard of feat of endurance—refueled and were in steaming Cairo late that afternoon. I was back in Cairo when Italy surrendered, some weeks later.

CAIRO, *September 10, 1943*

I HAVE gotten into a hell of a row with British censorship. Four days ago I had lunch with members of the *émigré* Greek government. They were discussing the proposed armistice Italy is about to sign. The Greeks as well as other Allies are naturally being consulted. Prime Minister Tsouderos afterwards showed me a draft copy of the agreement, and I confirmed its details with King Peter. This is all Top Secret and has not been announced. However, I have worked in Algiers enough to know when a communications jam is going to arise. Therefore, on September 7 I wrote a very brief dispatch giving the main terms of the proposed armistice. I brought this down to Colonel Stevens, chief British military censor, and told him the story was to be approved and held by his office until the armistice was announced. I explained that I merely wanted to send this piece from Cairo to backstop our staff in Algiers. Steve understood completely. He sent my story up to General Scobie, Jumbo Wilson's Chief of Staff. Scobie was astonished that the news of the armistice had leaked. Nevertheless, he played ball, approved the story and sent it back to Steve to be held.

On September 8 the armistice was announced by Eisenhower in Algiers, and Steve released my story immediately. To my astonishment—and also to the great embarrassment of Steve and Scobie—Eisenhower did not announce the terms but merely the fact that a cease-fire had been signed. I had not foreseen this eventuality. I had addressed my dispatch to NYKTIMES LONDON. The British held my story up in London and refused to forward it to New York. Yesterday a cable marked "MOST SECRET. OFFICER ONLY" was sent from the Chiefs of Staff to the commanders in chief, Middle East. A friend gave me a copy of this cipher message, which was marked "MOST IMMEDIATE."

"Cable was received in London last night for *New York Times* from Cairo giving alleged text of armistice terms. It has been stopped here but may have been routed some other way as well as through London and, if so, stop should be imposed."

In those days I saw a great deal of Jugoslavia's young King Peter, who was watched over carefully by the British and prevented from either returning to his country, as he professed to wish, or from exerting much influence on a situation that had already begun to develop into open civil war between the claimants to Hitler's fading power. On Oct. 15, 1943, I wrote in a diary:

> Lunch with King Peter today. He said of Mihailović: "I haven't been very satisfied that he has been fighting enough. I also gave directions to avoid any conflicts with the Partisans from his side and only to fight if he is attacked."
>
> Peter claims there cannot be a settlement in Jugoslavia until there is complete British-American-Russian understanding. He saw Eden yesterday noon and told him that if the Russians would restrain the Partisans, Mihailović would follow British desires in terminating the civil war. Eden said he regretted but Britain did not feel it could defend Mihailović's actions in the forthcoming conference with the Russians (at Moscow).
>
> Peter complained that M.O.-4 (the British intelligence agency handling these Balkan operations for SOE), held up all messages to him (King Peter) from Mihailović between the dates of August 4 and September 29 and only brought the accumulated batch of telegrams to him yesterday, a half-hour after Eden had left.

CAIRO, *October 16, 1943*

SAW King Peter again. He says he is working on a scheme to have the few Jugoslav "Liberators" (American B-24s) organized into a flight that would parachute him into the country.

Afterwards I saw David Balfour, now a British major attached to the Greek *émigré* government. David has been all kinds of things in his career, but I suspect only, in the end, an intelligence agent. He was a Greek Orthodox priest until just before the Italians attacked in 1940 and confessor to the royal family. He next showed up with beard shaved off in a major's uniform. He tells me a real civil war broke out in Greece October 8. The struggle is between the ELAS (Communist) and the EDES (rather Royalist). ELAS grabbed most of the Italian arms when they surrendered last month at the time of the armistice.

CAIRO, *December 1, 1943*

THE big Middle Eastern event of 1943 was a series of summit conferences held in Cairo and Teheran. As president of the Middle East War Correspondents group I was placed at the head of a committee that sought to obtain better facilities for the press than the unpromising blackout threatened in the name of security.

Apart from an engraved silver cigarette case graciously given me by the other correspondents as a reward for beating my head against the bureaucratic wall, the one reward I received for my efforts was a long talk with

Churchill. This was the first time I had occasion to meet the British war leader.

Lampson, the British Ambassador, was kind enough to arrange for me to have a drink with Churchill. He seemed extremely fatigued and spoke in a tired voice. He was wearing a tan suit and brown shoes. He had a heavy gold chain in his waistpocket. He solemnly shook hands, invited me to sit down, and reminded me that his grandfather Jerome had been an owner of *The New York Times.* Churchill reviewed with evident satisfaction the plans he had helped so much to materialize, not only for victory but also for safeguarding its permanence. He was prepared to take an even money bet that the Germans would not be able to last out the present winter. He continued: "In Palestine there should be enough room for both Arabs and Jews. I personally, as you know, have been Zionist from the beginning. But I believe there is enough for all. I have helped the Arabs and put Feisal on the throne of Iraq, Abdullah in Amman. Some people tend to underrate the great services of the Jews. They have made cities in Palestine where there were hamlets and orange groves where there was nothing but glistening sand. Their money flows in from abroad available for developments which would not otherwise exist."

CASERTA, *January 20, 1944*

WHEN I reached Caserta, enormous royal palace of the Kings of Naples and Sicily where General Mark Clark then had his Fifth Army headquarters, there was a big commotion. In an effort to outflank the stubborn German defense line based on Cassino, an amphibious landing was being made southwest of Rome at Anzio and Nettuno. I was invited to go along with the commander in chief, Sir Harold (later Lord) Alexander. I took the following notes:

> We traveled together on the destroyer *Kempenfelt*; I joined Alexander at Caserta. Early in the morning I had stumbled through darkness over the plowed fields to his private train. Alexander came in and very cordially invited me to breakfast with him and his chief of staff. Then we drove down to Naples where we boarded *Kempenfelt* and zigzagged off through the bay, cutting high plumes of spray because it was pretty windy. One after another, we passed swaying, heaving convoys heading up to the beachhead.
>
> General Al Gruenther, Clark's chief of staff, was in the party. Gruenther described the Anzio landing with much enthusiasm. He said: "We prevented the Germans from knowing of the expedition largely by the use of our air power. This operation will be studied in the future. Nevertheless the Germans have been very skillful. They have already brought reinforcements up to the high ground and are massing there, although they are probably not yet ready for attack."

Anzio was really rather a disaster. It didn't achieve its objective of turning the Nazi line. Even Alexander displayed less warmth toward the

Americans once the initial advantage of surprise wore off and the beach-head became a dead end. Subsequently he was to complain: "Mark Clark switched his point of attack north to the Alban Hills, in the direction of Rome. If he had succeeded in carrying out my plan the disaster to the enemy would have been much greater; indeed, most of the German forces south of Rome would have been destroyed. I had always assured General Clark in conversation that Rome would be entered by his army; and I can only assume that the immediate lure of Rome for its publicity value persuaded him to switch the direction of his advance."

Alas, I can fully confirm the implications of Alexander's remark. I spent most of the next three months in and around Cassino and often talked to Clark, a rangy, hawk-featured man who looked much like the sheriff in a Wild West movie. Clark was fearless; but he never impressed me by his brilliance, and he was certainly obsessed with vanity. He always talked about "When I take Rome." Once, when I had been complaining to him about the particular stupidity of his Fifth Army censors, he put his long arm around my shoulder and said: "Cy, when we make our breakthrough I want you to ride in a jeep with me. I'll see to it when we get there that you can tell the world just how Mark Clark took Rome."

⋦§⋟

WHILE in Naples I saw Count Carlo Sforza, the renowned anti-Fascist who was to become Italian Foreign Minister. He wanted a free port in Trieste under joint Italian-Jugoslav-Austrian-Czechoslovak-Hungarian administration. He added: "I do not believe in the future of colonies. The moment will come when it will not pay to have any colonies. But I think it would not only be ungenerous but unwise to take from a democratic Italy her own pre-Fascist colonies. There is a supreme necessity to avoid creating new myths about injustice and violence."

CAIRO, *April 26, 1944*

TODAY I had an extremely interesting talk with Ambassador Lincoln Mac-Veagh, American envoy to the *émigré* Greek and Jugoslav governments. MacVeagh, very worried about the eastern Mediterranean (an English sphere), where we have no concrete policy, suggested to Roosevelt in the early spring of 1944 that the Allied expedition which goes to Greece must at least be headed by an American general, since we suffer neither from fear of Russia nor distrust of Britain. The idea was turned down. Mac-Veagh would like to see real buffer states between Russia and England (there is no other European power) established in the Balkans, with the United States actively aiding.

Churchill is now personally responsible for Britain's Jugoslav and Greek policies, and it is hard for the Foreign Office to advise him and keep him from blurting out difficult remarks.

CAIRO, *June 23, 1944*

ONCE again I have been having a hell of a time with the British about a story. On June 19 I submitted a piece to the censorship which began: "Initial steps toward outlining zones of 'initiative' in the Balkan peninsula have been agreed upon by the British and Soviet governments, under which Greece is definitely recognized by Moscow as within the British military sphere of influence and Rumania is likewise recognized by London as within the Soviet Union's military sphere of influence."

The story was submitted to the military censorship, which passed it on to the political censorship. Kit Steel, in charge of these things, demanded to know where I got the information. I refused to give even a clue.

As a matter of fact, I got it from MacVeagh, who wanted the news of this private deal between London and Moscow, dividing up Eastern Europe, to be known. Churchill was shown a copy of the story cabled in code from Cairo, and he is reported to be enraged. (I was to learn later that on June 23, 1944, Churchill drafted a "Personal and Top Secret—Prime Minister's Personal Telegram" to Lord Moyne, who had replaced Casey as Minister of State for the Middle East. The message, which was corrected in the Prime Minister's own handwriting and classified as "Personal and Private," made no effort to deny the information I had obtained. However, recalling that his own grandfather had been a former *New York Times* owner, he asked me to be most careful about using it and urged me to consult Moyne in advance. Churchill contended the Anglo-Russian deal was only temporary, that it was in no sense a permanent arrangement for spheres of influence. Curiously enough, after all the precautions of classification and the trouble taken by the Prime Minister to amend the telegram in his own hand, it was never sent. I now possess a copy. The importance of the Anglo-Soviet deal cannot be exaggerated. First Roosevelt conceded to Churchill the control of Anglo-American affairs in East Europe and the east Mediterranean, apparently as an exchange for British acceptance of the politically popular [in election year America] policy of unconditional surrender. This arrangement itself was so secret that, months later, Secretary of State Hull summoned the British Ambassador, Lord Halifax, to complain that certain equipment had been sent by London to Turkey without first consulting Washington. With some embarrassment, Halifax said the auction accorded with the Casablanca agreement. Hull himself had never heard of it.)

Subsequently, I flew back to Italy and drove to Rome, where I was given a heartwarming reception by my old friends Tomajuoli and Alfio Russo, who pawned silver and other possessions to give me a magnificent party. I have always been impressed by the staunch faithfulness of Italian friendships.

While in Rome I heard that the Ardeatine catacombs, where more than three hundred Italian hostages had been slaughtered by the Nazis, were about to be opened. I decided to take with me to the dismal scene an American colonel who maintained that reports of German atrocities were manifest propaganda.

We drove out on a baking hot day and scrambled through the hole that had just been opened into the cave of abomination. The stench was unimaginable. Each batch of prisoners had been machine gunned, falling on top of its predecessors. Some victims were not yet dead when Nazi engineers blew in the entrances.

The colonel said nothing as we jeeped back into Rome, but from then on I noticed a striking change in his references to the Nazis. I sent my uniform out to be dry-cleaned and my clothes to be laundered. Nevertheless, that night I awakened, overwhelmed by the oppressive Ardeatine stench. It came from my shoes, which I had failed to put outside for fear they might be stolen.

3

JIMMY JAMES, MANAGING EDITOR, REQUESTED ME TO RETURN TO New York and help plan postwar foreign coverage of *The New York Times.* I had agreed to join the paper only in case of a war and for the period of hostilities plus two weeks. However, James offered me the job of chief foreign correspondent in charge of all our overseas coverage. I was not yet thirty-two, and I accepted. James told me that he would back any project I suggested, and, if I was right, he would give me credit; if I was wrong, he would fire me. While waiting the judgment of events he would endorse all my recommendations to the publisher, my uncle. This suited me fine.

I resolved to wind up the war with the Russians. The Red Army had borne the heaviest burden and would obviously be the first to enter Berlin. I hoped that I could manage somehow to be with it. First I went to London, Paris and Rome to consult with correspondents. Then, to facilitate my plan, I persuaded Joe Davies, the American diplomat, to send a letter on my behalf to Molotov. He wrote:

"You will doubtless recall that on the occasion of my visit with Marshal Stalin and you at the Kremlin, I spoke of Mr. Sulzberger, who was a correspondent of *The New York Times* then in Moscow, and his desire to fly over the battlefront. The matter was left with the suggestion that you would take it up with the military authorities and see if it was feasible. I then said that I had a very great respect and admiration for Mr. Sulzberger, and felt that he was a friend of the Soviet Union. He is now very anxious to have an interview, if it is possible, with Marshal Stalin."

I had hoped not only to see Stalin but to obtain his approval of my plan to accompany his army to Berlin. Nothing, alas, came of this careful planning. But when I flew back to Cairo, en route for Russia, to spend Christmas with my wife and new daughter, I was brimful of optimism.

CAIRO, *January 2, 1945*

SIR Hughe Knatchbull-Hugessen, British Ambassador to Turkey, signed a secret armistice for the Allies with the Hungarians. It provides that when "the proper time" comes Hungary will turn against the Germans as Italy did. The accord was signed late at night, September 9, 1943, on a boat in the Bosphorus, but was never activated. The Nazis occupied Hungary March. 19, 1944. In September, 1944, Admiral Horthy slipped a general into Italy asking for another secret pact before the Russians thrust in. The Allies decided not to trust him.

TEHERAN, *March 7, 1945*

TODAY I again saw the young Shah, Mohammed Reza Pahlevi. He claims Iran deserves complete and sympathetic recognition by the United Nations and above all by the Great Powers for the part she has played in World War II as "a faithful ally since 1941." That seems like a rather strange argument. Iran was occupied by Soviet and British troops.

MOSCOW, *March 11, 1945*

JOHN Davies, the new secretary at the American Embassy in Moscow, told me a fascinating story while we were together in Teheran waiting for a plane to Russia. He had been political adviser to General Stilwell in China and had a run-in with Major General Pat Hurley, the new American Ambassador to China.

According to Davies, the Chinese Communists, who have the seat of their government at Yenan, formally requested the United States government to turn over to them all arms and munitions captured by American forces from the Japanese. The purpose is stated to be to enable Communist troops and guerrillas to increase their activities against the Japanese occupying forces.

Apparently the United States accepted this idea, but Chiang Kai-shek, who heads the Chungking Kuomintang government, has refused to permit shipments of this material across China to Yenan territory. Chiang is afraid the Communists will get too strong.

MOSCOW, *March 23, 1945*

GEORGE Kennan is Harriman's Number Two at our embassy, a brilliant man but resentful that Harriman hid from him everything connected with Yalta. Kennan argues that the war was far more costly to the population than the purges, but easier on the bureaucracy. National self-confidence was immeasurably increased. War pulled regime and people together and strengthened faith in the future. Says Kennan:

It revived the hope, latent in every Russian soul, that the scope and daring of the Russian mind will some day overshadow the achievements of the haughty and conventional West. It dispelled some of the suspicion, equally latent in every Russian soul, that the hand of failure lies heavily over all Russian undertaking.

Stalin will logically seek to increase the power and prestige of the Russian state in the world. A good guess is he will seek to increase fixed capital and maintain the military establishment rather than rapidly improve living standards. After the war, it is probable the Kremlin will revert to the basic program of military industrialization in which it was engaged from 1930 to 1941.

MOSCOW, *March 27, 1945*

THE East European leaders are starting to make obeisance as the war nears its end. Saw Masaryk and Beneš. Masaryk has little faith in being able to keep Czechoslovakia from being Communized. Beneš, on the other hand, seems quite businesslike and relatively optimistic. So embittered by what the French and British did to him at Munich, seven years ago, that he seems willing to put some trust in Russia.

Beneš said he was "neither entirely satisfied nor entirely dissatisfied" with his visit. Stalin told him there was absolutely no thought of setting up any sort of puppet German government (like the Hungarian one).

Before leaving London Beneš got a written pledge from the British that they would support the pre-Munich frontiers including Ruthenia. He got an oral pledge from the United States. My feeling is that Czechoslovakia may be shoved a bit west, giving it some German territory as "ancient Slovonic land." Poland is getting up to the Oder. Beneš said, "Czechoslovakia would be ready to absorb such additional lands if it was later decided by the allies this would be for the good of Europe and the general peace." As for the Ruthenia, for the moment Beneš says it is Czechoslovakian. But, "if the people there really want it they can join the USSR." He seems to know the wind is plainly blowing that way.

MOSCOW, *April 5, 1945*

TODAY I had a talk with Maxim Litvinov, vice-commissar for foreign affairs and for many years commissar. His most recent important assignment was as wartime Ambassador to Washington. I have known him for four years, and he appeared more bitter, unhappy and aged than I have ever seen him. He is white, lined, nervous, fat and uneasy. He was wearing the new uniform of Soviet government officials. He looked rather less like a general than anybody I have ever seen. His gray uniform was rumpled and unpressed, and there were food stains on the lapels. He was extremely frank but obviously pessimistic about the world situation, and it was entirely clear that he is not being consulted on any important decisions.

He said he is now working solely on postwar problems, with the exception of reparations. Also, that nobody listens to his advice or pays any attention to him. He seemed utterly convinced things were developing badly among the Allies and for a world security organization.

Litvinov seemed cut off from all news. To my knowledge he did not know Tito was coming here, although at the time I spoke with him Tito was due at the airport. I do not believe he knew the Japanese pact would be publicly denounced in two hours' time and that Molotov has already spoken to Satō.

The situation is developing badly. First, he said, the Allies make a mistake and rub the Russians the wrong way; then the Russians make a mistake and rub the Allies the wrong way. He was a regular Jeremiah, full of gloom.

Moscow, *April 13, 1945*

At about 2:00 this morning, Harriman learned of Roosevelt's death (which occurred at 11:45 P.M., Moscow time). Immediately he went to see Stalin. Stalin was clearly moved and worried about implications. He held Harriman's hand for a perceptible time, saying nothing. Then, with Molotov present, they talked. Harriman wished to explain how very important to the American situation and therefore to the international situation this tragedy was. He put it up to Stalin point-blank that Russia must cooperate strongly now. Stalin clearly recognized this, and a number of problems were settled right then and there. Stalin wanted to know all about Truman.

Moscow, *April 15, 1945*

Today for the first time I saw Marshal Tito in the Yugoslav Embassy, which has been awarded to this movement by the Russians. He is a stocky man of medium height and rather good-looking, with blue eyes and a resemblance to Goering. He was wearing the marshal's uniform the Russians had flown in to him last year. He was very friendly. Although we had a long conversation, there remained much ground to be covered, and he asked me to come and see him in Yugoslavia. He told me he knew I had been trying to get there during his campaigns but was blocked by the British.

Tito wants southern Carinthia, including Klagenfurt, to which he refers as a Slovene city; all of Istria, including Fiume; all of Corizia, including Trieste. I doubt if Macedonia will be an issue for some weeks anyway; maybe not until they get Greece ripe for trouble. I asked him if now that he has his treaty with the USSR he wanted to sign pacts with all or any of his neighbors. Not at this time, he said.

He had asked for—and obviously was positive of receiving—permission to hold a military zone of occupation in Germany. He specifically used the word Germany (Nemachka) rather than Austria, but I am confident he was referring to Carinthia.

Moscow, *April 16, 1945*

ATTENDED Tito's reception yesterday evening. Everyone drinking heavily. Tito invited me to down a few vodkas with him and Marshal Budenny, a squat figure who was pouring it between his handlebar mustachios.

Tito introduced me to Milovan Djilas, the tough, moody Montenegrin who has attracted Stalin's affection by his reputation as a guerrilla and his ability to recite poetry. Djilas looked at me stonily, said: "Ah, you are the American who writes that our Tito is slaughtering Serbian peasants with American rifles." He turned his back. Tito chuckled, pounded me between the shoulders and said: "Don't pay any attention to him."

Moscow, *April 17, 1945*

PAT Hurley, on his way to China as our Ambassador, saw Stalin from 10:00 P.M. until after midnight last night. Hurley was asking Soviet cooperation in resolving Chinese differences. This evening he invited me for a drink. Leaning against the mantel, glass in hand, he said Stalin was in a receptive mood. Hurley claims he said Stalin had an unfair advantage, because Communist cells are allowed to operate in America but no democratic cells are allowed to operate here. He thought freedom was a logical necessary development of history and that any progressive country would face that fact. Stalin disagreed. Hurley replied that after all Stalin could only judge by Russia and Russians. Stalin laughed. Hurley curiously maintains that he had far less difficulty selling the idea of a free and united China to Stalin than to Churchill. "I had no trouble with Stalin," he boasted. "He played ball." Personally, *I* would trust Churchill.

Moscow, *May 1, 1945*

THE May Day parade in Red Square was massive; but despite the excitement on the eve of victory, the usual strict guards were out, and nobody was admitted without a permit. The people couldn't see their own parade. I saw old Litvinov standing below the diplomatic bleachers. I asked him why he wasn't allotted a seat. "I was," he said dourly. "But I prefer it down here with the masses." He never once looked up at Stalin and his lieutenants standing atop Lenin's tomb. He just stared out at the low rows of cannon and marching troops.

LONDON, *May 14, 1945*

I WAS in Moscow during the rather incredible celebrations of V-E Day. The Soviet radio announced the German armistice only when it was official and had been signed by their military delegate. When it became known in Moscow, people began to pour out of their homes in all kinds of costume from pajamas to fur coats to rags. They came out by the thousands. There was a good-sized crowd in front of the British Embassy, but the assemblage before the American Embassy was enormous. This may be because our embassy is right off Red Square and the Kremlin, or it may be because we are emotionally far more popular than the British. At any rate, the Moscow authorities kept sending out new squads of NKVD police. But the crowd was too massive for them. It is the only demonstration I have ever seen in Russia which was so huge that the police didn't matter. By the time a hundred new policemen showed up, there were five thousand more people. They pushed and swayed in all directions, demonstrating sheer joy. I doubt if America has ever been applauded with such tremendous enthusiasm in Russia before. I came out of the embassy shortly after George Kennan, chargé d'affaires, made a speech in Russian to the crowd. I was picked up by hundreds of jovial and sympathetic hands and tossed and carried around until I could shake myself loose.

It was hours before the police could restore order and drive the poor Russians back into their groove. But it was done; the machine began to grind again.

I left on General Hap Arnold's private plane, which had come on a special shuttle mission to Moscow. We were supposed to fly to Scotland by a devious route via the Mediterranean. However, thank God, we had no Russian navigator aboard. We went up high, and then our skipper said the hell with it and set a path straight across the southern Baltic and northern Germany, and we made a nonstop flight to Prestwick, disregarding all Russian threats. At Prestwick I was able to bum a ride on a British plane down to London.

LONDON, *May 16, 1945*

IN the first dispatch of my Russian series I said the USSR would attack Japan in about ninety days from V-E Day. The admiral in charge of British censorship, Thompson, called up and asked if I was sure of my facts. I said I was but had written it "on my own" so it could look speculative. He passed it. But a stupid editor, although it was passed by the chief theater censor personally, resubmitted the dispatch to Washington under United States voluntary censorship (which doesn't apply to material already approved abroad). As a result, it was killed.

LONDON, *July 27, 1945*

THIS is the day after the British election in which Labor gave Churchill a terrible drubbing. I went to see King Peter in his modest two-room suite at Claridge's.

He received me in his bedroom. Queen Alexandra was sitting up in bed in a bed jacket and their ten-day-old son was lying in a basket covered with silk beside the bed. Princess Aspasia, Alexandra's mother, kept popping in and minding other people's business. She did, however, succeed in obtaining some liquor from what she called "the wine cellar"—a closet in which Peter had a few bottles stored away. She kept telling me and Peter that she hoped to have a great deal of influence on Peter when he got his throne back. Peter told me that he had to play his hand very cautiously now, but that he still felt that his people would back him if they were given free expression and that he hoped that the Allies would stay by his pledge of this. He told me that President Truman had sent him a letter three days previously promising that he would do his best to see to it that full liberty prevailed in Jugoslavia.

I saw King George of Greece at 3:30 P.M. He seems to be doing rather better than Peter, but, after all, he has been a refugee before. He has a big comfortable office suite in Claridge's.

George was friendly as always and full of gossip. If he were not a king, he would be the kind of fellow people call upon at the last minute to fill up a dinner party or a celebrated gossip columnist in the American press.

He was convinced neither his position nor his plans had been changed by the British elections, that Stalin spoke perfect French(!), that he, George, was constantly being visited by Communist agents, that American businessmen were vitally interested in developing chromium and lead mines in Greece. Every time I talk to him, he impresses me as an amiable idiot without any feelings for Greece, its people or for politics. He seems to think of Greece as of a potential area for exploitation by J. P. Morgan & Company. George is obviously determined to get to Greece at the earliest moment.

PARIS, *August 24, 1945*

GERTRUDE Stein kindly invited me to tea: a fat, most amiable old woman who lives in a strange combination of sloppy comfort and a modern art museum with her friend, the cozy, hideous Alice Toklas. Stein is writing a new novel, *Brewsie and Willie*, about GIs and how they worry and how she worries about them and how they worry together about their worrying:

"Are we isolationists or are we isolated is what I want to know," she said, munching excellent cookies. She went on:

I am worried. And the GI is terribly worried. He is quite as worried as I am. We are quite worried together. I am worried as they are worried and they are worried as I am worried. I am trying to get our worries down in my new novel. It is written simply as those boys talk. I know them well and what goes on in their minds.

I am completely drowned in the American army and I eat, think and sleep GI so my French friends are disgusted with me. I am almost the only American woman in civilian clothes these boys see and I am an older woman and many of them talk to me as if I were their mother. I pick them up in the street and bring them home to talk.

The GIs are worried. Their minds are being deadened. They lack spiritual courage. They lack interest in home politics except locally. They don't believe anything is true. It is kind of a dark picture. Compared to Europeans they don't take any active interest in things. They have a leadership complex. I say to them: "Can any of you lead yourselves? Do you all have to be told?"

PARIS, *August 30, 1945*

SAW Léon Blum. He says de Gaulle will be the next Prime Minister but after that temporary government, he doesn't know what will happen.

He denied that he had committed himself not to accept the premiership if the Socialists win the elections. He would take it but would prefer not to, since he wants to retire. Says he is tired.

LONDON, *September 18, 1945*

MOLOTOV said today (in an interview at the Soviet Embassy): "We feel, and we have sufficient grounds for this, that in Rumania, Bulgaria and Hungary there exist democratic governments enjoying the confidence of an overwhelming majority of the people of these countries. We feel that it is a great merit of these governments that they have established order and tranquillity, which did not exist in those countries before these governments were set up. You, as well as I, know well that not everybody is pleased with the existing governments of Bulgaria and Rumania, but I don't think that there are any governments with which everybody is pleased."

LONDON, *October 6, 1945*

AZZAM Bey (Abdul Rahman Azzam), Secretary General of the Arab League and old personal friend, called me around today and explained that to his regret he couldn't go through with the scheme he'd cooked up with Weizmann and in which I was middleman. Both men knew I was a friend of the other. After various conversations the Zionist leader and the Arab leader agreed it might be useful if they could meet (they never have) and consult in secrecy. I offered them my house in Barton Street. Guaranteed to get everybody there even including our housekeeper out on any day if they gave me advance notice. I would give each of them a key and they could just go in and meet in an empty house.

They were both intrigued. But Azzam told me he had had second thoughts. "I am followed by the British," he said, "and I assume Weizmann is also. If anyone sees me going into your house—and then Weizmann—they can ruin me. One picture of such an event and I could be blackmailed out of all influence. I am sorry but you can see the point, my friend."

Too bad. It might have been useful. I see no way of avoiding the Palestine storm.

LONDON, *October 24, 1945*

ATTENDED the baptism of Alexander, Crown Prince of Jugoslavia, in Westminster Abbey. Certainly the only time the old Slavonic of clerical Serbia has echoed through the Abbey. The Patriarch of Jugoslavia officiated together with the Archbishop of Canterbury. George VI, King of England, carried the baby three times around the baptismal font while the Patriarch was tossing incense merrily around. Alexander howled like a stuck pig when he was dipped in a basin of cold water. The King looked exceedingly embarrassed and held the baby as if it were a hot egg.

"Doth thou," the officiant asked the sponsor "renounce Satan and all his work and all his angels, and all adoration of him, and all his pomp?" The "officiant" was the Patriarch. The "sponsor" was George VI. When the officiant instructed King George: "Blow and spit at him," Alexander squealed. The Patriarch was allowed in England for only two weeks and was told that if he overstayed his visa he might be subject to a labor draft.

OSLO, *November 15, 1945*

SPENT an hour with King Haakon VII. His palace is well situated on a small hill, comfortable, electrically heated, ugly. It was built early this century. The atmosphere is quite informal.

Haakon is very lean and tall. He was dressed in an admiral's uniform, wearing two rows of ribbons. His office is cluttered with naval souvenirs like torpedo warheads, ship bookends, etc. His desk was a mess of newspapers, books, papers and dozens of family snapshots. He sat in an armchair and talked steadily for an hour. He waves his hands in a curious, loose way like flippers, and his body is very agitated while he talks.

He said he advised his government not to be irked about small nations not being invited to make international decisions: "I tell them it is just like in school and they shouldn't get complexes. In school the senior boys make all the decisions and then tell the younger boys. The younger boys may complain and they may have very sensible ideas, but the senior boys say it's too bad, all the decisions have been made and it will be done accordingly."

He criticized de Gaulle although recalling that he was the "only" Frenchman to resist. He said de Gaulle had a big-power complex but "we must say to him, show us if you are a big power, and he can't." De Gaulle should have tried to organize a bloc of small nations led by France and including Holland, Belgium, Denmark and "myself" and then insisted on speaking as a unit in international councils.

STOCKHOLM, *November 20, 1945*

THIS afternoon saw Count Folke Bernadotte, the King's cousin and president of the Swedish Red Cross and the Swedish-American Society: tall, distinguished but not handsome, ruddy face and graying hair. He is conceited and self-assured.

He said:

> There's no doubt such a thing as a war crime exists but it is wrong to try high officers such as Keitel and Kesselring merely for preparing their country as best possible for war. In a military job one must do as much as one can to build up one's forces. As for diplomats such as von Papen, they could be considered war criminals if it is proven they violated international law. If a diplomat follows instructions violating international law rather than risking his career to refuse to obey them he could be classified as a criminal. Similarly an officer might risk death in order to avoid violating the Hague conditions but it is sometimes difficult to know where the lines are drawn.

LONDON, *December 22, 1945*

DINED with Adlai Stevenson, his wife, Andrei Gromyko (Soviet Ambassador to Washington and delegate to the UNO Preparatory Commission here) and Wilder Foote, who works for Adlai. Marina sick in bed and couldn't come.

Stevenson is a most agreeable, talkative liberal; witty, amusing but rather weak. He doesn't lack for ambition and seems to be searching for some goal. Stevenson believes small nations in UNO are not eclipsed and have the opportunity of gaining enlightenment by their example to the big powers. He says UNO is of course predominantly a big-power organization because "this is a big-power world."

I suggested Berlin should be UNO's seat. "Why," asked Gromyko. "Because," I continued, "it is the best example of what happens without international order. You should build a round tower as headquarters and each floor should have a wide balcony all around it. Then, if there is any disagreement, the statesmen can adjourn their talks and go out and see what happens when statesmen disagree." Stevenson smiled. Gromyko grunted. No one thought I was serious. But I was.

PARIS, *January 5, 1946*

SAW Maurice Thorez this afternoon, a stocky, red-faced former miner who is now boss of the French Communist Party and Minister Without Portfolio in de Gaulle's Cabinet.

Thorez was very optimistic and thought the Communist Party next spring would have a majority to take over the government. As Premier he would complete the task of nationalization (at present only half done in banks, railways, and so on). He favored credits for the army. He is against all blocs. He would like UNO and alliances with each of the Big Three. France is a big power still but not in the grandiose way de Gaulle thinks.

PARIS, *January 9, 1946*

VISITED André Malraux, now de Gaulle's brilliant Minister of Information. He is extremely nervous, very thin, with dark shadows under his eyes and a long nose and face.

He is assertive and sure of his opinions. He told me he knew Tito in Spain. He said Tito operated under the name of "Antonio" and was political commissar to Division Commander Lukacs. Lukacs was a Hungarian who became a general in the Russian army. He said Tito had a good record, that he spoke Russian with Lukacs and that he knew Spanish. (I don't believe Tito was ever in Spain.)

He said Thorez had gone to Russia in 1939, through Switzerland, aided by the Germans. Thorez is a very brave, vigorous, religious Communist, as compared with Tito, who is a military Communist.

GSTAAD, *January 20, 1946*

LONG talk in his chalet with the exiled Belgian King Leopold, a rather handsome, weak-faced man with blond-brown hair and slightly watery eyes. His wife is extremely pretty. Leopold speaks excellent English, but complains he is out of practice. He was wearing checked sports jacket, red necktie, ski pants and ski boots. Leopold said:

I don't want to impose myself in any way or to go against the desires of the Belgian people. I wish to remain a constitutional monarch, faithful to the constitution and to my oath to respect the spirit of the constitution, which is democratic. The interests of the country naturally transcend my own. I am by right the King of the country and I shall abdicate only if I know that this is the wish of the majority of the people. So far there have been no indications that such is the wish of the majority.

But no government can compel my abdication—this can be done only by the people. Last July the government asked me to go. I refused. There must be a new law permitting a referendum or plebiscite and I will abide by its decision. There will be no hesitation. Furthermore, the question of my return has nothing to do with the type of political government Belgium would have. I have often heard reports that the King of the Belgians is no true democrat. I refuse to accept that.

ROME, *January 24, 1946*

TODAY I saw Premier Alcide De Gasperi, a rather strange looking man with thick lips, heavy spectacles, pleasant, grave demeanor. Devoutly religious, De Gasperi is especially close to the Vatican. He comes from the North and before World War I was in the Austrian Parliament under the old empire.

He said: "No democratic government signing away Trieste could last and a resurgence of the worst form of nationalism would be inevitable." But he was ready to cede the Dodecanese and hoped, as a result, to restore good relations with Greece. He foresaw an Austrian demand for the Alto Adige but feels especially strong against any cession there because of his birthplace, Trento.

Rather to my surprise, De Gasperi made a strong plea for the Italian colonies. He said:

Either these are to be taken away for punitive reasons—and it has been said that the Allies do not wish a punitive peace—or our contribution must be recognized. We appeal to the United Nations Organization to study our pre-Fascist contributions in North Africa. We gave a constitution to Libya before Mussolini.

One should not question our morality or our capacity to govern. We would like a UNO commission to go to Libya and judge our work. We sent Venetian peasants to Cyreniaca to win back the desert. Mussolini pulled them out during the war and, when the Italians withdrew, the desert returned. The natives have demonstrated that they cannot cultivate the land. I want to rebuild ancient Africa, which requires people who wish to emigrate, and there are no others. Even Tunisia is full of Italians.

ROME, *January 26, 1946*

THIS noon I had a long talk with Prince Umberto, Lieutenant General of the Realm. Umberto told me that should the Italian people vote to retain the monarchy, it is understood he wishes to remain above politics and is equally willing to reign without political interference over any government of any political complexion, Communist, Socialist, liberal or conservative. If they vote for a republic, he will be quite happy to abide by any such decision. Like Leopold; the time for royal arrogance is past.

MADRID, *February 19, 1946*

TODAY I lunched with a thirty-three-year-old man who operates under the name of Felipe and who is chief of the propaganda section in Spain for the clandestine Communist Party. He is a well-dressed, prosperous-looking youth with glasses and a small mustache. He studied at medical school for two years until the Civil War came, when he was mobilized into the Republican army. He was a member of the Socialist Youth, which united with the Communist Youth. He became a Communist. He rose to battalion political commissar. After the war he fled to France and traveled around South America before he secretly came back to Spain. His family does not know he is here.

We ate in a restaurant opposite the main bull ring. Establishing contact was rather Hollywood. I had had a letter (from France) which I had delivered to someone in Madrid. I was advised yesterday to be in front of my hotel at 11:00 A.M. A respectable middle-aged man came by for me in a taxi and chatted about trivia in French as we drove along. He left me at a street corner, and a girl picked me up there and took me in a bus to another district of the capital. There I was picked up by another man in a taxi, who delivered me to the bull ring restaurant where Felipe introduced himself. All to avoid the police.

Felipe explained in excellent French that the party's Central Committee (of which Dolores Ibaruri, *La Pasionaria*, is the chief) had a three-man delegation in the underground here. All are less than thirty-four years old. Felipe is the member of the trio in charge of agitation and propaganda. He says the party has an active membership of about 25,000; 3,500 in Madrid.

The Communists have a very small quantity of arms. That is their biggest weakness. "But we are going to solve this problem" and bring them in, presumably from France. There are between nine thousand and twelve thousand guerrillas of all sorts in Spain today. The majority are Communists or under their influence.

The Big Three of the party in Spain are known to party members as the *"Delegacion."* The party runs things from Toulouse, which they regard as the acting capital of Spain.

Should Franco make a deal and quietly hand over the government to Don Juan, the Communists will take no precipitate action. First they wish to study the objectives and program of the new outfit. They have nothing either for or against Don Juan as an individual. However, in April 1931, the Spanish people made clear their views on the monarchic question. Therefore it is evident the CP is flatly against a monarchy as such. Nevertheless it is ready to negotiate with monarchists and all groups opposing Franco. However, the party will not accept a plebiscite except after Franco's disappearance and the establishment of representative provisional government.

Asked if Moscow or Madrid came first Felipe said: "I am first a Spaniard—above everything. I want to defend my fatherland but I do not wish an aggressive fatherland."

Despite its weakness he says the CP is the strongest opposition party.

"It is the center of anti-fascist activity. The longer Franco stays in now, the better, because the Communists are skillful at organizing underground while none of the other opposition parties are. So the Communists will eat up the rest."

MADRID, *February 20, 1946*

TODAY I saw Franco: a small, dainty, fat little man with natty uniform, big red sash, good boots. He is very neat, has a plump, weak olive face and a rather youthful, slightly pathetic smile. He looks as little like a dictator as did Metaxas. The Generalissimo talked earnestly and at length, continually emphasizing points with his nervous, small hands. He said, "When the Spanish people are consulted on their future form of government, I believe they will accept the monarchical method which they recognize as more stable than the republican. Of course, when the time for such a decision comes, the Spanish people can have another type of republic different from previous ones, if they so choose. However, I am a monarchist. The traditional methods of Spain are monarchic. A modern form of monarchy could achieve the methods of a presidential regime and still conserve the advantages of stability."

Admitting that his own government could be regarded as "transitional," he would give no clue as to when such a "transitional" period would terminate. He said that must depend entirely on the course of events. Speaking of that unknown day when he would complete his functions as chief of state, the Caudillo said: "That will be my happiest day—when I no longer need worry about the problems or future of my country."

I asked if he believed in the principles voiced in the Atlantic Charter and if so, whether they shouldn't be applied in Spain. He replied:

Yes, the principles are sound. My aim is to apply them basically as far as possible. But these principles must truly be practiced everywhere. I understand that some nations have complained they aren't being practiced towards them.

I reemphasize Spain's peacefulness. We have remained out of the last two world wars and we don't wish to increase our territory. We can only hope that others will learn this lesson. And as far as the Atlantic Charter goes, internally the people must take care to distinguish real democracy from false democracy and not to permit loose governmental fabric which allows the Trojan horse of communism to enter. We have had a sad experience in the past and we know what communism is and that we must prevent it.

You must realize that following our Civil War—which ended seven years ago—it is difficult to restore all the liberties as may be done in other lands which have not had civil wars of their own. We certainly don't want to give permission for parties to work openly for another Civil War. This is a delicate situation.

MADRID, *February 23, 1946*

I GOT ahold of the catechism used in most Spanish schools today, the seventeenth edition of *Nuevo Ripalda* as published in Barcelona this year by Editorial José Vilamala. Among other things little children are forced to learn is that principal errors condemned by the church are, in this order—naturalism, Darwinism, atheism, pantheism, deism, rationalism, Protestantism, socialism, communism, syndicalism, liberalism, modernism, masonry.

That catechism favors censorship and says it is a grievous sin to subscribe to "liberal" newspapers. Nevertheless, a note in the text specifically states that there can be a reason for reading part of a liberal newspaper: for example, the stock exchange reports—an odd aspect to the religious instruction of young Spaniards.

NUREMBERG, *March 6, 1946*

HAVE attended a couple of sessions of the War Crimes trial. The first session was a strange experience. My seat was up in front of the courtroom, and as I walked down the corridor, the prisoners filed in on the other side of the barrier, accompanied by their guards. Von Papen happened to be just across the low wooden barrier from me—only a few feet away. We nodded, as if to say, let's have a chat as soon as we've shaken hands with the hostess. Then he turned left to sit down, adjust his earphones. I turned right.

LONDON, *April 23, 1946*

TODAY, Foreign Minister Bevin told me he hoped India would remain in the British Commonwealth as a free member for the sake of its security and to avoid civil war. Civil war in India could start a world conflict.

Bevin said Russian policy toward China in Manchuria was a great mistake and might push China and Japan to unite as a huge Asiatic power.

He does not want a quick settlement of European peace so much as a just settlement and is prepared to see some form of *modus vivendi* in Italy and the Danubian countries rather than an unfair peace.

PARIS, *May 7, 1946*

SAW Bedell Smith, new Ambassador to Moscow. Smith asked Stalin how much further does Russia intend to expand her frontiers. Stalin replied "only a little further." He refused to elucidate.

Smith considers Molotov the most irritating man in the world. He says at least Vyshinsky is human and shows his emotions. It is Smith's guess that when Stalin dies, the likely order of succession would be: Zhdanov, Andreiev, Malenkov.

TRIESTE, July 11, 1946

RIOTS and shooting every day, Slavs against Italians. Just before lunch the sky is so filled with bricks and stones that it looks like the Battle of Crécy. Then time off for pasta and a long siesta.

The Mayor is an amiable, paunchy individual. He perspires as he eats fresh-caught scampi from the Adriatic. Outside there is no longer any noise because the rioters have returned to their homes for lunch. The Mayor says: "It is terrible. I am perfectly certain terrible things are going to happen." His wife adds: "But not until late this afternoon. Now they must take their siesta."

PARIS, August 11, 1946

GEORGE Andreichin invited me for dinner with Vassili Kolarov, Bulgarian Prime Minister and former head of the Comintern, a tough, squat little man. George, who is Trotsky's former secretary and spent years in a Soviet jail, was also once the adopted son of King Ferdinand.

To lighten things up, George told Kolarov I had just come back from Greece where my son was born. "What did you name him?" asked Kolarov. "Basil the Bulgar Slayer," said I (Basil being the famous Greek Emperor and savior of Constantinople). George roared with laughter. Kolarov was furious.

Next day George sent me a huge box filled with various kinds of Bulgarian cigarettes.

BELGRADE, October 14, 1946

IN the spring of 1945 Tito had promised to see me, and when I got to Belgrade I sent word that I was here. Despite the horrible relations between our countries he agreed to receive me.

He saw me in his villa, and when I was taken into his office, not a very large room, he was wearing his full marshal's uniform, including black boots and all. He greeted me coldly, and reminded me that it was only because he was a man of his word and also because he knew that I was an old friend of Jugoslavia that he made an exception. He waved me to a chair and started walking ponderously up and down, up and down, delivering himself as he did so of a tirade against the United States.

However, I had a friend in the room, Tiger, his large old German shepherd dog. Tiger was an SS dog captured by the Partisans during the war and retrained as Tito's personal pet. He was lying sprawled out on the

rug in front of his master's desk, and his liver clearly wasn't functioning;
or perhaps he was simply very old. At any rate, as the dictator strutted
about expostulating, Tiger lay there farting loud and clear. I couldn't help
grinning. Tito looked at me shrewdly a moment, his light blue eyes gleaming. Then, without a word, he walked to the desk, pushed a button. A
moment later, in came a tray with glasses and *šlivovica*. Still without a
word, Tito poured out glasses. Then he suddenly smiled, lifted his hand in
a toast, and the storm vanished. We had an agreeable and interesting talk.
Here are some excerpts:

> We will never collectivize. Our farmers have a cooperative system.
> The Communist Party is the leader of the National Front, which it con-
> stituted and created. Other parties were taken in. Although not listed, it is in
> the National Front. It is unnecessary to list it with the other parties of the
> Front. I want to add the following. The National Front was not created by
> formal agreement between parties as in other countries. In our case it was
> created during the war. During the fight against the enemy the Communist
> Party proclaimed the Front to all honest citizens without respect to their
> parties.
> I know that there is an opposition and that it often employs illegal meth-
> ods. I know it will never become stronger—only weaker. We do not envisage
> any change in our attitude towards the opposition or any change in our
> measures against it because we know their methods are discredited before
> the masses of the people.

I inquired: "What is the origin of your name, 'Tito'?"
Answer: "This is not a *nom de guerre*. I took it before the war as my
illegal name in party work. It is just an ordinary Croatian name. I have
had other names such as Rudi and Georgi."

KOZANI, GREECE, *October 21, 1946*

AFTER completing my dispatches from Belgrade I got the jeep overhauled
for roads ahead and took off. I had been summoned by the chief spook at
the British Embassy and warned there were rumors an attempt would be
made to assassinate me in the mountain passes to the south where there
are said to be Cetnik bands still wandering (anti-Tito) so that a plot could
be camouflaged. I paid no attention save to borrow a Colt forty-five revolver from the American military attaché. This would be of no use except
to protect the jeep. (I have a few gold coins such as I always carry in the
Balkans; for it is the only currency the peasants value.) Also obtained
through Tito's office a permit to cross into Greece via the Monastir Gap
(Bitolj-Florina), which is a forbidden area.
Half-way through no-man's-land we saw little figures ahead disappear-
ing into what later turned out to be slit trenches and dugouts. They must
have imagined a jeep, with windshield down (against mine fragmentation), the forerunner of some attack. There were a couple of warning

shouts and I halted. We sat there with our hands up. A patrol slunk furtively toward us, covering each other, until they got near enough for me to shout "*Demisiographos Amerikanos*." There were hollers of joy, and about ten of them clambered aboard the poor jeep, patting us on the back, grinning, waving their Sten guns. We lumbered on into Greece.

We spent the night in Florina and then set off for Kozani despite warnings from the garrison commander that we should wait for the next armed convoy (in two days) because most of the area was uncertain, at best, or in the hands of Communist "bandits." Now we are in Kozani and stuck for an indeterminate period because the commanding general simply won't let us go on. "For our sake," he says.

ATHENS, *October 26, 1946*

TODAY I had a long talk with King George. It was the first time I have seen him since his return to Greece. He is kind of fidgety and asked me to come in the back door of the palace on Theohari Street, from which I was smuggled into his office in front. He was sitting alone looking rather insignificant in his study. A fire was going.

He is obviously very lonely and extremely uncertain as to what he should do or what is going to happen in his country. As usual he is full of all sorts of rumors about what the Russians are up to—some of them correct and some of them obviously false. He is convinced the Jugoslavs are training left-wing Greeks and Slavs from Greece and slipping them across the border. He says the Yugoslavs are now sending in arms. This is done by a special Russian outfit working in Jugoslavia and Albania, where there are two Russian brigades and considerable Russian equipment.

ATHENS, *October 28, 1946*

HAVE been staying with the family in Marina's little house in Maroussi. Marina and Nursie are quite unconcerned about the chaos. Yesterday when I drove home from Athens I had to take the back road. Alexis (my brother-in-law) called and said lots of shooting was going on in front of the house near the main road. But all was quiet when I got there.

Big tragedy today. The damned jeep, having been brought all the way from Rome through Jugoslav anarchy and a Greek civil war, was stolen. We parked it just by the British Embassy, where there are both soldiers and armed police. Furthermore, had a thick, heavy chain and padlock around the wheel and removed the distributor cap. Nevertheless, when we went for it, it was gone. Not even a grease spot.

DHAHRAN, SAUDI ARABIA, *November 30, 1946*

MODERNIZATION is retarded by the strictly conservative and fundamentalist religious traditions of Saudi Arabia. Its Wahhabi dynasty frowns on smoking, drinking and other modern fads. The religious courts of the Koran are still *the* law. Thus, for example, when Ibn Saud wished to lay a telephone line from Mecca to Jidda he met strong objections among the old judges of the Ulema (religious courts).

It was only when the old King commanded a chapter of the Koran to be read over the new-fangled instrument that his religious counselors saw its value and withdrew their objections. Ignorance is still rife and perhaps 95 percent of his subjects are illiterate; the social system is strictly feudal. In many regions the arrival of the airplane predated the arrival of the wheel.

The rigorous penalties of Saudi Arabian law appear crude. Adultresses are stoned to death. Thieves have their hands chopped off and the stumps plunged into burning oil, which serves as an effective cauterizer. Yet Arabs are horrified at the idea of imprisoning thieves for years; they consider their own punishment code more humane. Furthermore, they point out that its harshness is required by the geographical situation. A vast desert land cannot be filled with police.

Aramco doctors have obtained permission from the Emir of Al Hasa to slightly humanize the system of amputation for thievery. Now the cleaver used in the region is kept in a sterilizer in an American hospital at Dhahran. When Saudi Arabian officials send for it, the doctors know what's going to happen. A medic goes along and, before the victim is punished, the doctor injects an anesthetic. After the amputation, instead of cauterization in boiling oil, the culprit is taken to the American hospital, where the wound is treated and sewn up.

If oil drills get stuck some four thousand feet below the earth, the Moslem crew, which may often include liberated black slaves from Oman, usually concludes that a *Djinn* has clutched the tool and *Mashallah*, praise God, it will be released—as eventually it is. What did, however, astonish the wary *bedou* was the miracle of chicken incubators.

JIDDA, *December 2, 1946*

I SPENT the day with King Abdul Aziz Ibn Abdur Rahman Al Feisal Al Saud of Saudi Arabia. Early this morning I drove with the Syrian who is Foreign Minister in Jidda (Mecca is the King's capital) to the white pillar marking the frontier of Mecca—beyond which the non-Moslem is not permitted to pass. Then we got out of the car at Shumaisi, which is a small stop-off beside the Hudaybiya mosque on the road from Jidda to Mecca. It was at the Hudaybiya mosque that the Prophet Mohammed signed his first treaty with the unbelievers. There is an ancient cemetery through which we walked, not even knowing we were strolling over graves because the

Wahhabi sect permits no effigies or images, and there were just some unmarked rocks atop the graves.

After realizing this was not where Ibn Saud proposed to set up a tent city to receive me, we went back a couple of miles to a resthouse on the pilgrimage route just a little outside Mecca, a place on the fringe of a green oasis near Wadi Fatima, named for the Prophet's daughter. Some tents had already been erected by the time we got there, although it was still early morning. They were filled with comfortable chairs and luxurious Oriental carpets. New tents were constantly being put up, and furniture was being unloaded from trucks driven from Mecca. There were several companies of soldiers in khaki, wearing green headcloths and drilling in anticipation of their sovereign. Servants and slaves were broiling large panniers of food on fires beyond the tents.

Ibn Saud drove up in a Mercedes Benz cabriolet, his favorite car. It was given to him by Adolf Hitler. The King of England gave him a Daimler, but he apparently feels more comfortable in the Mercedes. He moves with great difficulty nowadays and suffers from all kinds of illnesses which leave him stooped, halt and lame. Despite that, bent over as he is, he is still over six feet in height. They say he was six feet, six inches in his youth. He is a massive man, although now it is largely fat. He has one bad eye obscured by a cataract, and heavy, slightly Negroid features, a quiet, gentle voice and manner. He was wearing the plain brown robe with a slight golden edge that marks royalty in Saudi Arabia and a red headcloth with golden *igal.*

He was accompanied by a group of nobles, sheikhs, members of his court and beautifully garbed warriors from his bodyguard carrying rifles, pistols and gold and silver daggers and scimitars, wearing crimson, golden, blue and yellow robes. After his troops had saluted, Ibn Saud and his principal courtiers, including his brother, Prince Abdullah Ibn Abdur Rahman, congregated inside the royal tent. The King rested while a northern breeze began to ripple along the desert, curling the palm fronds in the oasis.

Jeeps and other vehicles protected by machine guns drew around the periphery of the encampment to protect the King. Ibn Saud joined his private imam and, facing Mecca, rendered his prayers, kneeling and bowing in the direction of the sacred Kaaba four times. Everybody else including the soldiers did the same. A signal was sent from the royal tent to my tent that the King would receive me. Seated in a large armchair and gazing rather blankly through his dark glasses, the King started a general discussion of world affairs. The basis for this had been prepared in a series of questions I had submitted from Jidda, the answers to which, written in a beautiful Arabic script, were given to me here. The interpreters sat on rugs at the foot of the King and translated.

Back in my tent, the court chamberlain informed me that Ibn Saud was awaiting me at dinner. I went to the banquet tent, where a long table had been set with European-style plates and silverware—as contrasted with the usual bowls of pilaff eaten with the hands according to the dictates of the Koran. Some thirty royal princes and sheikhs were present. It was a nine-course dinner during which the King spoke through an interpreter who stood behind him and translated his remarks and those of his brother, between the two of whom I sat. The interpreter was a large Negro slave who spoke with an English accent.

On the other side of the King was another huge Arab slave with Negroid features who broke morsels of food into small pieces and laid them on the King's plate. These he ate with his fingers—the only man present not to use a knife and fork. He explained that he was only "a simple Arab" and ate the way the Koran said he should. He had some difficulty because the middle finger of his right hand (the Arab never eats with his left hand, which is used for other purposes) had a knuckle swollen and broken decades ago by a Turkish bullet.

Conversation did not flow easily. The King made a few remarks such as that his land was barren of all but patriotism and religion. He remarked that the water which was served at the feast (mainly chicken preparations) was his favorite water; not only was it exceptionally fresh, but it came from the well where the Prophet had drunk.

While sharing with me his plate of sliced oranges from Taif, he spoke of his exploits when, with twenty warriors, he had descended from Kuwait to start his conquest of Arabia by capturing Riyadh in a surprise night raid in 1900. He recalled wounds, including that which has greatly weakened his leg, and pointed to the gnarled finger which had been cut by a Turkish bullet.

As a matter of fact, the Emir Bin Jiluwi told me a few days ago at Dammam the full story of that raid. Bin Jiluwi had been one of the handful of loyal followers exiled to Kuwait with the Saud family and who returned with Abdul Aziz to attack Riyadh. They climbed ladders over the walls of the city and crept over the housetops to overcome the sentries. According to Bin Jiluwi, Ibn Saud was dangerously wounded in a very personal portion of his anatomy. Old Bin Jiluwi said to his chief, "Ah, Abdul Aziz, you have gained a city, but you have lost something more precious." Ibn Saud, to prove that nothing important had happened to him, ordered one of his soldiers to bring a woman in the middle of the battle and proceeded to demonstrate that he was unimpaired.

At the end of dinner ewers of water were taken around the table, and everyone washed his hands. Ibn Saud then, leaning on his simple cane, limped to another tent, open to the desert on one side. Numerous little cups of coffee flavored with cardamum and poured from long-nosed brass pots were served. We sat on two chairs side by side. The interpreter squatted on a carpet before us. The bodyguards sat in a semicircle outside the one open wall of the tent. Their eyes and teeth and the damascened work on their weapons glistened brightly, reflecting the light of the lanterns. Occasionally a fox barked in the stillness.

Over the coffee Ibn Saud said he had great esteem for the late President Roosevelt. He was touched by the President's gift of a duplicate of his own wheelchair and then by the present of a luxurious airplane. When they had met in Cairo in 1945, they exchanged jokes about their infirmities. Ibn Saud indicated rather directly he did not admire President Truman because of his attitude on Palestine. He said, however, he would not accede to pressure from other Arab states and cancel his oil concessions to the United States. He feels he cannot break his pledged word, and anyway it would be ridiculous to boycott America, which is now only "three days" away by air.

The King has a very interesting way of talking in parables. He told me one he had related to Churchill when the Prime Minister had started to discuss Germany with Ibn Saud. This is the story:

> Once there was an old sheikh. A tiny serpent came to him and said, "There is a wolf hunting me and I crave protection." The sheikh put the serpent in his bosom, but the serpent said he did not feel safe there because the wolf might reach up and scratch him. Therefore he asked to be put in the sheikh's mouth, and the wolf went away. Then the serpent said to the sheikh, "Now I shall reward you for your kindness. I am going to bite you. But I shall offer you a choice as to whether I bite you in the tongue or on the palate." That is the way of an enemy. It is the way of Germany and one must take care.

Finally in the dark night after the audience concluded, I returned to my tent, and a group of attendants came through the door shortly afterwards bearing cushions covered with presents. These were a royal Saudi Arabian costume, a portrait of Ibn Saud with an Arab inscription, and a magnificent gold Swiss wristwatch with gold bracelet with the King's monogram on its face. They dressed me up in the costume and then, finally, my car was brought nearby, and we drove down the road from Mecca to Jidda. Foxes slipped across the desert stalking kangaroo rats in the moonlight, and occasional returning pilgrims wandered toward Jidda and Medina.

CAIRO, *December 4, 1946*

I GOT out of Saudi Arabia by signing on as navigator of one of King Ibn Saud's airplanes carrying pilgrims from Jidda to Beirut. The pilot was an American who spoke nothing except English. The copilot was an Arab who spoke a few words of Italian, having been trained to fly in Italy at the time of Mussolini's attempt to make headway in the Arab world. I was navigator on the basis of the fact that I spoke a few words of Italian and could translate between pilot and copilot. The plane was overloaded to an excessive degree, but the American pilot pointed out this happened every time. He was just about fed up. The King's few planes, used on this pilgrim run, are operated under the control of a colonel whose previous experience has been with the camel cavalry. He had noticed that although a truck filled with benches could hold perhaps twenty people, if you jammed everyone together standing up, it could hold perhaps fifty, and the truck would still operate. He figured aircraft function the same way.

Hell of a time taking off but finally got into the air. We had hardly gotten up a thousand feet when there was a terrific banging in the back of the bucket-seat DC-3. "They want to know where Mecca is," said the copilot. As navigator, I told them. More banging. The pilot asked me what was going on. I went back and found everybody praying toward Mecca, damn near upsetting the plane. I also noticed right after the prayer that some of the female pilgrims had hauled off their veils and were looking somewhat less Wahhabi now that they were getting away from puritanical influence and going back to the fleshpots of Beirut.

Last Saturday morning there was a public execution in the square near Jidda customs house. The victim was a man who had become drunk and run amok. Alcohol is prohibited in Saudi Arabia, and therefore the crime was double. The method of execution is simple. The man is stood up, bound, between two executioners. One jabs a knife into his side. As his reflexes make him bend over toward the side from which the pain is coming, the other executioner knocks off his head with a backhand scimitar blow.

There are plenty of odd contrasts in Jidda. A few miles from the Africans' mud huts you can see 1946 American automobiles belonging to wealthy sheikhs pulling in at tiny taverns where their owners gather for coffee or the high-priced deep-well water. Heavily veiled women patter down alleys with burdens on their heads and orange henna stains on their bare feet. Behind shuttered harems the less religious puff forbidden cigarettes. I remember going into the office of the Syrian Foreign Minister who handles Ibn Saud's contacts with diplomats. After we had gotten to know each other, one day he locked the door of his office and pulled open a drawer and offered me my choice of cigarettes—Camel, Chesterfield, or Lucky Strike. As we smoked, he took off his headdress and talked longingly of Damascus, which he had not seen in thirty years.

The slave trade continues in a dying trickle along the Persian Gulf. One day while I was fishing near Bahrein, a little slave vessel came in at Al Khobar, a Saudi Arabian village near the oil centers, filled with children bought or stolen from the Baluchi coast, who were being peddled. The boat found no customers, so it loaded with dates and water and took off. I saw a letter last week written by a sheikh asking the oil company to give jobs to two of his liberated slaves. He granted them freedom because it cost too much to feed them.

4

I SAW LÉON BLUM, PRIME MINISTER, THIS MORNING AT THE HOTEL Matignon. At the entrance to his office, he paused to look longingly out over the lovely garden of the Matignon saying it was a pity one had to work and could not just look at the garden. On his desk was a vase of roses with exceptionally long stems, and there were two pink azalea plants in his office, which is dominated by a huge tapestry.

The great thing that has occurred, Blum says, is the reestablishment of France's parliamentary tradition. Perhaps one hundred and fifty out of the more than six hundred deputies have previous parliamentary experience. Past governments were made up of coalitions, and when the majority parties had decided upon a policy, their deputies in the assembly more or less automatically voted to support them without much question. However, Blum's Cabinet represented a minority party. Every policy step had to be explained to the deputies and argued out. This brought a true resurgence of the best and most useful type of parliamentarianism. Parliament now stands upon its feet in the French political picture.

LONG talk with Chaim Weizmann, Zionist leader. He is most gloomy. He fears the return of six thousand English women and civilians from Palestine will spread anti-Semitism in the British Isles. He deplores the terrorists and says that while there are reasons to believe the Stern gang is made up of misguided idealists, there are many ordinary racketeers in the Irgun. He calls Ben Gurion "that damned fascist."

He thinks the position of the Jews in Palestine is worse than it has been at any time since World War I. He fears the terrorists may force an eventual conflict between the British and the Jews in Palestine and that it would lead to a situation similar to that of the war between the Romans and the Jews. At that time the Jews held out for three years against the Roman Empire, and the survivors shut themselves up in the fortress of Masada, where they fought for many months and finally slaughtered each other rather than surrender. He says that in the British Cabinet, Bevin is becoming increasingly anti-Semitic. He says there is a split in the Cabinet and Attlee is Bevin's man. He has not seen Churchill for months. He blames the government for an entire lack of policy and thinks that partition is inevitable but that Britain missed the opportunity to impose it. The Jews would have accepted it and he is sure Azzam Pasha would have counseled the Arabs to accept it. Now the situation has gone from bad to worse. He says that just at the time Lord Moyne was assassinated, the Conservatives, including Churchill and Moyne, were working out a sound plan for partition.

PARIS, *February 10, 1947*

THE five peace treaties were signed with Italy, Rumania, Hungary, Bulgaria and Finland. Signature was in the Salon de l'Horloge of the Quai d'Orsay on the table where the wounded Robespierre was stretched out before he was guillotined. There was strangely little joy either in the room or in Paris itself, which greeted the event with supreme indifference.

PARIS, *February 11, 1947*

THIS afternoon I saw Prime Minister Ramadier, a friendly, unassuming man, with a small pointed beard. Discussing the hostilities between French and Vietnam forces (of Ho Chi Minh) Ramadier said:

> The French government was the victim of an aggression. The December 19 attack was premeditated and prepared in advance. It was accompanied by the sudden massacre of French, Eurasians and Indochinese friends of France. Therefore, we cannot treat with Ho Chi Minh until we receive adequate guarantees that the terms will be respected. It would be difficult to undertake any serious negotiations under such conditions and until we have further information on developments within the country and within the Viet Minh. We have made all concessions possible. In the interim, while waiting we must continue our military efforts. These are now showing positive results.

MOSCOW, *March 5, 1947*

ARRIVED here today on Ernest Bevin's special train from London—a memorable trip. On the stretch through Poland the Poles put on a special restaurant car, and I was among those drafted to go and have dinner with Bevin and his Polish hosts (about twenty of us, all told) around an oval table in a very old-fashioned diner. It was an absolutely enormous meal, and there were endless quantities of Polish vodka. Bevin's doctor was sitting next to me and kept leaning forward and telling his corpulent patient, who has a bad heart, not to eat, not to drink. Bevin just grinned—and gulped. The doctor ended up by determinedly getting plastered.

Moscow, *March 17, 1947*

I WAS sitting quietly in the cold lobby on the mezzanine floor of the Moskva Hotel this morning when John Foster Dulles, the Republican adviser on Marshall's delegation, came along, nudged me and suggested we go for a walk. Out in the street he reached into his pocket and drew out a paper. It was marked "Secret." "Read this," he said, "and be sure to be careful when you return it to me. Give it back to me personally this evening." Later I read it: Marshall's instructions to the American delegation: how to behave, to beware of tapped telephones and devices in the walls, never to discuss important things except in the streets, walking around; not even in the embassy. I wrote a story on it and gave it back to Dulles, who was very pleased with his own indiscretion.

Moscow, *Early April 1947*

MOLOTOV gave a reception for the foreign ministers at the House of Soviet Aviation. I had a long argument with Vyshinsky, who started by saying he was glad to see me but that he still waited to read an article by me which was favorable to the Soviet Union. I replied that he had no need to worry about that whenever I was in Moscow because the censors took care of it. He said censors were there to help correspondents; to guide them toward the truth.

I said I preferred to agree with Pushkin, who wrote: *"Tsensura Dura"* (All censors are idiots). Vyshinsky said of course Pushkin was referring to the Czarist regime. I answered I accepted a literal interpretation of Pushkin's words; that all censors were idiots. I asked if he was a censor.

He replied angrily, his face flushing, that he had many functions in the Soviet government: that he was a member of the Supreme Soviet, was chief prosecutor of the state, was Deputy Foreign Minister, was an editor —and also a censor.

He said I should consider myself lucky that he was only my censor and not my prosecutor. I told him that it was rather easy for a prosecutor here to have a good record of convictions—when there were sufficient bayonets behind every prisoner. Stunned anger. But he started it.

MOSCOW, *April 25, 1947*

AFTER forty-five days of increasing stalemate, the Council of Foreign Ministers closed. There is no peace for Germany in sight, and relations are abrasive between Russia and the rest.

It was Boris Izakov's birthday, and Yuri Zhukov gave a party for him in his apartment. He invited me and anyone I wished to bring along. So I asked Elisabeth de Miribel, a handsome girl on the French delegation.

Elisabeth came around to my rooms while I finished typing. Then, well after midnight, we drove to Yuri's. There was a table heaped with food and drink and about sixteen shouting people around it, all plastered. They insisted we pay the "traditional" penalty for being late. Each of us was given a highball glass which was then carefully filled with vodka to the exact brim. We had to stand and lift the glass without spilling a drop, drink it all straight, then turn it upside down on the table. To my astonishment and much to the admiration of the Russians, Elisabeth accomplished this without blinking.

The dinner went on and on. Whenever a Russian passed out two others would pick him up like a log and dump him in the bedroom next door, where a stack had already been piled. Yuri made a long toast, saying there must be no war. I replied that if there was one, Boris, Yuri and I should look out for each other and families if we fell under the other's sway. We pledged this in another toast.

Elisabeth was taken home relatively early by a relatively sober Soviet diplomat. I stayed on to the end. A Russian drove me home, but it was by then daylight. When we got to the Bolshoi, across the square from my hotel, I hopped out. It seemed an excellent idea to get taken to the Lubyanka prison, about which I had heard so much. So I marched (tottered) up to a cop and, startling him, demanded that he arrest me and send me pronto to the Lubyanka. With friendly *politesse* and some amazement he summoned a companion, and the two of them delivered me to my suite.

WARSAW, *April 30, 1947*

WAS received by Jakob Berman, one of the top Polish Communist bosses. He said that although a disastrous depression will engulf the world within a relatively short time, it will not destroy the Western capitalist system. Capitalism and communism can survive side by side, at peace in this ideologically turbulent era.

I asked Berman whether Poland would be prepared to sign as strong an alliance with any Western country as it now has with the Soviet Union. He replied: "Yes, if they would guarantee our frontiers and the security of Poland. It is no secret that we are now carrying on just such negotiations with France."

PRAGUE, *May 4, 1947*

MET Premier Klement Gottwald, the stolid chief of the Communist Party. He said Czechoslovakia's system of bilateral alliances with Russia, Poland and Jugoslavia is aimed solely at a possible recurrence of German aggression and is open to Western nations willing to undertake similar obligations.

Gottwald insisted there was no reason why capitalism and communism should not live side by side in peace. However, he foresaw difficulties between Moscow and Washington as long as the German question remained open. He saw no logic for a "compromise ideology" combining various features of Marxism and capitalism, but he pointed out there were differences between the Communist-led states in Europe and Russia: "each country has its own traditions and requirements and one cannot impose the same system everywhere."

PRAGUE, *May 6, 1947*

LONG talk with President Beneš. He said Czechoslovakia was not interested in an alliance with France. The Czechoslovakian people remember Munich and what happened to their last alliance with France. If France's interests were with Czechoslovakia in another war, France would support Czechoslovakia whether there was an alliance or not. If France's interests were not with Czechoslovakia she would probably not help Czechoslovakia, regardless of any alliance. Actually, Beneš's views are not necessarily final, because Czechoslovak Communists are working hard for such an alliance.

PARIS, *May 30, 1947*

TODAY I had a long talk with de Gaulle, the first since the war. He received me in his small suite at the Hotel Lapérouse, not too far from the Etoile. He was very friendly and talked quite freely.

De Gaulle said:

I am convinced that it is necessary to re-create a Europe. If this is not done, the world will be divided into a rivalry between Russia and the United States. That would lead to war—a horrid war.

To re-create Europe the first condition is that France should be on her feet. France is a Western power, and Europe is a symbol of Western civilization. Europe, to be restored, must be built upon occidental civilization. Such a Europe would be an element of strength and equilibrium.

To rebuild such a Europe would be impossible without outside help which, practically speaking, must come from the United States. This American help should take the shape of a treaty and not a bargain. On the French side, the interest is in reconstruction. From the American side, the interest is in the reconstruction of an occidental France and by that I mean an occidental Europe.

I asked if political parties would be permitted if the RPF (his French Popular Rally) came to power. He replied: "Naturally in a democratic system, such as I favor, there will always be political parties, but what is wrong at present is that the parties have all the powers—executive, legislative, etc. As a result of party disputes, therefore, there is terrible confusion. The RPF is not interested in parties—only in men and in their policies. Naturally, we are willing to receive men from all parties."

I asked de Gaulle how he planned to come to power. Would he accept the prime ministry if Auriol offered it to him early in the winter? He replied: "I cannot forecast such things. That is a question of tactics. If events force such a choice, the Constitution will have to be amended." I said to de Gaulle that would take some time—a few weeks. He answered: "Some events such as those of 1940 show that a constitution can be changed quickly, even in one afternoon."

PARIS, *June 12, 1947*

LUNCHED again with Jacques Soustelle and Malraux. Malraux used to know Maxim Gorki, who was the only "mammoth" he ever knew besides de Gaulle, a heritage from man's ancient past. He said Gorki was a huge man, but had the teeth of a six-year-old child, small, white and evenly spaced. He was astonished when Gorki opened his mouth to laugh.

The one time he met Stalin was at Gorki's house. He said Stalin adores Shakespeare and never misses a performance. His other hobby is the dance —to watch other people dance. Stalin told him that the way he destroyed Trotsky was by making him write.

Malraux said Gorki paid a pension all his life to four old friends. One was a waiter in a café at Capri. Another was a Romanoff princess.

He said the greatest intellect of the revolution was Trotsky's.

WASHINGTON, *November 4, 1947*

SAW President Truman this morning. He seemed very sincere and quite self-confident. He asked me a lot of questions, but I tried to keep him answering rather than asking. He asked me if I would inform him directly of my impressions as I traveled around the world. I didn't commit myself, but I am no Presidential agent.

When I asked what his basic foreign policy was, Truman described it as: "Peace in the world. Anybody can have any government they want but no one has the right to impose their own form of government upon anyone else. We do not care if Russia wants a totalitarian state. But we do not think that Russia should be allowed to impose such a form of government upon anyone else—such as Poland for example."

What would his view be if public pressure at some future date should press for a meeting between him and Stalin. He replied: "Stalin can meet me right here. I won't go anywhere to see him. I told him at Potsdam I would like to see him here and if he wants to meet with me he knows where he can do it."

Truman said: "Stalin made a number of agreements with me at Potsdam in 1945. He was very amiable and very easy to deal with. The British were far more difficult to deal with. They would make an agreement with me one day and then, the next day, they would start arguing about it. But, since Potsdam, Stalin has broken every single one of these agreements. Maybe it's not his fault. After all, he is only secretary of the Politburo and has his troubles with the other thirteen members just the way I have my trouble here with my Cabinet and the Congress."

He said Henry Wallace, during the summer of 1946, just before he resigned, attempted to explain Russian policy by stating that the Russians feel national interests are more important than life itself; that the Russians are that way; that we must accept this as a condition in dealing with them.

Truman said he asked for Wallace's resignation right then and there. He said that this never came out and was still confidential, but that there were two witnesses to the event. He did not say who the witnesses were.

Truman considered the Russian system exactly like the Nazi system. He thought it did not require much of a change for a Nazi to become a Communist. That was the big problem in Germany, because German nationalists hoped to use Russia in a quest for German world domination.

He defended the Truman Doctrine very strongly. He said: "If Russia gets Greece and Turkey then they would get Italy and then France and the iron curtain would extend all the way to Western Ireland. In that event we would have to go home and prepare for war."

LONDON, *December 4, 1947*

I HAD a talk with Prime Minister Attlee this afternoon in the Cabinet room of Number 10 Downing Street. Attlee is a very small, rather withered man. His speech is sporadic. He halts, then blurts forth quick bursts of words. He thinks extremely rapidly. He is not impressive looking, but is unquestionably intelligent, and very sincere. He has extremely kind eyes in a worn and wrinkled face.

Attlee said that a socialist revolution had now begun in England. But he said there would always be two parties in England. There would be the Labor Party, and a Party of the Right. He did not think it would change its name from "Conservative" because "here in England we do not change names very often."

He believed the world tended to sell Great Britain short as a power and pointed out that not only is the British empire a possessor of the secret of atomic fission, but also influences the vast imperial importance of Africa. He felt that the United States tends to consider England either in terms of

George III or Victoria. "We have a different King George now," Attlee said, "and this is the Twentieth Century."

Attlee expressed the hope that when British recovery has been completed, socialist England, leading the socialist states of Western Europe, will serve as a bridge between capitalist America and Communist Russia. England has economic parallels with Russia and parallels of liberty and mutual conception of human rights with the United States. He hopes that some day England will be able to help bring the world together by exercising an economic influence upon the United States and a humanitarian influence upon Russia.

Attlee was very bitter about the American attitude on Palestine. Britain had been well on the way to establishing a satisfactory solution on a cantonal basis in Palestine last year when Truman made his speech demanding the immediate entry of some hundred thousand Jews. He said that now there was no question about any alternative to Britain's intention of withdrawing all troops next year. He feared considerable bloodshed and thought it would be very difficult to protect the Jewish colony living inside Arab states, such as the eighty thousand Jews in Iraq.

LONDON, *December 5, 1947*

THIS morning I saw Foreign Minister Bevin in the Foreign Office. He looked rather better than in Moscow: neatly dressed in a pin-striped dark blue suit. Throughout the conversation he kept his cigarette in the corner of his mouth, and the ash kept falling onto his vest. It did not seem to bother him.

He said there had been no discussion between Britain and the United States along the lines of what became the Marshall Plan before Secretary Marshall made his famous speech at Harvard. However, Bevin had been considering these matters for a long time and was delighted when he heard Marshall's words, and he felt that was the moment to act.

Bevin with great pride recalled that Britain had "stood like a rock" in 1940 and 1941. Britain must now, economically speaking, "stand like a rock."

ROME, *February 18, 1948*

I TALKED at length with Pope Pius XII this morning. He looked extremely fit and remarkably energetic for a man of his age. Although he is well over seventy he has delicate and extraordinarily youthful hands.

I asked him what would be the position of the Vatican if the Communists came to power in Italy. He thought if the Communists ever did come to power in Italy they would stay long in power, and he admitted quite frankly that the church was doing everything possible to prevent this. He spoke very enthusiastically about Archbishop Stepinac, who is in prison in Jugoslavia, and said he was a brave and dignified man. In Poland the persecution was not as severe yet as in Yugoslavia, but the Communists obviously were determined to destroy the church everywhere. Before the Revolution, although the Czars of Russia were by no means favorable to the Catholic church, they did permit the establishment of four Catholic bishops in Russia as well as various priests; but now there were only two or three priests in all of the Soviet Union.

I asked him why he believed that communism was so determined to stamp out the Catholic religion. He said this was because there could never be compromise between Catholicism and communism, between materialism and spiritualism. He greatly admired the way the United States was now battling against communism on a temporal basis.

I asked the Pope if it was possible for a good Catholic to be at the same time a Communist, having in mind certain French Communists who said they are believing Catholics. The Pope replied that it was absolutely impossible.

ROME, *February 19, 1948*

COUNT Sforza, the Foreign Minister, told me that if the Marshall Plan succeeds, the Soviet Union will some day regret its failure to participate in it and will recognize that decision as an error.

He added: "Proof that the Marshall Plan was really a great historical idea is given by this fact: in Europe now, amid the confusion of languages and ideas which characterizes the political atmosphere everywhere, the only way to determine what a man or a nation really stands for is to know whether he is for the Plan or against it."

MILAN, *April 17, 1948*

SINCE there is a real threat that in this election crisis the Communists may seek to cut Italy in two (across Tuscany and the Romagna) I am covering the North and leaving our bureau in Rome to cover the South and the government.

Today government officials here showed me what they claim is Communist Plan "K" for an uprising to start in three days. Having just blasted one fake document (Protocol "M"), how much faith should I place in this one?

The security authorities, however, believe that Tuesday the Communist Party will announce in its press—before the official election results have been made known—that a solid electoral victory has been obtained by the Communist-led Popular Democratic Front. The fundamental purpose of this tactic would be to denounce the final results tabulated in Rome— which will be known on Tuesday night and Wednesday—as fraudulent and "fixed."

About two dozen well-known Milanese political leaders and journalists have been privately advised by the police to seek refuge on Tuesday with Archbishop Cardinal Schuster, whose properties are believed to be safe from mob attack. Stiff orders have been given to the police and carabinieri and army to take the toughest action if necessary, and to shoot—even against women if trouble comes.

It is expected—if the Communists strike—that they will attempt to seize all trucks available to transport their goon squads. As a result, today the Falck industrial concern, one of the most important in Milan, sold all its trucks en bloc for fear they might be seized.

MILAN, *April 19, 1948*

ACHILLE Marazza, Under Secretary of the Interior, who has secret microphones planted at various Communist centers, told me that Communist Party leaders were having a conference in a room of the Milan Town Hall in order to discuss further plans. Among those present, he said, are: Longo, Pajetta, Montagnani (whose sister is married to Togliatti), Mazzali, Alberganti (a tough and battle-minded Communist labor leader) and Troilo. Marazza is the government's boss if military action is needed and the North is isolated from the South. He served drinks and chatted while from time to time, aides rushed in with typed reports from the bugged Communist strategy meeting.

Marazza said he thought that because of the strong government position now demonstrated, the Communists would not attempt to put through their "plan K," for forcible takeover of power. He said: "I believe the plan has been abandoned. We obtained a copy of the plan written in Serbo-Croatian when it was slipped to one of our counterespionage agents. It was a very logical plan, but the Communists must fully realize now that if they make any move they will face a most energetic opposition."

LONDON, *May 25, 1948*

TALK with Ernest Bevin. He said: "I can get along with the State Department but what can I do when that blessed President of yours and the State Department have different policies?"

In Palestine he had sought a plan calling for four cantons, two Jewish, two Arab, with a central administration in Jerusalem. Bevin wanted this tried for five years without definite commitment by either side and with the right of secession. But in the United States election campaign, Truman decided to issue a Palestine statement to forestall Dewey. The statement asked Britain to grant 100,000 extra immigration certificates to Jewish DPs.

Bevin said partition was won because America told China she wouldn't get a loan if she didn't vote for it in the UN. This was "thoroughly wrong." In the last days before the mandate ended, Bevin had sent in combat troops so as to clear the way for settlement along partition lines—that is to say he stopped the Jews in Jaffa—drove them out of Acre, and restored order in Jerusalem.

Zionists want to crush the Arabs, he said. Jews and Arabs can live together, but not Zionists and Arabs. He is convinced the Arabs would not have a chance under the Zionists. He sees the Zionists as Fascists or Communists ruling the Arabs.

PARIS, *June 1, 1948*

PRESIDENT Vincent Auriol told me in the Elysée that he was deeply concerned over the question of freedom in France and in Europe and for the peace of the world. In France freedom was threatened by the Communists, but he also spoke of de Gaulle, saying that he wished a type of authority that was incompatible with free institutions. Auriol felt obliged to steer between these two threats.

ROME, *June 10, 1948*

SAW Pope Pius XII this morning together with Myron Taylor, Presidential representative to the Holy See. The Pope looked weary. He expressed his usual concern over communism and showed great interest in the American elections.

Taylor has apparently been going around trying to get religious leaders together to work for peace. He says the Protestants in America and Belgium have been most uncooperative. Taylor said he saw Franco on instructions from the White House. He seems to think a lot of Franco and says we may need him "in the war" against Russia. Franco told him: "After all, I am the only man who really fought communism. I fought it and defeated it in my own country."

ATHENS, *June 12, 1948*

LUNCHED with King Paul and Queen Frederika. Should war ever come again, the King and Queen will remain in Greece no matter what happens. In case of occupation they will send their children abroad, but they will stay on. "We are sick of being treated like honorable refugees," the Queen said, referring to their Cairo experiences.

Paul said he had wished to return to Greece by parachute in 1943 and secured Churchill's agreement during the Cairo Conference at the end of that year. However, after his brother, King George, had agreed to the project, Churchill, who was then in England, reneged on his promise.

Frederika thinks that possibly the meeting at Teheran after the Cairo Conference changed Churchill's mind. At Teheran the decision was reached to support Tito in Jugoslavia.

The Queen also said there were two countries in the world where it is not necessary for any third country to have an intelligence service. One is Japan, where it is impossible to find out anything. The other is Greece, where it is impossible not to find out everything.

ATHENS, *June 16, 1948*

JUST completed a tour of forward headquarters lasting two days. Went up with General Van Fleet and General Yadzis, chief of the Greek general staff, in Van Fleet's plane. Yesterday morning, we flew to Janina. We were briefed by commanders of two Greek divisions. Two things struck me. The first was the GNA's (Greek National Army) difficulty because it cannot fight near the frontiers under orders of the government. If the rebels get up to the edge of the border, they can usually slip away. The GNA is often shelled from Albania, Jugoslavia, or Bulgaria, where guns support the rebels; but it cannot fire back. The other thing which strikes me is the position of the Americans. Actually, they appear to be in charge of operations although everyone pretends it isn't so.

ANKARA, *July 1, 1948*

TALK with President Ismet Inönü. His policy is not to give interviews. However, I hauled out my notebook and started taking notes. After a while he smiled and said: "I never give interviews—not even to my own cabinet ministers. But go ahead." And he patted me on the back.

He would very much like an alliance with the United States and is afraid that American interest in Turkey is not a permanent factor. That he cannot say publicly, though, for fear of disturbing people.

CAIRO, *July 15, 1948*

VERY long talk at Arab League headquarters this afternoon with my old friend Azzam Pasha (he has been promoted from Bey by Farouk). After about an hour his aide came in and whispered, somewhat nervous. Azzam grinned and whispered back. When the aide had left Azzam said: "He told me the Grand Mufti is waiting outside for me and is getting impatient. I told him to tell the Mufti I was busy—with an American Jew."

Azzam proposed a three-point formula for the establishment of a long-term truce in Palestine by placing the contested area within an international *cordon sanitaire*, and thereby "freezing" the situation in *statu quo* until the basis for a satisfactory permanent settlement can be obtained.

"My objective would be to let the people of Palestine live together for a while peacefully, totally disarmed and sealed off from the world. With no more arms to fight with, and with therefore an end to fears, a solution could eventually be arrived at by democratic methods even if it took many years."

TEL AVIV, *July 21, 1948*

THE provisional government of fledgling Israel will not accept any limitation on immigration but is prepared to take in "millions" of new citizens from among world Jews. This statement was made today by Prime Minister Ben Gurion. He received me in Israeli general headquarters, an area well guarded by roadblocks, sandbags and bronzed young men and women of the national army carrying Sten guns. He said:

The position of Arab refugees from Palestine would depend in the final settlement on the treatment meted out to Jewish populations in Arab lands.
Israel insists on its claim to the southerly desert area of Negeb and will not barter that area for any other piece of land.
Israel pledges guarantees to all inhabitants of freedom of religion, assembly, and so forth and those civil rights generally accepted by Western democracies.
The government is determined to put down any efforts by extremist minorities to grab power by a *coup d'etat*. It will insist by force that if and when a peace is signed and the frontiers for a new state are fixed, these borders will be respected.

TEL AVIV, *July 24, 1948*

A MOST extraordinary thing happened today. I was typing in our hotel room, and Alexis (my brother-in-law) was still in bed with the sheet wrapped around his head to keep out the light. A knock at the door and a message was handed to me: a name I didn't recognize. Downstairs were two handsome, tall young fellows in khaki shorts and light-colored shirts. They shook hands and suggested we go out for a coffee because they had something to say. It turned out they were South African Jews who had come here since the war and were not only ardent Zionists but members of the Stern Gang. They told me not to bother remembering their names (including the one on the message) because the names were phony.

They discussed the aims of the Sternists and, among other things, horrified me by warning that the organization intended to assassinate Count Bernadotte and other advisers on the UN mission just the way Sternists had murdered (my word, not theirs) Lord Moyne because it was necessary to frustrate the UN effort to confine Israel within artificially constricted borders. At first I couldn't believe them. When I was convinced I took them upstairs, awakened Alexis and, as I pulled him up by the hair, said: "This is my brother-in-law. He works for UN and I don't want him murdered by mistake; he's not important enough for any deliberate murdering. Remember this face." Alexis looked bewildered. My visitors nodded amiably and departed.

I suggested he tell the UN people, and I intended to pass it on to Reuven Zaslani (later Shiloah), Ben Gurion's high muckamuck in secret service and dirty tricks.

ATHENS, *July 27, 1948*

LONG cozy chat and drinks with King Paul today in the air-conditioned little study of his Athens palace, sitting face to face in the armchairs beside the fireplace. What he told me—and authorized me to write as an interview—is bound to create a commotion and, above all, a lot of trouble with the British. He suggested that if Cyprus, now a British crown colony, were united with Greece—that is to say, given to Greece by Britain—this country would offer the British rights to establish military bases in Crete or elsewhere, in exchange. The news that the King has asked for Cyprus is bound to inflame both the Cypriots and mainland Greeks.

PARIS, *October 5, 1948*

LUNCHED with Trygve Lie, UN Secretary General. He impresses me as being anti-British. Also, in contrast with the last time I saw him, when he was still Foreign Minister of Norway, he has become rather anti-Russian. Lie said that there is no longer any debate about putting UN headquarters in New York. The foundations are under way.

PARIS, *October 11, 1948*

LUNCHED with Foster Dulles, Republican member of Secretary Marshall's delegation to the UN Assembly. He will almost certainly be Secretary of State if Dewey is elected President—which appears probable.

I asked point-blank if Dulles would be Secretary of State. He said: "I haven't yet decided. Nothing has been formally fixed." He was not certain whether he wanted the job. He might prefer a position like Harry Hopkins, under Roosevelt, or Colonel House under Wilson who had "much more fun." Dulles complained the Secretary of State is too tied up with political maneuvers and party obligations.

PARIS, *October 15, 1948*

HECTOR McNeil, British Minister of State, dined at the house last night. He was indiscreet enough to indicate that one of his jobs is to serve as liaison between the Cabinet and British Intelligence. We were talking about Intelligence and he said: "I ought to know about it, it is my job."

Later on, I needled him about the way British Intelligence employed newspaper men. He said: "Oh no, we only hire them in the Middle East."

MADRID, *November 10, 1948*

THIS afternoon I saw Franco in the Pardo palace. I went out with the Marques de Lema, an amiable career diplomat, whose father was Foreign Minister under Alfonso. We were kept waiting a long time and sat chatting in a large waiting room lined with tapestries for which the designs had been made by Goya. The Pardo is a small hunting palace started by Charles V and finished in the eighteenth century.

Lema told me the following about "Franquito," as the skinny little major was called in his Morocco days: There was a mutiny of the Spanish Foreign Legion at Melilla. Franco strode along the lineup of angry men who were holding their mess kits. The riot had been about food. One legionnaire took his mess kit and hurled the contents at Franco, saying "How do you expect us to eat stuff like this?" Franco calmly drew out his handkerchief, wiped his face and uniform, continued the review. Then, he summoned the captain in charge of the mess and ordered him to bring him a plate of the stew. He tasted it and found it horrible. He then demanded a new meal cooked and fed to the men. After the meal he ordered a new formation. In front of the men he bawled the captain out for serving such foul food and then ordered him to go to the barracks and consider himself under arrest. Franco then reviewed the men again. When he came to the man who had hurled the food he summoned him three paces forward. Then, before the other men, he had him shot.

In our talk Franco said Spain desired improved ties with the United States. He wanted a loan and suggested $200 million. He also urged a defensive coalition and said: "Spain would be willing to take part in such a Western alliance."

He started chatting about himself. He said: "I started working when I was fourteen years old. By the time I was twenty-one I was commanding 14,000 men. I have always had responsibilities higher than those I have desired." He went on: "In a certain way we feel ourselves to be American. In these days the seas tend to unite nations more than the land; there is no intervening nation between. Nevertheless, there has been a certain mutual lack of comprehension between our two countries concerning their problems. This has been more true in the case of Americans than with us. The United States has not quite understood the problems we have faced and those we have to face."

He said Spain had suffered much during the Civil War and then lost its commerce with Germany and Central Europe and needed funds to replace outmoded industrial equipment. Its gold reserve had been stolen by Russia (sent there by fleeing Republicans), and Spain needed dollars. When Franco suggested a loan he added: "Spain is a very good investment. Even during our Civil War we paid all our debts promptly." He said Spain didn't want to join the Marshall Plan "for the reason that the other nations participating in it do not seem to want us and make it appear as if we would be stealing their food. The United States is a curious nation. It provides the money but lets the recipients state the conditions. Spain prefers to deal directly with the United States and thus avoid political confusion. When nations help each other they increase mutual love. Spain, as if emerging from a ditch by its own efforts, has felt lonely." He added:

> The only way to avoid war with Russia is to make certain that Russia feels she cannot win such a war. If the West is prepared, this condition will be met. Russia will not gamble the outcome of a war on the toss of a coin. More dangerous than a potential Russian military aggression is Russian political aggression. Until now Russia has preached the contrary of what she has actually accomplished. It has been possible to demonstrate that, despite Russian propaganda about social welfare, the standard of living in Russia is lower than elsewhere. But one must take into account that if, when Russia was economically so much worse off than other countries she was nevertheless able to exert so much international influence, this will become still greater when Russia is better off. Russia sacked and drained the wealth of twelve countries and took their riches and industrial assets, from Europe to Manchuria. She took their mechanical devices and their scientists. Within a few years Russia can raise her standard of living on that basis. Then she will certainly exert a much greater influence. During his recent conversations with visitors, Stalin has said: "I will not permit any country bordering on Russia to have a higher standard of living than that of the Russian people." As Russia develops her wealth she will have an increasing influence not only in Europe and Asia but also in South America, which is not as wealthy as the United States.
>
> To us, socialism and communism are the same thing. If you practice socialism fully you arrive at communism. Therefore, to combat this growing Russian influence, we must meet our social problems ourselves and in non-Marxist ways that will preserve the bases of Western civilization.

ESTORIL, PORTUGAL, *November 16, 1948*

THIS afternoon I talked for about an hour and a half to Don Juan, Count of Barcelona, pretender to the Spanish throne. He is a huge, tough fellow who looks like a football end, with heavy shoulders and a beak of a nose. He has the bluff, easy manner of a British naval officer—which he was. Over whisky and soda he expressed his ideas on Franco and on Spain.

He talked to Franco about the necessity of improving the social and economic lot of the masses. However, Don Juan doesn't want to come out and state this as a program, because it would gain him the opposition of some monarchist leaders supporting him in Spain today. Don Juan blames Britain and the United States for ruining his chances of going back in 1946. He said: "I was all ready. Everything had been fixed up."

Franco is a tricky horse trader and continually shifts his position. He believes he impressed Franco greatly, for Franco continually told him he had been "misinformed" about Don Juan. Juan believes he will go back within three to five years. It is hard to budge Franco from his position at the top. He says he will not deal with Franco and allow him to keep an important post under the monarchy.

Don Juan sees the Spanish as crazy, violent, anarchic people. He doesn't think much of the Portuguese but says his ancestors had to give up Portugal in the seventeenth century (Philip II acquired it in the sixteenth) when faced with the choice of hanging on to Portugal or putting down a French-backed revolution in Catalonia. He adds: "Naturally the King of Spain, as he always is, was too poor to raise a big enough army to face both problems; so he chose Catalonia in order to protect the Pyrenees frontier."

Juan says he wants a liberal constitutional monarchy with full freedoms, freedom of the press, and so on. I doubt this. He is a Bourbon who never forgets and never learns. He assured me: "The only good things ever done in Spain were done by the Kings of Spain."

CASCAIS, *November 18, 1948*

THIS morning I saw former King Umberto of Italy, who lives in a simple seaside house at Cascais.

Umberto said he would always be prepared to return to his country as its ruler if the Italian people desired, and that the traditions of Italy clearly did not exclude the possibilities of a future plebiscite on that question despite the present constitutional assertion that the country is permanently a republic. However, he would not engage in any "intrigues" or "maneuvers" to encourage his own return.

Umberto, a tall, quiet man, has been in Portugal since the Italian referendum of 1946. He says: "If the nation so desires, we are content to remain quiet. We will not participate in any underground manipulations. If the majority wants us we are ready to return and will always be so. If not, we will naturally remain apart as we are. Things are really very simple."

LISBON, *November 18, 1948*

THIS afternoon I met Dr. Antonio de Oliveira Salazar, Prime Minister and for twenty years dictator of Portugal, in his rather simple, comfortable office in the Parliament building. He is on the short side, thin, very worried and grave-looking although with a nice smile which infrequently lights up. His voice and manner are quiet and careworn. His face is sad and rather religious; he is very devout and was educated by the Jesuits. He was simply dressed and, curiously enough, wore high-button shoes.

Salazar favors an Atlantic military alliance from the Iberian peninsula to Scandinavia and sees that as "the salvation" of Portugal and the West.

He wants the United States to play a dominant role in organizing Europe's resources. When an Atlantic bloc is finally organized he believes the Portuguese empire can offer a valuable contribution. The United States already has a base in the Azores.

ATHENS, January 3, 1949

THIS evening I had a talk with King Paul for one hour and a half at his country palace of Tatoi. We sat in front of a log fire and talked. He said that he was going to throw out the present Greek government. He would offer the chance to the political parties of forming a coalition of all parties. If they refuse to agree on this, he would suggest a nonparty cabinet with General Papagos, the hero of the war against the Axis and present Minister of Court, as Prime Minister.

If Parliament refuses to accept the government, King Paul would dissolve Parliament. Legally, he is permitted to dissolve Parliament for forty days. However, Paul has resolved to continue this dissolution indefinitely under technical loopholes until the crisis is over.

He would guarantee, in a speech to the nation, that there would be free elections at the end of the crisis. He would like the United States to support his program and to formally guarantee supervision of such free elections at the end of the crisis. King Paul plans to go on the air and explain all this to the nation. The tenure of the present government expires February 1. However, Paul would like to take all these steps before then.

He says he told all this to Ambassador Harriman two days ago and that Harriman approved. Harriman told King Paul that Congressional Committees would commence hearings on the Greek aid program on February 1. Paul is in a great hurry to get his idea launched.

I told him I thought it would be very difficult to "sell" such an unconstitutional move to American public opinion and that it seemed to me to be especially risky to take such a step just at the time Congress was considering the new Greek aid program. I recalled that Communist propaganda links Spain, China and Greece and that there was a risk that the Communists would make many Americans believe that this contemplated step confirmed their accusation of "Monarcho Fascism."

Ambassador Grady, who just returned to Athens today from Washington, has been consulting about these proposed measures, King Paul said. Before going home, Grady told him he would support any move King Paul made. King Paul said it was imperative to improve administrative efficiency in Greece. He said that if it were necessary to dissolve Parliament and name a Papagos government without Parliament's approval, "this is the last step."

Paul thanked me for the article I wrote on an interview with him last summer in which he demanded the return to Greece of Cyprus. When Sir Clifford Norton, the British Ambassador, returned from London, Paul asked if Bevin had talked to him about Cyprus. Norton said no, but King George VI had asked him why Paul had made such a declaration. Paul explained to Norton that I had asked him to express his views on the subject. Norton said, "But did you authorize him to publish them?" Paul said, "Of course." Later, Paul said, King George sent word berating him for wanting to take apart the British Empire.

My impression of all this is that Paul, urged on by his able but ambitious wife, wants to assume personal rule of the country instead of remaining a figurehead, constitutional monarch. The two chief men in the proposed Cabinet would be Papagos and Markezinis. Papagos is Minister of Court; Markezinis' last job was that of a court functionary, and he is therefore very closely tied up with the King.

Obviously Paul hoped I would tell him all this would go down well in America in the name of "efficiency." I didn't. Quite the reverse. I wonder if he will take this view into consideration. After all, he asked for it.

PARIS, *January 4, 1949*

I HAD a long talk with Harriman about the Greek situation. He denied that he had approved King Paul's program to dissolve Parliament and appoint a nonparty government. He said he hoped for a government with seven ministers and then a sub-cabinet of more ministers, which would improve efficiency.

5

I SPENT MOST OF THE DAY WITH JOHN PATON DAVIES, WHO HAS JUST completed drawing up a new American policy on China. It was finally passed by the National Security Council and approved by the President. The long-term aims are these: 1. We want a China truly independent and free from foreign control. 2. We do not want a China which is an instrument of Soviet policy. 3. We want a friendly China.

The United States is waiting to see how the process of disintegration in China is finally completed. We don't know definitely whether we wish to meddle with this process or not. The Russians have been benefiting in an imperialistic way from the breakup of China. In northwest Manchuria, near Chita, a Russian-controlled unit has been set up. This is the Huilibor Mongol regime with its headquarters at Hialar (an administrative unit consisting of a Stalinist Mongol regime set up by the Outer Mongolian Republic).

In northern Manchuria at Harbin the dominating military leader has been Lin Piao. He is an attractive little man who loves dancing and is an excellent general. The nonmilitary political boss of Manchuria is Li Li-San, the man who wished to base the Chinese revolution on the support of city proletariat. Li Li-San's theory lost out, and Mao Tse-tung, who based his theory on the support of the farmers, won. Li Li-San, after losing his dispute with Mao, was in the Moscow "deep freeze" until 1945. He is now believed to be the Stalinist representative in Manchuria.

Mao's agrarian movement gathered momentum during the 1930s. Mao built up his own apparatus of party, secret police and army—fifteen years before Tito did the same thing in Jugoslavia. This insulated him against liquidation: thus Mao is in a position to call his own tune. There is no question but that Mao considers himself a Marxist. Maybe that ideology is the only tie between Mao and the Kremlin, and maybe it will not keep him amenable to Kremlin policy. We must wait and find out.

The Kremlin suspects human nature. It does not want Mao to take all of China without the application of certain checks to be sure he will be kept in line. The Russians fear he might become a massive Tito. Therefore, it is believed they wish to establish a regime in the south to play against Mao and to force the north to depend upon Moscow. Also if the Communists move south they would be in direct contact with the Communists of Southeast Asia. This huge bloc would no longer depend upon Moscow.

The Russians are confused and are taking no chances. Stalin is gun-shy in China and has been so ever since the failure of the Borodin venture in 1927. Stalin, an Asiatic himself, realizes just how slick the Chinese are. The United States in some ways is now in a position in China comparable to the position during the summer of 1948 vis-à-vis Jugoslavia.

The Russians have been embarrassed by China just as much as the United States. They obtained no steel or production centers of importance, but only a mass of misery and an area of potential famine. They acquired an area of potential Titoism too large to handle.

The United States must wait until the distintegration process in China has been pretty well completed before we know what materials we have to work with on our Chinese policy. The dust must first settle. We cannot afford to commit American support to anything yet. We have now virtually disengaged ourselves from the policy of supporting Chiang, which proved bankrupt. Our military supplies were useless. All they did was to bring us hatred. In effect we armed the Communists because Mao captured or bought our material in vast quantities. Since V-J Day, according to American military authorities on the scene, the Nationalists never lost a battle for lack of equipment.

GENEVA, *May 8, 1949*

LAST night Marina and I dined with King Leopold of Belgium and his wife, the Princesse de Réthy, at Leopold's spacious and comfortable house at Pregny, just outside Geneva. His second daughter and the two boys (including eighteen-year-old Crown Prince Baudouin) were at dinner, and the girl stayed afterwards. The boys appear bashful and timid, rather weak. Leopold corrected their homework and called them backward, in front of us; not very tactful.

Leopold is quiet and grave, a tall, handsome man. He is extremely badly informed and gives me the impression of being naive and reactionary. For example he asserted that there were so many Communists in England that England could not go to war because there would be crippling strikes in all key industries. Leopold has such an extreme distaste and contempt for political parties that it is unhealthy. Leopold told me: "I want to go back and put things straight. Then if the people do not want me and are unwilling to cooperate in a government. I am prepared to go away. But it is unconstitutional to forbid me to return. The law which bans me at present was passed in 1945 and refers to the "impossibility" of my reigning because of "enemy action." Such "enemy action" no longer exists and it is up to parliament to recognize this situation."

OSLO, *June 30, 1949*

AT noon today I had a long talk with King Haakon in the royal palace, an awkward building overlooking the town from a slight hill. It is strictly Victorian and encumbered with clumsy furniture, bronze ornaments and statues and little knickknacks. He is as skinny as ever and filled with vitality. He waves his arms around, grins and gesticulates constantly, and at one point imitated the barking of a fox terrier to show how the little *émigré* governments during the war nagged at the British government in London.

The people seem to like him greatly. He said he calls the Communists the "Royal Communist Party" because they not only never attack him but local mayors speak flatteringly when he visits them. He recalled a dinner in his honor at a hotel in Hankø two days ago where he said he was surprised the owner had managed to get tablecloths and napkins of linen for everyone. He said all such equipment had disappeared during the war, but he supposed the owner had managed to gather enough together from other hotels in his chain. "I am used to paper napkins," he said. Haakon said the people weren't working hard enough. He attributed this to the fact that during the occupation it was patriotic not to work for the occupiers, and employers congratulated their workers when they did nothing.

He said he personally had urged the government strongly to join the North Atlantic Pact. He wants to make it clear to all and sundry who their real friends are now so they can never be fooled during a war. He said it was known who the fifth column was—and there *would* be a fifth column in another war—and in a threatened period they would have to be watched carefully and even locked up. He said he was trying to consider all these questions in terms of a fifty-year period. He would not be here, but he was thinking of his son and grandson.

TURKU, FINLAND, *July 2, 1949*

I SPENT this afternoon with President Paasikivi at Kultaranda Castle, which is twenty kilometers from Turku. We sat on the terrace under a sun shade. Russian tea was served in glasses together with cakes. He was wearing a gray flannel, old-fashioned suit, a pink shirt with a stiff white collar, and horn-rimmed glasses. After the sun shifted and his head was exposed, a servant rushed out of the large stone house and set a panama hat upon the president's head.

The president said,

> Our position has always been and of course remains pro-Western despite our geographical proximity to Russia. We remain a democratic and occidental country, and the last elections showed that our people are determined we shall remain so.
>
> When the Czechoslovakian coup took place we were again astonished that the Czechoslovakian people were so weak. Of course, Beneš, although he was ten years younger than I, was very ill and lacked force. Also the Czechoslovaks are Slavs. We were astonished when Hitler took over Czechoslovakia and was not opposed by a single shot. That could never happen here. They had a good army and an excellent munitions industry.

He commented: "I am a good friend of Russia, but I am a Finn. I know Russia. It is another world. The mentality and principles of life are utterly different."

BAD HOMBURG, *July 13, 1949*

THIS morning I had breakfast with John McCloy, new American High Commissioner for Germany. He said it was a great problem how to integrate into German life former Nazis who have been cleared by the courts or who have served their sentences. We are using all the real democrats we can find. We must let former Nazis play an economic, social, and political role, or otherwise they will sit on the sidelines and sulk, perhaps become more dangerous.

Germany was like an infantry company in which 10 percent of the people were heroes, 15 percent were cowards and "the rest follow the leader." In the same way, there is a percentage of Communists at one extreme, and a percentage of Nazis at the other.

PRAGUE, *July 25, 1949*

LUCA Dainelli, of the Italian legation, arranged a meeting at his house with the Reverend Father Silar, Father Provincial of the Jesuit order in Czechoslovakia, who has the clerical rank of archbishop and is the most important man now free and active in the Czechoslovakian Catholic hierarchy. He leads the underground against the government.

Dainelli brought Silar around. Silar apparently rode on his bicycle to the home of a contact of Dainelli, wearing ordinary civilian clothes, and then came here by car with his clerical garb in a briefcase. He went upstairs, changed, and descended clothed as a priest, for a drink and some highly tough talk. It strikes me as rather naive of Dainelli not to assume his place is wired for sound. But this clearly worries neither of them. Silar plunged right in: a fanatical-looking man with thin face, thick glasses, brilliantly red ears and lips.

He said only twenty of Czechoslovakia's seven to eight thousand priests supported the government's new Catholic Action movement. However, since 1925 the state had been granted the right to pay priests' salaries directly, and this gives it a huge advantage today. The government is now demanding that each priest and each church should prepare lists of the faithful and should also prepare complete inventories of church property. So far, the church has refused to do this because it fears confiscation decrees. He continued: "The Pope based his excommunication decree upon the effort by the state to take control of the church through a lay organization, the Catholic Action Committee, which was created by the state. The decree was directed against all members of the false Catholic organization, both priests and laymen, or all those who acted actively in collaboration with them and such people were excommunicated *ipso facto*. Probably not more than two hundred or three hundred laymen had been excommunicated. Their names have not been published and nobody really knows who they are."

BELGRADE, *September 5, 1949*

I HAD another long talk with Tito today, in his villa at Dedinje, the Belgrade suburb. At the end of our conversation he gave me a stony glance and said: "You did not interpret my remarks very accurately last time we met. If you want relations between us to remain as they are, you had better be more accurate this time." Obviously he was referring to a series of articles I wrote criticizing him and his regime. His idea of "accurate" is, I fear, somewhat different from mine.

Tito said: "A few days ago I said in a conversation and I still maintain today that I do not think there is a possibility of war in the world. I do not for a moment suppose that any nation would desire the recurrence of such an international conflict as that which ended recently or for that matter one which would be even worse. The threat of such a catastrophe prevents the possibility of war. The consequences of the last war are still too close to us to admit the thought of a new one."

PARIS, *October 26, 1949*

THIS afternoon I had a long talk with General de Gaulle. He started off by saying that naturally his first effort would be to change the Constitution in France if and when he comes to power.

I asked him if he would agree to participate in the French government if President Auriol requested him to. He replied haughtily:

Such an idea is a joke. The only way I will participate is after the people have expressed themselves in elections. Unfortunately, there is no way of forcing the deputies to dissolve. The constitution permits the deputies to remain in office right up to the moment of catastrophe, because the constitution was devised by the parties now in control. If catastrophe comes, the deputies will vanish. But they sit waiting for a catastrophe just as in 1940; and that is what I fear.

In an ordinary parliamentary regime dissolution comes from the government itself. In France, unfortunately, this depends upon the deputies.

De Gaulle said the first thing he would do when he came to office would be to revise the Constitution. He said it would be almost exactly like the American Constitution. The powers of the president and of Parliament would be fixed and limited. "Dictatorship would be impossible under such a constitution," he said. "My enemies say I wish to be a dictator. I had all the power in my hand, once. Was I a dictator?"

De Gaulle said the North Atlantic Pact was a good thing in principle but that the aid foreseen under the military assistance program is insufficient. He added: "I told my supporters that France must first count upon itself independent of foreign aid."

He added further: "All of Europe faces insufficient aid from America and we must always live as if war were just around the corner."

As far as Germany was concerned:

I am for an independent Germany. The Bonn system is not good, but it exists. I am for an arrangement between France and Western Germany on the basis of equality. This has nothing to do with the East German state. I have always had this idea, even before the Russians created the new East German satellite. A French-German accord could balance the effect of the Russians' East German state. This would stabilize the situation. The reason for which I was against the Washington and London agreements on Germany and the Bonn system was because they hinder a direct agreement between Germany and France. The creation of the Bonn system in Western Germany was supported by the British primarily to prevent the strengthening of France.

De Gaulle was very bitter about the attitude of the present French government toward him. The entire French problem is that the regime considers itself only as an apparatus against General de Gaulle and works exclusively against General de Gaulle. "The entire regime is constructed against me."

LONDON, *November 8, 1949*

LONG talk with Prime Minister Clement Attlee at 10 Downing Street. I like Attlee and feel he has far more quality and tensile strength than indicated by his modest appearance, that of a wise version of Tenniel's dormouse. Tamping his pipe, talking in calm bursts, he made much sense. I asked if he thought Britain could really integrate its economy with that of

Europe. He replied: "This is difficult for Britain. We cannot do the whole thing along the lines apparently desired. We are not strictly a European power. We are a member of a Commonwealth. We have to consider that and our responsibilities to it more than Europe and our obligations there. We are in a different position from all European powers, even those with large foreign possessions; different even from a country like Holland. Furthermore, one must always remember that the nations of Europe have long traditions of individuality, and you cannot expect to scramble all these eggs either successfully or in a hurry."

BONN, *December 19, 1949*

JUST after 1:00 I saw Konrad Adenauer. An indication of how hard the Germans work is the fact that he and his entire staff were working right through lunchtime. They nibbled sandwiches at their desks.

Adenauer is a tall, elderly man with sad, pale face and inscrutable, red-Indian features, a weary, kind look. His voice is soft. His thin figure was attired in a dark blue suit.

I started the conversation by asking what he considered the role of West Germany in the defense of Western Europe, not as of today, but in the future. He replied:

We must always make a distinction between two things—the cold war and a war which is not cold. In the cold war, the psychological and economic situation of the German population is of importance. In the cold war we can hold our position only if the United States continues to aid us at the same rate as is now the case. In the second instance—a real war, our only wish is that God may prevent it.

The Western powers must give the population of our Republic a feeling that they stand a chance of being defended against aggression. This can only be done by some public assurance that we will be defended.

On one side of us, the Russians are rearming. On the other side, the West is rearming. In between, we are 48,000,000 Germans without arms. We hear that plans are being discussed to defend the Rhine; that only temporary holding operations would start on the Elbe. Everyone would fall back to the Rhine, leaving us exposed. Sometimes I feel that military men are thinking in terms of a war like thirty or forty years ago. The Allies are preparing to blow up the Rhine bridges, but such strategy was proven worthless in the recent war.

I don't want to say a word about rearming Western Germany. However, I think the Western powers already are considering the economic assistance of Germany in European defense and the alteration of the Allied attitude on dismantling is perhaps a part of this. On the subject of rearmament itself, there are many possibilities for eventual development, but the more one speaks, the worse it is both for the Germans and the rest of the world. We must keep a place for potential war industry, but we hope we will never need it for such a purpose.

I asked Adenauer how the Allies could ever trust Western Germany not to turn Eastward and make a deal with the Russians? He replied: "I believe if you treat the Germans fairly they will never turn to the Russians again."

He said: "I wish the United States would push Europe harder on the path towards integration. I have already expressed in my view that the Americans are the best Europeans."

PARIS, *January 20, 1950*

DINNER last night with Averell Harriman. He said Stalin had told him there is only one man who could unify China, and that was Chiang Kai-shek. Furthermore, Stalin said the only country which could develop China economically was the United States. What a contrast to present trends.

PARIS, *February 11, 1950*

LAST night dined with Averell Harriman. I asked him, since he knows all the great men of our time, who was the greatest. Without any hesitation he said Stalin. He describes Stalin as ruthless, brutal, direct, extremely intelligent, very well informed and expert on many matters, including military affairs. He is ready to sacrifice anything to achieve his objectives, whether millions of men in a battle, or a country. He treats Molotov and his other colleagues the way an autocrat treats servants. Molotov fawns before him. Molotov, incidentally, bullies his own inferiors. Stalin is completely frank. He breaks his word whenever it suits his convenience and openly admits that he has changed his mind. He roared with laughter once when Harriman, in Molotov's presence, told him that Molotov had lied to him. Stalin agreed. He has absolute control of himself and of Russia and, as a result, is not overbearing, pompous or vain the way Hitler or Mussolini were. Frequently he says "I think" or "I have decided." At other times, he refers to "my associates" or "we." When Harriman told Stalin that an atomic bomb had been dropped at Hiroshima, he asked him what he thought this would mean to the future of the world. Stalin said such a weapon might make war impossible. Then he added that this would provide an excuse for the Japanese to capitulate. This was before Russia had invaded Japan.

ROME, *February 23, 1950*

THIS morning I had a talk with Monsignor Montini (later Pope Paul VI), who serves as the Pope's Acting Secretary of State. I said to him that since the world was in a cold war, divided between materialist and nonmaterialist elements, it would seem to me useful if the groups recognizing the spirit could associate themselves more closely; that all religions, Christian and other, should announce agreement to combat materialism. I asked if the Vatican would not take some initiative in this.

He replied that this was extremely difficult and delicate. He explained the church considered itself the only true church and that naturally this view is combated by Protestants, the Orthodox, Jews, Islam, among others. It was a difficult project to execute, and there was no use in embarking upon things which stood no chance of success.

TIBERIAS, ISRAEL, *March 18, 1950*

TODAY I drove down to this ancient town on the Sea of Galilee. It was a lovely spring day, and the fields were full of flowers. In many of them Arabs in their headdresses were calmly plowing. A pass is still required to drive through Nazareth, a center of Arab Christians still specially protected.

At a little resort hotel I had a long interview with Prime Minister Ben Gurion. He was much fatter but far more relaxed than when I last saw him (1948). He is full of visions combined with an energetic practicality and great willpower.

He bitterly attacked communism as "another name for Russian chauvinism." He said there had been a change in British public opinion "but I don't know if the Foreign Office has changed. Certainly Bevin never will."

Ben Gurion claims Israel wants to negotiate formal peace with all its Arab neighbors as quickly as possible and on the basis of present de facto frontiers. He insists it harbors no present or future intention of expanding into adjoining territory. He said:

Peace is of paramount interest to our policy. We must develop the country. The North was ruined by the war. The South, Negeb, was ruined by sixteen hundred years of neglect. It requires a tremendous effort to rebuild and that in itself is a paramount reason for peace.

Furthermore, we face an urgent problem of immigration. If, for example, Iraq really opens her doors for departure of Jews we must take them in. Even if there is nothing—no houses, no jobs awaiting them we must take them in.

Supposing Rumania were suddenly to say "You can have all our Jews who wish to emigrate providing you receive them immediately," we would take them—regardless of economic difficulties. This requires peace.

If there is one Arab state which should fear us it is Jordan. We have no quarrel with Egypt. We do not covet the Sinai Desert or the Suez Canal. Our frontiers with Jordan are long and complicated. Still, there is a real possibility of peace there.

Turning to long-range problems, he continued:

Our fundamental policy is one of unlimited immigration. We are especially interested in absorbing as rapidly as possible the Jews from countries where they face persecution or threats their emigration will be restricted in future.

Our present population is 1,200,000 of whom 1,050,000 are Jews (the rest Arabs). In ten years, we will probably have a population of 3,000,000. Therefore, we must work to develop our agriculture and industry to provide more jobs.

We will irrigate the Negeb—where experts say there is oil. We are planning to develop chemical, textile and metal industries including steel—for which we will import coal and iron. With hard work and determination our country can support a big population.

Look at the way Switzerland has developed itself with far less riches than are ours. Or Belgium, which is a little bigger than Western Palestine and yet supports 8,000,000 people. We can work as hard and as skillfully. We intend to develop maritime industries—shipping and fishing. Not many Jews have experience in these fields. Yet, few had had agricultural experience and we proved they could do the job. Experts—even our first pioneers—said it would take generations to make a farmer. We proved you could do it in a year. These things can be done and will be done. In ten years we will have tens of thousands of sailors and fishermen. We will send them to Norway to learn. Everything depends upon brains, ability and determination, not on heritage and habits.

TEL AVIV, *March 19, 1950*

THIS evening I drove out to Rehovoth to see Dr. Chaim Weizmann, first president of Israel. Poor Weizmann has been very ill and looked it. He is seventy-five and is just running down. His heart is bad. He received me in his bedroom, where he was sitting in an armchair in pajamas, dressing gown and blanket. He looked like a dying man, thin and with drawn yellow face. The conversation was quite without interest save for one point.

He said Eddy Jacobson, Truman's Jewish friend from Missouri, had told him on the long distance telephone that Truman would welcome a visit by Weizmann. He asked what I thought about it. I said that he should wait for a better clue as to the President's real desires. He replied that the State Department would try and block it. I thought it was not a propitious time for a visit; that Washington was pressing the Arab states to negotiate with Israel; that if he went to Washington the Arabs would all suspect a Jewish plot. He suggested perhaps it might be better after the Jordan negotiations conclude successfully, but that he would have to go before the Washington heat became too intense. He seems to want very much to go and said his last trip was very profitable for Israel.

ISTANBUL, *March 22, 1950*

INTERESTING visit to the Patriarch of the Orthodox church, Athenogoras. The Patriarch lives in the old quarter of the Phanar in a relatively simple home-office. He has a signed picture of Truman beside him—under a cross. He is a huge man—at least six feet three, under a towering black "pope's" hat and wears a long gray beard like Michelangelo's Moses. He speaks good American English, having lived in America almost twenty years.

He said it is a tragedy that religion cannot make peace in its own family. "How can the spiritual world face conflict with the materialist world when it cannot agree with itself? Religion is behaving criminally. It is at war in Christendom." He had sent a message of greeting and regard to Pius XII that was not even answered.

TEHERAN, *March 30, 1950*

THIS evening I saw Shah Mohammed Reza. The Shah said there is no indication of any Soviet buildup indicating a threat of aggression against Iran. There is a softening of the Soviet attitude in terms of propaganda. He mistrusts this and thinks such trends sometimes forbode ill.

It is an economic burden to the country to maintain an army of 136,000 men, but it is necessary. There are 2,500 kilometers of frontier with Russia alone, and even that cannot be manned. The Russians are creeping southward and in fifty years have occupied a strip of about forty kilometers of Iranian territory.

America is under the misconception that Iran is another China—therefore hopeless to defend and salvage. That is ridiculous. The country is in far better and more united shape than China ever was.

Iran has no illusions about being able to form any military alliances with her neighbors. She is too weak. But she hopes some day the United States will extend its already existing commitments and incorporate Greece, Turkey and Iran ("the right flank") into the Atlantic bloc.

KARACHI, *April 11, 1950*

I HAD a talk for an hour and a half with Liaquat Ali Kahn, Prime Minister of Pakistan. I saw him in his home, and we sat around having highballs, an unusual thing in the Moslem world. He proposed that British Commonwealth nations should issue a collective guarantee of the territorial integrity of Pakistan and India in order to ease tension.

A bland fifty-five-year-old Oxford graduate, Liaquat furthermore suggested it would be "useful" if Britain formally declared that any infringement of the Durand line, Pakistan's border with Afghanistan, would be automatically considered as a violation of a "Commonwealth frontier."

Liaquat is calm, soft-spoken. He thought the United States should encourage guarantees of India and Pakistan in order to allow them to spend more on economic improvement and aid to the poor, which would help keep out the potential menace of communism. He admitted that popular feeling in Pakistan against any threat of Indian domination is so strong that some people would rather be conquered by the Soviet Union than reconquered by India.

KABUL, *April 14, 1950*

I FLEW to Kabul, Afghanistan, with Lieutenant Colonel Miller, American air attaché in Karachi and Kabul. He was flying up about a ton of ammunition and emergency rations because the political situation is believed to be very hot here, and foreigners, in an emergency, might have to barricade themselves in their compounds. The Americans have made plans for such an eventuality, choosing a compound that has its own source of water as their fort.

Louis Dreyfus, the quiet, cultivated American envoy, and his charming wife insisted on putting me up in the residence. She said the Kabul Hotel wasn't even fit for insects.

KABUL, *April 15, 1950*

TODAY I had a long talk with King Mohammed Zahir Shah. He is a tall, saturnine fellow in his mid-thirties whose French is fluent. He was quite friendly but not especially at ease. This was the first interview he—or, for that matter, any Afghan ruler—had ever granted. Mohammed, who was wearing a double-breasted blue suit and striped shirt, had just returned to Kabul five days ago (because of the rumors of conspiracy to oust him) from a long trip in Europe and the Middle East. I suppose one might say he was quite friendly and informal, considering his autocratic powers. He is dark, lean, brown-faced, brooding, with mustache, bald head, crooked features, crooked nose, crooked smile. I would not trust the man behind that face.

The audience occurred in the Royal Palace in the center of Kabul, a large nineteenth-century building in a walled compound guarded by tall Pathan sentries wearing German-type helmets and carrying rifles and packs. The sun was just setting behind the barren crags which surround this city, and a blooming apple orchard in the royal compound glowed pink.

I was escorted to the King's study by formally attired servants wearing Karakul caps, a heritage from the days of the Mogul emperors. The King said Afghanistan required assistance, experts and capital from friendly nations, but did not wish to grant any individual concessions. Mixed capital enterprises controlled by Afghanistan would provide a better solution.

Turning to foreign affairs, the King said the Saadabad Pact, of which Turkey, Iran, Iraq and Afghanistan are members, still "exists in spirit." He said that to strengthen the bonds of Islamic countries, however, many mutual problems must first be ironed out. He referred especially to Afghanistan's present dispute with Pakistan. Relations with Iran were "based on full friendship and we hope in the future will be even better," but "an impasse exists at present with Pakistan," which borders both countries.

We chatted about Paris, where he once went to school and which he loves. When I expressed admiration for Afghan hounds, the magnificent local dog, he promised me one. What the hell will I do with it?

KABUL, *April 16, 1950*

THIS morning I saw Prime Minister Sardar Shah Mahmud Khan, brother of the last King, uncle of the present one. It was curious in a chat after the interview to hear him referring to his family as "My nephew, his Majesty the King; my brother, His Royal Highness so-and-so; my nephew, His Royal Highness so and so."

He urged creation of a new independent country of Pushtunistan (or Pathanistan) embracing all of Pakistan's northwest frontier province and part of Baluchistan, including the famous cities of Peshawar and Quetta. Such a state would extend from Chitral, at the northwestern tip of Kashmir and just below the high Pamir passes, to Chinese Sinkiang and on down to Sind in the south. Its western frontier would be the Durand line, the present border between Afghanistan and Pakistan. Its eastern frontier would be the Indus River. He said: "We regard the inhabitants of Pushtunistan as our brothers. There is no difference between us in culture or language. Years ago (first by the Sikh Empire, then by the British) they were divided from Afghanistan by force. Now that the entire world favors the freedom and independence of subject people, Pushtunistan should benefit. Pakistan, which only recently threw off British subjection, should not wish to be the master of Pushtunistan."

When I got back to the residence there was a great clamor going on. The master of the royal kennel had shown up with about fifteen Afghan hounds; I was to take my pick. They were splendid, huge animals, but, rather to my astonishment, they were poorly cared for and even had ticks. To my regret I had to refuse (although there was one I dearly wanted: a golden-colored male, lean and shaggy). Obviously it would have been hard to take a huge hound around the world from Saigon to Tokyo to Alaska to Paris; and I doubt if *The New York Times* would have enjoyed on my expense accounts items listed as food and transportation for One Afghan Hound.

JALALABAD, *April 17, 1950*

I CAME down here by bus; a hair-raising trip. Broken-down vehicle, overloaded with bearded, ragged, turbaned Afghans; rather high-smelling and given to furious debate, shouts and laughter. The bus spent the night in this eastern Afghanistan town, and I found there was a Pakistan consul who was delighted to see me. He is completely isolated and watched like a criminal because of the bad relations over the Pathans. He gave me a burning hot curry, lots of whisky, a bed and a whirlpool of gossip about the Afghans, none of it favorable. His consulate is rather down-at-heels, but Jalalabad is a pleasant, ramshackle town with lovely orchards and gardens, a pastel-shaded background.

I confess I am fascinated by the Pathans and their claims to statehood (somewhat like the Kurds or Armenians). Their Pushtunistan propaganda is of a curious sort, generally in poetry. Here are some recent excerpts:

> The bulbul is complaining regarding his life. The cruel foreigner does not allow the bee to come near the foreigner . . . Heaven does not permit the lovers to have a sound sleep and a laugh.

> Pathan. I am addressing you. Get up. Get up with all your gallantry . . . You who are renowned throughout the world as a warrior; whose heritage is a sharp sword.

The most important warrior of the border, who has been raising hell for fifteen years, is Mirza Ali Kahn, Hadji Sahib, the Faqir of Ipi. A splendid name for a little man who lives in a cave.

PESHAWAR, *April 20, 1950*

ARRANGED a car and driver to go through the Malakand Pass up to Swat, a semi-independent principality. Its ruler used to be called the Ahkund, leading to a rhyme: "Who or why, or which, or what is the Ahkund of Swat?" Now there is a Wali.

It is a lovely drive through mountains, past rushing rivers in which I occasionally saw the rising backs of great fish and on to Saidu Sharif, capital of Swat, on the edge of snowy peaks that point toward China. Bees hum amid the honeysuckle. Horses are garlanded in jasmine. Poppies stud rippling wheat fields. Bubbling streams abound in mahseer, a handsome, firm-fleshed fish. Fierce-looking Pathans wear roses behind their ears. Children squat in the bazaars, nibbling sugar cane, while their mothers spin wool that comes from fine Merino sheep.

All around are mountains, shutting off Pakistan's plains in the south, the little lands of Dir and Chitral in the west and north—and the Soviet Union beyond them—and troubled Kashmir in the east, leading on to China. Swat is not the land of Cockayne, where sugar buns grow on trees, but it is as near as one can get.

The ruler is the Wali, Mian Gul, Abdul Haq Jahan Zeb. Wali means "ruler" in Arabic. Mian Gul means "descendant of a saint." Jahan Zeb is a glorious Mogul imperial name. The Wali, who is forty-two, received me in his up-to-date little one-story palace, which is patrolled by a natty body-guard of seventy-five men, well drilled and uniformed in British style. From above his desk, Jahan Zeb seemed dressed in ordinary English tweeds, but when he rose to offer me a cigarette I discovered that instead of flannel slacks below his jacket he had on something like a large white diaper. He speaks good English and was most affable, saying:

> Who would exchange democracy for autocracy? The trend of the whole world is toward democracy and that is the trend in Swat. We used to have an autocratic state but now it is a true democracy. Our *jirga*, a council of elders, meets whenever it wants and I and my cabinet of four abide by all their wishes. If they wanted a republic I would resign. But they seem happy; and I am pleased.
>
> My people have more than enough to eat—and good things—wheat, rice, barley, sugar, ghee, honey. Nobody has any major problems. There are less than ninety people in jail. Everyone comes to me if he has worries.

NEW DELHI, *April 22, 1950*

TODAY I had lunch with Ambassador Loy Henderson. He said the following:

> Nehru has certain inner secrets. He is strongly anti-American. This stems from several things. His governess when he was a boy came from the British middle classes and regularly hammered into his head the concept that Americans were vulgar, second-rate people. This, as his sister has confided, had an effect. Whenever an American was invited to the house, the governess would alert the children and then comment on the visitor's manners afterwards in a critical way. Secondly, Nehru is by nature a tremendous introvert and automatically resents the normal extrovert manner of Americans. Furthermore, he tends to look down upon them as cheap and nonintellectual. Nehru has been bitterly disturbed by American race attitudes and this has led to a strong and perhaps subconscious reaction of pride. All of this was reinforced in one way or another by his education at Harrow.
>
> Nehru is by conviction a Socialist. He used to be a Marxist but now tends more towards the British form. Harold Laski had a very strong influence upon him. Nehru does not like the autocratic system of Russia but probably in his heart of hearts he is less anti-Russian than he is anti-American.

NEW DELHI, *April 26, 1950*

YESTERDAY evening I had a talk with Pandit Jawaharlal Nehru, India's Prime Minister, and one of the heroes of the national struggle for independence. He received me in his private residence, a large, comfortable building which used to be the home of the Commander in Chief of the Indian army during the days of the British raj. We sat in a sitting room on the second floor. Orange juice and cigarettes were served.

He was friendly in contrast to my first meeting, when he was irked about some stories I had written from Pakistan. He has a curious way of talking. It is indecisive and indirect. You ask him a question and he begins to answer it by talking continually in his famous "thinking aloud" method;

but just when he seems to have reached the climax he stops. I was not exceptionally impressed. I started off by asking him what he thought should be American policy in Asia, and he replied with the following oblique answer:

By force of circumstances the United States has an economic responsibility to face. I can only tell you rather generally how we for our part try to act wherever possible. We think that generally speaking the problems of Asia cannot be solved by military means. However, they might be affected by military measures.

It is obvious that the people of Asia are in a state of acute mental change. They are more politically conscious because of the changeover from the period of colonial rule. Their first national reaction is to expect a betterment of their economic conditions. Primary problems of these underdeveloped areas are things dealing with the primary essentials of life. Other matters are relatively theoretical.

Another primary urge is what might be called the nationalist urge. This, after the colonial stage, is strong.

That economic urge tends to make people inclined towards any policy or proposition that tends to realize or improve that condition—whether it is or not is another matter.

Where the nationalist urge and the economic urge join, that produces a powerful movement. Where they tend to split up, there is weakness. It should be our purpose, therefore, to help and encourage the nationalist urge, plus giving it the economic content of future betterment.

The strongest "anti" feeling in these countries is the relic of colonial days and it is against any retention of colonial forms of control. These are the basic factors out of which we feel policy should grow.

Since Nehru had not answered my question on what American policy should be, I repeated it. He replied:

If you apply that it means encouraging national elements as such and helping them in so far as possible towards economic advance. These elements are split up. If sufficient incentive is given to national feeling plus economic advance that would attract many people.

I should imagine most intelligent people don't regard the United States as a colonial power. But I suppose there are plenty of people who have rather vague and undefined suspicions, mainly because the United States is a very powerful country economically and in other ways. Take the relationship of England and India today; there is not a ghost of a chance of their imposing any policy on us. I am not in the slightest degree afraid of such. But past suspicions remain.

I asked him about Russia and he replied:

There has been in India an impression on the one hand that in the past, chiefly in central Asia, the Soviet Union was a liberalizing force that raised the tone. Partly that was because of the frightfully backward conditions prevailing which gave a relative feeling of appreciation for cultural advances in that area. There were many people here who admired the cultural achievements of the Soviet Union but who do not like at all the tendency towards the suppression of individual freedom which apparently is growing more and more into what might be called a nationalist expansionist policy rather than the old style concepts of communism. This has created an adverse reaction among many people in India including many who were previously struck by cultural advances of Russia.

RANGOON, *April 30, 1950*

LAST night I had dinner with Burma's strong man, General Ne Win (later dictator), who commands all army and police forces. He is a good-looking young man (forty) in the Chinese fashion; clearly very vain and ambitious, by no means brilliant, obviously an opportunist (he fought with both the Japanese and the Allies), certainly energetic. We sat up until 3:00 A.M. talking and drinking. He is short, stocky, has a good sense of humor and ready laugh, but I am told he has a quick temper and can be cruel and brutal; is given to coarseness.

Ne Win predicted that Burma's complex civil war would be ended by a government victory before the end of this year. He said negotiations were now going on secretly between leaders of the Karen rebellion and the government and that "more than half the Karen rebels will come over to our side soon. The Karen revolt will be over before the monsoon ends in September." The monsoon season of heavy rains and bad campaigning starts this month.

SAIGON, *May 8, 1950*

FRENCH Intelligence has received information indicating that Ho Chi Minh's rebel Vietminh "government" has concluded a secret military agreement with Mao Tse-tung's Communist regime in China. It is believed this provides for accelerated arms deliveries. Chinese Communists captured sixty thousand rifles as well as other large stocks of equipment at Hainan, much of which might be useful to the Communist cause in Vietnam. France is strongly urging the United States to speed up deliveries of arms and especially of aircraft to its forces in Vietnam.

The French feel they are the only fighting force on hand to oppose the extension of dynamic communism toward Southeast Asiatic areas of vast interest to the West. Therefore, they argue the least Washington can do is to make available more equipment and economic aid.

SAIGON, *May 9, 1950*

SAIGON is a tranquil city of assassination. Late every afternoon sidewalk cafés fill up. Restaurants, dance halls and gambling establishments do active trade. French and Vietnamese housewives shop in well-stocked stores. Coolies pedal their bicycle rickshaws through complicated patterns of traffic. French, Vietnamese, colonial and Foreign Legion soldiers stroll leisurely—bearing no sidearms.

And yet, almost daily some individual on Ho Chi Minh's "death list" is suddenly murdered by a chosen executioner. Hand grenades are rolled down movie aisles or pitched into unsuspecting groups of innocents. And at sundown, on the city's outskirts, the crump of mortars and occasional rattle of machine guns remind this nerveless city that right on its borders guerrillas are ready to carry out their nocturnal trade.

From a military point of view this combined "terror" and hovering menace of formal operations is not regarded as important by the commanders of the French and Vietnamese forces. They do not intend to be swayed from their major plan of cleaning up the key Red River valley in Tonkin and strengthening defensive positions near the Chinese border.

But politically, the continual threat of Vietminh reprisals keeps the Vietnamese population in a constant state of agitation. Early this month, when Premier Long and his successor, Huu, were speaking at Saigon's Town Hall on the anniversary of Bao Dai, a champagne cork popped. Everyone present ducked instinctively.

SAIGON, *May 10, 1950*

THERE is no doubt that soft-voiced little Ho Chi Minh, a man of simple personal habits, undoubted bravery and vast stubbornness, has captured the mind of a vast number of Southeast Asian peoples still struggling to shrug off the last vestiges of nineteenth-century colonial subjugation. There is also no doubt that Ho Chi Minh is a Communist.

Ho Chi Minh, whose name means "The one who shines," adopted his *nom de guerre* (Asiatic equivalent of Tito or Stalin or Lenin) shortly after Japanese troops occupied French Indochina in 1940. His real name is Nguyen Tat Thanh, and like many other professional revolutionaries he has had various pseudonyms in the past—at least seven of which are known.

He was born about sixty years ago in the small village of Kim Lien in North Annam. Annam, which has been amalgamated by the French together with Tonkin and Cochin China into Vietnam, is traditionally famous for producing rebels. He was brought up in a revolutionary environment. His sister, Nguyen Thi Thanh, and his brother, Nguyen Tat Dat, were both sentenced by the French for aiding revolts.

In 1911 Ho (Nguyen Tat Thanh) shipped aboard the French merchantman *D'Artagnan* and visited France, Britain and the United States. In 1919 he settled in Paris and worked as a photographer's assistant. He dabbled in journalism and novels and became acquainted with the French Marxist leftist leaders of the period including Vaillant-Couturier and Marcel Cachin, now dean of the French Communist Party. When the French Socialist Party split, he went with a group joining the Third International (Communists). He left Paris for Moscow in 1923 as a delegate to the Peasants International Congress.

After two years in Moscow he went to Canton as interpreter for the Borodin mission seeking to establish a Soviet state in South China and while there created the "Annamite Section of the League of Oppressed People." Although by then well versed in Marxism, Ho stressed nationalism in his propaganda on the grounds, as he explained in 1927, that "no one would understand the meaning of the word Communism in Indochina."

Even if the situation remains only static, it is clearly to Ho's advantage. He has on his side an immensely popular slogan created by the Japanese: "Asia for the Asiatics."

SAIGON, *May 12, 1950*

BAO Dai, chief of state of Vietnam and former Emperor of Annam, received me in Lagrandiére Palace: a plump, sleepy-looking man. I wouldn't die for anything he sponsored. He told me that, as soon as this country has been "pacified," he would call for a national referendum on its political future. People would be able to freely express their choice of government. He is prepared to accept any popular decision; republic, monarchy, or other administrative form.

"I don't want to impose any kind of regime," he said. "I left the country in 1945 for precisely that reason; I wished the people to have a chance to decide. I came back only to facilitate the liberation of the nation, and when that has been accomplished, the people themselves must decide on the type of regime they want—freely and openly."

TOURANE (LATER DANANG), *May 13, 1950*

LINGUA franca at Tourane is German (Foreign Legion). The French liaison officer explained to me that the place was going to pot (it isn't as bad as all that); that grenades and shells would go off at night (they didn't, although there were plenty of noises); that the Germans (legionnaires) were the best troops they had around but that when they came to town they raped, they looted and murdered; that the French army out here was lousy and all spit and polish (I saw regrettably few signs of spit or polish).

TOKYO, *May 18, 1950*

VERY long talk with General Douglas MacArthur, former Chief of Staff, hero of the Pacific war and now Supreme Commander for the Allies in Japan. He is a remarkable physical specimen. Although he is a few months past seventy, he really looks fifty. I am told he dyes his hair. Be that as it may, he is a handsome, well set up man filled with youthful energy. He is taller than I expected, eats and drinks sparingly but does no exercise. In a uniform he cuts a very lithe figure. He apparently smokes only pipes and cigars because he was gassed in World War I and does not inhale, but he smoked a pipe throughout our conversation, one which continually went out and he kept lighting. In the interim he played in a fidgety way with a box of matches.

I started off by telling the general I had heard him quoted as saying there was not much chance of a new world war in the near future. He replied:

The basic reason I have for concluding that there will not be a war soon is because of the changed nature of war. The scientists of the world have developed to such an extraordinary degree the processes and ways of accomplishing mass killing that war is no longer rationally a means of settling international problems. Its destructiveness has become so great that there can be no winner. Both sides lose. It is almost a form of mutual suicide. Therefore, it is not an acceptable rationalized means of settling international quarrels. (The Korean War came in the next month!)

During the last 150 years, if you look back, you find that international wars were invariably preceded by a period during which one or the other side—and sometimes both sides—became prepared and believed that if they were successful in war they would triumph thereby. They looked upon war as a short cut to power. Thus always one side or both sides were relatively prepared not only in the sense of military force but in a psychological sense; public opinion approved and that was of great importance.

At the present time that is not the case. The public realizes all too well in terms of the last war that there can be no real victory in a future war. Therefore, on neither side is there psychological preparation. The Russian masses are probably just as opposed to a shooting war as the Anglo-Saxon masses. Therefore, many incidents have taken place during the last few years which in the past would have led to war but which have been passed over.

I don't believe that war is imminent because the people of the world would neither desire it nor would they be willing to permit it. That goes for both sides. That is the basic reason for my belief that war is not upon the doorstep.

The Soviet is a patient man. He thinks in terms of decades or centuries. He is not an Occidental but an Oriental. He is white; he is partially located in Europe; he has our gregarious instincts. But at heart he is a Tatar. He is like Genghis Khan. It is an Oriental trait to be patient. They deal in decades or centuries. This is against our nature. When we want a thing done we want it done right away or tomorrow. But the Russian will lay down a railway that he wants to use in twenty-five or fifty years.

We must never forget that Asia includes perhaps 1,250,000,000 people and maybe 60 percent of the assets of the world. Yet it has the lowest standards of living perhaps in the whole world. It is manifest destiny that the effort of future civilization will largely be an Asiatic problem devoted to raising the standards of that huge area.

I wish there was more effort to face the fundamental problem of doing away with war. For example, the United Nations should look squarely at the problem of *abolishing* war. Yet the United Nations continually asks for its own armed forces. It talks of *fighting* to maintain the peace. That is a ridiculous anachronism.

In this respect the Japanese are ahead of their time with the Constitution outlawing armed forces. Someday the rest of the world must catch up. The public opinion of the world is against war because the masses of the world realize its futility.

NEW YORK, *June 27, 1950*

ARRIVED yesterday after crossing on the *Ile de France*. Aboard ship I had several talks with Lieutenant General Alfred Gruenther. We were playing bridge one day and Al was called to the phone. Gone some time. Came back with a quizzical look. Said nothing. Finished the hand, then, as he was shuffling the cards, remarked with a deadpan: "Cy, you'd better put your soldier suit on, North Korea has invaded South Korea."

Gruenther said he was convinced that, if the Russians did not intervene, the South Korean army would be able to hold its own. I think he is too optimistic. Furthermore, he thinks that if the Russians want to risk a world war, they will do it in Germany, because it makes a better propaganda issue for them and has more appeal to their satellite allies.

6

LONG AND EXCEEDINGLY INTERESTING INTERVIEW WITH MARSHAL TITO in his simple villa on Užice.

I asked what his country's stand would be should a deteriorating situation bring about hostilities between the United States and Communist China. He replied: "If such a situation as you mention should develop, we would take a stand against any and all aggression. I should not like to be misunderstood. It is the United Nations itself which must decide who is the aggressor. Our stand will be the same—that of the United Nations. We will adhere to that body's decision."

Tito recalled his country had agreed to recognize Peking. There had been no reply from China. "We know why. It is the same in the case of all countries having a close relationship with the Soviet Union. They all have a uniform policy on Yugoslavia, because Soviet policy toward this country has not changed, and they cannot have an independent view."

Jugoslavia is ready to purchase arms from the Western powers for national defense, and in an emergency would ask for material aid wherever she could obtain it. Despite Moscow's propaganda, Jugoslavia does not consider that the Marshall Plan has been "catastrophic" for Europe; instead, it has afforded "great help" to certain countries, such as Italy and France.

If this country, for its own security, requires material from a Western power, it will seek it. "I can say this," Tito observed. "We won't care what anyone says. If an opportunity comes to obtain arms to defend Yugoslavia —material which we cannot manufacture at home—we will accept it. The Soviet Union has received equipment from Great Britain, including jet planes and strategic raw materials. If it is a question of our own security, we'll buy materials wherever we can, although no negotiations on such matters are going on at present."

I told Tito I had two favors to ask. What were they? First, I wanted to see the Chief of Staff, Colonel General Koča Popović. Why? To get a briefing on the military situation around Jugoslavia's borders. O.K., said Tito. This pleased me. Our military attaché never sees anyone higher than a colonel.

Favor two: I wanted to see Stepinac. Tito said he was well; I wanted to see for myself. There were millions of Catholics in the United States, and all of them were deeply interested. Tito took this one rather dubiously. He thought a while, then he walked up and down, a stony look in his blue eyes. Finally, "You will hear from me," he said. "One way or the other." We shook hands and I left.

BELGRADE, *November 9, 1950*

GENERAL Koča Popovic is small, dapper, and wears no decorations on his handsome uniform. He received a degree in philosophy at the Sorbonne, speaks fluent French and German and was a surrealist poet before the war. He received me surrounded by great folders of data to which he referred. Every now and then we were interrupted with Turkish coffee.

Popović charged that Bulgaria, Rumania and Hungary, the Danubian states that were allies of Hitler during World War II and are now Soviet satellites, were violating the military clauses of the 1946 Paris peace treaties and building up large armies in excess of the limitations specifically fixed.

ZAGREB, *November 11, 1950*

I HAD a fascinating yesterday. Late on the previous day, my phone rang and I was told to go to Zagreb to report to the local Interior Ministry and get my permit to see Archbishop Stepinac. Then the phone rang off. I drove off as early as possible on the new autoroute; and everything worked O.K.

Even before I was officially advised to go to Zagreb, the Jugoslav public, because of the prominence given in the local press to my conversation with Marshal Tito, was discussing the projected interview.

Orthodox Serbs of all political shades came up and growled: "Stepinac should have been hanged. It was he who condoned the murder of thousands of the Orthodox."

"The only good thing this regime has done," said those in opposition to it, "was to put the rascal in jail."

Croats—virtually homogeneously Roman Catholic—beckoned me aside in secluded places and whispered. "You should know before you see the Archbishop that no matter what they tell you we adore him. He is the great hero of the people and no slanders launched against him are believed. He is our martyr."

After spending a night in Zagreb, I called yesterday morning at the headquarters of the Ministry of Interior for the Republic of Croatia. It must be remembered that this is popularly conceived as a dread organization. When one mentions the ministry—known locally as the UDBA, a combination of the initials of the ministry's name—it is *sotto voce*. A revolution always brings with it popular fear of its dynamic and brutal qualities, and this is exceedingly true in Croatia.

At the entry bureau I requested a guide to the office of the Croatian Minister of Interior. The young man at the desk was perplexed by this and asked for my *legitimacia*, or identification documents. I replied that I was an American and had no such papers. An old gentleman, sitting on a bench with a group of petitioners for various favors, stood up and said: "Comrade. The American comrade has no *legitimacia* because anyone knows that in America you don't need such things."

This seemed to satisfy. The youthful official showed me politely upstairs to the office of the Minister's Cabinet chief. The latter asked: "When do you wish to see Stepinac?" "Immediately," I replied. "Where is he imprisoned?" The answer was "Lepoglava."

In Jugoslavia, Lepoglava has deep connotations. It is a prison some fifty miles from Zagreb that was built when Croatia belonged to the Austro-Hungarian empire. Patriots and opponents of all the regimes in the bloody history of this region have suffered there. Under the Hapsburgs, hundreds of Slav nationalists paid for their ideals in Lepoglava. Under the Karageorgević dynasty both Marshal Tito and Moše Pijade, a member of his Politburo today, were incarcerated at Lepoglava.

During World War II the Fascist Croatian Ustaši and the German Gestapo perpetrated horrors within its walls. Since Jugoslavia's liberation by Marshal Tito's Partisans, fearful rumors have seeped through the country about Lepoglava. Its very name throws a dark shadow, although it means "beautiful head."

The Croatian Minister of Interior entered the picture at this moment and politely asked me if I knew the way to Lepoglava. I replied that I did not. He asked if he might send someone from his office to escort me and I agreed. Shortly thereafter a young man named Anton Sobotinćić, wearing the long brown leather coat often associated with members of the UDBA, entered the room, and we departed.

We drove off through the lovely countryside of the Zagorije region of Croatia, where Tito was born in a small peasant house. It was an exceptionally beautiful autumn day. The sun lay softly on the ruddy mountains and velvet green fields.

After chatting at length with the amiable Sobotinćić, who describes himself as not a Communist but a sympathizer (improbable, or modest, for a functionary in the Interior Ministry), we finally arrived at Lepoglava, a small village nestling below the mountain massif of Ivansčica. This hamlet is dominated by the prison that has made its name famous. Virtually the first sight is a series of white walls punctuated with square watch-towers, each of which is guarded by armed peasant boys in blue militia uniforms.

Sobotinćić told the sergeant of the guard that we wished to see the prison commandant. We were taken to his office, and shortly afterward he strode in, a friendly, if perplexed, tough-looking functionary wearing jack-boots, brown leather overcoat, and the type of visored cap that twenty-five years ago was popular in America among motorists and golfers. Today it is fashionable among some members of the political bureaus of Eastern European countries. He was introduced as Josip Spiranec, a former major in the Partisan army of Marshal Tito, a war hero, and undoubtedly—a member of UDBA.

When the purpose of my visit was described by Sobotinćić, Spiranec appeared a bit doubtful. When I asked him how many prisoners were in Lepoglava he seemed still more so. Sobotinćić then said that, first of all, Marshal Tito had himself approved this trip, and, secondly, the government had nothing to hide. At this, Spiranec brightened up.

We went into the sunny courtyard, examined the village church which abuts upon the prison, and he said there were about a thousand persons locked up here with only one "special prisoner"—Archbishop Stepinac. The others live in dormitory rooms, which I did not see, and work eight hours a day, six days a week in neighboring fields and workshops. The Archbishop has exceptional quarters and treatment.

Accompanied by the assistant prison director, we walked down the village street past groups of idling militiamen and UDBA troops to the actual prison gate. A young soldier with a tommy gun flung this open, saluting the commandant, who entered first. We three followed, passing more guards in blue uniforms in a courtyard, going through still another gate, and then climbing a stairway to a brick building. Just inside the doorway we halted in a corridor on each side of which was a row of wooden doors. In each was inserted a tiny peephole, covered by a wooden disk.

Spiranec said something to his assistant. He then took a key from his pocket and entered the first door on the right. Sobotinćić urged me to follow. I went in.

We found ourselves in a room about nine by fourteen feet. The window was barred but not in such a way as to exclude the light of day. The room was warm. The furniture was simple: a cot with sheets and a pillowcase as well as blankets; one table and one chair; a bureau upon which, among other things, were a wash basin, a pitcher and a tin vacuum bottle. The floor was bare wood. From a series of hooks hung some clothing and a towel.

Having worn dark glasses because of the bright sun in the courtyard, I needed a moment to adjust my vision. Then I saw a slender man of medium height standing behind the table, looking first at Spiranec and then at me. It was Archbishop Stepinac.

The Archbishop is a man of pale but evidently healthy countenance, fine features, thin brown hair, and a facial expression that clearly denotes a tremendous inner passion. He stood there for a moment, looking at me, his left hand holding open the pages of a large book upon the table, his reading glasses set beside it. It was then that I realized he had not the faintest idea who I was or why I was there. His contact with everyday affairs is slight, and Spiranec had not had time to explain the circumstances.

The Archbishop's four visitors stood awkwardly for a moment, clutching their caps and hats. Then I told the prelate who I was, how I happened to be there, and that with due respect to the circumstances of the interview and to his own desires, I wished to report to the world any messages he might care to send on how, in general, he felt about his physical treatment and psychological condition.

We spoke in French, which no one else in the room understood. The Archbishop apologized for his mistakes, saying he was far more fluent in Italian and German. Nevertheless, he has mastered the language.

"Monseigneur," I said, "could you tell me what the state of your health is?"

He replied still standing: "I feel well. I am in no way ill. I have lost no weight since I came here four years ago."

I then asked the Archbishop how he occupied his time. He said he devoted many hours to prayer, contemplation and, at the moment, to the translation of a work on the lives of saints. He is studying church history. He showed me the work he was engaged in examining: a Latin tome on the Franciscan order by an Irish prelate named Wadding.

I asked whether it was difficult for him to receive reading material. My three escorts stood silently by, and I am convinced they understood not one word of the conversation. As for the Archbishop, it became evident as the interview progressed that he could not care less if they did.

He told me he received books continually. Most are brought by his sister, who visits him every month, he said. He complained, however, that all the reading material, even ecclesiastical, was first scrutinized by prison censors. He had no access to newspapers; he especially missed *l'Osservatore Romano*, the journal of the Vatican, which he described as "prohibited."

I asked if he was in touch with the world outside the prison walls. He replied, "Letters are not strictly forbidden. But they are all subjected to censorship. Therefore I do not write."

I then explained to the Archbishop what Marshal Tito had said to me concerning the possibilities of his release either to a Roman Catholic monastery within Jugoslavia or to exile—on condition that he should never return.

He stood there silently for a moment, dressed in his black clerical garb, one hand upon Wadding's ecclesiastical history, absolutely motionless. Then, in a calm and quiet voice, he replied: "Whether I go to a monastery, or whether I remain here, or whatever should happen to me, I am utterly indifferent. Such things do not depend upon Marshal Tito. They depend only upon the Holy Father, the Pope and upon no one else."

I asked the Archbishop if he had any kind of message he would like to transmit through me to the world outside the walls of Lepoglava. Again, after slight deliberation, he replied: "I have nothing to say. I am content to suffer for the Catholic Church. Whether or not I shall ever resume my office depends only upon the Holy Father."

I then asked, "Monseigneur, are you well treated?"

"There were some difficulties," he replied. "It is better than I should not speak of it." He added that he received plentiful food and that his cell was heated every day.

All this time, the Archbishop was standing before the one chair in the room. I asked if he would not please sit down. He remained on his feet and said: "I am sorry that I have nothing to offer you. I regret that I cannot even ask you to seat yourself."

I asked if he was able to perform his religious services and to take communion. He pointed to another wooden door opening on to one wall of his cell and said: "There is my chapel. You may go in." I opened the door and saw another cell, slightly smaller, dominated by one table covered with a white cloth and serving as an altar. Archbishop Stepinac explained that there were two other Roman Catholic priests imprisoned in Lepoglava who were permitted to pray with him daily.

"I am completely indifferent as to the possibilities of my liberty," he said again. "I know what is at the root of this matter. It is a question which only the Holy See can resolve. My freedom, or what I may do afterward, is not for this government to decide. I am completely indifferent concerning any thoughts of my liberation. I know why I suffer. It is for the rights of the Catholic Church. I am ready to die each day for the Church. The Catholic Church cannot be, nor will it ever be the slave of any regime.

"If Marshal Tito wishes to free me he should speak with the Holy See. The Catholic Church cannot be the slave of anyone or any country."

After this conversation we bade each other farewell and, led by Spiranec, walked out of the building, out of the prison compound and into the sunny village street. "What did he say to you?" asked Spiranec with considerable curiosity and a gleam in his hard, intelligent eyes.

I precisely recounted the interview. He thought for a moment. Then he said:

That is not entirely true. For example, he has never asked for that paper, *l'Osservatore Romano.* What he asks for he gets. Why, he lives better than the guard here.

In the morning he gets coffee, bread and butter. For lunch he has soup, meat, dessert and half a liter of Dalmatian wine. In the evening he is given either a schnitzel or eggs and half a liter of coffee. Every day he has either šlivovica or a liqueur. We give him between one and a half and two liters of šlivovica each month to drink when he wishes.

How can this man complain? We can never forget the crimes he committed, we who fought this war. It was under him that thousands of Serbs were butchered because they were not Catholics. It was he who collaborated with the enemy. It was he who hid gold and valuables in his church, contravening our laws.

On the way back to Zagreb, after a very considerable silence, a conversation began between myself and Sobotinćić. He described himself as a strongly proregime Catholic who went regularly to church. He contended that Archbishop Stepinac should be where he is and that the Roman Catholic people of Jugoslavia had largely forgotten about him. But he confessed to an admiration for the prelate's obdurate courage. At this moment my Montenegrin chauffeur, who is of the Orthodox faith, muttered: "They should have killed the pig."

PARIS, *January 2, 1951*

ON Saturday night, December 30, I had a small dinner party at home. Those present were: Chip Bohlen and Bill Tyler of the embassy (later U.S. Ambassador to Holland) and Yuri Zhukov.* Zhukov had expressed the desire to meet Bohlen. I told this to Chip. George Perkins, in charge of European affairs at the State Department, approved the project. Zhukov apparently called off a New Year's weekend trip in order to come. Tyler was there, so that the dinner party would not look too obviously arranged as a get-together between Zhukov and Bohlen.

During the general conversation in French, and later in a direct talk in Russian with Bohlen, Zhukov indicated that:

1. Russia would like very much to have a two-power talk with the United States.

2. If this is impossible, Russia wants a "real" Big Four conference and not just a propaganda meeting.

3. Russia is not really getting on too well with China, and the economic problem of aiding China is enormous. The United States has made a propaganda present to Moscow on the subject of China by continually calling Mao Stalin's stooge.

What will come of this talk, I don't know. I am not sure just what Zhukov's position is in addition to being Pravda's correspondent. Unquestionably both sides will report it at length to their governments and probably attribute more significance to it than is warranted. Zhukov and Chip had a long private *tête-à-tête* in Russian in the corner—on Korea.

* (Soviet journalist—and more.)

I was at Chip's house Sunday evening, New Year's Eve, and he took me in a corner and expressed the feeling that the meeting had been a very useful and interesting evening. Clearly Zhukov was acting as Moscow's messenger and not as a journalist.

PARIS, *January 12, 1951*

LUNCHED today with Randolph Churchill. He said his father is perhaps not 100 percent sold on Eisenhower. He never forgave Eisenhower for not sending air support to Jumbo Wilson during the Dodecanese campaign. The campaign had been agreed upon at the Quebec Conference and started just after the conference ended. Wilson, after committing his troops, needed P-51 fighter planes—at that time the only Allied fighter with sufficient range. Eisenhower refused to send them on the grounds that the Combined Chiefs of Staff had not recommended this, and he needed them for the Salerno operation.

As a result, Churchill really wanted General Marshall to command "Overlord." However, being a good student of psychology, he allowed the impression to be given that he did not want Marshall, and that has become the historical version. When Eisenhower was appointed, Churchill "cottoned up" to him strongly and did a deliberate "snow job" on him.

Randolph thinks Roosevelt was in many ways a greater man than his own father and that, above all, he was the greatest politician who ever lived, one who really *knew* public opinion. Roosevelt was always a little bit hurt that Churchill did not remember him from the days of their first meeting in 1919, when Churchill was first lord of the admiralty and Roosevelt was Assistant Secretary of the Navy. Nevertheless, two days after Britain entered World War II, Roosevelt telephoned Churchill from the White House. Churchill thought it was a spoof, told the butler to keep these "damned correspondents" off the phone. A few minutes later, the butler came back and said: "It is really the President." Over the open wire, Roosevelt said: "Winston, we are all for you and I hope you can keep me informed on what is happening." Churchill reported this to Chamberlain (at that time Prime Minister), and Chamberlain gave him permission to do so. Churchill wrote to Roosevelt almost every week afterwards—long before he became Prime Minister.

Churchill always tried to use Harry Hopkins, of whom he was very fond, to put across ideas toward the latter part of the war. He cabled Hopkins more often than Roosevelt. Hopkins would plant the idea in Roosevelt's mind and then FDR, sold on the project, would try and convince Churchill as if it had been Roosevelt's own idea. That, at any rate, is Randolph's account.

He says his father has a curious reputation for drinking much more than he actually does. He really does not know much about food and nothing about wines; he drinks less than a bottle of spirits a day. However, he used to have a whisky and soda at Cabinet meetings and often calls for one at 10:00 A.M.; but it is always a very weak highball, and it may take him three hours or more to finish it. He merely likes to toy with it.

He told me his father recently said to him that he had simplified life at Chartwell by arranging that nothing but champagne should be served at lunch as well as dinner—and only Pol Roger. The old man figured that would save him the trouble of worrying which drink should be served, whether it should be beer, hock, claret or Burgundy. Randolph says his father has a horrible fear of brandy, which is, he says, "the drunkards' drink." He will never take more than a couple of brandies.

PARIS, *February 7, 1951*

LAST night, the Jugoslav Ambassador gave a reception for Milovan Djilas. Djilas has aged considerably since I last saw him. Although he is only forty, he has grown gray and thin. He said to me: "You never come to see me in Belgrade. You always go straight to Tito." I told him the reason I did not go to see him was that he had never been very friendly; that in 1946 he had publicly announced his intention of hanging me.

Djilas said it was true; that I had written that Tito was killing Serbian peasants with American rifles. I reminded him that when Tito had first introduced me to him in the spring of 1945, Djilas had said: "Ah. You are the man who writes that our Tito is slaughtering Serbian peasants with American rifles." He then turned his back. Tito patted me on the back and said: "Don't pay any attention to him."

Djilas remembered this. He said: "Tito remembers the good things as well as the bad things. Maybe I just remember the little things." He suggested that we should have a drink, forget everything and start out afresh. "Times have changed."

PARIS, *March 6, 1951*

LUNCH with General Eisenhower. Eisenhower was in an extremely good humor, full of beans. He has gained a bit of weight and aged somewhat since I last saw him but is very vigorous. He chafed at the diet set for him by his doctor, General Snyder. He appears to be on the water wagon and doesn't smoke. He is eager to relax and suggested playing bridge Thursday afternoons. He is also anxious to arrange a golf foursome.

He asks: "What would have happened had Moscow started war last year? or the year before?" He answered his own question by citing current military preparations of NATO. Admittedly, SHAPE headquarters is still undergoing birth pangs and has not yet even moved into its permanent buildings. Nevertheless, the basic deterrent exists: American nuclear superiority plus the ability to deliver this where strategically required. Therefore the prospects of a Soviet invasion are in all probability remote. The new NATO armies cannot be considered a threat to Soviet security in any sense.

We are working for a limited number of Western divisions in the general area of the Rhine. At best they could be employed in battle around the Elbe. It is ludicrous to fancy they might be conceived as a force to assault the Oder; still more ludicrous to imagine them fighting on the Vistula; beyond all reason to think of the small army being planned ever getting involved in combat further eastward.

This army is conceived solely as a defensive force safeguarding nations which have reason to feel themselves threatened. In *no* sense can Moscow or anyone else regard it as provocative. Therefore it is not only *not* accelerating the possible imminence of war; it is achieving the opposite. In the end it will serve as a deterrent to any imperialist thoughts entertained by Moscow which might otherwise be attracted westward by a vacuum.

Eisenhower has been painstakingly explaining to political leaders that the Allied forces being assembled have only one fundamental objective: the preservation of peace. The subsidiary *raison d'être* is, of course, to afford the best possible military defensive prospects should war recur.

Eisenhower says NATO protects the *national* freedom of its members and of any nations which may later choose to align themselves, in one way or another, with the alliance. It is not NATO's business to mix in any way into the political or ideological affairs of other countries. It is concerned with the independence of nations as such. But Eisenhower emphasizes the intrinsic importance of personal liberty within the framework of national liberty.

He said he cannot personally approve of governmental systems that make of the individual citizen a slave or servant of the state. But he has a clear idea of the authority he holds as NATO commander, and that does not impinge upon the realm of political philosophy. He feels it is absurd for Americans to expect all other nations to model their governing systems upon our own—one which took some three centuries to mature in its special surroundings.

This world cannot be divided into realms of "black" and "white." There are large "gray" areas: regions where for different causes various philosophic concepts and economic conditions have arisen.

Eisenhower has been deeply impressed by all he has heard of the fighting spirit and determination of Greece and Turkey. He thinks it would be excellent, from a strategic point of view, if the eastern Mediterranean were strongly braced and if any conceivable threat of attack on Western Europe were to be menaced by a problem on Russia's left flank. He recognizes that Jugoslavia is, politically, a Communist state, but it has already asserted its intention of defending its *national* integrity. Therefore he favors granting all necessary assistance to Marshal Tito to preserve economic viability and to improve his military potential. He would like to demonstrate that the United States is doing more to aid the suffering Jugoslavs than the Soviet Union is doing to alleviate Hungary, Rumania and Bulgaria—lands stricken by drought last year.

Eisenhower feels that all nations wishing to join in strengthening Western defenses against aggression should be encouraged. Nevertheless he recognizes special political problems are presented by Spain. One European statesman told Ike that Franco would welcome an invitation to join NATO because it would give him pleasure to spurn it. Eisenhower admits there would be difficulty in associating the Franco government with Britain and France. It is certainly not worth risking offending two of NATO's principal members on this issue.

Therefore he thinks it might be wise to make some preliminary military arrangements with Spain before any political compact. He would like to coordinate some of Spain's particular defensive problems with the overall common task of Western Europe.

Eisenhower kept stressing that a soldier must have a clear feeling he is fighting for a worthy cause. One of the tasks of NATO governments is to disseminate among their populations the moral principles of NATO: freedom, peace, self-defense. Ike recognizes the immense importance of morale and hopes the NATO governments will coordinate their propaganda.

Ike is bearish on the European army. He emphasizes the technical difficulties of command and organization, the complexities of interplay between governments that might have contingents assigned in mixed units. He recalls that in past history individual national units fought together on foreign soil—such as the mercenary English and Swiss "companies" that sold their services in medieval and Renaissance Italy. But the problem which would be presented today bears no comparison. Good soldiers might indeed be found among *émigrés* in Europe or among adventurous-minded Germans. But they would have to be organized in some form of foreign legion. This is different. A European army would be difficult to work out. In a sense, it would be "putting the cart before the horse," because it would represent a political unity that does not yet exist.

Eisenhower complained of intergovernmental wrangling. He said he doesn't care if governments are red-faced. What would distress him would be to see populations white-faced. He does not consider assignment of positions in SHAPE headquarters in the category of political plums or gestures toward national pride. These jobs are not kudos. Rather than being a "wreath of roses," such an assignment is more truly a "crown of thorns."

Ike says he is a good soldier and works for an American administration —as well as for Allied governments. But this does not necessarily identify him with the social or political philosophy of the administration. Nevertheless, he is on record, he recalls as favoring unity among nations menaced by aggression, and as recognizing the necessity of combating communism economically if that threat is to be overcome. He wants the West's workers and farmers to feel that NATO is conceived to help preserve them and their way of life.

He confessed that in political prejudices he has a far greater community of views than disparity of views with Herbert Hoover or with Senator Taft, despite their vigorous disagreements on the subject of NATO. But he is not thinking as a political man today, only as commander of an Allied force. He does not believe an army—any army—should mix in politics.

During World War II, it was suggested to him that he should pioneer social reform in the United States by ameliorating relationships between Negroes and whites in his units. Regardless of the good intentions of such a suggestion, Ike felt it was not the role of any army or its commander to spearhead social reform in the government to which it was responsible. Any American general who conceived his duties as such should be fired.

PARIS, *March 12, 1951*

LUNCH with Eisenhower, Chip Bohlen and Bunny Carter at Morfontaine Golf Club; then we played. Ike was in a fine mood. It was the first opportunity he had had to get away from his office. Nevertheless, a French secret police guard followed us around at a discreet distance. Eisenhower plays an amiable, steady, unsensational game. He made an eighty-eight and was very pleased with himself.

Eisenhower thinks that Zhukov is a really "good" Russian with whom the West might have gotten along, but the Soviet system prevents any such possibility of an individual rising to such a position. In August 1945 Eisenhower was visiting Moscow. As an exceptional honor, he was invited to join Stalin on top of Lenin's tomb during a review in the Red Square of gymnastic formations. Eisenhower was allowed to take Harriman and his military attaché, General Deane, with him. It was killing business to stand up there for five hours, but the review was impressive.

Ike said he thought perhaps the most disastrous decision ever taken by makers of American policy was to abandon Chiang Kai-shek because he refused to allow any Communists in his government. (An oversimplified view, indeed! say I.)

PARIS, *March 16, 1951*

LUNCHED and played golf with Eisenhower. Morfontaine is usually closed Mondays, but they opened the course for us and arranged caddies. Nobody else there. He made a ninety-one (with a nine); I made an eighty.

Eisenhower, at lunch, compared Montgomery and Patton. He said Patton did not know how to stand and fight a set battle but was a genius at pursuit. He liked to make headlines, and the best way was by registering the deepest advance. Montgomery could fight a methodical, planned battle and knew how to get the utmost out of the British Tommy.

Incidentally, Ike says the Tommy will fight harder under worse conditions than any other soldiers except Germans. Our soldiers have to be convinced that the fate of the nation depends upon this or that particular effort in order to equal the Tommy.

Montgomery is not a good strategist. He moves too slowly. During the Normandy breakout, Montgomery failed to utilize to its full potentialities the Falaise "killing ground." Montgomery thought he had done well, but Eisenhower says he missed a great opportunity.

I asked Ike if he would have fought the battle of El Alamein the same way Montgomery did. He said Montgomery protected his tanks with infantry during the initial penetration stages. Eisenhower would have first attacked the German mine field with "scout" forces of tanks. Then, the infantry and reserve tanks would have been used to exploit the opening. This would have saved lives. He got up in the empty Morfontaine dining room, gathered salt and pepper cellars, sketched a battle map on the paper tablecloth and moved his "divisions" around. Like a fool I didn't pinch the table-cover map—"Eisenhower's plan for El Alamein."

BELGRADE, *April 3, 1951*

LONG and excellent chat with Milovan Djilas, Minister Without Portfolio and member of the Politburo, Number Two or Number Three in the country.

Stalin told Djilas in 1947 that Albania was the "weak point" in the Communist structure. He now realizes just why Stalin was content to keep it weak. However, he is worried about outside interference in Albania. Jugoslavia would like to see Albania free—but within its present boundaries. It opposes Greek desires to gain southern Albania. What is the use of risking the entire democratic structure (with possible Soviet reaction) for the sake of two poor provinces? Venizelos (Greek Prime Minister) recently proposed to the new Jugoslav Minister in Athens that the two countries should partition Albania. This was vigorously rejected.

Jugoslavia is pleased with American generosity and the way the food assistance program was carried out. It trusts Washington and knows the United States has no intentions on this country, politically, militarily or ideologically. America must follow its policy of giving things for the common interest but not demanding political concessions. That would be fatal. The people would resent it and fail to understand. Jugoslavia has not embarked upon a course of democratizing its political system just to please America or in gratitude for food. Nevertheless, its social system is growing closer to that of ours. It would be foolish for Jugoslavia to join the Atlantic Pact. It is valuable to keep Jugoslavia an independent socialist country.

Nevertheless, it is apparent that our countries must work out a basis for mutual aid. In a sense they are already allies. Some day a system can be arranged for joint declarations of mutual policy; this would be different from a formal alliance such as NATO. Negotiations for arms aid from America must come about (I gathered some such talks have started). It is necessary to have certain equipment for training purposes. But naturally such negotiations must take place in secret, without publicity.

It is necessary—before a war—for Jugoslavia to work out a common defense plan with Greece and Turkey. Diplomatic relations with those countries are now normal. Each must know how many divisions the other can provide on a particular sector in case of emergency. Such arrangements must be made *before* a war breaks out. Djilas thinks the chances of war this year are remote—because of the popular attitude in the Soviet bloc, which cannot be counted on. Therefore he feels there is time to make common defense preparations.

The most important part of our talk came at the end. Djilas said he understood I was going to Greece. I said yes. Would I see the King and the Chief of Staff? Yes. Would I please tell them Jugoslavia was willing to join in mutual defense talks, perhaps an ultimate alliance? I asked if this was *just* Djilas' personal idea or if he spoke for Tito. "The latter," he said, looking me straight in the eye. "Very well," I said. "It's not my regular work but I'll transmit the message."

ATHENS, *April 12, 1951*

I VISITED King Paul this evening. Paul wants the Balkan area to be considered in terms of a possible offensive base—not just defensive. Generals Cannon and Van Fleet and Admirals Sherman and Carney approve of this concept. But General Collins, Army Chief of Staff, opposes it.

Paul would like Greece's traditional two big parties to reorganize themselves on a popular basis and put an end to the innumerable splinter groups now confusing Greek politics.

I told Paul about my talk with Djilas and the latter's assurance that the alliance bid comes from Tito himself. The King was excited but wary. But he promised to explore the idea with care and discretion.

PARIS, *May 11, 1951*

THIS afternoon I had a long talk with de Gaulle. I asked him if he would outlaw or limit the activities of the Communist Party if he came to power. He replied: "Certainly. They are already illegal in many ways. They are acting in the trade unions, but this is against the law because the law specifies that trade unions must only be professional and not political. It is easy to prove they are political. Up to now, the law permits the expulsion of the Communists from unions. The legislative position vis-à-vis the

Communists must be further defined. You cannot have a state within a state. We cannot prevent people from being for the Soviet Union, but we can prevent them from favoring the Soviet Union against France."

De Gaulle said France must be revived militarily. This was necessary for France and for NATO: "Therefore we must have true responsibility in the Mediterranean. If France has a greater responsibility towards NATO in Europe and in North Africa, it will have more interest in working for the coalition."

I asked if de Gaulle thought France should contribute more divisions for the defense of Europe than are scheduled at present and he replied: "Certainly yes; not only divisions, but also a greater contribution in sea and air power." He explained that France cannot at present make much more war material, but it can certainly produce more manpower units—both active and in reserve—and could also increase its arms production. He asserted that with American equipment many more French divisions could be provided, but that it was necessary that France should have more interest in making this greater contribution by having more responsibilities.

I asked de Gaulle if he thought West Germany should be rearmed. He replied that it should, but on condition that West Germany should never be permitted to have an army in Europe stronger than any other army in Europe—above all that of France. He dismissed the idea of a "European army" and said that only national armies could be formed, although an international expeditionary corps could be selected from such armies. The idea of a "European army" was a "joke of the politicians."

PARIS, *May 12, 1951*

THIS morning I had a talk with Field Marshal Viscount Montgomery of Alamein, Eisenhower's deputy commander. Montgomery said it was imperative to include Spain in NATO. It is ridiculous to leave that country out, especially since it is surrounded by NATO members: France, Portugal and French North Africa. Spain may be a Fascist state in the eyes of the politicians, but at any rate it had already fought and defeated communism. It must be brought into NATO as soon as possible.

I asked Montgomery what he thought of the chances of war. He said he did not believe there was any chance of war this year. However, by the end of 1952, there must be a decision one way or another. The Russians believed that they had enough superiority available in the West not to fear Western rearmament until Germany began to rearm in cooperation with the Western powers. At the moment, the question of German rearmament was "under the table," and nothing was being done on it. However, if the subject becomes current again and active steps are taken, the danger of a Russian attack will increase.

PARIS, *May 29, 1951*

I PLAYED golf today with General Eisenhower and General J. Lawton Collins, Chief of Staff of the United States Army. Afterwards, lunched with Eisenhower, Collins, Gruenther and Biddle.

Collins and Eisenhower told me they had agreed the constabulary setup by the American Army in Germany, although it has the strength of an armored division, is not to be considered as a division. This will permit the Army to build itself up stronger than the six-division limitation fixed by Congress. In actuality the Defense Department could build up American strength in Germany to the equivalent of seven combat-strength divisions by including the constabulary and not listing it as a division. Collins begged me not to write anything about this because it would put Congress on its ear and damage the chances of the plan.

PARIS, *June 27, 1951*

LUNCH with Eisenhower, then played golf. Ike said the greatest disaster in American foreign policy was the fumbling which resulted in handing China over to the Russians and giving them 400,000,000 people to use as they saw fit. It now looks as if the second greatest disaster is about to occur— the loss of Iran.

He said Montgomery had done a great thing in reviving the spirit of the defeated Eighth Army in Egypt. Montgomery had something of Cromwell about him. However, he had all kinds of complexes. He did not come from the same top level of society as Alexander. He had not gone to the best public school. He was a little, insignificant fellow as a young man, and had never been popular. Eisenhower preferred Alexander, who was a better man to work with.

Ike said he is going to London July 2 for the ceremonies in memory of American Air Force personnel who lost their lives in England. He is going to make a speech at the English-Speaking Union in which he will point out that argument and disagreement between democratic allies are necessary and useful but should not be staged in public. He will recall that during the war he had bitter arguments with some of the people present (at the dinner), but they did no damage because the world never knew about them. He will be referring above all to Churchill. He is going to stress the imperative need to unify Western Europe. He believes the greatest thing Anglo-American policy could accomplish would be this.

He sees no reason to wait for years to accomplish this in a series of slow steps. After all, when a person goes to a hospital for surgery, the doctor does not operate 10 percent each time. We should set a goal for unification within six months or a year and work hard for that immediately—not talk of the vague and distant future. He is thinking, as a first step, of trying to bring about one state for West Germany, the Benelux states, France and

Italy. England could not be included at this time because England remains primarily an imperial rather than a European power. He wants agreement to do away with all customs barriers; to create one currency, one nationality and one passport in a real union of Europe, which would then be open to other nations to join.

PARIS, *July 4, 1951*

YESTERDAY Eisenhower made the speech he had talked about. I must say he watered it down a lot from his original plan. It was by no means as strong and urgent an appeal for quick action on European unity as he had promised. But he did ask for "the establishment of a workable European federation" and requested that the problem should be attacked "by direct and decisive assault with all available means."

7

THIS MORNING I HAD A TALK WITH WINSTON CHURCHILL AT HIS home, 28 Hyde Park Gate, a charming brick house with a lovely garden. After a moment, I was taken upstairs to Churchill's bedroom by a manservant. The old man was propped up in bed, his arms resting on a bare breakfast tray that had legs on it. He had two sponge pads on which to ease his elbows. He was wearing a cream-colored nightshirt and smoking a long cigar. He did not have glasses on. The first thing he did was ask if I wanted a whisky and soda (this was 11:30 A.M.). I replied in the affirmative, and he asked the servant to bring me one and to "bring me another" startling me by handing out an empty glass. However, the highballs were pale, and I noticed he sipped about twice; the drink was really almost full when I left. Likewise, I don't believe he puffed his cigar more than eight or ten times in forty minutes.

He was extremely courteous and friendly. He has aged a great deal since I first talked with him eight years ago in Cairo. He seemed rather dreamy and not thoroughly alert. I am told he really perks up only in the evening. It is sometimes difficult to follow his conversation. First of all, he speaks very softly and frequently rolls his words around his large cigar. Furthermore, he sometimes begins to talk about something then remains silent for some seconds, and you believe he has finished what he was about to say; then he recommences.

Churchill said the United States has every right to negotiate a private bilateral agreement with Spain, and he intends to say so soon in public. (I may recall that today and all this week there has been a great furore in the British press because of Admiral Sherman's visit to Madrid and the announcement that America intends to seek an agreement with Franco. We are being bitterly criticized by most British papers, and Britain is catching it for "interference" in the American press.) Churchill, however, said Spain should not be admitted to NATO. He thought that the present argument would soon blow over. He warned that America should beware of making any deal with Franco on Gibraltar.

Churchill spoke strongly in favor of a European army. Each of the European members of NATO should have its own national army, which would then contribute divisions to an overall European army. Germany should likewise contribute divisions to such an army. Britain and America would send divisions from their armies to Europe to be added to the European army, which thus would become the force under Eisenhower's command.

He claimed the Labor government was sabotaging projects for European unity, and he said, "Of course, you know how I feel about the need for such unity."

He said a European army was necessary, above all, in terms of the day when, if our policy succeeds, the United States will eventually withdraw its troops from Europe, when that continent is strong enough to stand upon its own feet. He thought that Britons scattered around the earth plus 150 million Americans together were strong enough to face anyone and to press for the desirable goal of European unity.

It was rather a shame the United States had never had any colonies because it did not appreciate the problems posed. The French were doing a very good job in Morocco, and it would be most damaging to NATO if French control were removed. The United States criticized England for years about India. Now a disaster is occurring there. A half-million people have been killed in the Punjab alone (Churchill's figure is a gross underestimate), and terrible growing pains are being felt. The situation is bound to get worse. There is little advice we can give India and Pakistan, because their leaders are intelligent men who were trained and educated in England and "know all the tricks."

British and American policy is, of course, to get strong enough so that eventually we can negotiate a settlement with Russia and force Moscow to abide by it. Russia must evacuate the eight captive capitals of Eastern Europe. But the most dangerous situation is while we are getting stronger —not when we are finally strong. Russia might feel it necessary to risk an attack during the process of our rearmament, before we are really strong.

Russia fears our friendship more than our enmity. The Soviet dictatorship could not stand free intercourse with the West. We must make Moscow fear our enmity more than our friendship.

PARIS, *July 23, 1951*

LUNCH today with Pierre Bertaux, head of French Sureté. He asked if I could get a message conveyed directly to Marshal Tito. He had tried to send the message through the British but was not sure the British had direct enough contact. The message is this: The Soviet Ambassador in Paris recently told certain French Communist leaders that they need not worry about Titoism. Russia was confident it could have Tito assassinated whenever it wished, but there was no need for it at present. The Russians had agents so close to Tito that the latter could not possibly suspect it. One French Communist leader asked the Ambassador if he was not being indiscreet. The Ambassador laughed and said: "Not at all. If Tito got suspicious and started a purge he would do half of Russia's job for Moscow."

PARIS, *August 24, 1951*

INTERESTING talk with David Bruce. He said the meeting between Eisenhower and the Jugoslav Chief of Staff, Colonel General Popović, took place in the embassy. Popović said Jugoslavia had 400,000 men under arms plus 800,000 men trained as partisans and a mobilizable reserve of 400,000 additional soldiers. He believed the Russians would attack Jugoslavia only if they thought they could get away with it without a world war.

PARIS, *August 30, 1951*

LUNCH with Zhukov. Yuri intimated that Malik's peace-in-Korea speech was a result of the dinner party where I brought Zhukov and Bohlen together. He said: "Didn't you see how Malik followed the line Bohlen gave about settlement on the thirty-eighth parallel?" I recalled to Zhukov that for more than a hour he had sat at one end of the room with Bohlen talking in Russian while I sat at the other end of the room chatting with Bill Tyler, the only other person present. Therefore, I did not know all that went on. He then said Bohlen had intimated a settlement could be reached around the thirty-eighth parallel. I asked if this had anything to do with Malik's reply, and he said "of course." Obviously Zhukov passed on all of Bohlen's remarks to Moscow.

Always by innuendo, he indicated Russia was having a great deal of trouble with the Chinese. I said I thought the Chinese wanted a settlement in Korea. They were losing a lot of blood and their best human cadres just at the moment they needed such elements to carry out the final processes of their revolution. I had heard through Indian sources that the Chinese really wanted a settlement. He agreed that China needed such a settlement. I could not understand why the disciplined Russian Communist system did not order it. He said there were difficulties—but I "could not understand."

Zhukov was extremely worried about Jugoslavia. He was convinced the United States was planning an attack on Russia through Jugoslavia. Not less than three times he asked me if Harriman had not gone to Belgrade to arrange such an attack. I said he was crazy and I was sure the situation was the reverse, that there was every reason to fear a Communist attack on Jugoslavia.

PARIS, *September 25, 1951*

LUNCH today with Eisenhower. He is distressed at the way the American public permits politicians to bring about national policies on a basis of purely selfish personal interests of individuals thinking of votes. He would like very much to see committees or centers established in cities and towns throughout the country where businessmen, lawyers, farmers and other citizens would get together and discuss issues and make up their own minds what is in the national interest, then try and exert public pressure accordingly.

Eisenhower said it was a shocking notion on the part of some American politicians that the United States should cease all trade with Russia and her allies. It was similarly ridiculous to expect other nations to cut off trade with the Russian bloc. The only result of such a policy would be to force all foreign nations to make a choice between trading with Russia or trading with us and in the end possibly to choose the Soviet bloc. In order to survive, all nations must have foreign commerce. Bernard Baruch, during World War I, even maintained a secret trade for certain vital materials with Germany. It is folly to assume that we can force other nations to cut all foreign trade to suit our political interests.

We talked at length about General Marshall. Eisenhower said Marshall had been very strongly influenced by "Black Jack" Pershing, a stern disciplinarian. This, he thought, was the reason that Marshall's staff was always terrified of him. As a result, Marshall was horseback riding on December 7 when the Japanese attacked Pearl Harbor, and his staff was afraid to notify him as quickly as should have been the case. Eisenhower said Marshall was shocked when he first heard his staff was afraid of him. Eisenhower said loyalty was not a sufficient quality to introduce into one's staff; an element of personal friendship and contact on a human basis was also required.

We discussed General MacArthur. Eisenhower admitted that when he served with MacArthur in the Philippine Islands, MacArthur always underestimated the role of airpower in war. Apparently this was true even during the initial period of World War II. Quezon told Eisenhower that when the Japanese attacked Pearl Harbor MacArthur was convinced for some strange reason that the Philippines would remain neutral and would not be attacked by the Japanese. For that reason, presumably, MacArthur refused permission to General Brereton to bomb Japanese bases on Formosa immediately after the attack on Pearl Harbor. As a result, the American airfields in the Philippines were badly bombed by the Japanese, more than twenty-four hours after Pearl Harbor, because all our planes were still on the ground.

Ike said the biggest problem facing the world today was one simple question: Are the fourteen men on the Politburo truly ambitious dictators or ideological fanatics? If the former is the case, their primary ambition would be to retain personal power. If the latter is the case, it means inevitable war.

PARIS, *October 2, 1951*

LAST night, at the home of Margaret Biddle, dined with the Duke and Duchess of Windsor (formerly King Edward VIII). The Duke had just come back from London, where he stayed during the critical operation on the lung of his brother, King George VI. After dinner we were sitting together talking, and every now and then he would look across the room at the Duchess and say: "It's so wonderful to see her. You know, I have not seen her for a week. Isn't she charming?"

After dinner there was a pianist. The Duke was transported with joy. He sang a few songs rather badly and joyfully imitated the playing of various instruments such as the cello and the violin, waving his arms around like a happy schoolboy. He knew a few Spanish and German songs partially. I asked him what languages he spoke, and he said: "German, a little Spanish and a little French."

He talked steadily. At one point the Duchess leaned over the table and said: "You promised you were going to listen tonight because there are a lot of brains around but you are talking all the time." He replied: "I have to talk or otherwise I would fall asleep."

He made it clear that he still feels strong sympathy for the Germans as a people. He recalled that he has German blood and many German relatives. He said he understood the Germans, and that "we must have them as allies."

PARIS, *October 15, 1951*

YESTERDAY we went to a surprise birthday party for Eisenhower, who was sixty-one. The whole thing was a plot by Gruenther. Ike is a great lover of birthday parties. Al decided to kid him. When General Ike woke up, nobody congratulated him. He was astonished when Moaney, the Negro sergeant who has been with them for years, seemed to have forgotten his birthday. Mamie said nothing. When the general got up he asked whether she wanted him to wear anything special. She said no, anything that would be comfortable to play bridge in. Gruenther had invited him for cards that afternoon.

Averell Harriman, Secretary of the Navy Dan Kimball, and I had been invited to play at 3:00 P.M. at the Gruenthers. We were all in on the plot. When Eisenhower came nobody mentioned his birthday. We just sat down and played. Both generals were wearing ordinary civilian clothes. Grace Gruenther was downstairs in the kitchen supervising the cooking. Gruenther had seen to it that no letters or telegrams congratulating Ike were delivered. All telephone messages, including transatlantic calls, had been stopped.

As we were playing bridge, the plot took shape. A few other friends, including Marie Harriman, Marina, Mrs. Perle Mesta (American Minister in Luxembourg, who came down with a birthday cake she'd baked) gathered at the Eisenhowers'. Here they learned a song which Grace had written for him. At 6:00 sharp, while we were playing bridge, and Eisenhower—with his back to the surprise—was sitting gloomily as dummy, the whole group tiptoed to the entrance of the room and suddenly began singing the following song, to the tune of "When You Wore a Tulip":

> Oh, Ike had a birthday, a big, happy birthday,
>   But nobody told him so.
> Not even Moaney, Admiral Capponi,
>   Or Mamie seemed to know;
> Instead of being cheery, the day seemed so dreary,
>   And poor Ike felt so alone.
> We're sorry we ignored you, for really we adore you,
>   Happy birthday from one and all.

The general was astounded. He turned around blushing a little with delight. Then the party started. Cocktails were distributed while Eisenhower sat in an armchair and his presents were brought in, plus his cables, letters, and so forth. I gave him a bottle of Przovka (pepper vodka). He said the last and the only time he drank it was with Stalin. The Gruenthers gave him an apparatus with which to make sauerkraut. The Harrimans gave him a book, *The Cruel Sea*. Among the cables he received was one from President Truman. He sat like a little boy grinning from ear to ear as he went through his presents and messages.

PARIS, *October 30, 1951*

LUNCH and long talk with Eisenhower. He is under immense pressure to run for President. He pointed to a pack of letters on his desk, either congratulating him upon his alleged decision to run—which has not been made—or begging him to run. The mail also included brochures from various "Ike for President" clubs.

He pointed affectionately to some pressed columbines, which he had received from Denver. The columbine is the state flower of Colorado, and he has named his new plane for it. We had a glass of sherry with Gruenther before lunch.

Ike said that before he announced his decision not to run for the Presidency in 1948, President Truman offered him the opportunity to run on the Democratic ticket and added to this that he, Truman, would step down and run for Vice-President. After Eisenhower's public announcement that he would not run for political office, he said that he ranked about "as high as Saint Peter" with Truman.

Eisenhower looks back with horror upon the confusion and lack of coordination in our planning and defense spending immediately after the war. He recalls that Admiral Ernie King visited him at his SHEAF headquarters during the spring of 1945. Eisenhower said to him: "Well, Ernie, you will be glad to know that this show is going to be over soon and that you can have the whole damn British fleet to help you out in the Pacific." King replied that he did not want a single British ship. Since he (King) had been a little boy, the British had been trying to plant the white ensign on the islands of the central Pacific, and he damned well was going to prevent it. Eisenhower asked him if he meant by this that the United States was planning to build the huge tonnage in extra shipping to do the job all alone without British aid. King said that was exactly what he meant. Eisenhower was horrified by the enormous waste of money required to build these strategically unnecessary ships and said: "That certainly is a hell of a way to build a democratic system in the world."

On the subject of rearming Germany, Eisenhower said he had told Hallstein, Secretary of State at the Bonn Ministry of Foreign Affairs; General Adolf Heusinger, military adviser to Adenauer; and General Hans Speidel, formerly Rommel's Chief of Staff and now one of Adenauer's military advisers, that there must be no attempted German blackmail seeking to get better terms out of the West by playing off the threat of the East. The Germans must realize that their bread is buttered on the Western side; they must take a real part in the Western community.

Eisenhower thought it was necessary to explain day after day with enough repetition to drive the point home just what American foreign policy is. He recalls that after the British advised us they could no longer support Greece and Turkey, Truman decided we would have to do so—the so-called "Truman Doctrine." But Truman told Eisenhower we wanted to announce he would support any country against communism. Ike told the President it was the wrong way to go about it; we should promise support to any country prepared to defend itself. We could not embark on a straight anti-Communist campaign around the world, but we must encourage independent nations to fight for their independence against aggression.

Eisenhower admitted he was a member of the Republican Party; that he had voted for Dewey as President in 1948 against Truman; that he had voted for Dulles in 1950 as Senator against Lehman. He agreed to allow a statement to this effect to be put out in America by his brother Milton. He does not seem to wish to run for President. However, he may be forced to do so.

PARIS, *November 10, 1951*

LAST night I attended the annual reception at the Soviet Embassy in honor of the October Revolution. It was crowded with Russians, satellite diplomats, and various Communist delegations to the United Nations Assembly. General Slavin, a member of the Soviet delegation and a burly, thick-set man with hands like a blacksmith, forced me into a corner with an overly affable vodka toast, saying: "You people want war and if you insist we will give you war—and smash you." I thought this a somewhat eccentric bit of hospitality.

PARIS, *November 12, 1951*

THIS afternoon I had a very good talk with Eden. He said that in his speech before the Assembly today he had demanded that Italy be admitted to UN in order to "rehabilitate" his own name in Rome. He is not yet too popular on account of his noble attitude during the Ethiopian War. Eden admitted he would be happy to see a "package settlement" on UN admissions, letting in such Western countries as Italy, Portugal and Eire, together with such Russian puppets as Rumania, Hungary and Bulgaria. However, he drew the line at Outer Mongolia.

Eden said the great difficulty in the Middle East was Palestine—not so much the mere fact of Israel's existence as an independent state, but the tragic situation of the Arab refugees. Now that King Abdullah of Jordan was dead, it was more difficult to deal with this.

PARIS, *November 13, 1951*

LAST night I attended an extraordinary dinner party given by the Duke and Duchess of Windsor. Aside from Senator Warren Austin of the UN delegation and his wife and Prime Minister René Pleven and his wife, a weird collection of social derelicts was there. After dinner and dull conversation, Pleven departed, rapidly followed by Austin. I was anxious to go but the Windsors insisted we stay.

The Duchess caught Marina by the hand and said, "Don't go, it's so nice to have brains to talk to." She sat down and we began speaking of the world situation. She kept repeating, "I do hope really nothing is going to happen, because we do want so to buy a house."

Then Marina and I were treated to an extraordinary conversation. In essence, it comprised a tragic lament about the British royal family. The Duchess kept insisting she would never go back to England because "the Duke," as she always calls her husband, had been treated so shabbily.

They told the following story. The Duke had worked nobly and patriotically for Britain while Prince of Wales and, briefly, as King Edward VIII. Between 1918 and 1936, he averaged one speech every day. It was untrue to say that Winston Churchill had been his "ghost." He had no ghost, wrote all his speeches himself, and was very proud of it. This, he insisted, was true of his famous speech of farewell to the British nation— although I must say I have heard from other eminently responsible sources that he got a good deal of help from Churchill on that one, at any rate.

The Duke was furious over the following incident. He had prepared a lengthy speech designed to boost his book of memoirs. The thing was recorded for a publishers' dinner, but Buckingham Palace ordered it stopped on the grounds that it was no time to make such a speech because of the King's illness. On the afternoon before the speech was to have been delivered, Princesses Elizabeth and Margaret went to the races. Both the Duke and the Duchess kept repeating that the two "nieces" had gone "to the races," while, at the same time, the speech was banned because of King George's illness.

The Duchess said: "Why don't you play them your record?" The Duke protested: "Oh, no, no, I can't." Then we were escorted downstairs where they have a long-playing phonograph.

The Duke's speech said he now "knew why Job said 'I wish my enemies had written a book'." It was a great honor for him because "it is the first time in fifteen years that I have spoken in England, which, in spite of everything, is my country and my home." The speech continued: A lot of people had been nasty about the book, there had been criticism, but he didn't see why, just because he is an ex-king, he wasn't allowed to write. He brought in a lot of examples of English rulers who had written books— Charles II, Henry VIII and Queen Victoria. The speech ends with the remark: "My book is not a novel, but it is a romance, and all I can say is that I hope it can end like most fairy tales—'and they lived happily ever after'."

The speech was very pleasant but we were told he had never been allowed to make it. The Duchess kept saying, "What nonsense! What hypocrisy! What jealousy! When I think that very day, the girls went to the races and the Duke of Gloucester went to a dinner party!"

PARIS, *November 16, 1951*

REMARKABLE dinner party last night given by Marie Harriman in honor of Averell's sixtieth birthday. Averell looked extremely happy and nowhere near his age. He kept wandering around like a little boy saying: "I'm astonished to be sixty. I am not sixty. I won't be sixty."

It was a distinguished gathering, way out of my league: Dean Acheson and his wife, General Eisenhower and his wife, General Bradley (Chairman of the Joint Chiefs of Staff) and his wife, General Gruenther and his wife, Ambassador Bruce, Admiral Kirk, Ambassador to Moscow, and a few others.

After Averell had blown out the birthday cake candles, Acheson made a very pleasant little speech on behalf of "all of us around the table who have come together this evening because we are so fond of him." He recalled that he had first met Averell in 1905. (They were schoolboys together at Groton. Acheson told me afterwards that Averell was two years ahead of him.) Then he went on and talked about what a great public servant Averell was.

Harriman got up and recalled that he had coached the Yale varsity crew while Acheson coached the Yale freshmen. He said Acheson rowed Number Seven on the freshmen at 149 pounds, and that he was willing to wager there had been nobody that light on the Yale freshman crew before or since. He said Acheson's advice had always been good, although it was once responsible for the two of them getting "fired" together in Paris when they were youngsters. I didn't catch this one.

Then Averell turned to Eisenhower and said he wanted to take particular notice of him, as he was the most important man here and the most important man in Europe today. Averell has been a Democrat since the days of Al Smith. I think the party bosses would have run him out of the ranks after hearing this—although Averell was sincerely talking about Ike's value to Western defense and had no thoughts concerning politics.

PARIS, *December 11, 1951*

THIS morning I had a talk for an hour and a quarter with Eisenhower. He does *not* want to run for President. He has never wanted to run for that office. From a personal point of view he has nothing to gain from it, but that, of course, is not the fundamental reason for his attitude. It's a hell of a life and would be very grim for his grandchildren. He detests the idea that they would always have to be followed around by Secret Service men.

Eisenhower said, furthermore, that being in politics placed a man in a very uncomfortable personal position. He said, for example, that he had recently given a few thousand dollars to an old friend of his in the oil business to invest in a new well. Some of this money had been invested in the name of his son and grandchildren. He did this just as a "fling," he said. What would happen if the well came in and he made many times his original investment? Were he in politics, people could attack him and attempt to create a scandal, although he was merely hoping to make something for his family. He would like to continue the job he is doing and eventually to become a sort of "elder statesman" who would be completely free from any political attachments and therefore would be in a position, if necessary, to advise or influence people and events for the sake of his country. He feels that it would be a useful thing in our political system to have two or three such men utterly free from politics, who would thus be in a position to speak for the United States and the American people, rather than for any political party.

He is now determined to stay on as commander in SHAPE unless he is given another responsibility. In other words, he has no intention of resigning and returning to Columbia or to any other civilian job unless he is drafted as a candidate for the Presidency. (In the past Eisenhower has said that he does not believe an Army officer should run for the Presidency and indicated he might therefore resign this position and return to America to permit his nomination. He no longer feels this way.)

He has no intention of making any move to help those political leaders who are seeking to draft him as the Republican candidate. He is, of course, a Republican and always has been. He is against many aspects of the New Deal and particularly the trend toward centralization of government power. However, he does not believe the clock can be turned back. Our Constitution is a living thing, but it must adjust itself to changing circumstances as the world evolves.

He is fully aware there are many people who would like him to run. But he feels there are many possible candidates and he does not intend to make any move in that direction, either covert or overt. Many of the political leaders of the Republican Party, such as Dewey, Taft and Lodge, are continually requesting him to come out and declare his colors. He will not do this. If the American people draft him as a candidate, he would respond to a call of duty, but he hopes this will not occur.

Since 1943, there have been various movements trying to get him interested in politics. In 1948 (he told me before that Truman offered to stand down and run as Vice-President if Eisenhower would accept the Presidential nomination for the Democratic Party in that year) all he had to do was to promise political leaders that he would "keep my mouth shut." The situation now has altered only in the sense that "I'll keep my mouth utterly and permanently shut." Now he has a position of vast responsibilities to the American people and to their European allies. He does not intend in any way to jeopardize the movement toward constructing the democratic alliance.

If he were to make a statement now that he was a Republican, it would immediately split American opinion in terms of backing NATO. As I know—he has said this to me often—he is strongly in favor of changing the regime in America because twenty years is too long for any party to be in power. Corruption has set in. Although Truman is a fine man in many ways, the only thing he knows is politics. Every inch he has moved up the ladder has been on the basis of winning elections. As a result, men have been appointed to offices who are not fit for those offices.

It would be a good thing to "clean out the stable," Eisenhower thinks. I remarked that I thought Truman had at least shown good judgment in appointing Acheson and standing by him, and that it seemed rather gallant on the part of the President to remain loyal to the one member of his Cabinet who was a great political liability. Eisenhower smiled and pointed out that if the President were to fire Acheson now, it would be an admission of failure of his own policy—which Acheson was pursuing.

Eisenhower talked strongly against Taft. He said Taft was a very stupid man. He might have a memory—that, the general did not pretend to know—but he had no intellectual ability, nor any comprehension of the issues of the world.

He had in his possession a letter Taft had sent to somebody else that said Taft was prepared to back the principle that six American divisions should be stationed in Europe and that even this amount could be increased by "bits and pieces." But Eisenhower said he would not place his trust in Taft as a man.

Eisenhower said some of the liberal Republicans were very worried about the way Taft was muscling in on the party machine and lining up delegates. Eisenhower could not help this. The politicians told him he would have to make some move pretty soon to give them a clue. He refused to do this. I pointed out that Willkie had managed to gain the nomination in a whirlwind last-minute finish without benefit of the political machines. Ike remarked, "That, of course, was a different matter," and he went on to say that the party was looking for anybody at that time who could possibly capture public imagination and gain office on behalf of the politicians. (Of course, it was also very different because Willkie campaigned strongly for the nomination.)

Eisenhower said that he would respond to a "call of duty" only if it were demonstrated by the country, forcing a convention to nominate him. He knew the limitations of the American political system and that sometimes politics was a pretty "sordid" business, and big issues were settled in "smoke-filled rooms," but, nevertheless, it was our system, and he had no intention of making any move himself.

He said there were some Republicans who felt that if Taft was nominated as the candidate of their party, the Democrats would then draft Eisenhower immediately afterwards at their convention. At this point he repeated that he was a Republican, even though he would make no statement to that effect now because he wanted to remain entirely outside the political picture.

PARIS, *December 13, 1951*

DINNER last night at the Eisenhowers. Eisenhower said we had to assume the Russians were dominated by a group of men following one of two possible philosophies. Either they were dictators who were out to hang onto their jobs and stabilize them; or they were fanatics whose actions could never be predicted and who would inevitably force another war. His own thought was that the former is the case.

He blames Churchill entirely for the political division of Germany which gave Russia such a large share. He said Churchill never had any faith in "Overlord"—the invasion of Normandy. Churchill had already told Eisenhower that the capture of Pantelleria in the Mediterranean was a "miraculous" military operation. When they were planning "Overlord" in England during the spring of 1944, Churchill said that if Eisenhower moved thirty-six divisions across the Channel into France to control the Brest and Cherbourg peninsulas, it would be the greatest military operation in all history; that if he also gained control of Le Havre, it would be an operation without any historical comparison and that he (Churchill) would be the first to get up and announce this. Eisenhower said that he expected to be on the frontiers of Germany by Christmas. Churchill kept shaking his head and said that this was entirely out of the question.

As a result of Churchill's skeptical attitude, unsound political decisions were taken. In fact, in a final briefing Eisenhower had before the start of "Overlord," Churchill was extremely pessimistic. All the high Allied officers plus the King of England and Churchill were present. After Eisenhower had finished his briefing, Churchill said before the group that his attitude toward "Overlord" was "hardening." Eisenhower commented: "That was a hell of a way to inspire faith in my officers."

Eisenhower said he had absolute confidence in the ultimate success of his plans but he could never convince Churchill. Churchill came to him once and started explaining what a terrible tragedy it would be if the operation failed. Tears began to roll down his cheeks, and he said that in such a case, he would have to present his resignation as Prime Minister to His Majesty. Churchill kept building up logical arguments as to why the operation would fail, but he always based them upon an unsound initial premise.

Unfortunately, Eisenhower said, Churchill forgot all about his promise to get up and announce what a great victory and unprecedented success "Overlord" had been, after France was overrun. In March of 1945, the Allies were all ready to close in on Germany. They were still about three hundred miles from Berlin. The Russians had no more rivers to cross and had a powerful bridgehead across the Oder. As a matter of fact, the Allies could have gone much further east than they actually did. When they met the Russians, the latter proved to be a battered, rag-tag, bobtail outfit, and, Eisenhower said, "We could have licked the hell out of them." But he had to stop at the Elbe, which was already far to the east of the political line dividing Germany which had been fixed by the political leaders.

This line was chosen largely because of Churchill's pessimism. Churchill refused to believe that the Western armies could even get that far into Germany. If Churchill had had confidence in Eisenhower's armies, the line dividing Germany between east and west could have been moved much nearer to the Elbe or on the Elbe itself. Eisenhower could not have taken Berlin, because the Russians were in a position to surround the city before he could get there. He had to draw a battleline where the Eastern and Western armies would meet in order to avoid confusion, because there was a tremendous paucity of interpreters on both sides, and friction had to be avoided at all costs.

The Russians told him when he was in Moscow that the Russian soldier always fought well for his motherland. In fact Eisenhower said he thought there was more patriotic love of country in Russia than in any other land. While he stood on Lenin's tomb beside Stalin, reviewing Red Army units, Stalin kept saying to him that America and Russia must be friends because Russia needed help from the United States.

Eisenhower said the Russians would certainly not be provoked into attacking the West by the defensive preparations of NATO. They had a marvelous intelligence system, and they knew perfectly well that the scale of our preparations was only defensive and could never be considered useful for an offensive. Furthermore, he added that a preventive war or an attack on Russia would be insane because Russia could never be defeated by an invasion. He cited the cases of both Hitler and Napoleon.

There was, of course, no doubt that Russia could overrun Europe very swiftly at present. However, he was confident the Russians were sufficiently realistic to recognize that this was inadequate in terms of winning a war. They would embark upon a war only if they were confident of total victory. This was out of the question. The Russians were fully aware that a long war would be a question of relative production ability, and we alone had three times their economic capacities. For that reason they would certainly not start a war.

PARIS, *January 7, 1952*

SENATOR Lodge has caused a great sensation by announcing that Eisenhower has given permission to have his name listed in the New Hampshire primary as a member of the Republican Party.

MADRID, *January 23, 1952*

THIS morning I had a long interview with Generalissimo Franco. My interpreter was a Foreign Office official named Juan de las Barcenas, an amiable but rather pompous individual who speaks extremely good Oxonian English.

Among the most important views expressed by Franco were the following:

Spain would welcome the stationing of United States military missions here to instruct this country's armed forces in the use of new weapons and new techniques if the proposed bilateral agreement between Washington and Madrid is enacted.

Spain would be willing to accept the philosophical premises of our Mutual Security Act and the Benton amendment (providing for acceptance of the principles of free trade unionism, encouragement of private enterprise and discouragement of cartels). Franco said Spain already fostered private enterprise and sought to check cartels. He thought support of free trade unions was "merely a matter of definition." However, he said later on that he regarded such American labor institutions as the right to strike as "archaic," so I think that little point of "definition" is going to raise a bigger stink than he foresees.

Franco thought a bilateral agreement with the United States would be a step on the road to fuller cooperation between Spain and NATO. He said the Iberian peninsula was a "natural geographical area" of Western Europe. Britain was another. France, Germany and Benelux comprised still another. They all had fundamental common interests. A bilateral Hispano-American accord would serve as an "indirect agreement with other NATO members." Franco said there would be little difficulty if a NATO naval unit, including non-American ships, wanted to use Spanish port facilities. He was confident that vessels of all Allied nations could enter Spanish harbors.

He stressed that it was to Spain's interest to assure the defenses of Western Europe as far to the east as possible and dismissed the idea that any neutrality in a war between the United States and Russia would be respected by Moscow or that "neutralism" as a concept had any validity. However, he added that the possibility that Spanish armed forces could be contributed to any defensive coalition north of the Pyrenees would depend upon conditions yet to be reviewed.

LISBON, *February 16, 1952*

LUNCH today with King Carol, former sovereign of Rumania, and his wife, Magda Lupescu, who now calls herself Princess Helen. He has a slightly missing chin and an obstinate face. His forehead is exceptionally narrow. He is a fairly big man, who inclines to plumpness, speaks English with a noticeable German accent and has the unfortunate habit of spitting and drooling. I talked with him at length, and he has everything worked out very simply in world affairs. According to him, the United States is much stronger than Russia so we should send Moscow an ultimatum, in a year or two or, otherwise, attack. He considers himself the ruler of Rumania because he never abdicated as did his son and successor, Michael. When we were discussing the German situation, he said the only solution for Germany was monarchy, and the obvious choice was the eldest son of the late Crown Prince.

Carol said there was a good type of democracy in Rumania where the peasants were not servile but were respectful and took their hats off. He thought it would be better if there was more of this type of democracy in the United States.

AL Gruenther sent me Eisenhower's first and surely only annual report to the standing group of NATO. He wants my comments. I have read it very carefully this afternoon and am going up to see Gruenther with some suggestions for alterations. Then we are going on to the Eisenhowers'.

YESTERDAY afternoon after I had finished working on Eisenhower's report I drove out to SHAPE and spent thirty-five minutes going over it with Gruenther and Colonel Pete Carroll, one of the bright young colonels Eisenhower brought over with him. I had several minor and a few major suggestions, and I think they are going to be incorporated into the final version. Gruenther and Carroll agreed with my insistence that we should stress defense against "aggression" and "Soviet imperialism" instead of the draft's mention of "communism." The latter, after all, includes Tito.

Gruenther and I then drove over to Eisenhower's house, where there was a female canasta game and a male bridge game. We started playing at 6:00, stayed on for an excellent steak dinner, and then played again until 11:30.

Yesterday was the day of the New Hampshire primaries. The eyes of the entire United States and a good deal of the world were turned on this small political test. Nevertheless, we never mentioned the subject last night except to make a couple of kidding remarks to the general.

EISENHOWER is going to return to the States in May or June and "run." That is the big news today. I had lunch with him.

For some time Eisenhower spoke about President Roosevelt and indicated more of an antipathy than I had suspected. He said Roosevelt, whenever he had talked to him, had used the "vertical pronoun" far too much. At the time of Casablanca, Roosevelt kept telling Eisenhower what "I" plan to do. Roosevelt had said that "I" do not know what "I" will recommend for the future of such capitals as Algiers and Tunis because "I" don't know what France will be capable of after this war. To Roosevelt it seemed like a potentially weak power. He gave Eisenhower certain "orders" for North Africa and West Africa which Eisenhower said he could not accept because he was an Allied commander and not merely an American commander. Roosevelt then agreed with Eisenhower and said he was right, but within a few minutes started talking of "my" wishes again. Nevertheless, Eisenhower admitted he was *for* Roosevelt in the 1944 election; he had been against him in 1932, 1936 and 1940. He had been against the third term above all; but when it came to the fourth term,

Eisenhower felt so many things were at stake that it was too risky to change leadership.

Eisenhower admitted he had more or less made up his mind to ask for relief from his job but did not quite know how to do it. He admitted President Truman—who he said had always been very square with him—should have sufficient advance notice of the general's departure date in order to choose a successor and have enough time to get agreement in the United States and from the other NATO Allies. At this juncture, Eisenhower said he thought Al Gruenther was obviously the man, and he had found an increasing acceptance of that point of view from the European countries recently.

Eisenhower talked about his political ideas. He was against centralization of government and, above all, against overwhelming federal taxation; for example, state schools should be supported by state taxation rather than federal grants for education. I told him he sounded very much like a Jeffersonian Democrat, rather than a Republican, and he replied that he thought it would be better to describe him as a "Jeffersonian American" and that the Democrats had diverged too far from Jefferson's ideas.

He said his greatest hope was to achieve a form of cooperation between labor and capital in the United States, with the government remaining in the position of "referee" between the two forces, because they simply had to collaborate with each other in order to preserve a common front against the Soviet danger.

He thought there was a great danger of the military messing in politics in the United States, and that was one of his most serious problems at present, since he remained a military man. His conscience troubled him considerably. This is the primary reason why he has now decided to quit his present NATO job and eventually to resign his commission. He thought it would be disastrous if there was ever a chance of American officers being appointed to commands on the grounds of their political opinions.

PARIS, *April 2, 1952*

LAST night Eisenhower's report was finally made public. One suggestion I had made was that the adjective "Communist" should not be used throughout when describing the Soviet threat, but that "Stalinist" and "Soviet imperialist" should be substituted. Al Gruenther, last week, showed me a semifinal draft which had followed this suggestion also, but the final version reverted to the original and stuck fairly generally by "Communist" and "Communistic." (Later I found this was for political—Republican Party—reasons.)

PARIS, *May 5, 1952*

MAURICE Schumann invited me for lunch at the Quai d'Orsay in honor of Foster Dulles. I was able to eavesdrop on the conversation, sitting, as I was, across the table from the guest of honor. Schumann speaks excellent English but made the mistake of saying to Dulles that, of course, the latter spoke French. Dulles smugly agreed. From there on a crisscross of misunderstanding developed, with conversations like: "Do you think German rearmament is a good thing?" being answered with observations such as "I am sorry she isn't here." I was sitting next to André Maurois who was equally fascinated.

PARIS, *May 12, 1952*

LUNCH with Eisenhower today, and then we played golf out at Morfontaine. Afterwards in the locker room he was saying rather regretfully, "Anybody is a damn fool if he actually seeks to be President. You give up four of the very best years of your life. Lord knows it's a sacrifice. Some people think there's a lot of power and glory attached to the job. On the contrary, the very workings of a democratic system see to it that the job has very little power."

PARIS, *May 27, 1952*

TODAY the six Foreign Ministers of the European Defense Community signed the EDC (European army) treaty, and Acheson and Eden, who were also present in the Clock Room at the Quai d'Orsay, signed the separate guarantees the English-speaking world is giving to that organization.

Adenauer sat stonily throughout the whole performance. His expression did not change except when Eden, who was in the neighboring chair, leaned across and made a wisecrack which caused a faint, Mona Lisa-type smile to flicker for a second on the German's face. It was odd to recall that Schumann, who was the principal figure at the ceremony, served in the German army during World War I.

PARIS, *May 29, 1952*

LUNCH today with Lieutenant General Hans Speidel, former chief of staff for Field Marshal Erwin Rommel and one of the brightest generals in the German army. Speidel is a schoolteacherish type of man. He has an intellectual face and wears glasses. He studied French, Latin and ancient Greek in university and says he still reads and writes both Latin and Greek.

He said the most important thing in Germany was to sell the youth on the necessity of defending their homes and families and defending the civilization to which they were accustomed. It is no longer a matter of national patriotism to defend the borders of a country which can be flown over by a jet plane in less than an hour. Something bigger is required. He thinks the young men understand this fairly well. They are violently against war and don't want to join any army, but they see no other choice. The only alternative would be to be occupied by Russia and sent off to Siberia without a fight.

He said the two best wartime American generals were Patton and Bradley. The Germans never knew what they were going to do, and they handled their troops extremely well, although Patton made a fool of himself in the public declarations he made. Montgomery, he thought, was a terrible general. You could always predict exactly what he would do, and you knew that he would rest and draw things together always after so many days of battle. He had only one maneuver—a left hook. He is a charming man but a lousy general, Speidel thinks. He thought Zhukov and Koniev were the best Soviet generals. Timoshenko and Budenny were awful.

Speidel said the Americans were better than the British on the attack, but the British were better on the defense and held fast more doggedly. He had no way of judging the French. In 1940 the Germans went through France much faster than he expected.

8

I ARRIVED HERE THIS MORNING—THE DAY BEFORE THE REPUBLICAN
convention starts. The first thing I did after checking in at my hotel
—which took an hour and a half because of the queue—was to go
over and see General Lucius Clay at his suite in the Blackstone, which is
where Ike is living. The usual trays of drinks were well in evidence.

Clay was very disturbed about the use of the words "retaliatory striking
power" in the draft of the national defense plank of the proposed platform.
He thinks this implies that a Republican administration would rely solely
on long-range atomic bombing or, in other words, the "fortress America"
concept of Herbert Hoover. Clay wants a more active foreign and strategic
policy expressed. For example, last autumn, word was received through
Radio Free Europe that we could stage a revolution in Czechoslovakia any
day we wanted to. We had to tell our friends in Czechoslovakia to lay off
because they would have been crushed and there was nothing we could do
about it. We must evolve a policy warning the Russians that if there is any
revolt by free forces in a satellite nation, we will not permit the Soviet
army to intervene. We cannot keep calling off possible revolutions, or all
our friends will either get fed up with us and give up the ghost or get
locked up by the Communists.

Clay is a kind of chief of staff for the Eisenhower forces. He stays in the
background very deliberately, above all to avoid having Eisenhower tarred
with the brush of an Army "cabal." As a matter of fact, Ike is so worried
about this that he has left his closest aide, Colonel Bob Schulz, in Denver
and has left General Howard Snyder, one of his best friends and his
doctor, in Washington to avoid having military folks around.

Clay told me Dulles was now enthusiastically for Ike and actually would
have declared so publicly had it been so desired by the Eisenhower strategy

board. Dulles was the Number One choice for Secretary of State as things now stand.

After leaving Clay's office, I went upstairs one floor to Eisenhower's suite. I was just making myself known when Ike and Mamie came down the corridor returning from church, and they asked me in for a drink, which developed into a couple of drinks and a buffet luncheon. All told, I was there about two and a half hours. Ike looked fine—far better than when he left Paris last month. Mamie admitted to me, however, that both of them needed a rest.

I asked Ike what he thought of the foreign policy and national defense planks of the platform draft. He had not seen the actual text but Dulles had come to see him yesterday, shortly after Eisenhower had arrived in Chicago, and had given him a verbal outline. No particular reference was made to the theory of "retaliation." Eisenhower is dead against this and said he simply would not accept it. When carefully interpreted, it really means abandoning the concept of NATO in favor of sole reliance on strategic air power. He went so far as to say that he not only would not take it in the platform, but that he would rather not run than accept it. He made no secret of the fact that he is very worried about this critical issue, which is one very few people seem to understand. He got red in the face as he does when he's angry, put his tray aside, walked up and down and said: "I'll be damned if I run on that." Wow. Here was the candidate saying he wouldn't run on the party platform.

After I left, I hunted up Foster Dulles. He asked me in for a drink, and I told him about Ike's reaction on the retaliation business. He was very surprised and said, "Does he still feel that way after what I outlined to him?" I said, yes, and I expect Dulles will be hearing more about it. Dulles, of course, is really the author of the theory of "retaliation," but he explained to me that he conceived it in a broader sense as merely "one of the means" of safeguarding the free world and preventing Russian expansion.

CHICAGO, *July 9, 1952*

DULLES told me that reference to "retaliation" has been taken out of the platform draft, although the latter has not been made public. Dulles saw Senator Millikin, chairman of the Resolutions Committee, and asked him what the national defense subcommittee had recommended. Millikin told him. Dulles said Ike would insist on eliminating reference to retaliation.

The national defense plank as it then stood commenced as follows: "On the prudent assumption that Communist Russia may not accommodate our own disgracefully lagging preparedness, we should develop with utmost speed a force in being, as distinguished from paper plans, of such *retaliatory striking* power as to deter sudden attack or promptly and decisively defeat it." (The italics are my own.)

Dulles explained that Millikin did not understand the importance of the reference to retaliation. "He was too dumb to know what it was all about and thought it was only a matter of semantics," Dulles said. Of course, in fact, it was the difference between the foreign policy advocated by Eisenhower and Hoover's concept of "fortress America." Millikin agreed to get the offending words removed.

(P.S. Much later. Dulles is a confusing man. Together with Admiral Radford, he invented the policy of "massive retaliation." He got it into the platform. Then, when Ike balked, he got it out again. But when the campaign developed, most of Foster's declarations advocated "mass retaliation" once more. Ike, who was ready to withdraw on the issue, either didn't notice or didn't care.)

CHICAGO, *July 11, 1952*

EISENHOWER was nominated today as the Republican candidate for President. When the morning session of the convention started, I went over to Clay's suite in the Blackstone Hotel and watched the performance on television together with Clay, Cliff Roberts and Harold Talbot, who is one of the team put together by Ike's staff. When Ike got up to 595—just before Minnesota swung its delegation from Stassen to Eisenhower—I rushed up one floor, and Homer Gruenther shoved me in the door to Eisenhower's apartment and said, "Why don't you see the show?" Victory came with the Minnesota change, thus nominating Ike on the first ballot.

Ike seemed to be in a curious mood of dazed elation. He rushed in to see Mamie, who was in bed with a bad case of neuritis, which kept her up all night. Then in a few minutes he went over to see Taft on a courtesy visit, which also represented an appeal for party unity that the two men made on television. The few of us who were in his suite started drinking to his victory, although it was probably not even luncheon time. They included Clay, Bill Robinson, Cliff Roberts, Senator Carlson, Senator Seaton and the four Eisenhower brothers. In the middle of our toasting, Ike came back. Curiously enough, there was a moment when he was sitting all alone on the sofa as if he were an invisible man. For a couple of minutes he sat there looking rather pale and stunned with his thoughts obviously far, far away, while we all drank to him as if we didn't even know he was there. I went in to see Mamie, who was sitting up in bed in a pink bed jacket, and gave her a victory kiss. Although she had obviously been suffering pain from her neuritis, she was visibly elated. Her mother was sitting beside her.

CHICAGO, *July 12, 1952*

NIXON was nominated today as Vice-President. I understand Ike likes him primarily because he is young (only thirty-nine), and the general wants to capture the imagination of American youth—an idea he has expressed to me before in Europe.

CHICAGO, *July 21, 1952*

I FLEW in here at lunchtime for the Democratic convention, which opened this morning. I was amused that the first demonstration I should see was a rather motley-looking band followed by a gang of singing youngsters waving Harriman flags and singing "I've Been Working On the Railroad."

CHICAGO, *July 22, 1952*

I SPENT two hours today watching Averell Harriman work as a politician. I spent some time in Averell's headquarters and then rode with him in his official car behind a police escort to the Palmer House. His personal bodyguard, assigned by the City of Chicago, had been Taft's bodyguard at the Republican convention. He told me Taft had openly broken into tears the minute Eisenhower was nominated; the detective swore he had seen this with his own eyes.

I asked Harriman, as we were riding back to the Blackstone, if he would agree to run as Vice-President on a ticket headed by Kefauver or if he would serve as Secretary of State were Stevenson to be nominated and elected. He turned on me with a very pale face saying, "Don't insult me by thinking I would make any deals for second place or any other position. I am in this fight to the finish. I am the man to put through this program."

WASHINGTON, *August 22, 1952*

GOOD talk with Bedell Smith over in his office at the C.I.A. He is concerned about the possibility that Moscow might use its huge gold reserves as an economic weapon to smash Western economy. He agrees that the Russians have a vast annual production and don't use much of their gold. The hoard is mounting. We know they use it occasionally to finance foreign missions, including the UN, and to pay for subversive activities. Once a shipment in a box broke open at the Paris airport, and gold coins spilled all over the place. Whether the Russians use bar gold or mint their own fake sovereigns or Napoleons (the way the Bank of England mints sovereigns for the Greek government) we don't know. However, a good deal of these costs listed above are handled by the Russians with platinum. This is smuggled abroad from Moscow in Soviet diplomatic pouches.

The Soviet gold supply is enormous. They could do two things with it. Moscow could suddenly establish a gold backing to the ruble, making it a real currency, which would then attract foreign investments and could also be used to make purchases abroad, breaking the Allied blockade on strategic materials. Or the Kremlin could order the dumping of huge quantities of gold on foreign markets at an artificially low price. This would break the economies of many countries with vital but dwindling gold reserves, such as England or France.

ROCQUENCOURT, *August 28, 1952*

TODAY I had my first talk with General Ridgway, who replaced Eisenhower as SHAPE commander last June. All in all, Ridgway seems an extremely high-minded—one might almost say noble—sincere democrat who takes his responsibilities with immense seriousness. I doubt if he has much sense of humor or a light side. As long as he has the brilliance of Gruenther at his right hand, he should be able to avoid any major problems.

PARIS, *October 17, 1952*

THIS afternoon I had an excellent talk with Montgomery. He said:

> We are today at war. It is called the cold war. No one knows how long it will go on. Yet no one handles this problem. We handle a hot war. We have armies and headquarters and commanders and councils dealing with that possibility. But there isn't any Allied organization for the cold war.
>
> Why don't the nations come together with a declared unity of purpose and coordinate their psychological warfare and propaganda? Of course, this is a civilian thing. It has nothing to do with us soldiers. But we must get the truth over to the enslaved peoples—and get it over quickly. Right now look at the situation. The other side puts out something—say the Moscow radio. All our nations have to hold meetings and consultations on how to answer. They ask each other. Finally they reply a month later. By the time we answer the effect of the other side has sunk in. That's no good.
>
> We should answer the same night—at once. But you can't do this unless you have a setup handling it. Right now fourteen nations are handling it in fourteen different ways. There is no single directing mind of the free nations to fight this insidious enemy.

BELGRADE, *November 8, 1952*

I HAD a conversation with Marshal Tito in his villa on the Rumunska which lasted about an hour and a half. I asked him first why, since Jugoslavia founded its policy on UN and strongly supported collective security, it did not send at least a token force to fight in Korea. He replied that it would do more political harm than good since "no other country is as threatened as we are."

I asked if he had any thought on how the Korean War should be ended since Jugoslavia maintained that as long as it continued, China would remain dependent on the USSR. He replied:

I have no concrete proposals. Korea should be returned to the *status quo* so that the Korean peoples can settle their own destiny under UN supervision. I wish to emphasize that the UN should supervise this and insure against further aggression.

I believe that China's participation in the Korean War was partly the result of faulty Western policy. The West's support of Chiang helped Russia to push China into the Korean conflict. It is difficult to say how this can be rectified now. We think it would be a good idea to recognize the Chinese Government in order to make international cooperation possible and stop China from being a tool of the Soviet imperialists.

Talks on regional security measures with Greece and Turkey will start soon. In a sense military talks have already begun. We are trying to reach agreement on what should be done to defend the Balkans. This involves what kind of mutual help should be pledged, which bases conceded, and technical preparations and plans.

After such agreements have been reached, it will be perfectly easy for us to write down such obligations. I would like to say also that people looking at these problems from the outside naturally want speedy results. But it should be remembered that we have not had friendly relations with each of these countries for a considerable period of time. But great progress has been made recently.

Was Jugoslavia prepared to accept obligations vis-à-vis Asiatic Turkey as well as European Turkey? He replied: "There is no difference, for there is no real boundary between Asia and Europe as aggression is not limited to geographical frontiers. We consider Turkey as a whole."

ATHENS, *November 15, 1952*

LONG talk with King Paul today at Tatoi Palace. Despite the fact that to-morrow is election day, he seemed unconcerned and relaxed. He was dressed in an admiral's uniform, and we sat around informally before the fireplace in his study.

The King expressed confidence that the Communist underground was now licked in Greece. He said the police are very efficient and keep a sharp eye on all conspiracies, moving in on the plotters if and when necessary. He expressed the belief that there was a definite split between the EDA (existing legal *locum tenens* of the Communist Party) and the Moscow Cominform leadership. EDA continually disobeyed Moscow orders and took independent action. I asked if by this he meant that they were "Tito-ists." He didn't seem to know much about this, but thought it was just a question of disobedience.

He said the Jugoslav mission, which had visited Greece in September, was made up of "a bunch of thugs." He was obviously very skeptical about Tito, and at least three times asked, "Can we trust him?"

The King said he was rather embarrassed by having to entertain General Tempo, who had been the Jugoslav representative with the Greek Communist rebel army, but, he added, Tempo had the tact not to mention the subject. The King said he expected he would probably be entertaining Tito in the Palace one of these days, but added, "I certainly shan't like it."

NEW DELHI, *November 21, 1952*

THIS morning I had a talk with our Ambassador here, Chester Bowles. Bowles read me a letter he recently wrote to Secretary of State Acheson requesting the formulation of a long-range policy for India. The letter said substantially as follows: We are not facing up to the fundamental crises in Asia. A free India is vital to world peace and to our own security. We must build a program to meet the requirements of the situation. The choice in India is between the present democratic government and communism. There is no other organized force. It would be a catastrophe if the present government fails. One-sixth of the world's population lives here. In the last war India provided an army of three million. A Communist India would help communism to dominate southeast Asia. India has rich mineral resources and a strategically important location. It defends South Asia. In Communist hands it would block the Suez Canal route to the East. India's loss to the West would cause Moscow's prestige to soar. Millions around the world would join the Communist bandwagon.

The Chinese have sold themselves well here. India needs United States aid to accomplish its five-year plan. This should come on the scale of aid to Greece. It would take less than $1 billion to get the five-year plan through. There is a need for village and land reform before communism goes into the villages. And communism *is* moving in. The youth must be given a sense of participation in progress. But the Congress Party is too far removed from the people.

The Chinese have given their people a sense of participation. *We* don't understand the appeal of communism out here. At the lower levels the Communists do a good job of what passes for democratic participation. The people ask, "What shall we do?" The Indian universities are turning out Communists.

NEW DELHI, *November 22, 1951*

THIS evening I had an interesting talk for about an hour and a half with Jawaharlal Nehru, Indian Prime Minister and the only dynamic force in the country. I saw him in his residence, former home of the British commanders in chief. We sat in a relatively small study decorated with carved ivory. The two of us were perched upon a comfortable stuffed sofa. Nehru is so delicate and graceful that he makes one feel awkward. He was dressed in a long russet-brown Indian jacket and white leggings. He seemed relaxed and affable. Coffee was served, and we smoked occasional cigarettes.

But although he was cordial, I had a constant feeling of his mental arrogance and assumed contempt for the intellectual capacities of most Americans. Time and again I asked him questions concerning ideologies, Marxism, and so on, and he gave me rather childish and, I thought, contemptuous—certainly unsatisfactory—replies. He is a confused man who is unquestionably enveloped in a cloud of his own egotism, which is obviously kept charged by surrounding admirers. That he is sincere, intelligent and potentially dynamic is beyond a doubt. Nevertheless, I had the feeling that he is groping his way through many difficult problems without a very clear idea of where he is going and without any preconceived plan, either moral, political or economic.

We started off with a discussion of Marxism. He said that when he had read Marx and books by Soviet leaders, he had been very impressed, but it was "not the dogma I adopted." He continued:

> Marxism is an analysis of history. The present-day Communists have changed this about a lot. Therefore I take what helps me from Marxism and discard the rest. Socialism as such is naturally making its way in the world through economic doctrines. Progressively in each country there is more and more social control by the state—even in the United States.
>
> Thus in India there is a definite tendency for the state to assume increasing control. But this is limited by a paucity of financial resources and of available administrative personnel. The state needs to control the key strategic vital sectors such as transportation. Thus the railways are owned by the state. Motor transport is largely state-owned. Air India is one-half state-owned although privately operated.

This was a rather vague and amateurish definition—if such it may be called—of socialism. I asked him if he felt himself socialistically inclined, whether he considered having the Congress Party adhere to the Second (Socialist) International; I pointed out that Marshal Tito had just told me he was contemplating having his People's Front join it. Nehru answered that the Second International was merely a trade union organization. He said, "Our trade unions might some day join it, but the question has never come up."

I asked if India thought of signing any strictly defensive alliances with any powers or joining a mutual defense coalition of a regional nature. He answered, "No alliance is contemplated. After all, what is a strictly defensive alliance? A defensive alliance automatically becomes a military alliance, and the purpose of a military alliance is to deal with preparations for war. We are obviously interested in what happens along the regions near our borders; thus, for example, we are interested in what happens in Burma or Pakistan, but we are not resolved on any concrete policy of what to do."

Could Nehru explain to me in his own words just what it was that held India together as a state against the various centrifugal forces operating in this newly independent country? He replied: "In one word, it is a certain nationalistic sentiment. This goes deeply into the past. Throughout history you will find that, politically, India was often divided but it remained more or less a unit. The same ideas coursed through India, the same background of culture. The people never attached too much importance to politics. That was for the kings and emperors. Now to this matrix of a common past two or three germs of politics have been grafted. I must say that one of the politically unifying forces was the British occupation."

After a while I thought it was about time to go, but Nehru was in a mood to talk some more in that curious and occasionally effective manner of his that some describe as "thinking aloud." He said: "We based our five-year plan upon what I might call present advantage. The choice is between present advantage or future development. The Russians, in their five-year plans, have chosen the latter. But to do this requires an authoritarian government. We also want to plan for the future but our first requirement is to plan for the present and this makes for a sort of juggling act. We must deal with a heavily populated country. There is not enough land to go around as there is in Russia."

KARACHI, *November 27, 1952*

TODAY I had a long talk with Lieutenant Colonel Iskander Mirza, Secretary of Defense (later dictator). Kashmir and water are the two big problems with India. "Get us a Kashmir decision and water," he said, "and I'll be the first to approach India on staff talks for joint defense of the subcontinent. We want to be friends with India. The future of each of our economies and everything else depends on the two countries pulling together. We would have staff talks and plan a regional defense—save for that blasted Kashmir thing."

TEL AVIV, *December 6, 1952*

VERY interesting talk today with Ben Gurion, the Israeli Prime Minister, in his Tel Aviv house, which is crammed with books in many languages on many subjects. He seemed in vigorous shape for a man his age (sixty-six) who works so hard and who is said to sleep only four hours nightly.

He said Israel desperately wanted peace with the Arabs and then economic and military cooperation. He first thought Naguib was conciliatory but now doubts it. Ben Gurion won't tolerate the return of any of the Arab refugees or any territorial changes except minor frontier adjustment trades. He fears the recent Prague trials mean official anti-Semitism by Moscow under the guise of "cosmopolitanism" and that in case of war the Russians will "exterminate" their 2 million Jews. "After all, they killed millions of their own peasants when it was deemed convenient."

CAIRO, *December 13, 1952*

TALKED with General Mohammed Naguib, who ousted King Farouk last July and established a semidictatorship. He complained about Western support for Israel; said we had created a state of 1 million and thus lost the friendship of 50 million Arabs and their oil. He didn't trust the Israelis, who had ignored UN resolutions and created a "bad stain" by expelling 1 million Arab refugees. Egypt could trust Israel only if it paid the refugees an indemnity and returned them to Israel.

He complained bitterly that the US had pushed Germany to pay reparations to Israel for the Nazi Jewish victims, and with this money Israel was getting stronger militarily while Britain held back even on delivering jet planes, which Egypt had paid for on the excuse of priority delays.

He opposed change. Change damaged economic stability. He had abrogated the Constitution to modernize it. On the whole I had the impression that Naguib is not the "strong man" he is made out to be. I would not be surprised to see more revolution and more fireworks before the next year has passed.

ADDIS ABABA, *December 18, 1952*

THIS morning I had an audience with His Imperial Majesty, Haile Selassie I, the Conquering Lion of the Tribe of Judah, Elect of God, and Emperor of Ethiopia. This is a very formal business. I had to borrow a cutaway from a fellow at the embassy.

Ato Tafara Worq, the Emperor's secretary, came along and escorted me to H.I.M. On the way he explained I must bow three times: at the entrance, half-way through the room, and finally when shaking hands. This I did, without too much grace, and then the Emperor motioned me to sit on his right-hand while Tafara Worq sat on my other side.

The Emperor knows English quite well, thanks to his exile in Bath, and speaks fluent French. Nevertheless the interview was gravely held in Amharic. His Imperial Majesty is small, thin and has a dark, rather handsome countenance, with black beard, aquiline features, sad eyes, and a thinning mane of black hair which, as with so many Ethiopians, seems to grow out like a bush of wire. He was wearing the summer tan uniform of Commander in Chief, spattered with ribbon decorations. He sat on a sofa. Beside him were two small tan and white dogs, something like spaniels, who slept throughout most of the audience.

The Emperor declared that his country not only wished to join any projected Middle East defense organization, but was anxious to have an American military aid mission established here in order to modernize the army and help establish a navy. This country, although not strictly Middle

Eastern in a geographic sense, thus becomes the first nation of the region to apply for MEDO membership without prior conditions.

Speaking as head of the Coptic Christian Church, he said that while

the forces of materialism are at present increasing in the world, they are still weaker than those led by people dominated with spiritual beliefs. According to my understanding, the religion first preached in this world was to serve the purpose of God and preach His word. Unfortunately its ways have changed. Religion is frequently used by different countries for their own national purposes. It is a fact that the materialist philosophy of communism is a grave danger to world peace. But it is very hard for the Russians to prosper here in Ethiopia. Communism succeeds where there is poverty. Thank God we are not so poor.

NAIROBI, *December 25, 1952*

WE have been in Kenya several days. There is only one topic of conversation—Mau Mau. Almost everyone we know carries a hand gun; either in his wife's bag or strapped around his middle, in a shoulder holster or even a pocket. Everyone locks his doors and windows at night and locks the servants out (they live in separate huts anyway) until morning. Nevertheless, life seems surprisingly normal.

NAIROBI, *December 26, 1952*

ED Dorz, U.S. consul general, very kindly asked us to a Christmas party. Good, old-fashioned colonial style; all the men in white dinner jackets, women in summer evening dress; lovely and friendly, plenty to drink; the decorations looking a bit out of place in the tropical air of a prosperous Nairobi suburb. Next morning we learned that three native Kenyans had been murdered by Mau Mau within a three-hundred-yard radius of our party. Most of the murders are against natives—to instill fear.

ZANZIBAR, *December 27, 1952*

ZANZIBAR is filled with clove forests, but many clusters of trees instead of being heavy green have gone gray with a blight called "sudden death" that has destroyed thousands of pounds worth. The fruit trees are incredible: jackfruit, baobab, vast mango trees, coconut palms, lemon, all set off by brilliant red flamboyants. The first dhows are now coming in on the northeast monsoon from Muscat and other Arabian ports (they go back in a few months on the southwest wind). Dhow captains with silver J-shaped daggers in silver scabbards thrust into their belts, bearded and fierce looking, stroll about the streets or wander past squatting Indian and Parsee shopkeepers in the narrow bazaars. Humped Zebu cattle graze amid banana clumps. African workmen, with colorful skirts and white skullcaps, walk in and out of the forests near their villages of daub and wattle huts, thatched with palm leaves. In the bazaars the first African agitators from the mainland are said to be stirring up whispers of racial resentment.

SALISBURY, *December 30, 1952*

FEDERATION of Southern and Northern Rhodesia and Nyasaland is the hot issue: Europeans fear a future British government may force through universal suffrage for the Africans; therefore they want federation now, before the blacks get a break. Everyone knows their ability. In 1946, the Goromonzi secondary school was established for Africans. In Cambridge examinations the Bantu boys did better than the whites.

CAPE TOWN, *January 17, 1953*

THIS morning I had a two-hour talk with Dr. Daniel F. Malan, seventy-eight-year-old Prime Minister and head of the Nationalist Party, in Groote Schuur, a few miles out of Cape Town. It is a lovely house, built in the old Dutch style, with magnificent grounds. The original house was built in the eighteenth century for the Dutch East India Company. Cecil Rhodes lived there, and he bequeathed it to the Union as a residence for prime ministers.

I asked Malan if he intended to establish a republic should the Nationalists be reelected, and if so, whether such a republic would remain within the British Commonwealth. He replied: "Do you think it abhorrent for a party to desire a republic in South Africa? Is it not only natural? The most important parts of South Africa, the Transvaal and the Orange Free State were republics. A very considerable number of people alive today took part in the struggle for these republics and independence. Thousands died for it. Is it strange, or only natural, that a considerable number desire a republic? I think it is not strange."

I asked Malan if he had any thoughts concerning a sound racial policy for the entire African continent. He answered: "Africa must belong to the Africans, just like Europe for the Europeans, America for the Americans and Asia for the Asians. The first claim to a large part of Africa, anyway, belongs to the indigenous people. Of course, they are divided into tribes, as Europe is into countries. They are primitive. You cannot expect a primitive people to rise to a European level in one or even in many generations. Africa must develop, but the African must be assisted and guided in the direction of European Christian civilization. He must be protected against the infiltration of the Asiatic."

LOURENÇO MARQUES, *January 21, 1953*

IN 1951 Mozambique was changed from a "colony" to a "province" of Portugal. The former Minister of Colonies is now called Minister for Overseas. The Portuguese theory is that these overseas provinces are a part of Portugal, just as if they were on the mainland. The people of Mozambique are inhabitants of Portugal under this theory.

Not all inhabitants here have citizenship rights. But anybody, regardless of color, can become *civilizado* or "a civilized one." If he becomes *civilizado*, he is just as eligible for citizenship as if he were a white man living in Lisbon. The *indigena*, or native, is governed by a different set of laws. He is not regarded as "civilized." Everyone in Mozambique is in one of two groups:

1. All whites, all Portuguese citizens, all Indians who are Portuguese (Goans), all Macaoans who are "civilized," all mixed bloods recognized as "civilized," all the civil administration.

2. The others—meaning the overwhelming majority of blacks.

A native who meets certain requirements is recognized as "civilized", he becomes what is called *assimilado*.

LEOPOLDVILLE, *January 27, 1953*

A GLIMPSE of the Belgian Congo has proven pessimistic. We stayed with Mulloy, a very nice United States consul general and wife who put us up in great comfort. They talked admiringly of the Belgian colonial officials, but I was depressed and felt contact with the vast native population was almost nonexistent. Despite Mulloy's assurances that the natives were happy, had a high standard of living and vast numbers of bicycles, I sensed disquiet. Blacks must be locked up in their native quarter each night. The Belgians have given them absolutely no preparation for self-rule. This is a powderkeg. It looks nice on the surface, but appearances are deceptive.

One day we went across the sluggish, vast Congo River, filled with islands of floating vegetation, to see our old friend Bob Mason, British consul general in Brazzaville (French Congo). The French may not give as good a life to their charges as the Belgians in terms of economic statistics, but they treat them as human beings.

Mason, who goes across the river often, says he invariably shocks the Belgian businessmen there. At one after another party someone inevitably comes up, as Topic A is discussed, and says to Bob: "Quite right, monsieur, but after all, how would you feel if your sister married one of these types?" Bob's reply: "As a matter of fact she did."

ACCRA, *February 5, 1953*

TALK today with Kwame Nkrumah, Prime Minister of the Gold Coast. He is an affable, youthful chap with a rich chocolate complexion and a loose-lipped mouth. He seemed quite amiable but did not impress me very much as an intellectual.

He wants to work for a West African federation extending from the Congo to Dakar, but this is obviously an eventual hope, and there is nothing imminent about it.

I asked him why parliamentary democracy was assumed to be the best form of government here. He said no other form had ever occurred to him, but he favored parliamentary democracy because it was workable, lasting and guaranteed free speech, press and religion.

He wants independence for the Gold Coast as soon as possible, and steps are being taken to negotiate constitutional changes. The Gold Coast should stay in the Commonwealth as an independent state because then it would benefit from the advantages of mutual defense, economic assistance and participation in the sterling bloc.

9

T EA WITH FIELD MARSHAL EARL ALEXANDER, NOW SECRETARY
of State for Defense. When we got to the subject of Russia,
Alexander picked up the telephone and asked General Strong,
head of British Intelligence, to come in.

Alexander said (and Strong agreed) that Russia would not be provoked
into war. They simply were not ready to accept provocation. They intended to go along in search of their goals in a patient, long-sighted,
Asiatic way. They wouldn't be provoked even if we bombed Manchuria or
even if China and the United States formally went to war or even if the
EDC treaty started to rearm Germany—unless they were ready for and
desired war at the time. Then they wouldn't wait for provocation. What
Alexander fears as a possibility, however, is that a series of incidents might
lead into each other. We might bomb Manchuria and finally decide this
wasn't achieving enough; then decide to bomb closer and closer to Russian
territory until we begin to hit it.

The two men had no faith in Chiang Kai-shek. Alexander made the
point that much of Chiang's army was made up of overage soldiers; many
had served with Alex himself in Burma during World War II. If they ever
landed on the mainland, a great number would simply desert and disappear.

It was absolutely imperative that an agreement on Suez be reached. The
Suez base had cost 3 million pounds (then close to $1.5 billion), and even
if another piece of geography could be found there is neither the time nor
money to build. Furthermore, there is no such other piece of geography.
Suez can be approached from west or east by sea and from north or south
by land. Alexander, who has troops all over the earth, would like to get the
two divisions out of Suez for use elsewhere. But a large number of technicians and experts would have to remain to keep the base going. The

Egyptians simply aren't competent in terms of engineers. This goes for the operation of the French canal company as well as the base itself. Not only must the Egyptians agree to leave foreign technicians in adequate numbers, but they must make firm agreements on MEDO before a Suez evacuation is accepted.

Both Alex and Strong felt that as long as Stalin was around there was little risk of war. Stalin undoubtedly knew not only of America's atomic superiority but of the immense destructive power of the bomb and the fact that we had the means of delivering it. No man of seventy-three was going to start a war and risk seeing all he had built up around him destroyed.

PARIS, *March 24, 1953*

THIS evening I had a couple of whiskies with Eden. Eden said he now felt exceedingly optimistic about Europe—although he always qualified this with pessimism concerning other areas.

His visit to Washington had been highly satisfactory, and that full agreement had been reached on the Middle East. Dulles had reassured Eden that if Mossadegh turned down the latest offer on Iran, the United States would stand together with England. Furthermore Eden and Dulles agreed that the United States should formally take part in the Suez negotiations in Egypt.

Now things were going badly, and Eden is worried about a new crisis in Egypt. This is of vital importance to the whole world. We must keep Suez defended and open to the West. The French, for example, are particularly interested in this. If Egypt had full control of Suez and decided one day not to permit French ships to traverse it, that would mean that all vessels bound for Indochina would have to go around Africa, and there simply is not enough shipping to support the Indochinese war in that event.

PARIS, *April 21, 1953*

LUNCH today with General Speidel. Speidel told me he had been in Russia in 1930, when Germany was secretly manufacturing tanks and aircraft there. In 1932, Marshal Tukhachevsky attended German maneuvers on the Oder River, and Speidel was with him all the time. He was impressed. Tukhachevsky spoke good French and was very free in his observations, which were extremely intelligent. Tukhachevsky always wore an immaculate uniform and was a smart officer. At a party one night he got drunk and announced he would lead the Russian army into Istanbul and he did not care a damn whether it was under the Red Star or the Cross of St. Andrew.

Speidel said German intelligence information was so good at the time that when Stalin purged Tukhachevsky and most of the principal Red Army leaders, the Germans never believed that this crippled Soviet military potential. It was a mistake to consider the Russians rigid and unimaginative in military strategy; Zhukov was a first-class general, and Koniev was also good.

PARIS, *April 28, 1953*

DRINK this evening with my old friend Panayotis Canellopoulos, Greece's Defense Minister. He was astonishingly indiscreet. I asked him how the negotiations with Turkey and Jugoslavia were going. He told me:

In case of war there will be no joint Greek-Jugoslav offensive against Albania. Rather, it is hoped that within between two and nine months a *coup de main* can be staged there (this year) getting rid of Hoxha and prying the country from Soviet grip. I gather American troops, if necessary, will be used to "maintain order" after a local coup. The Greeks have agreed to keep out, and the Jugoslavs have been more or less warned to do so.

Nevertheless, even if the coup doesn't come off, it is figured (and Admiral Carney approves) that no occupation of Albania is necessary. Thus a large number of Yugoslav and Greek divisions are being freed for use to the north and east—troops that otherwise would have to invade and do occupation duty.

LONDON, *June 3, 1953*

QUEEN Elizabeth was crowned yesterday in an extraordinary ceremony. Despite the discomfort of sitting in the Abbey from 6:00 A.M. until after 3:00 P.M., hungry and thirsty and cold, in a tailcoat, I was extremely moved.

At almost precisely half past twelve the Archbishop of Canterbury, wearing a cope of cloth of gold faced in cobalt, placed the heavy crown of Edward the Confessor upon Elizabeth's head. For a brief moment a hush fell across Westminster. Then a fanfare of trumpets sounded. The peers and peeresses of the realm donned their coronets and a sharp chorus broke forth, "God save Queen Elizabeth." And through the tall gothic windows, over the heads of those determined servants of the crown—the Queen's field and air marshals, generals, admirals, and, most redoubtable of all, the Queen's Prime Minister, Sir Winston Churchill—came the dull boom of guns from the venerable tower fortress down the Thames.

BUDAPEST, *June 19, 1953*

ATTENDED a couple of dreary sessions of the World Peace Council. In speech after speech, regardless of the orator's language, there were continual references to "Li Sin Man" and that always brought roars of rage. Finally discovered this was Syngman Rhee (South Korean president). Ilya Ehrenburg was the hottest Soviet contribution. I have known him for years, and he has entertained me at his Moscow apartment. But when I went over to chat he gave me a disdainful, fishy stare. Obviously it is not the chic thing to speak to Americans now, and he goes with the wind.

PARIS, *July 11, 1953*

LAST night I dined with Bohlen. Poor Chip has had to call off his plan to drive down with me to Majorca on Tuesday (where our two families are sharing a house). He was summoned back to Washington urgently and had to leave from Orly at 11:30 P.M. He thinks Washington's reaction to the Beria purge is wrong. Washington is saying that Beria represented a "soft" policy and that this now means a tougher dictatorship and cold war. Chip points out that since Beria's arrest on June 27, there has been a continued series of events indicating the "soft" policy has been accelerated rather than dropped.

PARIS, *July 17, 1953*

THIS morning I had a good chat with Adlai Stevenson. He is very worried about the internationally bad effect on the United States reputation of McCarthyism. He was surprised at the extent of French disillusionment on Indochina and their desire to get out of that situation. He is trying to point out to the French that now particularly they must keep containing Soviet dynamism in that quarter. We have neutralized Russian pressure in Europe. We must prevent the Sino-Soviet bloc from outflanking India.

BONN, *August 17, 1953*

THIS evening I talked for more than an hour and a half with Adenauer in the Schaumburg Palais. I asked if the McCarthyist purge of American officials in Germany had in any way affected German regard for American democracy or the German opinion of American qualifications to teach democracy. He replied:

The American occupation Army here at first had a number of Communists in important positions. Then there was a purge—prior to and without McCarthy. It is certainly true that neither the regard for nor the respect for the United States and its democracy suffered from this.

Now there are some things going on which we cannot understand. I met a number of very honorable men recently in Chicago who admired McCarthy greatly. I met a number of equally honorable men in New York and Washington who condemned him strongly. Here in Germany we have a proverb that one should not wash one's dirty linen in public.

BONN, *October 19, 1953*

I LUNCHED with Adenauer today in the Schaumburg Palais. Adenauer, waited until the waiters had finished serving and actually left before anything was said of a serious nature. He explained *sotto voce* later that the Soviet intelligence service was exceptionally good and might well have one of the waiters in its employ. To my surprise he said that now the Germans, thanks to their experience in Russia, had the best intelligence. He added there were many patriotic Germans in East Germany who provided information for no payment at all. I was amazed that he should in effect say that this demilitarized country had the best intelligence in the world— which he did.

When I asked him what should be done if EDC fails, he said he had in his mind a map including the United States, Germany, England, Spain and Turkey. In other words he was for busting up NATO and for a separate scheme of alliances. He implied France should not be permitted to frustrate a United States–Germany alliance. Although France was in NATO and an occupying power in Germany (with those two vetoes), Adenauer recalled there had once been four Allied occupiers in Germany; they split, but the Big Three kept on with their policy. The Big Two, if necessary, he implied, should go ahead regardless of France. If France doesn't ratify EDC, there must be an immediate alliance between Germany and the United States. It would be better if England joined also. But if there is any indication England would delay the project and slow things up, the United States should go ahead anyway, because delay would be fatal to the psychological atmosphere in Germany.

BONN, *October 20, 1953*

YESTERDAY evening I dined with Theodor Blank, head of the West German defense office. General Heusinger, Blank's principal military expert, was there.

Heusinger was present when the briefcase bomb went off at Hitler's headquarters on July 20, 1944. He had been substituting at briefings for a few weeks because General Zeitzler, Chief of Staff, was ill. Heusinger knew there was a plot being concocted against Hitler. Tresckow, his army contact in the plot, tried to sign him up. Heusinger refused to go along unless the plotters got a flat guarantee from Britain and America that they would stop the war as soon as Hitler was dead and Naziism overthrown; that they would then pitch in with Germany against Russia. I observed to Heusinger that this was a difficult pledge to expect enemies to make against an ally, which Russia then was. Heusinger didn't join. He fought on and was a prisoner at Nuremberg for two years, where his testimony was valuable in the War Criminals Trial.

When Colonel Stauffenberg (who carried the bomb) entered headquarters on July 20, he was confident this was the day. Heusinger was standing next to Hitler when the bomb in the briefcase left by Stauffenberg beneath the table went off. Fortunately, he says, they were in a temporary headquarters above ground while Hitler's underground bunker was having more concrete added. Also there was a heavy oak table, which absorbed the shock of some of the blast. Heusinger's aide was killed. But he found himself on his back with a map burning above his head. He fumbled about and felt his hand in a mass of hair as he struggled to rise and get out. The hair was Hitler's. He complained that Stauffenberg hadn't tipped him off on the bomb. "Why should he?" I asked, astonished. "You had refused to join."

Heusinger admitted it would be far handier to have twelve German divisions in national corps and armies than an EDC—from the point of view of military efficiency. He also admitted that from the standpoint of plans it would take no time at all to shift the blueprint for remilitarization from a supranational to a national basis. The only important thing would be supplies, said he. Since the United States is going to provide the basic equipment anyway, I don't see the problem there.

VIENNA, *October 24, 1953*

LAST night I dined at Tommy (Llewellyn) Thompson's; he is now Ambassador here. Karl Gruber, the Foreign Minister, came in after dinner. He has just returned from a political tour of the Tyrol, where local elections are to be held tomorrow. Gruber told me that if there is any plebiscite around Trieste, there must also be a plebiscite in the South Tyrol to decide whether that area should remain Italian or go to Austria. This rather astonished me, because it was Gruber who personally negotiated with De Gasperi the settlement allowing the South Tyrol to remain Italian after World War II and merely securing certain autonomy rights for the German-speaking population and a sharing of such things as hydroelectric power.

PARIS, *October 30, 1953*

THIS morning I had a talk with Prime Minister Joseph Laniel at the Hotel Matignon. He said that without the Indochina war the French would have a magnificent army in Europe and would not fear German rearmament so much, that there was nobody to negotiate a peace with because you need two to negotiate. He could not tell whether the Korean armistice had made the situation in Indochina more dangerous, because so far there had been no concrete reaction by the Chinese. The morale of the Vietnamese (Saigon) troops had been greatly lifted. They were the same people as the Vietminh, but there was no doubt that the Vietminh had far more fighting spirit. He thought General Navarre's current operation had forestalled a Vietminh offensive. If China were to invade Indochina or interfere in a more direct way, the war would be internationalized; he had obtained agreement to that by his trip to Washington.

PARIS, *November 12, 1953*

I DINED last night with Chip Bohlen, who just came in from Moscow. Chip had a lot of interesting gossip about things in Russia. The November 7 reception given by Molotov on the anniversary of the October Revolution was incredible.

As the evening wandered on, Molotov sent word that he wanted Marshal Zhukov to join the table. Chip says Zhukov is by far the most popular man in Russia, and feels that he actually outranks Vassilievsky in importance, although Vassilievsky is listed as ranking higher in the army setup. Zhukov joined the group and behaved with extraordinary dignity. He did not participate in the vodka-drinking race. Chip had the impression that he was looking with great disapproval at some of the others who were throwing the stuff down. Several toasts were exchanged, and Chip made a toast in favor of "justice among the peoples of the world." Zhukov was later on asked if he would make a toast. Chip overheard him replying to his neighbor and saying, no, he would not make a toast, but he was glad to associate himself with the toast of the American Ambassador. This is a very extraordinary statement, even though it was just muttered in an aside to one of the Party boys.

Chip is convinced the Russians are stuck with their foreign policy whether they want it or not. Even if they are trying to change over from Stalinism, they have to hang on to the basic essentials of his policy. They cannot possibly discuss getting out of Germany, because if they lose East Germany, they are likely to lose their satellites. They don't want war, but they can't have real peace. As far as Stalin himself goes, Chip says the process of deflating him now seems to have ended. He makes this analogy. He refers to the Peruvian Indian habit of shrinking human heads. Stalin's head has now been shrunken to its final size. He is no longer a god but just one of the idols of a series of idols in the Soviet Valhalla. He is now Stalin, the great successor of Lenin and part of the Marx–Engels–Lenin–Stalin legend; but no more.

Another extraordinary development in Russia is the fact that the secret police have stopped following ambassadors. Ever since Bullitt first went to Moscow in 1933 the American Ambassador (and all other ambassadors for that matter) had been openly followed by a police car, generally with four cops in it. Now the MVD tails have stopped.

WASHINGTON, *November 23, 1953*

INTERESTING set of visits in the White House. Major General Howard Snyder, the President's doctor and close personal friend, asked me if I wouldn't like to go up and see Mamie. We rode up in an elevator to the private living quarters and went through a hall on the walls of which were a couple of recent paintings by Ike. Mamie greeted me like a long-lost friend. She was sitting up in bed in a pink bed jacket. She stretched out her arms and kissed me on both cheeks, sat me down beside her and we started to chat. The bedroom which she shares with the President (although he has his own bedroom and study next door) is the room where Abe Lincoln used to sleep. Lincoln's bed has been replaced by her pink double bed. Outside the window is the nice small park and lawn where the President practices his golf shots.

When Montgomery was their guest, she took him around. Monty showed eager curiosity about everything, but when he had finished his sight-seeing tour, he said, "Mamie, it's certainly a fine house. But you know, it is smaller than Buckingham."

While we were chatting, her secretary came in and said the President was waiting for me, so I had to rush off.

I told him I had just dropped in to say hello and I certainly didn't want to disturb him. But he seemed quite relaxed and started gassing about all kinds of things. Among others, he talked about the following:

Pakistan wants to help the cause of the United States and the Western powers, but in order to do so needs military aid. The Pakistanis are vital, brave people like the Turks and the Greeks. However, India and Afghanistan object to the thought of our giving help to Pakistan. Afghanistan is worried that Russia might use this as a provocation and excuse to do something against the Afghans. India, on the other hand, is just being "a nuisance." Several times the President referred to "Nehru and his tribe."

The President said, "We must have EDC." He emphasized the vital importance of the European army project to Congress. "I have had two visitors in the past two days who told me that it will go through—shortly after the French elections," he said. I told him I was pessimistic about its chances. This irked him. He expressed great confidence.

He didn't expect any news at all or any real developments at Bermuda. The whole idea was Churchill's, and he was merely trying to be agreeable. He couldn't imagine why I wanted to go down there, because there certainly wouldn't be anything doing. He had investigated and heard the weather was bad. As a result, Mamie was not going. He began to wonder aloud as to whether he should take his golf clubs or not. I suggested no, recalling his clouding political mirror. Finally he said he guessed he wouldn't do it, although he had heard the Mid-Ocean course was pretty good.

The President developed an idea I've never heard him express before. He wanted to outlaw the Communist Party. The Communist deputies should be taken out of the French Chamber. He thought there was no point in keeping the Communist Party respectable and allowing it senators and deputies. The Communist Party was like an iceberg and only a bit of it showed above the surface; the really important part was invisible and secret. Nevertheless he thought it would be useful to render illegal and destroy the "respectable" part that was "visible."

Eisenhower shoved his chair back and got up and started to walk around. He said he detested the methods of McCarthyism, but nevertheless it certainly was necessary to fight communism and fight it hard. It was silly to think that the liberties of the United States were being endangered merely because we were trying to squash communism, but he disapproved very strongly of the methods by which McCarthy himself was trying to conduct that battle. Again, as he strode up and down, the President said that at Bermuda he would like to suggest that the Big Three should severally and together outlaw the Communist Party.

WASHINGTON, *November 24, 1953*

THIS afternoon I had a talk with General Matthew Ridgway, the first time I saw him since he took office as Army Chief of Staff. He told me it is absolutely essential for Jugoslavia, Greece and Turkey to coordinate their military planning, and in the end to tie it up with Italy so that Southern Europe can be properly defended. Taking me over to the map, Ridgway pointed out that Salonika and Istanbul must be held against any possible attack.

WASHINGTON, *November 24, 1953*

THIS afternoon I had a long talk with Foster Dulles. This is what he told me:

The United States does not intend to admit Britain into the ANZUS agreement. We don't want to band together with the old colonial powers in any kind of regional agreement that would lay us open to the charge of joining up with the imperialists. What we are hoping for now is the emergence of some Asian leader who could take the initiative in bringing together an alliance of the free Asian nations which we could support, but which would not be dominated by the Western powers.

Syngman Rhee is far too involved politically and emotionally to qualify. Chiang Kai-shek is an *émigré*. The mere fact that he got tossed out of his own country disqualifies him for leadership of an international coalition. Yet there must be someone who can tie together the anti-Communist nations of Asia, Japan, Formosa, Korea, the Associated States of Indochina, and even Indonesia. Perhaps the best, and indeed only, man for the job is Ramon Magsaysay, who has now emerged as a definite Asian personality.

I asked if there was any truth in the rumor that we were shifting our policy on China more to accord with the British in the hopes of a split between Mao and Moscow. He said emphatically that we are *not* changing our policy at all. Sharp differences remain between Britain and the United States on the subject of China.

It is absolutely essential to American foreign policy that the EDC treaty should be enacted. Under existing United States law 50 percent of the present aid program pledged to the six countries supposed to be united under the European Defense Community is pledged to EDC itself as an organization. Not even Eisenhower's prestige can get more aid out of Congress if EDC fails. If it is not enacted, a definite revision of United States foreign policy—especially as applied to Europe—would almost inevitably be brought about.

As far as Southern Europe goes, we have definitely worked out a policy. As soon as a Trieste settlement can be arranged, every effort will be made to bring about full cooperation between Italy and Jugoslavia and to get Italy's complete adherence to the existing treaty among Greece, Turkey and Jugoslavia. In that way a true link could be established between the east Mediterranean area and the rest of NATO.

WASHINGTON, *November 24, 1953*

AT dinner tonight with Alice Roosevelt Longworth, I mentioned the fact that I had always looked upon her father, Theodore Roosevelt, as the American equivalent to Churchill since he was an author, an adventurer, a soldier and an explorer, to say nothing of having a particular personality flair. She agreed, and then added something interesting. She said her father had always hated Churchill during the years he knew him. This was not only because Roosevelt and Churchill fought on different sides during the Spanish-American War, but because Churchill in his younger days had been arrogant, rude and generally insufferable—very much as Randolph is, unfortunately, so much of the time nowadays. This, above all, Teddy Roosevelt detested.

TUCKER'S TOWN, *December 8, 1953*

THIS morning Dulles said there had been few concrete issues "to which we could direct ourselves" during these Bermuda talks. He described the conference as "Churchill's inspiration." He said it wasn't designed to resolve concrete problems. After the conference was called, the Soviet Union reversed its tactics on a proposed four-power meeting in Berlin, and therefore this became the one concrete issue of the Bermuda talks. An early meeting is probable.

TUCKER'S TOWN, *December 9, 1953*

LUNCH with Hank Byroade, Assistant Secretary of State for the Middle East and Africa. He foresees a gloomy future in his area. Byroade fears

imminent disaster in Egypt. He has only had a chance to speak briefly to
Dulles since he came to Bermuda and saw the President but for a moment
at a large dinner party. In other words, he really didn't get his views across
to anybody. Nor does he quite know whether Eisenhower really wants to
push for a military assistance agreement with Pakistan or not.

He fears that before January 1 the Egyptians are going to start guerrilla
operations against the British forces in the Canal Zone, and the situation
might very well deteriorate into formal war. In that case, of course, we
would have to stand by the British, who are our allies. Byroade muttered
the last with singular regret.

Byroade mistrusts the series of secret tête-à-tête conversations in bathing suits on the beach between Dulles and Eden. He fears Dulles is too
ignorant on the subject of the Middle East and that Eden might get away
with things.

❧

Drinks and a long talk this evening with Anthony Eden. He had the
following to say:

This Bermuda conference has accomplished little. The bathing parties
of Eden and Dulles together were more important. The two men got to
know each other. Eden professes to like Dulles a lot and finds him a good
man to work with. Their exchange has been exceedingly valuable. Eden,
however, confided that he detests Hank Byroade. He says Byroade knows
absolutely nothing about the Middle East. "He has only spent five minutes
there."

Eden said he and Dulles had actually reached an essential agreement on
China. Each recognizes the other's internal political problems. Dulles saw
clearly that Britain cannot "de-recognize" the Peking government. On the
other hand, Eden saw clearly why the United States could not "re-recog-
nize" China. Eden said he understood what an important role China had
always played in American history since the days of the Yankee Clippers.
American individual traders and clergymen had spent their lives in China.
Many fortunes had been made there. In a sense it was like the British
tradition in the Sudan over the years—something, Eden added, that was
not generally understood in the United States.

Returning to the meeting, he described it as "Winston's conference." It
had no real use. Most of the time, as far as three-power meetings had been
concerned, was devoted to the tripartite note replying to the Russians on
the proposed Berlin conference. Eden said Bidault spoke too much, too
often and for too long a time on subjects "we all knew about anyway."

When I brought up the subject of Egypt, Eden half jumped off the sofa
we were sitting on, splashing his drink on his suit. It is obviously something he is really worked up on. He admitted there were only two points at
issue between London and Cairo, but these were all-important, and Britain
could make no further concessions. The issue of uniforms for the British

technicians to remain in the base area if an agreement is signed is not merely a matter of prestige. It is only being used by Egypt to obscure the most important point, which is the agreement on Britain's military "reentry" into the Zone in case of crisis. Dulles, Eden said, had written out a formula last spring governing reentry which would still be perfectly acceptable to Britain. But it is no longer acceptable to Cairo, and American policy seems to have changed.

He said Britain would indeed be glad to have its troops out of Egypt. More than two divisions (totaling approximately eighty thousand men) are now stationed in the Suez Canal Zone, while the United Kingdom itself is bare of defense.

PARIS, *January 21, 1954*

I HAD not seen General de Gaulle in a long time, so this afternoon I spent an hour with him at his headquarters. He offered cigarettes and told me to go ahead and take notes if I wanted to, even though he stressed this was off the record. He said, "It is you, and I have confidence in you."

I turned the conversation to Indochina. I asked what solution he could see. "Solution?" he asked, shrugging his shoulders:

> I can't see anything but evacuation of Indochina or a continuation of the present situation. For a military solution a new method and a new effort would be required. But France does not want to make that effort. We have no really direct interest in Indochina. What is taking place there now is merely a prestige war. Not even the prestige of France is involved any more. Indochina is of international interest more and more and of French interest less and less. There are only two real authorities in Indochina—France and Ho Chi Minh. There is nothing else. There are no other "authorities." The dynasties of Bao Dai, Cambodia and Laos are nothing now. They are only an appearance. Ho is a reality. He represents independence, nationalism, communism, Asia. France is a reality. She represents the occident. Now there is no more French authority in the country. Everything has been given up. Therefore, inevitably the French must get out. They will get out when they have had enough. We will regret it greatly, but we must go. In 1863 Napoleon III went to Mexico. He supported Maximilian. But all the United States was against him. He had to get out. It is the same thing in Indochina.

I asked him what he thought might come out of the Berlin conference starting next week. He said,

> I don't think any *real* entente is possible between the East and West as things now are. But I think for a certain time each can coexist with the other and trade with the other. Neither the United States nor Russia wants to make war now. As a result the cold war has become insupportable. It costs too much. It weighs on the budget, business, the spirit. A cold war cannot be continued if nobody wants it to lead to a hot war. There must be a *modus vivendi* even if nothing is signed. It will provide for more exchanges—

tourists, students, athletes and goods, and it can last a long time. After Berlin there will be many other conferences. A détente is beginning, a *modus vivendi*. It started already in Korea. The dangers of war at present are less and less. The decisive point in Korea was the quarrel between MacArthur and Truman. This showed that the United States did not want war. After Truman said no to MacArthur's proposal to attack China, war was excluded. The English want business with Russia. The French want an arrangement in Indochina. The United States wants export markets. These are the imponderables that make for a *modus vivendi*. This is not an entente; it is armed peace.

This is the first time since 1946 or 1947 that I have heard de Gaulle talk about the chances of some form of peace or, at any rate, not war. In the past, he has always talked about the imminence of world war and how, when it comes, France will need him.

I asked if he had any new proposals on how to deal with Germany. He said, "The first question is to finish with EDC." He said that this was an

entreprise manquée, an error, a stupidity. It was invented by some French politicians who aren't France. When it was submitted, France said no. Finish with the system. That is the first thing. It is absurd from a national, an international and a military point of view. Finish with it. It is absurd.

But we must incorporate Germany into the West. I have always said that. How? By a very wide European arrangement—Britain, France, Germany, Scandinavia, all of free Europe in an alliance, a confederation, in which each would safeguard its own individuality. You cannot suppress nationalities. Within such an organization you can have common arms. See the way Britain has just accepted the NATO rifle. You can have a progressive rearmament of Germany. But it is an absurdity, a dream, a fantasy to think that you can suppress France and French nationality.

The United States has walked along with this idiocy. Now you must extricate yourselves. If you put your money on a bad horse, you are lunatics if you keep throwing it away on the same horse. I guarantee that EDC will not go through. I will do everything against it. I will work with the Communists to block it. I will make revolution against it. I would rather go with the Russians to stop it. It won't go through. I repeat, I will make revolution to prevent it.

I asked de Gaulle what reliance he thought France should place upon the Soviet Pact he signed in Moscow in 1944. He replied, "France must not lose its independence to anyone. I prevented the Communists from grabbing power in France in 1944 and also in 1947 when I started the RPF. We cannot lose our sovereignty to Russia." This is doubletalk.

He continued by saying the Germans would be rearmed without French permission if the French held back too long. On this issue the Soviet Pact could have a useful influence. He then said: "If one rearms Germany and France does not approve of such rearmament, the Soviets also will object. Then the Soviets may occupy West Berlin. What would the French do? The French would not object, under the Franco-Soviet pact." I pointed out that if West Berlin were occupied, the Allied garrison would be taken prisoners by the Russians. The general replied, "France could have its troops repatriated by the Russians."

He continued that there was "no chance of any serious policy being based upon the Soviet pact. We must have the United States' alliance. We also want Germany with the Western world—but without the simultaneous disappearance of France. Everything but that."

I asked what he thought of Eisenhower's proposal to take citizenship away from persons accused of conspiring against the government—namely, Communists—and whether he thought the Communist Party should be outlawed in France. He replied, "You in the United States have a different problem. You have not been invaded as often or had as many revolutions as we have. You don't have as many Communists because you have not had fourteen revolutions and thirteen invasions in 150 years." (I must say, I don't quite follow his history when he uses these fourteen and thirteen statistics.)

> The real remedy in France is a great France, *une grandeur française*. Now there is despair here. Those Frenchmen who are despairing go to the Communist Party. That is why you need a great French policy to eliminate communism. This is not easy. But on this we have not received much support from our allies.
>
> During the war I made war. I finished by success. Now France is divided again. In 1947 when the Communist Party was dangerous, I made the RPF to stop them. Now that they are not so dangerous, the French are again dispersed—the RPF also. [This latter was a curious admission.] Now all I want to do is to prevent stupidities like EDC. I cannot achieve *positive* progress all alone, but I can block absurdities.

I asked de Gaulle what his personal program was now. He said, "The age of giants is over. Giants can do nothing now. Churchill is the only survivor and he can do nothing. I like Eisenhower. But he is not a giant. Roosevelt is dead. Stalin died—too late. This is the epoch of Malenkov, Fanfani and Queuille."

BERLIN, *January 28, 1954*

LUNCH today with Yuri Zhukov, now assistant director of *Pravda*. After sparring around with polite opening remarks, Zhukov suddenly drove in. He said: "Well, it is quite a while since you and Bohlen and I arranged the Korean armistice."

I replied obliquely that I remembered an interesting dinner party at my house at which he and Bohlen had been present. He said "Yes, we arranged the armistice quite successfully. After all, they followed the terms that we discussed. Don't you think it is about time that we should have a similar agreement on present problems?"

He thought what was needed was realization by both the United States and Russia—the only two really great powers here—that neither one nor the other wanted war. This Berlin meeting could achieve an armistice in the cold war, and future meetings could achieve real peace. Bilateral talks between the Russians and the Americans were absolutely imperative in order to arrive at a real understanding.

He then stressed that conversations could be held under the cover of being negotiations on atomic issues such as have already started between Russia and the United States. Under this guise of "atomic affairs" everything could be talked over from Indochina to East-West trade.

He assured me Russia had *no* desire for further territorial expansion. I said that this might indeed be true, but surely anyone reading the newspapers would be fully aware that the United States was concerned about the expansionist tendencies of the Soviet bloc and international communism. I pointed out, for example, that even if he thought a Ho Chi Minh Indochina would not be another republic in the Soviet Union, from the United States point of view it would be a gain for the Communist bloc and, in my opinion, would not be tolerated.

He said such things could be arranged. I remarked that as far as I could see, the only way they could be arranged would be by Russia telling China to stop sending arms to Indochina. He said Russia could not tell the people of other countries and the Communist Parties of other countries what to do and could not order them to cease fighting for their independence. I replied this might be true but that in my opinion a basic fact remained, and that was if Russia told China to stop sending arms to Ho Chi Minh, it was probable a solution could be arranged in Indochina. Zhukov replied, "Maybe such things can be arranged."

I pointed out that it would be a very difficult thing, it seemed to me as a journalist, for the United States to embark on two-power negotiations with the USSR, because after all it had obligations to its allies France and Great Britain. Zhukov replied that he understood this, but after all France and Great Britain were not really great powers as were the USSR and the United States. I then said that it seemed to me pretty evident that the Soviet Union was just trying to split France and Britain off from the United States and to divide us. He said, "You mean to drive you into isolationism?" I said, "Precisely." He said, "Well, one must always have alternatives. If our negotiations with you do not succeed, naturally we must seek alternative policies."

I didn't think it would be possible under any conditions to come to an agreement on the unification of Germany because I felt, among other things, that the Soviet Union was too scared of a unified Germany to permit it, even if it was a Communist Germany.

Quite obviously Zhukov had something to do with shaping the Russian decision on the Korean armistice. Also quite obviously he figures that I am a kind of Jeffersonian Zhukov because I happened to be the host when he was talking with Bohlen. Therefore he is putting out what appears to me to be a most important Soviet "line," although naturally I am in no position to judge whether this is for propaganda purposes, for the purpose of trying to get us to swallow some bait and divide the Allies, or in a sincere effort to arrange a *modus vivendi* along the only lines the Russians understand, namely, power politics.

BERLIN, *January 31, 1954*

LAST night I dined with Chip Bohlen. He gave me a good definition of democracy—a word the Russians flaunt all the time. In the Soviet lexicon a "democratic government" is one with at least 20 percent Communists in its composition. A "progressive democratic government" is one with at least 40 percent Communists in its makeup. A "people's democratic government" is a Communist dictatorship.

BERLIN, *January 31, 1954*

THIS afternoon Dulles summed up his impressions of the first week of the Big Four Conference. Of Molotov he said: "I have personally known most of the diplomats of this century. As a boy I attended the second Hague Peace Conference in 1907. I would classify Molotov as tops. He is very skillful. But his skill is directed against two things he cannot surmount— the pretty solid unity of the West and the fact that world opinion is sick and tired of Soviet propaganda. [Of course, Dulles hopes to master Molotov, outdo the "best."]

PARIS, *February 10, 1954*

THE Berlin Conference is a fraud, and I left Clif Daniel in charge of our large staff there and beat it. Dulles keeps insisting he won't agree to a Far East conference and dealings with China; yet it is evident this is about all Berlin will produce. He goes out of his way to build up Molotov as the greatest diplomat since Talleyrand—so, if he, Dulles, manages to worst him, he'll look even better. And he acts as a kind of P. T. Barnum presenting Bidault as a brilliant statesman and chief spokesman for the West—even comparing him to Abe Lincoln, a ridiculous *non sequitur*. Bidault goes along with us, above all on Indochina, but French politics are shifting sands, and it is silly to build any policy castles on them. The Russians are working for a French sellout; and they'll get it. The French don't even dare draft recruits for Asia.

I have decided to make a tour of Italy to confirm or deny Clare Luce's asseverations to Washington that it is going Communist unless we intervene. I think she's nuts and merely wants to make a big name for herself as an activist in her first diplomatic job. I mistrust her judgment.

BOLOGNA, *February 23, 1954*

GIUSEPPE Dozza, Mayor of Bologna and president of a League of Democratic Communities, is one of the handful of top Communists in Italy. He is an extremely popular and intelligent man. He received me in his Mayor's office in the Palazzo del Municipio, a beautiful medieval building on the main square of Bologna. He is heavy-set, smiling, with sharp features, a shock of white hair and the powerful nose and jaw of a *condottiere*.

When I asked why communism was so strong in Italy, Dozza replied that the tradition of Italy's labor movement had been violently interrupted by fascism. He said: "If I were an anti-Communist, I would not counsel anyone to take exceptional measures against the party such as outlawing it. Look at the way the Communist Party grew during the fascist repression. We never gave up the struggle and by our sacrifices we gained leadership of all antifascist movements, not just our own. Unknown youths imprisoned for ten or fifteen years educated themselves in their cell and assumed leadership over older and better-known prisoners. When these people emerged from prisons and from hiding, they gained the confidence of the masses."

CONSUMA, *February 27, 1954*

I DROVE to Consuma on the snow-powdered Tuscan hills to see Professor Giorgio LaPira, Mayor of Florence, who is taking a brief vacation here. He is an extraordinary phenomenon of modern politics: a saintly little man who lives permanently in Florence's San Marco, the Dominican monastery with frescoes by Fra Angelico, where Savonarola lived. He said: "There are only two choices in Italy at present—Christian Democracy or communism. We must polarize Christian Democracy towards the left. You cannot apply pre-Fascist democracy to post-Fascist people. The need now is for dynamic democracy. Unfortunately the leaders of our party mistrust the ability of the younger people. We must rely more upon youth. Communism is a danger to Italy, but not yet a mortal danger. We must be aware of it and take steps to curb it, but we have time and ability."

ROME, *March 2, 1954*

GIUSSEPPE Saragat, head of the Democratic Socialist faction (future president of Italy), says: "To combat communism a good social policy must be instituted. The problem in Italy is not like the United States where communism is merely a small police problem, and not social and human, as it is here. The difference of standard of living between the classes is far too sharp in Italy. It is hard to know what can be done because this is not a laboratory where you can do what you want. We are dealing with people and history. The Italian *bourgeoisie* is unenlightened and backward."

ROME, *March 4, 1954*

AMINTORE Fanfani (past and future Prime Minister) is authoritarian, but now a member of the extreme left-wing group of the Christian Democratic Party. Industrialists attack him as being a "white Communist." He was Prime Minister early this year, but his government was not confirmed by the parliament.

He told me the maximum strength of the Communist Party had been reached before the June 1953 elections. It was dangerous to give the impression that either Russia or communism was too strong. That helped the possibilities of communism conquering the country. The Italian people were frightened and weak and were much impressed by appearances of strength.

ROME, *March 5, 1954*

DE Gasperi, now only running the Christian Democratic Party, survives remarkably. He is almost eighty, and I must say he looks a good deal younger than his comrade, Adenauer. He is full of energy, health and good humor. He said he is limiting himself to party affairs because it is of paramount importance in the struggle against communism to get the party into good shape.

De Gasperi said the problem now is not so much the revival of communism as it is the strengthening of the extreme right. "The two together represent a return to the shadows of the past. In a sense, what has hurt the center has been anticommunism (the right) rather than communism." He almost wept when complaining of Mrs. Luce's efforts to encourage the right in a misguided anti-Communist move.

It is difficult for us to form a government with the Monarchists, as your ambassador wants. That poses the question of the regime which is very important. The danger comes more from a rightist revival than from communism. You cannot expect us democrats who fought fascism to join with fascism. There are two methods of defense against communism. Either all the moderate anti-Communist votes should be rallied, or we must depend upon the Monarchists. It is a question of one or the other. But, if the Monarchists come in, the Saragat Socialists and Republicans will work with the Communists, and they will be lost forever.

PARIS, *March 25, 1954*

LUNCH with Exintaris (Greek envoy to NATO). He told me American policy on a Balkan alliance has changed. In January Washington suddenly began to exert diplomatic pressure on Greece and Turkey *not* to sign a military pact with Jugoslavia. The United States—and Britain seconded the motion as the result of Washington's pressure—suggested to Athens and Ankara that the project be staved off for awhile. This was very embarrassing to the Greeks and the Turks.

The United States wants things delayed in order to point out to the Jugoslavs that it would be easier to get such an agreement if the Trieste question first were settled. Exintaris thinks the Italian government has exercised influence upon Mrs. Luce, the United States Ambassador, who in turn has applied pressure on the State Department. Exintaris thinks this is a disastrous move.

PARIS, *April 7, 1954*

LUNCH today with Gaston Palewski, Minister and old friend of de Gaulle. He first met de Gaulle in 1934, when de Gaulle was a major and was drawing up a scheme for armored divisions for the French War Ministry. Palewski at the time was working with Reynaud. He said de Gaulle was more affable and less distant in those days. He also said at that time de Gaulle was rather fond of women. I asked if he meant that de Gaulle actually was able to carry on a badinage and flirtation in the approved French fashion, and he replied that de Gaulle seemed more intent on proving himself than in enjoying the process. His was "the technique of the heavy cavalry."

PARIS, *April 12, 1954*

LUNCH today at General Pierre Billotte's with General Paul Ely, Chief of the French General Staff. Ely said it was impossible for France now to lose Dienbienphu. The place had no military value. Its only military importance was during the invasion of Laos last year. However it has become a political symbol of such importance that it cannot at any cost be lost. It is impossible to relieve Dienbienphu by ground.

As a result, the only way of holding on in Dienbienphu is by expanding the area held by the French. Ely estimates the Communists have lost, in terms of permanent casualties (dead or totally crippled) twelve thousand. To expand the French position it is necessary initially to get a large enough area to reopen the airfield so that troops can be flown in.

Ely is going to see Premier Laniel this afternoon, in anticipation of the Dulles visit (Dulles arrives tomorrow) to request that the French be prepared to accept American air assistance. That does not mean merely aircraft but also crews.

PARIS, *April 14, 1954*

SAW Dulles this evening before he took off for Washington on the conclusion of a two-day trip to London and a one-day visit in Paris trying to straighten out Big Three teamwork on the eve of the Geneva Conference. I think he has done a pretty good job, considering that the situation is hopeless. His neck is in a noose still, but he has got some soap on the rope.

Before Dulles, I had a chat with Walter Robertson, Assistant Secretary of State for the Far East. I asked Robertson whether the French had finally requested American land-based and sea-based air support and told him about my conversation with General Ely. He said they hadn't really clarified their own point of view yet. He was very distressed by French ineptitude. At hysterically urgent French prodding he and a group of American experts had sat up until 3:00 A.M. arranging a special airlift to Dienbienphu because the French said it would fall otherwise. When everything was arranged, they got word from Pleven that it really couldn't start operating until the middle of May because it would interfere with vacation schedules of pilots.

Dulles looked tired but in good humor. He is going to be back here next week. Over a whisky and soda he said the reason for his trip was that: "We foresaw at Berlin that if the subject of Indochina was put on the agenda of the Geneva Conference, it would probably lead to intensified military efforts by the Communists in Indochina in order to try and help their bargaining position. Precisely that has happened, and they have been pushing hard with extravagant wastage."

Without a defense agreement it is quite conceivable that the countries of the region would be lost to communism one by one—first Vietnam, then Laos, then Cambodia, then Thailand, then Indonesia. A threat to the Philippines, New Zealand and Australia would develop, and the entire western Pacific position would be menaced if there were no agreement on unity of action covering the area.

Dulles said the Communists must be made to realize they are up against "something strong enough" to force them to abandon their plans to extend their rule over Southeast Asia. He did not think this would precipitate a war. On the contrary, the Communists were capable of starting a war whenever it suited their book. They would not be provoked into war.

Dulles hoped practical arrangements to prepare for a Southeast Asia alliance could be started very soon. It was of the utmost importance that "the stigma of colonialism" be removed from this enterprise. (Personally I don't see how on earth he is going to remove such a stigma with the French and the British as partners. After all, the British have Malaya and nearby Hong Kong, which is a crown colony; and the French have Indochina. I don't think Nehru, for example, is going to fall for the idea that this is not a colonial enterprise.)

10

TODAY APPEARS TO HAVE BEEN HISTORICALLY TRAGIC IN TERMS of the position of Western democracy. Obviously the United States is now convinced Dienbienphu is going to fall and nothing can save it; that as a result either Indochina will be conquered or we will have to intervene—and nobody wants to intervene with us. We feel that the loss of Southeast Asia would cripple our world position.

I had dinner with Walter Robertson, Assistant Secretary of State for Far Eastern Affairs. He said April 22 had been one of the worst days in United States history. He compared the present situation in a rather illogical way with that of Washington at Valley Forge and said we simply could not abandon our position. What he was referring to was news that had been received that Dienbienphu is apparently gone. It hasn't actually fallen, but the area is now so small that aid cannot be effectively sent to it. The airlift we arranged last week with the French is too late—if not too little.

We must recognize that it is impossible for us to lose Southeast Asia, which would follow the loss of Indochina. Our whole civilization would be affected. We must intervene. The loss of Southeast Asia would not only represent an enormous loss of face, but also of vital raw materials and rice coveted by China. What is the difference, Robertson asked, whether the Communists start a war of aggression or we lose our civilization because we have failed to take a sufficiently powerful stand? Yet from that position he hastened on to say that any kind of war means the end of our civilization. He remarked that the national debt is now $275 billion, and another war would bankrupt the country.

There is no point in our arguing that we will intervene in one way but not in another way. If we are going to intervene, we have to intervene wholeheartedly. This is a time to tighten our belts, for unpopular decisions and higher taxes—not for a soft, easy, luxurious life.

The Navarre Plan in Indochina has been a complete failure. The Indochinese hate the French and with reason. Robertson recalled the bombardment in 1946 of innocent Indochinese civilians by a French cruiser which killed "thousands" of them. We are stuck, he said, with the "horrid little Bao Dai," whom he described as useless and cowardly. He said that although Bao Dai claims that malaria keeps him away from visiting the front, it does not keep him away from big-game hunting and the Riviera. He is a "rotten little Japanese collaborator," and if he, Robertson, were an Indochinese, he would have no use for him at all. If only Ho Cho Minh were on our side, we could do something about the situation; but unfortunately he is the enemy.

PARIS, *April 24, 1954*

THERE is considerable fear among the Americans that we are hovering on the verge of World War III. This evening I had a talk with Dulles over at the American Embassy, where the top members of the American delegation for Geneva had gathered for a quick buffet supper before taking off a half-hour later in Dulles' plane. Admiral Radford, Chairman of the Joint Chiefs of Staff, had just finished conferring with Dulles when I saw the Secretary.

Dulles told me the French had requested the intervention of American aircraft manned by American crews. It had been explained that it was impossible under United States constitutional authority to intervene that directly. Such would be an act of war, and the President could not take such a step under his peacetime executive powers. Dulles said the French simply didn't seem to understand American law very well.

He had pointed out, however, that the request might be regarded differently if there were actually an operational Southeast Asia alliance with France and the United States as members. Congress would have to approve American participation—probably by a resolution. Then, perhaps in a fashion similar to Korea, where the United Nations intervened, the United States might be able to intervene.

Dulles admitted the prospects for Geneva were by no means good.

PARIS, *April 24, 1954*

TONIGHT I wrote:

France has asked for direct large-scale intervention in the Indochina war by United States aircraft manned by American crews.

However, she has been told it is impossible for President Eisenhower to sanction such a grave move in peacetime.

It has been explained that the United States has gone to the limit of assistance within the prerogatives of the President's existing peacetime authority in furnishing technicians to keep aircraft operational and in flying paratroopers from metropolitan France to Indochina bases outside the combat area.

There was no mention of ground forces in the request, but it included both land- and carrier-based aircraft.

The French have been advised that if a united front can be established through the creation of a Southeast Asian alliance, as suggested by Secretary of State John Foster Dulles, the legal status of their request for wholesale "air assistance" may be regarded differently.

GENEVA, *April 25, 1954*

SAW Dulles this afternoon—on the eve of the Geneva Asian conference. Right now there is absolute confusion on policy among the Big Three and on procedure among the Big Four.

He doesn't expect to stay here long and hopes Bedell Smith can take over the delegation leadership within a week. He admits to no optimism. He warned that whenever the USSR gains a "temporary" advantage over an area, it doesn't relax its grip; and therefore partition would be a dangerous solution in Indochina. There is also little hope of expelling the Communists from North Korea.

Dulles thinks he'll be gone before Indochina comes up as a topic. It will be mainly up to the French to decide whether priority should be given to consideration of Indochina because they are doing the fighting. The United States will be guided primarily by French views. In Korea we always insisted that those with troops on the battlefield should be responsible for basic decisions. We will thus be guided largely by the French on whether they want the Vietminh represented here or not. Of course Paris will consult us.

Dulles explained the United States had taken all steps short of war to aid France in Indochina, but there was no present reason to foresee that we would cross the line of belligerency. We don't want to see Indochina fall, but sometimes things *do* occur that we don't like. The Administration's policy is to avoid belligerency.

Dulles said he didn't expect to see Chou En-lai here "unless our automobiles collide."

GENEVA, *April 28, 1954*

LUNCH today with Humphrey Trevelyan (later Lord Trevelyan and Ambassador), British chargé d'affaires in Communist China. He left there April 3 (via Hong Kong). He thinks the United States' policy is insane. It is far more important to have representatives in a country you dislike than one you like. He can do little for British subjects held by the Chinese and even less for Americans. America must expect no favors after its savage attacks on China. Chiang has no more influence in China; he is finished and done for, even as a symbol.

BLED, *May 7, 1954*

TODAY I saw Tito at his summer house in Bled. He is up here for a fortnight or so, following his official visit to Turkey, shooting *auerhahn*
(capercaillie); the season is in the beginning of May.

Tito's dog Tiger is now dead, and I saw no animals. He received me in
an awful-looking salon, the walls of which were all hung in heavy dark
blue velvet curtains. The furniture was massive, square and certainly not
comfortable for my build. Tito was wearing a blue suit with a modest
figured necktie clasped to his shirt with a ruby and diamond bar pin. He
had a large solitaire diamond ring on his left hand and a gold bracelet
wristwatch. He said there were "no more obstacles" in the way of a full
military alliance among Jugoslavia, Turkey and Greece and that this
would be a "firm guarantee of peace in this part of the world."

"Neither we nor the Turks see any reason why such a full alliance
should not be formed. That is why I am going to Greece next month.
Everything has already been done by the three general staffs preparing for
the alliance. All that is needed now are formal arrangements to give formal
approval to what already exists."

Tito said the alliance would have to come in the form of a military
annex to the Treaty of Ankara and that this would have to be ratified by
the parliaments of the three countries. The annex, he said, would of course
be "the most important part of the treaty." It would "give it its true
character and be a binding obligation."

He said: "If the base of EDC is broadened, Jugoslavia will be ready to
join it." This is all, of course, a lot of crap. Tito clearly doesn't even
understand just what EDC is (or was) but he is being very shrewd about
using it for propaganda.

I asked Tito, considering that he was pressing for alliance with Greece
and Turkey, both members of NATO, and was talking of maybe joining
EDC, which would be part of NATO, why he didn't wish to join NATO
himself directly. He said that while it was necessary for Jugoslavia to
cooperate with NATO "to a certain extent," he didn't want to join that
organization.

ATHENS, *May 13, 1954*

TODAY I lunched with King Paul at his country residence in Tatoi, about
twenty-three miles out of Athens. Paul was very irked with the British on
Cyprus. With a smile and a puff at his cigarette holder, he then looked at
me and said: "Remember, we started that one, didn't we? King George of
England sent me word that he didn't want me breaking up his empire. He
sent word by Norton" (former British Ambassador here). King Paul was
referring to an interview I had with him a long time ago on the matter.

He blamed Eden largely for the present crisis but added: "Of course everybody knows how disagreeable Eden is." He said when Eden was recuperating from his operation here last year, Papagos had asked to see him on Cyprus and Eden had been exceptionally rude. That had put Papagos' back up.

ATHENS, *May 17, 1954*

I HAD a good talk this morning with Field Marshal Papagos, the Prime Minister. Papagos said he had always been "a partisan of military alliance" with Jugoslavia and Turkey and that a political understanding—as under the Ankara Treaty—was not enough. I told him what Tito had told me about his hopes for a military annex providing for automatic assistance if any party were attacked, and he said: "I am completely in accord with Tito."

IZMIR, *May 28, 1954*

LONG talk with Lieutenant General Paul Kendall, commander of headquarters, Allied Land Forces, South East Europe (ALFSEE) here in Izmir. Kendall, who is friendly, rather overbearing, and by no means subtle, continually referred to the Turks and Greeks as "the best damned mercenaries I know. We've bought ourselves some damned fine mercenaries and they're cheap at the price. We get five times as much soldier for our money here than at home." Et cetera.

He thought the Turks were better mercenaries than the Greeks because there were more of them and they were cheaper: they got paid (the *"Asker,"* or private) only about 15 cents a month plus two uniforms, one winter and one summer, for their two-year service. They ate little, and when told to stay in a hole they remained there and fought until they died.

PARIS, *June 15, 1954*

LUNCH with Bill Gibson of the American Embassy. The military situation in Indochina is absolutely disastrous. It is far worse, says Bill, than it looks. It is a ridiculous joke to think that Cambodia and Laos can be saved even if Vietnam goes. There is no will to resist anywhere in Southeast Asia. Almost certainly Thailand will make a deal for collaboration with the Communists just the way they collaborated with the victorious Japanese during World War II. The French are in desperate straits in the Delta. Chinese intervention is now on a massive scale with convoys of thousands of vehicles coming over the border. The Vietminh not only gained a tremendous moral ascendancy after Dienbienphu but acquired a vast new amount of equipment, which they know how to use very efficiently. Vietnamese troops fighting for the French are virtually useless. The way the French use them, Vietnamese soldiers are mixed up with French soldiers in the same units. This makes it all the easier in times of crisis for an entire unit to disintegrate and collapse.

The new Prime Minister just chosen for Vietnam, Ngo Dinh Diem, is a virtually unknown individual. By sheer chance Gibson knows him well and is probably the only Westerner who does. Ngo Dinh Diem is a rather mystical Catholic of an impractical sort. He has been studying at a Catholic retreat in Bruges recently and is now in Paris very much incognito. The Ministry of the Associated States here didn't even know a thing about him when he was named. He is staying at a third-class hotel in Paris, and Gibson is his only contact. He calls up Gibson under a code name, and they meet in places like park benches. He is a completely unreal figure, but at least he is scrupulously honest.

PARIS, *June 23, 1954*

LUNCH with Speidel. He was very gloomy about the prospects of EDC. That very morning General Edgard de Larminat, president of the military committee for the organization of EDC, with much embarrassment, for the first time in the history of these Franco-German negotiations at the military level, suggested a "solution de rechange" for EDC. As Spiedel understands the Larminat suggestion it would be an end of the supranational army idea.

The most important thing Speidel said to me today was that if Germany had to start planning a national army instead of European army divisions, it would take only about "a couple of hours" to change the blueprints around. But the most significant event of our meeting was an extraordinary kind of ballet in which all the players were unaware of their roles.

I arrived at Lucas Carton a few moments ahead of him and told the waiters to send "Le Général Speidel" to my regular table. So they knew who he was (although he always wears a gray double-breasted suit and looks like a well-fed professor, with his glasses and earnest expression). Some of the waiters must have known him from the war, when the principal occupation officers, including Goering, Rundstedt, Rommel, Choltitz, Speidel and others, often ate at Lucas. Malraux once told me the ground floor here was the favorite restaurant of the Nazi military brass, so Resistance leaders often gathered in the private dining rooms one floor up. Gestapo tails were put off if they followed a suspect through the revolving doors and came face to face with Goering.

Because of Larminat's ominous news, Speidel was flustered, nervous and did the rare thing for him, accepted a preprandial cocktail. This was unusual enough and confirmed his conviction that EDC was finished. But then his nervousness showed as he was eating his soup later and spilled a bit on his lapel.

Immediately, before my astonished eyes, the occupation was reenacted. Speidel grew taller and taller, straighter and straighter, his belly drawing inward, his chest expanding, as he sat up stiff and summoned the maître d'hôtel, the sommelier, the waiters, as if he owned the place, ordering salt, hot water, vinegar, and so on to remove the foul spot. And the waiters, for their part, became smaller and smaller, stooping and cringing obsequiously before this suddenly military figure. They formed a kind of parade, each with his napkin, salt or lemon, performing menial services and whispering apologies as if it had all been their fault. Finally, the stain was out. Speidel relaxed, his chest caved in, his stomach sagged out, he subsided into civilian comfort. And the waiters, pleased with themselves, grew taller, cockier, more self-confident.

I sat there with my eyes popping. Nobody playing his role in that sad and grim enactment had the faintest idea of what a spectacle was taking place.

PARIS, *June 29, 1954*

GIBSON of the American Embassy told me he had spent the day with Don Heath, who has now flown to Washington with the mission of shaking the United States loose from its support of Bao Dai and shaking Bao Dai loose from Indochina. Bao Dai now claims he is ill and has to go to Vittel for a cure. The French apparently are in agreement, and it appears that Bao Dai is never going to go back home. Why the hell we couldn't have done this five or six years ago, I don't know.

PARIS, *July 1, 1954*

GOOD talk with David Bruce this morning. Bruce took apart the Radford theory of strategy. He said some of its advocates had obviously wanted to intervene with tactical atom bombs at Dienbienphu as a way of getting the United States engaged first in Indochina and then in China; that to conquer China more than the forces of Chiang Kai-shek now on Formosa would be necessary. This meant engaging American land troops. If the Soviet Union were to intervene in this war between the United States and China, these people wanted to blow up the Soviet Union with hydrogen bombs. Bruce said that if one wished to accept the logic of Radford's theory, it didn't make sense anyway. Radford's theory was that the relative advantage now held by the United States was slipping, and the Russians were gaining every year, holding their own advantage in conservative forces and weapons and catching up on new weapons. Therefore, according to some theorists, a preventive war was necessary. However, as Bruce points out, if this logic is sound, there is no sense in going through the performance of intervening steps involving China. If the theory is sound, war should be started right away against Russia. The other approach is dishonest, because it seeks to get the United States involved in a war with China without letting the people know that.

NEW YORK, *October 5, 1954*

THIS morning I had a satisfactory talk with Dag Hammarskjöld, Secretary General of the United Nations. Hammarskjöld said that when he became Secretary General he considered he had completely dropped his national passport as a Swede. A country of origin does not exist either for himself or for other international UN servants. But one cannot change one's heritage or personality. The political training he received naturally had a special flavor and derived from a background with a certain tradition which, despite Sweden's so-called neutrality, was extremely Western—"more western than that of certain other nations in the West," he added.

He did not think present American "loyalty" concepts necessarily conflicted with these views. A man who is patently disloyal to his country lacks integrity, and therefore is of no use to an international body. If a man is regarded as an enemy by his own country because of his own *intellectual* views—either in the United States or the Soviet Union, for example—it does not necessarily constitute the type of disloyalty to his country to which he was referring. He could imagine a man in the United States having intellectual sympathy with Communist philosophy and still not being disloyal to his country; thereby retaining his integrity as a UN servant. There are two entirely different concepts of loyalty; but a basic lack of loyalty to one's own country would be a serious disqualification. Political dissenters of any sort cannot be permitted to let their beliefs influence their national attitudes in the UN.

WASHINGTON, *October 8, 1954*

TALK with Foster Dulles. I must say, he shows physical signs of strain. He has the appearance of a tired man and a slightly unnatural flush.

I asked if he thought it possible to arrange terms for coexistence between the United States and Russia. He replied:

> I take a somewhat philosophical approach to this question, just as the Soviet leaders do. With their materialistic approach to problems, coexistence means to them merely physical coexistence in the sense that everybody would be alive together in the world at the same time and following a particular pattern. Their idea of coexistence is to have a completely ordered universe, patterned completely according to a harmony set in terms of total conformity. Everybody and every nation would move in a fixed orbit the way planets do. I can understand what they mean from a purely materialistic point of view.
>
> But we believe in a spiritual view of the world. We believe in a world that

is governed by more than material things. People are entitled to their individual beliefs in their own minds and to their individual spiritual faiths and loyalties. The differences of their opinions not only represent the theory of freedom, but they are a source of richness in themselves. This is the exact reverse of the conformity desired by the Russians. Such conformity breeds sterility, whereas individual differences in thought breed freedom.

The Russians do not and cannot admit that type of coexistence which is basically contrary to their own fanatical beliefs. When we are talking about coexistence, we are talking about something entirely different from the Russians. I can give you an example of this. When I spoke to Molotov at Berlin earlier this year, I asked him why he wasn't prepared to give the Germans their independence the way we granted independence to Japan. Molotov said he didn't trust them and that they could not be relied upon. Freedom would be dangerous for them because the Germans have already shown in the past how they abuse it. The Russians mistrust freedom. There is a basic philosophical difference between their conception and our conception of coexistence.

This doesn't mean that you do not and cannot settle matters. It is, of course, necessary for nations to adjust themselves and make compromises on international problems. We can coexist with the Russians under our own system as long as we don't abandon basic principles in the sense that we can live together at the same time. That kind of coexistence is possible, but always on a limited and provisional basis. We must recognize that our two systems are inherently incompatible.

WASHINGTON, *October 14, 1954*

THIS morning I had an excellent discussion with Dean Acheson at his law office. I wanted a precise comparison of his views with Foster Dulles'. Acheson said:

Coexistence is not different from "peace" as a word. But the problem is different. The phrase is "peaceful coexistence." This is a flabby and unrevealing phrase. Really, one might call it "competitive coexistence." The world has seen something develop that is not explained solely by the development of the Soviet Union—which has upset the balance of power. More than that is involved. It is more than a question of differing ideologies. Now we are faced with a direct challenge to all the values of civilization. These values are moral, spiritual, and ethical. They have been the underlying element of society and civilization for hundreds of years. Now they are called nonsense by this new system. That challenge is perhaps more important than the challenge of the Soviet state.

The truth of the most fundamental beliefs of the free world is now denied—not merely in propaganda—but in fact. They deny the goodness of truth. They regard everything as an instrument. They want only to produce results. There are no basic values—like the individual human spirit—important to them. They see as fundamental their immediate objectives. And they twist the human spirit by the will of the state.

Such a challenge has two sides—the vigor and strength of both the challenger and the defender. Is our civilization strong enough and vigorous enough to resist? No. Our civilization must reinvigorate itself.

Behind the new barbarism is a combination of a powerful state and its allies plus a powerful doctrine. In the light of this, we must examine coexistence. It is a little bit more than working out an adjustment between two competing systems. Coexistence has various sides—political, military, and moral. This is a matter of moral strength. We must build up economic and military cohesion. But we must translate our moral beliefs into practical expression. McCarthyism and totalitarianism challenge here and undermine our moral worth. These challenges occur both within the country and within the individual. McCarthyism denies the truth of ourselves and of our country. It undermines us in the world's concept. Other people are losing faith in us.

What is coexisting? We must maintain western civilization while in the same world there exists a new barbarism that cannot be confined to the distant reaches as in the days of the Romans. We must have a rebirth in ourselves and in our ideals.

It *can* be done. But it is very difficult. And this is a competitive affair, competitive coexistence. It is like two cabbages in a field that exist if they are not planted too close together.

We and the Russians must recognize that we *do* have a capacity to destroy each other. We also must recognize that China is a pretty ominous thing. The Russians must be aware that if they get into a dogfight with us, their Chinese neighbors might inherit the earth.

WASHINGTON, *October 15, 1954*

THIS afternoon I went over to the Pentagon for a talk with Admiral Radford, Chairman of the Joint Chiefs of Staff. He scares the hell out of me. He's the American equivalent of the Soviet mechanical man.

I asked what Radford thought were the chances of working out a system of peaceful coexistence. He replied that based on the public writings of their Soviet leaders, they will coexist only until they are ready to strike us. Their objective remains conquest of the world, and they have never deviated from this. This does not necessarily mean armed conflict—provided that we are willing to give in. But if we don't give in, it does. He said the leading Communists, such as Lenin and Stalin, have predicted the inevitability of armed conflict, and the pattern of their armed forces today indicates they still believe this. Unless there is a change in this pattern, we cannot assume anything else about the intentions of Soviet leaders.

Radford considered that we were now in a state of war—only without shooting. A military solution will come "only when the Russians are convinced that their other offensives have failed." If you follow Radford's thinking to its logical conclusion, the moment we begin to win the cold war the Russians will start a hot war.

WASHINGTON, *October 19, 1954*

I SPENT two and a half hours in the White House. Ike looks markedly older and his face and neck show new lines and signs of worry. He thought a President ought to have a Congress controlled by his own party in order to achieve his foreign-policy goals. As chief executive he had to use his power as head of the dominant party. To gain his objectives through Congressional approval, he had to be in a position to influence and cajole logrolling congressmen. He had such influence and authority within his own party, but not within the opposition. The Democrats were, of course, patriotic and would support the national interest on any major issues such as national defense. But he thought they would try to hamstring him on anything not of top importance, and this included foreign policy.

Wilson, Hoover and Truman had all been crippled at times by the lack of Congressional support. (I recall that Truman did get through the Truman Doctrine and Marshall Plan plus the Korean War.) Hoover had warned Ike when the latter said he intended to have a middle-of-the-road, moderate government that he would inevitably be unpopular, because the extremists of both left and right would oppose him. Yet he intended to pursue this course. The country needed calm and cleaning up. Just like the Tories in Britain hadn't tried to return to everything of pre-Labor days, he didn't want to make over what the Democrats had left—entirely. But he wanted a moral cleanup and was getting it slowly. He was proud that his policy on McCarthy had proven right. McCarthy's name is mentioned now much more rarely; his influence is slipping. He had always been determined not to attack McCarthy personally and thus build him up as the single symbol of opposition to the President; he didn't want to give him that importance.

PARIS, *November 10, 1954*

INTERESTING talk with General de Gaulle. He looks old, gray, and is more cynical and pessimistic than ever. He told me he stays almost all the time in Colombey-les-Deux-Eglises.

De Gaulle says the real trouble with France today is that Frenchmen were used to glory and prestige. They are disinterested in what happens to their country or government now because they have the habit of thinking in terms of French grandeur; and there is no French grandeur. He told me: "The United States made a great mistake by not pursuing a policy of war. When you took your stand in Korea the free world was with you and was ready to be led into war. But you cannot expect other nations to adopt a real self-sacrificing military attitude if you do not pursue a policy of war. You had your opportunity when you had a definite atomic lead. You should have followed MacArthur's policy. But now it is too late. Neither

America nor Russia is ready to pursue a policy of war and therefore a modus vivendi for a long time is inevitable."

He now sees absolutely no future for Europe, the world, or for France. He says war is inevitable, although a period of coexistence and modus vivendi will continue for a considerable time. This is demonstrated in the improved relations between England and China, by Malenkov's soft talk, by the new attitude toward Jugoslavia, and by Ho Chi Minh's efforts to develop good relations with France. Post-Stalinist power contests were shaking the Kremlin, de Gaulle remarked that Russia is "just exactly as it was under the Czars, still a dictatorship tempered by assassination."

All of Indochina is gone now, and it is folly to think otherwise. There were only two *real* forces in Indochina—Communist nationalism and the French army. The French army is now being pulled out, so *all* of Indochina is lost.

He told me: "The big trouble with France is that in one hundred and fifty years it has had thirteen constitutions and has been invaded six times. This only covers the lifetime of two old men."

PARIS, *November 17, 1954*

LAST night we attended a small dinner party where the Windsors were present. He ingratiated himself to me all over again by announcing that he thought Joe McCarthy was a wonderful fellow. He added, "Of course I don't approve of *all* the methods he applies, but, after all, he has taken the lead in showing you people what is wrong with communism and we cannot let the Communists get away with it."

PARIS, *November 18, 1954*

I HAD an extremely interesting and stimulating conversation this morning with Bidault at his home in St. Cloud. It is a simple little suburban house, furnished without luxury and looking just exactly like what you would expect of a professor's home: bookshelves completely filled and extending to the ceiling, other books piled all over the place, papers scattered about, and a broken photograph frame on his desk mended on the back with a strip from a cigar box.

The situation in Indochina is rotten. Bidault is convinced this is due to the treason of at least two members of the present French government. A formula had already been arranged to sell out Indochina before the Geneva Conference convened last spring. Even then, he said that only four days would have sufficed to make the rotten deal that Mendès-France accepted. Bidault said Bao Dai was a corrupt, contemptible coward.

The present Prime Minister of Vietnam, Ngo Dinh Diem, was an obstinate idiot who could not get along with anybody, adding: "I say that even though he is a good Catholic."

Bidault said Mendès-France deliberately sabotaged EDC. At Brussels the experts had agreed upon a compromise solution, but Mendès personally changed this with his own handwriting and then said that unless his amendments were accepted, he would not take it. Bidault clearly detests Mendès and says that if he lasts six more months he will have accomplished the ruination of France.

PARIS, *November 23, 1954*

LAST night we dined at Pamela Churchill's. She told me old Winston is a pronounced agnostic. Once, she asked him whether he believed in an afterlife. He said no, he thought there was only some kind of velvety cool blackness. He then added: "Of course I may be wrong. I might well be reborn as a Chinese coolie. In such a case, I should lodge a protest."

LONDON, *December 3, 1954*

THIS morning I called on Harold Macmillan, Minister for Defense. He will almost certainly be foreign secretary when Eden becomes Prime Minister. He said:

> Despite the particularly dreadful implications to a little island like Britain of the hydrogen bomb, there has been no change in policy which remains founded on the awareness that Britain must keep strong. The offense has a large advantage over the defense. Therefore, Britain's greatest protection is the knowledge by an enemy of British striking power. This has a great deterrent value in preventing wars.
>
> The theory now is that if a war were to come there would be a brief and terrible period during which the two sides would exchange atomic bombardment. After that would come the "broken-back" phase. Millions of Russians would be swarming around Europe like the Goths, but without any lines of communication back to their own country. These would have to be driven out by more traditional methods.

BONN, *December 13, 1954*

TODAY I had a long talk with Adenauer. There is no alternative to joining the West and rearming, Adenauer said. He did not think there was a danger of militarism. During the recent local election campaign he addressed many meetings himself, and the audiences showed a reasonable attitude "with no trace of militarism." But he added: "They are convinced we cannot avoid becoming soldiers again. We must consider the situation as it is today. We are supposed to get twelve divisions. This is a ridiculously small force compared to the United States or Soviet Russia. It is absolutely unimaginable that Germany could again become a military state and lead a militaristic future. When Germany was a strong military power we had our own factories to support our armies. Such is no longer the case. The past will no be repeated—*Das ist alles vorbei*."

PARIS, *December 25, 1954*

THIS Christmas morning I went over to see Prime Minister Pierre Mendès-France at his apartment on the fourth floor of 23, Rue du Conseiller Collignon, near the Muette. Poor Mendès had taken a bad beating last night when the Assembly voted him down on German rearmament.

He is not having a very merry Christmas, poor fellow. He and his wife had a *réveillon* last night in the form of a quiet *tête-à-tête* dinner with water. It was the first time they had been alone together for months. They never drink wine when they are alone "of course," he said. He added: "But I am not against a drink and sometimes I lift a glass of champagne with friends." Today he was planning to work all day.

I told Mendès some of his advisors say it would be a good idea if he were ousted from office after the German rearmament agreements are ratified in order to better prepare his popular position while in opposition and thereby to come back stronger in general elections. Mendès said he knew they felt this way, but he did not agree. He added: "I want to continue my fight in the government and I don't want to be thrown out even if it would enable me to make propaganda."

VIENNA, *January 5, 1955*

I WAS taken through the complex corridors and staircases of the Ball-hausplatz (from the antechamber in which Dollfuss bled to death) to the office of Leopold Figl, former Chancellor and now Foreign Minister. He looks like a dressed-up fox with spectacles.

Figl thought Moscow's initial goal, vis-à-vis Austria, is to try and neutralize the country in order to prevent it from becoming a member of any Western European bloc or grouping, even economic. Moscow hopes eventually to gain economic control of Austria and then bring it slowly into its political orbit; much as it is patiently trying to do with Finland.

KARACHI, *January 31, 1955*

IN the early evening I went to see Ghulam Muhammad, who is Governor General. He said:

> [American capitalism is] selfish and narrow. It hasn't enough energy or broadness of concept. America hasn't met its global responsibilities properly yet. You take five years to think about a problem and then three years to act. This process costs too much. Look at China or at Vietnam. In threatened countries you have two choices: Either you must defend them against Russia or you must build up their economies. You are always too late. You

are going to lose many things. You are going to link us up in the mess too. You must end your policy of half measures. One curse of capitalism is that it always wants to be efficient in terms of dollars. By the time experts have computed an efficient cost, things have already gone too far.

KARACHI, *February 5, 1955*

THIS morning I saw my old friend Iskander Mirza, who is now a major-general (lieutenant-colonel when I first knew him) and Minister of Interior. He is the "strong man" of the government and probably is going to make a play for dictator one of these days.

Mirza said the country had been "ruined" by complete adult suffrage for all men and women. "You can't have suffrage on that scale with 86 percent of the population illiterate."

NEW DELHI, *February 8, 1955*

NEHRU is an intellectual snob who dislikes most Americans as "uncouth." When Nehru came to the United States on an official visit in 1949, he felt there was much too much ostentation. At a dinner given for him by a group of bankers, the host boasted that so many billion dollars were represented by the people around the table. Nehru shuddered. At a White House dinner he sat on Truman's right, Vinson on Truman's left. Most of the meal was taken up in a debate between Truman and Vinson on the relative merits of Maryland and Missouri bourbon whisky.

BANGKOK, *February 21, 1955*

THIS evening, Jack Peurifoy, our Ambassador, dropped in to see me at the hotel where I've been laid up with gout. He says this is the "most pro-American and most corrupt government" he's ever seen.

BANGKOK, *February 23, 1955*

THE SEATO Conference opened today in the Throne Hall of Ananta Samakom Palace, a curious and gaudy bit of Oriental baroque with lots of gilt, marble, curlicues, and twittering sparrows flying around inside. Outside, gangs of schoolchildren marched up and down waving paper flags and bearing slogans such as "SEATO for Democrat" and "Democrat Asia."

Dulles arrived during the afternoon. He told me:

I have been working a long time to bring about a cohesive security arrangement for this part of the world. We talked about this while fighting was still going on in Indochina. But the President didn't have the necessary authority from Congress to intervene then and there was no assurance that we would have had any allies if we had acted. We hope to do away with such impediments through this treaty. This area is demonstrably important to the United States and the treaty assures our interest in it and assures that we have allies here.

To us there are three strong points: South Korea with its strong army of 500,000; Formosa with its army of 300,000; and the SEATO powers. This creates a situation so that if there is aggression in this area there could be retaliatory action in other areas. China would face a war on three fronts. China wouldn't like this. When the Chinese fought in Korea they didn't activate the fronts in Formosa or Indochina.

There will not be any permanent committal of United States ground forces in this area. We rely primarily on sea and air power and retaliatory action at places and by means of our own choosing.

BANGKOK, *February 25, 1955*

THE SEATO Conference ended today—not with a bang but a whimper. Everybody is glad to get out of this miserably hot, overcrowded, inefficient town.

Dulles said: "The conference was a complete success. Everything we hoped for came out of it and nothing that we feared. I am glad to say that the presentation I made on the first day swept away the last vestiges of efforts to have specific forces allocated to this theater."

I was appalled by his remarks. The Conference did nothing. He brags about getting the words "international communism" mentioned once in the communiqué. He is getting caught up in the political semantics of a holy war.

SAIGON, *March 2, 1955*

LUNCHED today with Lucien Bodard, *France-Soir* correspondent: a big, awkward fellow with thick, dark-rimmed glasses. There are growing indications Diem won't agree to elections. Diem can claim he's not a party to the Geneva agreement. Also that freedom doesn't prevail in the North. But if there is no election in 1956, says Bodard, there will be either open war or a real coordinated subversion effort. It depends how far China, which controls Ho, will let him go.

The Vietminh is now busily organizing the villages of South Vietnam. Their agents take pictures of Ho Chi Minh and Bao Dai around and ask the peasants "Which will you vote for?" Naturally they say Ho—because Bao Dai is detested by everyone. "Don't forget that," warn the agents.

The Cao Dai and Hoa-Hao sects are split into segments. They have men in the government in order to assure income, and they have factions opposing the government to prevent it from becoming too strong.

Bai Vian (or Le Van Vian) is head of the Binh Xuyen gang. This is not a sect but simply an organization of tough racketeers. He was named chief of police for all Vietnam by Bao Dai. Previously Bao Dai had rented him the concession for Le Grand Monde, the famous and incredibly rich gambling concession at Cholon, outside Saigon.

SAIGON, *March 3, 1955*

RANDOLPH Kidder, United States chargé d'affaires, says it is reported the Binh Xuyen paid 41 million piasters for control of the police; quite a concession!

PHNOMPENH, CAMBODIA, *March 6, 1955*

I am just winding up a brief visit to Cambodia. King Norodom Sihanouk abdicated suddenly Wednesday. The King is a young man with a martyr's complex. He thinks of himself as a royal Robin Hood. He wants to go to the country and come back to his throne as a popular hero. In the interim, while his father rules, there will be no basic change in policy.

Cambodia is a sort of oriental Graustark. The political experience of the people is not far beyond that of the Bronze Age. There is very little means of spreading information. The country claims 40 percent literacy, but this is an exaggeration. The priesthood is archconservative.

SAIGON, *March 7, 1955*

THIS evening Ed Stansbury, who runs USIS, said one of Diem's chief weaknesses is that he trusts no one. Therefore he himself insists on signing all entry and exit visas. He has to do this at night, his only spare time, and everything is hopelessly delayed and fouled up. He wants to prevent the departure of people against whom corruption charges might later be filed. And he wants to prevent his opponents from entering. The result is nobody can get any sort of visa these days.

TAY NINH, *March 9, 1955*

I spent an extraordinary day at Tay Ninh, headquarters and holy city of the Cao Dai sect, a curious melange of religion, free masonry, secret society, and private army. The Cao Dai religion was founded thirty years ago and is a blend of Buddhism, Taoism, and Confucianism with an organization and hierarchy like Catholicism. Cao Dai runs what is virtually a feudal state near the Cambodian border. They have their own flag, arms depots, military insignia, and ordnance factories where they make Sten guns, automatic pistols, and rifles out of retempered steel. Their organization includes male and female priests and priestesses, bishops, cardinals, and a "Superior." There used to be a pope. However, after his death, no new pope was elected, so the Superior acts instead.

The Superior, Pham Cong Tac, a smiling, intelligent-looking man who appears to be about sixty, said there were more than 2 million Cao Daiists. They have three ministers in the Diem government. Their private army numbers more than twenty thousand. The Superior wound up his confusing talk by saying: "Diem is unpopular and only the Catholics have any use for him."

I then drove off some miles to the Cao Dai military headquarters, where I lunched with the operational general and his staff, several colonels, two majors, and a captain. The captain, obviously European, turned out to be Walter Schumann, late of the German Wehrmacht and the French Foreign Legion. He eventually married a Vietnamese, has several children, became a converted Cao Daiist, now bears the name Nguyen Thanh Duo, and is an instructor in infantry tactics at their military school.

The general, who spoke excellent French, complained that Diem was trying to force unification of the private armies too fast. He said soldiers of the regular Vietnamese army were selling their arms to the sects. The country is in a state of anarchy, and Diem does not control the non-Catholic communities.

SAIGON, *March, 11, 1955*

IN the afternoon I had a long talk with Diem at the President's Palace. He speaks excellent French. But as he gets warmed up on a subject both his voice and his gaze seem to drift far away; he takes on an almost drugged expression (although his only vice seems to be cigarettes, and he is so puritanical that his enemies say he doesn't even know what a man looks like).

He made no secret of his skepticism about elections in 1956. He claimed that the Vietnamese there were even more disgusted with the hypocrisy of Vietminh than with the tyranny of communism; that they resented more the continual lies along the path to communization than a frank and brutal dictatorship.

I came away rather puzzled. Diem seems to border on the fanatic, and doesn't appear to be very bright.

MANILA, *March 15, 1955*

LUNCHED with President Ramon Magsaysay at Malacañan Palace. It is an old Spanish residence which the Spanish government took over as the summer palace for its governors in the early nineteenth century; then it served the American governors and now the Filipino presidents.

Magsaysay is large for a Filipino—about five feet ten, strong, with heavy shoulders. He has a broad face with a big jaw. His manner is affable. He seemed moderately pessimistic. He complained about the amount of work he has to do. He obviously knows little about foreign affairs and doesn't have much interest in them. For the most part he is still working to stamp out communism. Its military apparatus has been squashed, but land reform and corruption remain to be rooted out. There is still corruption in the army as well as in civil life. He said he freely used bribery to beat the Huks: so much per dead Huk. He bribed informers with automobiles. He used to distribute doped Coca-Cola to be given to Huks by peasants who would then murder their visitors to collect head money.

TAIPEI, March 16, 1955

THIS afternoon I visited General Chiang Ching Kuo, elder son of Chiang Kai-shek. Chiang Ching Kuo lives in a rather modest Japanese style house (although he has a handsome Cadillac), and the room we sat in, built for diminutive people (low door frames) contained hardly any ornaments aside from a gold athletic trophy and a large portrait of his father. He resembles the old man but is far less distinguished looking. In his forties, the son has a bland, inexpressive face with a sullen mouth. He lived for years in Russia (when he didn't get on with his father), was a Communist and has a Russian wife. He broke with Stalin and came back to China; acted as his father's agent in Manchuria when the end of World War II came. He is now Assistant Secretary General of their equivalent of a National Security Council. Actually he is in charge of morale, political commissars in the army, some aspects of the secret police, and security, etc.

TAIPEI, March 19, 1955

TODAY I flew down to Kaohsiung in order to spend the day with Chiang Kai-shek. He has a simple house outside Kaohsiung on a beach at Sitzewan. He has been there several days because he has had a cold and is resting up. I went down in a special plane used for government VIPs, accompanied by Samson Shen, Chiang's official interpreter.

Chiang Kai-shek's house is a large, unattractive establishment. The sitting room where we sat before and after lunch was square, particularly ugly, filled with hideous, comfortable chairs and sofas covered with artificial leather.

A few moments after my arrival the Generalissimo and Madame Chiang came in. He is a good deal shorter and smaller than I expected, no taller than five foot six, slender: a trim-looking man who is certainly extremely fit. He was wearing what the Chinese call a Sun Yat-sen uniform, a military-looking khaki garment with high collar similar to the sort of uniform Russian Communist leaders often wear. It bore no insignia. Madame Chiang was wearing a long, cylindrical black Chinese dress. Although she may have been beautiful once, now she has a rather evil and tough face.

Our conversation took place in three sections. At first we sat around before lunch and I asked a series of questions. Then, during lunch, at which we were joined by his military and civilian aides, thus making a table of six, the conversation was general. Again after lunch, we repaired to the sitting room and continued. I asked Chiang if this were the lowest point in his long personal career of fighting to establish a unified government over China. He replied that the nadir of his fortunes came in 1926, just before he took off from Canton with less than five hundred followers bearing arms. "Now we are in a much better position—especially concerning the psychology of our people," he said.

I asked if the United States had ever formally guaranteed to defend the offshore islands of Matsu and Quemoy. He suggested I should rephrase my question and eliminate the word "formally." He then answered his own rephrased question by saying, in a series of oblique sentences, that he had only agreed to evacuate the Tachen Islands because he understood the United States would defend Matsu and Quemoy. (This, of course, all adds up to nothing. I don't believe any specific guarantee of any sort was ever given, and that is why Chiang is being so cagey.) He said:

> It would not be fair to try and force us to give up the offshore islands without a fight. That would be contrary to all international justice and to the obligations of our allies. The United States should not accede to British ideas on this. Whether the United States joins in the defense of these islands or not, she should not try and compel free China, an ally, to give them up. Under no circumstances will our forces withdraw from them. We shall not yield to any pressure. We are determined to fight to the last man. It is a mistake to think that because we evacuated the Tachens we will evacuate Matsu and Quemoy. We will certainly fight for them. And this may turn into the decisive battle for China.

I told Chiang I had heard he believed World War III would start in 1956. Why? He replied:

> That is correct. I think that next year Russia will be ready for war for the following reasons: You will remember that as soon as the Russians had completed the Trans-Siberian Railway they started their disastrous war with Japan fifty years ago. Russian strategy depends upon railways. According to Communist planning, new railways linking China and Russia across Mongolia and Sinkiang will be ready. As soon as these roads are finished the Russians will figure that the moment has arrived for war. And at the same time, economic and agricultural conditions are such that if Russia and China don't start a war in 1956 they will risk collapse.

TOKYO, *March 22, 1955*

THIS afternoon I visited Ichiro Hatoyama, the Prime Minister, at his home. The Prime Minister, who is seventy-two and partially paralyzed by a stroke, received me in his study; a strange, crowded room filled with books, snapshots, and odd little souvenirs and trinkets accumulated over the years.

I started off by asking if Hatoyama would not raise Japan's budgetary contribution for national security. At present only 2½ percent of the gross national product is assigned to defense. This represents 13 percent of the annual budget and covers Japan's own defense forces and its contribution to the maintenance of the U.S. security force. We are trying to prod Japan to increase this to 4 or 5 percent of the G.N.P.

Hatoyama indicated he has no thought of playing ball on this. He argued that the Socialists had demonstrated in last month's elections a gain in strength which must be checked. To do this the government had to settle the housing problem and for this: "We must reduce our share of the defense costs."

KYOTO, *March 27, 1955*

CAME here last night from Osaka and stayed in a Japanese hotel called the Dai Monji. This hotel has had only one other American visitor during its fifty years' existence. I dined with Sei Wada, deputy editor-in-chief of *Asahi*, at the Ichiriki geisha house, which was built in the late seventeenth century and is the place where Oishi, leader of the 47 Ronin, used to get plastered with his favorite geisha while plotting his conspiracy. We had a long and complicated discussion with the geisha girls about what the American occupation had done to Japan. The geishas are unabashedly slaves, and if they run away they are brought back by the police; except they don't run away.

None of the geishas had the least bit of interest in the changing world. All said they voted, but it was clear they didn't know what this meant and, if they had no current boy friend to instruct them, they cast blank ballots.

SEOUL, *March 29, 1955*

ARRIVED in Seoul as Ambassador Ellis Briggs' guest. Briggs says Syngman Rhee wants to free *all* Korea—time is getting short. Rhee wants World War III. He admits frankly he would have started war himself if he hadn't been rationed on gasoline.

CHIN-HAE, KOREA, *March 30, 1955*

FLEW here this morning on a rough trip in a tiny air force plane to see Syngman Rhee at his summer hideaway. Chin-hae is the South Korean naval base, but Rhee built himself a place here. It used to be a big Japanese naval base, and it was from here that the Japanese fleet steamed out in 1905 to destroy the Russian navy in the battle of Tsushima.

Rhee is a little old man with a face like a squeezed orange, covered with wrinkles. He has snow-white hair and smiles constantly. He was wearing a rumpled blue suit with a cardigan over his vest. I started the conversation by asking whether he agreed with the idea Dulles had voiced at Bangkok of a three-pronged Asian strategy that would be launched against China in the event of any Chinese aggression elsewhere in Asia. Rhee said he thought this was fine.

He said: "The Communists are trying to conquer the world whether you Americans still believe this or not. We are on the frontier in Asia. We don't believe we can coexist with communism. The United States sent an army here to defend us. Therefore, this all-for-one-and-one-for-all spirit prevails in our war against communism. We want to help to defend other areas. As a matter of fact, we offered to send twenty thousand soldiers to Vietnam just before the Geneva Conference. Someone in Washington turned it down."

Did he think we should start a preventive war against the Communists, and if so, where and over what issue? He said the war was already on. "The Communists are advancing all the time. They improve their position daily. How long will you let them keep on? My proposition is, as I told General Eisenhower, that the sooner we cripple Communist aggression the easier for the whole world. Preventive war is the only solution. You have to protect yourself forcibly against gangsters trying to break into your house."

I must say that it is astonishing how belligerent this amiable-looking little old man (eighty now) seems to be. He said: "We would have driven to the Chinese border on the Yalu River in 1953, if you had permitted us. But you control all logistics. Our gasoline and ammunition are locked up; we have only two days ration. Have you ever heard of such a thing? What kind of a world is this? The sooner we stop these gangsters the better. You people are too afraid of world war. If war is the worst thing you can imagine, then you should surrender everything, give up Washington. Give up your stocks of atom bombs. The only alternative is to stop the Communists and the sooner the better. Fewer lives will be sacrificed."

Rhee was getting very excited. His voice rose to a scream, and he started waving his hands around. His wife, a plump little Austrian woman around sixty, tried to calm him down.

At this point the telephone rang and an aide came in. Rhee rushed out. We all looked at each other as we heard Rhee's anguished screams into the phone. It apparently was functioning as most Asian telephones do. After some minutes of obvious lack of communication he came back with his hair all rumpled saying: "I hate telephones. I would like to tear them all out and use the wire to strangle the man who invented them."

PUSAN, *March 30, 1955*

WHEN I left Rhee the Defense Minister, Admiral Sohn Won Il, invited me
to join him, the Foreign Minister, Young Tai Pyun, and the Chief of Staff,
General Chung Il Kwon, in the ride over to Pusan on a Korean navy PT
boat. This suited me fine. We had a glass of good Korean beer and were
driven down to a pier and piped aboard an old U.S. PT boat, taking off in
a tremendous gale at thirty-six knots. As we plunged from roller to roller, I
stayed on the bridge trying to see Tsushima; but it was far away.

When we got to Pusan a navy car met us, and we were taken fifteen
miles to a dilapidated hotel with a natural steam bath. We squatted down
on the floor. Odd characters, both male and female, kept coming into the
room and jabbering away in Korean. I was in one round tub with all the
top brass—the most high-level bath I shall ever have.

Finally around 6:30 P.M. we were taken to another room where a
magnificent banquet was set out on a low, long table. Three Ki Saing
(Korean geisha girls) were already squatted on cushions by the table to
serve and amuse us. The poor things looked like the original prototype
peasant women and didn't have any of the charm of their Japanese
equivalents.

HONOLULU, *April 4, 1955*

LONG talk at his Pearl Harbor headquarters with Admiral Felix Stump,
United States commander in chief for the western Pacific and also chief of
U.S. naval forces in the whole Pacific area. He said we were at a permanent disadvantage vis-à-vis the Communists because they know not only
that they can start a war at any time but that they can also stop it any
time, as they did in Korea. Because of public opinion and our political
organization, we do not have the initiative in any respect.

11

Lunch with Speidel. Speidel thinks Indochina is lost completely and the Asiatic situation stinks. The Russians must be getting worried about the Chinese now, and certainly the Chinese are no satellites. One reason Khrushchev is trying to force hundreds and thousands of people to settle in the eastern parts of the Soviet Union is to build up a protection against Chinese expansion in that area.

Paris, *May 7, 1955*

This morning I visited Edgar Faure, present Premier, in the Matignon. I asked if he thought it possible to save Vietnam now. He did *not* think so; it was too late. It was even too late for Bao Dai to return to Saigon.

Paris, *May 8, 1955*

Yesterday evening Dulles told me (*chez* Dillon): "We are disposed to support any Saigon government there which is competent, honest, nationalistic, and anti-Communist. Diem, in our opinion, has been doing a good job building an anti-Communist state there. But we don't pick and choose the government of Vietnam. We see no particular reason to throw Diem out. But we don't have a closed mind. We are not supporting an individual as such. We are supporting a cause. If someone else comes along, we don't consider any individual indispensable. Our support is not for any single individual."

PARIS, *May 11, 1955*

LUNCH with Walter Robertson, Assistant Secretary of State in charge of Far Eastern affairs. Robertson said he knew Mao Tse-tung quite well and spent a weekend with him once. Mao is a devout, sincere, fanatical communist who wants to give his fellowmen the things that poor people now lack. He is utterly ruthless in seeking this goal. Robertson considers Chou En-lai one of the most charming men he ever met; one must know him well to realize what a tough fellow he is. He has killed people with his own hands and then emerged calmly smoking a cigarette. When General Marshall went to China after World War II to try and promote a coalition government, Robertson warned him against Chou and his charm. But nevertheless, Marshall fell into the trap.

I asked if he had heard any reports about difficulties between Russia and China. He said he had heard none. Furthermore, he added, even if there were difficulties on a local basis, they would be unimportant. The interests of the two countries lie together. Robertson claims that already in 1940, Mao Tse-tung was writing that he wanted to support world communism under *Soviet* leadership.

The situation has changed greatly since 1940; I wonder if Mao would be as interested in Soviet leadership now as then.

Robertson said he recently told Dulles there is no hope whatsoever of Mao Tse-tung becoming a "Titoist." He told Dulles that Mao is as loyal to his own principles as Dulles is loyal to the principles taught him by his father, a Presbyterian preacher.

LONDON, *May 19, 1955*

TONIGHT I had a fascinating and very moving experience. I followed old Churchill around on what will almost surely be his last campaign. I was struck by the similarity between the issues he raised this evening and those he spoke about in his first by-election campaign in 1899, at Oldham.

This afternoon I went over to Randolph's and thumbed through *My Early Years* by his father. I found references to his speeches in 1899, on "Tory democracy" and "Never were there so many people in England and never before have they had so much to eat." He said almost exactly the same thing this evening.

Churchill gave his delighted audience the business. He said: "The state is the servant and not the master of the people." He said: "We have a higher standard of living than ever before. We are eating more." Then, *sotto voce*, regarding his tummy, he added: "And that is very important."

Afterward, I had a brief chat with Winston. He sat down in a little room and lit one of his enormous black cigars. He looked old and tired when he got off the platform. Looking at young Biggs-Davison, the Tory candidate,

Churchill nudged me and said: "From the cradle to the summit—I just thought of that. On my feet I thought of that."

BELGRADE, *May 27, 1955*

LAST night I dined with Prica, Number-Two man in the Foreign Office. He says the Russians are stupid, Byzantine, and hidebound. Russia is scared of China and can't afford to pay China's needs. It fears the day when the United States and China get together. It fears an independent and "Titoist" policy in China. Therefore, it is moving population eastward into Asia.

BELGRADE, *May 29, 1955*

LAST night Tito gave a reception for Khrushchev at Beli Dvor, the White Palace of the Karageorgevićes. It was a rainy evening, and the blossoms of the pink chestnut trees lining the long entrance driveway were beaten onto the road.

The assembled diplomats, political leaders, generals and admirals of Jugoslavia massed in a couple of small reception rooms, and then the stars of the occasion arrived, walked in, and stood at attention while an unnecessarily loud band boomed out the Jugoslav and Soviet anthems. In front came Khrushchev and Mrs. Broz. Khrushchev, in an astonishingly badly cut Soviet sacksuit that looked as if it hadn't even been pressed, stood like a little gypsy dancing bear, staring dully ahead with his jaw hanging slack and his belly falling down beneath the four buttons of his jacket. A single decoration dangled incongruously from his lapel. Tito's wife, Jovanka, in a white evening gown, towered over him, a handsome, large woman with gleaming black eyes and short black hair, regular features, and white teeth. Behind them stood Bulganin, in gray uniform, with somewhat bleary, kind blue eyes, smiling behind his beard and looking for all the world like the bandmaster in a small German spa. Then came Tito, sunburned, stocky, in a dandy's uniform, with a faint smile upon his face, and Shepilov, a huge, sardonic-looking Russian with a sour sneer; then Gromyko, Mikoyan, and a pack of body guards.

The Jugoslavs looked infinitely more impressive than their visitors, and one would have thought that the great military power was represented by the handsome marshal and his tall, well-groomed commanders, rather than the stubby little dictator and his guardians. Vladimir Popović, a former Partisan general and newly named envoy to Peking, a towering, handsome man, remarked with ill-concealed arrogance: "I suppose this is the first time Khrushchev has ever been about among the people." Certainly, he observed, it was the first time he had ever been submitted to the badgering of photographers as was permitted here.

After midnight, the performance ended. The burly, gruff Soviet plain-clothesman outside the door of the sanctum moved away and the massive

Soviet lieutenant-general and immense Jugoslav general chatting there opened it up. Khrushchev was boiled and tottered out, clearly a victim of the power of *šljivovića*. Bulganin looked foggy, and Tito himself was peering through a mist. They pushed through a cleared alley in the crowd, stood blinking while the band played anthems and photographers flashed bulbs, and then went out on the rainy porch where they bade good-bye. (Khrushchev, balancing uneasily, kissed Jovanka's hand; Tito gave her a husbandly buss.) Then the Russians piled into their cars for the station and Brioni. Khrushchev had to be loaded into his car physically.

ROME, *July 4, 1955*

TODAY I visited Giovanni Gronchi, newly elected second president of the Italian Republic. Gronchi said: "We have only three political movements in Italy with a future: the Catholic social movement expressed in the Christian Democratic party, the Communists, and socialism. It is my hope that we can separate the Left Socialists from the Communists. This has been achieved in other European countries—why not here? What is needed as a first step is agreement of the Christian Democrats on a government with a program leading to such social and economic reform that it must inevitably provoke a *crise de conscience* among the Socialists."

CAIRO, *August 10, 1955*

THIS morning I talked for an hour and forty-five minutes with Nasser in his office at the headquarters of the Revolution Command Council. Nasser is a handsome, tall, powerfully built, and vigorous man, who resembles the massive statues of Rameses II. He speaks English fluently. I started out by asking: "What is the ideology of your revolution?" He replied:

I have read much about socialism, communism, democracy, and fascism. Our revolution will not be labeled by any of those names. We seek to meet the needs and requirements of our own people and we are not trying to copy anybody else's ideology. We have many diseases and shortcomings in our country and we wish to overcome all of them. We began our revolution with principles, not a program. We find that sometimes we have to change our methods.

We must liberate the individuals of Egypt. Only then will the country be totally free. To do this we must limit land ownership and liquidate the domination of the landlords. We must replace the present system with co-operatives to help the small farmers and to aid them in the distribution of their crops. Only in these ways can we make the farmers feel free.

I know how these people feel. My family are farmers. I can now tell as I visit areas affected by our revolution that the farmer feels his own master. Before the revolution the people always felt that the government was their enemy. I know. I used to feel this myself. The government used to take from the many and give only to the few corrupt, wealthy people. Now the people must be made to feel that the government is not taking from them but is working for them.

All our western desert is ready for cultivation. The only thing it needs is water. Something will have to be done. We have a big problem of increasing population as a result of scientific advances. According to statistics, we are now in a position to double ourselves over forty years. New hygiene and medical measures are reducing infant mortality. What will happen when we are forty million people limited to five million acres of the Nile Valley and Delta?

I asked what the philosophy of his foreign policy was and whether it could be described as neutralism. He replied: "Neutralism only applies during a war. If you mean neutrality in a cold war, it is difficult to define. Only if there is a war does the question of neutrality arise."

I changed the subject by asking him how the Palestine war could be ended. He replied:

Once I thought there could be peace. I said to my troops and officers in Palestine that we must do our best to have peace in this area. They disagreed and said Israel would not agree to peace. I replied that I had guarantees from England and the United States. But after the bloody Gaza incident, when I saw the same officers, I felt responsible for the deaths of those thirty-two men. There had been no Egyptian troops at Gaza except for administrative units. They lived in their billets without defenses—no barbed wire or trenches. They were killed in cold blood. What could I say? I said I was wrong and responsible for the lives of those people. I said if you see any Jew kill him. You are responsible for yourself and for your land and we can no longer rely on guarantees.

Fear dominates the area. What do you think I feel when I hear that the Herut party in Israel wants expansion from the Nile to the Euphrates? This was said in Herut speeches in the recent election campaign. And they said that the Arabs must be pacified by force. And after that the Herut party gained eight seats. Now they have seventeen. And at the next election they may have seventy—all of them for expansion. We live in fear and as long as there is fear there cannot be peace.

What did he want in the way of relationships with the United States? He replied that in 1946, America had been very popular in this part of the world as a result of wartime declarations.

But, by 1948, all this popularity had gone. Still, after the Israeli war, people began to hope again for America. Again they started to think the United States was working for liberation and had no colonial objectives. At the beginning of our revolution we informed the American embassy, the only embassy we informed. At that time I had only two main hopes: The agreement with Britain to evacuate her troops; and a policy of friendship with the United States. I was able to attain the first but not the second.

What is the meaning of friendship? For the army it is equipment. For the people it is help against domination and help to improve their standard of living. The army is a basic factor in Egyptian life. The Communists have made many efforts to penetrate the army. They say I am working for the United States and the United States refuses to help us. I have felt this propaganda in the army. Friendship, for the army, means equipment. Our revolution was stimulated in the army by a lack of equipment. If our officers feel we still have no equipment they will lose faith in the government.

I tell your people you spend millions of dollars on propaganda; please divert some of it to the material side. People receive all these free pamphlets but they do not read them. I know. I receive them and I do not read them. We are asked if we intend to use our equipment against Israel. I reply that I am not interested in waging war; I want to build my country; I want to raise our standard of living.

Two years ago when Naguib was still head of the regime he sent a letter to President Eisenhower pledging that any equipment we received would be used only for the defense of the country. We sent that letter because you asked for a commitment that no equipment should be used against Israel. But we have received nothing. There are still negotiations. But public opinion in the army has been poisoned.

ANKARA, *August 18, 1955*

TALK with Prime Minister Adnan Menderes. He said Turkey had not received its fair share of American aid. The total on a per-capita basis amounted to only $19 for each Turk, whereas Greece had received $228 per capita. Even Ireland and Sweden, who are neutral, had received more proportionate aid. (This is claptrap.)

I asked what Turkey would do if it did not get the aid. He said: "Rest assured we will not collapse." Turkey requires an effective industry to support a modern army.

ATHENS, *September 18, 1955*

YESTERDAY afternoon, I went out to Tatoi and saw King Paul at his summer palace. He had just returned from his official visit to Jugoslavia.

Tito had stressed to King Paul that he would never go back to the Soviet bloc; once was enough. He didn't intend to associate with any bloc in the future that did not include *both* the United States and the USSR. By this he meant he would not support any security organization in Europe that sought to eliminate or ostracize the United States. Tito wants to attract the satellites away from their outmoded concepts of Stalinism. He told the King he detested Stalin and "always had."

The King said there is no doubt Marshal Papagos, the Prime Minister, will die very soon. At present he feels the only man he could ask to form a government if Papagos dies is Caramanlis, the Minister of Works, an honest and popular man.

ATHENS, *September 20, 1955*

TALKED this morning to Constantine Caramanlis, the bright young man of the present government. I asked him if he should be called on to form a government, what his foreign policy would be. He stared at me in amazement. "If I talked about a policy for myself," he said, "I would look ridiculous. And I would rather die than look ridiculous."

Caramanlis said from $150 million to $200 million in gold is still hoarded in the country because the people lack confidence in the currency. There is a paucity of capital. Lenders demand 40 to 45 percent interest. As a result, there are no new investments.

NICOSIA, *September 28, 1955*

I SAW Archbishop Makarios III in his office in Nicosia. Once a theology student in Boston, he is head of the church and also ethnarch (national leader) of the Greek Cypriots. The leading ecclesiastic has always been the Greek ethnarch here. The Cyprus church ranks high in Greek Orthodoxy and has three special privileges granted by the Byzantine Emperor Zeno. The Archbishop is allowed to sign his name in red ink. He wears a purple mantle. And, on ceremonial occasions, he carries an imperial scepter instead of the usual staff.

Makarios has an El Greco face, long and ivory colored, with long, prominent nose, long narrow eyes, black beard slightly streaked with gray, the whole ensemble rendered more Gothic by the tall, orthodox stovepipe hat. He wore a black robe, and around his neck was a heavy gold chain, on the end of which dangled a bejewelled religious medallion. He sat at his carved walnut desk on a thronelike walnut chair given him by a Cypriot artisan two years ago. On its back was carved the Byzantine imperial device of the double-headed eagle.

Makarios admitted he often preached political sermons. The church was very nationalistic. It had a great history. That's why it was called *Greek* Orthodox, not just Orthodox. Interference of the church in politics is a Greek phenomenon. The church had led all unfree Greek territories to liberty. Cyprus was the last. Makarios described his technique as something similar to Gandhi's—"under very different circumstances." His passive and EOKA's (National Organization of Cypriot Fighters) active resistance policies "led to the same end." He personally was for passive measures, but EOKA was activist and underground. A large section of the Cypriot population favored EOKA. "When the island is free the church will quit politics and I will lose my job as ethnarch," he added.

NICOSIA, *September 29, 1955*

LAST night, a rather interesting experience. After a series of carefully arranged and discreet contacts, I had established contact with the EOKA underground. I was called up by an unknown voice, after two days of secret exchanges, and told to be in front of Electra House at 8:00 P.M. A car with the license number J— would drive up at precisely that hour. I was to get right in beside the driver and go off.

I followed these instructions. At 8:00 P.M. on the dot, two cars came up out of the night. J— did not stop but seemed to be wandering around looking for security agents. Behind it was another car. I hopped in and off we went. There were two other people besides the driver. I did not get a good look at their faces, because every time I turned around they hid them behind briefcases.

Some miles out we turned off the main highway and down a narrow road and finally came to our destination. A chunky EOKA character was standing at the gate. He greeted me amiably and conducted me into a funny little room decorated with pictures of archbishops and icons.

After a few minutes, another door opened and I was summoned into a dark room. I stumbled to a chair and sat down. When my eyes got accustomed to the darkness I could make out a couple of figures. One of them was clearly very nervous. From a crack of light under the door I noticed that he was wearing dark glasses, although we were sitting in the pitch black. He was taking no chances on my being able to recognize him again. He did most of the talking in rather good English but with a stilted imitation Oxford accent.

The men I talked with said they were members of the central committee of EOKA. Whether they included Dighenis (Grivas), I do not know. They told me:

> We are at war with Britain, but we have nothing against the British as a nation. After all, we are very pleased with the attitude of the Labour party on Cyprus. Therefore we have not killed any English people. Our program has been to frighten the British, but not to kill them. We kill only Cypriot traitors. But soon, we fear, we will have to kill the British too.
>
> The central committee is called Kendriki Epitropi. Under it is a series of groups and subgroups, each of which is called an *Omas* or team. Dighenis is called the *Archigos* or leader. Each Omas is headed by an *Omadarchas*, or group leader. All the leaders use *noms de guerre*. Many do not know the real names of their colleagues. The system is supposed to be that nobody knows anybody else out of his own Omas, except for the group leader. Therefore, if one Omas is discovered, its members cannot betray other groups.

JERUSALEM, *October 5, 1955*

THIS evening I had a stimulating talk with David Ben Gurion, former Prime Minister and again Prime Minister-elect, and still Defense Minister. He is a grand old man, sixty-nine years old, beginning to show signs of age.

Ben Gurion, upon hearing that I had been in Greece recently, complained that he could no longer get any decent classic texts from Athens, which had ceased printing them. He went on for some time discussing Sophocles. A local company had put on *Oedipus*, but the Israeli people simply could not comprehend the idea of Greek tragedy; the idea of fate unjustly controlling man's destiny and man having no influence thereon.

It was only with some difficulty that I brought Ben Gurion back to modern times. He turned to the recent Soviet promise to sell arms (through Czechoslovakia) to Egypt. For the time being, Ben Gurion said: "The deal is only being carried out through Czechoslovakia, but Russia may eventually appear openly as a munitions salesman."

He said at first he considered Nasser a decent fellow, but now realized "He is a crafty, deceitful, Arab type." He added that Nasser has three aspirations: to be head of the Arab world; head of the Muslim world; and head of the continent of Africa. "Meanwhile," he sneered, "he has lost the Sudan." Ben Gurion suspects the British are trying to push Nasser's interests northward toward Israel in order to keep his mind off the Sudan.

I inquired what Israel would do if it were discovered that the Egyptian arms purchases are as extensive as he suspects. He replied: "If it turns out to be true that they are receiving between eighty and one hundred MIGs, as it is reported, we will have to smash them." I said that this would mean war, a preventive war. Ben Gurion said, "No." He thought ten Israeli planes could stage a sufficiently accurate raid to end the whole matter, and it could be done without war. He explained Russia's arms sales as an effort by Moscow to obtain a footing in the Middle East. This had been Russia's aim for three hundred years.

Ben Gurion said there could be no peace with the Arabs until Egypt was prepared to sign with Israel. No other country would make the move until after Cairo had done so.

PARIS, *October 14, 1955*

THIS morning I went to see General de Gaulle at his office on 5, Rue de Solférino. He hoped it might be possible to save some connection with North Africa by working out a new structure for Tunisia and Morocco. But the situation is different with Algeria. Algeria was never a state. De Gaulle likened Algeria to a heap of dust—*"une poussière."*

From North Africa, de Gaulle branched on to France itself. He said he had twice tried to save France. The first time was during the war. The second time was by organizing the RPF. Now he says: "I know of no third way."

The consequences of the present French crisis would eventually be seen in a great change in French psychology, especially vis-à-vis foreigners. The French would inevitably become very xenophobic because of their misfortunes. It was hard to see where this would lead in twenty years, but xenophobia was already mounting. As a result of this, a violent French nationalism would ultimately set in.

"The United Nations already means nothing here," he said. "Nations will come and go, enter and depart from it. But it is finished. Soon the same situation will develop in NATO."

I asked de Gaulle on what terms or in what condition he thought he could return. He said: "I would never come back except with real power. That would require a dramatic situation. While things remain as they are it is impossible. This regime can only offer the Presidency of the Republic—which means nothing—or the Prime Ministry—which means nothing. It is impossible to do anything in either of these positions. These are not for General de Gaulle." He had concluded that even the top position in France—which he had previously indicated he would be willing to accept—no longer suited his purposes.

He continued: "Present events are not dramatic enough; they do not press hard enough. This regime must first vanish—as the regime vanished in 1940." The general then spread his long arms and hands and said he was desolated, desperate, but what could he do? He did not mean by this that France would "disappear"; its national vitality remained very great. But it was too disparate and had been terribly weakened by past events. National opinion had become nonexistent, and France was becoming detached on everything. Indifference was growing as a national characteristic. This seemed to him to be unbelievable, but it was true. He had personally tried to shake off this national indifference; the Communists had tried; but nobody could budge the French from this mood. Nevertheless, "in France nothing is ever definitive—not even impotence."

Regimes never reform themselves. They simply fall. They collapse. France has had thirteen regimes in the last 193 years. (Note how the statistics change.) None of these ever reformed themselves. The monarchy did not know how to reform itself. It fell to the revolution. Then the revolution and the *Directoire* did not reform themselves. They were succeeded by Bonaparte. Then Bonaparte did not know how to reform himself and he was wiped out by Waterloo. When the Restoration monarch came, he fell because he did not know how to reform things. The same was true afterwards with Louis Philippe. Napoleon III, who could not change things, fell at Sedan. The Third Republic also fell at Sedan (in 1940). Then came Pétain; and then the more recent period.

Looking toward the future, de Gaulle said that when France had completed paying these "debts to the past," present events would contribute to a new French nationalism. He was sure this would be a disagreeable form of nationalism for the world, including the United States, but it was inevitable.

PARIS, *October 22, 1955*

LUNCH with David Bruce. He is still technically an "adviser" in the State Department. If the Democrats win the 1956 elections he would be very anxious to become the first U.S. Ambassador to Communist China. Under present conditions it is impossible to recognize Peking. First the Chinese must make conciliatory gestures and behave themselves. However, recognition is ultimately inevitable.

PARIS, *October 25, 1955*

TODAY I saw René Coty, president of the French Republic, in the Elysée Palace. He said he had done a very audacious thing at Dunkirk October 15, when he made a speech stating that the French Constitution needs reforming. After all, he was the guardian of the Constitution; yet he was demanding that it be changed. The last president who had ever ventured to do a similar thing was Millerand, in 1924, and he had to resign as a result.

Nevertheless, it was absolutely essential that there should be a change. He does not favor the Gaullist type of Constitution with more powers for the president. What he wants is a stronger Prime Minister with the ability to dissolve the Assembly and call elections when necessary, so that the government will no longer be subject to the deputies' whims. The presidency of the Republic has adequate powers now to operate behind the scene.

GENEVA, *November 12, 1955*

THIS evening I had a long talk, more interesting than usual, with Dulles in his suite at the Hotel du Rhône. He seemed cheerful and energetic and walked restlessly up and down as he talked, occasionally stopping for a handful of nuts from the table on which drinks were laid out. Only at the end did he settle into a chair and relax.

I asked whether he thought Molotov's unexpectedly stubborn attitude at this foreign ministers' conference might reflect some change in the Soviet internal political situation. He replied:

That is possible. The "Geneva spirit" has certainly been in some ways inconvenient for the free world by melting the glue that has been holding us together. But perhaps there are even more serious consequences within the Soviet orbit. It encouraged there a desire for more independence and more tolerance. And the whole Tito affair put ideas in the heads of the people in the satellites which are still being ruled by Stalinist governments.

The opportunity seized by the Soviets to move into the Middle East strained the Geneva spirit. If you add all this together it is possible that the people in the Soviet Union indoctrinated in the old Stalinist line may have swung the balance. Tito pointed out to me that there are many people emerging at the top in Russia now who were brought up on Stalinism and still believe in it.

I asked how long he thought we could go on with a divided Germany splitting Europe; could the entire Western coalition adjust themselves to the idea and keep the West Germans from making their own deals. Dulles replied: "We are going to have to live with it for quite a while. We don't see a chance of a united Germany until the entire Soviet relationship with its satellite empire changes. . . . Eventually this will change—in a year, or ten years, or more. Either a different type of government will evolve in the satellites, or the people in those countries will become so indoctrinated that they willingly accept their regimes. When either of these situations develops the German Democratic Republic won't be as symbolic of the satellite position as is now the case. Only then will Russia be able to afford to unite Germany."

PARIS, *November 23, 1955*

LAST night we went to a dinner party at the Norstads. Larry says Nasser has been extremely clever about his handling of the Russian arms deals. He asked the United States to supply B-26 bomber planes. This was turned down. Then he turned to the Russians and got his arms deal through. He now is actually flying some IL-28 twin-jet light bombers and is rapidly assembling MIG fighters. Nasser was asked why on earth he had requested B-26s from us when he knew they were outmoded. Nasser replied that he knew they were not classified, there were plenty of them, and they were of no use to the United States. Therefore, he reasoned, if he were not going to get these he wouldn't get anything out of us. In such a case he would turn to Russia.

MOSCOW, *November 28, 1955*

WE have been here since Saturday evening, staying at the Bohlens. The city has changed considerably: vast new skyscrapers of overornate architecture; batches of neon lights on the main streets; a traffic problem—minor compared to Paris or New York, but nevertheless Moscow's first. The standard of living has risen.

There is a curious fast set of youngsters who study up on American jazz in the Lenin library, bootleg records, wear suits replete with zippers wherever possible, and speak to each other in phrases of Latin or English. This gang is called the *stilyagi*—"stylists" or "style-hunters." There is, among young Russians, a tremendous enthusiasm for jazz. Recently a concert of Gershwin music was given. There is an immense vogue for the translated writings of Dreiser.

(British Ambassador Sir William) Hayter has a young secretary who, after picking up a Russian girl, has been introduced into Moscow's youthful high society. They are continually intermarrying and divorcing among

themselves. One of them, son of a rather bad musician named Duna-
chaievsky, inherited two apartments, three dachas, four automobiles including a German Horch, and a huge bank account. The smart thing
among these youngsters is to go abroad; they try and get jobs in even the
lowest capacity on state visits, or do things such as driving foreign cars.

Chip thinks gradually the party administration will ease up on Communist parties abroad and relax the monolithic control system; also that
for a long time to come they won't worry about ideology in such countries
as India and Egypt; just try and line them up on their side.

MOSCOW, *November 30, 1955*

LAST night we dined at the British Embassy. John Morgan, the young
secretary with connections in the youthful smart set, was there. He said his
group has great esteem for Molotov. They seem to have a split view on
Stalin. They realize things are much better now, but they still regard Stalin's period as a "golden age."

The group dresses well, preferring foreign clothes. These are brought
back by friends from official overseas trips; or, more often, each has a
commission shop where clothes, jewelry, and other articles are pawned.
The shop boss will send a discreet message when he thinks something of
interest to the client shows up. Then they meet at a selected rendezvous,
and the deal is consummated. The shop boss will make a profit of about
300 percent. Vishinsky's daughter, who adores foreign clothes, paid
3,000 rubles just to be introduced to a dressmaker capable of cutting
modern-style dresses.

The group lives well. One has an apartment which, although small, has
magnificent silverware ("The finest I've ever seen; heavy solid silver; better than in a duke's house") and china, including Sèvres porcelain. The
group seems to have so much money they can't spend it all. They keep it in
savings deposits at a 3 percent interest rate. There is considerable snob-
bism, and most are children of important officials or artists. The only
apparent exception is the son of a country doctor. The group has no
connection with the *stilyagi*, who are far below them in class. There are
only one or two restaurants and nightclubs they consider chic. They drink
(but not too heavily), have a roaring sex life, don't play cards, and never
talk politics.

Chip and Hayter agreed that Malenkov is by far the most able and
intelligent of the Presidium, a real intellectual force. Hayter says he not
only uses some Latin phrases but has a considerable knowledge of Turkish. Chip says there is a rumor he is half-Tatar, half-German, that Malenkov is not a real Russian name, and that he was born Klein. (I have often
heard he was half Bashkir.)

MOSCOW, *December 12, 1955*

LOUIS Joxe, French Ambassador, came for dinner last night. Joxe said that when Leopold Bravo, recent Argentine Ambassador, saw Stalin shortly before the latter's death, he expressed polite pleasure at the honor of being received. Like some old Mongol Khan, Stalin replied: "In this country even the shepherds are well treated."

TASHKENT, *December 18, 1955*

WE had a huge "brunch" in the dining room at noon and then set out to see the Mufti of Central Asia, with whom I had a 2:00 P.M. appointment. Tashkent was taken (from the Emir of Kokand) by the Russians in 1865. A "new," or Russian, town was then built beside the old Turki town. Apart from some large and ugly administrative buildings, the airport, and parks with silvered statues of Lenin and Stalin or nude athletes (covered with singlets), the Soviets seem to have built little. There is one large Soviet textile plant to use up the local cash crop, cotton.

The city is situated attractively. Today sunshine gleamed on the Tien Shan mountain range in the background. The range is a barrier leading toward China (Sinkiang), India (Kashmir), and Afghanistan.

In the home of the Mufti (now ninety-five years old and bed-ridden), we were taken to the main room and sat down around a table every square inch of which was crammed with food: round flat loaves of bread; dishes of somewhat withered-looking, sweet grapes (kept over from the autumn), apples, pomegranates; plates filled with yellow clustered crystals of sugar candy; dishes of raisins and nuts.

Our host, the acting Mufti, Al-Hafiz Ghazi Zia-ud-Din Babahanoff (a Hadji), the son of the old Mufti who serves as substitute, was a pleasant, Turkish-looking man wearing a tan robe and white turban. Across from him sat Ghazi Pazil Hodja, Chinese-looking, with wispy white beard and white turban. Both were Uzbeks as well as a capped (Uzbek skullcap) Russian-speaking civilian at the end of the table.

Babahanoff said there are about 30 million Muslims in the USSR; that there were about 30 million before the revolution. (I doubt very much if there are even fifteen million practicing today.) The name of the old Mufti (his father) is Ishan Babahan Ibn Abdul Mejid Khan, born in Tashkent in 1861, when it still belonged to the independent Khan of Kokand. Every year about fifteen to twenty (pilgrims) go from the USSR to Mecca. They apply to the Council of Religions in Tashkent or Moscow, and the council helps those it approves to get passports, visas, and foreign currency. Babahanoff said the number of pilgrims is so small "because it is very expensive and we are very far from Mecca."

He says that in 1917, Tashkent had three hundred mosques and a population of 600,000; now, with a population of 1 million, there are only eighteen mosques.

After our lengthy lunch and conversation, Babahanoff took us into the old Mufti's bed chamber. Ibn Abdul Mejid Khan was sitting up in a chair, dressed in a black, flowered robe and flat, honey-colored turban. He has a wispy beard straggling down from his toothless jaw, a brown face, dull old brown eyes, and a fierce hawk nose. He muttered a few words of blessing, but he wasn't too aware of what he was saying or to whom: merely traditional Muslim courtesies. The old man looks like something out of Omar Khayyám.

BOKHARA, *December 19, 1955*

BOKHARA was the capital of an independent emirate until the Bolshevik Revolution, when the Emir fled to Kabul in 1920 and reportedly went into the rug business. Its population (largely Uzbek) was noted for savage and fanatical Muhammedanism, and its emirs were renowned for their cruelty. The market for slaves was notorious. The bazaar was once famous for products from China (on the old caravan silk route), India, and the loot Turkmenian robbers stole. The prisons were particularly disagreeable. In the old jail, one cell was sunk into the ground and called the vermin pit. It was filled with sheep lice said to have been habituated to a special diet of meat so they could happily nibble away at prisoners.

This is the shabbiest Asian town I have seen in some time; completely run down, everything crumbling into dust, the only clean-looking people are the few battalions of Russian infantry from the garrison who march through every now and then, swinging their arms and singing beautifully: European recruits, striding through their Asian colonial subjects like British regiments in Kipling's India.

In the Bokhara restaurant we watched drunks falling into their beer while a pathetic three-piece band (one woman) of violin, drum, and accordion made loud music, some of which was faintly recognizable (one piece being a weird version of "J'Attendrai").

Outside was an old mosque, now used as a poolroom, where there were three spirited games and walls of pictures of Bolshevik leaders and exhortatory posters such as: "If you get drunk you won't be able to fulfill your norm."

SAMARKAND, *December 20, 1955*

SAMARKAND is painted in pleasant blue, green, and gray pastel shades and filled with plane trees and poplars. The Russians captured it in 1868 from the Emir of Bokhara, and it seems still like a nineteenth-century Czarist garrison town.

The open-air bazaars are pathetic: few goods, shabby, sad-looking people. Nevertheless, there is real charm to this city with its blue-tiled mosque domes standing out against the nearby foothills of the Tien Shan range. There is a fine blue dome over Timur's (Tamerlane's) tomb, which we visited.

We went to the ruined mosque of Bibi Hanum, favorite wife of Timur and daughter of the Emperor of China. In 1399, Timur returned from India with much loot, including slaves, elephants, jewels, and gold. He decided to build the finest mosque in the world and ordered his architects to erect it in five years. As a result they couldn't build it as they wanted, and time and earthquakes have laid it in almost total ruins.

Timur specified that he wanted the main portal to be fifty meters high. His architect warned him it would soon collapse. But Timur insisted. Bibi Hanum, then alive, used to watch the construction. Timur went off to the wars again, and the architect decided to build the portal only forty-three meters high. When Timur returned he ordered it rebuilt. It was.

The architect asked but one favor of Bibi Hanum, a kiss. This was so sweet and burning that it left a mark like a red rose. When Timur returned from a campaign and saw this he knew what had happened and had the architect killed. He went to his death smiling and was turned into a dove who sang to Bibi Hanum every morning.

TASHKENT, *December 22, 1955*

SHORTLY after we boarded the train for Tashkent a short, fat, enormously wide woman with broad, brown, smiling Asian features, wearing a garish print dress came into our compartment and introduced herself as Vice-President of the Tadjik Soviet Republic. She bore a melon, long and yellow, done up in a reed net, as credentials of goodwill: Comrade Saida Khalikova of Stalinabad, born in 1909, a Tadjik deputy in the Supreme Soviet's Council of Nationalities, now on her way to Moscow for the Supreme Soviet meeting.

She sat down in our compartment, joined us in a cigarette, and gushed away in bad Russian with fierce gestures of clenched fists, shaking her powerful arms. She was born in Stalinabad when it was still called Dushambi, a village on the territory of the quasi-independent state of the Emir of Bokhara. When she was a girl, women were the slaves of their husbands and had to wear the veil. "Look at me," she boasted. "I was brought up as a slave behind a veil. Now I can wear anything I like and go where I please and I'm vice chairman of our republic. Before the revolution women couldn't even leave their houses, now I have a grown son and he is married to a Russian girl. When I was a child, the Emir ordered all girls to start marrying at nine."

This morning we visited the Tashkent museum. The most interesting thing was a wax reconstruction of Timur's head, based on his exhumed skull. Decked out in helmet, pointed beard, and drooping moustache, he looked rather like a muscular Chiang Kai-shek.

LENINGRAD, *December 27, 1955*

CAME up for the opening of *Porgy and Bess*, the first American stage production in Russia since the Revolution. The arrival of the cast created quite a stir—the sight of flashy Negroes in this white city. One of the actors wears a nutria coat and hat and has special holes in his gloves so his rings can show through. The opening was, I thought, lousy: A poor company hampered by a bad theater. Yet it seemed to go down very well—except the prudish Russians were shocked by the sex.

MOSCOW, *January 4, 1956*

GOOD talk with Molotov in his office on the seventh floor of the Foreign Ministry skyscraper. On the walls were pictures of Lenin and Stalin.

I told Molotov that, as he undoubtedly had heard, Dulles thought that in all the years he has personally been connected with diplomacy the ablest statesman he had ever witnessed in action was Mr. Molotov. Who did Molotov consider the ablest Western statesman he had dealt with? He smiled and said: "I should not dwell upon the subject. The statement about me is an obvious exaggeration. As for western statesmen, that is a difficult question. There are many experienced diplomats in the West. In the United States, Cordell Hull was certainly an experienced diplomat. I had occasion to meet Mr. Hull here in Moscow in 1943, and, during the previous year, in Washington in 1942. Also, there is no doubt that Mr. Eden in Great Britain is a very experienced diplomat." [Notice: He left Dulles out.]

I said, in Soviet proposals for the amalgamation of the NATO allies and the Warsaw Pact members I had noticed no mention of similar proposals for economic cooperation on that particular, if somewhat artificial, basis. He said: "Of course that could well be discussed. But the question that has decisive importance is that involving the NATO pact and the Warsaw Treaty. First we should arrive at a political decision. *Then* questions of an economic character could be brought up."

Those observations led me to ask a question which is puzzling many Americans: How is it possible to build a true basis for coexistence between two systems when one of them (communism) openly proclaims its determination to triumph ultimately over the other? Molotov replied:

> Well, after all, that was first said over one hundred years ago by Marx and Engels in the *Communist Manifesto* published in 1847. Communism thinks it is scientifically true that history is moving ahead from one social system to another, to a more perfect social system. We think communism is a better system, a more progressive system, and that it will historically triumph. This

is our conviction. We merely consider it a well-founded conviction. It reflects historic processes.

According to the doctrine of communism, one of two systems must be victorious and must prove it is more progressive and in accordance with modern requirements. We believe communism is that system which can bring to peoples of the world more favorable material and spiritual conditions of life. This does not mean that no important changes are taking place within the capitalist system. These changes *are* taking place. Changes are also taking place within the Socialist countries engaged in building communism.

The essential part in this historical process, as we see it, is that communism is called upon to take the place of capitalism eventually as a more progressive system. Nevertheless, we recognize that not everyone shares our views.

You see, basically the two systems are contradictory. Capitalism is founded upon a system of exploitation of one people by another people, one class by another class, and one person by another person. Communism rejects the theory of such exploitation of one man by another man. In that sense the two systems are incompatible. But the change-over depends upon historic conditions. We should like the change-over to communism to be as painless as possible.

WARSAW, *February 22, 1956*

WHEN I reached the hotel a pleasant and exceedingly pretty young woman from Orbis, the travel agency, named Danuta, placed herself at my disposal as guide-interpreter. Danuta guided a group of Russians recently. They were very nice but pathetic. The girls locked themselves in their rooms to smoke; they were afraid of being caught. They envied Danuta's pants at Zakopane, the ski resort. They envied the lipstick, powder, and styles of the Polish girls. And the Russian boys complained: "Why aren't our girls attractive?"

WARSAW, *February 23, 1956*

CALLED on Acting Foreign Minister Marian Naskowski, a plump man with a sad, pale face. He said: "The West doesn't understand our policy well enough. It is not imposed by Russia. There is nothing in this thesis. If on the principal questions our policy is identical with that of Moscow this is for the simple reason of common interests. Our road to socialism is in many ways different from that of Russia or of China. For example, there are different percentages of collectivization. But our general direction is the same—the socialization of production."

GDYNIA, POLAND, *February 24, 1956*

LAST night I came up by train (with Danuta) to Sopot, a seaside town which was part of the old free city of Danzig (Gdansk).

We lunched (enormously) in a restaurant with a group of local editors. Toasts were drunk to "friendship of Polish and American journalists." The conversation was affable but obscured by slogans, i.e.:

The only real Germans seem to live in West Germany, where Adenauer is almost a new Hitler because he covets Silesia. It was terrible for the West to rearm West Germany. But the East Germans are democratic and therefore not dangerous. It is OK to give them guns.

After we were well filled with hooch, a big shot in the Gdansk Communist Party suddenly dropped all pretense about good East Germans and bad West Germans.

He shouted at the puzzled journalists. "Maybe all Germans are the same. For my part I hate them all, ours as well."

WROCLAW, POLAND, *February 25, 1956*

TOURED Wroclaw (Breslau) extensively and was astounded at how "slavicized" it has become. The Germans are gone, and Poles from all over— but especially the eastern areas ceded to Russia—have been moved in.

In the cathedral I was guided about by Father Jan Kowalski, who speaks excellent French. At the end, saying farewell, he asked: "Do you ever go to Madrid?" Puzzled, I said, "Yes." "Next time would you say hello to my sister?" "Who is she?" "Lady Mallet, wife of the British ambassador."

He says Wroclaw is now "*très croyant*"; despite great cold the churches are always filled. "I think the reasons are evident," replied Kowalski.

CRACOW, POLAND, *February 26, 1956*

ARRIVED here after an all-night third-class train ride. On the train, Danuta and I had a few drinks with a man from Zakopane who had spent two years in Dachau during the war. He asked me my impression of Poland now. I told him—frankly. He disagreed; said everything was rosy. When Danuta went out to get some coffee for us, he leaned forward and whispered in German: "You're right. Don't believe what I said. I don't dare talk. But I agree with you. So do 99 percent of the people."

WARSAW, *February 28, 1956*

ROMUALD Poleszczuk, acting chief of the Foreign Office press section, requested me to come around. When I went downstairs to order a taxi through Orbis, I noticed I was being openly followed. A fellow in a felt hat standing beside a nice new Mercedes got in beside the driver when I took off. They came along behind to the Foreign Office.

Poleszczuk said the Polish government was very disturbed and disappointed with the first column I had written (published Saturday, February 24). The government found it offensive. As a result he had been instructed to tell me no more appointments were being made for me. I replied that I found it extraordinary that they censured a correspondent for being objective when that was what they said they wished. I proposed to do no favors for Poland: I would write as objectively about this country as I wrote about any other, including my own.

PRAGUE, *March 3, 1956*

THIS afternoon I spent two hours sightseeing with a Czech woman guide who in no time was savagely denouncing the regime. Said it was a joy to have a Westerner to talk with as she no longer dared even to give her views among her friends for fear of some stool pigeon.

We passed the huge, grim Stalin monument above the Vltava planted about with trees from Georgian saplings. The ice pack has broken on the Vltava; how much of a thaw will there be politically? My guide complained: "We need schools so badly. But instead they spent millions of crowns on this statue." Masaryk supposedly said here: "I went to Moscow a free man and came back Stalin's servant." My guide says people aren't allowed to see the room from which Masaryk jumped. She sadly recalled Jan Hus' words: "*Pravda vitezi*—Let the truth prevail."

PRAGUE, *March 5, 1956*

WENT to the Satirical Theater to see a play called *Caesar*, first produced as a satire on fascism in 1932 and revived this winter with some mild new jokes against the present system added. It has had enormous success. The author, producer, and main actor is a huge, bearded Czech named Jan Werich who looks like the perfect Falstaff.

After the show I went with Werich for supper at the Budapest Restaurant on Vaclavski Namesti. Later he led the way to a tiny wine joint in the old part of Prague, and we sat up for hours talking. Here is what he said:

"They" is the key word here (as elsewhere in the orbit). Everyone has his "they." "They" refers to the all-powerful inner circle, the direction. But it is an invisible "they." Nobody really knows who "they" is. "They" is bureaucracy. "They" is the system. But "they" is also something else—it is the excuse for refusing to take responsibility, for inaction ("they" wouldn't like it, etc.). Once, Werich was talking with one of the highest Politburo leaders here, and he made reference to "they" wouldn't like it. "My God," said Werich, "you don't mean to tell me that even you have a 'they'." President Zapotocky came to see *Caesar*. He told Werich after-ward: "The play is okay. We have decided to have satire. Since we have to have satire, I approve *Caesar*."

Werich says regretfully: "The truth is that the Czechs are not a fighting people. We have never really fought since the Hussite wars of the fifteenth century. The Hapsburgs took over complete power in 1621, after the battle of White Mountain. From then on Czech mothers brought their children up in a passive tradition. They were taught: 'Don't speak up what's on your mind. There is no need for people to know what you think.' The result has been Schweikism. This is a method. But it is no good as a national philosophy."

The Good Soldier Schweik by Jaroslav Hasek depicted the stupid, bumbling but shrewd peasant mentality, always going along but passively resisting.

PRAGUE, *March 7, 1956*

TODAY was T. G. Masaryk's birthday. One would never know it. No men-tion in the press of the republic's founder and first leader. *The New York Times* secretary, a pathetic Jewish woman with the tattoo of Auschwitz concentration camp on her arm, recalled the occasion and says they have removed almost every trace of Masaryk. His name has been obliterated from streets, schools, and hospitals. She also sadly recalled that today is the anniversary of the date her mother was put in a gas oven at Auschwitz.

In the afternoon I went to see Antonin Zapotocky, president of the republic, co-founder of the Czechoslovakian Communist Party, member of the Politburo, and first Secretary General of the party.

I observed to Zapotocky that Beneš had sought to make of Czecho-slovakia a bridge between East and West; what did he, Zapotocky, think of the idea of following such a policy? He replied: "Czechoslovakia is cer-tainly willing to develop friendly relations with all countries regardless of their regimes. But if by the term 'bridge' you mean a policy of fence sitting, we certainly do not wish to do this. We wish to build socialism here and we must base ourselves upon Socialist countries. The capitalist coun-tries clearly wouldn't want to help us any more than we would seek to build up capitalism in countries elsewhere."

At this point Zapotocky developed a truly extraordinary lie with every external indication of sincerity. Today, Masaryk's birthday (which he seemed unaware of), he said: In Czechoslovakia you may see a number of memorials to T. G. Masaryk. *None* have been taken down. It is clear that Masaryk will remain a historical figure in Czechoslovakia even though our political ideas are different.

BUDAPEST, *March 11, 1956*

TODAY (Sunday) I went to see Matyas Rakosi, Secretary General of the Hungarian Workers' Party and Communist boss. He received me in his office in party headquarters in Pest, not far from Parliament. Everywhere pictures of Stalin—despite his "demotion." Rakosi is astonishingly short (barely over five feet) and very broad with a huge, powerful chest. He is built like a small ox and must be exceedingly strong. We spoke in English, which he knows fluently. He told me he also speaks (in addition to Hungarian) Russian, German, French, and Italian. Once or twice he interjected Latin quotations; obviously a well-educated man.

He spent nineteen years in prison, but his health didn't suffer because "my parents were very healthy." When in prison he kept himself fit by using his table as a weight for setting-up exercises. He read such books as the prison censor permitted and as were smuggled in by friends.

What, I asked, was the historical position and reputation of Stalin as a result of the Twentieth Congress? He replied (dutifully): "We hold exactly the same opinion as Khrushchev and Mikoyan. Everybody makes mistakes. Lenin said that even the most clever men, even geniuses, can make mistakes—especially when they get old. This was the case with Stalin."

Rakosi said: "To measure a man's historical value you must be able to look backward over a certain distance in time. For example, in the case of your American presidents, some of your historians thought Coolidge was a wise, strong, silent man; wise simply because he didn't speak. But he is no longer considered so smart by your historians. [This is an odd comparison —Stalin and Coolidge.] There is no doubt that Stalin had very great historical merits even though he committed blunders also. We Communists measure historical figures both in terms of their merits and their demerits."

I then turned to Tito and Titoism. Did Rakosi think the quarrel with him had all been a big mistake. He said: "We were misled on Titoism. This was one of the works of Beria and his group. He sought to create a situation that would weaken the bonds of Socialists and the quarrel with Tito was part of it. Khrushchev spoke of this in Belgrade last year. Now we are trying to forget this disagreeable episode and to improve our relations with Jugoslavia."

Rakosi said he was born with the name of Rakosi; it is not a *nom de révolution* like Lenin, Stalin, or Molotov. He was exchanged to the Russians in 1940 for battle flags of the Hungarian revolution of 1848–1849.

BUDAPEST, *March 12, 1956*

LUNCHED with Joszef Szall, head of the information section of the Foreign Office. He told me Rakosi's name at birth was Roth and that he changed it while a university student; it was a "Jewish name."

SOFIA, *March 22, 1956*

MARIA Popilieva has been out of work for six years. Her crime: working for *The New York Times*. She spent three years in a concentration camp under the Nazis and has suffered all over again from the present outfit.

Her brother has become a Communist Party member and is practicing law. But Maria will have none of it and for eighteen months has refused to speak to him—despite the fact that they live in the same two rooms with their mother. Maria has no work; they refuse to give her permission to get a job. She earns about 150 levas a month embroidering and is almost starving. "But I'm tough," she says. Goes around in a worn old dress, frayed coat, and shawl about her head; but chin held high.

Last night I dined with Maria in a small joint where I used to go for tripe soup after a night out. No more tripe soup now. Three youngsters sat down at our table. They talked timidly but frankly after cautioning me: "Whatever we say is secret." One, the nephew of an Orthodox bishop, asked, "Is it true that there is bad prejudice against Negroes in America?" I said there was but it was getting better. But, said he: "I saw an American ship once and the sailors, black and white, were sitting happily at the same table playing cards."

SOFIA, *March 24, 1956*

RUSSIANS doing jobs here are paid ten times the equivalent of Bulgarians. They are forbidden to have relations with Bulgarians. They have a restaurant above the diplomatic restaurant to which no Bulgarians are admitted.

Bulgarians always asked for "Grandfather Ivan from Moscow." Now they've got him. They are interested in the Khrushchev new look. But, says Maria: "We have a proverb—the wolf can shed his skin but not his habits." Should be the bear.

Attended a dinner in my honor at the journalists' club at which the host was Vladimir Topencharov, editor-in-chief of *Otechestven Front* ("Fatherland Front"), brother-in-law of the late Traicho Kostov, and himself once in prison as a Titoist. They have broken him. I asked him about Georgi Andreitchin and he solemnly assured me he wasn't in jail but alive and well. (He's dead.)

BELGRADE, *March 29, 1956*

TALK with Veljko Vlahović, chairman of the Foreign Relations Committee of the Socialist Alliance, the main Jugoslav ideologue: a six-foot-five-inch Montenegrin with a shock of black hair. He is very lame and walks with a cane as a result of a wound while fighting with the Republican army in the Spanish Civil War.

I asked him to outline for me the differences between Jugoslav Communist and Soviet Communist ideology and practice. He said:

> We have tried to base the authority of the state upon individual citizens. We have workers' councils, factory councils, and much discussion at the lowest level. We try to have ideas worked upward from the bottom. Thus, for example, there are many candidates in our elections. The selection comes at the bottom. Any citizen can be a candidate. There is discussion of the choice before he is nominated, although once he is nominated he is generally elected.
>
> Russia is highly centralized. We are based on local workers' councils. A factory council cannot only change the directors of the factory, but it can also alter the actual program of that factory.
>
> Our conception is that you cannot socialize agriculture by force. We have many cooperatives similar to the Soviet *kholkhoz*, but we also have other forms of cooperatives. We have allowed our peasants to leave cooperatives if they desire. And the small private landowner can remain a private landowner.

Vlahović says 17 percent of Jugoslavia's arable land is socialized now, whereas in 1950, about 25 percent was socialized. In other words, the trend is away from collectivization. In Russia, 100 percent of the land is socialized, and the peasant has no choice.

I 2

PARIS, *April 21, 1956*

MELAS, NEW GREEK AMBASSADOR TO NATO, WAS AMBASSADOR in Cairo before coming here. Upon paying his farewell call on his Soviet colleague he mentioned Greece's population problew and the need to seek areas for emigration. The Russian said: "What kind of a population problem do you think that is? In China there are fifteen million more people born each year than die. That is a population problem." Melas concludes that Russia is very concerned about the continual growth of a huge Chinese state on its borders. He wondered if it was not possible that in ten years or so Russia might be seeking alliance with the West against China.

PARIS, *May 7, 1956*

LUNCH today with Stanislaw Gajewski, Polish Ambassador. The famous Khrushchev de-Stalinization speech has been issued as a text and widely printed, distributed to all top Communist officials. It has been labeled "for party use only." Gajewski has a copy in his safe but regrets he cannot let me have it.

However, eighty thousand copies were printed in Polish in Warsaw, distributed to party leaders, and read before local conclaves. It is about fifty pages long and takes two hours to read. "Because this was done in Poland," he says, "a lot of black market copies were run off." The eighty thousand original copies were all numbered and therefore could not find their way into the black market without risk to the man who resold them. But, being Poles, the printers ran off several thousand extra unnumbered copies for the black market. The original price per copy was 500 zlotys (125 dollars). But so many copies found their way to the black market that the price has fallen to 300 zlotys.

Khrushchev said Stalin prepared his military strategy from a school-room globe of the world; that Stalin contended Zhukov founded his strategy by sniffing a handful of earth, deciding whether or not to start an offensive from the smell. Gajewski added: "We know this is obviously not true. Why does Khrushchev say these things?"

Khrushchev reported that something like 80 percent of the Bolshevik Central Committee in 1934 was shot by Stalin. Several of the old Bolsheviks wrote letters to Beria and Stalin an hour or two before their deaths, expressing confidence that if Stalin only knew about these injustices he would save them. These letters were found among Stalin's papers. He had ignored them. Stalin told Khrushchev he had but to move his little finger and he could destroy Tito. Khrushchev added that he was unable to move his little finger.

Gajewski told me he had heard of my troubles in Warsaw and was embarrassed and shocked. "They couldn't expect you to write Marxist propaganda," he said.

PARIS, *May 31, 1956*

THIS afternoon, I spent an hour with General de Gaulle. He admitted: "We can't have peace very quickly between the Arab world and the West. In Algeria, Tunisia, Morocco, and the Middle East, the Arabs are working all together. There would have been a possibility for France to find a solution with the Arabs, but it is not possible in the present situation. The Arab question is a world question, not just a French question."

Yet in no sense did this imply—as his enemies were later to adduce—that de Gaulle was an Arabophil. He elaborated:

Who are the Arabs? The Arabs are a people who, since the days of Muhammed, have never constituted a state successfully. Muhammed made a state because of Islam. After him there has been nothing but anarchy. Have you ever seen a dam built by the Arabs? Nowhere. It doesn't exist. It has never been seen anywhere. It has been like that for centuries. The Arabs say that they invented algebra and built huge mosques. But this was entirely the job of Christian slaves they captured [a strange distortion of fact]. It was not the Arabs themselves. We French tried to do much with them. And the Russians before us tried. But they can't do anything alone.

At the time, I noted: "I don't quite know what de Gaulle meant by 'the Russians before us'; I suppose he may be referring to Islamic Central Asia; that is a mere conjecture."

De Gaulle assured me: "It is impossible to reform the Constitution now. The politicians won't do it. I cannot imagine *any* circumstances under which I could come back into active political life. This regime will not reform itself. One needs a drama first." I asked what he meant by the word "drama" and he said: "Not necessarily a war. Revolution or some form of tumult might be the answer. It is not always necessary to have a war.

Charles X and the Restoration disappeared without war. Then there was a revolution. The 1848 Republic disappeared without a war. But we *do* need a drama."

I remarked that I found him particularly pessimistic today. He said: "The present is pessimistic. I live in the present, not in the future. Who knows what the future will bring. If someone drops an atom bomb, that will change all."

I asked how he foresaw the future. He said:

> For the next two or three years there will be coexistence. But it will not be sincere. There will be exchanges of visits, of ballets, of football teams, and sporting groups. During that time the Russians will continue to develop economically and to progress. And they will progress further in the Arab world. But I think they will have psychological difficulties and also political difficulties with the slave peoples—Poland, Czechoslovakia, Rumania, Hungary, and the Baltic peoples. Maybe even in the Ukraine and Caucasus.
>
> Europe is confused and sad. It will stay like that for some time. And what will come of this? I don't know; but surely something. I must repeat, it will not be gay for the next few years. There is no West now. It is finished. There are westerners but no West. The United States is against the West everywhere. If you could replace the West, all right. But you can't. You Americans are part of the West, not the West itself. And meantime Europe will vegetate. The Germans won't do much. They have already remade their life. But they have remade neither their power nor their ambitions. And Britain is no longer very vital. This is also unfortunately the case for France.
>
> From the western side I think the U.S. will remain uncertain. You won't attack. You will make a coexistence—but without satisfaction. That is not a policy, it is just a series of ideas. The future of NATO depends entirely on Russia. If Russia threatens, NATO exists. If Russia does not threaten, NATO will die.

PARIS, *June 23, 1956*

I READ a summary which French Ambassador Dejean sent in a telegram to the Quai d'Orsay of a conversation French Socialist visitors had with Khrushchev, Mikoyan, Shepilov, and Suslov. Khrushchev admitted that agriculture was the big problem. He was seeking to stimulate production by encouraging private initiative and the development of private family plots attached to the *kolkhozes*.

Khrushchev said it would be useless to form an opposition in the USSR. He asked: "Do you wish that we should form a second party now? My children would say to me: 'Papa, have you lost your mind?' "

He continued: "There are no more classes in the USSR. Our society is monolithic. To create an opposition would be to put a flea beneath the shirt. One does not need that to fight bureaucracy. It is sufficient to stimulate self-criticism within the Communist party."

At this point, Mikoyan joined in. He said that as a youth he had wanted to be a priest but had not succeeded. The Communist Party was atheistic but respected the religious sentiments of the population.

Khrushchev interrupted. He said: "Some Communists don't believe in God at party meetings, but they do believe in God at home."

LONDON, *July 10, 1956*

TODAY I had a fascinating, wonderful, and moving experience. I spent five hours with old Winston Churchill down in the country at his home, Chartwell, in Kent. I had lunch alone with him, Lady Churchill, and a young man from the Foreign Office named Anthony Montague Browne. Montague Browne has been loaned to him to keep him in touch with foreign affairs. He shows him cables and keeps him generally advised so he will understand the reasons for government decisions; this is under the guise of Churchill being a privy councillor. (It is partly for humanitarian, generous purposes of keeping him in touch; and partly so he won't bring the government down by some speech objecting to a policy he doesn't understand.)

After lunch Lady Churchill slipped off and for three hours, I was either alone with the old man or young Montague Browne was with us as we sat and smoked and talked, as Churchill read from one of his books, or as we wandered around the estate while he admired his cattle, his gardens, and fed his huge, fat goldfish. (He is most proud of a little pond of twenty-five-year-old golden carp.) The greatest impression made on me was of his infinite courtesy and gentleness. He was generous in his references to every figure we discussed—save Hitler. He insisted on rising and tottering off to escort his wife downstairs. He lifted his wine glass in a little private toast to Lady Churchill across the table. And, as we were wandering back to the house after our little stroll, he saw a tiny dead bird. He pointed at it with his stick, very sadly, tears in his eyes, muttering.

Chartwell is a large, rambling brick house situated on the edge of a fine valley in Kent. Churchill, staring out through the mists of this overcast day, kept murmuring about what a pity it was I couldn't see the wonderful view—"the whole weald of Kent." I said that today with the mist it looked as if the sea were only a mile away. "Thank God not that," said Churchill. "Our island is small enough as it is." Above the house was flying Churchill's private flag as Warden of the Cinque Ports. When I arrived (greeted by the young diplomat) I noticed rows of paintings in the hall. Churchill pointed one out later (some Pierrots) which had been painted by Royal Marine prisoners of war during World War I and given to him. On the table in the hallway were small bronze statues of some of his racehorses. I went into the living room, Lady Churchill joined us, and we chatted over sherry (she took tomato juice).

Then the old man came in. He was dressed in his "siren suit"—sort of a battle dress cut of dark blue flannel with a narrow gray pinstripe. It has a zipper down the front. He wore black shoes with zippers and a silk, nineteenth-century French artist's shirt with long (about eight inches) pointed collar tabs sticking out over his siren suit like a dressed-up schoolboy. He looked like a comfortable old teddy bear, above all after lunch, when he'd been puffing away at his cigar and ashes had trickled down his front.

He was very torpid at first: couldn't follow the conversation; wasn't using his hearing aid; didn't seem to understand anything. His wife would repeat things and almost translate them to him, but he sat slumped in an armchair, uninterested, confused, gazing sullenly out of his rheumy, blood-shot eyes while Lady Churchill tried to carry on a gay conversation, only dealing him in when he seemed to resent being left out in the cold. Clearly he was hungry and only interested in lunch.

We then went to lunch, the old man (despite his temper and his hunger) politely seeing me through the door first. He mounted the one flight to the dining room in his tiny, exceedingly slow elevator, which Lord Beaver-brook gave him. We walked up the fine oaken stairway with rough wood steps. The hall outside the dining room is lined with Churchill's paintings, mostly Mediterranean scenes and some quite good.

He took three glasses of wine, two of port, two of brandy (in huge, balloon goblets which really give one an overpowering bouquet), and two cups of coffee. Finally the cigars (his immense black ones) were passed. He seemed astonished when I refused. By the time he was into his cigar, with the wines and brandy and coffee circulating about his system, he began to revive. But until then the conversational going was hard. He seemed half-asleep, staring a bit greedily, looking like a great, pink, hungry baby, far more interested in the food (and such things as where was the mustard) than the conversation.

The rest of us chatted about Chiang Kai-shek, Russia, Tito, the Middle East, and only occasionally he would butt in with a question; the answer would be explained to him, repeated, then he would subside back into his chair. Lady Churchill clearly has a nice catty view of Madam Chiang Kai-shek (which I strongly endorse). She asked me if Madam was still so beautiful. I replied that the evil was now more visible in her face than the beauty. This delighted her. She said she couldn't abide her. Mrs. Roosevelt had told her that when Madam was staying in New York once, she and Mrs. FDR had returned to Madam Chiang's hotel rooms and found the two FBI agents outside the door fast asleep. Next day Madam asked Mrs. FDR what had become of the agents. Mrs. Roosevelt said she assumed they'd been reprimanded. Madam said: "In China it would have been this" (drawing her hand across her throat). "Rather rude to her hostess, don't you think?" inquired Lady Churchill. Lady Churchill said her husband hadn't met Madam Chiang until the Cairo Conference. Once before, when he was in Washington seeing FDR, the President said to him: "I want you to meet Madam Chiang; she's a beautiful woman." So FDR called her up to invite her for lunch the next day with Churchill. Madam Chiang refused unless Churchill first called upon her. Lady Churchill also observed that

although she dressed Chinese fashion, she had her gowns and jewels designed in the West by the best firms. (Every now and then Sir Winston
would mumble into the conversation: "Formosa? What's that? Where's
that? Ah, yes. I see," with a lisp.)

Lady Churchill asked me if I thought Eisenhower would run again, and
I said certainly yes. She asked if I was pleased. I said that I admired
Eisenhower and was a friend of his, but I was very worried about his
health and the possibility that Nixon might have to succeed him.

After Lady Churchill departed, we sat down in the sitting room again,
he plonked himself into an armchair, ashes over the front of his siren suit,
and suddenly, slowly came alive; not just the shreds of a great character
and the impeccable courtesy of his personality, but the old flame and
wisdom began to emerge.

He put on his tortoise-shell spectacles, called for the sixth volume of his
memoirs, read several pages to me with commentary, made sage and often
profound observations on the world abroad and English politics, puffing
contentedly and pondering for more than an hour. (I shall list some of his
observations afterward.) Then he suggested we go for a stroll. He
crammed a battered old gray homburg on his head (I noticed his light tan
sombrero on the hatshelf), refused a coat (later he gladly accepted one
brought to him), grabbed one of his many walking sticks from a stand,
and off we set. He tottered out in energetic but unsteady fashion, and I
feared for him. A man appeared who seemed to be either a guard or male
nurse. But nobody offered the old man aid, and off we went, down pretty
steep slopes, up again, down uneven rock steps (he explained he had the
rock brought from Wales and put in to set off the fish ponds), across
steppingstones through a pond, through a field of high grass, up other
slopes, through the rose garden, into the Marlborough pavillion ("I built
this; my nephew Jack Churchill painted the charming frieze of the Battle
of Blenheim and the Duke, the Duchess, Prince Eugene, and Queen Anne,
in the four corners"), through a box hedge to the croquet ground, up some
more steps (here he tired, sat down on a brick wall, and we rested), and
then back into the house, where we sat in the hall and talked about his
American ancestors and racehorses.

He is astonishingly pink. His hands are quite delicate and not terribly
large or strong; nor are they as aged in appearance as one would expect.
His eyes are bloodshot but kind. His vision is good; a bit far-sighted but he
can read anything (with glasses). During our stroll, he spotted in the
distance and pointed out to me his black swans on a pond and a calf born
last week. He is proud of his black and white cattle: "They don't need
anything. They look after themselves. We don't have to bring them in,
even during the winter. They don't need any help in calving—only a bull."
He is devoted to his two ponds of fish; assured me they weren't goldfish
but golden carp (*Orfes*). (I think all goldfish are carp.) He tapped on the
edge of the pools when we arrived, and his nurse or detective reached

down for cans of food sitting there; the old man flung great gobs of it to the fish, who ate merrily while he watched them in proud silence.

Back at the house, while we were sitting there alone in the hall, his daughter Mary (young and pretty, who lives nearby) came popping in the door, gave him a buss on the head (now almost bald, with thin strands of snow white hair), popped off again after agreeing to come for dinner with someone helping him on his book. He has finished Volume II of the *History of the English-Speaking Peoples* (it comes out in November) and is determined to do Volumes III and IV. He doesn't have much new work on them (mainly editing and cutting), but he is including an entire new section on the Renaissance in Volume II. Churchill told me that he was both surprised and delighted by the enormous sales of his book in the United States. The first volume has been a best seller for weeks.

He wanted me to sign his visitor's book. Then, before I could even find out where it was, he forgot, rambled off on something else. You could see age and fatigue gripping him again. He got up to say farewell to me; gravely stood at the door, shook my hand, said "au revoir, au revoir" several times, waved to me, and was still standing at the open door when the car drove out of sight.

By far the most interesting part of the day and that which endured longest was when Churchill entered into a discussion of the present-day state of the world and what it might have been had his advice been heeded. He asked Montague Browne to bring him Volume VI of *The Second World War*, and then he read to me from Chapter XXXVI (pp. 522–527), commenting as he went along, looking up over his spectacles ruefully. In the end he maintained sadly that had his advice been followed, both peace and Western civilization would now be less menaced. He read to me at great length and in a strong voice. His basic thesis was that we went to Potsdam with a bad hand of cards; that the meeting should have been held earlier, while we were at our full military strength in Europe; and that we should not have agreed to reduce that strength without adequate and compensating concessions from the Russians.

Churchill admires Truman a lot. But Truman knew nothing when he first came in—although he learned fast. It was a tragedy that he had the initial ignorant period. It was then we lost Eastern Europe. Ike never understood or made any recommendations. We should have taken Berlin and Prague (where the United States had two armored divisions stranded for days just three days' march away). Following are some other topics Churchill discussed.

America should be temperate and wise about taking time to solve its Negro problem. "After all, you can't take twenty million of them into your belly just like that. Nonsense to say the black is the same as the white." He called for a copy of this morning's *Daily Sketch* with a picture of a Negro Salvation Army singer followed by a white Salvation Army lass. "Is that what they are going to have in Heaven?" he asked. "Is that what I am going to find there? If so, it is no place for me. I don't intend to go to a place like that."

There is, said he, no serious anti-American feeling here. People like young Amery are "bloody fools." Our destiny is together. "I'm half American, you know. You people pushed us out of Egypt. It was a mistake. But I harbor no resentment."

Undoubtedly in a decade or two China and Russia will be at odds. But he doesn't think China will be a tremendous power ever: It's never shown the capacity to develop so.

It is a profound mistake to back the Arabs against Israel. Turkey, Iraq, and Israel should be backstopped. Nasser is nothing. He is working with the Russians.

Woodrow Wilson was largely responsible for the crazy development of self-determination which is parcelling up the world. What about the Russian empire and colonies, the satellites and Baltic states? But the Baltic states are finished; they have been under Russia too long; too many hundreds of thousands of Balts have been deported or slain.

Churchill accepted getting out of Egypt (as a result of our pressure). But he never agreed on Sudanese independence; thinks it a bad thing. "Why should they have the same vote in the United Nations as us?"

He thought Nehru was not up to much good. India chose to go its own way. "Nehru has never done anything good for us." He is sure Nehru would never help England in another war; and might even be induced to join the Communist bloc against the West, through Russian and Chinese pressure.

The Commonwealth will get worse, not better. No point taking in all these Blacks like the Gold Coast. They will go their own way. And in another generation the Indians will be even more Indian.

He thinks Stalin was a great man; above all compared to Khrushchev and Bulganin. "Stalin never broke his word to me. We agreed on the Balkans. I said he could have Rumania and Bulgaria; he said we could have Greece (of course, only in our sphere, you know). He signed a slip of paper. And he never broke his word. We saved Greece that way. When we went in in 1944 Stalin didn't interfere. You Americans didn't help, you know."

How about the Civil War, I asked? Didn't Stalin double-cross him? No, that was local Communists.

He thought Khrushchev and Bulganin agreeable. He sat next to Khrushchev at dinner one night, and he was very pleasant. But not a great man; not like Stalin. Khrushchev and Bulganin had done their cause "measureless harm" by denigrating Stalin. They would never recover. It was an immense mistake. They could not maintain communism with liberty. And it would be much harder for them to return to dictatorship, because they had proven it wrong. (Bulganin told Churchill he had urged Khrushchev to make his anti-Stalin speech.) The Russians were now faced with the necessity of becoming really European, having a European policy. Inevitably that would lead to the satellites slipping gradually away.

He thought the Poznan revolt in Poland significant. But he didn't think anything of the 1953 East German revolt. (Of course, he was in power then and could do nothing; I suppose that's why he downgrades it.)

He thinks Tito is a big man; tough, intelligent, able.

The French were up against a great crisis. They were now showing more vigor and courage. But the challenge of Algeria would be their supreme test. As for himself, he thought the French should go ahead and reconquer Morocco and Tunisia.

He thought Dulles was "quite right, quite right" to declare Goa a Portuguese province and stand against Nehru.

He spoke at length about the virtues of "our aristocratic" heritage in English leadership. He was proud of Parliament as "the oldest and most important" organ of representative government in the world—"and the most powerful." He thought it shocking that MPs are not paid more. Then and there he decided he would speak Thursday (in three days) favoring an increase to 1,500 pounds a year in MPs' salary. "The House must face these facts courageously. There is nothing to be ashamed of. What does an American Senator receive? Ah, you see." (Then he decided ruefully he would not make the speech after all; didn't want to embarrass Eden.)

Spain? "I was with Franco, you know, when he started his revolt; not physically with him, but supported him. But when he accepted German and Italian help, that was different. Step by step I changed my policy. But Franco has given Spain two decades of stability."

He thinks the basis for policy now should be firm agreement among the United States, Britain, and West Germany. If the French want to come in, all right. Also the Lowlands, or Scandinavia, or Italy, anyone else. But that is the heart of it.

Adenauer "is a fine man. But the Germans are turning against him. He's the best they'll ever get." Maybe the Germans will turn sour again; who knows?

He asked me about Selwyn Lloyd's view on Cyprus. I told him. "Nonsense," said he, "that's no policy." But he wouldn't elaborate.

He is very proud of his few racehorses. "My grandfather, you know, founded Jerome Park in America." One horse won a good race; now has a bad fetlock; but he hopes to run him next month in a pretty rich German race.

He recalls his family association with *The New York Times*. "When the Irish [I suppose he means the Tweed ring] threatened my grandfather, he set up guns in the office and told them to come ahead; they didn't dare."

In summation, the thing that struck me most perhaps was the thought of talking all day with this kindly old man who had seen the last Dervish charge against Kitchener in Omdurman and had fought with the Spaniards against the Cuban insurrectionaries.

My final impression was an extraordinary experience of seeing him come fully alive and then, tired out by the effort, by the walk, our long reading from his work, the conversation, the entire physical and mental effort, to see all that dynamism fade away. It was like watching a very strong light bulb during an electrical crisis: First a faint reddening of the filament, then a flickering, then a glow, and then a brilliant blaze of light. Finally, after being blinded by the sustained glare, again flickering, subsiding, just a red filament; then nothing.

LONDON, *July 11, 1956*

PLEASANT talk with Lord Attlee in the House of Lords. I asked what his own feeling was concerning Khrushchev and Bulganin. He replied: "We thought Malenkov was a bigger man. Khrushchev is noisy and speaks a lot. Bulganin is more cautious. One thing that strikes me is that the Communists have always thought of the Kremlin as a Vatican. What the Pope said went. But Pope Stalin is gone. Today, in their own right, Mao Tse-tung and Tito are bigger figures in the Communist world than anybody in Russia."

I asked if he himself—and he had talked with Stalin many times at Potsdam—thought that Stalin was a great man. He replied, somewhat to my surprise (Attlee is small and mousey), "Stalin was not a big man. I saw him often and he did not impress me. Of course, he had control of his show, but he was not a man of any great foresight. He was a successful dictator but not a world statesman."

However, Attlee added hastily: "Khrushchev and Bulganin were on a much lower scale than Stalin. Stalin had the talents of an oriental despot. He had what is necessary to make a man dominate. But he had no grandeur of personality."

PRINCETON, NEW JERSEY, *August 1, 1956*

I SPENT the day with George Kennan, who is now out there at the Institute for Advanced Study. I lunched at his house, and afterward we sat around in the garden analyzing the world.

I asked Kennan if he thought if was possible for a man to be a good American Secretary of State both at home and abroad. He replied:

It's hard to be good both abroad and vis-à-vis our Congress, but possible to be successful abroad and vis-à-vis the American people. Certain political forces playing on Congress make it less able to understand good statesmanship than the people at large. Dulles has not played to United States opinion in general but to an influential part of that opinion—the right-wing Republicans—centering around Senator Knowland. Dulles could have been a good Secretary abroad and at home if he had stated the case frankly and reasonably at home, but he preferred only to convince Knowland.

The actual policies of the Eisenhower administration are very little different from those of the Democrats before. But the words have been different.
There is a general insensitivity to foreign feelings in this government.

I then asked what Kennan thought should be the relative roles of the
President and the Secretary of State in the formulation of foreign policy.
He replied:

The two positions are in tandem. Both encompass the same responsibilities
in the field of foreign affairs. But the Secretary is only an assistant to the
President in foreign affairs. The President's is the basic responsibility. At
some time in the future of this country, the President will have to concentrate in one person all subordinate responsibilities in the entire field of
foreign affairs. This can be done either by setting up a Deputy President or
Prime Minister in charge of all aspects—military, foreign trade, propaganda,
diplomacy, etc.—or to make the Secretary of State what he was probably
supposed to be under the Constitution. That envisioned him as the senior
Cabinet member, with a predominant position in all foreign policy.

The system we have today is a system of self-paralysis. There is an
extreme dissipation of the means to make and execute policy. This is deeply
wrong. In fact, the bane of the performance of our government lies in the
committee system. We tend to tell these committees that anything they agree
upon will be OK. The alternative to this, instead of allotting responsibility to
committees, would be to pick one official and make him ultimately responsible for decision. He could arrive at this decision anyway he wants, consulting with committees or individuals, while his individual responsibility would
be rigidly fixed, and he would stand or fall by his decision.

The main frustration in foreign policy in Washington is the feeling of
never being able to manipulate through the labyrinth of conflicting responsibilities and committees. We don't act enough because of this paralyzing
system, and time and again reality passes us by.

I told George I was interested in his observations that racial prejudice as
expressed in the United States hurt our prestige abroad. But how did he
propose to eliminate such prejudice? He answered:

There is no answer but courage and political self-sacrifice on the part of
our leaders. They should say to Americans that we cannot hope to aspire to
any position of moral leadership for this country unless we can succeed in
giving a happy place in our own life to the colored people here. Look at the
people around the earth. Compared to most denizens of this world, the
American colored people are gentle and good-humored. They are intensely
human. They have a good sense of humor and a warm sensibility. Their
innate courtesy towards each other is greater than the courtesy of the whites.

There shouldn't be any problem of absorption. Fortunately for this country they are not difficult people like the sullen Peruvian Indians. Think of
what things would be like if our Negroes had organized something like the
Stern Gang in Palestine. Save for a few intellectuals, the Russians never
succeeded in taking them over. But they are deeply unhappy. They don't feel
admitted to equal citizenship. They have been asked to make the ultimate

contribution by joining the armed forces, but they are not totally in our society.

There are few people in conspicuous positions of government now who combine forces of intellect and character. One must combine both. Truman was very much a man of the people. People like myself actually were more different from him than from Eisenhower and Dulles. But Truman had more good-natured acceptance of intellectuals. An intellectual could work under the Democrats. This quality has been sacrificed to the Mammon of internal security, to the concept of the colorless man.

At this point, Kennan remarked with a sour grin: "It took Foster Dulles to make a Democrat out of me. I never thought of being expelled by the State Department. I never thought I would be dropped by our government after being expelled from Moscow. Surely, this must give the Russians the feeling that they managed to eliminate me as a force in our government."

I asked what George would do, taking things as they are today, if he were responsible for planning United States policy on the Suez Canal and Nile River issues. He said it was, of course, difficult for him to answer this because he no longer had access to State papers. But then he went on:

> For years I have felt strongly—and five years ago I wrote Loy Henderson on this—that we were making a great mistake playing up to these Middle Eastern tin-pot dictators. Today, the chickens are coming home to roost. These men are not our friends. Concessions made to them in return for nothing earn nothing for us. I would like us to stick right by France and Britain on this Suez quarrel. We must stand up to Nasser in the strongest possible way. After all, we were very influential in getting the British out of Suez.
>
> Sooner or later, the United States government must recognize that what our oil companies do in the Middle East is so much the concern of our national interest that it must be controlled by us. The financing and the profits of these companies can remain a private matter, but the government must supervise their interests. We can't pass out such huge sums without considering it a part of our foreign policy. The royalties paid to the Arab sheikhs are not too little; they are far too high. The theory of giving 50 percent to the owner of a natural resource when someone else develops it totally—and this 50 percent is net, not gross—is absolutely cockeyed. Look how we corrupt these sheikhs.

WASHINGTON, *August 5, 1956*

WHEN I was in Eastern Europe earlier this year, I applied in seven separate capitals for a Chinese Communist visa—Moscow, Warsaw, Prague, Budapest, Sofia, and Belgrade. Today, to my astonishment, I received a cable from Peking instructing me to pick up my visa—which had been authorized—either in Hong Kong or Moscow. I have decided to go via Hong Kong, after the San Francisco Republican convention.

Legally, I am forbidden to go by the State Department, but I think this is a pretty good test case. After all, we had no relations with Bulgaria when I went there, and correspondents were also ordered to stay out of Hungary. But I visited both, advising the Department I would do so ahead of time, and I wasn't even slapped on the wrist. I intend to take this up with the Department, at least unofficially.

WASHINGTON, *August 6, 1956*

THIS morning I went to the White House. Eisenhower looked thin and pale but quite healthy, considering what the poor fellow has been through. He started right off talking about the Middle East and the Suez crisis. A few days ago it looked as if things were going to blow up, "but I put my foot down and stopped the drift." He sent Dulles over to London and tried to persuade the British and French that things must, if at all possible, be settled at the conference table.

But he realizes that the British and French people want action. He understands their viewpoints. The French think they can bail out their North African situation by getting tough, and the British are worried about oil and the entire Mediterranean.

Ike is furious at Nasser. He says we were willing to play ball with him on the assumption he was trying to help his position. We were fully behind the project for the High Aswan Dam and were going to really assist him in financing this. But we had to call a halt when he started flirting with the Russians.

Eisenhower did not see how Nasser could possibly figure on getting $100 million a year out of the Suez Canal to contribute to the building of his High Dam project. Even if he raised Canal tolls—which he will probably do—the total income (gross) of the company last year was less than $100 million.

To date, we have no positive information that the Russians put him up to the Suez nationalization, but they are clearly trying to "fish in troubled waters." It's too bad we don't have the old Turkish (Ottoman) empire. They still had plenty to give up, if necessary, under pressure. But none of the little successor states do. Take Syria, for example. What have they got to give up? (A curious view.) Why, a Turkish empire could have been the third great power today!

A situation has come about in the world where the weaker powers find it possible to blackmail the stronger through their very weakness. Wilson's theories of self-determination have let loose a movement whose end cannot be seen. Last year Eisenhower prepared a speech in which he said the United States was behind self-determination for any people that wanted independence and was capable of economically supporting it. His advisers jumped on this phrase and made him strike it out. They said everyone would hop on his back if he put in that economic qualification.

But it was necessary. Take the Central American countries, for example. Panama has a population of only 900,000. Its annual income is only $50 million. Most of this comes from the Canal. It couldn't support itself otherwise. Yet it manages to keep ambassadors all around the world. How? The President can't figure it out. There isn't, he says, a single Central American country capable of living economically or politically entirely by itself and without aid.

Swiveling from side to side in his desk chair, Ike (as he so often does) kept thinking aloud. He said it was of course possible that the Arab countries would cut off oil supplies and the pipelines, which they could easily do. Then the only thing that would happen would be of benefit to the Russians. England probably has a six-week oil reserve on hand; the Continent about four weeks. We could shift everything, open up our supplies, mobilize all available tankers, put ourselves on gasoline rationing, and help the situation along. Meanwhile, the Arab states would collapse without the money. But who would benefit by this?

Yet if war comes, it would be hard to limit. Ike is convinced the Russians fear war dreadfully and, in the end, would do anything to prevent it. But it is hard to calculate their estimate of the situation. Some kind of order must be established, but it is difficult to see what it can be; or will be.

Eisenhower has little respect for the Russian leader. He thinks Khrushchev is about the equivalent of "a drunken railway hand." Bulganin "looks like someone who does what he is told."

I lunched with Bob Murphy, Deputy Under Secretary of State. Our main conversation was about the Chinese visa issue. Quite unofficially and as a friend, Bob said that in my position he would be sorely tempted to go. But, he added, the government had in no way changed its attitude banning such trips by Americans. He talked with Dulles about it this morning. They were against anyone going. If it were January (in other words, after the elections), their attitude could be less tough, but this is a hot political question.

Bob promised: "If you get locked up, at any rate, I'll send a few newspapers to you—if you go." I told him I favored going. This was a competitive business. How would I feel if a rival columnist went? Bob allowed that maybe in my position, were he abroad, he'd already be on the way. But there would be no official change in attitude.

CHICAGO, *August 12, 1956*

THIS afternoon, I had a talk with former President Truman in his suite at the Blackstone Hotel, specially papered with the seals of the various states and territories. He looked spry, full of confidence. Yesterday, he threw support to Harriman and opened up the Democratic convention.

He regretted that Dean Acheson wasn't here (hadn't been invited). Acheson was "the greatest Secretary of State we ever had." On Spain, he said he would only like to see it in NATO "when it gets a free government. But I don't like Franco and he knows it." On Germany, he said it was "only common sense" to keep enough American troops there for an adequate time until West Germany is rearmed.

I asked if he favored a "liberation" policy for the satellites. "Do you want a world war?" he countered. "There's no other alternative. Anything else is hooey and for political purposes." How about trying to encourage some form of national communism or Titoism there as a first step, I inquired. "You can't do that," he said. "How are you going to get behind the Iron Curtain and operate? You'd get your neck sliced off. That's hooey too. You find out how you can do this; and then it could be done. But it can't."

CHICAGO, *August 13, 1956*

I SPENT the evening with Adlai Stevenson in his Blackstone suite with just a few of his friends and family. We watched the second session of the convention on TV. Adlai was both amused and amusing about Governor Clement's keynote speech, a real old-fashioned rabble-rouser. At one point, Clement spoke of the unity of the party. "Let us pray," observed Stevenson. When Clement said: "It's better to serve in the house of the Lord than to sit in the seat of the mighty," Adlai said: "I'm not too sure of that."

SAN FRANCISCO, *August 23, 1956*

CALLED up Uncle Arthur to say good-bye. "Where are you going?" he asked. "China," I told him. "My God, you can't do that." "Why not? I have a visa, and quite unofficially I warned Bob Murphy I would do so."

Then the whole sad story came out. It seems that in a moment of mental aberration Uncle A. promised Dulles he wouldn't let anyone from *The Times* go to China before Dulles gives his okay. "I know I was a damned fool," says A. "But I gave my word and there's nothing we can do about it. And just think, if it were broken by someone with my own name!"

I agreed he was a damn fool and we were stuck with it.

WASHINGTON, *October 17, 1956*

LONG talk with Foster Dulles. He greeted me in a most friendly way despite the fact that I have been rather needling him in recent columns. "Why come here?" he asked with a grin. "I thought nobody in this office knew anything about foreign affairs." This morning I had written that the anger of France and Britain over the Suez situation did not yet seem to have percolated through to the State Department.

I asked what he had to say about U.S. policy in Eastern Europe. He replied: "On the whole there is a growing desire for nationalistic forms of government in that area. Above all, this is true in East Germany, Poland, Czechoslovakia, and Hungary. The example and influence of Tito is very useful. He has prospered under this. His example tends to make the mouths of the satellites water with envy. We have sharp differences with Tito on domestic policy. But his attraction on the satellites is useful. There is a parallelism there in our interest. We are not giving him aid to please him or vice versa. But it helps both our purposes."

On the Middle East, he said:

It is almost impossible to foresee a satisfactory solution. The decision to carve Israel out had a great deal of merit but it raised an equal number of problems. I have studied many of these jointly with the British. But we need a period of relative quiet during which the emotions must be calm. The Jews and the Arabs got along for a long time in many areas. The problem is not inherently insoluble.

But we must first get emotions to die down. Then Israel can become an important supplement to the rest of the Middle East. It is better equipped for industrial activity than the other countries. A solution theoretically can be seen. But it cannot be brought about during the present instability. And, of course, the Suez crisis has made everything worse.

There is a great tendency on the part of the French and the British to assume that because they are allied with us in NATO we will support them everywhere. However, I can show you the report of the Senate Foreign Relations Committee in 1949, before NATO was ratified, in which we pointed out that we were not allying ourselves in colonial areas with the NATO powers, but only in a specific NATO area.

NEW YORK, *October 22, 1956*

LAST night, dinner with Averell and Marie Harriman at their New York house. Averell was bitter about our foreign policy. He thinks our world position is sagging; Eisenhower simply refuses to make decisions, and anyway, he doesn't know what is going on because nobody tells him. Dulles is a disaster as Secretary of State.

Harriman, by the way, thought my idea of naming the defeated Presidential nominee as our next ambassador to NATO was excellent. He is deeply worried about what is happening to NATO. The terms of reference and powers of the American Ambassador have been drastically cut.

COLUMBIA, SOUTH CAROLINA, *November 2, 1956*

I CAME in here last night in order to see James F. Byrnes. I wanted to ask two things: Whether it is inherent in the office that a Secretary of State should be unpopular; and how one could reconcile the Southern racial situation with American overseas propaganda and diplomatic interests. He replied:

> Any effort of the Secretary of State to please a local situation is bound to be disastrous. This makes for unpopularity in his office. I don't recall any effort to fix foreign policy to meet the political needs of a community, with the exception of the case of Israel back in 1945. Both parties were then trying to please groups interested in raising the number of immigrants to Palestine. Ernie Bevin told me representatives of the Arabs and Jews were at that time in London. Bevin assured me he had learned their conversations had been very amicable. Attlee and his Cabinet hoped real progress was being made toward satisfactory settlement in Palestine—satisfactory to both sides. The main issue at that time was the number of immigrants allowed in.
>
> But Truman cabled Attlee, telling him the U.S. position: between 200,000 and 300,000 Jews should be immediately permitted to enter Palestine. He wanted me to reiterate this to Bevin. It was nice of Truman to tell me this and he added: "I hope I haven't thrown a monkey wrench into your machine."
>
> I asked the President if he had already sent this request to the British. He replied in the affirmative. Truman further told me that Yom Kippur was starting and he had heard that Tom Dewey was going to make a speech in the following week advocating the same thing. He wanted to make his speech before Dewey.
>
> I remember Bevin telling me he knew I had nothing to do with this. But he added: "You can't run foreign policy to meet the needs of your New York elections. There are too many of them." He was referring to the fact there were mayoralty and gubernatorial elections as well as presidential ones.
>
> This sort of thing cannot be done. You must keep in mind the interests of the people as a whole rather than the interests of any particular group of the people. Our Polish friends have always been enthusiastic for Polish interests. There are lots of Poles in Michigan and they managed to make life miserable for poor old Arthur Vandenberg. In New Jersey there are lots of Ukrainians and they have been very outspoken. As these various groups press their interests, the Congressmen and Senators often try to pass the buck to the Secretary of State and the President rather than offend groups of constituents and thereby lose votes. A man can introduce a resolution favorable to such pressure groups of constituents just to gain popularity.
>
> The Secretary of State must be a whipping boy. He must be strong enough to resist demands from various groups having at heart some particular or local grievance. But the pressures should continue. That is the way our democracy works. There is no way of preventing this nor should there be. But some person in office must be strong enough to say no. That is the Secretary of State.

I asked Byrnes how he could relate our position and prestige abroad in terms of Jeffersonian democracy with the idea of segregation at home. He replied:

There is no answer to this save the facts. The difficulty is that the Northern press so distorts the facts concerning the people from the Potomac down to the Gulf. And the information of the Northern press is what goes abroad —not the point of view of the South.

The Negroes have money. They are in the banks, the stores, business. They are lawyers. There is, of course, still a shortage of Negro doctors. I am helping two Negroes myself to study to become physicians. But this economic well-being is not reported. The Negroes are making wonderful progress. Negro schools are often better than white schools because they are newer. We should prevent a picture from going abroad that is limited to the Northern viewpoint.

PARIS, *December 12, 1956*

THIS afternoon, I went over to de Gaulle's headquarters. The general began one of his usual gloomy tours d'horizon by stating that nowhere in the world does any government or any statesman seem to know what he wants. As a military man he was astonished by the ineptness of the Suez operation. It should have been planned to accomplish its objectives within two days on a lightning basis. Instead of that, there was a ridiculous long-range, tedious, drawn-out plan for something the equivalent—in terms of logistics and the length of time—of the Normandy landing.

De Gaulle said neither the Eastern powers (meaning Russia) nor the West have any policies in Europe. Here too, they are simply reacting to events as they occur. When the revolution in Hungary developed, Washington and Moscow were surprised. Neither knew what to do about it.

The fact is that the dictatorship of communism is a thing that is ending. It doesn't correspond anymore to today's requirements. It was possible in Russia after the Czars because Russia had been beaten and had to organize its economy at all costs. The price was, of course, immensely high. Millions of people lost their lives. But that is not important in Russia where they have such an enormous population. They succeeded in organizing their economy and finally, in the last war, in beating Germany.

But now they don't need communism anymore. Even Khrushchev knows this. To complete the defeat of Germany, the Russians had to control all of Eastern Europe. But now this is done. Germany is no longer an important menace. There is no need for communism in Poland anymore and all the Poles know this, even Gomulka [at that time a nationalist-minded Polish Communist who had been brought to power from the jail where Stalinism sent him]. Even Nagy [the Hungarian rebel leader, also a nationalist Communist, who was hanged by Khrushchev] knew there was no longer any need for the Russians or for communism in Hungary.

In the future, there is bound to be a world war. This is the future of the world. When or how it will come I don't know. It will come whether there is a revolt in East Germany which drags in the West Germans; or whether there is no such revolt. There will be a danger to the world brought about because Prussia revolts against Communist and Soviet domination; or, equally because Prussia does not revolt. War is a law of the human species. What Boussuet called "providence" is responsible. War is the law of the species. The moment for this war will come when the people of the world wish to destroy themselves, or to risk that by changing things. But, the pretext for such a war or the men who will start it cannot be foreseen. After all, the assassination of an Austrian archduke was surely not an adequate pretext for World War I, with all its casualties.

He added:

I don't believe in NATO. What real worth has it shown? The atomic bomb has big value. There is also real value to the friendship between the United States, Britain, and France. These are the things that kept Russia back in Europe. But NATO? Pooh! What value has that? Where are NATO's divisions? The reason the French don't mobilize is NATO. What reason is there to mobilize forty divisions if General Norstad is in charge of France's defense? You can't take away from people their own responsibilities for themselves. Yet this is what NATO has done and this is why it is failing.

He said:

There is no hate for the United States in France. France remains friendly to the United States. But the French people don't like the American people. The United States is our friend and will remain so; but the American people are not regarded sympathetically. Nevertheless, the United States will remain our friend. From time to time, when moments of great danger arise, then only the United States and France will remain and people will tend to forget the Americans and French who do not get on so well. Of course, during intervening periods, the fact that our interests are not really the same will continue to appear more obviously.

He made plain that he was increasingly pondering the possibilities and circumstances of extra-legal violence as a means to personal power and national reform. He said: "It is true that the more complicated affairs get and the more apparent the danger seems, the more people will come to recognize that the French regime lacks force, willpower, or popularity. Naturally the French people will then be inspired to look elsewhere. But so far any such development is purely speculative, not political. How it develops in the future depends upon events. We need responsible men in power. Small men cannot answer to the responsibilities of the world. Small men cannot handle great events."

I inquired whether the French army could be considered a potential political force. He replied (interestingly for a general, a career officer): "The army in France has no political force. It is, of course, always for order and *la patrie*. It is also always against weak governments. But that does not suffice for the army to wish to be the state. No revolution in French history was ever made by the army. The eighteenth-century revolution was made by the bourgeoisie. The people made Bonaparte. Not even

Pétain was made by the army—that was Parliament. And de Gaulle was not made by the army."

He said: "Revolutions in France must be made by the people. When the people *desire* a change, such a change is brought about quickly. This has been true each time there was a revolution in our history." I inquired how one could know in advance that the popular mood was ready to demand change—for example a return of de Gaulle? He answered: "That will not be difficult to see. You will even see it in the newspapers, bad as they are. When the people wish change you will see this reflected in the newspapers because the newspapers are always ready to sell themselves to the new authorities." He considered that there had not yet been any more than faint intimations of this, but he knew enormous shifts in public attitude could develop very quickly. Thus, he told me, he had recently read a collection of newspapers from the year 1815, when Napoleon came back from Elba and marched northward from the Mediterranean to Paris (a fascinating insight into de Gaulle's thought patterns some eighteen months before he regained power after an army coup). The general recalled that at first, papers were saying in their headlines: "Order restored on the Mediterranean coast." Then, when Napoleon reached Lyons, headlines read: "Tyrant arrives at Lyons." Finally, according to de Gaulle, when Napoleon got to the capital, the same newspapers printed in their headlines: "His Majesty the Emperor in Paris."

To conclude this colloquy, I asked the general if he thought it necessary to have a period of chaos in France before he could come back. He replied "Yes" and added: "We must have some chaos first. This regime was made against me. Therefore it cannot call upon de Gaulle to save itself. De Gaulle is not prepared to save this regime." Did he think, I inquired, that chaos would be accompanied by bloodshed? He replied: "Blood? There is always a little blood. There is blood being shed in Hungary today. *Hélas. Que faire?*"

PARIS, *December 14, 1956*

THIS afternoon I had a talk with Franz-Josef Strauss, Federal Defense Minister for the West German Republic, a burly, powerful-looking young man. He recalled—which is true—that he had had a strongly anti-Nazi record. Our conversation roved over many subjects.

Strauss is very disturbed by the moral situation in which the world finds itself. Are we to remain helpless to save decent people in the Soviet bloc merely because of the fear of total war? If this is to be the case, doesn't it prove that Hitler was really right? If Hitler had had atomic weapons in 1939, he would have been allowed to get away with everything and murder anyone he wished. Not even England would have dared to go to war against him if it meant global destruction. If the present logic is followed to its conclusion, it means only that the Soviets can do things equally horrible merely because they are stronger and the weapons in existence are more dangerous. Were the war criminals of Nuremberg hanged because of their crimes or because they were not powerful enough to commit them? This is a grave moral problem. Was it a question of the Nazis' power or their wickedness?

PARIS, *December 15, 1956*

YESTERDAY evening Dulles invited me in for a drink chez Dillon. Dulles said the main problem facing us now was this: if all our eggs are in a nuclear basket, the Russians can do things and get away with them because it simply would not be worth dropping the atom bomb in order to stop them. We have to be prepared to reply in degree according to the offense. He said: "I always wanted us to have the *capacity* for nuclear retaliatory power—but not to depend totally upon it." (I think he is revising his policy a bit here.)

Later I had lunch with Bill Tyler, head of the Western European Division of the State Department. As far as Washington knows, it was originally planned Israel should attack Egypt on November 7—the day after our elections. This date was moved up as a consequence of the Hungarian uprising when it was figured that Russia would be occupied in Eastern Europe and UN attention could be focused there. The French and the British, who were obviously in collusion with Israel, had drawn up a list for a dummy government of Egypt. Nasser clearly got wind of this and rounded up and shot forty-five Egyptian officers, including the chief of the air force.

PARIS, *January 17, 1957*

WE invited the Dillons for a farewell lunch at a little bistro. Ernest Hemingway was there and joined us for champagne and coffee. Hemingway was charming. He thanked me for all the assistance I tried to give to D, his former bodyguard, later jailed as a collaborator. He agreed there was nothing to do for the poor fellow; he had thought about it a great deal and was trying to imagine writing about him; but in the end, when he boiled it down, there was nothing to write. The tragedy was the fellow did have a police record. If D had been in the British army he would have gotten the DSO—probably the Victoria Cross. Unfortunately, here, he got nothing but a kick in the pants.

I asked about his days in Paris when he was an intimate friend of Ezra Pound and whether it was true he used to box with him. He said he tried to teach Ezra how to box, but it wasn't much good. He couldn't move very well. He has immense admiration for Pound, although his political ideas are simply terrible. Hemingway and T. S. Eliot had just sent a letter to the U.S. Attorney General requesting that Pound be released from St. Elizabeth's Hospital. After all he is "just a crazy—the kind of crazy you find in towns all over the United States. When he lived up in Nantucket he was regarded as the local crazy."

Hemingway said any poet is crazy. He pointed to his head as he said that. The world would be a sad place if we didn't have crazy poets in it. He thought Ezra Pound should be sent back to Italy to spend the rest of his days there writing more beautiful poetry. And if Pound started to talk to people about the necessity of "killing all the Jews," he was "prepared to tell Ezra in advance that I will go to Italy and spank him personally." After all, nobody paid any attention to Pound except as a poet.

I asked him if Buck Lanham was the model for the hero in *Across the River and into the Trees*. He said it was largely Buck and also a fellow named X. "You probably don't know X. He was before your time. But I fought with him long ago. He was in the Foreign Legion and later on he organized an English outfit." He said X was somewhat eccentric and was always ordering people shot. He would tell Hemingway: "Take so-and-so out and shoot him." Hemingway would take so-and-so out, but would not shoot him. Later in the evening, X would ask Hemingway: "Did you carry out my orders?" Hemingway would say yes. Still later in the evening (after a certain amount of alcohol) X would say: "I wish I hadn't shot so-and-so." Hemingway would say: "I'll bring him around in the morning, Sir." Hemingway remarked: "This was an interesting experience for a kid."

I asked how his book was coming—*The Great Project*, a novel about World War II. He said it was almost finished; it would only take about two or three more years. He had been working on it eight years. He gets up at 6:00 every morning and forces himself to write. He added: "You can't write if you don't practice discipline."

Hemingway didn't drink much, but as soon as he had a few glasses of wine, his speech became even more pronouncedly slurred. If he didn't have such a magnificent constitution, I think he would have died long ago from too much alcohol. I only hope he lives long enough to finish his book.

PARIS, *January 18, 1957*

OUT to SHAPE for a long talk with Field Marshal Montgomery. He is browned off by the fact that he was never consulted in advance about the British invasion in Egypt. It was evident he would have liked to have commanded the expedition himself.

Monty said Russia had carefully reckoned the cost of aggression in the West and decided that, because of the existence of NATO, it was impossible. Therefore, Russia wanted to outflank Europe, going through the Middle East by purely cold war means.

> Moscow has no intention of direct attack. It is just trying to exploit the chaotic situation in the Middle East. The principal trouble there is the Israeli-

Arab problem. That is the guts of the whole thing. And of course Arab nationalism is very heady wine. Also there are rivalries among the Arab states.

I think Britain was quite right to go into Egypt. But they did it in the wrong way and at the wrong time. In a military sense, the needs of that area are as different from those of western Europe as a village cricket match is from a test match. In western Europe we could only have a test match. But the Middle East is village cricket.

The Israelis hit Egypt for six. It only took them three days. We should have let them finish the job themselves. The only people who can fight in that area are the Israelis. The rest are no good. They have no unity. They are jealous of each other.

Monty dismissed as a lot of bluff the Soviet threat to use rockets with nuclear warheads against England and France if they didn't get out of Egypt. He added: "Russia never had the slightest intention of rocketing England. Russia is physically capable of doing this, but we could do the same thing back. Physically, they would be destroyed in the end. The Russians haven't the slightest intention of doing anything that would bring on a war."

Monty said:

Diplomats don't seem to understand that the game being played is poker. They play it as if it were chess. There are three players in the game and all of them have got some good cards. Israel had a good deal of Egyptian territory. Nasser had the Suez Canal. And Britain had a good buildup of military strength in the Eastern Mediterranean.

When the United Nations told us to stop the expedition, we should have played it like poker. We should have said: "OK, I'll see you." Just like poker. The game could have gone on. And if we had been frightened about going on, we should have let Israel go it alone. The Israelis would have had the Canal in no time.

He was convinced that the Russians would not send volunteers to fight in the Middle East. That was only propaganda.

They never had any intention of doing it. The Russians will take no steps leading to war. Russian manpower couldn't sustain a war.

The only reason there has been no war since 1948 is because of the strength we have built up as a deterrent against war. I mean NATO.

Rule one of war is, Don't march on Moscow. That is rule one of war. Lots of people have tried it. But nobody has succeeded. Napoleon got there but he had to get out. Hitler didn't even get there. You can destroy Moscow without invading it. You can destroy it with atomic rockets. The function of an army is to hold. The offensive is for the air.

Rule two of war is don't march on China. China is like a sponge. You can squeeze it and everything is forced out of it. Any army that gets into China will be squeezed and forced out. Just like a sponge. You have to stand back and pound China with rockets. There is no point in getting into it.

13

ATHENS, *January 25, 1957*

I WENT OUT TO TATOI TODAY TO SEE KING PAUL AT HIS COUNTRY home. Paul is quite pro-Tito now (an interesting contrast with his views a few years ago). He has full confidence in Tito's honesty, friendship, true neutrality as between blocs, and alliance. He thinks Jugoslavia would move if Bulgaria attacked Greece—"Although of course you never know; the Jugoslavs didn't act in 1940. But that was a different team."

The British were being particularly obtuse about Cyprus. When Lord Halifax was here last Easter (1956), Ambassador Peake brought him to the palace. Paul told Halifax: "This is something to be settled by statesmen, not politicians. You should run up a Greek flag over the island and right away I would be prepared to give Britain base rights at the three finest naval bases in the eastern Mediterranean—Agostoli in Cephalonia, Milos, and Suda Bay in Crete. Why the harbor at Milos can hold all the navies of the world together." But Halifax paid no attention. "He just sat there, looking glum, holding his head in his hands. And he never passed my proposition on. Why don't they have sense instead of trying to treat us like a bunch of white niggers?"

ATHENS, *January 26, 1957*

AN hour's chat this morning with Caramanlis, Prime Minister since October, 1955. He was wearing a tweed suit and, instead of smoking, played constantly with a string of amber beads.

He said he was a man "of the West" and would always remain so, even if he were the last in Greece. He had won the 1956 elections handily, but all sixteen opposition parties (some in Parliament, some not) were gunning for him on Cyprus. He was standing for moderation. He would not allow riots against the British, and he tries to keep the lid on parliamentary discussions. He was seeking a reasonable solution, recognizing that while justice was on Greece's side, political expediency must also be considered. But his opponents were screaming for Greece to leave NATO, quit UN, become neutralist. He was confident his government could ride out the storm. But if the UN debate goes sour—above all if the United States doesn't make an adequate stand for Greece—things could change swiftly. The Greeks are very volatile.

KARACHI, *February 3, 1957*

THIS afternoon, I went over to see my old friend Iskander Mirza, who is now president of Pakistan, and, although his constitutional powers are limited, remains the recognized strong man. We strolled around his garden while he talked.

He thinks Afghanistan is down the drain. Prince Daud, the Afghan Prime Minister, is unduly influenced by the Russians. Mirza told Daud during his visit to Kabul: "You people are a novelty. Communism is usually introduced from the bottom. You are introducing it from the top." The Russians are all over the place. They are building two broad military highways south from the Oxus border to Pakistan. The King's uncle has gotten Mohammed Zahir interested in women—and as a result he has lost any faint interest in political affairs. Mirza mused: "Why is it that royal families vary so? His father was an able man. He is a useless weakling."

He still favors "controlled democracy" and fears real democracy with universal suffrage would wreck Pakistan—"which I won't permit."

He hates Nasser and mistrusts him.

> Why didn't the British plan a decent operation? If they'd had the sense to go on forty-eight hours more, Israel would have done the job for them. Then they could have pretended to save Egypt when they intervened. The British made a mess of it. The Israelis fought magnificently. They are a good, modern army. They are brave and have a cause. [Odd from a Muslim statesman!]
>
> When King Saud was here he started to tell me about Nasser's victory. I told him he was mad; that he didn't know the facts; that he just listened to Egyptian sources. What kind of an army wins a victory, I asked him, by losing to half its number? Thirty-eight Egyptian MIGs took refuge on your Saudi Arabian airfields. Is that the way to fight?
>
> Twenty thousand Israelis smashed forty thousand Egyptians. They could have taken Ismailia and Suez if the British hadn't messed things up. That would have cooked Nasser. I asked Saud—Who do you think is trying to upset your dynasty? Is it England or France? No. It's Nasser. Yet you employ Egyptian officers to train your army. That made him think. The Arabs are worthless. If God and 120,000 prophets couldn't make something of Arabia, certainly they can't.

PESHAWAR, PAKISTAN, *February 9, 1957*

STURDY tribesmen stride in from the mountains before their camel trains, greeting each other solemnly with a *"Stare Mashe"* (May you never be tired), and replying *"Khowar Mashe"* (May you never be poor). In the storyteller's bazaar a bearded old Pathan smokes a pipe of hashish, and, tears rolling down his leathery cheeks, tells how Alexander the Great searched for the fountain of youth. When he found it and was about to drink, an ancient cripple hobbled over and warned him against it, "Lest you become like myself, five-thousand years old and neither able to live nor die."

Yesterday we drove to Swat, crossing a bridge of boats over the Kabul River at Nowshera and turning north. The people of Kaffiristan (between Chitral and Afghanistan) are so primitive they still leave their dead out unburied.

In the village below Malakand are vain old men with beards dyed red and eyelashes shaded black. Swat, on the other side of Malakand, is a pleasant, high valley with green fields and grazing flocks. It is rimmed by snowcapped mountains and filled with orchards of olives and oranges. On the Swat River is a ferryboat of inflated goatskins.

Execution in Swat is curious. A convicted murderer can bail himself out if the dead man's family agrees to accept a fixed sum of blood money. Otherwise one of the murdered man's family is assigned to shoot the murderer—before an approved group of police officials.

PAKISTAN, *February 10, 1957*

SPENT the day in the Afridi country around Kohat Pass. Each mud or stone house in the tribal territory is built like a fort with a wall and shot-tower (just in case). The villages are administered by local maliks who arm their own Khasildars. Afridis stroll along the road with rifles slung across their backs.

At the village of Darra is a fantastic "cottage industry" of arms production. They make everything from revolvers, rifles, and shotguns to tommy guns, machine guns, and three-inch cannon. All is done by hand with hand-turned lathes and little bellows furnaces. The steel used to be stolen from railways (possibly still is). In each weapon is stenciled the name of the foreign firm from which it has been copied—British, American, and Russian (often misspelled). I saw a little can of these stencils. Darra makes 250 rifles (303 bore) a day plus other weapons and has been in this backyard business for eighty years. I bought a little Webley-Scott .32 revolver (90 rupees, or about $18) made in "Birminoam London." Everything, even the screws and bakelite (from stolen rubber tires) for butts is made here. The eighty-five-year-old chief, Malik Samand Khan, of the

Zarghun Khel Afridi tribe, told me: "Give us an atomic bomb and we will copy it."

KABUL, AFGHANISTAN, *February 12, 1957*

THIS morning I had a talk for an hour and a half with Lemar-e-'Ali, Sardar Mohammed Na'im, first cousin of the King and Foreign Minister. He is tall, slender, aristocratic-looking in his early forties.

I said I had the impression that Afghanistan's foreign policy during the nineteenth century and until the outbreak of World War II was primarily to try and balance off Russia and Great Britain. If this were correct, wasn't Afghanistan now seeking to have the United States fill in the vacuum caused by Britain's disappearance from the Indian subcontinent. He replied: "Presently there is no power except the United States to create a balance against the Soviet Union."

KABUL, AFGHANISTAN, *February 14, 1957*

THIS morning I called on Prince Mohammed Daud, Prime Minister, cousin of the King, and strong man. He has a forceful, intelligent face, long nose, heavy jaw; is very sure of himself.

He said: "I can assure you that this will be the very last country in the world to become Communist."

NEW DELHI, INDIA, *February 19, 1957*

LUNCHED and talked for two and a half hours with Nehru under a peach tree whose pale pink blossoms drifted onto our plates. Afterward, we admired his pet panda. Black, white, and wooly, like an expensive toy, it is kept in a large net cage built around a tree. We went in and he fed it dates and bamboo leaves and played with it. Its mate died a few weeks ago. Nehru clearly loves animals. Has a delightful golden retriever pup which he caressed fondly. The only people there were Marina and myself, his niece (Madam Pandit's daughter), and her husband.

Nehru was wearing a white Gandhi cap which he later took off, exposing a sudden bald head much paler than his sunburned face. Also white, tight pants and a buttoned, homespun jacket. A rose was inserted in the second buttonhole.

I asked if he really had written (under a pseudonym) the analysis of Nehru published in a Calcutta review in 1937. He said yes, he had written it for his own amusement then sent it to a woman friend. She passed it to someone else, who published it. Nobody guessed he had written it, and Gandhi was even indignant, thinking some enemy was attacking Nehru.

I asked if he would stand by the self-analysis today; that the weaknesses of character he had attributed (tendency to dictatorship, etc.) had not come out in his political administration. He said that, after all, if a man could see such character weaknesses in himself and discuss them, that was proof in advance that he would never succumb to them.

He spoke of jail with a certain nostalgia. He was in a group of twelve, and they shared the cooking chores. The only thing he ever learned to cook was "various preparations of eggs." Incidentally, he said he usually prepared the salad dressing at home, but today he allowed his niece—for the first time—to do so. Quite good.

Nehru thought Chou En-lai a brilliant man, one of the greatest he ever met. He gives the impression of being very open-minded; whether he is or not, that impression is most important. Of course he is obviously a sincere Communist ("I don't discuss this with him."), but he seems tolerant: "Perhaps, more conservative than the others." Nehru thought China showed more composure and confidence than Russia; that it had a greater cultural tradition and deeper internal roots. I asked if he saw any contest between Peking and Moscow for leadership in Asia. He said perhaps.

He agreed that the Hungarian repression had been terrible. It was too bad it came at the time of Suez. Otherwise, he thought the Russians would have been forced to let go as they did with Poland. Nagy had made a mistake in openly appealing to the West. The Russians were convinced (wrongly of course) that the United States had touched off the Hungarian revolt and approved the Anglo-French venture in Egypt. Tito was now on the spot.

I remarked that in his early days Nehru considered himself a Marxist-socialist, but his administrative record certainly did not confirm this. What was his dogma today? He said:

> Marxism or communism or Leninism—call it what you like—first impinged on my mind just after the Russian revolution, when here in India we were in the thick of our own movement. Of course I was completely absorbed in Gandhi. We welcomed the Russian revolution and thought it a good thing. Later on, however, I read Marx when I was in prison. I was much fascinated by his brilliant analysis of the changes wrought by the industrial revolution in England—although I never had much interest in his theory of surplus values.
>
> But we were all so impressed by Gandhi; we thought he was following a more correct path than Marx and Lenin. Later on I said once that if I had to choose between communism and fascism I would choose the former. But that was a reaction to fascism, nothing more. Both communism and fascism have the same evil features: violence, cruelty, and oppression. But communism at least aims at something better. It is unfortunate, if inevitable, that communism has become so tied up with violence and suppression. As a pure economic theory it would have been more attractive. And we must remember that when Marx evolved his theory in the first half of the nineteenth century, there was no real democracy. He had to think of violent means of upsetting the controlling oligarchy.

I asked him, in the Indian revolution now, what were the relative roles of the individual and the state, of public and private enterprises and ownership. He replied:

> In the modern world, everywhere, there is a conflict between an increasing centralization which makes for less individual liberty. It is hard to draw the line. But we would like to preserve individual liberty even at the risk of slower progress in the economic field. I refuse to accept any doctrinaire socialism. Our main objective is that all the people of India should have equal opportunities. And this they certainly don't have yet. It would be absurd to apply to India today the nineteenth century theories of Marx evolved with respect to England.
>
> Ours is a pragmatic, not a dogmatic revolution. It aims at equal opportunity. Gandhi was not a Socialist in the real and generally accepted sense. But he always identified himself with the very poorest. He left with us the idea of identification with the poor and the suppressed. He used a fine phrase about himself once. He said: "I should like to wipe every tear from every eye."

I asked what, in his opinion, was holding India together; not politically —except during relatively brief periods of strong rule such as the Moghuls —but internally. The concept of India was always there, and strong conquerors always thought to subdue India.

> Culturally, we are remarkably united. In a sense, it is like the old idea of Christendom in Europe—but even more intense. Political divisions didn't upset the idea of a common culture here. Our chief places of pilgrimage are widely separated—south, east, and west; there were constant streams of pilgrims coming and going to them from all over India.
>
> Another factor that was very important in the past is Sanskrit. This language has not been spoken since the days of Buddha—2,500 years ago. But it is *still* the language of the learned.
>
> And then, the modern theme of unity was, strangely enough, brought about by Britain. The British enforced their unity. And our opposition to their rule was a unifying force. The Congress party started seventy-one years ago as a small movement, but it was always aimed at *all* India. Today we are politically and intellectually united. But we are not yet emotionally integrated. When something happens, passions break loose. India would be completely united against an external danger. But when we get complacent internally, then we fall out.

I noted that in one of our previous talks I had asked him on which side India would be in case of war. He had replied reluctantly that in the end it would be with the West because of a common political tradition and a dependence on maritime commerce.

> Did I say that? Really? Well, most of our economic contacts are certainly with the West—our intellectual contacts also. And the mere fact of English being used and known here as a language and in our periodicals and books is

important. Furthermore, of course, there is the bond of our governmental and parliamentary system.

But in the event of a war—I just don't know. We would certainly try and keep out of it. And what developments would lead into—I don't know. Geographically we are favorably situated. We are outside the normal way of war.

KATHMANDU, NEPAL, *March 5, 1957*

NEPAL, as a country in the real sense, is only seven years old. Until 1950, it was merely a vast feudal estate. It had neither budget nor treasury system. The only services provided by the ruling Rana clan were police, army, and tax collectors. The last Rana Prime Minister, opening a school there, said: "This is the beginning of the end of the Ranas."

Soldiers are an important export. Several thousand a year go to Britain and India. Some of the money is allotted home; plus pensions. Retired Gurkhas are an element of stability.

The Will Mullers (acting head of USOM) gave us a party. Among those present was Field Marshal Kaiser Shumshere Jang Bahadur Rana, brother of the last Rana Prime Minister and a relative of the King. Kaiser is a funny little old man (sixty-six) with a black Nepali cap and coat, white leggings. He was Ambassador simultaneously to London, Paris, and Washington. He gave me a long lecture on the use of the kukri. To chop off the head of a buffalo in one shot you need a double-handed grip on a heavy, two-handed kukri. For a human head it is better to use the forehand; but a good backhand can do it. There is also a neat upward disemboweling stroke.

KATHMANDU, NEPAL, *March 6, 1957*

LUNCHED at the Price's. He is head of the UN mission, a charming American, born in China. Price told us that when the late King Tribhuvana died, the present King Mahendra, to safeguard his father's soul, got inside the body of a newly slain rhinoceros and prayed for his parent. This is an ancient custom.

After lunch, as we sat on the terrace, Mrs. Price suddenly turned her head and said: "Look! Look, here it comes." And as we stared at the immense peaks stretching into the sky we saw, coming through the clouds above them, the breathtaking bulk of Everest, advancing slowly and then vanishing backward into a new bank of mist.

COLOMBO, CEYLON, *March 15, 1957*

THIS morning I went to see Prime Minister Solomon West Ridgway Bandaranaike at his comfortable, unpretentious house. On the porch, dozens of hangers-on lounged about, including numerous orange-robed, shaven-headed Buddhist priests. We sat in an ugly hot salon. A brown grey-hound lay panting.

Bandaranaike, a small, thin man with spectacles and curiously thick tufts of hair emerging from each ear, seems tricky and speaks in pompous, platitudinous English in a lilting, high-pitched voice. He said: "As one of your Americans once said, This is the age of the common man. It is a period of transition in world history. The emphasis is on the needs of the masses. In our country the common man lives largely below the poverty line. I mean to say, he has a very low standard of living. We feel it is not possible to solve the economic question purely on capitalistic lines. We follow socialistic lines of economic development. The repercussions of this situation produce our concept of neutralism. We want to be friends with everybody, to borrow from both East and West, from both capitalism and socialism."

JUFAIR, BAHREIN, *March 21, 1957*

WE have been staying with Sir Bernard Burrows, British political resident for the Persian Gulf. Any British official in this area has the authority to free slaves. If a slave shows up at a residency or consulate and requests his freedom, this can automatically be granted, and the slave is given a paper declaring him free. About twenty slaves a year are still freed here in Bahrein. Mostly they are Saudi Arabs.

PARIS, *March 29, 1957*

DINED at Elie de Rothschild's. Jean Cocteau was there plus a young man who was supposed to be Cocteau's boyfriend and an extremely attractive woman supposed to be the boyfriend's girlfriend. After a great deal of rather uninteresting badinage, Cocteau really began to talk. These are some things I remember.

"The great tragedy of France is that its politicians are unsuccessful writers and its writers are unsuccessful politicians."

Cocteau says the trouble with our time is not that this is a lying epoch, but it is an epoch that is lied about. He referred to Napoleon and quoted him as saying: "Any man who thinks is my enemy."

LONDON, *May 6, 1957*

EXCELLENT talk with Prime Minister Harold Macmillan in the Cabinet room at No. 10 Downing Street. He greeted me with his usual courteous urbanity, waved me to a seat, and then pulled up a chair: a large, imposing, handsome Edwardian figure with a shock of gray hair, puffing a slender cigar.

I told him I had heard people describe the philosophy of his government as a "Tory revolution." Did he consider this an accurate statement? He reflected for a moment, puffing his cigar. Then he said: "Yes, I suppose that is exact. Certainly socialism is out of date. Likewise, the old capitalism is dying. You in America have already done a great deal toward creating a new capitalism. I think you will agree that this must be both dynamic and creative. We must have equality and opportunity. Privilege must disappear—but not to be replaced with the false privilege of egalitarianism. But this does not mean leveling people down from the top. It is more important to pull other people up than to let them pull down the rest."

I said the broad outlines of Macmillan's policies of "Tory revolution" were becoming evident in terms of defense and budget reforms. However, would there be any changes in foreign policy? He replied:

No, there will be no change in foreign policy except in this sense—it must be an Elizabethan policy rather than a Victorian policy. During the Victorian age, England, as a leader of the industrial revolution and the richest country in the world, was able to muddle through. We were not very intelligent. But we managed because of our wealth and power. Perhaps we were in the same position as America today.

But during the Elizabethan age we were a small country—only about two million people. The skill of the great queen enabled us to hold an important place in the world.

Of course, you must have a certain size or you cannot be an important power. Thus, for example, San Marino could never be a great country. An ant can never be much of a thing. But mere wealth and size are not necessary for greatness. You can be too big—like an elephant. Man is a reasonable size and perhaps that is why he has succeeded so well. He is neither dinosaur nor bee.

Our great periods have been those when Britain has made its mark not by size or wealth alone. Remember the days of Marlborough, when there were only six or seven million English and twenty million French. The proportions remained about the same during the era of Napoleon. We don't need to be frightened of the Russians or the Chinese just because there are a lot of them.

PARIS, *May 20, 1957*

ADLAI Stevenson came for breakfast. Said that during the first twelve days of the Hungarian revolt—when the rebels were largely in control—he thought it shocking that the United States did not send in aid, including troops. We could have gotten away with this, and it was our moral obligation. Unfortunately, because he made this suggestion in public during the height of our election campaign, Eisenhower was not able to act upon it for political reasons. Stevenson said any man who makes good suggestions during a campaign automatically negates their chances of success.

Our breakfast for Adlai was quite an event. We invited Bill and Susan-

Mary Patten. Grat, our butler, was exceptionally flustered, even for him. Marina usually takes only toast and tea, and I have a cup of hot milk, but we decided to entertain proper American-style: fruit juice, eggs, bacon, coffee, toast, marmalade, etc. Grat started things off by serving one piece of bacon all around. Then came coffee. Then marmalade. Then toast. Then eggs. Then, as dessert, fruit juice. By that time we were all as confused as he, poor fellow. When the phone rang, he rushed off to answer: "Madame is busy. She is receiving guests . . . yes, of course. In this house we receive at any hour."

PARIS, *July 19, 1957*

THIS morning, I had a long and extremely interesting talk with de Gaulle. He said he didn't foresee a "catastrophe" in Algeria. And also that it was obvious the existing parliamentary parties would never summon him back. Very well, I asked flatly, how about a *coup d'état*?

"Why not? I have already staged two *coups d'état* in my life. In June, 1940, I staged a *coup d'état* when I established our movement in London. In September, 1944, I staged a *coup d'état* in Paris. When I came back to Paris I established the government. I was the government. The only thing is that one should not stage a *coup d'état* unless public opinion demands it. Public opinion must be entirely behind you—like Napoleon with the eighteenth Brumaire." I asked him how, in this complicated age, public opinion could express itself in such a way as to satisfy him the moment had come for a coup. He said he wasn't sure. Many things could happen. For example, the army could decide no longer to obey the government or its officers. Or there could be a general strike provoked by exterior events— like Algeria. He didn't know exactly how, but there had to be some such expression before any coup could be considered. He did not think that another man could stage a *coup d'état* for him.

(This was the final crystallization of his views on the subject—some ten months before an actual coup destroyed the Fourth Republic. It is to be noted that: The very first of the necessary preconditions he outlined occurred in May, 1958—the army decided not to obey the government; and, although, for the record, the coup was made by leading French officers in Algeria, many top Gaullist agents were there, helping and inspiring them, and *de Gaulle himself did not think there was any man who could stage a coup for him.*) [Added later]

He said that in Russia: "Communism is finished. They have lost faith in themselves. They still, of course, call themselves Communists, but it is no longer the same thing. The bureaucracy in the administration is made up of Communists; but they have no faith in their movement. They saw that they could not conquer Poland. They saw that they could not conquer Hungary—morally, I mean. Therefore they realize that they have lost their dynamism. They can no longer dream of conquering Germany, of conquering France, of conquering Italy. They cannot even hold what they have."

De Gaulle said one thing of interest when discussing the absence of "giants" from the present political scene. He said this fact indicates a real détente in the world situation because it is only in times of crises that nations throw up "giants." They do not need them in normal times.

I asked him if Stalin had really impressed him as being a big man when he met him during the war. "Yes, undoubtedly. He was certainly a big man. Of course he tried to be affable and almost charming. But even that was merely an exterior. And sometimes he didn't even show that. He was a grand figure, a tyrant, a real czar. He controlled everything. He had absolute authority and absolute confidence. He did everything himself. Yes, there is no doubt that he was a great man."

I asked him if he had met any other men of similar stature. He said yes; Churchill was a great man "during the war years. Not before the war and not after the war; but during the war he was a great man, despite certain deficiencies."

He then went back to his old theory that there are no longer any giants. And he saw none on the horizon. He said that now we had an era of Eisenhower, Macmillan, and Khrushchev. I reminded him of his phrase, used three years before, that "The age of giants is over; this is the epoch of Malenkov, Fanfani, and Queuille." I remarked to de Gaulle that I thought his original phrase had been somewhat more euphonious.

BONN, *August 6, 1957*

LONG talk with Adenauer in the Schaumburg Palais. At eighty-two he still looks remarkably energetic with astoundingly youthful gait. I noted he believed Khrushchev was a small man who would not remain in power long. How did he feel about the present gyrations in Russia? He said he had had a list prepared for me of all the purges from Lenin's time on. He went on to say: "These so-called purges are invariably connected with dictatorship. Much has been forgotten, but when you read it all again, you see that this is permanent. We still really do not know—at least I do not know—whether Stalin wasn't killed before being purged. That's not established. A process of that nature harbors certain dangers, of course, for the surrounding world, but it also gives rise to a certain hope. Such a system can never calm down internally and people will realize that one day. What lesson can we draw from this? Not to lose patience, to keep on the alert!"

I asked if he thought the purges had now stopped and that there might be a further contest between Khrushchev and Zhukov and others. He said: "Suppose you were a dictator, Mr. Sulzberger—that would require a good deal of imagination—and you were together with somebody else who is in command of the armed forces. I feel sure you wouldn't feel altogether comfortable about it."

Only one man since Stalin's death had held military power outside the army—Beria.

> That was why they liquidated Beria, but Beria could only be eliminated by the armed forces, by Zhukov. Zhukov could only be eliminated by another marshal. This would mean that the army was split, while in the case of Beria the whole army was against him.
>
> For some time now we have been informed that Bulganin and Khrushchev together stir the marshals up against each other. Zhukov has come to the forefront, but may I remind you of one thing. In *Red Star* there appeared some time ago a picture of Khrushchev and Bulganin on the front page with Zhukov in the background. Shortly afterwards, the editor of *Red Star* was dismissed.

I inquired whether this implied Zhukov was in the background or what? He answered:

> For having shown his picture at all! At that time he was not yet one of the top rank. I was in Moscow in Autumn, 1955, and a great reception was given in our honor. One thousand people were invited but not one marshal!
>
> Six months later the French Premier and the French foreign minister paid an official visit to Moscow. When I was there, Bulganin and I occupied the chair in turn, Khrushchev not at all. When the French were there, some time later, Khrushchev occupied the chair and not Bulganin. At the great reception we were given, there were no marshals; at that given for the French, there were many. There had obviously been a change during the seven or eight months in between. This development has not yet come to an end; of that I am firmly convinced.

I asked if he thought Khrushchev and Zhukov would win the fight. He replied: "At present Khrushchev and Zhukov are like this. [The Chancellor made a gesture with his hand to show that they are on the same level.] At the end of the year they will be like this. [He crossed one hand over the other to illustrate that Zhukov will be above and Khrushchev below.] And that is as far as I can see. Who would be likely to come after that? Then we would have a dictatorship of the army! That may well be, but we cannot be sure. Zhukov is in any case no better than the others."

I then asked Adenauer who—of all the men he had met during his lifetime—were those, if any, he considered truly great. He replied:

> I definitely consider Churchill to be a great man. He saved his country when it was in a very difficult situation. But take de Gaulle for example. He saved his country, but afterward he was a complete failure as head of government. In the United States there are a few men to whom I attach very much credit for having realized—and acted accordingly—that the power that America obtained rather quickly and its wealth create the obligation to be a real leader among the nations.
>
> That is in my opinion the greatest achievement of the United States in our time. History will someday reveal who contributed to this or who played a

leading part in it. In general, wealth makes people blind. Thank God that has not been the case with America.

I told Adenauer many people, including Churchill, had compared him with Bismarck. What did he think of Bismarck? He said: "Bismarck was a great foreign politician but a very poor home politician. He persecuted the Catholics and he persecuted the Socialists, thus preventing the creation of a large liberal party in Germany. As a result, the German people in my opinion were not politically strong enough to bear the power which they suddenly obtained. And that is what led to our collapse."

TOKYO, *October 9, 1957*

PRIME Minister Nobusuke Kishi received me in his office near the Diet, rather unattractive but comfortable. He said Japan has no intention of seeking diplomatic relations with Communist China at present. However, Japan would like to promote trade. The best solution to the impasse is the so-called "Two Chinas" formula. This would prevent Peking's control of Formosa—a threat to Japan. However, Chiang Kai-shek and Mao Tse-tung object to the "Two Chinas" formula, and America opposes it.

Japan could simply never permit the communization of Formosa and Korea. It would render this country helpless. Japan thinks it would be desirable to unify North and South Korea. But the reunified country could never become Communist. The best solution would be to have a neutral, unified Korea. It is impossible, however, to solve this problem locally. China and Russia are behind North Korea. As long as the great powers are split, Korea must remain divided.

TAIPEI, *October 16, 1957*

FOREIGN Minister George Yeh told me that under the secret letters he exchanged with Dulles in December, 1954 (eight days after the Mutual Security Treaty was signed)—only the "substance" was published—Chiang agrees not to invade without our prior permission. But we (and this wasn't published) promise to make no substantial reduction in our Okinawa forces without first consulting Chiang. So he has a hold on our Japanese policy.

This evening went out to President and Madam Chiang Kai-shek's for tea and a long conversation. I asked why, since he advocated limited war as the only way of liberating China, he didn't take off. He said: "You know the answer. It is the United States." I asked why he had handcuffed himself by such a commitment. He said the subject had never come up during negotiations for his American treaty. However, after it was signed, Washington asked him to make such an agreement in subsidiary letters so that Congress would swallow the treaty.

I asked if he would have to consult the United States before, for example, landing a battalion on the mainland from Quemoy. He said the treaty wasn't that precise; but he would keep our people advised of everything. Would he be able to move in quickly without waiting for consultation if a rebellion broke out on the mainland opposite Quemoy? Yes, but he'd tell us as soon as possible.

What did Chiang consider as an alternative to coexistence except war, I asked. Nothing, he said. The present situation of coexistence was like Trotsky's "neither war nor peace."

I told Chiang I had read his memoirs with interest. Was I right in interpreting his beliefs as seeing only war as a solution. Yes, he said. But he was sure Russia wouldn't come in. Then he leaned forward, always with a grin in which his Hapsburg underlip protruded, and said: "Now let's speak plainly and without hesitation. What do you think? Will the American people support me in a limited war?"

I said: "Frankly, I don't think so. Until 1945, that would have been possible. But since the atomic age began most people don't care to risk a nuclear war which would destroy civilization. They don't think war can be limited."

"I am afraid you are exactly right," said Chiang to my surprise. "That is an accurate statement of the American view."

QUEMOY, *October 17, 1957*

Took off at 6:00 A.M. in a typhoon for this small offshore island. We had a nice little DC-3 with a crew of three majors, a captain and a sergeant. Also Admiral Liu and Sampson Shen, chief of the government information office, came along to brief me. We had to fly so low we almost touched the waves. Deathly ill, Sampson and two of the majors vomited ceaselessly.

Everybody talked of war, but I didn't see a single artillery piece. I was taken to well-built defensive positions which would sweep roads and beaches—but I saw no machine guns. Hardly anybody carried sidearms, and only the sentries had rifles. It was a most unwarlike atmosphere.

TAIPEI, *October 17, 1957*

This evening I dined at the Generalissimo's: most lavish for his Spartan regime. Started off with champagne. Then we had a Chinese dinner served European-style with knives and forks.

When saying farewell, a strange thing happened. Madam Chiang came up, gripped my hand between hers, looked me in the eyes earnestly, and said: "Never trifle, always be in earnest."

"Yes," I said, puzzled. "Did you hear me?" she inquired. "Did you hear what I said? Never trifle, always be in earnest."

RANGOON, *November 9, 1957*

THIS afternoon, I visited U Nu, the Prime Minister, at his house. He and the other ministers live in a compound surrounded by barbed wire and sentries armed with tommy guns. This is practical in a country at present engaged in fighting eight civil wars and where murder and violent robbery are the norm. In 1947, a prime minister and almost his entire Cabinet were wiped out by tommy gunners at a routine Cabinet meeting.

U Nu is a nice-looking man of medium height and sturdy build, affable, poised, speaks good English. "Neutralism is a very simple thing. It means that you don't join any power bloc, but at the same time you try your level best to bring the two blocs together as quickly as possible. This we are trying to do in our own humble way."

WASHINGTON, *December 4, 1957*

LONG talk with Dulles. I started off by asking how we were to avoid the dilemma of the relative importance of our alliances and of our different allies. He answered:

Maintaining alliances is quite an art. There is no simple formula. The miracle is actually that they are maintained at all. In the Federalist Papers our early leaders contended that alliances could not be kept up except during wartime. Of course it's hard to keep alliances alive. There are many stresses and strains. But, I'm glad to say, nothing has actually cracked yet—touch wood.

Issues must be resolved in general terms. Thus, it is obvious the United Kingdom is the most important ally we have. But we even went against Britain on Suez. We felt it would destroy UN if they went on; that it was better to strain our relations with the U.K. than to accept the destruction of UN and get into the morass of war in the Middle East, from which none of our people could see a possibility of extricating ourselves without the loss of much money and prestige.

We must decide each question on its merits. There was the question of relations with France and sending police arms to Tunisia. France is more important than Tunisia. But we had to consider the issues. Everyone felt the Tunisians were entitled to get some arms; this even included the French. We could not repudiate the concept of independence and throw North Africa into the arms of the Soviets.

PARIS, *January 29, 1958*

LUNCHED today with Pierre Courtade, foreign editor of *Humanité* and a member of the Central Committee of the French Communist Party. He was in Moscow recently and says that if Molotov had been either a brutal dictator or a good politician he would have licked Khrushchev. When the Presidium met at Molotov's behest to bounce Khrushchev in 1957, two-thirds of the members present supported Molotov. Molotov intended to become Secretary General of the party or Prime Minister, and he had drawn up his Cabinet list. Shepilov was to be Foreign Minister and Khrushchev had been assigned as Minister of Agriculture. But Molotov had no pipelines to the party apparatus in the countryside. Zhukov placed his planes at the disposal of Khrushchev, who flew in a stacked Central Committee which supported him two to one over Molotov. Zhukov supported Khrushchev in the whole fight. But Khrushchev fired him because this was Russia's "MacArthur case." Zhukov was getting too big for his boots, and Khrushchev had to reestablish civilian control of the army.

PARIS, *February 20, 1958*

THIS morning, I had a good talk with de Gaulle in his office. I told him I had the impression that France was heading slowly but immutably toward disaster. Was there any way of stopping this trend? He replied:

I don't know how to stop it. If I were in power—without this type of regime—something could be done. But the only thing that can be done is to give this country back its independence. How could that be achieved? It could be achieved by ending NATO.

I would not enter into a dispute with the United States and Britain. But I would quit NATO if I were running France. NATO is against our independence and our interest. Our membership in NATO is said to be for the protection of France against a Russian attack. But I don't believe that the Russians will attack at this time. Of course, one cannot say that this will be the case forever, but there is no fear now of a Russian attack.

The development of Soviet missiles, as demonstrated when Sputnik was launched in 1957, reinforced his argument. He said:

The Russians now have long-range weapons. If one of their explosives were to fall on France the United States would not fight for us. It would not go to war immediately. It would only fight immediately if a bomb fell upon the United States. If a bomb fell on France the United States would merely protest in the United Nations and make all kinds of diplomatic moves.

Thus France is not defended by NATO. And, on the contrary, NATO prevents France from serving her own interests. NATO prevents France from acting in Algeria. Under one pretext or another NATO will deprive us of Bizerte in Tunisia; and we can never forget that Bizerte is a primordial French interest.

France must take back its independence. But this regime is incapable of leading. The consequence of this is both that we will lose Africa and stay in NATO, which is meaningless to us. NATO prevents France from believing that she is responsible for her own defenses. The French people think that it is the Americans who are now responsible for the defense of our country. This is very bad. If a war came, the French would not fight. They expect the United States to fight.

NATO is no longer an alliance. It is a subordination. This is very bad. Alliance, yes; that is all right; but subordination, no. After France has regained her own independence perhaps she will be linked with the western countries in formal alliances. France can be connected with other countries which are under the same threat. But we cannot accept a superior, like the United States, to be responsible for us.

I reminded de Gaulle that the last time I had seen him a few months ago, many people were talking about the chances of his return, and he referred to *coups d'état* he had engineered in the past. What were the chances now of his return? He replied:

The situation is worse now than it was a few months ago. But it is not yet dramatically bad. The French people eat well. They are contented. They do not suffer. That is the trouble. Because, in the meantime, if this regime [meaning not just the Gaillard government, but the entire system now prevailing] continues, France will lose all North Africa.

Alas, only a disaster can change things. The French people must *personally* suffer before there can be a change. They don't know what misery is. They must experience disaster and personal suffering the way they did during the German occupation and the war. Perhaps a serious economic depression could accomplish this. The regime could not stand up against a big depression. A big depression would bring anger and suffering among the population which would throw out this regime.

De Gaulle thought the Algerian mess might—but by no means necessarily would—aggravate the situation sufficiently to bring about a change. He doubted if enough people would suffer to cause a revolution or coup d'état. The army was restive, but as things stood it would not rise up. And the general reminded me: "The army in France has never been a political force. The army has never made a *coup d'état* in France. Sometimes a military man has made a *coup d'état* but not the army. Even Bonaparte, when he made his coup, made it himself because the country wanted a *coup d'état*. It was not the army that made it. I made two *coups d'état* myself. That was because the French people wanted them. The army did not make them. It only followed after I had succeeded."

I asked how he thought the countries of the West should stand up against the Russian menace. He replied:

The countries of the West must be for themselves, each should be for itself. France must be for the French. Nations cannot be suppressed as individualities. But NATO suppresses them as individualities. One reason for the success of Soviet pressure now is that the Russians have changed a lot internally. They are no longer the Bolsheviks of other times. They keep communism in an economic sense. But in an intellectual or perhaps a spiritual sense they are no longer Communists. There is an internal trend within Russia that is going toward liberty—above all liberty of the spirit. Russia used to be an ignorant country. But now it is educated, even if it is not impartially educated. And the educated people—above all the elite—are working toward liberty. This fact alone is incompatible with the old-fashioned Bolshevism. The Russians are pushing toward liberty, pushing toward the sun. They crave contact with the West. This is no longer the Russia of twenty years ago.

They have kept the economic and social system of communism. This won't change, and we should realize it will not change. But in terms of the spirit, they are seeking and obtaining more freedom. Their politicians—and we should never forget that they are politicians—represent this trend. This is the current of the moment.

BELGRADE, *February 28, 1958*

THIS morning, I visited Marshal Tito at his home. Madam Kveder, wife of the former Ambassador to West Germany, interpreted, and a private secretary took shorthand notes. We sat around a low table in the president's study. Turkish coffee, *šljivovića,* and a fruit juice were served. Tito smoked cigarettes in a gold and ivory holder.

I asked if Tito considered the Balkan Pact linking Jugoslavia with Greece and Turkey still valid and active. He replied: "From the military side, the pact no longer exists. The threat which occasioned it no longer exists. The main importance was that it helped us establish close cultural relations with Greece and to improve relations with Turkey. Of course, relationships between Greece and Turkey are not of the best at present and this makes the pact invalid from a tripartite point of view."

I asked if Tito wanted a neutral, demilitarized zone in Europe and whether he favored a neutral bloc as a diplomatic force in international affairs. He said it would be unrealistic to feel that the creation of a neutral zone could be achieved in the sense that member countries would renounce their existing alliances. The only realistic possibility would be to create a denuclearized zone. Such a zone would include countries belonging to the two alliances. We could not expect Western Germany or Italy to leave NATO, but they could be included in a denuclearized zone.

I asked if he thought it possible for a Communist state to be as neutral in world affairs as a non-Communist state considering, after all, the close ideological ties of communism. He answered: "It is impossible for any country, including a Communist country, to be neutral. All countries are members of the world community. It is not possible for any country to be indifferent to the world situation. There can be no neutral countries today. But a Communist country does not have to be a member of a bloc. It can cooperate with anyone—even though abstract neutrality is impossible."

I told him I knew he objected to the American distinction between "national communism" and "international communism," but that some form of differentiation is necessary. What did he think of the future of national versus international communism in this sense? He laughed heartily. He answered: "National communism simply doesn't exist. Jugoslav Communists are international. Our point of view is that communism in various countries builds socialism with different methods. We have our own methods. We don't have different systems, but we do have different ways of building systems. We have our own point of view here on how socialism should be built and we don't try to force this on other countries abroad. Jugoslav Communists don't shirk from the general aspirations of communism. *We have never renounced* the international obligation of communism, but we don't interfere with other countries."

I then asked what were the main differences between the ideology of communism in Jugoslavia and Russia. He answered: "There is no difference in ideology. There is only a difference in method."

I told Tito that when I last saw Molotov in 1956, I asked him who was the greatest diplomat he had ever met and Molotov answered "Eden." Tito remarked, with a sour smile, "I am surprised he didn't say himself."

PARIS, *March 8, 1958*

DRINKS with Bob Murphy. He is handling the U.S. "good-offices" mission between France and Tunisia. He asked if I would take a leave of absence and take over the second (Algerian) phase of the negotiation. I told him it was more fun to write about the mistakes diplomats make.

CAIRO, *March 23, 1958*

LAST night, I talked with Nasser for two and a half hours in his home, a comfortable and quite luxurious villa on the road toward Heliopolis. Nasser said:

> We are a simple people. Our historical background is based on morality and sincerity. Christianity came into this area—based on moral and material action. Then Islam came by just moral actions. The three main religions in the world came from this area.
>
> Saladin, a Syrian, came from Syria with a Syrian army to help Egypt overcome the crusaders when they reached the outskirts of Cairo. After that he was appointed here as a minister.
>
> When Syria was in trouble after that, Saladin helped Syria with Egyptian troops and his object was to protect the area from foreign domination. This is the same objective everyone in the area now seeks.

I asked what was the present condition of relationships between his country and the United States? He replied:

> The Baghdad Pact was a turning point in our relations with the United States and with the West. We believe defense of the area must depend on its people. We are not the same as western Europe. The historical development of the West was different. When Hitler invaded, the U.S. helped western Europe. Again Europe faced the danger of the threat of communism after World War II. It was clear the danger was communism and that there must be an alliance with the U.S. for defense.

But in this area we were suffering from western colonialism. Therefore, any new form of defense which constitutes any sort of western influence will be a new sort of colonialism.

The second thing was the Israeli aggression in February, 1955. This was also a main turning point. From 1952, when we took power here in Egypt, to 1955, there was no tension on the borders. Everything was quiet. We felt we were perhaps in a period of peace. But suddenly in February, 1955, there was this Gaza incident. Many people were killed. We felt the danger of Israel. Then after that there was the election campaign in Israel. The Herut party demanded expansion. This was headed by Menachem Beigin.

They said in election speeches that their Holy Land extended from the Nile to the Euphrates. This meant that if their party ever took power, the result would be war. Mr. Ben Gurion's policy was based on forcing settlement. But to force a peace also means war; you will begin by war and try to defeat your opponent before you can reach peace. This, to us, is also a threat.

Israel claimed it had been able to fulfill two-thirds of its armament program by supplies from the West—when we were not able to get any supplies from the West. This led to our arms deal with the Soviet Union. That was the second turning point in our relations with the U.S. There was a blockade against us—and the press campaign, especially in *The New York Times*. They say Nasser is a Communist, that Nasser works with communism.

But these are not Communist arms. Any weapons we receive from the outside become Egyptian weapons when we receive them, when they reach our ports. And we look to the Israeli danger with more concern than ever. We sought arms because we were facing a threat.

There were various pressures after the arms deal—until we were faced with the withdrawal of the High Dam offer. It was said in the newspapers that Nasser was playing the East against the West. We were not. We were working for the interest of our country. We asked the West for arms. We got none. We were negotiating with the West for the High Dam when the East came to us and offered help. I said no thank you.

It was the withdrawal of the High Dam offer which led to the nationalization of the Suez Canal. It was not because of the withdrawal itself. This was your right. It was because of the way it was done. The meaning of Dulles's statement was clear—to undermine the government. So we nationalized. We feel that in spite of being a small country, we must not accept anything against our dignity. Then came the Eisenhower Doctrine. This means that the U.S. wants to influence this area and to have agreements to defend the area against aggression from the Soviet Union. But we had seen, all of us, that aggression was not from the Soviet Union but from Israel and the West. Its object was to isolate Egypt.

I inquired: "What is your ultimate policy toward Israel? Do you think it should exist as an independent state and in what relationship to its Arab neighbors?" He said:

What I feel important is the rights of the Arabs of Palestine. As long as the Arabs of Palestine are deprived of their rights there will be a problem.

They were expelled from their homes, property, and land. Now they are refugees. One million live around Israel, while Israel receives 100,000 Jews a year from abroad.

The second question concerns our security—Arab security. Israel needs $1,000,000 every day just to continue. Suppose this aid ceases? What will be the result? The result will be expansion. We have to prepare ourselves to face any ideas of expansion.

I asked whether, over the long range, some kind of relationship could be worked up between Israel and neighboring states. He answered:

Every day we wait for news that Israel has invaded Egypt. On October 28, 1956, we were celebrating the birthday of one of my children when they brought in a message. It said Israel had invaded Egypt. This was 1956. One year later, on October 28, 1957, they again brought me a message. My first impression was that this must be another invasion. But it said there had been a bomb attack against Ben Gurion in the Knesset. Every day I wait for news of another invasion. This is the condition today—fear, no trust and no confidence. Tomorrow I wait for invasion.

BONN, *April 28, 1958*

TALK with Brigadier General Werner Panitzki, chief of staff to General Heusinger, inspector-general of the army. Panitzki is a big, blond, brutally handsome fellow with a thick scar on his forehead. He was a Luftwaffe bomber pilot. Now forty-seven, still air force, he looks like a bad dream in his gray uniform.

To fulfill its role, Germany will and must have tactical atomic weapons. It would be impossible to equip this force differently from the allies fighting beside it. The enemy would break through at any point where it realized it was not being opposed by tactical nuclear weapons. This would split the front and make inevitable the use of strategical nuclear bombs on German soil.

PARIS, *May 12, 1958*

SPENT yesterday with Tommy Thompson, Ambassador to Moscow, golfing and lunching. Tommy said Khrushchev is certainly still the boss. But many party leaders disliked his plan to dissolve Machine Tractor Stations. At this moment, it is an ideological step backward. Moving from state ownership to collectivism is a retrograde step in Communist ideology.

Khrushchev cannot let liberalism continue to grow without an eventual blowup. The intellectuals have become bolder in the new atmosphere. Many writers summoned to recant have obviously done so with tongue in cheek. Liberalism cannot be rationed, and someday Khrushchev will have to crack down on it and move back in the direction of Stalinism.

The reason for the attack on Titoism is that Khrushchev now realizes he can no longer tolerate the heresy of a Communist state making independent decisions without first clearing them with Moscow. When Khrushchev was in Hungary, he became acutely aware of where this ultimately leads.

PARIS, *May 15, 1958*

I had coffee with Raymond Laporte at a café outside the National Assembly. Laporte is now Chef de Cabinet for Maurice Faure, Minister of the Interior. Raymond looked up at the cloudy sky and said: "Thank God for the weather. This will make an airborne assault on Paris difficult."

He told me the following: General Ely, Chief of Staff, resigned this morning. The security forces last night tried to arrest his two principal assistants, General Challe and General Martin, without even advising him. There is no commander of the French army at this moment. Nobody knows whether the air force is loyal, but it appears dubious. General Chassin, a leading air force general, is in hiding.

The Ministry of the Interior does not know who precisely started the plot. There is no evidence that de Gaulle promoted it, but he is fully aware of it.

De Gaulle is under protection of security forces, on the grounds that his life has been threatened by the left. I asked Laporte if either the Communists or the Gaullists had arms available for fighting. "Everyone has arms," he said sadly.

It would be easy for the military rebels in Algeria to send four or five thousand paratroopers to Paris because almost the entire Air Transport Command is down there. The crowd, including the police, would go wild over them.

PARIS, *May 16, 1958*

THE last time de Gaulle threatened to come out of retirement and seize the helm one of his supporters complained: "He marched us to the Rubicon; and then he told us to take out our fishing rods." This is no angling party. Paris appears *insouciant*. But danger rumbles underneath.

There is undoubtedly a deep conspiracy. Mysterious arrests are taking place. De Gaulle's old hatchet man, Soustelle, is under surveillance. Thanks to efficient police dispositions, Paris has been rendered safe, although many political cliques have arms. But what about France? The bulk of the army and all its striking force are in Algeria. So are the Air Transport planes.

PARIS, *May 22, 1958*

THIS afternoon, I went to see General Ely in his apartment in the Ecole Militaire. His face looked pale and almost like a skull.

I asked if the army was behind de Gaulle, behind Pflimlin, or split in its opinions. He said: "The army is for de Gaulle as the only solution. This is not for reasons of sentiment, but for reasons of logic. The army was not especially Gaullist before. But de Gaulle is the only man now who can heal the break. He would only come in for a few months, but he could do it in that time."

14

VERYTHING SEEMS OVER WITH THE FOURTH FRENCH REPUBLIC save for the shouting—or the shooting.

Today, while Pflimlin and his legally constituted government were still in office, de Gaulle was already issuing a statement of far more significance and impact than anything promulgated by the Assembly or the Premier. The first act draws to an end.

During a confused fortnight, whatever initiative Paris might have gained by ruthlessness was dissipated by inaction. For the sake of avoiding bloodshed the regime chose to appear as if it supported the intrigue against itself. Premier Pflimlin was in the position of a man who finds a burglar rifling his safe. At gun's point, he tells the intruder to continue. Later he announces: "I wasn't burgled. The man was acting on my instructions."

PARIS, *June 16, 1958*

LONG talk with André Malraux: terribly tense, pale, and electric. Since he thinks even faster than he speaks, his tongue is always racing to catch up with his mind. After five minutes with the brilliant Malraux, who by then is speaking a kind of French shorthand, I long for the composed paragraphs of de Gaulle.

Malraux said de Gaulle would prepare a "presidential constitution something like the American Constitution," and a "social reform something like the American New Deal." Above all, he said there must be a swift and extensive improvement in workers' conditions. I asked him about de Gaulle's old idea of labor-capital *associations*. He said, "That idea, that word, has not been mentioned from the government camp. Algeria, peace in Algeria, is the only question of the moment."

Malraux made the odd remark: "Communism destroys democracy, but maybe democracy also destroys communism. We will beat the Communists by doing what they didn't do. But if we don't do this, we won't beat them."

As I was leaving I remarked to Malraux that I presumed he wasn't writing these days. "No," he said. "This is no time for literature."

PARIS, *June 17, 1958*

TODAY, Maurice Thorez, the French Communist boss, received me in party headquarters, a large building on the edge of the banking district, almost a fortress. Even the front door is opened by a tough character who regards you carefully before he unlocks.

I asked why the Communists called de Gaulle a Fascist. He replied:

> We do not call him a fascist, although he formed a government, in abnormal circumstances and on an illegal basis, which is in reality a personal dictatorship. He came in by force and is maintained in power by the military. Such a situation can lead only to fascism. But it is not yet fascism. Fascism is a regime of open, violent dictatorship that is at the same time demagogic.
>
> I knew de Gaulle, of course. And I am convinced that he does not have the same conceptions as other people of the republic or of democracy. All his ideas are different from those of bourgeois and worker republicans. And his ideas and methods can only lead to fascism.
>
> When de Gaulle relinquished power in 1946, he summoned all his ministers one day to the Matignon. He said: "Sirs, I am going." There was no explanation. That was all.

PARIS, *June 18, 1958*

LAST night, at dinner, George Ball told me a fascinating story. During the 1956 Presidential campaign, the Democrats wanted General MacArthur to come out for Stevenson. Ball and Chet Bowles called on him in his suite at the Waldorf Astoria and spent the better part of two days trying to arrange this. MacArthur was just as sweet as pie. He said: "If Eisenhower is reelected President it will be the greatest disaster in American history. I know just what will happen. He will go off to the golf courses and the trout streams of the country and then he will just disappear. There won't be any American government at all."

FONTAINEBLEAU, *June 20, 1958*

LUNCH with Speidel. At last he has his own house in Fontainebleau—after having long been given the cold shoulder.

As a young officer, in 1932, Speidel was present at German maneuvers, which Marshal Tukhachevsky and a group of high Russian officers attended. He was immensely impressed by Tukhachevsky, one of the best military men he ever met. Tukhachevsky had been a lieutenant in a Czarist guards regiment. He was only in his thirties when he came to maneuvers as commander of the Red Army. An insolent German general asked him how old he was. According to Speidel, Tukhachevsky replied: "Old enough to lead my armies to victory if necessary."

Tukhachevsky spoke excellent French and quite a lot of German. He and all the other Soviet officers drank like fish, but Tukhachevsky never showed it—although the rest were staggering around.

PARIS, *June 25, 1958*

PRINCE Paul of Jugoslavia was at dinner: very civilized and polished. Paul told me about his negotiations with Hitler. He was received by Hitler alone with Ribbentrop. Hitler wanted Paul to sign a proclamation urging peace, together with Mussolini. Paul said: "How can you expect me to sign anything together with that Italian who murdered my cousin, King Alexander?"

WASHINGTON, *July 25, 1958*

THIS morning, I had a long talk with Vice-President Nixon. He has a curious, heavy jaw which gives him a puffy appearance. I found that when I looked down at my notebook and did not look at him, his personality came through more strongly. For he has a resonant, good voice.

I started by asking what he considered to be the aims, basically, of U.S. foreign policy. He replied:

I would say that our foreign policy begins with the major consideration of protecting the independence of the U.S. We recognize that the independence of our nation and the freedom of our people cannot be considered as separate from the independence and freedom of other nations.

Therefore, especially since World War I, we recognize that when the independence of our allies is threatened, we have a stake in helping them to defend it. This was a primary consideration in both world wars and in the Korean War.

Let me summarize my ideas of policy. First of all, we should protect the independence and security of the U.S. Secondly, we should give military support to those nations who will stand beside us. Thirdly, our economic program should shore up the independence of other countries. And fourthly, we must recognize that any world war would destroy or warp our freedom, and, consequently, we have the obvious objective of finding useful solutions to international problems; that is why we support UN.

The people of this country and perhaps its policy makers cannot stress too much that we are devoted to peace at almost any price. And there is an important ingredient of our foreign policy which we have not adequately conveyed abroad: We are not wedded to the status quo. We recognize that the world, above all the world outside the West, is in a process of change and that the popular masses want a better way of life. Unfortunately, the image we present to many people abroad is precisely the opposite of this desire on our part. We are not for change merely for the sake of change as Russia is, but we do not oppose change.

In the Middle East, we are presented as taking a position of opposing change in the status quo and opposing Arab independence and economic improvement. This is not true. Regardless of ideology, I think we should aid any independent nation. The security interests of the U.S. require this. Therefore, for example, I am for helping Spain and Jugoslavia. My own view is that we should take chances like granting economic aid to Poland to encourage the independence forces in nations that are not really independent.

I asked if Nixon would give me three names of men he would consider eligible for the position of Secretary of State if he should be elected President in 1960. He looked a bit coy. He said: "It would be presumptuous of me to comment on anything I might do if I were elected President. I don't even mention such things to my wife. In those terms, I can't answer your question. I don't like to speak of names."

But then, somewhat to my surprise, he went on and answered: "As a Secretary of State I think that first of all, a man should be able to talk to various people and get their various views on foreign policy, even though the Secretary of State should have the final word." (I took this as a jibe at Dulles, whom Nixon dislikes.) He continued:

A President should have several broad-gauge men sophisticated in international affairs in his Cabinet. There is a continual and extensive political campaign in the world. The propaganda and political struggle is constant. Therefore, just as in wartime, when several members of the War Cabinet participate in making decisions, a President nowadays needs to call on the best men in his administration to help guide his decisions on foreign policy. For example, such ministers as the Attorney General, the secretaries of Commerce, Treasury, and Defense, should join with the Secretary of State, the head of the Atomic Energy Commission, the head of the CIA, and others in making decisions. All of them can contribute something to the thinking of the chief executive.

(I was very interested to see Nixon put the Attorney General at the head of the list. His own closest personal friend in the Cabinet is Bill Rogers, the Attorney General.)

WASHINGTON, *July 28, 1958*

I HAD an extremely interesting lunch in the office of Senator Clark with Senators Fulbright of Arkansas, Humphrey of Minnesota, and Sparkman of Alabama.

Fulbright was much concerned about the attitude of our military leaders. He said both General Twining, present Chairman of the Joint Chiefs, and Admiral Radford, his predecessor, favored preventive war against Russia. They felt that the balance of power was still in our favor, but in a few years time it would be in Moscow's favor, and therefore we should strike now. Fulbright thought it most significant that the only military man Eisenhower consulted before going into Lebanon was Twining, who "wants a war anyway."

Fulbright complained that our system of government could only work in the present world when a really strong man was President, and yet it was a total accident if a strong man were elected, because the best-qualified candidates in terms of getting the nominations were those who had never taken a stand on any controversial issue.

WASHINGTON, *July 29, 1958*

THIS morning I talked for an hour and a half with Senator Jack Kennedy, who, at the moment, is way in the lead as Democratic candidate for President in 1960.

I started off with my standard question: What should be the essential aspirations of U.S. foreign policy? He answered: "Our policy should obviously sustain countries and help them to maintain their independence of the Communist system, at least as it is controlled by Moscow or Peking; by doing this, we can preserve the security of the U.S. Within these broad terms of reference, I think we should support countries regardless of their ideology. I would like to see American loans to nations behind the Iron Curtain in order to lessen their dependence on Russia. Those countries don't have to associate themselves with us. That would be self-defeating."

I asked Kennedy why it was that the Democratic Party seems so strongly opposed to our foreign policy while at the same time totally unable to exert any influence in order to change that policy. He replied: "Everything conspires against an effective role by the opposition party in foreign affairs. And you must remember that the President maintains a good deal of general support in the country on his foreign policy. It is not like internal political questions."

The upshot was, in my mind, that the President of the United States is now in a position to get us into war or to involve us in treaty obligations without the necessity of Congress declaring war or the Senate approving a treaty by ratification. And Kennedy seems to think this is a good thing.

BONN, *December 6, 1958*

LONG talk with Franz-Josef Strauss, German Defense Minister. I find him both the most impressive and depressive individual in Germany today. Someday, he is likely to be Chancellor. He could be a fine democrat, another autocrat, or even the man to make a nationalistic deal with Russia.

I asked what orders Strauss would give the Bundeswehr and/or the militia in case of another uprising in East Germany. He replied: "We will do all we can to keep the people quiet. For there is *nothing* we can do if they arise. That is to say, there is nothing we can do unless there is a NATO decision to act. There will be no special and specifically German action. Furthermore, any kind of armed interference would risk war."

I asked on what conditions West Germany would agree to forgo nuclear rearmament. He said: "We didn't ask for atomic arms until there was a NATO decision to equip all alliance forces accordingly. If the whole alliance is to be equipped with nuclear arms, as NATO decided, we cannot exclude ourselves."

PARIS, *January 20, 1959*

AVEROFF, the Greek Foreign Minister, told me a Cyprus solution appears to be in the offing and will be incorporated in an overall Greek-Turkish arrangement. Averoff asked me if I would be prepared to go to Cyprus and secretly contact Colonel Grivas, head of the EOKA underground, who has been hunted by the British for the last four years. Averoff thinks the reports he sends Grivas by present, uncertain contacts are watered down by extremist Cypriots (pro-Enosis). Averoff would advise the British of my trip in advance and said he was in a position to guarantee they would not use me as bait to capture or assassinate Grivas.

I think Grivas is too wise a guerrilla warrior to risk his neck on Averoff's promise. Nevertheless, I agreed to go. I told Averoff to get a message to me through his embassy stating he is anxious to see me in Athens. I would drop everything if I get such a message. I am not going to tell anybody in advance concerning this plan. But knowing how ruthless the British can be when necessary and how bitterly they feel about the numerous murders accomplished by Grivas, I don't bet much on any assurance they might give Averoff.

PARIS, *January 31, 1959*

THIS evening, I had a good talk with de Gaulle, the first since he became president of the Republic. I saw him in the Palais de l'Elysée, France's White House, which is busy as a beehive nowadays.

I asked de Gaulle if he would clarify for me the desires of France vis-à-vis the United States in terms of our alliances. He replied:

I told the United States and British governments that we must consider our relationships in terms of world security. NATO only covers the North Atlantic area. Together we must organize something for the whole world. This must be done by our three countries, as the three leaders of the free world which have global interests. These three leaders must organize world security both in a political and in a strategic sense. In this respect, NATO is a secondary question. It comes below and after the global problems.

NATO should be reformed entirely, to include Africa and the Orient as zones of action, as well as the Red Sea. That doesn't mean the countries in those regions should become members of NATO, but those areas must be considered in our strategic interest. Furthermore, NATO must be reorganized so as to stress cooperation rather than integration. The commands of NATO must be redivided. As things are, in case of a war, the French fleet in the Mediterranean area does not belong to France. It is intolerable. And U.S. policy in North Africa, politically speaking, is not our policy. That was demonstrated in the United Nations. There must be a world security organization among the three leading Western powers and at the same time NATO must be reorganized.

If the United States refused to go along with his ideas, I inquired, did he contemplate an alternative foreign policy? He answered: "There will be no change from NATO. We regard NATO as necessary [somewhat of a reversion from previous views] and France will not leave the alliance. But we will cease practicing our membership in the same way as we practice it at the moment. There are other ways."

But then he added a threatening phrase: "Only if there is no comprehension of our viewpoint, if there is no other way than war [meaning an intra-allied political dispute, not an armed conflict] will we join in the battle. We will take back our liberties. But I don't foresee this. All logic points towards an accord."

I asked if he thought the United States should or could grant more aid to France in connection with atomic weapons. He replied, lifting his shoulders in a shrug, stretching out his long arms, and raising his eyebrows: "That is up to you. Certainly France thinks there could be more such help. Of course, we do not know how this could be arranged with your Congress; but if there were better cooperation from you on this, it would save us much time and money."

I reminded him that after Stalin's death he had explained that the world situation was then against the return of dominating figures. I remarked that now that he was back in power, I wondered if the world situation had changed and whether he foresaw a new age of giants. He said: "I don't know. I suppose that depends upon the world situation. When that situation is grave the giants come nearer to a return. Also, you must remember, people grow in stature. One speaks of giants when it is all over. Sophocles said that one must wait until the evening to see how splendid the day was; that one cannot judge life until death."

MADRID, *February 4, 1959*

TODAY I spent more than an hour with Franco. Franco was wearing full uniform with a red sash about his middle. He's almost sixty-seven, plump, with delicate features, amazingly soft, warm eyes for so hard a character, olive complexion, quiet smile, soft, high-pitched voice.

To start things off on an easy basis, I asked about his relatively new hobby of painting. He said he had taken it up twelve years ago and enjoys it "when I find a free moment." He likes to paint wild animals and landscapes. In the country, he makes sketches and then paints from them on rainy afternoons later on. He also admitted to having taken up golf. But he is clearly no enthusiast. He said: "It takes up too much time."

I asked if it were correct that Spain, through the Portuguese alliance (and consequent tie to NATO) and the U.S. agreement, could still be considered a neutral. He replied: "Obviously Spain is no longer neutral; and for the reasons you point out. Nowadays neutrality is impossible for any country on the continent of Europe. This is especially true for a land with the strategic importance of Spain."

I asked if he considered the Spanish-U.S. accord "an alliance." He replied: "Up to a certain point, it is an alliance. It is certainly an alliance from the standpoint of our agreement to oppose a common foe, Russian communism."

I asked if Spain desired to join NATO. He replied with arrogance: "Spain would study the question if we received an invitation. Every time the matter has been raised in NATO [by Portugal], it produces the criticisms and vetos of certain members. Spain does not like to provoke such discord. And the matter is not urgent. We are in a position always to align ourselves with the NATO lands in case of war, thanks to the U.S. agreement. For this reason, in our conversations with the United States, we point out that we fulfill practically the same role as NATO members and that therefore we want the same amount and kind of aid."

I asked if, under the 1947 Succession Act, Don Juan was "the obvious and only heir to the Spanish throne." Franco said that undoubtedly Don Juan could lay valid claim to "all the rights of inheritance" of the throne. "He has the most natural rights and claims." But then he went on to say, "Naturally whoever succeeds to the throne must first accept all the conditions and stipulations of the Act of Succession. The monarchy would have to rest upon our prevailing laws. After all, they were accepted by more than 90 percent of the people in a plebiscite which established them as the laws of the country."

(This would certainly hang quite an albatross around Don Juan's neck.)

Finally, I asked him if he still felt—as he had told me in 1948—that socialism and communism were one and the same thing. He answered:

> You foreigners must understand that Spanish socialism is entirely different from such other kinds of socialism as, for example, British socialism. Here it is far more primitive and revolutionary than elsewhere.
>
> From our experience, we could not help but see that socialism and communism in Spain were practically the same. One of the tactics of the Communist party here was to penetrate socialism, to attract Socialist party

leaders to communism, letting them appear to remain Socialist, but actually using them as Communists. That is why, in 1936, communism spread so rapidly and so widely. Both parties had Marxist roots. Believe me, if you ever established a Socialist state in Spain you will end with a Communist state.

ESTORIL, PORTUGAL, *February 10, 1959*

LUNCHED with Don Juan, Count of Barcelona and (he hopes) future King of Spain. Don Juan is a massive fellow, about six foot one, huge, broad shoulders and chest; must be strong as a bull. He looks like a former all-American tackle; beak of a nose, heavy jaw, thin lips, a not-too-high forehead that slopes sharply backward.

He served very happily in the British navy, getting a royal commission from his uncle, King George V. He had eventually to resign this commission as Lieutenant Prince John of Spain because of a regulation introduced by Ramsay MacDonald's Labour government that only British subjects could command ships.

After the Spanish Civil War started, Juan slipped across from Portugal to join a Franco unit, but when it was discovered by higher echelons and referred to General Franco, he was sent back. Nobody wanted to (a) assume the responsibility for his life; (b) be stuck with the monarchic question.

Don Juan said: "Portugal is a republic where if you mention the word 'republic' you are clapped into jail. Spain is a monarchy where if you mention the word 'monarchy' you are clapped into jail."

He is discouraged about the future. Franco keeps talking about being a monarchist, but he does nothing to pave the way. He obviously intends to sit out his own life in power, come what may. "A real case of 'après moi le déluge'." Don Juan asked him if he wouldn't at least form a "government" with a Prime Minister. Got nowhere. Franco *is* the whole government. If he dies suddenly, Juan figures the only thing to keep the lid on is the army. He admits that "it will be a ticklish moment for me."

His idea of his future regime would be to install a system similar to the British monarchy. "We must move slowly to avoid chaos; Spaniards are anarchic people."

RABAT, *February 17, 1959*

IN the morning, I saw Mehdi Ben Barka, head of the left-wing Istiqlal faction that broke off from al Fassi's conservatives. (Ben Barka was later murdered near Paris by French and Moroccan agents.)

He said: "We have to build a state, not just run it. Morocco was three hundred years behind the rest of the world. The colonial heritage must be eliminated. Morocco had been skipped by the industrial revolution. As a result, our job is different from that of a Socialist party in Europe or a Communist party in Russia. The conditions for class war simply do not exist. We have three tasks: Form the citizen. Mobilize the nation; each citizen should be taught to feel what he must *do* for his country. Prevent the growth of the maladies of independence: nepotism and corruption."

RABAT, *February 18, 1959*

THIS morning, I was received by King Mohammed V. He expressed concern over the Algerian situation. Morocco felt friendship for the French people, but this was "an age of liberation," and colonialism simply did not fit in it. The basis for any solution must respect the desires for independence of the Algerian people, the economic and military interests of the French, and the status of the French people living in Algeria. Both in Morocco and Tunisia it had been demonstrated that such a basis could work for solution; why not Algeria?

MARRAKESH, *February 19, 1959*

ARRIVED yesterday evening in time to have coffee and brandy with Churchill on his last night in Marrakesh. We sat at his table in the corner of the Mamounia Hotel dining room. He was with Lady Churchill; Diana Sandys (his daughter, Duncan Sandys' wife); Anthony Montague Browne, the Foreign Office fellow assigned as secretary; and the British consul general in Tangier and his wife. Tomorrow, they plan to motor down to Safi where they are boarding the yacht of Aristotle Onassis for a trip to the Canary Islands.

He looked older; his skin is no longer pink but whitish and blotchy. His eyes are watery and dim. His hearing is even worse (as usual he wouldn't wear his hearing aid), and his voice is very faint. He is now really weak and can't get up without massive effort, has to be half-supported when he walks upstairs.

He offered me some marvelous brandy which Lady Churchill, with glee, said they had been permitted to bring in with them "duty free." When the servant offered me a cigar, I said I didn't smoke them. "That's a serious mistake," said Churchill.

He said he was going to America on May 4, for about ten days. First he will stay at the White House, then at the British Embassy, then with Barney Baruch, who, he said, was still in excellent health. "Probably better than Eisenhower's," I remarked. "Oh, I don't know," murmured Churchill. "The President seems to be on the golf links every day."

I told him I'd just been at our base at Nouasseur and had seen new fighters that go 1,500 miles an hour. "Ah, that's very swift, very swift," he said. "When I go to the United States in May, I shall attempt to find a plane that proceeds just rapidly enough, so that I can accomplish the journey entirely in the night and have my accustomed amount of slumber."

Churchill said he was sure the percentage of fatalities in air travel had not increased; on the contrary, they had decreased. "Otherwise I should have to reconsider," he added. It was odd to think of this old hero on death's doorstep talking about "reconsidering" travel means, in terms of safety.

At another point, we were talking about space rockets. I said I supposed in a few years men would be projected to other planets. "Oh, no," he said with some horror. "Why would anyone wish to leave this planet? That would be foolish. I cannot believe that."

Churchill was unexpected on Molotov. We were talking about how the Dutch had rejected him as Ambassador. "I like Mr. Molotov," he said. "I think he is a fine man, a nice man, a very able man." "Oh, surely you can't call Molotov nice," said his wife. "I do," he insisted. "I think Mr. Molotov is a nice man."

ALGIERS, *February 23, 1959*

THIS afternoon, I spent an hour with General Massu at his headquarters in the Caserne Pelissier. The building is rather crummy; surrounded by soldiers in jeeps. (Algiers itself looks like an occupied town with all the helmeted troops and police with tommy guns.)

Massu is tall, about six foot one, has a thin face, enormous arc of nose, long moustache, prognathous jaw, a few gold front teeth, large ears, thin-lipped mouth, rather brown eyes, low brow; an ugly man, not very intelligent looking, but with a pleasant smile. He was wearing jump boots and a regular uniform with a dark blue vest, the front of which was covered with a long row of gold buttons.

He started things off cozily by assuring me he mistrusted journalists. I told him there was a permanent cold war between newspapermen and generals, adding that he should realize there were newspapermen and newspapermen just the way there were generals and generals.

I inquired first what lessons in the art of fighting guerrillas he had learned in Indochina and from studying Mao and other Chinese partisan tacticians. He said:

> Everyone knows I won the battle of Algiers by being illegal. The system of justice must be adapted to the prevailing situation and to the mentality of the population. Technically, we fight a war in the regular way, using helicopters and other modern methods.
>
> A second observation I can make, after analyzing Mao's writings, is the need for double action against the political administration and organization of the rebellion as well as against their armed bands, the rebel companies. These are very different actions. Against the bands we employ classic means —night combats, ambushes; we have to surround the adversary before attacking and this requires sufficient numbers, artillery, and air power.

But against the political-administrative organization—against its political commissars, saboteurs, and terrorists—we are limited to the police action. We need *all* the police powers we can get. The military and police must be under one chief. We have to adapt ourselves to subversive war.

Did Massu think torture was still necessary in fighting the OPA aspect of the war? He said: "It is necessary. One can get nowhere with mere polite questioning. But I have given orders that neither the physical nor the moral integrity of a man should be damaged. I have ordered that this should leave no moral or physical trace on the person of the individual. [A curious phrase.]"

TUNIS, *March 5, 1959*

LAST night, I dined with President Habib Bourguiba at his home in Monastir, about one hundred miles away. A manservant brought in a steady series of bowls, which were left upon the table, and from these we helped ourselves—soup, grilled fish, pilaff, chicken stew, tangerines. There was flat Arab bread and nothing to drink but water.

Bourguiba talked a lot, starting on Algeria, which overshadows everything in this part of the world. He said:

> The situation is not ripe for settlement now. It will ripen; eventually it will have to ripen—but at what price? The French live totally apart from reality. They are fighting a full-scale war in Algeria with all their power just exactly as they did in Indochina and the result will be just exactly the same.
>
> They imagine they will win this war. They say it is a question of honor and prestige. They say that by winning it, they will be able to diminish the impression made on the world and on their own people by their having to leave Indochina, Syria, Tunisia, and Morocco. They still seem to consider the liberation of these countries as due to the treason of the *système* of the French regime.
>
> They don't yet recognize that this liberation movement is a natural phenomenon. After all, it happened to the British and the Dutch. It should be faced coolly and logically. The French think they are stronger and smarter than the British. How unclever they really are.

Bourguiba complained that there is a ridiculous situation in the world today. Dictatorships, such as Russia's or China's, which deny human rights to their own people, appear before the world as the champions of liberation, while the countries where true freedom reigns oppose such colonial liberation.

CARTHAGE, TUNISIA, *March 6, 1959*

ON March 4, I spent about eighteen hours with the FLN, the Algerian rebels. I had made my arrangements through Boumendjel, their permanent representative in Tunis. Some of the time I was with them in Algeria, across the border, some of the time at posts in Tunisia itself.

With us was the FLN hero Major Azzedine, wounded six times within thirteen months. He has twelve or thirteen holes in him, and six bullets still in his body. His right arm is gnarled; it contains an American explosive bullet fired from a B-26.

When he was captured for the second time by the French, de Gaulle sent a certain Captain Marion of the psychological warfare services to Algiers to seek his help in arranging a cease-fire.

Azzedine woke up in a helicopter on the way to Algiers. When there, he was visited in hospital by General Massu, whom he refers to as "the massacrer of Algiers." Massu told Azzedine: "We've been looking for you a long time." Azzedine told me: "I could understand this. I defeated Massu's men in the field. He had to write one of his defeats into his battle book."

He continued: "Massu said: 'You're a brave man. Your bravery is written on your body. I am happy to have seen you. At last I see you. But you can't win. We will win. The people are with us'."

Azzedine said he pretended to agree with Massu. When Captain Marion visited him in hospital he made certain proposals and said the French would release Azzedine so that he could return to his headquarters and arrange a cease-fire.

Azzedine replied he would transmit any proposals. He was released and went back to a rebel command post which joined in the game, telling him to give the French certain information, but not of a military nature. He went back to Massu, who said: "I am happy to see that the confidence we placed in you has been merited. You came back."

Azzedine told Massu his colonel was not at the command post but was attending a conference of colonels. Therefore he was not able to arrange anything and would have to go back. When Azzedine returned, rebel intelligence warned him he had better stay this time. So he did. The French proclaimed they didn't know what had happened to him.

Azzedine claims the best troops opposing the rebels are Foreign Legion paratroopers, the green berets. They are the most courageous and use the terrain best. The worst troops facing them are the conscripts. He says: "We call them *gateaux* [cakes]. At the first shot they quit." The French are still using Algerians in their units; about forty out of each four hundred men. Azzedine said: "We like this. Sometimes when there is a battle they fire on their own troops. The French are caught in Algerian cross fire. They don't realize their own men are shooting them." He said French troops often try to surrender and are shot down by their officers.

Azzedine claimed 80 percent of ALN losses were due to American equipment. He said: "I liked Americans. I used to work in an American factory. But when you have as many bullets in your body as I do and they are all American, things change."

LONDON, *March 24, 1959*

THIS morning, I had a chat with Harold Macmillan. Macmillan was his usual bland self, and sipped sherry while informally reviewing the world situation. He sat on a sofa in a reception room at No. 10 Downing Street, a Guardi painting of Venice behind him. He was wearing a fawn-colored Edwardian vest, a handsome, distinguished Edwardian figure himself.

Macmillan admits that Adenauer is very unhappy about what's going on but, "Where the tree falls, there the timber lies." What he meant, of course, was de facto recognition of East Germany.

LONDON, *March 26, 1959*

THIS afternoon I had tea and pleasant conversation with T. S. Eliot in his office at Faber & Faber on Russell Square, Bloomsbury. He has a very small, cluttered-up office filled with snapshots and other little mementos. There was an electric heater burning, although it was not cold. He served me with tea and biscuits.

I asked Eliot if he could explain why so many American writers, including himself, during the last thirty or forty years have chosen to live abroad. He replied:

I don't know if there is any particular reason. I don't know, for example, what Prohibition had to do with it. I have got a clean bill because I was living abroad before Prohibition was even thought of. I was encouraged to stay over here by Ezra Pound, who was the first man who managed to get any of my poems published, and was enthusiastic about them.

At that time, there were certain advantages for a young man in staying abroad. For example, I had to earn my living because I had no private means. It was easier for me to earn my living abroad.

Also, the American literary scene at the beginning of the century didn't seem to offer much encouragement to young men, especially for poets.

The influx of Americans into Paris came after World War I. I don't know exactly why. In many cases, it was just a question of a good deal of drift. You just go and find yourself in a certain position and then you find you are earning your living there.

There was a dull intellectual period then at home. This helped to push people abroad. But over in Europe, I met established literary people. Pound introduced me to Yeats. I got to know Virginia Woolf. People were interested in my poetry. I had never experienced that interest before.

That there is a definite moment of choice or a reason for emigrating in this way is an illusion. It is more a question of drifting along and a gradual readaptation. I don't think there is any single brilliant clue to my story, for example.

EAST BERLIN, *May 2, 1959*

APPOINTMENT with Walter Ulbricht, Secretary of the Communist Party
and boss of East Germany, at Central Committee headquarters, an ugly,
massive affair. Ulbricht, a short, solid man, was wearing a gray suit and
tie. A pointed beard (Leninist fashion) covers a slightly receding, half-
stubborn, half-weak chin. He wears rimless glasses, has a long nose, suspicious blue eyes. He was very friendly. Gerhard Eisler, his propaganda
chief and a well-known refugee from America, translated.

I asked Ulbricht what his reaction would be if the West turned over
control of West Berlin and the access lanes to Bonn's forces, replacing
those of the Big Three, when Russia hands East Berlin to the East Germans. He became indignant and said:

> There are no Soviet rights here in East Berlin; just the rights of the
> German people. We have a treaty with the Soviet Union. We have full
> sovereignty. 'Of course, we have accorded to the Soviet Union certain rights
> of transportation to handle the requirements of its military forces.
>
> The western allies have NO rights to hand over to Bonn in West Berlin.
> West Berlin is in East German territory. Any changes will have to be talked
> over and decided by four-power agreement with us. What you suggest is that
> West German tanks supported by the western allies should come to Berlin.
> That's no good. There is no question of what kind of West German troops
> should be in West Berlin. I can't imagine an American actually wanting
> them there. You know perfectly well it would mean war. Your theory leads
> me to the conclusion that you want foreign troops on our soil. West Berlin
> doesn't belong to West Germany and never has. You want to establish there
> a base for West German militarism.
>
> This question has only been made difficult by your refusal to recognize us,
> by the assertion that there is no German Democratic Republic. Yet anyone
> seriously wanting reunification would want talks between the two Ger-
> manies. Moscow has diplomatic relations with Bonn. The West should have
> diplomatic relations with us.

I asked Ulbricht what he considered the frontiers of a reunited Germany
should be. He said the existing ones, adding: "I can't imagine that Truman, Attlee, and Stalin agreed on these borders at Potsdam just to have
them altered later."

WEST BERLIN, *May 2, 1959*

THIS evening I went to see Willy Brandt, Mayor of West Berlin, at his
comfortable, modest suburban home. Brandt is a sturdy-looking character: a big, open-faced, hefty man who was a refugee from Hitler in Norway and came back to Berlin after the war as press attaché for the
Norwegian Berlin mission. He said:

Politically, I have always been doubtful about the West's position on Berlin's relationship to East Germany. I have never accepted the way the allies interpreted our reservations on West Berlin's position as a member state of the Federal Republic. The West says Berlin cannot be a *land* of the Federal Republic. But the GDR has incorporated East Berlin as part of the GDR. Therefore, there is no more reason for the allies to exclude West Berlin from being a portion of West Germany on the grounds of the Potsdam agreement.

However, I don't believe in substituting federal German troops for the allied garrison here. The danger would be much greater that trouble could break out if you had East German troops on one side of the Potsdammerplatz and West German troops on the other side. And politically speaking, the allies *have* rights of access to West Berlin despite Russian arguments to the contrary. There would be no similar legal basis for federal German troops to claim a similar free access.

WASHINGTON, *June 18, 1959*

DINED last night (at his Maryland farm) with Dean Acheson. Acheson was, as usual, charming, suave, witty, cynical, and somewhat bitter. I was no advocate of Dulles's policy, but I did find it offensive when he said, "Thank God Foster is underground."

We and the British had quite sensibly divided up the French effort during the war, he said. The British backed de Gaulle and we backed Vichy. The trouble was that Hull, "in his Presbyterian way," convinced himself that Pétain was right and was perfect.

Averell Harriman called him up before going to Moscow to ask him to represent Harriman as his lawyer in obtaining State Department approval for a Chinese visa. Averell added: "But please keep your price reasonable because I have a lot of expenses these days."

Dean called Bob Murphy and got a meeting arranged at the State Department. Murphy; Walter Robertson, the head of security; and others were there. Robertson objected. Acheson argued journalism was now Harriman's sole means of earned income and therefore Washington should approve his visa as a journalist. Robertson said other Asians might protest that Harriman was being secretly sent to negotiate with Peking. "You don't mean to say," said Acheson, "that you believe people abroad would think you fellows were really sending a Democrat to negotiate for you?"

WASHINGTON, *June 19, 1959*

DRINKS at the White House with President Eisenhower. The President said that on the whole his personal relations with political leaders were very good. He spoke warmly of Lyndon Johnson and Sam Rayburn as friends who were cordial and amiable when they came to the White House no matter what debate had been taking place at Capitol Hill. "As for Hubert Humphrey," he added, "why, he practically salaams when he comes through the door."

He said he had tried to have good relations with Truman (which wasn't Truman's version), but that the former President had always spurned these efforts. He felt that a former President could always be of help to his country as an elder statesman and that he would like to value their advice. But the trouble with Truman was that he simply wasn't intelligent or competent, and the counsel that he gave in public just wasn't useful.

Ike said he had now come to realize that the constitutional amendment preventing any President from having more than two terms was a good thing. For some years he had not thought so. He had thought it weakened the political position of the chief executive. But he saw now that this wasn't true. In fact, in a sense, it freed him by removing him from the political arena and allowing him to speak more freely for the entire country. He noted in this respect that as his own popularity seemed to increase in the polls taken, the popularity of the Republican Party decreased.

He felt automatically that any man who *wanted* to be a candidate for the Presidency was not qualified for the job. No man of any sense would aspire to the job; it had to be thrust upon him. He was inclined to oppose anyone who sought the job. He remembered how long it had taken when people worked on him to persuade him to accept the Republican nomination.

He said the first talk of running him for President started in 1943, and that in 1948, Truman had offered to him to run for Vice-President on any ticket headed by Eisenhower (as a Democrat). He said that when the pressure built up in 1951, he had finally gone so far in January, 1952, as to announce that he was a Republican.

He talked a lot about Churchill, who had visited him some weeks ago. He recollected that among the pictures hanging in the hall on the way to the room where Churchill slept (they always gave him the same room— the one he first had when he stayed in the White House as Roosevelt's guest) was one of Field Marshal Montgomery. He felt very strongly that despite the criticisms of himself uttered by Montgomery there was no reason to take his picture down. As he was conducting old Churchill down the hall to his bedroom one evening, Winston looked up and saw the painting of Montgomery. He suddenly came to life, emerging from his fog, and said in a low voice, "Aha! I see you still have that picture." Ike was clearly irritated by Montgomery's television appearance during which he had made unkind remarks about Eisenhower.

I asked about his painting. He said he still worked whenever he got any spare time, and at this point he took me into the studio. On the easel Ike had a painting of a golf hole on the Augusta National course—a short water hole. On top of a bookshelf to the left was a color photograph of the same hole from which he was working. Ike, who is no genius as a painter, always requires colored photographs as models.

When we went next door to join the ladies, Ike complained about the loneliness of his job. It was absolutely impossible to lead a normal life. The Secret Service is assigned to protect him and his family, and, of course, he couldn't interfere with their job no matter how inconvenient it is.

He showed great understanding for de Gaulle. Roosevelt had mistreated de Gaulle during the war and hadn't understood his pride and his determination to represent the noble things in France. This had given de Gaulle a complex toward us, and it made him difficult to deal with now. But he liked and respected de Gaulle (which, I might say, is a contrast to some of the things Ike has said to me before and some of the things he has written about de Gaulle).

He acknowledged sadly that there were many difficulties in keeping alliances among the democratic powers going because they all had to respond to their public opinion, and this was not an easy thing to resolve among many nations.

There was absolutely no doubt that Nehru needs aid in India and we must give it to him. He had been told the Russians were now offering Nehru between $600 million and $1 billion. This was a vitally important sector, and we had to react in our own interest.

WASHINGTON, *June 22, 1959*

EARLY this afternoon, I went up to the Capitol for a talk with Senator Lyndon B. Johnson, majority leader of the Senate and one of the more obvious Democratic candidates for the Presidential nomination next year. Johnson is tall, rangy, active, filled with energy. Once he opens his mouth, a hailstorm of words pours forth. He is an engagingly informal Jacksonian man, and several times during our talk, he tilted back in his chair to reach under his shirt and scratch his belly. He was neatly dressed in the Esquire manner, a rugged, tanned, handsome man with spectacles. His hair is thinning and graying a bit at the top. His expression changes with a varying assortment of wrinkles, and I noticed that he has large ears. He talks with extreme rapidity, but his Texas drawl is not overdone. He is certainly intelligent and charming, but I did not get the picture of a dominant mental giant. He is not overwhelmed by modesty and took pains to give me a photostatic copy of an honorary degree and citation he received on June 1 from Brown University which said: "Your skill as a politician has been notable, but you have subordinated politics to national interests, the service for which you will be best remembered."

He said:

The President must at all times be free to deal as our spokesman with foreign nations without having the country divided behind him. We ought to do things because they are right and not because they are expedient or to tide over an emergency.

New nations are being born all the time. Therefore status quo and laissez-faire attitudes are not sufficient to deal with a changing world. If we believe in free enterprise we must believe in this for everyone—for Asia and Africa, for the Philippines, etc. But we can't do this on the basis that "If you don't do something for Texas, Texas won't do something for such and such a foreign country." We have to meet the Soviet challenge and we must educate the public to this problem and produce some specialists on our own.

The Soviets have developed a new system that is really attracting people who need help and hope. We must make our own more competitive, and this is particularly true in terms of our foreign trade. If we do not compete more successfully in attracting the people of these nations they will look upon us as decadent. I have confidence that we can do this. I would hide in a cave if I didn't have confidence. Let's have an open-curtain policy. We have nothing to be ashamed of. Why, when Mikoyan was over here he wanted to see people and no Senator agreed to see him. But I wanted to be as close to him as I could. I can prove my own IQ. I welcomed him. I told him he should come to Texas and told him he should see San Francisco; he should see what we have and see what we do, take a look at our mines and cotton fields and our supermarkets. But he was pretty vicious. He said he'd been invited to see all kinds of glorious things, but that we didn't even want Russian children to have milk.

At this point Johnson had a telephone call, and when he hung up, amiably scratching his belly again, I tried to redirect the conversation to foreign affairs. Johnson said:

It's damned dangerous when a President takes on the Senate. Wilson and Roosevelt found this to be the case. Wilson lost out to a handful of willful men and that handful kept us out of the League of Nations and helped build the basis for World War II. Roosevelt lost out on his Supreme Court Bill, and after that he was only tolerated by the Senate through the war. Eisenhower should know that it's wiser to let dead dogs lie.

But you can't get this attitude of a united American opinion over to the outside world when your President is spoon-fed by Nixon and the Republican National Committee. We confirm Eisenhower's appointees except when honest men in the U.S. Senate think these appointees are not qualified, like Lewis Strauss [refused as Secretary of Commerce]. The U.S. Senate is not for sale.

Nevertheless, we can't have paralysis or stagnation in our foreign relationships. The President must have convictions and express them. However, he must also recognize that compromises are necessary in our political system. Take the question of the debt limit. Certainly it must be raised. Personally I think there shouldn't *be* any debt limit.

Our free enterprise system must compete with Russia's. Long-range planning is needed and we can't go ahead always budgeting on an annual basis.

EARLY this afternoon, I saw Chancellor Raab. He chatted away informally in his guttural Austrian accents. Raab talked mockingly of Tito. He said: "Tito's lifelong dream is to come to Vienna and stay at the Hofburg [the old imperial palace]. I'll invite him—when he signs the commercial agreement we're negotiating; not before. I'll even put him in the imperial apartments. After all, Tito was on guard duty at the Hofburg [when as a young man, he was in the Austro-Hungarian army]."

VIENNA, *July 24, 1959*

LAST night, I dined at Princess Hohenlohe's. The only people there were Bruno Kreisky, the Foreign Minister, and Gastone and Raffaella Guidotti. (Guidotti is Italian Ambassador.) It was totally informal; no servants.

We had drinks first in the small sitting room, then dined in the kitchen on goulash with dumplings that she had cooked herself. She is a merry, fat woman with glasses and bobbed hair, clever and nice, but she looks more like a Bohemian cook than a princess.

Kreisky is a droll-looking fellow with kinky, reddish hair like Harpo Marx, a sharp, long nose, humorous, bright eyes, and a very short upper lip. He is bright as a whip. He is a Jew (the first Jewish Foreign Minister in a Teutonic country since Walter Rathenau), the son of a wealthy family, number two in the Socialist Party. He was jailed under Schuschnigg and again under Hitler. When he got out, he escaped to Sweden, where he married and where both his kids were born.

Kreisky says Adenauer doesn't want a united Germany at all. He realizes this would be a Protestant Germany—which would offend his deep Catholicism.

DJAKARTA, *October 7, 1959*

TEA with General Abdul Haris Nasution, army Chief of Staff and Defense Minister. He is reputed to be anti-Communist and pro-American. Nasution, who speaks quite good English, is a clean-cut, handsome man who looks even younger than his approximately forty years.

I asked if he had any reason to believe the United States had given backing to the present rebellion against the government. He said:

I have proofs and documents certifying that there has been help from abroad, but for political reasons I have restricted publication of these facts. However, I did show one of your admirals a diary we captured and actual orders issued in Okinawa to one of the rebels. We have taken crates of new American equipment stamped certifying their origin as Clark Field in the Philippines and on Formosa.

Our army supports a foreign policy of "active independence." We don't want to be exploited by either side in the Cold War, and we resent interference from either side. During the first phase of the rebellion, it was perfectly evident the United States sympathized with the rebels. During the second stage, when war really began, there was physical assistance from your side. This included not only arms, but the training of cadres in the Philippines and Taiwan. But we spoke to your officials and gradually they began to realize that our policy was not pro-Communist. After we took central Sumatra in May, 1958, outside aid to the rebels ceased.

DJOGJAKARTA, INDONESIA, *October 10, 1959*

IN Djogjakarta, the intellectual capital of Java and first center of the anti-Dutch republic, I saw the Sultan, Kandjeng Sultan Hamengku Buwono Senapati Ing Ngabdulrachman Sajidin Panatagama Kalifah Allah Ingkang Djumeneng Nata Kading IX Ing Ngadjogjakarta Hadinigrat, usually called (thank goodness) Hamengku Buwono IX, or still more simply, the Sultan of Djogja. He is the only important royal figure left in the republic, which he supported from the start. He reigns as a kind of local governor.

The Sultan received me in his office, quite simple, dressed in half-Javanese, half-Western clothes. His pleasant appearance was marred by his upper jaw, which lacks all but the central two large front teeth, giving him the appearance of a smiling, earnest beaver.

He was gloomy. Expects serious trouble within the next three months. Says Sukarno isn't administering urgent executive problems. Skeptical about the potential ability of General Nasution because too many battalion commanders oppose him. Says the economy is sagging. Feels that most leaders are scared to stick their necks out.

DJAKARTA, *October 14, 1959*

THIS morning, I dropped in to see Ruslan Abdulgani, vice-chairman of the Supreme Advisory Council (Sukarno is chairman). His office is next to the presidential palace.

We hadn't been talking long when Sukarno came in and joined us. He was exceedingly friendly, and we had a long conversation. He made an infinitely better impression than when I saw him earlier. He took off his black fez, scratched his almost bald head, wiped his spectacles, sipped tea, ruminated, asked questions, thought aloud. But I found it possible to talk easily with him, interrupt, discuss anything, pose questions.

We discussed how statesmen relax. He said he never shoots. As a boy he had a shotgun. Later on, as an exile under the Dutch, he once shot an eagle (I think he means hawk) and brought it down. A friend who was with him cut off both the eagle's wings while the bird was alive. "I can never forget the look in that eagle's eyes," said Sukarno. "I can't kill anything. I won't even fish." He made his finger into a hook shape and jerked it up. "Of course, I eat fish and birds," he added with a grin.

He doesn't play cards, tennis, or swim. For exercise, he walks or dances. He doesn't paint, much as he loves it. He once painted a portrait of a Balinese woman; this hangs in his Bogor palace. But never again "because I have no time, like President Eisenhower. When I get three or four hours a week [clearly a minimization], I like to talk with my friends, to exchange ideas. Or I like to go to one of our shadow plays. It sometimes lasts all night and tires me out. But it clears my mind."

He claimed that his political ideas were different from those of any other leaders, suited to Indonesia. "There are points I have taken from Tito, Salazar, de Gaulle, Eisenhower, Nehru," said he. (This is baloney.) He said he had likewise been influenced by Marx, Engels, Jaurès, Sun Yatsen, Gandhi, Jefferson, and Paul Revere, all of whom he had read. "What did you read of Paul Revere?" I inquired. He skipped deftly on to other things.

He did admit that U.S.-Indonesian relations were now better. He was satisfied with our training of Indonesian officers, and they came back liking us. But we still failed to understand this country's national aspirations. Because of this, Eisenhower should come here. He had invited him directly and also through Nixon. "He should come. It would do him good. Why it would even do him good to dance. After all, Voroshilov was here and he is over seventy. You should not let the Russians always take the lead."

Sukarno didn't like Dulles. Things were now better under Herter. Dulles always considered anyone not actively allied to the United States as a Communist. He had to be pro-American or a Communist. Sukarno liked Nixon a lot. He was a good, direct man to do business with. He didn't care too much for Adlai Stevenson. Sukarno thought him too vague and "philosophical." He didn't think Adlai really understood things. He preferred Nixon.

DJAKARTA, *October 15, 1959*

TED Newton, the Canadian Ambassador, told me that on one of his plane trips with the ambassadors, Sukarno turned, as he frequently does, to sex. He asked each envoy how long he could do without a woman. The Russian, whose English is fluent but imperfect, said, "Two years." "Ah," sneered Sukarno, "you can't call yourself a man." The Russian, in a huff, retired early. The Pole was delighted.

CHRISTCHURCH, NEW ZEALAND, *October 20, 1959*

HURRIED down here via Australia to slip onto a flight to Antarctica while the relatively warm season is on. Lately, it has been very cold at our polar station, which is 9,200 feet high. The last week of September, the temperature at the pole has been 114 below zero. The Russian station at the pole of inaccessibility has registered the record low of 130 below zero.

MCMURDO SOUND, ANTARCTICA, *October 23, 1959*

AN eerie flight. En route, they turn off the heating gradually in the plane to acclimatize the passengers and prevent dashboard instruments from snapping. It's spring now and relatively warm—minus fifteen degrees Fahrenheit. Daylight all the time, the sun sets briefly around 1:00 A.M., but it's still light enough to read a paper. When everything isn't obscured by snow or blowing clouds, it's incredibly beautiful—a flat sheet of ice covering the Sound (the airstrip is on seven feet of ice and will break up around January), stark mountains rising behind, their rocky peaks bursting through the snow. This base is on Ross Island, a volcanic formation in the ice. Mount Erebus, some miles away, is still a live volcano.

Strange things. There is a snow mine—the place from which they dig out snow and bring it to the camp by machine to melt for drinking and washing water. This is rationed—only one shower a week. Men work always in silken gloves, and work ten minutes, warm their hands five. The silk keeps the hands from freezing to metal. My garb in this protected camp: two suits of underwear, one set of long-woolen; three pairs of socks; heavy, lined, rubber boots; heavy woolen pants; lined outer pants with waterproof exterior; double-thickness woolen shirt; woolen sweater; furlined parka with two hoods (over my woolen balaklava face helmet); either silk gloves plus woolen mittens plus leather mittens; or leather, fleece-lined mittens extending above the elbow and tied around the shoulder by a strap so as not to lose one when it's off; sunglasses, day and night, against snow blindness.

There are four poles, three at the North Pole: here, geographical, geomagnetic (marks earth's axis), magnetic (off the axis, center of compass attraction), and inaccessibility (point furthest from water on all sides). There is no inaccessibility pole in the Arctic, which is water surrounded by land, the reverse of the Antarctic. Shackleton's 1908 hut, nearby, still contains cans of food he brought—rusted only because of the sea voyage in. A New Zealander baked good bread recently from the fifty-one-year-old flour.

SCOTT BASE, ANTARCTICA, *October 24, 1959*

SCOTT is a New Zealand base near McMurdo in what the New Zealanders meticulously call the "Ross Sea Dependency." Rode over in a Sno-Cat. Afterward, went out on the ice and watched three sled teams (Greenland huskies weighing about 110 pounds each) come in from a long trip (thirty-five miles a day), their leaders' beards white with snow. The ice was magnificent. It was windless but twenty-five degrees below zero; so cold that your nose froze, despite parkas and woolen helmets, and your hands hurt within seconds if you took a pencil out. Wandered around the ice with a New Zealander testing the way with a long pick, looking for crevasses in the snow. Whenever it whined through we went around the cracks, heading toward two enormously fat seals lying sluggishly against the white background and mauve, blue and rose mountains in the distance.

SOUTH POLE, *October 26, 1959*

THE South Pole is marked by a circle of fuel barrels about fifty yards in diameter, set amidst an enormous, flat, empty plain of snowy waste, pockmarked and rippled by the wind. I spent an hour here this morning, circling overhead in a cumbersome C-124. We dropped fifteen tons of fuel products by parachute to our seventeen-man pole station and then waited while another C-124 dropped an equal load. All told, we circled the pole eight times, thus making eight trips completely around the world.

The flight lasted ten hours. We had good, full sunshine all the way. It is now six months continuous daytime at the pole, where there is only one day and one night each year. We flew along the frozen Ross Sea by volcanic Mount Erebus and tranquil, snowcapped Mount Terror, up the sloping flat plateau to Beardmore Glacier, then up the glacier for about an hour, between its towering borders of harsh, craggy mountains rising high above us on either side. We then reached the high polar plateau, extending, it would seem, infinitely to the pole itself, 9,200 feet above sea level.

The pole is on a great, flat ice desert; totally featureless except for pocks and ripples whipped into the snow by the howling wind. It looks like a perfect, incalculably large airfield (surely bigger than all France).

CANBERRA, *November 5, 1959*

EXCELLENT talk with Robert Gordon Menzies, the Prime Minister, at his office in Parliament House. Menzies said: "We won't break the line with the United States; we won't see Formosa handed over to Peking. We are anxious about the effect on the overseas Chinese if recognition is granted on any terms that might appear to concede a victory to Red China. This is not a juridical problem. It is a hard, current, political problem."

KOROLEVU, FIJI, *November 11, 1959*

FIJI is lovely. The people are Melanesian: tall, extremely sturdy, with muscular legs and enormous feet. The climate is astonishingly cool but humid; it rains virtually every day. Fijians ride horseback along the beaches just like Gauguin's painting of the Tahitian boy on a pink horse. The sea is filled with magical beasts and shells; the air is redolent with heavy flowers; and the moon seems larger and nearer than in other places.

PEARL HARBOR, *November 14, 1959*

BRIEFING at navy headquarters, with Admiral Ramsey, Chief of Staff. The Russians appear to be doing to Mao what we do to Syngman Rhee. They give Mao enough equipment to defend himself, but not enough to take off on his own in a war that would involve the United States.

NEW YORK, *December 1, 1959*

SAW Jack Kennedy today. He is an attractive man, but, I must say, he continues to look awfully young. He admits that is one of his big political difficulties: People say he is too young to deal with the men who now dominate the world scene.

He indicates that Catholicism doesn't bother him politically. It is a disadvantage in many ways, but an advantage in others. The political climate is more tolerant than in the days of Al Smith, and, realistically speaking, there are more Catholic voters.

He will formally announce his candidacy in early January. If he runs ahead in the primaries and maintains his lead in the public-opinion polls, he thinks he can get the nomination, but the tough thing is dealing with the politicians, not the public. He will not accept the Vice-Presidential slot if he goes into the convention with a substantial lead and is merely jockeyed out of position by the politicians in a smoke-filled room. He is confident he can lick either Nixon or Nelson Rockefeller, but would still prefer to run against Nixon.

He thinks foreign policy will be the main electoral issue in the sense that the Republicans will be attacked for letting the United States slip backward in the power race. He thought any Democratic nominee if elected (provided, of course, that it isn't Stevenson himself) would be delighted to have Adlai Stevenson as Secretary of State.

15

PARIS, *December 16, 1959*

LUNCH WITH CHIP BOHLEN. CHIP HAS BEEN STUDYING CHINESE-SOVIET relationships and is convinced there are major centrifugal forces in their alliance. China is now in the same position Russia was in when Stalin was collectivizing the land—only worse. Stalin needed a whipping boy to divert public attention in those days. China needs a whipping boy now. But Soviet society has evolved, and Khrushchev no longer requires one. In fact, because of nuclear arms, he probably thinks it undesirable to excite people too much, although he still pursues the cold war. In China, on the other hand, they want to keep people stirred up.

PARIS, *February 4, 1960*

THIS morning, I had a long talk with the Comte de Paris, Bourbon claimant to the French throne. He says:

In France today, there is a king but no monarchy. There is no provision for succession. De Gaulle has transformed many things and he is giving the habit to the country of needing a chief. There is increasingly wide consent to this delegation of authority. The work he has started here and in Africa requires a chief to complete the task.

I don't think we will return to the parliamentary system and to the election of a president and the party system. Neither the right nor the left (which has some undoubted men of quality) can assert itself. And no man can be produced by the competition of right and left who would have the freedom to speak for France as a whole.

PARIS, *February 11, 1960*

THIS morning, I had an especially interesting talk with Pompidou, de Gaulle's former directeur de Cabinet. Pompidou told me that to his deep distress—"but I assure you this doesn't come from the Elysée"—there was a very serious plot to oust de Gaulle, a plot backed by American money. The scheme was to form a government, including Bidault, and eventually to bring in Pinay as president. The most fantastic aspect of the story is that Alain de Sérigny, an Algerian French leader and editor, was supposed to be one of the principal conspirators and money raisers. It is not forgotten here that de Sérigny actively conspired with Bob Murphy prior to the North African landing and had close American contact. Pompidou said it is apparent de Sérigny would not have been arrested and imprisoned recently merely because he attacked de Gaulle in his newspaper and called for an Algérie Française. He is suspected of something infinitely more important, and now the government is in the process of ascertaining the truth.

Pompidou never even inferred that he suspected the CIA, but I had a feeling that this was what he was getting at. According to his story, important circles in America had become so distressed by de Gaulle's attitude on NATO that they had resolved to oust him and bring in a pro-NATO government.

PARIS, *February 12, 1960*

YESTERDAY evening, I told Houghton what Pompidou had told me. He was very alarmed and recalled that he had written a letter to Alain de Sérigny some time ago saying he would be glad to see him next time he came to Paris. He buzzed his secretary and asked her to find the letter, but when I left one and a half hours later, much to Houghton's distress, it had not been found. I told him I calculated this document would provoke some interesting questions when they applied the thumbscrew to Sérigny.

He asked if I could arrange a very confidential luncheon with Pompidou, because he is worried. (I am dictating this on Friday after having arranged said luncheon for next Wednesday.)

PARIS, *February 17, 1960*

LUNCHED today at Ambassador Houghton's with Pompidou, just the three of us. I acted as interpreter. Houghton wanted it so secret that his own staff wouldn't know. Houghton reassured his guest that U.S. policy remained firmly behind de Gaulle.

Pompidou again gave an account of the rumors of a conspiracy aided by American money. He said it was now evident that the political plot involved in last month's crisis was far more extensive than anybody had believed. Everything was supposed to go off in March or April but was prematurely exposed.

According to the rumor, Pinay would have been made president to placate the Americans. The idea behind the conspiracy was that France would impose a policy of integration on Algeria and gain American support in exchange by reaffirming close ties with NATO. Alain de Sérigny was supposed to be a money-raising agent.

Pompidou advised Houghton to do nothing about knocking down the rumors. He thought it was easier to let them die a natural death. The only thing required was for the United States to officially reassert its support for de Gaulle. Our abstention in the last Algerian vote in the UN had raised serious doubts.

PARIS, *February 18, 1960*

LARRY Norstad filled me in at length on the secret Spanish-German negotiations. Last autumn the Spanish Foreign Minister, Castiella, visited Bonn, and the Germans told him they were interested in special military facilities in Spain. Castiella agreed, and negotiations were begun by military experts. When Norstad first heard about this at the time of the NATO meetings last December, he discussed it with General Heusinger. He expressed regret and said the matter affected NATO. The negotiations were temporarily suspended.

The Germans say they want special help for training their new air force, for supporting it, and for practicing with new missiles. Spain would afford useful facilities for such things as long-range practice flights.

Larry is very worried about the propaganda and psychological implications. While Germany can cite the special agreement of the United States with Spain as a precedent, it is treading on delicate ground.

PARIS, *February 20, 1960*

THIS morning I went to see de Gaulle at the Elysée. Did he think there was any means of assuring Soviet good faith in coexistence? He answered: "The Russians cannot be of good faith, nor can we. Russia can think that it is in its own interest not to continue the Cold War and to pursue a temporary détente. Perhaps, at that moment, it is in their interest; but they won't give up on major, long-range aspirations."

I then asked what Khrushchev expected from his French visit in April. He said: "Propaganda. Khrushchev makes propaganda. Perhaps also he hopes this might aid him in his present relaxation policy [*politique de détente*] and perhaps it is now in Khrushchev's interest in many respects to start détente. He might need this in terms of his internal position in the Soviet Union as well as in terms of his relationships with the satellite countries of Poland and Hungary. Perhaps he sees it as desirable to pursue such a détente for the moment. And a tour of this sort—his visit to France— helps propaganda. Of course, I will talk with Khrushchev. We will chat. But I don't expect anything."

De Gaulle still vaguely hoped some kind of a deal could be worked out with Washington along the lines of Big Three cooperation (United States, Britain, France), which he had suggested to Eisenhower and Macmillan soon after regaining authority. But, discussing his plan, he said: "I never used the word *directoire* [in his letters to the President and Prime Minister]. That is an invention of the press. But the fact remains that there are only three real powers in the West; three powers that have world-wide support. They also have a certain force of atomic power. As far as France is concerned, we do not have an atomic military force today, but we will have. Those three powers are charged with the defense and security of the West."

Then the general hinted very plainly that if his views on this were not heeded he would reply by reducing France's support of NATO—precisely as happened. I had asked if he thought Big Three accord might be facilitated by the fact that France had at last crossed the nuclear threshold. He said: "I hope so. This is indispensable." However, he continued: "If our wish in this matter is not granted we will no longer support the organization of the Atlantic Treaty. [Note the precision of the phrase: He would be against the *organization*, not the treaty itself; he would take the O out of NATO, the North Atlantic Treaty Organization.] We have taken back control of our fleet and certain other things. Also, we will take back our liberty in other respects if this is not granted. We will take back our complete liberty. We will, of course, remain allied; but we will only be an ally and fully independent. [This is precisely what de Gaulle's policy became six years later.]"

I then asked if the general wanted American nuclear arms to reduce France's economic burden and thereby to speed up its defense preparations. He answered: "The United States will not give us aid. France is not the United States and the United States is not France. We are not the same country and we will each keep our secrets. The United States will not modify the McMahon law. I have not asked for any such modification and I will not ask for it. This is perfectly natural and I understand the American point of view. We will make our own atomic arms. That is that. It costs heavily and it will take much time, but you can be sure that we will work out this program, and basically it is better that way."

We then talked about disarmament. I asked de Gaulle if he thought that France could play a more important role in disarmament talks. He came up with an interesting idea. He said:

> There is only one subject on which it is possible to make a practicable disarmament arrangement today, and that is in the field of missiles. Perhaps a reciprocal control on missiles could be worked out. After all, missiles cannot be hidden. They are localized and can be inspected. [I am afraid de Gaulle missed the point of the new mobile missiles presently being developed, such as our Polaris submarine.] If an agreement on missile inspection can be worked out, atomic arms will become less important. One can do something in this field. But I don't know if anybody *wants* to do anything.

All this talk about stopping tests is unimportant. Stopping atomic tests wouldn't stop atomic arms. The United States and the Soviet Union already have enormous supplies of weapons and they will continue to make arms if they stop testing. A cessation of testing will only hurt France, which has not yet got its weapons. There can be no nuclear disarmament unless stockpiles are liquidated and I don't believe this will be done. The only field is that of missiles. The only possibility of making things a little easier is in the realm of missiles.

PARIS, *February 28, 1960*

LUNCHED with President Manuel Prado of Peru and his wife. Spaak was there. He thought it was a good thing that the Spanish bases story had come out now rather than after the deal had been made. When he came into the room, he winked and said: "I see the Spanish say I gave you the information because I am a militant Socialist who hates Franco."

LONDON, *March 15, 1960*

THIS afternoon, saw Selwyn Lloyd. Our conversation began with his remark: "Well, you are the man of the Spanish bases story." He thought the piece had done some good and said Britain's relations with Spain had, strangely enough, been improved by the affair. He said: "I would like to see a code of conduct approved for peaceful coexistence. Khrushchev now continues to try and subvert and undermine the West wherever he can. That is Cold War, not peaceful coexistence. I wonder if you can establish a series of self-denying ordinances, doing such things as controlling propaganda and subversion."

PARIS, *April 5, 1960*

BREAKFAST this morning with General Paul Grossin, head of French military intelligence (SDECE). He says the Algerian FLN has no need for heavy equipment and aircraft now, but some of their pilots have been trained in China. China gave the FLN considerable money with which to purchase arms in Czechoslovakia. Many West German arms dealers sell to the FLN, although the Bonn government tries to stop it. The French terroristic Main Rouge hires professional killers for special murders of arms merchants in Germany.

Since 1956, the Russians have been warning the French that they had better settle the Algerian war soon. General Jougov personally said this to Grossin. Grossin asked him, "How?" Jougov said: "That is your business."

PARIS, *April 7, 1960*

DINNER with Prince Paul and Princess Olga, former ruler of Jugoslavia. When the March 27, 1941 *coup d' état* took place, young Peter was with

Paul and Olga all day long, although history says he made a broadcast to his people. In fact, they found another boy and put him on the air.

Paul considers monarchy an outmoded form of government and is sure it will disappear everywhere eventually. It still was a success in England and Scandinavia because they had long traditions and fine discipline. He didn't think Don Juan had any chance in Spain; and the Comte de Paris is an insignificant fellow who will never regain the throne of France.

Under the influence of Queen Frederika, King Paul of Greece is preparing young Prince Constantine badly for kingship. He is giving him an old-fashioned education, which is no good nowadays. A prince, to have any chance as king, should be stuffed with knowledge and should mix with all kinds of people to know what they are like and what they want.

PARIS, *April 8, 1960*

THIS afternoon, I visited Georges Bidault, former Foreign Minister, Prime Minister, MRP leader, and now one of de Gaulle's principal opponents, in his home at St. Cloud. It was watched over by two agents with tommy guns. Inside, the house was dirty, untidy, and smelled heavily of illness and fear.

He called de Gaulle "crazy." He says France is "finished" and "the game is over." He talked about being locked up behind machine guns (referring to the guards outside). He said he did not know whether he was going to be shot or whether I would be shot. "Of course they took your picture as you went in the door." Later he said the policemen were there to protect him from assassination by the FLN. Still later, he said he was entirely free and could go wherever he wished. At one moment, he said he wanted to make a strong political speech but the Elysée had prevented it. But he admitted the press was "fairly free" and that his articles in *Carrefour* were uncensored. He expressed contempt for everybody, saying France was being governed by a "madman" (de Gaulle) and an "idiot" (Debré).

He said de Gaulle had destroyed the French army. Six months ago, there were two real forces in France—the Communist Party and the army. Now there are only the Communists. The army was represented by the captains and the majors, and they didn't dislike de Gaulle—they "hated" him.

PARIS, *April 27, 1960*

LAST night at dinner, Pompidou had the following things to say:

There are no real problems—no problems of substance—between France and the United States. France has problems with Russia, Germany, and England—but not with America.

De Gaulle told Khrushchev that both Russia and France were happy to have Germany divided. Neither was afraid of his own Germany. Therefore they should agree to let the Berlin crisis alone and to discuss other things at the Summit.

Pompidou was amazed at the frenzied reception given by the United States to de Gaulle. He thought there was something strange about it—it was like a funeral paean; we seemed to speak about de Gaulle as if he were already dead and a figure of history.

Pompidou said de Gaulle reasons (and told Khrushchev): The world can have either war or peace; if it isn't war, it is peace—and that means negotiations.

PARIS, *May 16, 1960*

THIS morning, I had a talk with Yuri Zhukov at the Soviet Embassy. Zhukov says the situation is very grave. Khrushchev had come back from America favorably impressed, saying he was an "incorrigible optimist." He was convinced the American people and government wanted peace. The Camp David talks had been successful.

Therefore, the Russians were especially angered by the U-2 incident. They could not understand why May 1, their big holiday, had been selected for the flight. In the beginning, Khrushchev deliberately played down previous U-2 flights and isolated this one. He tried to leave a way out for the President by stating he was sure Eisenhower knew nothing about the flight.

Zhukov says that unless Eisenhower makes a statement apologizing for the flight, there will be no Eisenhower trip to Russia, and the situation will become even more serious.

PARIS, *May 18, 1960*

KHRUSHCHEV had an extraordinary press conference, which resembled a mass political meeting. Apart from the microphones and cameras there were about three thousand people present.

Khrushchev is a remarkable actor. He got immensely excited and red in the face, shaking his fists, stamping, recalling how his mother used to punish cats who stole cream and saying this had to be done in the United States. But at other times he was humorous and good natured. Despite his bluster, he didn't stick out his neck, said Russia still desired peaceful solutions to all problems, that West Berlin could remain capitalist, and that although he had a prepared draft for a separate peace treaty with East Germany, it was his secret when he intended to use it.

PARIS, *May 20, 1960*

PLEASANT talk with Chris Herter in the upstairs sitting room of the embassy residence. He looked well considering the strain he has been under. He is a true gentleman, and I like him a lot, but I don't think he is a very good Secretary of State.

There is no legal distinction between photographic satellites and U-2 reconnaissance. De Gaulle observed to Khrushchev, when the latter was yammering about the U-2, that the latest Soviet satellite crosses France eighteen times a day.

The Russians never brought up our U-2 aerial reconnaissance at any time before this incident. They have made several protests about American overflights, but never the U-2. We had always replied we were prepared to put any of those protests before the Hague World Court.

Herter said de Gaulle was extremely angry with Khrushchev. Both de Gaulle and Macmillan had suggested in their bilateral talks with Khrushchev, after the single explosive Big Four session, that everyone should wait twenty-four hours and try to patch things up. De Gaulle requested that nothing should be given out to the public about what took place, but Khrushchev insisted everything should be made public because his people had to be informed.

CADENABBIA, ITALY, *June 4, 1960*

THIS morning, I spent two hours with Adenauer, who is vacationing here in a villa above the lake. Talking about Khrushchev, he said: "Khrushchev has lost his mind. That happens to all dictators. [He was referring to the Soviet Prime Minister's recent crude remarks, in which he suggested Adenauer should be put in a straitjacket and Eisenhower should be placed in charge of a kindergarten.] Khrushchev is a good man. He always helps us. And he helps you too. Now you Americans will be in a position to get over the dangerous months while you are choosing your new President. I always fear that period. Thanks to Khrushchev's hard line, we don't have to worry anymore."

He explained Khrushchev's decision to torpedo the Summit Meeting accordingly: "I think it was a combination of things. To begin with, American planes had been carrying out flights over Russia for several years and the U.S.A. had good pictures of all Soviet military preparations. This fact shocked Khrushchev and his army. Therefore, he wanted to show the army that in spite of this situation he was not afraid of the Americans. Possibly, fright played its role in Khrushchev's attitude. One doesn't know this because he is such a good actor. In fact, he is the best actor I have ever seen."

During the whole conversation Adenauer paid special tribute to de

Gaulle. He thought his twelve years in Colombey had done him immense good and that now he was the ablest statesman in the West.

When I was about to leave and the old man came to the steps with me, I asked him what music he was playing here because I knew he had brought quite a collection of discs along. He replied that far and away his favorite composer was Haydn. After that, he liked Beethoven, Schubert, Mozart, and Vivaldi. Oddly enough, he didn't like Bach.

PARIS, *June 24, 1960*

THIS morning, Allen Dulles said China has a long-range policy of wanting to plant colonies of 5 to 10 million people in different places around the world, such as Algeria or Latin America. This would help get rid of their surplus population and would also increase their global power. Human beings are the greatest Chinese product. Overseas Chinese colonies could be established all round to help take over world power later on.

LOS ANGELES, *July 14, 1960*

JACK Kennedy got the nomination, and today I spent three fascinating hours in his suite at the Biltmore while the Democratic bigwigs and bosses were consulted, some in groups, others one by one, to decide on who would be the nominee for Vice-President. The business was transacted in the next room. In the larger sitting room, where I sat, the bosses, governors, senators, and mayors waited and talked with each other, drinking gallons of coffee until Jack called them in. I was the only newspaperman present.

I was there from 12 noon until 3:00 P.M. Earlier that morning, Jack had gone to see Lyndon Johnson in his suite and had offered him the Vice-Presidential nomination, which Johnson accepted. But I did not know this while sitting there, nor did any of those around me. Among them were Adlai Stevenson, Senator "Scoop" Jackson, Chet Bowles, Senator Smathers, Governor Abe Ribicoff, Governor Loveless, Governor Combs of Kentucky, and Governor Dave Lawrence of Pennsylvania.

Jackson assured me at about 12:30 (at least two hours after the deal had been made with Johnson) that the Vice-Presidential choice had narrowed to a contest between himself and Symington. Little did he know.

This afternoon, I had a nice but sad talk with poor old Adlai in his "Presidential Suite" at the Sheraton-West. He was drafting a statement on Lyndon Johnson's nomination for the Vice-Presidency. I asked if he would tell me who he had in mind as the Secretary of State in 1952 and 1956. He hesitated a moment and then said: "I will tell you this in strict confidence, but you are the only person who has ever known. I was thinking of Bill Fulbright, for whom I have great admiration, but I never even told him— then or now."

LOS ANGELES, *July 15, 1960*

THIS afternoon, I had a talk with Kennedy in his hideaway at the Beverly Hilton, where he was resting and preparing to make his acceptance speech this evening. Jack has hotel suites scattered all over this sprawling town.

Kennedy received us at the door of his suite, and I sat in the bedroom. Jack sat on the bed across from me. He is clearly a man who can make up his mind (unlike Adlai), and he does so quickly, without the slightest hesitation. He is bright and self-confident. He is frank to admit there are lots of things he does not know yet. He has a high, nasal Bostonian twang and speaks quite rapidly. Our conversation was limited to foreign affairs.

He told me he does not plan any trips abroad either before election day or, should he win, before inauguration day. I asked when he intended to announce his choice as a potential Democratic Secretary of State. "Right after the election," he replied. I asked if it were a fair assumption that either Bowles or Stevenson would be his choice, and he said this was "sound speculation."

He was determined, if elected, to choose the best possible ambassadors. These would not necessarily be diplomats from the Foreign Service, but he favored maximum use of career men. In any case, he would certainly try to get the best available. This would not mean the men who had made the largest political contributions, but the best available for the particular post.

He strongly favored lengthening the period of budgeting to permit the United States to accumulate larger sums for longer periods than one year for foreign aid, so that other countries we wished to help could plan on a long-range basis instead of a year-to-year basis.

I told him that once I had suggested to President Eisenhower that it might be of great help if the government were legally in a position to draft civilians for special service abroad; that Ike had heartily endorsed the idea, but had never done anything with it. What did Jack think of it, and would he do something? He dodged this and said only that he thought Senator Humphrey's plan for students to work abroad for a year after graduation was a good idea.

I then asked if he did not think that in this nuclear-missile era, it was wise to shorten the period of U.S. political campaigns in order to have a much briefer lame-duck period of government. Jack gave a practical politician's answer. He did not wish to see us give up our system of primaries and did not see how we could reduce the period without so doing. And, he added, a grin on his face, if it had not been for primaries, he would not have gotten the nomination.

NEW YORK, *September 16, 1960*

CARL Sandburg, fine, salty, immodest octogenarian poet, had three amusing stories to tell.

One of the current Presidential candidates (guess which) was asked, "Were you born in a log cabin?" He answered, "No, that was Abraham Lincoln: I was born in a manger."

Old Man Scripps left instructions that since he would probably die while voyaging around the world on his yacht, he wanted to insure that he was buried at sea. This is just what happened. When the news came in, a linotypist on one of his papers commented sourly, "You know why the Old Man did this? So that nobody would piss on his grave."

Sandburg swears the following is true, but he couldn't put it in his Lincoln book unless he bowdlerized it. It was told to him by one of the Hay family, Milton Hay. Lincoln, as a young man, was defending a man in court. His opponent attacked the sanity of Lincoln's client, saying: "He is a strange man. Why he even stands in his house and pisses in the street." Lincoln got up in rebuttal and said: "What's so strange about that? Wouldn't it be even stranger if he stood in the street and pissed into his house?" The case was dismissed.

NEW YORK, *October 1, 1960*

THIS morning, I had a long talk with Lord Home, the new British Foreign Secretary, in his Waldorf Towers suite. Home said the Russians and the Chinese were making a "dead set" at Africa and that Chinese penetration is "very serious" in both the Middle East and North Africa. He simply doesn't know whether the Russians are worried about this or not. However, he added, "There is a real Chinese-Russian row on now."

NEW YORK, *October 6, 1960*

LUNCHED with M'hammed Yazid, Minister of Information for the Algerian Provisional Government, and Abdel Kader Chanderli, their permanent representative to UN (as an observer), at the most expensive restaurant in New York, La Côte Basque.

I said I would be prepared, despite my dilapidated condition, to spend a week in FLN territory if they could arrange it on my terms. I couldn't spend more than a week because of my regular column commitments.

Yazid said they could arrange for me to go in from Tunisia or Morocco and make a "deep penetration." I said I was more intrigued by what Ahmed Boumendjel had suggested in early 1959: They could pick me up at the St. Georges Hotel in Algiers and get me out of the country without killing me. That would be a test of their ability to show they really ran the hinterland. After a week, they would have to get me to a communications point in either Tunisia or Morocco. Yazid said he would fix it up for some time during the month of November.

He asked me if there were anybody I could appoint as my confidential agent in the negotiation. (This began to smell like EOKA days in Cyprus.) I said: "You must call my Paris office where I have a secretary named Nancy Ross. But you will have to have an agreed means of communication. She shares an office with another secretary who might answer the phone. You must have somebody on your team call up and say, 'Hello, Nancy'."

He had to decide on a name for his agent (and himself). The agreed name is Gilbert. Somebody from their outfit is to call up and say, "Hello Nancy, this is Gilbert. Can you meet me for a drink at such and such a place?" Nancy will then arrange the next step along this labyrinth.

NEW YORK, *October 11, 1960*

JACK Kennedy came in to see me today for a first-class talk. Jack thought Nixon "was a damn fool to agree to debate with me on an equal-time TV basis." He could easily have prevented it by applying pressure to the big TV and radio chains. Now it is too late. It is a tough ordeal. Says Jack: "Just imagine if Eisenhower had had to do this against Stevenson in 1952 and 1956. He would have looked silly."

Nixon tried to use all kinds of tricks. For example, last Friday the studio temperature was down to sixty-five degrees so that Nixon wouldn't sweat before the camera the way he did the first time. Jack said there were little tricks with the lighting designed to operate against him and for Nixon. But he thinks basically it was an enormous break for him to have this debate. The press is largely pro-Nixon and has been building Kennedy up as a naive, inexperienced young man. Now he can come before the whole nation and show his true colors.

I inquired at length about foreign policy. Since he implicitly foresaw a period of crisis for years to come, would he bring Republicans into the Administration in important offices and in the interests of national unity. "Definitely," said he.

He criticized the Eisenhower Administration for failing to do this. To the best of his knowledge, David Bruce was the only Democrat who got any post under Eisenhower. Kennedy would like to do what Roosevelt and Truman did, and use Republicans whose basic thinking was close to his own in positions affecting foreign policy and national security.

I asked what kind of a secretary of state he was thinking of and whether he considered national legislative experience as a necessary prerequisite. He said this was too tricky to answer. Naturally, there were political considerations, for example, of such men as Stevenson and Bowles (he specifically mentioned both names). He said: "I consider it essential that the Secretary of State should be able to get on well with Congress. However, prior legislative experience isn't necessarily essential and could not necessarily guarantee effective relationships with Congress."

I asked if he favored the idea of a separate foreign affairs adviser or agent like Colonel House or Harry Hopkins. He replied negatively: "The Secretary of State should be the President's agent. Only when there is no harmony between the President and the Secretary of State—as with Lansing and Wilson, and Hull and Roosevelt—do you have these special agents or advisors. The President and Secretary of State should be on an intimate personal relationship and have full confidence in each other."

He would like to keep Allen Dulles on "for a while" in CIA but then replace him. There is no way of checking up to see how well CIA is going. A new man could give a new perspective to the job. He hoped to persuade General Max Taylor to take it over after Dulles.

WASHINGTON, *October 12, 1960*

THIS afternoon, saw Allen Dulles in his CIA office. We talked about Gary Powers. The CIA has a theory that no man should ever be ordered to commit suicide if captured, and this was not in contracts with agents. The CIA thought there was more chance of a man's individual nobility prompting him to such an act if there were no such advance order.

Allen said Powers had done nothing wrong and probably would have had a hard time committing suicide either by pistol or with his poison needle, even had he wanted to. First he was parachuted out and secondly he was in a cumbersome pressure suit. Thirdly, he was captured pronto on landing.

Nevertheless, Dulles left me with the impression he thought Powers should somehow have knocked himself off. He said Powers had been brainwashed or brain-conditioned prior to the trial. It was clear he had told the Russians more than emerged, because his previous "testimony" was always referred to.

PARIS, *November 24, 1960*

LUNCHED with Billotte. He says the following French generals are involved in conspiracy against the state: Marshal Juin, Generals Zeller, Jouhaud, and Salan. Pierre thinks that by February 1, there will either be a complete end to the continuing drama of plots and an imposed settlement of the Algerian conflict, or civil war in France.

PARIS, *November 25, 1960*

LAST night, I got a call from Lyndon Johnson's aide. Johnson wanted me to come around this morning to tell him a bit about NATO, before he went to see Spaak. I had to take my dog, Benjamin Beagle, because Marina was away and the servants were out. Johnson only wanted to listen. He sat there glumly pulling his long ears, but from the questions he asked I deduced that he was browned off at Norstad.

He asked: "Don't you think a man like General Norstad should have consulted Democratic leaders before explaining this plan here?" I blew my top, saying that after all, Norstad was a nonpolitical general. Obviously he was a member of the Eisenhower dynasty and close to the President, to whom he was responsible, but he had no politics. Furthermore, his principal responsibility was as a commander not just of U.S. troops but of all the allies.

He asked what I thought about keeping Norstad on here as commander. I thought it would be fatal to remove him. Furthermore, he should be kept here for at least eighteen more months so that a new general could be trained as his chief of staff to succeed him eventually.

Johnson asked me if I would please tell him how I interpreted the Norstad plan. I said: "Really, I would feel like a lunatic telling you what the Norstad plan is after you have spent the entire week being briefed by General Norstad himself." "No," said Johnson. "I would like to know what the thing means."

I had a feeling he didn't understand the plan and wanted it explained in kindergarten language. He sat there listening with an absolute poker face, and I couldn't tell whether he was testing me, trying to get elucidation, or what.

It was an odd meeting, and Benjamin's presence brought about a rather curious insight into his character. He told me he had eight beagles, that the first one had been purchased nine years ago in Virginia. When he had his heart attack in 1955, that dog, whose name is simply Beagle, sensed there was something wrong and used to put its head up against his to comfort him.

A friend of Johnson's told him that when somebody is unhappy, a hound's olfactory organs smell a special secretion, and the hound comforts his master or friend. Then Johnson said an extraordinary thing. He said: "Beagle always sleeps under my bed. But when I am sick or unhappy or feeling sorry for myself, or when I cry, he comes up on the bed and comforts me."

"My God," I thought, "only a heartbeat keeps this man from the White House." I was really struck by the big Texan casually saying, "when I cry."

PARIS, *December 6, 1960*

EXCEEDINGLY interesting lunch today with Pierre Mendès-France. He told me an extraordinary thing about de Gaulle. He said that once, when he was having a private conversation with de Gaulle during the war, the general had confessed to him: "One of my brothers, Xavier, is crazy. The other of my brothers, Pierre, is thoroughly normal. I am in between."

PARIS, *February 11, 1961*

LUNCHED with Fritz Nolting. He had just come back from Washington, where he had two long talks with Acheson. Dean told him that when Kennedy visited him and asked him if he would accept the post as Ambassador to NATO, Acheson inquired, "Did you get this idea from Cy Sulzberger's column?" Kennedy replied, "Yes." (Acheson declined the job. He preferred to stay in Washington and keep his finger in the pie.)

PARIS, *February 14, 1961*

THIS morning, I had a one-hour talk with de Gaulle. The general said it was perfectly apparent that during our age nations needed greater direction by their governments. Eisenhower had not given the United States sufficient leadership. Whatever his intentions, President Kennedy would find himself increasingly pushed toward strong government, and the U.S. economy would find itself increasingly pushed toward dirigisme. This was a necessity of our times. The United States would simply have to abandon its shibboleth of free enterprise and accept ever greater government controls for its economy. There was no escape from this. The problems and pressures of our era are simply too great to permit the luxury of laissez-faire. We were all finding this out, and we all had this reaction to the enormous events of our time.

I asked de Gaulle if he intended to ask for revision of the McMahon Act in France's favor, now that there was a new U.S. Administration. He said: "We doubt the value of making any approach. I don't intend to make an approach. The last administration never proposed any such revision. And, frankly I wouldn't do it if I were in your place. As for France—we will continue to make our own nuclear weapons."

I was very much struck by one thing throughout our conversation. De Gaulle continually spoke of Algeria in terms of a fully independent republic which could decide freely on its own whether it had any links with France or not. In other words, he has gone whole hog.

I then asked de Gaulle what kind of guarantees concerning the status and rights of the European minority would be satisfactory in case Algeria finally opted for complete independence.

To my astonishment, he replied:

We are not asking for anything, for any guarantees. That is up to the Algerians. Obviously the Europeans are very useful to Algeria. It is the Europeans with their abilities, their techniques, and their capital who can make Algeria work. Without them there would be economic misery. It is clearly in the interest of Algeria that the Europeans should remain. But it is up to the Algerians to make the decision. *They* must make the decision and they must offer the guarantees and conditions which persuade the Europeans to stay on.

It is necessary for Algeria to link its diplomatic destiny with France; but it is not necessary for France. France does not need Algeria, but Algeria needs France. Without association with France, there will be anarchy in Algeria.

Oddly enough, considering that he had just offered the Algerians full independence if they wished, the general insisted that France had won the war itself, the military campaign. He told me: "You may not realize it, but the war in Algeria is now over. You can go anywhere. There is no fighting. There are a few murders—perhaps six a day, four Muslims and two Europeans. But that is not a war. The only war now is a war in the press—not in Algeria. But that doesn't mean that serious political questions do not remain to be settled."

It was becoming increasingly clear that the general envisioned the use of his own small atomic stockpile as a diplomatic weapon against allies in peacetime and not as a military weapon against enemies in wartime. In the latter case he obviously relied upon the preponderant U.S. nuclear umbrella. But, prior to the last extremity, he could hold France's advantage over a nonnuclear West Germany and could insist on France's presence at any major international meeting because it was, after all, an atomic power in its own right.

This became plain during our conversation, when I asked if Bonn might get access to French nuclear weapons were it to invest in costly new French atomic plants. He said: "Germany is not investing in our nuclear plants. We see no reason to change. France is building atomic plants with its own money."

The general had by this time expanded and broadened his theory of another great war. He said: "If war does not come within ten years, it is possible that the white, civilized people may group together, but they will not group themselves *against* the other people of the earth. It will only be vis-à-vis them, in relationship to them, the civilized peoples banding together with respect to the less civilized." This was a vague basis on which to build an enduring alliance structure. But he blamed U.S. and British failure to accept his Big Three strategic planning formula for the lacuna, adding:

> Unless there is an organization system there is clearly no engagement for a common policy. Look at the situation. The West must have a common policy in the world. But there is no common policy in the Congo or in Berlin or in the Far East. Yet a common policy is a primordial necessity. It is a primordial necessity that there would be a western-world policy confronting a Soviet world policy. The whole world looks for a *real western* global policy. Because there is no such policy the whole world suffers. We need a permanent cooperation of the three main western powers. That is indis-

pensable. And these powers are the United States, Britain, and France. The others are less important. They would follow us; they would have to follow us.

He saw no chance of a deal between Adenauer and Moscow. About Adenauer he said:

Germans are Germans. One reason that we must try to make a united Europe is to enclose [*encadrer*] Germany. As long as Adenauer is in control there, there will be no deal between the Germans and the Russians. But later—I don't know. I am not so sure. There are important factors pushing the Germans toward Russia and the Russians toward Germany. The Germans manufacture great quantities of industrial equipment. Look at the Ruhr; look at Krupps. And Russia never has enough industrial equipment. Krupps is very alerted to this.

Reciprocally, the Germans need cheap agricultural products to feed their workers. These products must be cheap so the Germans can keep their prices down on the manufactures they want to sell. Krupps continues to push the idea of this as the basis for a German-Russian deal. This will not take place with Adenauer. He won't treat with the Russians. But after Adenauer things may change. Russia may work out a deal on Berlin and a federation of East Germany and West Germany as the basis for such a realignment. It is not impossible to envision this after Adenauer. That is why we must have a strong Common Market Europe.

I said I had heard that Macmillan had recently discussed with him the desirability of admitting Communist China to UN and the recognition by other Western countries of Peking. He said:

China in UN? It is all the same to us. We don't believe in UN. UN is anarchy, nothing but anarchy. It won't change if China comes in. If China comes in it won't bother us. It will just add one more orator to insult the West.

As for diplomatic relations between France and China—we are not so opposed to the thought. [In fact, he established the link in 1964.] After all, we have diplomatic relations with Russia. But we will do nothing ourselves to separate France from the rest of the West on this question. We are simply not against it. And, I repeat, as for UN—what is the difference if we bring still one more devil into it?

After a weekend of talks with Prime Minister Harold Macmillan, I asked if he thought London's policy toward the Common Market had changed and if the British now wanted to join. He raised his eyebrows skeptically and said: "British policy—no; British sentiment—perhaps. Britain is certainly less sure of the United States now than in the past and it is not sure of the health of its own economy. Therefore, some people in England seem to think that perhaps they should eventually make a deal with the Common Market. But this is only sentiment; it is not policy. As far as we are concerned, we shall continue to make the Common Market, to make Europe."

ANKARA, TURKEY, *February 21, 1961*

USEFUL talk with President Çemal Gursel at the Presidential Palace of
Çankaya. Gursel (chief of the provisional government) received me in an
ugly high-ceilinged, brown-paneled room. He suffered a stroke some
months ago, and although his mind functions well, he moves in a cumbersome way. His left arm is clearly not working. He had difficulty ringing a
bell for his secretary.

I said that I had been interested to read several times his words—
uttered before and again after the revolution—to the effect that the Turkish army must remain out of politics. Did he still feel this was necessary?
He answered: "Indeed I do. We have already put the army out of politics.
We have isolated it by specific orders which are followed in the sense of
rigid discipline. The army is out of politics." This is not strictly true,
because he, a general, is chief of state; a prominent member of the military
junta remains commander of the Ankara district; and several others retain
commands.

I asked what had been the reason for his revolution, why had the junta
considered it necessary to throw out the previous regime? He said: "The
revolution took place because the political situation had degenerated beyond repair. We were headed toward a dictatorship: a sectarian, party and
class dictatorship. Furthermore, the economic life of the country was stulti-
fied. The people of Turkey were rapidly dividing into two camps preparing
to fight each other in a civil war. Is that not adequate reason to justify a
revolution?"

ATHENS, *March 1, 1961*

LUNCHED with Foreign Minister Averoff. I recalled his request, before the
Cyprus peace, that I take a letter down go Grivas—which I undertook to
do as a journalistic experience. He told me he had not gone through with
this. At that time Grivas was holed up in a house near Limassol. He was
afraid that if I established contact with him the British might be able to
trace Grivas because they had a good idea of the neighborhood he was in;
it would have been disastrous for the Greek government to be linked with
this.

ATHENS, *March 4, 1961*

YESTERDAY evening, I had a long talk with General George Grivas, who,
under the pseudonym of Dighenis, headed the EOKA uprising against the
British in Cyprus. Although born in Cyprus, he has made his career as a
professional officer in the Greek army. He is now up to the ears in politics
and would like to overthrow the present government and become Prime
Minister.

He said in guerrilla warfare no system that works in one country is of any use in another. Flexibility is all-important. His permanent EOKA force in the mountains was never larger than two hundred, but the towns and villages were filled with hidden guerrillas. Grivas himself went back and forth between mountains and villages. During the struggle there were 40,000 British troops in Cyprus, which has a population of less than 500,000. The one essential for guerrilla success is to have widespread popular support.

CAIRO, *March 26, 1961*

THIS evening, I had a talk for two and a half hours with President Nasser at his home in Heliopolis. I asked what was needed to improve U.S. relationships. He answered: "One of the main obstacles is Israel. We want to see the U.S. fair on this. But if the Arab people see the U.S. taking sides and neglecting our own views, then naturally they get angry."

I said I knew his policy was what we called "neutralist" but that, in reading his newspapers and listening to his radio, I felt it was extremely *un*neutral toward the United States. He answered: "Neutrality is not an exact description of our policy. Neutrality applies only during war. Ours is a policy of 'nonalignment.' And our policy is perfectly fair. There is a plain reason for the fact that we do not attack the Communist bloc. We never read any attacks on us in the Soviet press or by Soviet statesmen. But the U.S. press attacks us and U.S. politicians attack us. I keep reading of American senators who want to blockade us because we don't allow Israeli ships to go through the Suez Canal."

I said I was appalled by the shortness of memory around here. After all, in 1956, the United States, which is always being attacked as "run by Israel," turned against its two closest allies, Britain and France, and forced Israel to retreat to its own borders. And yet we received no credit from this "nonaligned" government and "nonaligned" press and radio.

Nasser replied rather lamely that they had praised our stand against aggression following the Suez war and again in 1958. But that our Suez stand was "almost immediately followed by the Eisenhower Doctrine which ended all understanding with Washington."

I told Nasser that when I last saw him three years ago, I had asked his impression on religious freedom for Soviet Muslims, and he had said, "Ask me after I come back from my own visit." I now wanted to know. He said: "I can only tell you what I saw. I saw freedom. I worshipped at mosques in Moscow, Leningrad, and Tashkent. And there were many people in the mosques. Last year, the Soviet radio broadcast Ramadan services just as we do here. That is what I saw, religious freedom. But I will admit that I noticed the mosques were mainly filled with older people. I don't think the younger people are very interested in religion."

I reminded him that both in 1955 and in 1958, he spoke to me of his worry about an Israeli invasion and said that he feared war "as long as Israel exists." Did he still feel that way? He answered:

> Of course. It could happen any day or any night. That is our experience with Israel. Seven days before the 1956 invasion, Ben Gurion said publicly he wanted peace. I read in the Israeli newspapers that Israel is preparing again for war. Just a few days ago the Israeli chief of staff issued an order that his soldiers should be prepared. We fear the threat of a war madness beside us. And the French are arming the Israelis with the latest Vautour fighter-bombers and Mirages to replace their Mystères.
>
> Furthermore, we are suspicious that the Israeli nuclear plant is not for peaceful purposes because they built it secretly and first called it a textile factory. We told the UN about our own nuclear laboratories. France and Israel are cooperating in the atomic fields.

I then asked what he thought of the Eichmann trial. He said: "I hear that Eichmann is being moved continually from place to place and drugged. It is not Israel's right to try Eichmann. He should be tried in a German court. Israel didn't even exist during the period of the crimes he is charged with. The Israelis say Eichmann killed six million Jews. How many Jews were there in Germany or the entire world before the war and after the war? It is easy to check the figures and see that these claims are not true. Maybe one or two million were killed."

I looked at Nasser and saw him suddenly glance across at Mohamed Heikal, who must have made some sign, because Nasser then said: "But, of course, killing is killing, anyway. We merely think the figure is exaggerated for propaganda reasons."

PARIS, *April 7, 1961*

YESTERDAY evening, Gavin gave a reception for Vice-President Johnson, which I attended with Marina. When Johnson spotted me he rushed over and grabbed me by the arm and took me into a corner for a talk. He reached into his pocket and hauled out a document. This was a carbon copy of a cable from Finletter to the Secretary of State marked "Secret—Eyes only—for Secretary of State to be passed on to President." The cable reported that Johnson's speech had made a profound and favorable impression on our allies and had already considerably changed the atmosphere.

Tom Finletter was at the reception and later observed that other NATO ambassadors were most impressed by Johnson's speech. "Yes," I said, "I saw your cable." "What cable?" he asked. "The one you just sent to the Secretary of State." "Good God!" he said. "I just sent it. It was in the highest possible classification. How did you ever see it?"

MUNICH, *April 14, 1961*

DINED with Franz-Josef Strauss, dynamic young Minister of Defense and political boss of Bavaria. He interprets Kennedy's new defense policy as a return to the theories of Generals Max Taylor and Gavin, who resigned from the army when their ideas were turned down. Kennedy is now giving them what they originally asked for—a considerable buildup of conventional forces. At present, the "nuclear threshold" is really zero. We have no plan to fight a conventional war beyond the divisional level.

He told me, very off-the-record, that there are special military relations between Israel and Germany. Germany is now sending more arms to Israel than France is, but this is top secret and would cause a furor in the Arab states if it became known.

We talked about the whole Spanish deal. Strauss said he had learned a lesson from this. He said: "I marked my proposal to be classified as Cosmic and it was only later reduced in classification to NATO SECRET. Yet somebody leaked it. I know whom you play golf with, and I don't mean any generals. [Clearly he was thinking of Frank Roberts.] Golf is a good game and maybe I will take it up someday. But I have learned one thing from this experience. I will not confide any future major secrets to NATO."

16

ELARLY THIS MORNING THE NEWS CAME OF A NEW COUP D'ÉTAT IN
Algeria, and things look bad. Norstad called at 8:00 P.M. to tell
me it was very serious. He simply couldn't understand how General
Challe was crazy enough to get into this. No important politician has as
yet been implicated. The government is worried lest the French forces in
Germany declare for the rebels.

The government will try to quarantine Algeria and starve it out without
taking military action. The odds are against the insurrection, which can be
blockaded and cut off from food and money. In order to win they will have
to come and get de Gaulle. Challe knows that de Gaulle will give no
quarter to the leaders. However there is a big difficulty: Nobody can be
expected to fire on the paratroopers.

The new OAS (Secret Army Organization) is linked with the army.
Three months ago, a group of paratroop and Foreign Legion leaders were
organizing a conspiracy. The legion seems to be the main force of the plot.
General Salan has disappeared from Madrid and can be expected to show
up in Algeria. The *plastiqueurs* (plastic bombers in France) are increasingly active and seem to be directly linked to the conspiracy.

PARIS, *April 26, 1961*

NORSTAD called and we had a somewhat indiscreet telephone conversation.
Larry said things seem to be going better now for de Gaulle, but he "still
cannot exclude an invasion of France."

While we were talking, Tom Finletter came in to see me. He brought
with him a draft (marked secret) of his briefing for Kennedy for the
latter's visit to de Gaulle. Tom said this represented the combined effort of
himself and Gavin. (It looked to me like a slightly formalized version of

the precise ideas I had given Finletter in an informal "briefing" Saturday.) Tom, who was accompanied by Arthur Schlesinger, asked if I would read the draft and make suggestions. I did. I suggested first of all there should be a separate corollary paper analyzing de Gaulle's personality and the best way of approaching it. Tom asked me if I would draft this myself. I acceded and sent the following (condensed) to the White House a few days later:

SECRET

Memorandum on General de Gaulle

I am impressed by de Gaulle as a powerful personality and as a major and fascinating historical figure. But he is largely black and white by coloration. Many of his conceptions are, I believe, either false, outdated, or premature; at least not applicable to May 31, 1961.

Nevertheless, I have sought to show the man as I *feel* him to be and as a human reality we have to deal with—whether his ideas are convenient or inconvenient, sensible or totally without reason. The man is *the* fact of French politics today. And although we may well have to postulate a post-de Gaulle policy, while we deal with current France it means dealing with de Gaulle.

If in any way during these talks de Gaulle imagines he is being driven into a corner or even indirectly threatened, he will become politely but adamantly obdurate. The weaker he feels vis-à-vis his interlocutor, the more difficult he will become. . . .

De Gaulle deliberately modeled himself on past figures, most of them French, although in a curious way he is influenced by his classical education. In the latter respect, he is more Greek than Roman, and places an immensely high value on the individual qualities and capacities of superior human beings to influence their era. Technically speaking, his method of approach strongly reflects his early acquaintance with the philosophy of Henri Bergson and the mixture between pure logic and intuition. This aspect of intuition is most important to remember in any effort to influence the course of his thinking. . . .

Beneath his superior air and frequently disdainful manner, General de Gaulle is a rather shy and timid man. He is not noted for the slightest levity or any sense of humor, although he does indeed have elements of the latter. Whether it will emerge depends, I suppose, on the rapport established during these talks.

He has been known in the past to show to intimates a rather remarkable gift of mimicry. He can display a cruelly sarcastic tongue. In terms of humor, as in terms of gallantry, one of his old friends described de Gaulle's approach as "the heavy cavalry technique."

Before getting into further "psychoanalysis," I would like to say that I think de Gaulle is favorably inclined towards youth. In this regard both the President and Mrs. Kennedy have a certain human advantage that may strike a chord of sympathy. He likes young people. I would suspect that, in moments of relaxation between the major conversations, he might enjoy a bit of quiet gaiety and laughter, a rare atmosphere in his self-chosen, austere surroundings. . . .

De Gaulle and many people around him rely upon the U.S. as a protective umbrella which will prevent war and beneath which they can proceed with their own plans to recapture some of France's lost position. But they don't enjoy having to rely upon this implied protection. They resent this dependence which is never mentioned.

The General doesn't really like us and he suspects our motives, even when they are above suspicion. He is exceedingly sensitive in this respect. But he is inclined to mask his suspicions and reactions. It is highly unlikely that he will disclose them in any frank way as English-speaking statesmen often do. On the contrary, they will always be obscured by a mask of courtesy. De Gaulle is an astute poker player—but with the European "stripped deck." We must remember this and not deceive ourselves.

De Gaulle's feelings on America stem from two causes. There is an undoubted resentment at the fact that the United States is now the great power of the West—in Europe as well as elsewhere—while France has fallen to a tertiary role. In this connection he even exaggerates the very close relationship between Washington and London. He feels there is a kind of invisible Anglo-American conspiracy designed to keep France from recovering the prestige it held, above all, on the Continent, during and after World War I.

The second basic cause is that series of "incidents" between himself and Americans and between France and the U.S. dating back to World War II. De Gaulle has a long memory. He will never forget the policy of Franklin D. Roosevelt, first of all vis-à-vis Vichy and Marshal Pétain, culminating with Admiral Darlan; and secondly vis-à-vis himself and the ultimate effort to build up General Giraud.

De Gaulle feels strongly about Roosevelt. He also feels strongly about Truman. He thinks American policy worked deliberately to develop a "third force" which would prevent his return to power when he first tried this through his Rally of the French People (RPF). . . .

I think when the subject of North Africa arises naturally in conversations (and I emphasize the word "naturally" because I am not sure it should be introduced by our side), we must tread softly. While speaking with complete honesty, we should do so in the most delicate possible way. . . .

It is my thought that, when the serious exchanges begin, we should follow the formula, "first things last." In other words, I think a more favorable atmosphere could be created were the President to seize the earliest possible opportunity to steer the conversations to subjects where there *is* inherent agreement between Washington and Paris.

There *are* areas of agreement and political discussion should focus on these initially. Of those, the most important, perhaps, is Germany. Despite the Common Market and the close, if variable, relationships between de Gaulle and Adenauer, the General is still imbued with deep mistrust for Germany. And despite his distaste for clichés, he uses them when discussing this subject.

Unless West Germany is firmly tied to the West, he foresees a nervous period after Adenauer. He thinks Moscow will make a new offer to Bonn and that the post-Adenauer government (Erhard or Strauss) will be pushed by "Krupps" to accept some kind of unification deal, perhaps based on confederation, which would prize West Germany from the occidental camp.

It could do no harm to point out that one of NATO's fundamental political purposes is to ensure not only that Germany (and therefore France) has an adequate defense, but that Germany will be linked closely with France and the Allies, and thereby will be unable to launch any adventures of its own so long as the North Atlantic Treaty endures.

I fear at this time that there is scant hope for achieving any great advance on the project for integration of French forces in NATO. Yet we may usefully stress the need to continue encouraging Germany's political and economic integration into the alliance.

It is blatantly apparent that de Gaulle has little use for our conceptions of either NATO or the UN. The only change I have detected in his NATO attitude during the past ten years or so is that while once he had absolutely *no* use for the alliance and would have been prepared to pull out completely, he is now prepared to tolerate it—but with minimal support.

In this connection I think it might be psychologically appropriate for the President to ask de Gaulle a favor. That favor would be to mute France's public opposition to our efforts to strengthen the free world's cause in the UN.

(I specifically use the word "favor." De Gaulle is very human. I suspect he might feel flattered if asked to "give" something to a power which his brain, if not his heart, acknowledges as greater. In an Orwellian sense this might make him feel "more equal." Things might be easier if this feeling can be encouraged in the General's mind.)

Furthermore, while I dislike any thought of "buttering up" de Gaulle, it would be sensible to point out how pleased we are that the heritage of French culture (which, alas, may not last too long) in former French colonies in Africa has helped bring many of these to the support of western causes in the UN Assembly.

At this point, under ideal circumstances, it could be apt for the two Presidents to exchange ideas on "decolonialization." De Gaulle is particularly sensitive on this subject. He is in the astonishingly paradoxical position of having fought since June, 1940, to restore the entire French empire—largely against Mr. Roosevelt's concepts—and, since his return to power three years ago, has sought to yield this empire piece by piece, without wholly dislocating France.

Algeria is the last important area affected and the one on which, like every Frenchman, he is most sensitive. But even here his policy has been remarkably consistent over the last three years, despite apparently contradictory tactical public shifts.

Can the two Presidents usefully and tactfully discuss the problems of decolonization and how the West may insure that the fledgling Afro-Asian states, whether Algeria or Laos, can be kept free of communism? At this point it might be suitable for President Kennedy to "ask the General's advice" concerning not only Cuba but all of South and Central America.

We are no more bound to follow his advice than he is bound to follow ours. Nevertheless this represents his conception of consultation, what has been falsely called his proposal for a *"directoire."*

De Gaulle wants France to be accepted by Washington on a basis of complete parity with England. I think that, concerning the so-called *"directoire,"* he is far more interested in establishing Big Three consultative machinery for what he calls a "western policy" in regions *outside* the North Atlantic Treaty area, not *inside* it.

As for nuclear arrangements: This vitally important subject will, I venture to say, have to be raised by President Kennedy. If it is not, I doubt if it will ever be raised by President de Gaulle. Therefore, I think we should be very careful to choose what appears to be the most propitious psychological moment before the subject is brought up. And no matter how generous an offer we might suggest to the General (even after explaining the difficulty of U.S. congressional approval), we should be prepared for de Gaulle's statement that, in fact, he doesn't want any atomic assistance from us.

He has a dim prevision of vicious racial cleavage between the white race and other races—somewhat along the lines entertained by William Randolph Hearst in the 1920s. For some time he tended to think of the Soviet Union solely in terms of "eternal Russia" rather than in terms of a dynamic Communist power. He somehow felt that the white peoples dominating Russia would eventually accommodate themselves to the West; he regarded their ideology as a passing thing, because of the menace on their southern and eastern borders from a vast bloc of nonwhite nations headed by China and eventually aided by Japan.

To sum up, I would venture the opinion that in psychological relationships between the U.S. and France, four rules should be recalled by our Chief Executive in terms of maximum desire for a successful conclusion to these talks.

1. We, as the stronger power (and therefore per se at a disadvantage in conversations with this haughty man), must display a patient and willing interestedness to listen.

2. At no point during the conversations should we *press* de Gaulle. Rather it is wiser to seek to induce him into *mutual* discussion. He is most difficult when he feels weak and at a disadvantage.

3. We must never forget, no matter how friendly the atmosphere, that he *sus*pects the U.S. more than he *res*pects us—much as he knows he depends upon us. He feels that for geographical reasons as well as the logic of current history we depend almost equally on him.

4. In concluding, I urge that when serious conversations are started, if possible these should be begun on points where the policies of France and the United States are evidently in basic accord.

PARIS, *April 27, 1961*

THIS morning, I had a long talk with Norstad. He read me exchanges of telegrams he had had with Washington during the French crisis. His recommendation was that we should offer to be of assistance but be very careful not to "force" any aid on an "already sensitive and overburdened government."

What we did do—and advised the French thereof—was to issue special orders to U.S. units. We told air units that if there was any attempt to seize installations they should be blocked with obstacles but not with recourse to shooting. This meant that if an airfield radar system picked up indications that unexpected planes were coming, the field should be covered with trucks.

PARIS, *May 6, 1961*

LUNCHED with Areilza (Count of Motrico), now Ambassador in Paris and formerly Spanish envoy in Washington. He is delightful and extremely funny.

Motrico said he had been tipped in advance that the recent insurrection against de Gaulle planned as its very first move to assassinate the president Friday night while he was attending an official performance at the theater. He passed this information to Geoffroy de Courcel at the Elysée.

GENEVA, *May 14, 1961*

LONG talk with Dean Rusk, our first meeting since he became Secretary of State. The Laotian Conference is about to start. I thought the partition of Laos at the seventeenth parallel was preferable to a coalition government, and the only way we could save South Vietnam was by partitioning Laos. What was his feeling? He answered: "Partition won't solve the problem in South Vietnam. The Communists have been infiltrating South Vietnam through Laos already. Of course, if Laos becomes fully Communist, the infiltration problem would be greatly magnified. Frankly we prefer a neutral Laos to a partitioned Laos."

Long lunch with Averell Harriman, here as Rusk's right-hand man. When Rusk goes home, the baby will be left in Averell's lap, precisely the way Dulles left the Vietnam baby in Bedell Smith's lap in 1954. Averell is pretty gloomy and seems more inclined to a solution by partition than his boss. He confided: "I am not yet in the inner circle of this administration. I see all the telegrams—except I wasn't in on Cuba. But I am not really an intimate. I have known the President for some time but only slightly, and he always calls me "Governor," not "Averell." But I am confident that before things end up I will be in the inner circle. I started as a private with Roosevelt and worked to the top. And then I had to start as a private all over again with Truman and work to the top. That is what I intend to do again."

Averell would not accept any neutral Laotian government in which there was a Communist as Minister of Foreign Affairs, Defense, Interior, or Justice. The Communists could only have minor posts. And even these were dangerous. He had been told that a Communist Minister of Religious Affairs had succeeded in infiltrating the Buddhist Bonzes.

At one point during lunch Averell said he guessed his role here was as the "fall guy—the Bedell Smith." He thought the United States might have to put troops in Southeast Asia. If this happens we would like to get in Pakistani, Philippine, and Thai troops. The American contingent would neither be the largest nor the smallest in size.

PARIS, *May 30, 1961*

AT dinner, George Ball told me that when Kennedy went to see General MacArthur, the general said to him: "All the chickens are coming home to roost and you are living in the coop."

PARIS, *June 2, 1961*

THIS afternoon, I had a forty-minute talk with President Kennedy in his apartment at the Quai d'Orsay; the first since he entered the White House. I was looking out of the window of his secretary's office when a cortege arrived from the Elysée, where he had paid his farewell call on de Gaulle.

Right at the start he said: "I guess we had better settle on what basis this is. Is this for the record or background or what?" I said it would be a great break for me if he would let me put it on the record. He said: "Gee, Cy, I had better not. You know I have got all these fellows traveling around with me and this would just get me into a lot of trouble." Later on he added: "Please protect me on this. Don't indicate in any way that you have seen me and don't tell anybody. I haven't seen anybody. So please protect me."

He said the paper I had sent on to him was "invaluable" and "very useful." I had suggested that the best strategy—to prepare a favorable atmosphere for the tough questions—would be to discuss first things last. I asked Kennedy if this was what he had done and he smiled and said yes. They began with Berlin and then moved on to Asia, Africa, Latin America, etc., before hitting the more direct problems. He said that Berlin was easy because we knew in advance we agreed with each other.

I asked if we would give the French missile aid anyway, since this did not require amendment to the McMahon Act. He said this was being reviewed. We were considering making France eligible for such technical devices as guidance systems. But we would first have to see where we were going on the test-ban negotiations at Geneva. Although the question of missiles was not subject to the McMahon Act and not directly involved in Geneva, it was indirectly involved. It is all important right now that we should not seem to take the initiative in proliferating nuclear military power. Furthermore, if we give the French such help, there will be great German pressure to join in.

Were we now prepared to treat France, in terms of consultation both inside and outside the NATO area, on a basis of complete parity with the way we treat England? Without any hesitation he replied: "There is no doubt of this." He then said: "We will improve the consultation procedure in every respect."

Would we be prepared under any circumstances to enter into any kind of agreement with Khrushchev whereby both sides would promise to refrain from propaganda and subversion activities in each other's areas? He didn't think it would be in Khrushchev's interest to make such a proposal. He thought it was impossible from the Russian point of view, and when we had tried it in 1933, by the Roosevelt-Litvinov agreement, of course, it had not worked out.

I said that Khrushchev claimed to be opposed to war except for "wars of national liberation," which he favored. Couldn't this reservation entitle us also to say we favored wars of national liberation from our viewpoint? Kennedy said that this problem of local wars raised the question of "escalation." There was a danger of any such local war and external commitments growing into a major war. We were very concerned about this. The Laos crisis is an example of what can evolve from this kind of war. He said the talks with de Gaulle had been "very useful" and had been vastly helpful to himself (Kennedy). De Gaulle had explained in detail his views on France and his responsibilities and hopes. The talks also served to help give de Gaulle a real impression of American policy.

This process of consultations was particularly valuable because we and the French are involved in a great many places together. Kennedy admitted the French had a deep suspicion that we had a secret consultation treaty with England, but he said he had helped to alleviate this a bit. He added: "We consult in such an intimate way with England because the English are easy to consult with. We have a kind of community point of view. But now we are going to try to improve our own procedures of consultation with France which is involved in so many regions with us and where we are interested, such as Africa and Laos. After all, the French are in Laos under the Geneva agreement—we are not."

He returned to de Gaulle's suspicions of the United States and said: "You were quite right [in the paper I had sent him]. His anti-American feeling and suspicions go way back and are very deep-rooted."

It was only out of respect for French wishes that so little had been given out here in the form of background information "because you know how de Gaulle feels about the press. We had to go along. But I don't need to tell you this. You know de Gaulle very well."

PARIS, *June 5, 1961*

TOMMY Thompson and Chip Bohlen have returned from Vienna with Rusk to brief NATO on the Kennedy-Khrushchev talks. Chip is going with Rusk to the Elysée this afternoon to brief de Gaulle. Tommy told me I had been wise not to go to Vienna; it was a rat race. The only appearance of yield by Khrushchev, and therefore the only appearance of potential agreement, was on Laos.

Khrushchev made it clear that he intends to move on the question of an East German treaty and Berlin, but he did not fix a timetable. Kennedy warned Khrushchev we will not yield on Berlin because this symbolizes our entire position in Europe.

TEHERAN, *July 17, 1961*

THIS morning I had a two-hour talk with the Shah. He said:

> Personally, I feel that the stronger the United States and Russia become in thermonuclear weapons, the less danger there is of a global war. But I also feel that this very fact consequently increases the danger of local war.
>
> I don't question your good faith and your willingness to help us in case of a local aggression. But the United States simply would not have time to send troops here, nor would it be able to take an immediate quick decision to do so. It would have to consult all of its allies first, and this would take a few days. During those few days, our fate would be decided. The aggressor would grab as much as he could, benefiting from surprise, and who would be able to force him to withdraw?
>
> If Iran were more ready to defend itself against an enemy, that enemy wouldn't start things. I don't mean that we could stand up against the Russians. But suppose they used a proxy like Afghanistan to serve their purpose. And by keeping Iran weak, you tempt our enemies.
>
> Our neighbors, such as Iraq and Afghanistan, have modern Soviet weapons. We desperately need missiles and new planes. Our neighbors have greatly superior aircraft. We keep sending you shopping lists, but nothing happens.

I asked if he thought Khrushchev were planning some kind of coup in Iran while all the world was looking at Berlin. He answered: "For heaven's sake, don't write this, but I can tell you that if I were in Khrushchev's place, that's what I would do."

JERUSALEM, *July 23, 1961*

THIS morning, I went to one of the last sessions of the Eichmann trial. Eichmann is housed in a glass, bulletproof cage to protect him against assassination. Right behind him sit two Israeli policemen. The men who were on duty today were considerably less Jewish looking than Eichmann himself, the great racist.

In fact, Eichmann makes a very curious impression, like a figure out of a Kafka book. He is thin, definitely Semitic, dark, with an intelligent face, pinched features, glasses. A strained tenseness shows in the canted angle at which he holds his neck: a politely obstinate and curiously unctuous manner. He seems to have almost filial respect for the president of the tribunal, Judge Landau, a calm and courteous man.

Eichmann had odd things to say in today's testimony. For example: "An anti-Semite, I never was." He claimed he regarded the Nuremberg laws as laws that "would not be carried out." He said, with servile insistence: "I was not the one who sowed the seed of fear." At another point he added: "I was not a rude person, a driving and obnoxious man." When it was recalled to him that he had admitted grabbing a copy of the New Testament from his wife and tearing it up, he said with full earnestness: "I am not infallible, I must say." Later he made the extraordinary statement: "I tried as best as I could to live according to Kant's categorical imperative."

JERUSALEM, *July 24, 1961*

THIS afternoon, Ben Gurion received me in the Prime Ministry. I asked him what he thought of President Kennedy's present initiative with the Arabs aiming at the basis for a Palestine peace. He said that, unlike the Arab leaders, he had received no letter from Kennedy, nor had any special envoy been sent. He recognized that American policy seeks peace and that there was a great friendship for Israel in the United States, adding: "As human beings, all your presidents are nice men." On his recent trip to the United States, he had seen Kennedy and also Eisenhower and Truman. He lunched with Truman and told him he would be remembered not only in American history but in Jewish history. Truman was so moved that he wept.

But, Ben Gurion said, it was a delusion apparently still entertained by Washington to think that Israel can take back a large number of Arab refugees. The Arabs don't care about their refugees. During the Sinai war the Israelis lost only one prisoner to the Egyptians, a pilot. But they had captured six thousand. Nevertheless, it took a long, long time to arrange an exchange of one against six thousand.

For the Arabs the refugees were only a political weapon. Israel had taken in more than a million Jewish refugees, a larger number than the Arabs had driven from this country. Yet their Arab brothers did not integrate them into their own lands.

Ben Gurion predicted: "Nothing will change. The Arabs are out to destroy Israel. They only want to use the refugees to further that plan. And we are not insane; we won't commit suicide."

I asked if there were a written alliance with France. He said there was no written alliance and added:

Are alliances important? You can have written alliances that are broken and unwritten understandings that are kept.

We have no alliances in the technical sense of written alliances. But we have friends, and among these the first are the Americans. Your second President, John Adams, was the first to proclaim that the Jewish people would come back and build their own state here. In 1922, the American Congress supported the idea of an Israel. The U.S. government was the first to recognize our government. The first big loan came from the United States. But in terms of our defense, it is France. France saved Israel in 1956. Without French aid we would have been overrun by Nasser.

I asked him if he considered Israel a religious state or a racial state? He said adjectives were useless, but "my own adjective is Jewish. I now refuse to be called a Zionist. A Jew is a man who feels himself a Jew. No one knows why he is something—but he knows that he is. I have no quarrel with the American Jews, only the American Zionists. If they are real Zionists, they should come here."

JERUSALEM, *July 25, 1961*

SAW Mrs. Golda Meir, Israeli Foreign Minister, in the Foreign Ministry. We drank cold coffee, and I noticed that she smokes innumerable cigarettes. She is a homely but sympathetic-looking woman with a chignon of brown hair, heavy features, and a modest manner.

She said Israel would not take the initiative in seeking a French alliance because it did not wish to embarrass de Gaulle. A written alliance was unnecessary because France could do no more for Israel than she is already doing.

It seemed to me the only war Israel could afford to fight was a war it started itself, because of strategic weakness she had described. She said: "We will not start a war," but she admitted the sole deterrent to Nasser is the threat of another beating, and he must be made to know he is running a risk.

TEL AVIV, *July 28, 1961*

THIS morning General Moshe Dayan came to see me. He is a burly, sun-burned, youthful-looking man with a bullet head, strong cheekbones, large white teeth, and a rather merry expression, despite the black patch that covers his left eye, lost in World War II.

Dayan admitted the military situation was awkward but did not think Nasser was in a position to destroy this country by surprise attack. He said: "As the English say, nothing is ever as good or as bad as it seems. And that includes a surprise attack. We are a weak, small country. But even if Egypt attacked they could not prevent us from mobilizing. Unless they use atomic weapons they probably could not kill more than ten thousand people around Tel Aviv and in the morning the real war would start. And I don't think Russia is going to give Nasser atomic weapons now."

I asked if he thought Israel's future lay more with a Middle East confederation or with Europe and the West. Without hesitation, he replied: "In no way do we belong more to the Middle East than to Europe or America. I would like to see still stronger ties between Israel, the U.S.A., France, Scandinavia, and the Socialist countries of Africa. What do we have in common with Syria and Egypt? Nothing as compared with the western world. And in any Middle Eastern confederation we would be a minority. We would always be outvoted and forced to go along. We are not part of this Middle Eastern world. Geography by itself is not important."

CORFU, *August 7, 1961*

KING Paul invited me to Mon Repos, his summer palace, and I flew up at breakfast time. Corfu is pleasant and beautiful but too soft, muggy, and Italian. He referred to Cyprus, saying: "The present system cannot last. But something had to be done and this was a good arrangement to get over the trouble. Eden behaved very stupidly so that Papagos lost his temper and sent Grivas in while I was out of the country. Twice before, Papagos had tried to send Grivas, but I refused to give him permission. He waited until I was away."

He could not understand why Russia had pulled out of Albania and left it to Chinese influence. He said he had once told Tito: "Why don't you leave southern Albania to me and you take the north?" But Tito replied: "I already have a million Albanians—and that is too much."

King Paul said his gamble in putting in Caramanlis had paid off. The Queen said: "My husband gets on well with Caramanlis, but I do not like him. I like his wife and I like Averoff. But I admit the Prime Minister and his wife export well. They are beautiful and a good advertisement for Greece."

The King disclosed deep mistrust for Turkey. He had warned Washington fourteen years ago that, "If there is a war the Turks will never fight. You'll see, they will make some arrangement to remain neutral, just as they did last time." He did not know whether Yugoslavia would aid Greece if Bulgaria attacked this country, but a couple of times each year Athens and Belgrade exchanged "ideas on strategy."

At this point, the Queen said we had better go in to lunch and explained the house was filled with young royalty. There were about two dozen at table including: Paul, Frederika, Crown Prince Constantine, Princess Sophia, Princess Irene (very pretty and like her mother), Don Juan Carlos, son of the pretender to the Spanish throne, Princess Beatrix (heir to the Dutch throne) and her sister, Prince Michael of Kent, a Princess

Radziwill (no relation to Stash), and lots of the Queen's Hessian relatives.

The youngsters were cheerful and talkative. I was particularly impressed by the Dutch Princess Beatrix, plain but exceedingly nice and independent minded. She announced to me that all Dutch are Calvinists and Puritans, even the Catholics, and they all dress up in black and go to church on Sunday. She was very indignant with Frederika when the Queen said she refused to go and hear Maria Callas because Callas had twice let the audience down by refusing to sing. Beatrix insisted: "But she gives everything to art. She is a great artist. Once you hear her you forget everything." English was the lingua franca—although Juan Carlos does not speak it too well and has a marked accent.

King Paul said no emperor has ever lived the way Tito does. "Why, he has two or three palaces everywhere. He has his own heated, salt-water swimming pool where he swims a half-hour every evening. He certainly likes the good life. He could never go into the mountains again. He has gotten too fat and his health is bad—they say it is rheumatism." The King said once he was on a yacht with Tito and his principal advisers and told him: "You people are not Communist." Tito laughed, but the rest were quite angry.

We talked about what might happen when Khrushchev goes to Rome if he sees the Pope. The Queen said the Pope should line up all his priests with incense and when Khrushchev comes they should blow it at him. "You mean like chasing the devil away?" asked the King. "Yes," said the Queen.

Paris, *August 31, 1961*

SATURDAY night, August 26, I was in Spetsais, Greece, on holiday, when the village postman brought a cable saying: PLEASE FIND MR. CYRUS SULZBERGER AND ASK HIM TO PHONE ME MOSCOW 418580 STOP GEORGY ZHUKOV CHAIRMAN COMMITTEE FOR CULTURAL RELATIONS.

Moscow, *September 5, 1961*

TODAY, Khrushchev told me he is prepared to meet Kennedy again in another effort "to resolve pressing international problems." He hopes such a new encounter can be "fruitful" and that both sides "will display understanding." He would always be glad to meet the U.S. President to resolve urgent world problems such as those of peace and war. For this, he "would spare neither strength nor time." But the main thing is that such a meeting must be fruitful.

"In Vienna, we compared viewpoints. The task now is to find solutions for the major international issues causing concern. And if President Kennedy agrees to a meeting it will be important that both sides display understanding of the need to resolve such important matters as the signing of a German peace treaty and the solution on this basis of the question of West Berlin, as well as the problem of disarmament under strict international control."

Khrushchev said the Soviet Union had given no nuclear warheads or long-range missiles to Communist China or to Russia's Warsaw Pact allies. The only such weapons remain in the hands of the Soviet armed forces, and none are stationed outside Soviet territory except "perhaps in East Germany."

He proposed that it might be useful, in easing tension, for both East and West to revoke recent steps toward greater military preparedness and then, possibly, to discuss such ideas as the creation of a nuclear-free zone in Europe. But this did not include revoking of his own new testing program.

On the contrary, Khrushchev spoke of arming his forces with "several" 100-megaton bombs despite his acknowledgment that their destructive power is devastating. He indicated these will be manufactured in order to warn any other power against starting a war. At the same time, he promised Russia will never be the first to fight.

His attitude was tough and relentless, but he insisted that since 1958, he has been seeking agreement to his desire for separate peaces with each part of divided Germany and the creation of a free city of West Berlin under new statutes. Western dillydallying forced him to adopt a hard approach. He argued that the United States provided him with a precedent for unilateral action by its manner of signing a peace treaty with Japan.

He seems convinced logic is on his side, both the logic of history and the logic of power. In a strange Darwinian interpretation of the advance of nations, Khrushchev jokingly considers that the United States is still in the stage of "jumping" while the Soviet Union has learned how to "fly." This referred to the earth-orbiting successes of the Soviet spacemen, Gagarin and Titov.

Khrushchev believes absolutely that if it comes to a showdown, Britain, France, and Italy would refuse to join the United States in a war over Berlin for fear of their absolute destruction. Quite blandly, he asserts these countries are "figuratively speaking, hostages to us and a guarantee against war."

At two widely separated points in our lengthy discussion he mentioned a possible invitation to Kennedy to visit Russia when relations were better. Once he spoke of a possible state visit. Another time, jocularly, he suggested the President join him on a bear hunt.

When Khrushchev's Kremlin office door opened, it exposed a long, rather narrow room with plain, wood walls and simple furniture, the main articles of which were a large desk with a small table and two armchairs before it and a conference table covered with green baize and girded with chairs. At his desk and by Khrushchev's side at the conference table were twin sets of green and yellow telephones. At one end was a large engraving of Lenin; at the other a large engraving of Marx. This was once Stalin's office.

Khrushchev, who was sitting alone at the head of the conference table looking somewhat small, arose and came forward with a broad smile to shake my hand warmly. He posed beside me while several photographers took pictures. He then signaled the interpreter to the head of the table, seating me on the right and himself on the interpreter's left. When he noticed the sun striking my face, he arose and drew a ruffled yellow curtain. On the table was a tray holding mineral water, lemon soft drinks, and some green ashtrays. Late in the talk, when I asked if I might smoke, Khrushchev told me by all means and apologized for being remiss "because I am a nonsmoker myself."

Khrushchev was extremely well dressed in a fawn-colored suit, white, silk shirt with cuff links, and a gray tie. His pink complexion was mildly tanned by the Black Sea sun, where he had been taking a holiday. He observed that he had ordered all Soviet officials to take at least a month's holiday each year, but added ruefully: "As so often happens, the man who makes the rules is the first to break them."

I then plunged in. "Mr. Khrushchev," I enquired, "do you still believe war is neither inevitable nor desirable?" He replied: "Yes, and very profoundly, too. In spite of the acute crisis which, as you say, has now taken shape, I believe in the common sense of statesmen who bear the responsibility for the destiny of their countries. They cannot but understand that in our day wars must not be a means of settling any issue and I hope they come to the conclusion that it is necessary to resolve urgent international problems peacefully—first and foremost the German problem. This can and must be settled by conclusion of a peace treaty with the two German states now in existence."

I asked Khrushchev his reaction to the Kennedy-Macmillan cable asking an end to atmospheric nuclear tests. He opposed this idea vigorously. His essential argument was that such a ban would leave France free to continue testing—with American aid—on NATO's behalf and that there should be no new test moratorium anyway until there is an accord on world disarmament. He also claimed the West had carried out many more nuclear tests to date than Russia and therefore he felt he had a moral right to equal conditions.

Khrushchev said the 100-megaton bomb planned by the Soviet Union would indeed have immense destructive power but was needed "to make would-be aggressors think twice." He wanted this terrible weapon to warn "those who dare to attack that they will perish if they do so."

I asked if he favored some kind of East-West deal outlining and respecting spheres of influence. He scoffed at this formula as imperialistic and a cause of colonial wars, a policy that was outmoded. Instead, he proposed a nonaggression pact between NATO and the Warsaw Treaty bloc.

He suggested that, since Russia and America were now projecting satel-

lites above each other's territory, it might be desirable to negotiate agreements defining the frontiers of space. But cooperative use of space would
be impossible without a prior disarmament accord, since space satellites
are launched by ICBMs.

Khrushchev said Castro was "not a member of the Communist party" but
"a revolutionary and a patriot. If he does join the party, he would be a
worthy addition, but that depends on him." He made no blanket commitment, but did assert that "If Cuba were subjected to attack, it would have
every right to expect assistance from other peace-loving countries. There
is no treaty obligation, but we would certainly not ignore a request for
assistance."

During their Vienna talks, Khrushchev recalled, "President Kennedy
said to me: 'Our forces are equal. We have the ability to destroy each
other.' I agree with this, although privately I contest his analysis, as I feel
we are stronger. But certainly we should not start a war to find out who is
right. That would be savagery. Let us simply recognize that we are equal
and can destroy each other and draw from this the conclusion that together
we can guarantee world peace. Let us compete not in an arms race but in
the development of our economies and the material benefits of our peoples, and let history decide who is the victor—without a war."

He said there was not yet any fixed schedule for the landing of a Soviet
citizen on the moon. He gave this explanation:

> It is not a question of mooning him but of demooning him. Our national
> emblem is already on the moon, but we don't want to place a coffin beside it.
> We are now studying the possibilities of such a flight, but I cannot yet say
> when it would be scheduled. We can fly a man to the moon, but the
> difficulty is getting him away from there.
>
> We can now take off from the earth and land again. If we compare our
> development to yours, we believe it is a higher development. You remember
> Darwin's theories on the maturation of species—from those which crawled,
> like reptiles, to those which jumped and those which flew. Well, you are still
> in the jumping stage, while we have already learned how to fly, and to land
> again. But that is still insufficient. We still have to learn how to land on
> other planets and then to take off from them back to this earth.

Khrushchev then took off his bifocal glasses and said: "We want to be
strong in politics, but to do that you must be frank. I do not remember
who it was who said that a diplomat is given a tongue in order to conceal
his thoughts. He who does that is no diplomat but a cheap politician. His
policy is bound to end in failure. I do not belong to that sort."

After some reminiscing, Khrushchev expressed hope that the United
States and the Soviet Union would never fight each other and said he had
told this to Eisenhower. He said, "We are the strongest countries in the
world and if we united for peace there can be no war. Then if any madman
wanted war, we would but have to shake our fingers to warn him off. Now
the United States is arming and we are too. We are spending money and

energy in preparations to destroy people. We are making nuclear tests. But what the hell do we want with tests? You cannot put a bomb in soup or make an overcoat out of it. Nevertheless, we are compelled to test."

Khrushchev said:

Nothing can be resolved by war. I hope this crisis will be settled by the signing of peace treaties with the two Germanys. The most reasonable way to liquidate this crisis, as you put it, would be for those countries to bear the responsibility of putting an end to the state of war with Germany, to recognize the need for doing so, and to sign a German peace treaty.

To do this neither UN nor the neutrals are needed, since it is an elementary thing that after a thunderstorm there always comes a lull, a cool period; and after a war there always comes peace. Sixteen years have passed since the end of the last war and that is quite a sufficient period.

At one point, when we were discussing what was needed in the world, Khrushchev said: "The correct treatment for the militaristic spirit in the West is disarmament and disarmament alone. This alone would eliminate the danger of war and create conditions for peaceful coexistence."

My notes on his discussion of the 100-megaton bomb have him saying: "But if war is imposed on us and a threat is made to destroy our country and annihilate our people, we won't stop at anything to deal a retaliatory blow. Therefore it is useful to have *several* 100-megaton bombs to protect our country."

I then asked Khrushchev a somewhat philosophical question: "Don't you think that Communists, who by their convictions are atheists and do not believe in divinity and afterlife, might not fear war more than religious people, who by virtue of their religion believe in an afterlife following their earthly existence?"

He replied:

A very interesting question! I will be glad to answer it. I have lived a lot and seen a lot. I've seen war and I've seen death, but I have never seen anybody, even clergymen who consider themselves closer to God and, consequently, know more of the afterlife, who would be in a hurry to enter that afterworld. Imperialists, monopolists, colonialists, who also say that they believe in God, although they are sooner the devil's allies, are not in a hurry to enter the afterworld and prefer to send their soldiers to war promising them paradise after death, while they want to live longer on earth next to their safes and strongboxes of gold and dollars. So I have never noticed a special desire in religious people to get to so-called paradise in a hurry.

Soviet people, who are mostly not religious, although we do have our religious people, love earthly life and have no desire to get to paradise in heaven. They want paradise on earth. They want to live and work and enjoy the fruits of their labor, and we are quite successful in that. In forty-four years since the revolution, we have achieved great successes and now our road into a real, a Communist paradise is paved by the draft of our party's new program and we shall spare no effort to have this program implemented and make it come true. With the implementation of this program, we shall have crossed the threshold and will build communism.

As to paradise and heaven, we have heard a lot about it from the priests. So we decided to find out for ourselves what it is like there, and we sent up our explorer Yuri Gagarin. He circled the globe and found it nothing like paradise. So we decided to send another explorer up. We sent German Titov and told him to fly for a whole day. After all, Gagarin was up there for only an hour and a half and he might have missed paradise, so you take a good look. Well, he took off, came back, and confirmed Gagarin's conclusion and reported that there was nothing there.

All this, of course, does not mean that our people will not fight once there is no afterlife. Hitler, who unleashed a war against us, counted on the Soviet people refusing to fight for the Soviet Socialist system. But what was the result? The whole world sees that we are alive and prospering and are adopting a new program of Communist construction, while Hitler is gone and decayed and his associates have either been hanged or committed suicide.

So we Communists do not believe in afterlife and want to live and progress in peace. But if we are attacked we shall fight like lions against imperialism, against aggression.

Khrushchev said: "We have overtaken the U.S., but we are still poorer than you are. Yet we use the means at our disposal better."

Khrushchev gave me a long off-the-record analysis of the American political scene. He said:

I have said a lot about Eisenhower in my time. I consider him intelligent, chivalrous, and honorable. These are good qualities and were especially manifest during the war. When our troops were advancing on Vienna the Germans wanted to surrender to the Americans. But when Stalin advised Eisenhower of this he told the Germans to surrender to the Russians. For a general to do this, to make that sacrifice, shows him to be a man of high principles. He was later severely criticized in the U.S. for just this action.

There was a similar incident with Rokossovsky. The Germans he routed fled toward the British and Stalin approached Churchill on this—but Montgomery took them all prisoner. There you see the two men, Eisenhower and Montgomery. Naturally I don't know who took the second decision, whether it was Churchill or Montgomery. But Eisenhower's decision reflected his chivalry.

When I talked with Eisenhower I felt he was sincere. He didn't want war. He would never start a war. But due to his age and character he was indecisive. Dulles had a great influence on him. Eisenhower relegated all his work to Dulles. But Dulles was a man of a different sort and character, and this was not to Eisenhower's advantage.

American policy under Eisenhower was therefore far from brilliant. I have already spoken of the U-2 incident. I am sure Eisenhower knew of the overall plan for such flights. But I am sure also that he had no knowledge of that individual flight of Powers. That was something Allen Dulles cooked up. I just can't conceive of Eisenhower sending over a plane on the eve of the Paris Conference.

That was something done to put me in a difficult spot in Paris. It was supposed to show that the Soviet Union was incapable of protecting its own territory. This kind of position would embarrass any state. It was supposed to put me on the spot, but we shot down the plane and Eisenhower was put on the spot.

I am quite sure that Eisenhower wanted to apologize to me in Paris. When I proposed that Eisenhower should publicly voice his regrets he leaned toward Herter. My interpreter heard Eisenhower murmur to Herter: "I don't see why something like that could not be done." But evidently Herter said no and nothing was done.

The advantages Eisenhower had over Kennedy were that he was an older man, a hero of World War II, a man who commanded great respect in the U.S., and therefore if he said the U.S.A. should not go to war no one would dare accuse him of being afraid. And Dulles had also benefited from this prestige.

President Kennedy is in a different position. Politically he has a much broader outlook. When I talked with him in Vienna I found him a worthy partner. He himself conducted the talks without depending on Rusk the way Eisenhower always depended on Dulles.

At Geneva, in 1955, Eisenhower always waited for Dulles to scribble something on a piece of paper telling him what to do before he said anything. He took everything from Dulles and read it out. We were amazed. Nothing like that could happen here.

Kennedy formulates his own ideas. That is his superiority to Eisenhower. I had a feeling he understood things better. I am sure if Kennedy himself were able to decide matters he would not enter into any argument over Berlin and Germany. Views like those cannot be defended in an argument. It is opposed to common sense. No lawyer would risk defending that case in court. If he did, he would assume he would not stand much of a chance of winning. You cannot win that argument and Kennedy understands this. But he cannot break out of the situation. He is not a lawyer; he is a President.

Franklin Roosevelt would have agreed to our solution in Kennedy's place. He would have said it is foolish to fight over this. Many people would have opposed Roosevelt, but the population would have supported him.

Kennedy is too young. He lacks the authority and prestige to settle this issue correctly. He is afraid to take up that position and that is why he has induced those mobilization measures. But he doesn't want to fight. Only an idiot wants war.

But we will sign our peace treaty and arrange that access to a free West Berlin must be within the GDR. Macmillan, Fanfani, de Gaulle, and Adenauer all understand this, but nobody wants to be the first to say so.

The U.S. is the leader in the West. If Roosevelt were in power he would by now have appealed to the people. If Kennedy appealed to the people—if he voiced his real inner thoughts and stated that there was no use fighting over Berlin, no use losing a drop of blood—the situation would be settled quickly. All this talk of our desire to seize West Berlin is an invention.

Why? If Kennedy does the logical thing, the opposition will raise its voice and accuse him of youth, cowardice, and a lack of statesmanship. He is afraid of that. Eisenhower could have said this and no one could have accused him of being young, inexperienced, or afraid. Even though not understanding questions of state, Kennedy is probably abler than Eisenhower.

It is difficult for me to say how he will find his way out of this. If he musters up enough courage and signs a treaty, that is what's necessary and his prestige will be enhanced and he will undoubtedly be elected to a second term. Otherwise, the opposition will force him into a stand that will buy him no glory.

Of course, there will not be a war. Only men lacking reason want war. Kennedy is reasonable. Kennedy is reasonable but he is taking a very wrong stand now.

Here came the punch. Zhukov had told Khrushchev I had arranged his meeting with Bohlen, where the basis for a Korean cease-fire was worked out. Khrushchev now asked me if I would take a message from him to Kennedy.

If you are personally in a position to meet Kennedy, I would not be loath to establishing some sort of contacts with him to find a means, without damaging the prestige of the U.S., to reach a settlement. But on the basis of a peace treaty and a free Berlin. And through such informal contacts, the President might say what is on his mind in ways of solving the problem—if he agrees on the principle of a peace treaty and a free city of West Berlin. Otherwise there is no use in contacts.

If he does wish to make such contact he can express his own opinions on the various forms and stages of a settlement and how to prepare public opinion so as not to endanger Kennedy's prestige and that of the U.S.

I said to Khrushchev if he wanted such a message to go to Kennedy he should send it through Ambassador Thompson. He begged me to do it personally. He said: "Thompson is very able but he is an ambassador. He would have to send such a message to Secretary Rusk. Rusk would tell Kennedy what was wrong with it before he told him what the message was and Kennedy would end up wearing Rusk's corset. Kennedy could not get a fair initial reaction, and Rusk is just a tool of the Rockefellers."

My feeling was that Khrushchev really wants informal contact—not through diplomats—and he would like to circumvent his own Foreign Office and government and save his own prestige.

Zhukov then embellished again his tale of how he and Bohlen arranged the Korean peace in my house in Paris—and I had never written about it—a somewhat souped up version of what really happened. In some respects, Zhukov is a kind of Soviet Walter Mitty.

Khrushchev said: "Kennedy has spoken of the necessity of revising the position of your military bases and eliminating some of them. He is now actually taking scme steps in that sense. Many military men see the logic of this—men like Montgomery and MacArthur. This is a good trend. Also, some day, I don't see why we shouldn't have a nonaggression treaty between NATO and the Warsaw Pact—or some version of the Rapacki

Plan—and a gradual reduction of troops by both sides in areas outside their own countries."

I was struck by Khrushchev's continual use of the word "prestige." He spoke resentfully about how our signature of the Japanese peace treaty had harmed Soviet prestige. He said: "We must mutually take into account each other's prestige. You went ahead and signed the Japanese treaty and now you want to prevent us from signing a German treaty. We cannot tolerate that; we have rights of our own."

Khrushchev told me off-the-record: "I believe if we can settle the Laos question it will improve the atmosphere for Berlin and Germany. That appeals to Kennedy; it doesn't affect my position. I want to help Kennedy."

The sun had long since set, and, after a period of gathering darkness in the room, Khrushchev signaled for the lights to be turned on. In the sudden blaze he rubbed his eyes and looked a bit fatigued. He said: "We hope that we shall be able to resolve reasonably all the questions at issue between our two countries. Thereby the possibility would present itself for me to invite President Kennedy to this country as our guest. We will give him a warm reception and all the honors that are due to him as a President and a guest."

MOSCOW, *September 6, 1961*

THIS evening, the day after I saw Khrushchev, I went over to Ambassador Thompson's. I asked him to come out to the garden because there was less chance of the trees being bugged, although it is perfectly feasible to wire trees. I told him that I was in the embarrassed position of having been given a message for Kennedy by Khrushchev which he had specifically asked me not to tell Tommy about. I would request the President to deal Tommy in on it immediately. Tommy was very understanding and sympathetic about my quandary.

MOSCOW, *September 8, 1961*

SOMETHING happened in the Kremlin Wednesday, September 6, that caused Khrushchev to make a drastic shift in his cold war tactics. This can probably be linked to his talks with Nehru, which began that day.

Tuesday, Khrushchev told me: "We already have a 100-megaton bomb and we shall test it." This phrase appeared textually in the Russian transcript of our talk, taken down by a secretary, and in the official English translation.

Also, I originally wrote that Khrushchev saw "no use" in another meeting "at this time with President Kennedy unless the President is ready to agree at least to the essentials of a settlement along such lines"—meaning Soviet concepts for a German and West Berlin formula. I added: "I de-duce from Khrushchev's remarks that he considered a meeting with the President at this juncture would be untimely."

I prepared a dispatch including those remarks and then, Wednesday, September 6, went over it painstakingly together with Zhukov; Kharlamov, press chief; and Sukhodrev, the interpreter.

Thursday morning, Zhukov said two changes were desired by Khrushchev. One was in the official stenographic record. Here, referring to the 100-megaton bomb, he wished it phrased, "We already have such a bomb and shall test the exploding device for it." In other words, instead of announcing his intention to test the ghastly weapon itself, as he had first told me, he spoke only of testing its detonator, a vast difference. Also, he sent me a special statement dictated that morning and saying he "would always be glad to meet with the United States President to resolve pressing international problems."

These two changes are significant. As a result of the alterations, tension is less cruel than it might have become. I cannot pretend to know what caused the switch.

In my presence, the rewritten first page of my account of the interview was read over the telephone to Khrushchev. He expressed satisfaction to me personally.

PARIS, *September 9, 1961*

As soon as I got back to Paris, I went to see Cecil Lyon, chargé d'affaires. I explained that I had a top-secret message for Kennedy from Khrushchev. I had written it out in a sealed envelope for the President. Cecil put it in another sealed envelope with a letter to Mac Bundy and sent it off by swiftest courier.

I wrote Bundy in my own covering note that it might be wise to refer to the Khrushchev message in code henceforth so he could confirm receipt and ask questions through embassy cables without disclosing the subject. I proposed to call it "The Rockefeller Letter," since Mr. K claims Rusk and the State Department are Rockefeller tools.

WASHINGTON, *October 4, 1961*

THIS afternoon I went up to the White House for a talk with President Kennedy. He seemed extremely well, suntanned and fit, but his face is a bit puffy. Also, he looks a lot older than he did in Los Angeles last summer. He was friendly and relaxed. He said: "I met your wife at lunch." The Grahams had taken her to a *Washington Post* book luncheon honoring Harvard's publication of a volume of the Adams papers, and I knew they were going to take her to meet the President at a cocktail party before.

He asked: "Is she French?" I said, "No, Greek." "But then how can she be an Adams?" I said: "What do you mean?" He had thought most of the people at drinks were Adamses. I got the drift, explained we were staying with the Grahams (who later called Marina "the Greek Adams").

Then we started talking about serious things. First of all, he brought up the message Khrushchev asked me to give him and which I had sent. It was pretty hard to figure out just what it meant. I said that to me the only way to interpret this was in terms of Aesopian language; that one must stress the point of *prestige*, but wherever the word "Kennedy" was used the word "Khrushchev" must be substituted and wherever the word "Rusk" was used the word "Gromyko" must be substituted.

I asked the President if the Vienna Conference with Khrushchev had been useful. He said: "Yes it was useful for me in judging this man. One always has a tendency to think that reason will prevail in personal conversation, but now I have been able to judge him. Now I know that there is *no* further need for talking. The only reason to meet again would be to make the final arrangements in any previously prepared settlement."

Khrushchev was treating Berlin in terms of the sheer military advantage surrounding the city, and it was hard to shake him loose from that concept. I argued that the Russians had always taken the ground approach to strategy and had never studied naval or air strategy.

Kennedy said the American people must understand that, "We can't give what we haven't got." In other words, we don't have East Germany and it is not something we can bargain over. Furthermore, the American people should recognize how much de facto recognition West Germany gives East Germany, despite their propaganda against us on this point. He had no doubt at all that the people of the United States were ready to go to the brink of war on this Berlin issue.

At this point, he again said it was necessary to bring the Germans into any settlement, but also to bring them more solidly into allied defense in case there was no settlement, saying: "The chances of settling this without war are not yet too good."

It was very hard to explain to the American public such things as the fact that de Gaulle had already recognized the Oder-Neisse line (he pronounced this "Neesser") as Germany's eastern border. More than once when we were talking about Berlin he said: "If we push the button—if I push the button. . . ."

The President talked at length about the problem of negotiating with our allies as well as with the Russians. No solution could be arranged that the West Germans would refuse to accept and participate in. But the West Germans had to recognize their responsibility in terms of preparing for the alternative of war. It was much easier for foreign statesmen like de Gaulle to refuse to associate themselves with a projected settlement. If war comes, they can blame us. And if war doesn't come, they can argue we yielded too much in advance.

He talked about his difficulty in trying to help de Gaulle. Congress was very leery. They were concerned about the French security problem—both now and after de Gaulle. There had been a lot of trouble in trying to give the French the atomic submarine information.

Rather sadly, the President said that one of his biggest difficulties was that most Americans don't realize that we no longer have any overwhelming military advantage. However, Russia was not yet in a position to totally destroy us with long-range missiles. It simply did not have the capability. This was the importance of Khrushchev's statement to me that Britain, France, and West Germany were his hostages because he can pulverize Europe but not yet us.

The President thought the situation in Southeast Asia was getting rapidly worse, above all in South Vietnam. At least in Europe, over the Berlin crisis, it was perfectly plain how we would have to fight a war if war broke out, but it is far more difficult to face the problem of fighting a war in Southeast Asia.

I said Khrushchev had told me he thought the situation in Laos would soon improve. Kennedy believed this was the line Khrushchev was putting out, but he figured Khrushchev thought Laos might soon fall into his lap. At another time during our conversation, the President repeated it was more a clearcut problem to defend Berlin than to defend Southeast Asia.

17

THIS MORNING, I VISITED PRESIDENT ADOLFO LOPEZ MATEOS. HE
said Castroism was trying to gain support for its own revolution
in Mexico, but, "We will not permit any interference with our
government. Some leftists here sympathize with Castroism; we will permit
no foreign interference."

GUATEMALA CITY, *November 8, 1961*

THIS evening, we went to a farewell dinner by President Ydigoras for Ambassador John Muccio and his wife, who are leaving. An instant after we
met, Ydigoras startled me by saying, "As soon as the first atom bomb
drops, anywhere on earth, we will invade Belize [British Honduras]. The
British respect force."

PANAMA CITY, *November 14, 1961*

CREDE Calhoun, for many years our stringer here, an Old Panama hand
(now about seventy-five, retired), says one minister runs the biggest
whorehouse in Colon; another runs the biggest whorehouse in Panama
City. President Chiari is honest but unimpressive.

LIMA, *November 21, 1961*

CALLED on President Manuel Prado in his palace on the Plaza de Armas,
diagonally across from the old Spanish cathedral containing Pizarro's
mummified body. Prado complained the United States was too weak.
"This is not a moment for vacillation. You must choose whether you
support democracy or communism in Latin America. And how can you

apply nonintervention in Cuba while Cuba applies intervention everywhere else?"

SANTIAGO, CHILE, *November 23, 1961*

TEA in the presidential palace, called La Moneda, the Mint, with President Alessandri, a large, aggressive man with a surprising resemblance to Mussolini. I asked what chance the Communists had of coming in by vote. He began a tirade: "We must change our very bad political methods. The democratic institutions of the West are not adapted to the needs of the modern world. They lead to bad and dangerous political practices. Parliamentary powers must be limited. Deputies are too much subject to the electoral influence and interests of private groups. There must be more importance given to the real social needs of the community."

BUENOS AIRES, *December 1, 1961*

THIS morning, I had a long talk and drink with Juan Bramuglia, once Foreign Minister under Peron and now a Peronista leader seeking to recapture power. His last contact with Peron was two and a half months ago in Madrid. Bramuglia said: "I am more loyal to Peron's idea than I am to him." He said Peronism was not capitalistic but it stopped communism; it was a version of Christian socialism.

RIO DE JANEIRO, *December 9, 1961*

THIS afternoon, President "Jango" Goulart received me. Jango, as everyone calls him, is forty-three, swarthy, and looks like a smooth version of an old-fashioned Capone gangster. His comfortable apartment was filled with hangers-on, tough-looking ginks in shirt sleeves. He said. "Latin American sentiment isn't pro-Fidel; it is pro-small country. But the Latin Americans are Christian and not Communist. His declaration that he is a Communist did not help Fidel. It hurt him and helped the U.S.A. in Latin America."

PARIS, *December 16, 1961*

LAST night, I had an interesting talk with Dean Rusk at the embassy residence. I asked if we weren't being put in a position of disagreeing more and more with the former colonial powers on colonial questions like Angola, the Congo, etc. He replied: "On these colonial issues people cannot get it through their heads that the people of the United States really believe that governments derive power from the consent of the governed. It is only on this basis that decent relations can be worked out between different nations. But some of our friends don't accept this formula. That is the case of Goa. The best defense of Portugal would be to ask the Goans what they want. Portugal knows perfectly well that Nehru would not accept this. But they won't do it."

I said perhaps the Portuguese were concerned about the precedent because if there were a plebiscite in Goa they might have to have one in Angola. He admitted this but said the Portuguese had to face the changes in the world. "After all," he said, "there is more British money invested in India today than under the empire."

PARIS, *January 6, 1962*

AMBASSADOR Jim Gavin called up and asked me to stop by. Gavin showed me a long personal letter from Kennedy to de Gaulle dated December 31, and handed on by Gavin January 2. In substance, this said, in the most friendly way, that the United States simply had to explore the possibilities of a negotiated settlement on Berlin because American public opinion would not support going to war without first knowing everything had been done for peace. Kennedy said he was convinced that Khrushchev could not indefinitely put off signature of a separate peace treaty with East Germany —what de Gaulle had so aptly called "his treaty with himself." It was therefore better to arrange some kind of settlement before his treaty was signed.

Kennedy was sure that he and de Gaulle agreed on basic long-range objectives even though they disagreed on tactics. He then turned to the subject of nuclear arms. As politely as possible, he said that no country other than Russia and the U.S. could afford an independent nuclear deterrent by itself. For the present, Europe was well protected by the American deterrent, and Kennedy said U.S. policy on this was that we would use nuclear weapons to defend Europe and gave personal assurances that it was his own policy as well. However, someday it might be advisable to have some kind of group control over the nuclear weapons in Europe. The United States was opposed to the spread of nuclear powers. Had it not been for long-standing agreements with England dating back to World War II, Britain would be treated in exactly the same way as France, but of course the United States could not renege on an agreement. Nevertheless not even Britain was strong enough to arm itself with this kind of weapon.

If France persevered in its atomic capability, it was inevitable that Germany would seek to do the same thing, but this could not be permitted by the United States. There was still too great a memory and fear of Germany. He hoped de Gaulle would understand our view. Kennedy concluded by saying (after almost three thousand words) that he was sticking only to Berlin and nuclear arms because there was not space for anything else and these were the two most important matters.

PARIS, *January 15, 1962*

GAVIN showed me a letter from de Gaulle to Kennedy of January 11, replying to President Kennedy's letter to him. It is about three thousand words long and very cold although polite. De Gaulle says France cannot participate in any negotiations on Berlin at present and will not do so until there is reason to believe the Russians have changed their attitude. This would show weakness and greatly risks neutralizing West Germany, which is Russia's main ambition and, he adds, a neutralized Germany means a neutralized Europe, which would be dangerous for the United States as well.

De Gaulle sniffs at Kennedy's references to the dangers of giving nuclear weapons to Germany and says that France understood much better than the United States the dangers of a resurgent Germany. He wholly ignores Kennedy's plea that France should participate in a supranational NATO nuclear-sharing arrangement. He goes on to explain that France must maintain control of its own striking force. He recognizes that France has neither the money nor the space to develop a really powerful force of this sort. Nevertheless, it will continue in its present program. Russia might have ten times the killing power of France with such a weapon, but if France could demonstrate that it could "tear off an arm" of Russia, this might have a deterring influence. Anyway, France's national contribution would add to overall Western strength.

Then—rather to my astonishment—de Gaulle went right back to his September, 1958, directorate plan. He said the West should have regular, formal systems of meetings between the chiefs of government, the Foreign Ministers, and the Defense Ministers of the United States, Britain, and France.

PARIS, *January 20, 1962*

THIS morning I saw de Gaulle for an hour and twenty minutes. I asked if he attached much significance to the rumors of difficulties inside Russia. He wrinkled his nose, shrugged his shoulders, and said:

> Certainly there are difficulties inside the Communist world. This is no secret. Khrushchev himself advertises it. He has his difficulties inside Russia and also it is evident that he has his difficulties with China and Albania. The differences between Russia and China do not stem from conditions of ideology. They merely indicate the rivalry between two big neighbors.
>
> Also, certainly there is a progressive change in the life and the state of mind inside the Communist world. There are more and more intellectuals, more students and professors, and as a result they develop a more critical spirit. And, furthermore, the people want more liberty and a greater well-being. And today there is no war. There is no more war in the name of which the people can be repressed as in the days of Stalin. Khrushchev

realizes these truths. He weds himself to the popular desire for more freedom and well-being because, after all, Khrushchev is a politician.

I then said, "Mon Général, once you told me you thought Russia, regardless of its present ideology, was essentially a white, European, and western nation. Do you think that someday we can look to a true accord with Moscow and, perhaps, even an agreement between NATO and the Warsaw Pact?" "There can never be an alliance of that sort," he said. "NATO was created against Russia and the Warsaw Pact was created against NATO."

Nevertheless, he thought: "There *can* someday be a real cooperation between Russia and the West. And, indeed, there *must* be; otherwise there *must* be war. You cannot have a cold war for an indefinite period. I suppose that someday, in the vague future, we can imagine a concord among the white people against the colored."

Did he envisage the possibility of a unified North Africa, a unified Maghreb? Here, as usual, he waxed sarcastic and quite funny. Indeed, he has as great a gift for mimicry as Henri Tisot, who has made a fortune mimicking de Gaulle. The general said: "When one speaks of the Arabs one can never know what one is talking about. One can never be sure of what one says. They are always boiling. They are always unpredictable. Such is the nature of the Arab. They are nomads. They are anarchic; not anarchists, anarchic. They are engulfed in their own inherent rivalries. Nasser tried to create a union of the Middle Eastern Arabs. He couldn't. Nor will he ever be able to succeed. And who can do this for the western Arabs? No one, I venture to say. But the question is unimportant."

I inquired whether he expected trouble with the OAS, the Secret Army Organization led by General Salan in its effort to keep Algeria French and even seize France, should he make peace with the Algerian rebels. He sniffed:

The OAS does not make agreements. It is France that makes decisions. It is France that is seeking to make a peace in Algeria. France is finding a solution together with the rebellious Algerians, the FLN. The OAS does not matter. We accept the principle of an independent Algeria, but of course this can only be decided by a free vote in Algeria. Yet we know how this will result. [Later on de Gaulle said he was sure Algeria would have a neutralist government.]

But they, the Algerians, have difficulties. They are a poor people. They are not united. Each one of their leaders has his personal ambitions and his clan. Each one of them wants to be President. Now that they are on the verge of responsibilities instead of conspiratorial activities, they are overwhelmed by the prospect. Until now they have been agitators. But now they wish to be a government and, in truth, they are not very capable of this and they know it—and it irks them.

I hope soon they will prove able to recognize this new situation and to accept their responsibilities. I deeply hope so but I cannot know. If not, if nothing happens, we will have to act. We will then have to regroup the French in separate zones. This is not partition; it is regroupment. Partition means two Algerias; regroupment would first mean the establishment of separate zones administratively. And when that happens many of the French in Algeria will live. There would be one main zone running from the region of Oran to the region of Algiers. But there would be secondary zones, for example, in the region near Bône. But this would be provisional. It would not be a commitment to partition; it would be temporary.

As for the OAS [and here he spread his hands], the OAS is tedious [*assommant*]. The OAS is manufactured of passion and disorder. But it is not a political reality. It is not a political reality in France. And one must deal with reality. In Algeria the OAS is a sentimental reality. It is based on deep emotions. But it does not count in France. In France the OAS is made up of a few individuals who make plastic-bomb incidents.

What did he think the West should do if the present exploratory talks with Russia on Berlin should break down? He said: "Khrushchev seeks to neutralize Germany and if he neutralizes Germany that will mean the neutralization of Europe. And if Europe is neutralized the United States is lost. For you in the U.S. cannot continue alone, alone without Europe and without the third world of the neutralists. And if you lose Europe, you will completely lose the third world of the neutralists." He sniffed at rumors that he planned to restore the Royalist pretender, the Comte de Paris, to his throne. He said:

I don't think there is any tendency towards a restored monarchy in France at present. But the French people have the desire to decide for themselves who shall be their principal responsible chief. This is just the way the people of America elect their President and the people of England elect their Prime Minister. In such a way the people of France choose their President. Someday the Germans will have to adopt a similar system of directly choosing their principal executive.

There is no other way in which you can provide for the necessary continuity of government, and that is an absolute requisite. But, as for the monarchy, that is an illusory idea. I don't wish to say that one day it could not happen in France; that it could not happen, for example, that a member of the former royal family should be chosen as President. One should not exclude possibilities of this sort for the indefinite future. Now I cannot imagine any restoration of the monarchy. The idea seems to me most illusory.

His cultural tastes were highly conventional; what you would expect of any well-educated Frenchman of his generation. He said: "I am very fond of music and in the evening I often listen to it, both on records and on the radio. Certainly I like Beethoven more than Mozart—although I can say I am surely fond of Schumann and Schubert. Also there are moments—I say moments—when I like Wagner. I must admit to a liking for nineteenth-century French music like Debussy and Delibes. Unfortunately I am not a musician. I am not a qualified judge. I love and I seek music. I crave music. But I am not creatively competent. My tastes are difficult to define."

He said he had studied piano while living at home until the age of sixteen but that he had made no headway. He had not continued afterward.

When I inquired whether any single person had particularly influenced his life, his character or his personality, he replied:

I suppose it is something like music. No single individual. Many men took part. First of all, there was my father. He was a professor and he was very cultivated, very human. He contributed. He contributed much. Then, of course, looking through the past, there were many others. There were the Greeks, certainly, the classical Greeks. And then I suppose there were the Romans. There were the French classics. Above all, there were the tragedians—Corneille and Racine. And also, of course, Bossuet. There were all the French classicists who had grandeur. *Ça c'est toujours mon gout.* [He became enthralled by the idea, I noted.] Foreigners [as if to include the Greeks and Romans among Frenchmen]? Yes, there is Goethe and Shakespeare. Shakespeare! What grandeur. What power.

I continued this interesting colloquy by observing I had heard that Henri Bergson, the philosopher, was a good friend of de Gaulle's father and that the general had known him as a young man. He commented: "No, he was not a friend, but he was great. And before him August Comte. But you must know that in history I always admired *les gens efficaces.* Like our history. Clovis. Charlemagne. Jeanne d'Arc. Charles VII. Henri IV. The real statesmen, the people who accomplished something. Napoleon—*bien sûr.* And among the living, the people who were alive when I was alive, surely Poincaré and Clemenceau.

My notes run on: "At this point I couldn't stop him. He was dreaming away in a thoughtful and rather moving fashion, looking out of the window at the bare trees in the Elysée garden on a humid, warm winter day, when the entire world was talking about the agony of France and the imminent possibility of disaster [because of the OAS insurrection]." He continued:

And in America your great Presidents. Surely your great Presidents. Jefferson. Above all Jefferson. And then there was Washington, a very great man. I have big admiration for him. And my contemporaries? Theodore Roosevelt. He was a brave man who never hesitated. And I admit to an admiration for Franklin Roosevelt despite the differences I had with him. He had the grand manner.

And the English? Among the English, Churchill is surely a great man. And the Germans? Bismarck was a real statesman. He did great harm to France but one cannot forget the fact that he was a real statesman, that he accomplished something.

Hitler? Hitler, no. Hitler, no! Because of his crimes. Not because of his nationalism. Because of his crimes I reject him.

Since he had now met Khrushchev, I again asked him if—as a man who had had the privilege of knowing the great men of our time—he thought Khrushchev was a big man. What did he think of Khrushchev? He said:

I don't know. You cannot judge a man except in the light of achievement. When Khrushchev has achieved something I shall tell you. I can only give you the answer then. No man can finally be judged except in the light of achievement.

Stalin was a great man. He did something. He was a brutal man, but he created a modern state. Churchill was a great man. He forged a victory. And Franklin Roosevelt was a great man; although, as you know so well, I had many differences with him. He led the United States into war and through the war on to victory. He was a man of quality.

To be a great man, one must realize something. One must achieve something definite. If Khrushchev can achieve peace, he will be a great man. Or if he seeks war and can win a war he will be a great man. But if he does neither, he will not be a great man.

GHARDAIA, ALGERIA, *February 11, 1962*

SPENT three days on a French tour of the Sahara run by Olivier Guichard, Saharan délégué général. On February 9, we arrived at Hassi-Messaoud, main petroleum exploitation center. But there was an OAS strike, and we couldn't see much. It was the regular OAS system with which I became familiar in Algiers. An employee of a company is killed (sometimes by the FLN; sometimes by the OAS), then the OAS orders a strike for "more protection."

Today we flew off in our private plane to El-Goléa, an absolutely lovely oasis in the vast desert which was known to André Gide. Then we flew on to Ghardaia, principal town of seven Mozabite settlements in the Mzab dry level valley. The Mozabites are a heretical and fundamentalist Muslim sect who escaped from orthodox Arab persecution in the Middle Ages. Mozabite dignitaries did not seem very happy at the prospect of living in an independent Algeria.

ALGIERS, *February 16, 1962*

BILL Porter, U.S. consul general with whom I stayed, has an extensive radio tapping outfit (he is a licensed ham operator), and we used to sit around in the evenings listening to secret signals of the security forces. "Albatross" is the code name by which they contact each other, and "Alerte Chicago" is the sign of violence.

I have been rereading Camus and noted the following: From "l'Hôte" in *l'Exile et le Royaume*: "In this vast country which he had loved so much he was alone." From *La Peste*: "Stupidity has a knack of getting its way. We had nothing left us but the past, and even if some were tempted to live in the future, they had speedily to abandon the idea." In one chapter, a Jesuit priest in Oran, Father Paneloux, gives a sermon saying, "Calamity has come to us, my brethren; and, my brethren, you deserve it. We walk in darkness, in the thick darkness of this plague."

PARIS, *February 20, 1962*

CECIL Lyon called. He had just read my column on the OAS to the effect that their motto should be "Down with Intelligence, Up with Death."

He counseled that I should get a police guard at my house to insure against plastic bombs. The embassy would be glad to arrange this.

I thanked him for his concern but considered it was the duty of the city of Paris to protect its inhabitants. He commented that the city of Paris might be too preoccupied.

Marina, who is worried about the servants, is making them sleep upstairs in the children's rooms because, normally speaking, the bombs go off on the ground floor and could splinter them with glass fragments.

PARIS, *March 2, 1962*

LUNCHED with Jean-Jacques Servan-Schreiber and his charming twenty-four-year-old wife, Sabine (daughter of a professional army officer). Jean-Jacques, who criticizes the OAS, lives in a regular fortress: the fifth floor of an old-fashioned Paris apartment house. At the door to the building was a uniformed policeman who did not let me enter until I gave my name. Inside the door were two plainclothes characters who asked for identification. One took me to the elevator. At the fifth floor, a burly character again asked my name before he let me in. Standing in the corner was a .22 automatic rifle.

Jean-Jacques is a brave, intellectual, dynamic young fellow. I enjoy reading his magazine, but I cannot say that his logic impresses me. He hammers away at de Gaulle and yet admits de Gaulle is the only man who can save France.

PARIS, *March 5, 1962*

RECENTLY I have noticed some strange ginks hanging around my house. I mentioned this to Al Ulmer at dinner. He confessed to me that Cecil Lyon, after being turned down by me on his kind suggestion that my house should be guarded, asked Al to make arrangements with the French security to do just that—and not tell me. That is who those guys are.

GENEVA, *March 13, 1962*

LAST night, I had a pleasant talk with Dean Rusk. I found him all alone in his modest hotel suite, just finishing dinner, wearing a shirt and sweater, no necktie. He said:

> The Russians must think of West Berlin as if it were on the border in a normal sense and not as if it were an island inside their territory. We *are* there and we will stay there. If Khrushchev wishes to push us out there will be war.
>
> It is hard to analyze just why Khrushchev chose to start another Berlin crisis now. It is probably an effort to consolidate his East German position. East Germany has been a second-class province of the Soviet empire. And Khrushchev has treated his own Germans as second-class citizens.
>
> The westward flight of East Germans was not encouraged by the West. It was simply that Khrushchev could not keep them in. In fact, we preferred our friends to stay on where they were. But Khrushchev had a demonstrated failure and could not even hold his own people.

CADENABBIA, ITALY, *April 2, 1962*

DROVE to Cadenabbia on Como today and spent an hour and three-quarters with old Adenauer in his villa above the lake.

I mentioned de Gaulle's observation that Khrushchev's historic role could not be judged until we knew whether he intended to make peace or war and had succeeded or failed. He said: "In my opinion, Khrushchev will not make war. As a Russian nationalist he wants to be seen as the creator of Russia's economy coming, as he does, after Stalin's enormous expansion of Russia and after Lenin's development of Marxism. That is why he has no use for war. War would wreck the Russian economy. The second reason why he doesn't want war is the menace of Red China."

He then sat forward in his chair, rumpling his black suit, staring at me earnestly from a slightly tanned face, and said: "I was in Moscow in the autumn of 1955. At that time, at Khrushchev's invitation, I had intimate talks with him about China, where he frankly expressed his concern. He showed himself perfectly aware that in case of a war, whatever its outcome, Russia would be greatly weakened and China would therefore be much more dangerous."

I told him Djilas recalls Stalin saying that an army installs its own political system where it goes. Adenauer commented:

> Do you think that the present Soviet system is real, genuine communism? I think it has moved away and towards another dictatorial form of government in which a group, not an individual, has all the power. Khrushchev doesn't hold all the power.
>
> Russia has continued to develop differently from what Stalin had imagined. This makes an absurdity of the Stalinist doctrine. Even today, the East

German regime is much harder than that in Russia itself. The Russians venerate Marx as the founder of Communism. Yet Marx imagined a classless, stateless society. The present Russian social system is one of the omnipotence of the state, the exact reverse of Marx.

ROME, *April 5, 1962*

LUNCHED with Enrico Mattei, said to be the most powerful man in Italy and chief of the national fuel trust.

I asked him if it were true that he was really bitterly anti-American. He replied quite frankly: "Yes, I am anti-American. We need to work here. We need to export the product of our work. We need cheap oil. And yet you try to keep us out of markets abroad. Your policy is run by your oil companies. I agree with Khrushchev that the oil companies run American policy."

This evening, I saw Prime Minister Fanfani. He said: "The Americans have been very stupid not to contact Mattei directly. He feels like a hurt woman. I told President Eisenhower twice that I thought it would be a wise thing for the United States to invite Mattei on a visit. Each time Eisenhower agreed—but nothing was done. Then last year I said the same thing to President Kennedy. He agreed. But no one did anything about it."

PARIS, *May 7, 1962*

GAVIN has come back from Washington glum and disappointed. Both Rusk and Bundy produced long arguments against giving any nuclear aid to France. Gavin is very gloomy. He saw Professor Kissinger, who shares his views, and who told him he was positive the President would have to reverse himself within a year.

PARIS, *May 16, 1962*

I CALLED up Gavin this morning. I said I thought that he and I were being squeezed into a corner together. He chuckled and replied: "Let's add Kissinger. He told me when I saw him at Harvard during my recent trip home that the White House had asked him to come down to discuss policy. Kissinger said the hell with it; he disagreed with our German policy, our French policy, and everything else and there wasn't any point."

PARIS, *June 8, 1962*

I SAW Couve de Murville and asked him what had provoked the present crisis between France and the United States. He said: "We do not blindly follow U.S. policy. That is the real crisis. And, of course, we are the only country in NATO that takes this viewpoint—of not blindly following U.S. policy. All we can do is to live with our disagreement. Your people have already recognized that the best thing they can do with Russia is to live with their disagreement. Surely it is easier between France and the U.S. than between Russia and the U.S. to live in such a way."

He understood that the United States could not give its nuclear weapons to other powers and that France would have a similar attitude in the same position. But, this being the case, why should the United States object to its allies making their own nuclear weapons?

Received June 13, 1962
From Annecy-Geneva

Capitaine Clémence
OAS
Réseau Fidélite-Serment
GAAC
Dear Mr. Sulzberger,

I, as the chief of the Anti-Communist action group for France and Algeria, and in spite of my bad command of American language, I've to inform you still once that we OAS fight for the Free World against Communism.

Don't you see that this man de Gaulle is a danger for the free world, and for that we are hoping to murder him. Yes we want to replace him with a Pro-American and Anti-Communist government.

Yes we are to kill de Gaulle (that naughty old devil-inspired man). Yes we are to kill him in spite of HIM and of the Communists who thanks to their Soviet-manned spy group do inform de Gaulle of all they know about OAS. . . .

VIVE LA FRANCE et les U.S.A.

PARIS, *June 18, 1962*

MOST agreeable luncheon with Pompidou in his private dining room in the Hotel Matignon. I asked why the OAS wanted to assassinate de Gaulle. He said diehards wanted to kill de Gaulle for two reasons: to take personal vengeance on the man they blame for all their troubles and also to establish their own government.

Pompidou said that in a sense there were only two parties in France today—the government and the opposition. The opposition, apart from the Communists, was made up of the active Vichyists, including the Independents and part of the Radicals. He stressed: "When I say active Vichyists I mean *active*. After all, 90 percent of France was Vichyist at one time or another."

He said: "Let me tell you—not as Prime Minister but as a Frenchman. If the U.S.A. ever tries to turn against us—for example by trying to break our good relations with Germany—we will turn to Russia. This will be a third force. Such is the normal law of politics. If your friend turns against you, you turn toward your enemy. This is precisely what happened with the OAS vis-à-vis de Gaulle. The OAS decided that de Gaulle was an enemy so it turned toward its real enemy, the FLN."

PARIS, *June 25, 1962*

DINED last night with Professor Henry Kissinger. He was a private in the last war and didn't finish college until 1946. He started out as a professor of government. Tom Finletter sent him a letter some years ago via Arthur Schlesinger, and it was as a result of his reply to this that he was brought into the government as an adviser on nuclear strategy.

Kissinger told me he ceased being adviser to the administration because he simply could not bring himself to argue in favor of theories he didn't believe. Our nuclear policy is crazy, and we don't take into account basic political and human facts. There is absolutely no escaping the existence of a French national atomic force.

PARIS, *June 26, 1962*

SPENT yesterday with Couve de Murville, golfing at Morfontaine, then having gin and tonics, finally a late lunch. He thinks the only way the United States can solve the problem of gold leakage is by revaluing the dollar, sometime probably in one to three years. After all, the last revaluation was in 1933—almost thirty years ago.

Ultimately, he sees an inevitable Sino-Soviet split because of the conflict between neighboring great powers. But there is nothing the West can do to accelerate development of such a split. The big problem will ultimately be the question of Chinese immigration into the empty spaces of Siberia—the way they are now immigrating into Mongolia.

DUBLIN, *July 10, 1962*

I WAS received this afternoon by President de Valera in his lovely presidential residence in Phoenix Park, once the home of the English Lord Lieutenants. De Valera was sitting alone at his desk when I was introduced by his aide de camp. The poor old man is so blind that he extended his hand off at an angle. I shook it and he courteously waved me to an armchair beside his desk.

He is massive, although he is almost eighty, still well over six feet and, except for his eyesight, seems remarkably preserved.

His face is pale and long-featured, and he has a slight twitching of the cheeks when he talks. But despite this indication of nervousness he speaks calmly in a soft drawl.

I began by observing that the postwar era had been a time for old statesmen—Churchill, de Gasperi, de Gaulle, and Adenauer, to say nothing of himself. What did he consider to be the advantages and disadvantages of age in a national leader?

He replied: "The disadvantages are obvious because as one gets old one loses one's strength and energy and if by some freak chance you still retain these, none of those around you would be convinced. The advantages are, however, that if your faculties are all right you have a lifetime of experience behind you upon which to rely. You have seen all the moods of life and your judgment should be sound. Another disadvantage, of course, is that an old man is perhaps not very venturesome. He is not as inclined to take risks readily."

DUBLIN, *July 12, 1962*

DURING the afternoon, I had an excellent long talk with Sean Lemass, Prime Minister. Ultimately, he thought the whole problem of partition would fade away through the Common Market. The effect of membership would be profound upon both Britain and Ireland, and the change would inevitably lead to a new political climate. Lemass said the government of Northern Ireland would deny this, but he found in his contacts with the Belfast community a wide body of opinion which thought the existing division of Ireland would one day become anomalous within the Common Market.

LONDON, *July 16, 1962*

THIS evening, I had a talk and drinks with Prime Minister Macmillan. It was an interesting moment, because today he effected the biggest political execution Britain has seen this century, bluntly discharging over a dozen ministers with absolutely no advance notice. When I went in to see him at 6:30 P.M., the final slaughter was being announced to the press.

Macmillan received me in Admiralty House (No. 10 Downing Street is being repaired) in the Cabinet room, where he was seated at the long, green-baize council table with a whisky and soda before him. He promptly offered me one.

I reminded him of the time he said Britain's role was not to be too large, something between the bee and the dinosaur, and asked him how this affected its special position in the Common Market—if Britain is admitted. He said:

We cannot get into the Common Market on terms that are dishonorable to the white Commonwealth, to the EFTA [Free Trade Area] and to our own agriculture. We must protect all these obligations. If you took a purely intellectual view at this moment it would look only as if there were a fifty-fifty chance of our joining. Yet I feel in my knees that great world movements are irresistible. And there is a movement in what is left of Europe—

west of the Stettin-Trieste line—to develop into one sound unit. The negotiations may be very difficult. But when things finally begin to move it will be hard to resist the trend.

There is a confederating spirit, a spirit of the ages, the dynasts, that takes control. Sometimes that movement is for ill purposes and sometimes it is for good. Napoleon could not help himself when he was led on by the world spirit of revolution—to evil.

What are the European people? For 2,500 years, starting in the Mediterranean basin, they have been making what we call modern civilization. Some, like the English, spread overseas to what I call the Byzantium of New York. But what are the Americans but Europeans? I am half-American and I know.

There are two streams of thought and philosophy. One is from the Christian civilization based on a Judaic origin. One is from the great Roman tradition based on order. These have mingled to make the modern world.

Twice in my lifetime, by tragic series of events, the Europeans have turned on each other and destroyed themselves. It is because of this that they have lost their automatic predominance.

In the United Nations, the Europeans—and I include America—are no longer the predominant group. Even thirty years ago the Europeans governed more than half the world. But the whole background has changed. Since that time, there has risen the Russian colossus. It is a great power, even if that power is sometimes exaggerated, and half-Asiatic, half-European.

What do we do? What is left? All that is left of free Europe is a small appendix of some 200,000,000 people, very intelligent and energetic, who have been through all kinds of ups and downs after five hundred years of dark ages.

When I think of the Common Market I see that the economic side is vital. But it is not as vital as the political side. If we all work together, we can play a great role in the next stage of world development.

There will be 2,000,000,000 Chinese by the end of the century, even if you people don't seem to bother much about them. Napoleon said China was a sleeping giant and we should not wake it. But now the giant has been woken.

Your country and ours, and we are brothers practically, can play a role in the beginning of an enormous new period of history. But we want to work with Europeans so that they see our viewpoint—not because we are a proud people or want to keep an empire—but because we have something special to contribute. New countries are coming into being like mushrooms, some of them too soon. We try to teach them how to govern themselves. I want to keep an influence on them through the Commonwealth.

This is a completely new period of history starting now. There is an enormous change in the balance of power and also in the importance of power. In the end we must get the Russians into Europe. This will come very gradually. But they are gradually being corrupted by bourgeois influences. After all, they are ordinary chaps who want ordinary things, very decent people. We must just be very patient and avoid war and in a generation or two things will change. The Russians are civilized, intelligent people, but for the moment we cannot do much with them politically. They talk a lot of nonsense now but this won't go on forever. Our policy must be: never give in and never provoke.

GENEVA, *July 24, 1962*

DINED last night with Harriman at Le Lion d'Or above the lake. He leaves today, having finished the Laos negotiations and signed the accords.

Averell estimates it would cost about $7 million per annum to raise the annual Chinese calory intake by an average of 100 calories; 16 million tons of grain would provide the Chinese with about 1,500 to 1,900 calories. The shipping costs are immense. This means $1 per Chinaman per 100 calories.

He speculated about what might have happened had FDR lived and been well enough to stay on in office. He never would have allowed the Communists to grab China; it had been a mistake to force Chiang to collaborate with the Communists. Roosevelt "had his Dutch jaw stuck out on China," on which Churchill always disagreed with him. Averell says Stalin truly respected Roosevelt as "something new and different."

Averell thinks the United States must now retreat from "the front lines" in Southeast Asian policy and let others more visibly share the burden.

He says the CIA has gotten us into terrible messes and cites Burma, Laos, and Indonesia as examples (Burma being the Chinese Nationalist troops hodgepodge). We should have recognized Mao in 1949. Now we must wait and see what happens.

BONN, *July 26, 1962*

TALK with Franz-Josef Strauss, Defense Minister. I asked if he thought Taylor's new position (Chairman of the Joint Chiefs) did not bode changes for Europe. He answered: "Taylor in his book *Uncertain Trumpet* indicated that U.S. national survival was the only basic excuse for using atomic weapons. You can imagine how we feel about that."

RAVELLO, ITALY, *August 17, 1962*

SPENT a couple of days at the villa of Stash Radziwill, where Stash and Lee were entertaining her sister, Jackie Kennedy, for a fortnight together with her daughter, Caroline. Apart from myself and the above, the other guests were Gianni Agnelli and Marella, his wife, and Benno (Gilbert) Graziani and his wife, Nicole, a beautiful young blonde.

Jackie is a strange girl but quite lovely despite the fact her eyes are set too far apart. She is a good athlete, swims, water skis, and dances well, has a fine figure. She has an odd habit of halting consistently as she talks, a kind of pause rather than a stutter, so sometimes you think she's through saying something when she isn't.

We talked a good deal at various times, and here are some odds and ends I remember. She has immense admiration, love (and I felt a little fear) for her father-in-law, whom she refers to as "Mr. Kennedy." Says he can't speak at all since his stroke, and it is tragic when he tries to tell Jack something; the President keeps asking, "Do you mean this, or that?" and can't get through.

Mrs. Kennedy, Sr., and Ethel are immensely religious. I was struck by the fact Jackie herself went to mass almost every day. But she said with evident disapproval that Ethel goes with her children to the 7:30 A.M. mass every day of the summer.

She said Bobby is immensely ambitious and will never feel that he has succeeded in life until he has been elected to something, even Mayor of Hyannisport. Being appointed to office isn't enough.

She admires Malraux enormously. Thinks she made a hit with de Gaulle and is proud that at the Elysée dinner he leaned across the table and announced she knew more about French history than most French women.

Says de Gaulle told her to beware of Madam Khrushchev, who was "plus maline que lui." She thinks Mrs. K is hard and tough. But she rather liked K and likes his daughter, Mrs. Adzhubei, very much.

NEW YORK, *August 28, 1962*

LUNCH with Adlai Stevenson. He saw Tito this summer on his Adriatic island hideout and was overwhelmed by the imperial splendor in which he lives. He was received on Tito's seventieth birthday, and they drank copious quantities of wine, every bottle of which had been laid down in the year 1892, when the Jugoslav was born. They only rode around in a golf cart, ate, and drank. The wine was served in ceramic boots.

PARIS, *October 24, 1962*

I SAW Larry Norstad this afternoon. He thinks the odds are better than three to one against nuclear war over Cuba. Khrushchev must be muttering about these "mad Americans" and is somewhat nonplussed. He doubts if Khrushchev will try anything in Berlin, because anything serious would mean war, and he now realizes this.

We cannot let missiles continue in Cuba. The quarantine does nothing about overthrowing Castro. We simply have to take Cuba now—either by starting trouble on the island or starting some kind of a fake demonstration off the coast of Florida to give an excuse for a police action. And this would have to be total and extremely swift.

We cannot risk failure, and it would be a crime to stop. We have to follow through. But on the other hand, we should not push too far or too quickly, and this is against the American nature, which likes noise and action.

NATO has stood up remarkably well. Our actions against Cuba are not popular. But all NATO members are resolved not to be split by Khrushchev. De Gaulle has been particularly good.

PARIS, *October 25, 1962*

DINED last night at U.S. NATO Ambassador Tom Finletter's. On Cuba, von Walther, de Staercke, Boyesen (all ambassadors to NATO), and Alessandrini were convinced Khrushchev would not move simultaneously in Berlin, would initially pull back, and would force a negotiation on Kennedy which would ultimately prove embarrassing.

De Staercke said that when there is a negotiation it means that both sides must concede something. The blockade cannot continue indefinitely. The only way to remove missile bases from Cuba is to take Cuba, which would cause immense damage to the U.S. position in the world; or by getting the Russians to withdraw them. But the Russians could legitimately say they would not withdraw them unless we did something equal—such as dismantling our missile bases in Turkey. De Staercke thought we should take the initiative in making such an offer. After all, the entire concept of NATO now favored a maritime MRBM force which rendered such bases obsolescent anyway.

CAMBRIDGE, MASSACHUSETTS, *October 27, 1962*

ISAIAH Berlin came for coffee this morning. He had just been in Washington and dined with the President. Berlin says Kennedy is surrounded by a group of activists who are very stimulating but who are not long-range thinkers. Isaiah wonders if deep in the President's mind he may not have a presentiment that he may not live a long time because of his illness and that he must make his mark on history quickly.

NEW YORK, *October 31, 1962*

WE spent yesterday evening with Adlai Stevenson. The Cuba crisis had been "a gratuitous break" for the United States. Our position on Soviet perfidy had helped. The Afro-Asian nations had been taking a line of "a plague on both your houses," but when Khrushchev was exposed in Cuba it tended to confirm what we had been saying.

When the Soviet missiles were discovered, thirty-two of them were targeted on U.S. areas. How long could we have waited under this menace with a restive American public opinion?

WASHINGTON, *November 9, 1962*

MARINA and I dined last night at the White House. The atmosphere was extremely informal. The President looked well, calm and relaxed, and sat around chatting until 11:00 P.M. The rest of us stayed on another half-hour with Jackie, listening to phonograph records, including a folk song that has just been put out—"PT 109."

The President was extremely friendly and clearly wanted to talk only about politics or foreign policy. He made only rudimentary efforts to converse with the ladies at dinner and none before and after. When he greeted me he said: "You have come over at an interesting time," grinning from ear to ear. He said: "Nixon is a nice fellow in private and a very able man. I worked with him on the Hill for a long time, but he seems to have a split personality and he is very bad in public. And nobody likes him."

All the Russian missiles will be out of Cuba by Monday (November 12). "I am astonished at how fast they've been able to get them out."

There should be some way that the press can be answered back and restrained from excesses. "But we politicians can't do it. It is quite right that the press should take after us. Nevertheless, the uncontrolled attacks by the press should be stopped. There should be some means in the press itself to take care of this."

Kennedy said he could not understand why Khrushchev went into Cuba. If he had thought America wasn't going to fight in the heart of an area of its own vital national interest, he surely must have assumed we weren't going to fight in Berlin. Therefore, "Why didn't he go straight for Berlin?"

Several times Kennedy talked about his "terrible responsibility" in terms of making war or peace. "I know the figures," he said. "One-hundred million Europeans would be dead in a day—and eighty million here. A war can destroy humanity."

He complained that "Europe wants a free ride in its defense." What he meant was that the NATO allies weren't doing enough to build Western defense and were counting too much on our protection. He said: "Our press is too kind to Europe. They're not kind to us." I replied: "That is a pretty unkind cut, Mr. President." He grinned and said: "Well, maybe I didn't mean you, Cy."

Europe had to build greater conventional forces and refused to do so. The French had only one and one-half divisions in NATO. De Gaulle has no actual nuclear capability and cannot rely on atoms for defense. The Cuban crisis showed that large conventional forces are needed. We would have had to go into Cuba with conventional forces had we attacked. The Europeans want an atomic umbrella.

He thought the Russians, once they saw how determined we were, were afraid that we might capture some of their missiles in Cuba. The real alternative to a naval quarantine would have been a conventional assault on Cuba, not an air attack. There was too much danger that in the chaos resulting from an air attack, someone might have gotten excited and started off a terrible war.

Kennedy warned that it was always easy for the United States to make a deal on Berlin and avoid war. The Europeans should realize this and do more about arming themselves instead of relying on us. We couldn't go on forever carrying the burden largely alone.

WASHINGTON, *November 11, 1962*

SPENT the day at Paul Nitze's farm in La Plata, Maryland. Nitze told us the story of Dean Acheson's visit to Paris via London, where he spent a few hours briefing David Bruce and showing him the pictures.

When Acheson got to Paris he was smuggled into de Gaulle's office by an underground tunnel from across the street. Acheson went in alone except for the Elysée interpreter. De Gaulle greeted him, then said: "Je vous écoute." Acheson explained everything and added he had brought along pictures to confirm what he was saying. De Gaulle said: "It is not necessary to show me the pictures because obviously a great government like yours would not risk war for nothing."

WASHINGTON, *November 20, 1962*

THIS evening, I had a long talk with the President. I waited in the office of his principal secretary, Mrs. Evelyn Lincoln, hung with Presidential mementos. Macmillan had sent a large photograph and an effusive inscription revising the well-known quotation to read as follows: "Ask not what your country can do for you but what we can do together for all mankind." There were also quite a few cartoons. One of these was of Nixon and Kennedy and inscribed by Nixon: "To Jack Kennedy, my neighbor, wishing him the best success in almost everything. Dick Nixon." They were neighbors in the Senate office building.

I knew Kennedy had been at work since 8:30 that morning, and our conversation did not end until late; but he looked well and resilient. The only sign of nervousness was a fidgeting with an unlit cigarette. He was calm, collected, and moved easily from subject to subject across a broad spectrum. I am always impressed by his remarkable memory.

Despite his very considerable victory in Cuba (he had just announced that Russia was withdrawing its troops and bomber planes) and despite the Chinese-Indian cease-fire proclaimed today, he was by no means over-optimistic. I told him I did not want to waste his time because I knew he had had a cruel day. He grinned and told me not to worry, to take it easy, he had plenty of time. He asked me what I intended to do with my notes on what he said. I told him I wasn't entirely sure but I thought I would drop out bits of material in various columns during the coming weeks.

I inquired whether there had been the slightest advance toward a formula for disarmament. He said the deadlock remained unchanged. Likewise, there had been no new approaches on the subject of disengagement, and he repeated his emphasis that we were not engaged in any political talks with the Russians apart from Cuba.

In his recent letters to de Gaulle, had he ever answered the general's 1958 request for a *directoire*? Kennedy said he had not personally answered the *directoire* request but thought that it had been "bypassed by events." Anyway, the French request was "tied with Germany now." Furthermore, "De Gaulle has not brought it up lately. I guess that in a sense he has carved himself a de facto position already even if this is not formally acknowledged in just the way he would like. We'd better leave the matter alone."

Did we have any way today of checking as to whether the Russians had left any nuclear warheads in Cuba? He said quite flatly: "No, there is not any way, but I certainly assume they won't do so." I asked: "You mean they wouldn't leave such toys in the hands of such screwballs?" "That's right," he said.

I asked if the Yemen revolt were to spread to Saudi Arabia, whether it would be in our national interest to support the Saudi Arabian monarchy. He said this had tricky aspects. "If U.A.R. or Yemeni troops were to invade Saudi Arabia I think we would assist Saudi Arabia, but we would not have any obligation to do this if it were just a local insurrection and there were no evidence of an invasion. The real problem is the withering away of the Saudi Arabian monarchy. There is the same problem in Jordan. The wheel certainly turns quickly. Just a short time ago Nasser was in the ash can. Now look what he is up to."

Had we any intention of offering new inducements to our NATO allies to provide more conventional divisions? He shrugged his shoulders and said: "What more can we do? Sooner or later they will have to produce more conventional forces or otherwise there will be no sense to NATO." Did he mean that we would have to go through an agonizing reappraisal? He said: "If ultimately they do not produce more conventional strength, perhaps we will have to rethink our approach. Of course Berlin is the key to all this. We would need less troops without Berlin."

I was interested in what he had said about the problem of national security and the press and inquired whether he had ever considered trying to produce a U.S. version of an official secrets act. He answered: "I doubt if either Congress or the press would ever accept that kind of an approach. I talked with the newspaper publishers a year ago on this and on self-policing by the press in terms of security. But they wouldn't take it. They always suspect that this is a form of managing the news. I think somebody, like Columbia, for example, should take a look at how the press uses news and not just how we seem to use the news. Columbia should study this and I think they would find this was a very provocative subject."

I told him I wanted to ask a question I had posed to many other leaders: Who was the person who had most influenced him? Without hesitation he said: "I suppose you would say my father and the atmosphere he created around all of us as we were growing up. But there is not any special public figure."

I asked if there had been any particular philosopher or statesman who influenced him and he said, "No." He then continued:

As far as the presidency is concerned, nobody can really help there. Some people used to say that Nixon had certain advantages because he had learned a good deal and assumed responsibilities as Vice President. But being Vice President isn't enough. In this job there is nothing like experience. And that is also true in the Cabinet. It is unlike the British system, where you can have a Shadow Cabinet with different people working for many years and having knowledge about the government operations in particular departments. We suddenly bring men in and dump them into the situation. It is a very tough problem. And it would be hard to devise a Shadow Cabinet system here.

When you take over a job like this, you simply have to depend on the judgment of the men around you. And you don't know them at first. They may have good records and excellent reputations but their judgment may be lousy—generals and diplomats and others. And you can't tell at the start. Of course, after you have had a few months you gain a hell of an advantage.

I asked him if he had been scared by the immensity of the task and its responsibility at the start. He said with a grin: "No, not scared. At the beginning, you are protected by the value of your own ignorance. But I can do the job much better now and I could have done this much better earlier if I had had experience. Let me show you what I mean. After Cuba—the Bay of Pigs—we began to talk about maybe going into Laos. But all the generals and other people disagreed about this and you don't know whom to believe and whom to disbelieve. It is a very hard thing at first."

18

Dined last night at the Philippe de Rothschilds'. A very small dinner for Guy Mollet. Mollet said that just prior to the 1956 Suez crisis, Ben Gurion and the Israeli Defense Minister came secretly to confer with him in France. The British delayed for two months before agreeing to the Suez action and only on condition that they could run it militarily and politically.

PARIS, *December 16, 1962*

Last night, I had a long talk with Dean Rusk over at Bohlen's residence. The NATO meeting finished yesterday. I asked what the United States would do if NATO simply refuses to raise the needed conventional forces and whether we would consider some kind of "agonizing reappraisal" in our basic policy. Rusk said:

> If Europe doesn't stick by its promises, someday there will be a movement in the U.S. against the idea of the U.S.A. as a world policeman. *We* draft our men and levy taxes and suffer casualties in distant places like South Vietnam. Europe hasn't begun to plumb its capabilities. It is a matter of will. The Europeans haven't begun to approach the level of national effort they achieved in 1939, when they were quarreling with each other.
>
> We provide the cannon fodder as well as the nuclear produce and it is ridiculous for people to say that we should accept to serve as their cannon fodder. We have 400,000 men in NATO and are the only member that has met its agreed force goals. Why should we draft a Kansas farmer and send him to Britain where there is no conscription and where that same Kansas farmer sees Englishmen lolling about? This will become a political problem at home if something isn't done about it.

I then asked him if he thought secretaries of state were now "condemned" to travel. I pointed out that Dulles had been criticized by the

Democrats for traveling so much, and now here was Rusk hopping about like a traveling salesman. Was there any way to put an end to this? He said:

As long as the Under Secretary can serve as acting Secretary when the Secretary himself is away, it is not as serious a problem as it might be. But it might be desirable to have someone with the prestige of a Cabinet member to do the traveling job.

Truman tried to work out a system like this when he had Phil Jessup as ambassador at large. As a matter of fact, Truman once suggested that we should appoint a Secretary of Foreign Affairs—which was Jefferson's first title—and let him do the traveling.

One of Dulles's troubles was that he often took leaders of the State Department traveling with him and tried to run the Department from his vest pocket as he moved around. My theory is to leave the Department in the hands of the acting Secretary. Like General Marshall, when I travel I see myself as a kind of ambassador. Sometimes I even ask the State Department for instructions. I don't send instructions from abroad the way Dulles did.

PARIS, *December 20, 1962*

LUNCHED today with Alain Peyrefitte, Information Minister. He told me that he had had lunch at the Elysée with Eisenhower and de Gaulle in August, and that Eisenhower had told de Gaulle, "I am reading a book about you by Cy Sulzberger and I advise you to read it."

PARIS, *February 9, 1963*

DINED last night at the Alain de Rothschilds. After dinner, I sat in on an interesting dialogue between Pompidou and Bohlen. Pompidou recounted all the old arguments in favor of a French national "force de frappe" but then went on and said perhaps a "European deterrent" might be useful. Bohlen immediately urged him to go ahead with this concept, saying the United States had been eagerly requesting its allies to produce their own ideas.

Pompidou talked at length about the contrasts between Britain and the Continent. There was no escaping the fact that the British not only felt but thought differently. They were not truly Europeans and could not become such. I thought that this significantly hinted France would never let the British into the Common Market.

Pompidou made the interesting statement that India's fate is a much more important question than the French atomic "force de frappe." If India comes under Chinese domination, thus forming a bloc of one billion people, "We shall all be eaten in the long run."

PARIS, *January 22, 1963*

IN the morning mail arrived a plain envelope addressed in hand, which I thought was a bill. I ripped it open and found a two-page letter from General de Gaulle written in pen and ink on his personal stationery, a plain piece of paper headed in the upper left corner "Le Général de Gaulle."

It was dated January 20, and mailed yesterday, January 21, at 5:45 P.M. I note the time because on January 20, Adenauer arrived in Paris to sign a Franco-German treaty with de Gaulle which Washington is calling the "Bonn-Paris Axis." The letter said, in part:

> I read your book, *The Test*, with much interest. I will refrain from judging your opinions since you are passing judgment on me. But I must say that the facts you recount are, to my knowledge, exact on the whole and that your work is very vivid and very clear. Moreover, how could I fail to appreciate the sympathy toward me I felt in it.
>
> C. de Gaulle

Somehow it seems strange—in this age of teleprompters, ghost writers, electric typewriters, etc.—to think of a seventy-two-year-old chief of state writing a letter all by himself (despite his bad eyes), then addressing and licking the envelope.

BARBIZON, FRANCE, *January 23, 1963*

MOST interesting lunch with General Speidel. He says that France has a backward strategy while Germany has a forward strategy, and no meeting of minds is possible on this. The last French maneuvers were a disaster and entirely contrary to the meaning of NATO.

PARIS, *January 29, 1963*

LUNCHED today with John Mowinckel. He says Galbraith has such a high and mighty way of presenting his views to Washington that Rusk cabled him last Christmas: "Happy Birthday."

Baldwin, Ambassador in Malaya, cabled the Peace Corps over his signature saying one of the Peace Corps doctors wanted a rectal thermometer for buffaloes. He stipulated: "Require a seven-inch instrument. Five inches not enough." Shriver sent a deadpan memo to Kennedy, his brother-in-law, saying, "I think you should know what your envoy to Malaya requires."

PARIS, *January 31, 1963*

I SAW General de Gaulle this afternoon. I observed that a wave of anti-Americanism seemed to be infecting the mass media. "*Tiens.* You think that? I think just the opposite. Do you read the *Figaro*? I think the French press is very pro-American. I think the French press is very pro-American because it thinks de Gaulle is anti-American and this is the best way to be against de Gaulle."

Recalling a previous conversation, I asked if he thought the French people psychologically disliked the American people. To my surprise the answer differed considerably this time. He said:

> I am surprised that you should think there is anti-Americanism. I don't think such a thing exists. But you must remember that the French people, like most other nations, are xenophobic in this sense. They want to do things themselves. And they regret it very much when they cannot do things themselves. They don't like to resign themselves to letting others do things for them. That is all.
>
> It is very evident that during the war both the United States and Britain tried to control France and the affairs of France according to their own desires. And it is true that I opposed the United States and Britain in such efforts. I opposed them for the very reason I have just cited and I can assure you I did well. Just look at the facts. Supposing you had come back to France with General Giraud as a servant and a puppet. Giraud was a brave man but he never counted for anything and the French people knew this. He would have been quickly replaced. He would simply have been refused by the French people. And if he had been *your* man, seemingly responsible for French destinies, *you* would have been detested when he was removed.

To straighten out a matter that was becoming controversial and hurting the already diminished Franco-American friendship, I asked whether his original letter of 1958 to Eisenhower, suggesting the so-called *directoire*, had ever been answered, formally or informally. He again told me *directoire* was a word he had never used and added with a sour smile: "No, there has never been an answer. Not ever." This, I was subsequently to find out, was simply not true, yet it was believed not only by de Gaulle, but also by Couve de Murville and Ambassadors Gavin and, initially, Bohlen. I can only assume the text of Eisenhower's reply to de Gaulle was mislaid both in the French archives and the U.S. Embassy. Bohlen eventually dug this text out, and, with the authorization of Secretary of State Rusk, showed it to me.

Did the 1958 offer still stand, I inquired? He thought for a moment and looked skeptical. Then he said: "I ask myself if at present, things being what they are today, it would be workable. I do not think so."

I inquired whether he thought there could or should be such a thing as interdependence between Europe and North America. He said:

> Alas, first there must be a Europe. Right now it is very convenient for the U.S. There is a France and a Germany and an Italy and a Great Britain. And the U.S. plays each one against the other.
>
> But if there were a real Europe, that would be different. There would have to be a real Europe with its own economy, its own policy, and its own

defense. Once there is such a Europe, it should have an organized accord with the U.S., but what, after all, is interdependence? I don't know what is meant by this, and there must be "rapports" between Europe and America. That is interdependence, I suppose.

But certainly, in terms of defense, if there is a Soviet threat, Europe could not defend itself alone. Nor really could the U.S.A. The U.S.A. could defend itself with missiles but not in a moral sense and vis-à-vis the free world.

I asked him if—despite arguments between Paris and Washington—the United States could rely on full French support were there another crisis like the October, 1962, Cuba confrontation when France stood firmly by America. Without hesitation he said: "If there is a threat of world war France will be with the United States. *Evidemment. Evidemment.* That does not change."

At this point I asked the general to explain what seemed to me a contradiction in his thinking. In June, 1940, de Gaulle had endorsed the proposal of Jean Monnet and Lord Vansittart to unite France and Britain. This being so, I asked: "If you considered Britain a European country then, why isn't it European today?" He said: "Ah, but of course, Britain *can* be in Europe. It was European then. But it doesn't want to be European today. It was obliged by the circumstance of war to be European at that moment. Now it must come back to things in a European way."

Would he be prepared to see a demilitarized Germany in exchange for reunification? He said: "If Germany were neutralized, France would be quickly neutralized also. We are for a Germany allied to the West and militarily effective. Our view has not changed."

I remarked there had been rumors in some newspapers to the effect that he would like to make a deal with Russia of a private sort. The general said this was absurd; the Communist menace remained, and France remained attached to its ideals and obligations.

I brought up the subject of Bergson whose theory of intuition so evidently influenced the general. He told me:

> In fact, I was much influenced by Bergson, particularly because he made me understand the philosophy of action. Bergson explains the role of intelligence and analysis. He saw how necessary it is to analyze questions in search of the truth. But intellect alone cannot act. The intelligent man does not automatically become the man of action. Instinct is also important. Instinct plus impulse; but impulse is also not sufficient as a basis for action. The two, intellect and impulse, must go together.
>
> Bergson showed me that action comes from the combination, the combined application of intellect and instinct, working together. All my life I have been aware of this essentially important explanation. Pure intellect cannot by itself produce action and impulse can produce folly if it alone serves as a guide, whether in politics or in military affairs.
>
> The two must be linked and this is Bergson's theory of intuition. The great men have both intellect and impulse. The brain serves as a brake upon pure

emotional impulse. The brain surmounts impulse; but there also must be impulse and the capability for action in order not to be paralyzed by the brake of the brain. I remember this from Bergson who has led me here in my entire life.

But surely you will agree with me that philosophy has never changed anyone. Men are still what they are. Philosophy helps them to express themselves better and to understand each other better, but no man has ever been *created* a philosopher.

PARIS, *February 1, 1963*

FIRST-CLASS talk with Pompidou.

How did he envision the role of the United States and Britain vis-à-vis the kind of "Europe" France was looking forward to? He said:

> The role of Britain is evident. In the end Britain must be in. It is inevitable. The normal role for Britain is to be part of Europe because it is so closely linked by history and geography.
>
> But this will mean, undoubtedly, a great historical change for Britain. After all, the British are used to their links with the Commonwealth and the United States. Also it has been British doctrine for so long to prevent any European unity. This was the traditional British policy until 1940. But there has been a profound change in everything and it is perfectly clear that ultimately Britain will be part of Europe.
>
> As for the United States, the day will come when the U.S.A. and Europe must work together on an equal basis. Once this essential fact is recognized, we can plan and work together and end our current difficulties.

I then asked if he thought NATO was outmoded, or if France, in any case, was planning to withdraw from NATO. He said:

> I will give you my idea. This is only my idea, but I would like to tell you what I think. NATO is not outmoded at the present moment. But for us, NATO is still the United States. It is dominated and run by the United States.
>
> NATO will be in this sense outmoded when the United States no longer dominates it. But the forces exist to create another balance in the West.
>
> In the future, once a Europe has been organized, NATO will reflect a separate change, a repartition of strength, a more precise balance of forces. At that time, Europe will be able to defend itself in a better and more effective way—but allied to the United States. It would become an alliance of two powers instead of fifteen nations. But this is for the future.

What did he think Europe's ultimate role would be? He observed: "Naturally, we all hope, all of us, that Russia will become more civilized and will turn westward, cut off from China and establishing its own freedoms. I think Russia will turn toward us and eventually aspire to join with European nations just the way Poland and Spain are now turning toward us. Europe is certainly closer to Russia than the United States is, for example."

Did he consider Russia a more "European" country than Britain? He replied categorically, "Certainly not. Britain is certainly more European than Russia. It is more European than Russia ever could be. But on the other hand, Russia is probably more European than the United States."

PARIS, *February 26, 1963*

LUNCHED today with General Stehlin (air force chief). De Gaulle has explained his strategic concepts to him. Either there will never be another war on a major scale because it is too dangerous, or the entire world will be destroyed in such a war. Either way, you cannot plan for the results, so there is no need to worry about logical defense. But France must join the nuclear club. One member of the French Automobile Club may have a Rolls-Royce and the other a 2 CV (Mini), but one can't join the Automobile Club if one doesn't have the 2 CV. Furthermore, de Gaulle wants his force as a diplomatic weapon.

PARIS, *March 6, 1963*

COUVE, Pompidou, and de Gaulle himself have told me the general's 1958 *directoire* letter was never answered by Eisenhower. And Kennedy plus two American ambassadors "confirmed" this. The Americans, at any rate, hadn't taken the trouble to look into the facts.

At last I got the story from Chip Bohlen. Chip, who had been doing some homework, took me back to the embassy to show me the actual texts.

On September 17, 1958, de Gaulle wrote Eisenhower a letter a bit more than a page long—to which was appended a memorandum which was being sent in duplicate to Macmillan. The general said France understood the worries of the United States on Formosa (then a crisis) and suggested that an "organization"—the word *directoire* was not used—be composed of the Big Three Western powers to make basic decisions in all the world, including the use of nuclear weapons.

On October 21, 1958, Eisenhower sent back a letter by himself and marked as a NIACT (meaning urgent, night-action telegram) for Cecil Lyon (then chargé d'affaires) and Randy Burgess (then U.S. Ambassador to NATO) explaining the American viewpoint. It stressed the necessity of considering the viewpoints of other NATO allies in any political decisions. The letter was in the embassy files.

Chip had been startled to discover this answer only a week ago. Before then, he also had believed the United States had never answered de Gaulle.

PARIS, *March 15, 1963*

LAST night we went to a very small dinner Couve de Murville gave at the Quai d'Orsay. One of the troubles with American policy, he says, is the curious system we have inherited from our earliest origins. It is the habit in the United States to elect a man President who has had no governmental experience. When he campaigns he is surrounded by "experts" on different subjects and he brings them along to the White House after his election. This tends to create a kind of second Cabinet, where a man like Mac Bundy can have more importance than the Secretary of State.

France, on the other hand, has a long tradition of centralized authority, dating back to the monarchy. It has the habit of a small executive aided by a formal Cabinet of what the French call the "governement," and underneath the professional civil-service functions. The Cabinet carries out policy on orders from the executive, and in the case of de Gaulle the executive is an unusually strong man. But there are three or four principal ministers in the Cabinet among whom Couve—with no false modesty—includes himself, adding: "I have much more to do with policy than Dean Rusk has in the U.S.A."

LONDON, *March 20, 1963*

THIS afternoon, I saw Harold Wilson, new leader of the Labor Party. He is a small, pipe-smoking man, with an unctuous manner, a very middle-class accent, and bright blue eyes: the face of a halibut, with shark's eyes.

I started by asking if a Labor government would give up an independent deterrent. He answered in the affirmative and added:

> We cannot afford to experiment on missiles ourselves. Our policy is wholly against an independent deterrent. An independent British deterrent does not add to western strength. The western deterrent *must* be American. We are now using up, in a useless nuclear effort, resources which could be put into conventional forces where we are falling down on our obligations. Not enough is left over for brush-fire forces Britain needs.
>
> We are against a European deterrent without the U.S.A. We don't want a further division of resources in the alliance and a German finger on the trigger. All we want is more fingers on the safety catch.

LONDON, *March 22, 1963*

TODAY, I drove to Alton in Hampshire to see Field Marshal Lord Montgomery at Isington Mill, his little country home. His place is *really* modest and simple. When I returned to London, I happened to pass Apsley House, the enormous mansion (almost a palace) on Piccadilly given by the grateful British people to the Duke of Wellington after the Napoleonic wars. Montgomery did not do so well. Whatever one may think of him, he is undoubtedly the most famous British general since Wellington.

Monty was wearing a dark blue knitted sweater and over it an open leather windbreaker. He led me through the dining room upstairs to his study. The room was decorated with a lot of bad oil paintings, at least four of which were full-length portraits of Monty. Also hideous but not uncomfortable furniture and an enormous mass of knickknacks. Everything was in apple-pie order, including the desk. In a peculiarly ugly cage was the only other living thing in the house, a somnolent blue parakeet with a celluloid fake companion. There were at most twenty books on a shelf by his desk, and I imagine this comprises his entire library. Prominent were *Burke's Peerage* and the 1963 *Who's Who*. I could just imagine the old codger reading himself to sleep with those after his usual dinner of mutton.

Among the decorations in this study were several signed snapshots of King George VI together with Montgomery. There were also signed photographs. Churchill had inscribed his picture: "To Monty. Hard times; stern conflict; victorious commander! Winston S. Churchill 1946." Among the bad oil paintings were one by Churchill and one by Field Marshal Alexander.

Monty sat on a sofa opposite the stove. He seemed cocky, tough, positive, intolerant, ignorant, and unbelievably vain. He has a stubborn, grumpy face, but looks extremely fit for a man of his age. There is not an ounce of fat on him, and there is a healthy gleam in his cold blue eyes. I dislike him and think that his supreme military gift is confirmed by the fact that his own army didn't shoot him in the back.

I began by asking him what he thought of the idea of a multilateral force for NATO. He said:

> Nonsense. Absolute nonsense. Just assume you have a ship with a crew of one-third Belgian, one-third Portuguese, and one-third Danish. It won't work. Won't work. You might get over the language barrier. Politically maybe the idea seems good, but militarily it's poppycock.
>
> People fight differently. I know. I have commanded all sorts of people. The European army broke down on that issue. You must keep people together in national units under national control. The politicians don't understand these things. The politicians never fought or commanded troops in battle.
>
> Why, you couldn't even put the British and the Americans together on the same ship. They are different. Anyone is a fool to think the British and the Americans are the same. Our sailors owe allegiance to the Queen; yours owe allegiance to the President. We have a different kind of discipline. You could not have a people more different than the British and the Americans. I have commanded both. I know.

I asked if he thought Britain should keep an independent nuclear deterrent. He answered curtly: "Yes, naturally; the French are going to. You can't have England without one. You can't let the French be the only

European country with their own deterrent. Is Britain to be completely dependent on the U.S.A. for their deterrent? That would be ridiculous: Politics change; men change; people change. But we can't risk it. I am against being completely dependent on the U.S."

He said:

There will be no peace, no lasting peace, until you get the armed forces of different countries back behind their borders and get the Russians back into Russia. Keep the Germans in Germany. Get the Americans back to America, the Canadians back to Canada, and the British back to Britain. Then you can do something. I don't believe the people who say that once the Americans go home they will never come back to Europe in a war. I have never known the Americans to break their word. They have signed a treaty. They will stick to it.

And there is another thing. You can't give the Germans any kind of nuclear weapons. The moment you do this you will find that the Russians are likely to go to war.

If the Russians march west, that is war. At once. But you don't have to have the Americans and the British in front line. There are fifty million Germans and if you want to know what fifty million Germans are like when they are fighting, I can tell you. They will hold the NATO front. And there are fifty million Frenchmen. Why do they want us over here?

He told me: "Eisenhower doesn't speak to me anymore." This had occurred since Monty had published his memoirs.

I said some nice things about Ike. But I put on record our entire correspondence on the Normandy campaign. I told Ike if he didn't pull back Patton on the right and hit the Germans a smashing blow in 1944, the war would last until spring. But Ike didn't follow my advice. He lost a lot of lives. Eighty thousand American boys in the Ardennes alone. Damned fool Ike.

I don't know why Ike was angry. He wrote the first book after the war, *Crusade in Europe*. And he said some bad things about Alanbrooke and me. But I did nothing. I didn't mind.

Monty told me: "I know de Gaulle very well. He is quite right to avoid the domination of an Anglo-Saxon bloc. If Britain got into Europe through the Common Market, we would be pushed around by the U.S. That would prevent any chance of an agreement with Russia. And de Gaulle wants some kind of agreement. He is quite right. And he has given France back her soul. He chucked out the useless politicians. Now he has a proper setup in France."

PARIS, *April 23, 1963*

DINED at Bohlen's last night with Averell Harriman. Chip said the first thing that happened at Yalta—which has never been written—was that one day as Roosevelt was looking out of his window, he spotted a very

pretty lemon tree and happened to express admiration for its beauty to one
of the Russians. Next thing he knew the damn thing was dug up and four
Russians came in and told him Stalin had presented it to him. It was sent
home, but nobody knows what became of it. Chip said: "The Republicans
could have really made something of Russia handing out not just a lemon
but a whole tree of lemons to Roosevelt."

Averell said he was present when General Marshall, then Chief of Staff,
came to Roosevelt and told him that Bill Bullitt had leaked the information about the impending "Torch" operation to de Gaulle. ("Torch" was
the code name for the invasion of North Africa.) Marshall said intelligence had made a very careful check and found out not only that de
Gaulle had been tipped off but that it was Bullitt, and this was one reason
why he turned so anti-Roosevelt and anti-Democratic Party.

Averell admitted that the U.S. government now endorses partition as a
solution for Laos but doesn't dare say so. Diem has been for this for some
time. De facto partition has already been established. No decision has been
taken on whether we should send troops there or once again send an
expeditionary force to Thailand.

The very important thing was to insure that the Communists didn't have
access to the Mekong River, which is the real highway into South Vietnam. The so-called Ho Chi Minh trail is barely a footpath, and they can't
send much in the way of supplies over it to fight Diem.

Bohlen told an amusing story about Hector McNeil, late British Minister of State, and Guy Burgess, the British defector, who used to work for
Hector as personal assistant. Before Burgess went to the United States for
the first time, Hector said to him, "Guy, there are three things the Americans can't stand: communism, homosexuality, and the race question."
Burgess replied, "I see what you mean, Hector, I mustn't make a pass at
Paul Robeson."

WASHINGTON, *June 5, 1963*

LUNCHED with General Heusinger, former Chief of the German General
Staff and now chairman of the Permanent Military Committee of NATO.

I asked Heusinger if it would be hypothetically possible for some small
and well-disciplined group of German staff officers to secretly conduct
arms research in both Israel (nuclear) and Egypt (missiles). After all,
Special Group R worked for Seeckt in Russia in 1921, prior to the Rapallo
Treaty and without the knowledge of any civilian officials. Heusinger
gulped, then said he was sure this was not being done—but hypothetically
it could be.

Later, I had a very amicable chat with John McCone, CIA head. He
says the Israeli atomic plant at Dimona was started in the winter of 1956–
1957 with French aid, and the United States didn't learn a thing about it
until late 1960. We have seen the French design for the reactor. It does

not include a plutonium separation plant for potential military purposes. But the Israelis are very sophisticated and surely can produce plutonium for weapons even if that phase is not yet operational.

As for Egypt, McCone says the Soviets sent in a test reactor in 1958. This was similar to Russian help for such lands as Jugoslavia and Czechoslovakia. It makes only a small quantity of weapons fuel but could make chemical-type devices for radiation purposes. McCone does not think this chemical-type weapon is alarming. Cheaper and more effective bacteriological and chemical weapons already exist.

WASHINGTON, *June 6, 1963*

LONG and excellent talk with McNamara in the Pentagon. He has a huge office, one of the biggest I have ever seen. I was fascinated to note de Gaulle's three volumes of *Mémoires* (in English) right behind his desk. The man must be a masochist.

He said there was no doubt that in terms of a holocaust the United States could absorb a Soviet surprise attack, survive, and obliterate the Soviet Union. But we needed NATO in another sense. We can handle the extreme of holocaust alone. But we cannot handle anything less than that extreme alone. Without NATO, the Soviet Union could gradually destroy us by salami tactics.

NEW YORK, *June 14, 1963*

THIS afternoon, I went over to see U Thant, Secretary General of UN, in his office on the thirty-eighth floor. I inquired whether he thought anyone but a neutral could be an effective secretary general. He said: "To begin with, anyone who came from a country other than those that are nonaligned couldn't be elected."

I asked if he thought the secretary general should be "morally neutral" or if, despite his political neutrality, he had to take forthright stands on issues where he felt there was a distinction between right and wrong? Without hesitation, he answered: "I can't be neutral on moral issues. One cannot escape decisions on such matters. And take, for example, the case of my country. Burma has been neutral, or nonaligned, in the sense of not belonging to a military bloc. But Burma is neutral only in this and no other sense; only militarily. We have taken stands as a country on moral issues. In 1956, we denounced Russia on Hungary. Nevertheless, we never joined SEATO because we did not think that was in our interest and we were geographically exposed with our long frontier with China. No Secretary-General worthy of the name can ever afford to be morally neutral."

PARIS, *July 3, 1963*

JEAN Monnet, as usual, was exceedingly nice when I saw him this afternoon. Monnet said it was necessary to build a "European-controlled" nuclear force in partnership with the United States. At present the security of the West was assured by American strength. A European-controlled force remained, however, in the distance because it was so costly and technically difficult to construct. But one must always keep in mind the *objective* of such a force, which would work in conjunction with that of the United States.

BONN, *July 22, 1963*

THIS afternoon, I spent an hour with Chancellor Adenauer at the Schaumburg Palace. He said:

If de Gaulle put all his forces under NATO, this would end him in France because of military resentment. It is vital to remember this in assessing French policy. And if de Gaulle were not there in France all Europe would be Communist.

And I would like to tell you something that may interest you. I was in Moscow in 1955. At that time, when I talked to Khrushchev, Bulganin was present but he didn't say anything. Khrushchev said he could not master the Red Chinese. He was so serious about this that I often remembered that event afterward and I felt that one day its result would be the lessening of Soviet pressures on us.

And now that these events are coming about, I wonder if the U.S. will go the right way. There are many curious developments. The U.S., Britain, and Russia are all supporting India. Why? Pakistan says that if India attacks Pakistan, China will help Pakistan. The Kashmir problem is very hot. I only raise the question. I don't have an opinion on it. But of course this quarrel between India and Pakistan and China's support of Pakistan lessens Chinese pressure on Russia and therefore has its effect on Europe.

We should always look at what the Russians are doing in eastern Siberia. The Russians are building cities and are forcing population to settle in the area. Once the Russians develop eastern Siberia, a large new center of power will be established there. Then the Red Chinese will have against them a strong Russia plus an India strengthened by U.S. and Soviet aid. And the Chinese will be supported by Pakistan. I don't know how far U.S. policy will permit Russia to build up its strength against China.

I then told the Chancellor I wanted to pose the most indiscreet question that had ever been put to him. Although I was much younger than he, I was much interested in death and had written a book on it. I wondered if it would be possible for him to tell me precisely what he thought death was. He smiled sadly but then began to talk. He said: "No human knows that answer. If I could tell you that—but no one can. It is perhaps a gift of God that I myself have little if any fear. I think of death with equanimity. I cannot imagine that the soul, which is our life, could fade to nothing when death comes. Somehow it must continue to exist. Man is not permitted to know how—but it must. Because the origins of life, life itself, is as much of a mystery as death and we are unable to explain either phenomenon. The highest commandment has always been that which others hand on to us—to do one's duty."

These are not very profound expressions, but there was something most moving about his earnest, simple sincerity.

I asked if as a young man he had had any special ambitions, such as writing a play or traveling to a certain country, which he had never been able to achieve. He said: "You may think this funny; you may not believe it. But my dream was to live as a notary in the country with my family with just enough money to get along and not too much work. We cannot control our wishes."

PARIS, *July 29, 1963*

LUNCHED at the Bohlens' with former Vice-President Nixon, his wife, and two daughters. Nixon could not have been nicer or more agreeable. He rushed across the room when he spotted me and said that when he had been in Greece the Queen assured him that, although she was somewhat worried about her projected trip up to London, she and the King would at least get a fair break in "anything Cy Sulzberger wrote." I told Nixon I feared that they must have been deceived, because I wrote a piece saying it was a damn fool trip.

Nixon said he was, technically speaking, titular head of the Republican Party today as the last defeated candidate, and he proposed to use his influence when he gets home to achieve three things: 1. To insure that there will be an internationalist and nonisolationist foreign policy plank; 2. To insure that there is no retrograde racist plank; and 3. To insure that there is a sound economic plank, "because after all I am a free enterpriser myself."

PARIS, *July 30, 1963*

GOLFED with Nixon, Bohlen, and Cecil Lyon. Dick (we have now gotten to a first-name basis) and I beat the two diplomats by steady, undistinguished play. "We fived them to death," said Nixon happily. His form is more determined than stylish or powerful.

He was very cheerful and not at all depressed by what the uncertain world of politics had done to him. He said that one had to go on living no matter what happened. Furthermore, he said, anent the Republican Party, that it had to count on the solid center block of American opinion and not just on "the extremists" who favored Goldwater. Despite his own defeats, he expected to have a good deal of influence at the 1964 Republican convention.

NICOSIA, *August 17, 1963*

I PAID an agreeable visit to Archbishop Makarios in his air-conditioned presidential palace. He is vain (flattery takes on him), overconfident, naive. He likes the prerogatives of being chief of state.

I began by inquiring whether, as an ecclesiastical head, he found any conflict, in his dual role, between that which is God's and that which is Caesar's. He said:

> No, there is no conflict of interest. I am not really a party leader trying to create a political career for myself. I was asked to offer myself to the people during their first steps in this new life of independence and I thought it my duty to serve. I accept the office of President not to satisfy any ambition of my own, but only in order to aid our state in its difficult first steps.
>
> Perhaps, there are some advantages to having an ecclesiastic as a ruler. There might also be some disadvantages; for example, it takes time away from normal religious duties; but I find it doesn't really interfere. And, after all, even in politics there is no different standard of right and wrong from that in religious life. What is right in the latter is also right in the former. Something cannot be both just and unjust.

I asked if he thought religion were a good training for politics. He said, "Yes, religion teaches morality and morality should always lie at the base of political life, as it should in all other aspects of life."

CAIRO, *October 20, 1963*

THIS morning I visited the elderly rector of the Al Azhar University, outstanding figure in the world of Islam, Sheikh Mahmoud Shaltout, Sheikh el Islam. The Sheikh said: "There is no authority in Islam save for the *Koran* itself. There are some leaders such as the Rectors of Al Azhar and other universities, but they have no authority in a clerical sense. In fact, the Caliph never had any religious authority. This belongs to God alone as revealed in the *Koran*. There is no single man or group above others in Islam; each man thinks for himself. Islam has no formal directing organization or clergy. Every individual is God's vice-gerent on earth." [I thought to myself, how strange; Islam has God but no clergy; Buddhism has a clergy but no God.]

CAIRO, *October 23, 1963*

THIS evening, I had a long talk with Nasser in his Heliopolis house. I asked whether the thaw in world relations was not perplexing to the non-aligned countries. He said:

The philosophy of nonalignment means I must adopt a wholly independent policy, independent of the two camps, and not be influenced in my point of view. And I think this attitude on the part of nonaligned nations has done much to ease international tension. We are always for peace, for coexistence, for negotiations, and for improving contacts between the two camps. But we do not have pretensions.

The two blocs remain, NATO and the Communist camp remain. Should there be a war, all the members on one side or on the other side would stick to their blocs. We don't want to get involved. Nonalignment doesn't have the mission of mediation. We express our views whether these please others or not. But anything that is against peace we oppose. In this kind of a situation we try to help mediate. [This is a rather odd statement from a man who is sponsoring a military operation in Yemen and is backing one side in another military operation on the Algerian-Moroccan border.]

He continued: "We feel that U.S. Middle Eastern policy is based on good relations with all countries, all *governments*, despite the contradictions which are deep. On the other hand, Soviet policy seeks the confidence and trust of the *peoples* of the Middle East, despite prevailing contradictions. We feel that the U.S., despite complications, wants good relations with all governments, even though their ideologies may be contradictory—as in the case of Israel, Jordan, Saudi Arabia, Yemen, Iraq, and Syria. This is a clever policy."

I asked Nasser: "What have you personally learned as a result of the revolution and being in power yourself for more than a decade?" He looked puzzled for a moment and then he smiled in a rather disarming way. He said: "Well, I was always very patient. But one learns to be more patient. I always thought I was very good in dealing with people. But there, too, one learns more. One learns more tolerance and one learns better how to deal with people. I have also learned not to go to bed later than 2 o'clock."

AMMAN, JORDAN, *October 28, 1963*

TAXIED to the palace to keep a rendezvous with King Hussein. At the gate of the palace, my taxi was checked carefully for bombs; then a soldier with red headdress and khaki uniform, carrying a tommy gun, got in the front seat and rode up with me to the entrance. Inside, the door to Hussein's office was guarded by two well-built Circassians in black cossack dress with karakul hats, cartridge bandoliers across their breasts, and silver daggers.

The King was standing at the door: a very short man, although slim, powerfully built. He is a first-class athlete—fencing, rifle and shotgun, riding, sports car and go-cart racing. He learned recently to water ski very well.

Hussein is very brave and good in crises; but not at all intellectual, never reads, and mixes with a rather inferior group of young English men and women with whom he has go-cart races.

I asked if he thought a central, dominant figure—whether king or dictator—were necessary in Arab nations today. He said:

> A central, dominant figure is a sign of weakness in a nation, I believe. My greatest ambition is to create a system of government that has the solid support of the people so that Jordan will not be dependent upon me. It is a weakness when a nation feels it must put all its hopes on the life span or the ability of one leader. In principle I am against this.
>
> As for kings—naturally there are good and bad kings; and maybe the same is true of dictators also. Perhaps one might criticize Nasser and his regime for this, just as Nasser criticizes me. But I am not, as such, contrary to any particular form of regime. I believe in the freedom of each people to choose the kind of system they consider beneficial, but I like to see this done in an orderly manner.

Princess Muna, his wife, says the hardest thing for her to get used to in this new life was seeing her husband, when he got dressed, strap on a shoulder holster. Hussein is convinced he will not die a natural death and that when he is killed it will be by a man in uniform standing behind him.

AQABA, JORDAN, *October 30, 1963*

SPENT the night here after a most interesting trip by automobile yesterday to the ancient Nabatean capital of Petra. Shortly before you get to Petra there is a rich village called Wadi Musa (Moses), where Moses stopped on the way from Egypt. Petra, with its pink and red structures carved out of the walls of sandstone canyons, is a remarkable and dramatic ruin to which we rode on horseback after the road became impassable.

We reached Aqaba at 5:15 P.M., after driving through the most extraordinary desert filled with vast, abrupt, jagged peaks. We first spotted the Gulf in an extraordinary purple-brown landscape; sea and sky, mountains rumbling toward the Gulf from all directions. Aqaba is only swimming distance from Elath, the Israeli port. A good swimmer could, within a day, traverse Egyptian, Israeli, Jordanian, and Saudi waters: They all meet here.

Hussein was down in his simple villa water skiing and took us out in his new glass-bottomed boat to look at the fish.

SDE BOKER, ISRAEL, *November 10, 1963*

MOST interesting talk with Ben Gurion, who is now living on a kibbutz here in a particularly unattractive and barren part of the Negev Desert. His house is a bit better than the others: terrible, little, dirty, green wooden boxes, plunked down amid the dust. Ben Gurion's is somewhat larger and is outfitted with television, plumbing, good army telephone communications, and a sentry outside the door.

I asked if he thought basic French policy had been changed under de Gaulle. No he didn't, although France obviously wanted friends in the Middle East now. It was understandable that de Gaulle wished to restore French influence in this area, but he was convinced it was not at the expense of Israel; Israel can still count on France as a source of military equipment.

I observed that there was speculation as to whether the Israelis were experimenting with atomic weapons manufacture at their Negev reactor in Dimona. Ben Gurion commented: "In eight or ten years, atomic power will provide cheaper electricity for us than conventional power and we have to prepare and acquire the know-how. This was the purpose of the Dimona reactor. Nevertheless, Nasser is getting atomic help in his experiments from India. I know he is working for this goal of military nuclear capability. He has not given up on his dream of being the dictator of the Arab world. He has lost a good deal of prestige, but if he defeats Israel he can recapture that prestige and therefore he won't give up on this ambition."

He thought Nasser was working on nuclear weapons. When I asked again if Israel were doing likewise, he hinted as much by indirect innuendo, but added: "Nasser has a large desert in which to test, but we cannot test here."

I recalled that in May, 1963, he had proposed a Soviet-U.S. guarantee of the Middle East and in lieu of this a defense pact with the United States. I asked him how he felt about these ideas now. He said it was impractical to think of a Russo-American guarantee today, and he doubted Russia could come any nearer to the West so long as its Chinese problem continued.

Then he returned to his theory that only Russia and the United States together could impose a real détente in the Middle East and that Russia's view depended on China. He thought it was a great mistake that the United States did not recognize China.

I asked him about Russia's attitude toward the Jews and he said:

If Khrushchev now allowed the Jews out, I am sure one million would leave. And Khrushchev cannot admit that he runs a country whose population would like to leave. But Russia is gradually changing. Education is spreading and the standard of living is improving. This must inevitably lead to more freedom and the time will come when Russia cannot remain a dictatorship. No country with an educated population and good living standards can remain a dictatorship [a statement denied by history]. But anti-Semitism will remain among the Russian people and the Jews will continue wishing to leave.

He contended that Periclean Athens was great but that half its population was made up of slaves. The old Jews also had slaves but he claimed they were not badly treated. He continued: "We had prophets and prophets did not exist elsewhere. These were men who objected with passion against any quality of discrimination."

He admitted that Plato had not been a democrat, although he said it was unfair to call him a Fascist. Plato deserved greatness for opposing wars among the Greek peoples, although he regarded all non-Greeks as barbarians. But he insisted (without historical justification) that 3,800 years ago the Jewish prophets had spoken out passionately against all forms of discrimination and any distinction between Jews and pagans. They had always emphasized "justice and leniency" as primary qualities, although this is not the general interpretation of the law of Moses. "Our prophets taught that Jews and pagans were equal as human beings, whereas the Greeks considered themselves superior to barbarians and favored a caste system. Nevertheless, what we should do is base our civilization on Greek society, which includes science, plus the Jewish teachings of the prophets, which taught that all the people of the world should live in peace and justice, goodness and grace."

JERUSALEM, *November 11, 1963*

AGREEABLE talk with Prime Minister Levi Eshkol, an extremely decent man whom I had never met before. He said: "I cry with one eye when I look at our defense budget, as a former finance minister, but I smile with the other eye because I know I am giving security to our people. Our enemies want our blood. They have three or four times the number of tanks and planes we have, as well as rockets and missile ships. The Hawks [ground-to-air missiles] we bought from you cost $25,000,000. We need a low-interest loan from the U.S.A. Of course, we would prefer aid without a loan such as Nasser gets from Khrushchev but a long-range low-interest loan would help a lot."

TEL AVIV, *November 13, 1963*

THIS evening, I got to the root of the basic question in Israeli security. I dined with Professor Bergman, head of the Israeli Atomic Energy Commission.

He thinks that India—and if it goes ahead and aids Nasser, also Egypt—will be able to produce a kind of poison warhead from isotopes or nuclear "garbage" within about two years. This would not have great explosive power, but if one such warhead were to land on Tel Aviv, for example, the entire area would have to be evacuated and perhaps could not be lived in again for thirty years. Nasser is behind on guidance systems, but were he to aim ten missiles at Tel Aviv, it is a dead certainty that at least one would land in the necessary area. There would not necessarily be any heavy casualties when the missile landed, and there would be time for people to move out, because the warhead could be detected through Geiger Counters.

Ambassador Wally Barbour was present during the conversation. He told me later this was the missing link in all his dealings. The Israelis know that no matter how many ground-to-air missiles they have, they can't prevent such an attack. That is why they are demanding ground-to-ground missiles from us. It is possible they are working on a small kind of warhead, for their own deterrent.

PARIS, *November 22, 1963*

PRESIDENT Kennedy was murdered this evening! It is too soon to even imagine what it all means or who may have been behind it. Television adds a new instantaneous reality to terror in this age; how much of a change does this mean in the United States?

Poor Kennedy, he didn't really have a chance to get things moving as he hoped. And poor Jackie. This was the most attractive couple we have had in the White House. Now, so soon, before anything really happened, the dream is over.

PARIS, *December 12, 1963*

THIS afternoon, I saw de Gaulle at the Elysée. I asked if he wasn't in fact disappointed by the way the German alliance was working out. He answered: "Our alliance should not be exaggerated, as it often is by the press. This was primarily an arrangement to end a historic quarrel. And this has been done. It also had the intention of establishing closer contacts in all fields between France and Germany, particularly in matters of economics and security. The press and many people read into the alliance much more than was the actual fact, but Adenauer and I never exaggerated it."

I asked if, now that France's *force de dissuasion (force de frappe)* was coming into being, he was prepared to work out with Washington and London common NATO targeting agreements in the event of war. He said:

> We don't yet have our *force de dissuasion*. It does not yet exist. But when we have it—and this is not yet the case—we are perfectly prepared to discuss with Washington, and to a much less important degree with London, working out arrangements on the use and targets of such forces. We are prepared to discuss what each should do with his nuclear weapons in case of war.
>
> But this does not mean that we are, or necessarily would be, in accord on strategy. The United States wants to use its nuclear weapons later, in case of

war. We want to use our nuclear weapons soon, virtually immediately. So you can see that the concept of military strategy differs. But this is the nature of things.

I remarked that it seemed very difficult to me, furthermore, to contemplate any agreement between ourselves and France on the issue of nuclear forces since we preferred to strike back only at an enemy's military installations whereas France, as I understood it, would strike at an enemy's cities. "Yes," he said, "It is very hard to compromise, I admit. We certainly would attack cities." He said: "NATO should have a common strategy and I don't see any such common strategy coming. We French are not happy with U.S. strategy. Therefore, I think it is better to leave things as they are without deceiving ourselves about reality as it exists. I can't see how any fundamental reform can be achieved. In theory it would be better to destroy the alliance and reconstruct it, instead of trying to reform it."

I asked whether he contemplated further reducing France's contribution to the alliance if NATO's strategy continued to differ from his own. With astonishing self-satisfaction he replied: "France has already withdrawn most of its forces from NATO. A large part of the army, a large part of the air force, and all of the French fleet are out. And now our new strategic air command will be out. All we have left under NATO is a small army in Germany and a few aircraft units. For the moment I see no reason for withdrawing what is left."

Returning to the vital issue of nuclear cooperation, I asked if de Gaulle would be willing to sign the nuclear test ban treaty if, in exchange, the United States gave specific information and blueprints on thermonuclear weapons to France. He said: "I doubt it, frankly. To begin with, the United States cannot offer us such information and will not do so. If I were in the position of the United States I would not do so either. And if the Americans were to offer us such information they would obviously do it under conditions that would restrain the use of these devices. We could not accept this."

The general had just been in the United States for President Kennedy's funeral. Johnson was in the White House. I asked if de Gaulle expected to visit the United States in 1964 (as had been planned with Kennedy). "No, I will not go. I don't envision any such trip. I had been involved in negotiations arranging to see President Kennedy in February or March but, alas, he is now dead. The exact date had not been fixed, but it would have been announced in January. I owed President Kennedy a visit because he had been kind enough to make an official visit here. But I did not plan a state visit. I had already done that under President Eisenhower. I merely planned a working visit. President Kennedy, after all, had come to see me and I was happy to repay the courtesy; but now the poor President is dead."

He had made no move on Peking. But he confided: "We have considered this for a long time. I cannot tell you just now what we will do. But one day we will certainly have relations. I just don't know when. You must remember that the British already have such relations; and you acknowledge the existence of China and have a certain kind of relationship through the conversations you have with them in Warsaw [through the U.S. and Chinese embassies in Poland]. They represent a kind of acknowledgment, a form of diplomatic contact."

This geographical focus of our conversation encouraged me to ask his views on Southeast Asia. I inquired whether the area's best future lay in a neutral federation guaranteed by both power blocs. He said this was his view, adding: "I have pointed out that in the present situation of Asia and Southeast Asia armed intervention—and indeed, any form of intervention—simply cannot help. We French have experimented with such intervention and now you are doing so. But it doesn't work. That is a zone where the only possibility is to establish neutrality as between East and West. Of course, any such arrangement must be guaranteed by the Communist countries as well as by the West to have any validity."

I recalled that once when I talked to him about Khrushchev and inquired whether he thought he was important, he had said you could not assess a man in a historical sense until the end of his life, and he had quoted Sophocles to say that the day could best be judged only in the evening. In those terms, how did he now assess President Kennedy?

He answered: "I cannot really say. He was very likable and he certainly had great value. He wanted to solve problems, but, unfortunately, he lacked the necessary time. He wanted to solve enormous problems: the race problem in your country, the problem of the dollar, the underdeveloped lands, Latin America, Europe, disarmament. Those were and are enormous problems and they require a great amount of time. History will probably say of Kennedy that he was a man of great ability who lacked the time to prove himself."

19

PARIS, *December 15, 1963*

YESTERDAY EVENING I HAD A LONG AND EXCELLENT TALK WITH Dean Rusk at the American Embassy residence. Ambassador Chip Bohlen very discreetly left us alone in front of the fireplace of his downstairs study, merely sending in a servant with drinks.

Rusk said sadly that he thought de Gaulle was drawing to a bitter, isolated end and "this will probably turn out to be the final chapter of a very great man. Personally I deeply sympathize with any patriotic Frenchman who saw the experiences suffered by his country during all these years and who lived through these experiences himself. And I can understand de Gaulle's deep desire to restore all the prestige of France. He fought against the dry rot in this country not only during World War II but before it. But he hasn't got the strength available in France to build up prestige to the immense degree he seems to think the country requires. He has taken France down a road where he is increasingly alone. Had he thrown France into the leadership of an authentic European movement with full cooperation with the other side of the Atlantic, French prestige would be soaring. But the trend he has chosen may turn out to be tragic, especially for the dream he has himself desired to accomplish."

PARIS, *January 3, 1964*

LUNCHED with Motrico. He suggests the United States would be well advised to try and patch up its relations with Cuba, or at least to explore the situation through Spain. He points out that Castro comes from a Gallego family, as does Franco, and the Gallegos always stick together like Irishmen. This explains Franco's oddly tolerant view of Castro despite his communism.

PARIS, *January 16, 1964*

I MUST say, de Gaulle has a diabolical sense of mischief. He took pains to invite Chip and Avis (Mrs. Bohlen) to lunch on Tuesday, January 14—the first anniversary of his famous press conference when he vetoed British admission to the Common Market. It was a very cordial luncheon. Absolutely nothing was said having to do with serious matters.

The day afterward, yesterday, Couve de Murville asked Chip to call upon him at the Quai and told him that, as France had promised to do, we were being notified in advance that Paris had decided to recognize Peking. As soon as Washington had received Chip's urgent flash, Averell Harriman (Dean Rusk was out of town) summoned French Ambassador Hervé Alphand. Alphand protested that this was not really a very significant or important step. Harriman brutally said: "I have known you for many years as an intelligent and experienced diplomat so there isn't any use repeating such twaddle."

PARIS, *January 22, 1964*

AGREEABLE talk this afternoon with Vinogradov, the Soviet Ambassador. He said Mao Tse-tung was a far worse despot "even than Stalin," and that if anybody raised his voice to criticize the government "his head was knocked off." The Chinese lived in misery, and economically the country was a shambles. The Chinese were racists and hated every white man. He added that it was not just a legend but that—although he could not reveal his source—he knew it for a fact that Mao had said he wasn't worried about another war because 300 million Chinese could survive and rule the world.

I asked if he was concerned about the possibility that France might give technical aid or assistance to China in developing nuclear weapons. He admitted that Russia was very concerned about this, "just like the United States." He said Russia had no intention of giving China any aid on nuclear weapons, and then wanted to know if I thought the French had a thermonuclear weapon. I said I didn't think they would for eighteen months.

PARIS, *January 27, 1964*

THIS afternoon I spent a very interesting hour at the Quai d'Orsay with Maurice Couve de Murville (Foreign Minister). I asked whether he thought France, by its new policy, was developing the possibilities of a "two Chinas" formula. He answered: "No, we never thought of this. This is not our business. It is not for us to decide the future of the Chinese people. We are merely establishing diplomatic relations with *the* government of China and we are not in so doing indicating whether we think this is a bad government or a good government."

He added: "If you look for the last analysis in all of this, it is a manifestation of an end of the existence of two ideological blocs. That system of two blocs is finished. This is not a deduction; it is a fact. The world is now back to national policies instead of bloc policies. Germany is divided, not because of ideology but because the Russians decided as Russians that Germany should not be reunified. That is all. This is a national policy. It has nothing to do with communism."

PARIS, *February 20, 1964*

DIRK Stikker (NATO Secretary General) invited me to lunch. The Germans are trying a new approach on getting atomic weapons. Heinrich Krone came to Paris last month to ask de Gaulle for secret collaboration between the Germans and the French on nuclear weapons. He was specifically charged with this mission by Erhard (who would prefer to have Britain in on the deal but knows it is impossible; *and*—I emphasize this word—Adenauer.

ADDIS ABABA, ETHIOPIA, *March 7, 1964*

THE church here is the only church in the world that preaches that the earth is flat and canonizes Pontius Pilate.

There are only twenty-five qualified Ethiopian doctors, whereas there are 150,000 priests.

About 90 percent of the country—and this is only a guess—is illiterate. Even in the priesthood about 70 percent is illiterate.

The Maria Theresa dollar is still currency in many regions, and in parts of the interior salt bars serve as money.

ADDIS ABABA, ETHIOPIA, *March 9, 1964*

THIS morning I saw Haile Selassie in his "office palace," guarded by Imperial Guardsmen in natty tan uniforms and by two lazy tethered lions. He received me in a comfortable office, covered with Oriental rugs and a yellow bearskin, sitting on a stiff-backed throne-armchair with an embossed seal in the back. He wore a tan summer uniform stiff with ribbon decorations. His little Pekingese dog leapt up beside him as we talked. We spoke directly in French.

"Liberty produces difficulties," he said, "and to erase these troubles is difficult. It requires the help of the former colonizers. I told all the African chiefs of state we must live with the old colonizers and that they had done good things as well as bad; that the good things must not be forgotten. I hope little by little we can escape from our difficulties and find a unity of purpose based on friendship with the old colonial powers and secure their aid."

The continent cannot follow any single system. "Each African country has its own problems and there are big regional differences. De Gaulle has done much in France that was good and could be followed but he was not the sole useful model."

He said: "The colonialists left us many things, including frontiers that had been delimited. These should be continued because otherwise there would be a danger of war. We are all in favor of keeping existing borders in Africa."

NAIROBI, KENYA, *March 11, 1964*

HAD tea and a talk at State House this afternoon with Malcolm MacDonald, new Governor General (chief of state and representative of the Queen) for independent Kenya.

MacDonald said nearly all black states are now independent and "the fight against white colonialists is over. However, it continues in its filthiest and purely racial form in the Union of South Africa. All the independent black governments are bitterly opposed to the white supremacy of the white South African and they are prepared to overthrow it by war if necessary. The longer apartheid stays the worse its echoes will be, and this may land all Africa in a mess. The Chinese have no sense of responsibility and they are very racist in their propaganda. They accuse the Russians of being white and they have got it across that they themselves are not white. The Peking radio gets into parts of Africa where no other radio is heard and it broadcasts in African languages."

DAR ES SALAAM, TANGANYIKA, *March 18, 1964*

THIS morning I went to State House to see President Julius Nyerere, a slender, slight man with a high forehead, a head that slopes suddenly backward, a small Chaplin moustache, rather high but pleasant voice, a bright manner and agreeable way of speaking excellent English. I asked if, because of his name and also because he had translated Shakespeare's *Julius Caesar* into Swahili, he was particularly fascinated by the character of Caesar. He said: "No. No particular fascination. My translation of Caesar was accidental. It happened to be the set book for the Edinburgh University exams when I went in and I had to study if fairly thoroughly. Actually, I have read little about the historical Julius Caesar. Shakespeare makes him into a rather arrogant old man and he doesn't appeal to me much. The character in the play for whom I have got respect is Brutus—a man of great principle."

I then asked, apropos of his own brochure, *Second Scramble for Africa*, whether he had any formula for keeping Tanganyika and Africa out of the cold war. He said: "No, there isn't any formula. We can but struggle all the time and it isn't an easy thing. The big powers are anxious to get us involved. And whether or not we take sides, we are still involved. Were there a formula to stay out, all the African countries would have applied it."

I asked him if, in view of the legacy of racial hatred left by colonialism, he thought his concept of a multiracial society in Tanganyika stood a good chance of success. He said: "One can only work for this because it is the only possible good. In this world we are all multiracial countries. There is no monoracial country in the world. Our racial groups in Tanganyika are more visibly different because they came in recently. But what chance have we got if people don't learn to live together in a multiracial world? What is the alternative? Extermination."

BUJUMBURA, BURUNDI, *March 25, 1964*

LAST night British Ambassador John Bennett, our host, gave a dinner party. Quite a crisis. The Mwami and his French doll, dubbed the Tutsi Roll, were invited. In the afternoon the palace calmly called up and said they weren't coming. John protested to the doll, on palace advice, and she said keep two places in case the Mwami changed his mind. He didn't.

KAMPALA, UGANDA, *March 29, 1964*

THURSDAY, March 26, we drove up to Kigali, Rwanda, with Bennett. Near Gitarama we left the main road for a British (Anglican) mission which has been having trouble. The mission runs a school for Tutsi and Hutu boys. They claim the Tutsis are much brighter and therefore do better— both in school and in later life, which is why they had all the cushy jobs. After the recent troubles many of the Tutsi boys' families had been slaughtered. The boys in school have split up and throw rocks at each other.

Rwanda is a paradisical place, green, wooded, lovely flowers. But the missionaries say occasional killings still take place in the vicinity and that a Tutsi was laid out on a hill nearby just a few days ago and had his hands and feet chopped off by Hutus.

Easter holiday was coming up, and twelve Tutsi boys had asked the missionaries for advice. Should they go home for holiday? (Some no longer had homes.) If they went, they might be killed en route. If they stayed, they might be killed. (The mission's only arm was a .22 rifle to kill mad dogs.) If they stayed next term to get their diplomas they might be killed. (All boys between sixteen and eighteen.) One said: "I know I'm going to die; I only hope it's a bullet, not a spear."

☙❧

FRIDAY, March 27, I saw Rwanda's President Gregoire Kayibanda in his office, a little reddish stucco building protected by two guards with helmets and tommy guns. Kayibanda is a small Hutu (about five feet, three inches), skinny, with a small head and intent expression.

He described the Tutsi situation as "tranquil for the present, but that depends on the actions of the Nyenzi" (the Cockroaches who lead the Tutsi refugees and who, according to the missionaries, are preparing a new invasion for April).

Kayibanda says the fact that the Cockroaches have automatic arms proves they receive financial aid. He does not know for sure from whom this comes but he claims it is "not the communists"; he blames "the church—above all the Protestants."

Kayibanda says, "The missionaries interfere to a certain extent in internal affairs. With some individual exceptions, this is not true of the Catholics but of the Protestants. Of course, I am a Catholic, you know."

❧

LONG talk with Milton Obote, Prime Minister and chief of government in Uganda today. Obote is very dark, with flat nose, high forehead, angular, intelligent face. He speaks very good English (with African accent), has a sedate, grave manner which clearly masks a very passionate internal personality.

I asked if he was worried about Communist activities and propaganda. He said: "I think that is inescapable. Propaganda is evident but other activity is less open. They are more interested in pamphlets and circulating papers. They are trying to cultivate friends and agents as a first step. This refers to both Russia and China but people are more worried about China. Chinese propaganda is especially anti-Western and antiwhite, which also hits the Russians."

I asked Obote if he was working for a multiracial society. He said: "I can only work for liberty, the liberty of individuals residing in Uganda. This is regardless of race. There should be a square deal for everyone and this idea is popularly accepted. There are, of course, small interracial quarrels. But the broad masses want peace and tolerance."

SEMLIKI, UGANDA, *April 4, 1964*

DINED with a bunch of "old boys," former British officers whose leader should be memorialized by Somerset Maugham. Colonel "Bombo" T.: a white, bald, strong superintendent of national parks, named for the town where his battalion of the old King's African Rifles was headquartered.

T. tells of how hyenas attack newborn elephants by continually circling the herd and finally snatching the helpless creature while it is still tied by its umbilical cord. Packs of wild dogs hunt down antelope bucks, each one tearing off a piece of flesh. T. saw one buck still loping along when he had no more flesh and hardly any muscle. He once saw a buffalo kill a lion who missed in his first leap to break the buffalo's neck. Lions hunt in pairs. The male roars and tries to terrify the prey while the female sneaks up behind and does the killing. The male eats first.

Obscene little pygmies just inside the beginning of the vast Ituri forest, standing there with evil eyes and smiling faces, clutching their miniature bows and steel-tipped poison arrows which look like toys but can kill an elephant. Black hunters, members of the Waliangulu tribe on the Kenya coast, have been collecting vulture feathers. This is what they make a special glue with to hold the poison for their arrows.

NAIROBI, KENYA, *April 7, 1964*

MR. Samuel, our affable black guide in the game park, drives us up to a pride of lions sleeping in the sunshine. "Squeaky," a castrated lion, huge and maneless, ambles up. Looking at Squeaky, Mr. Samuel says: "What are you doing? What are you doing? Gentleman, what are you doing?"

RABAT, MOROCCO, *April 21, 1964*

LATE this afternoon I was received by King Hassan II in his palace offices, where his father had received me five years ago. He waved me to a seat before his desk. A servant appeared with orange juice and mint tea.

At the very end of our conversation Hassan said in beautiful French: "I understand you like to shoot and fish." We talked about this a bit and he boasted of the trout, mouflon, wild boar, partridge, and ducks. He asked "When can you come and hunt with me?" I said not before October. He said: "That's fine. The season will just have opened. We can fish too." I asked about the trout season. "Don't worry," he said. "They're *my* streams. There is no season."

Our conversation started on territorial claims. He said that, vis-à-vis Algeria "the big problem is to make the Algerians realize this is a question for the future, not now."

ALGIERS, *April 27, 1964*

DINED last night at the home of General Jean-Louis de Rougemont at Alger Plage, about twenty-five kilometers out of town, eastward, on the beach. He commands the twentieth division which, at one time, had all eastern Algeria under its administration. It is now pulling out.

The only sensible French decisions vis-à-vis Algeria, says he, were those of Charles X in 1830 to invade and end piracy, and that of Charles de Gaulle to grant independence; everything in between was folly. The French *colons* tried to sway French policy in between. They were disagreeable, tough, unsympathetic people. The army resented them and sought, in its last years, to protect the Moslems from them and raise their standards, but it was too late.

Jean-Louis says Algeria won't go Communist although it may develop an even worse system of its own.

PARIS, *May 5, 1964*

LUNCHED today at (former Premier) Edgar Faure's. Faure was recently in China. He says Chou is now the real boss and he is the absolute boss in foreign policy. Mao is a kind of fossilized, tired symbol who speaks for the party but no longer runs things. Chou even read a newspaper while they were talking to Mao. Faure said: "Imagine reading a newspaper in the presence of General de Gaulle!"

THE HAGUE, *May 13, 1964*

DRINK and chat with Dean Rusk today. On Vietnam, I said it seemed to me that logic dictated that ultimately we would have to accept either a de Gaulle (neutralization and abandonment) or Nixon (northward attack) policy. Rusk said neither he nor McNamara was yet prepared to concede that South Vietnam, with our help, cannot win the war. There is not as yet "any objective reason to conclude this. The French tell us you can't do with fifteen thousand men what we couldn't do with two hundred and fifty thousand. But things are different. In general the people of South Vietnam don't want a Vietcong [Communist] solution. Sure, they're tired of twenty years of fighting. And the countryside is largely apolitical. When people are terrorized by the Vietcong at night they won't cooperate with the government in the daytime. They're scared. Security is an indispensable problem. We don't believe we have to make a choice between the extremes you mention."

PARIS, *May 25, 1964*

AN hour with Couve de Murville at the Quai d'Orsay. I asked him at what point France thought the United States should encourage the prospect of negotiations over South Vietnam.

Couve said:

I discussed this at length with Rusk and I said that, after all, in Algeria we had had a kind of guerrilla war that was no more pleasant than the one in South Vietnam. We knew that it was a losing affair and that in the end there would have to be a political settlement. We therefore decided that the Algerian people would have to choose and this meant independence.

Of course the situation in Vietnam is by no means just the same. But thinking of taking a political road or seeking a negotiation does not mean you have to abandon everything and stop fighting immediately.

The big difference in Vietnam is that, contrary to the situation in Algeria, things are deteriorating all the time from a military point of view. In Algeria the military situation was much better in 1962 than in 1959, although we granted independence in 1962. In South Vietnam time is not running for the West, for the U.S.A. or for General Khanh.

To establish some kind of stable military situation is theoretically the correct approach but I am not sure that what is theoretically right is practicable or possible. There are many ways to start a negotiation. The normal way is simply to explore, to explore the possibility through other countries and with other countries. I really doubt if I can say any more about this.

France would like to get South Vietnam established as a neutral and independent country, as envisioned ten years ago. Obviously the question of North Vietnam remains for the future because we cannot hope to neutralize it now. We must take our chances. But surely it is better to have a neutral South Vietnam than to continue with the present situation.

PARIS, *May 26, 1964*

THIS noon I had a very pleasant talk with Prime Minister Pompidou. Pompidou said: "We consider that our nuclear force is now operational. If there were a war we would launch nuclear explosives. It is a mystery to no one that during the rest of 1964 and part of 1965 we will complete the first phase of our nuclear weapons program based upon the Mystère IV."

I asked whether de Gaulle had ever given him any hint or indication that he considered Pompidou as his *dauphin* or successor. He grinned and said: "That is a rather embarrassing question." I repeated it. He said then: "If de Gaulle does not run for a second term, I will. And I will run with his blessing."

PARIS, *June 2, 1964*

HAD drinks and dinner last night with Bill Benton, who has just come back from a whirlwind trip to Moscow, where he saw Khrushchev. Khrushchev said: "South Vietnam is aflame and you are in a morass. U.S. policy is doomed. The same is true in Korea except that American troops can walk the streets of the cities without trouble. Why do you always ally yourselves with the reactionary forces? You call any revolution communistic even though there may be no communist party in the country involved and the leaders may never even have heard of Marx and Lenin."

PARIS, *June 8, 1964*

YESTERDAY I played golf with Couve de Murville. We then lunched together and sat around gassing. The French think it would be a terrible mistake for the United States to escalate the war by attacking North Vietnam. We would accomplish nothing by bombing North Vietnam except to bring China into that country.

The United States has immense military power and could surely fight a war against China and maybe kill 100 million Chinese. But what would that accomplish? The United States could not occupy China, and after the slaughter the entire world would be against America. And this, of course, has nothing to do with the very real danger that Russia might feel forced to defend China and thus start World War III.

NEW YORK, *June 26, 1964*

THIS morning I went to see Prime Minister Ismet Inonu of Turkey at his suite on the thirty-sixth floor of the Waldorf Towers. He has been over here for several days at President Johnson's invitation to discuss Cyprus.

He said the United States seemed to have no formula for settlement. The United States merely wants to "manage" its two allies who find themselves on the brink of war. American policy was obviously to prevent such a war and to keep the alliance alive. The question was how to accomplish this.

Inonu said that the phrase "self-determination" was now being used by the Greeks instead of *enosis* but it means exactly the same thing. All Turkey would accept would be a "double *enosis*," which means partition.

NEW YORK, *June 30, 1964*

Z., OF the CIA, says Israel has probably attained the capability of manufacturing two small nuclear warheads per annum. Under the original arrangements, in which the French helped the Israelis build the Dimona reactor, a core was provided by France for the reactor but it was always sent back to France to extract plutonium, in order to prevent Israel from making weapons materials. Now the Israelis have bought uranium from South Africa and mined some themselves and probably have the material for a very small scale weapons program. They deny that they intend this, but it is obvious that their strategic situation is ultimately very dismal vis-à-vis the Arab world and they must have some means of striking back.

NEW YORK, *July 20, 1964*

DINED last night with the Norstads (General Lauris Norstad, former NATO commander). Larry said that on October 27, 1962 (just before Khrushchev knuckled under in the Cuban crisis), Kennedy called him in Paris and asked him what he thought of Khrushchev's (then latest) offer. This was to trade Russian withdrawal of missiles from Cuba against U.S. withdrawal of missiles from Turkey. Norstad said he thought this was a very dangerous idea.

WASHINGTON, *July 22, 1964*

LONG talk with McNamara. I asked whether he had elaborated any kind of doctrine to oppose revolutionary warfare and, if so, were there any books or papers prepared on this for our war colleges? McNamara said we had no such doctrine because "this is not primarily a military operation. It is political and economic and only uses military operations as a subsidiary tool." I found his observations on this subject both naive and uninformed, and this frightens me. I don't think he understands what revolutionary war is.

I asked McNamara if he wasn't alarmed by the recent statement of General Nguyen Cao Ky (of the air force) demanding a direct attack on North Vietnam. McNamara said he didn't know why Ky had made such aggressive statements. General Ky "had better shut up or they will find themselves with a new air force commander." (This doesn't sound precisely like a U.S. policy of "advising" the Vietnamese on how to fight the war, but not intervening.)

WASHINGTON, *July 23, 1964*

THIS morning I had a forty-five-minute talk with President Johnson. He could not have been more friendly, but the experience did not make me very happy.

He spoke in a very low voice. When I was waved into his office—ten minutes early—he was on the telephone and, even with my good ear turned toward him, I found it difficult to understand him. He was in the process of bawling out somebody about what he called six major misstatements in today's press and television reports concerning himself.

When he had finished his telephone conversation, he came over and sat beside me. He asked: "How are you planning to handle this conversation? You know, I have 1,500 of you fellows around here and I don't find the time to see very many. I have a letter from the managing editor of the *Washington Post* right now asking to see me and I can't do it. I hope you won't quote me directly but just say something like 'the president believes' or 'friends of the president say'."

I started off by saying I was very concerned about the effect during the next one hundred days of the Goldwater campaign on both our friends and our adversaries overseas. All the experts said that Goldwater stood no chance of winning the election, but the mere fact of his candidacy was disruptive and seemed to be disuniting our allies and uniting our enemies.

Johnson said: "I am concerned by this problem of the effect of Goldwater's position not only overseas but also at home. But we always have problems in American election years. Remember that Wilson campaigned on a platform to keep us out of war and Roosevelt promised that he would not bring us into war—despite the signs of the times that they could very well see. The farther you are from the central scene the more likely you are to be concerned, but the American people have a way of infiltrating a candidate and getting him on balance and we will hope for that in this case. There is no question but that the views of some of the Goldwater people are very curious. There is this talk about the effect of fallout on the milk of children producing sterility when they grow up, or two-headed babies."

If these notes stray from subject to subject, it is a faithful rendering of the conversation. Johnson kept talking with absolutely no interruption or pause but there were continual sharp switches in subject matter. He said:

> If we had given the military a free run in Vietnam we would have been at war and bombing China all over the place long ago. Even the military didn't want a free run. They like a little check themselves.
>
> But the polls are running very well for me. The latest poll in Kansas, which is a rock-ribbed Republican state, has things going two to one for me. All this may soften Goldwater up. And it may catch some of the rich, financial quarters who will bring influence to bear and that will help.
>
> Nevertheless, what you say is true and at present our enemies are being encouraged and our friends discouraged.
>
> I would not want you to write this in any way, so please keep it completely off the record, but I thought that Scranton would be harder to beat than Goldwater and Mac [McGeorge] Bundy agreed with me. But it would have been a better campaign from the viewpoint of the national interest.

I said it seemed strange that the Republicans should choose foreign policy as the main issue. Imitating the Democrats in 1960, they selected "prestige" and a "weapons gap" to emphasize. Johnson replied: "He will get off of that. But Goldwater wants us to get in trouble in Vietnam so it can help him. He also wants race riots in this country so it can help him. He has said this on TV himself."

Johnson then buzzed Jack Valenti, his appointments secretary and one of the "Texas Mafia." The President had been reading from a piece of paper. When Valenti came in, Johnson said: "Take out this business of 'the Kennedy-Johnson administration.' Just make it read: 'the four years from 1961.' Take out all reference to 'the Kennedy-Johnson administration'." I gathered that this was going to be in a speech. Obviously what Johnson was doing was inferentially building himself up by omitting references to Kennedy. But he turned to me with a knowing look as Valenti left the room and said: "I am trying to take all politics out of this." Baloney!

I asked if he had any plans for a meeting with de Gaulle after the elections. He answered: "De Gaulle gives us our problems—above all in Vietnam. We would be glad to move out of there if anyone could guarantee its independence. But I understand de Gaulle and I know, just like in Cuba, that he is with us when the chips are down."

NEW YORK, *September 9, 1964*

DINED last night at the Norstads'. Present were Fritz (Frederick) Nolting and his wife. Nolting used to be Ambassador in Saigon.

Nolting says the United States really should not be in South Vietnam, in a military way, but now that it is there it cannot get out. Our only chance was to deal with a real government and try to build up political, economic and social unity and reform. That chance was ended when we decided to dump Diem, and there has never been a government since.

Norstad complains—and Nolting agrees—that at no time has there ever been a decision that helping South Vietnam might require an ultimate war with China. In fact the subject has never officially been discussed. Nolting says that there have been contingency plans drawn up involving China but never a decision on whether under any circumstances they might be implemented.

Nolting concedes that if the United States now resolved to put five divisions in South Vietnam in order to hunt down and squeeze out all the Vietcong guerrillas, we would end up by having the entire Vietnamese population unleashed against us on a national and anticolonial basis.

NEW YORK, *September 17, 1964*

CABOT Lodge told me Kennedy's instructions to him when he went to Vietnam were that he should not do anything to "thwart" an attempt to overthrow Diem. Lodge thinks the ideal solution would have been to throw out his brother Nhu—who was impossible—and to reform and keep the Diem administration. But things had gone too far, and the secret police were already brutalizing the population.

NEW YORK, *September 29, 1964*

TALK with Nixon. He thinks the situation in Vietnam is drifting more and more and that if we don't come out with some kind of a policy we are going to lose it within a year or two or have no chance to influence the outcome. Then, through Indonesia, communism would threaten the frontiers of the Philippines and Australia.

PARIS, *October 9, 1964*

BREAKFAST today with Dirk Stikker, former NATO Secretary General. Last July, when he was still at NATO, he saw (Pierre) Messmer, French Minister of Defense. Messmer told him that shortly after he had taken office under de Gaulle in January 1960, (Franz-Josef) Strauss, who was then German Minister of Defense in Adenauer's government, had asked him to implement the secret French-German agreement on nuclear weapons.

Messmer was startled and said he knew of no such agreement. Strauss then told him that he and Jacques Chaban-Delmas, Minister of Defense in the Fourth Republic government of Felix Gaillard from November 1957 until April 1958, had made a secret accord under which Germany agreed to help finance and manufacture nuclear weapons to be kept in storage on French soil, some of them allotted to German ownership and control. (The Western European Union Treaty stipulates that Germany cannot "manufacture" such weapons but does not precisely ban assistance in fabricating them outside the country.) Messmer told Stikker that he had said to Strauss that France could do nothing about such an undertaking. It was not the policy of France to give Germany nuclear arms.

LONDON, *October 15, 1964*

DINED last night at the Bruces. David told me General Marshall had persuaded Truman to offer the post of Ambassador to France to Mrs. Roosevelt. Very wisely she turned it down and said she thought it would be most "unsuitable."

HAVANA, *October 24, 1964*

CUBA has diabetes: too much sugar in its blood stream, and no economic or political insulin has yet been invented.

Like all revolutions, this one is convinced in its heart that *it* is really the very first. Yesterday I went to the revolutionary museum in the Martí monument, filled with gruesome photos of Batista tortures, slaughters, etc.; homemade or primitive weapons, including a bulldozer-tank; bloody uniforms; and even a shot-down U.S. U-2. My guide was appalled when I said it was almost exactly like the IRA museum in Dublin, which has an anti-Black and Tan display.

HAVANA, *October 25, 1964*

LAST night called Celia Sanchez, Castro's closest woman friend, to inquire about my appointment. A recorded announcement replied: "After seven o'clock in the evening, don't call. If it is not an urgent matter, don't call. If you are calling to discuss personal matters, relating to housing, expropriated lands, a house on the beach, furniture, refrigerators, automobiles, automobile parts, scholarships, exit visas, or prisoners, address yourself to the proper organism. I do not work in any of those departments."

The announcement is repeated twice. Initiates merely hang on to the phone, and then Celia or someone else eventually answers.

HAVANA, *October 26, 1964*

LUNCHED with two Foreign Ministry officials, taking them to a place called 1830 where a moderately good lunch set me back $70.

Among current jokes they told me: Khrushchev and Johnson are playing a chess game to settle the fate of the world. Khrushchev is astonished to find what a good player Johnson is and gets into a pickle. He calls time, gets on the phone and telephones Mikhail Botvinnik, world champion. He explains the board position and asks what to do. "Sacrifice the horse," says Botvinnik. (Horse is one of the nicknames for Fidel and also is what the piece we know as the knight is called in Spanish.)

Another: Fidel goes to a Chinese restaurant and orders dinner. "I'd like some prawns to start," he says. "So sorry," says the owner, "we have no fish." Fidel then orders sweet and sour pork. "So sorry," says the owner, "we have no meat." Then he orders chicken chop suey. "So sorry," says the owner, "no chicken today." "Never mind," says Fidel, "soon we will have everything: fish, meat, and chicken." "Are you planning to quit?" asks the Chinaman.

HAVANA, *October 30, 1964*

JUST before midnight Fidel Castro showed up in the Hotel Riviera and came to my room for a conversation which, before it had ended, lasted six hours. He would have been ready to go on indefinitely, but I had to catch my airplane to Mexico.

Ramiro del Rio, chief of the Foreign Ministry press section, arrived at the hotel himself at 11:30 P.M., and Juan de Onis, our correspondent, went down to greet him. A few minutes before midnight there was a knock on the door. Before I could open it (the key was in the latch) it swung in, and Castro and his crony, Dr. Vallejo (a veteran of the Sierra Maestra campaign), strode in, followed by del Rio and de Onis. Outside, in the quiet hallway, I saw uniformed guards, some with rifles and some with tommy guns.

Del Rio was wearing an ordinary civilian suit, but Castro and Vallejo were in full uniform with paratrooper boots and side arms in holsters and ammunition pouches. They each wore military caps. They shook hands, without removing their hats, and I waved Castro to an armchair, where he sat, slightly ill at ease. He only removed his cap after several minutes.

Vallejo and del Rio perched on the ends of the twin beds. De Onis sat in a chair near Castro from which he interpreted, and I took the other armchair. Castro lit a huge cigar, and we served cognac, a bottle of which I had brought to de Onis from Paris. Castro drank very little. As he smoked, he allowed his cigar ashes to fall all over the carpet around him.

Without paratrooper boots I would say he was a bare fraction over six feet. He is heavily built and getting thick around the middle. He has very broad hips. His skin is pale and clear, both on the face and hands, which are small, above all for a man who likes to fancy himself as a baseball pitcher. His wrists are unusually slender. His face is broad, but this is counteracted by his scraggly beard which makes him look a bit, from an angle, like a Hasidic rabbi. From other angles he looks like a football guard in fancy dress.

He said although his bedtime is irregular, he always sleeps six hours and then tries to take a nap after lunch. He eats only twice a day and generally tries to do this at 11:00 A.M. and at 7:00 or 8:00 P.M. He tries to keep fit by doing physical exercises, taking hikes in the mountains, skin-diving, and occasionally playing baseball (which he apparently does in the same army uniform and boots). With juvenile pride he told me: "You know, I am a better pitcher now than I was at the university. I have a better curve and more control," he continued, making a pitcher's motion with his cigar. I could not help but wonder if opposing batters tried to hit him as hard as when he pitched rather unsuccessfully for Havana University.

I began our serious conversation by asking Castro what man, alive or dead, had most influenced him. He thought for a while, rubbing his beard. He leaned forward in the chair pondering and puffing his cigar. He said: "I don't suppose there is any single living man who has had a particular influence on me. But in my youth I suppose it was mainly the influence of Cubans who had fought for our independence. I read much by and about José Martí and was devoted to him as a revolutionary, an intellectual and a human being. I also had much admiration for General Antonio Maceo as a warrior. But if I ask myself I can't think of any single person who really influenced me."

I observed that he had had the opportunity to meet many prominent world leaders since coming to power; who among them would he consider the greatest? He answered: "There aren't many. Of course, among them, I had most of my dealings with Khrushchev but perhaps this is not an opportune moment to answer you about Khrushchev and to give you my views on him. But I will answer anyway. Khrushchev was certainly a very intelligent man. [He had just lost power in Moscow.]"

I asked when he first became an outright Communist and why. This touched off a long, hand-waving and confused speech.

Castro said:

Before becoming a communist I was a Utopian idealist. I began to study political economics at the university. There I began to form ideas about a different form of organization, of society, than capitalism, even though I was studying capitalistic forms at the university.

Later on, as a more advanced student, I first read the *Communist Manifesto* and was strongly impressed. Why? I always had many social and economic impressions and opinions of my own. But I was especially struck by the eloquence and clear logic of this document.

Above all, this made up for the unclear works I had previously read and it

had great polemic force. One phrase struck me especially—that the bourgeoisie accuses the communists of trying to abolish private property, but
private property was already beyond the reach of nine-tenths of the population. I understood this myself because I had been raised in a property-
owning family surrounded by those who were landless.

Naturally one document doesn't make a communist. The primary thing in
a revolutionary is the sensitiveness of a man toward contemporary events,
his capacity for feeling the sufferings of others. Naturally abstract ideas have
a great importance, but the coming together of a man who himself has
revolutionary feelings with a revolutionary abstract idea completes a revolution. This is not an abrupt event like a revelation. It is a long process and it
took a long time with me.

I had been reading other interpretations of history but none of these had
convinced me. I then began to read more Marx and I was impressed by his
French Civil War and *Eighteenth Brumaire of Napoleon Bonaparte*. Then,
while I was still in university, I read some Engels and some Lenin.

Before this I had principally been influenced by Martí and, as a romantic
revolutionary, I had read several histories of the French revolution and
Lamartine, even before entering the university. I also read a history of the
Spartacus rebellion. But as a student I did not pursue philosophical literature
that preceded Marxism such as Hegel or Feuerbach.

I was much more attracted by the concrete aspects of political action than
by pure philosophy. But my two years in prison, after the Moncada Barracks
fight, allowed me to read much history and to start a more systematic
approach. I tried to amplify my knowledge. I read Plato and I read Kant,
whom I found very difficult. But I was more interested in political literature
—Plutarch, Suetonius, Livy, Demosthenes, Cicero.

Whenever I had to choose between reading history and philosophy, I
chose history. I read Machiavelli's *The Prince* with Napoleon's notes. I also
read biographies. I read the biographies by Zweig and Ludwig. I read a
biography of Bolívar.

In my final student stage at university I had come a long way reading
Marx and Engels but I couldn't call myself a communist. I was an individual
seeking the truth. I did not belong to the Communist party. My analysis was
basically idealistic. I did not conceive of methods of action in the classical
Marxist fashion. But I did realize that you could not change a society
without holding power. Therefore I began conceiving methods of attaining
power by revolutionary means based on popular support. I recognized the
simple logic that a revolution had to be made for the people and by the
people. And I had decreasing faith in the chances of solving Cuba's problems by peaceful methods such as elections. The powerful vested interests
that ran the country were supported by a professional army.

My mental process was moving forward. I could distinguish between
social revolution and a movement merely seeking to improve conditions
within the existing framework. I progressively became more separated ideologically from the merely reformist program. I became convinced it was
simply fooling the people just to promise a better life if the basic circumstances hindering their progress were not removed.

From that time on I struck out along my own road. I wanted to lead the party into a more revolutionary attitude. But then the Batista coup came along. At first I hoped there would be a united front by all elements to overthrow Batista and I talked with the different opposition leaders and told them I was willing to fight with them, under their leadership, as a soldier in the ranks. But time passed and the leaders divided and their forces broke up. I lost all hope and, with no resources, no party, barely known by the people, I decided to form a revolutionary organization myself. That was at the end of 1952.

By then I clearly understood that a revolution could only be carried out by the exploited and against the exploiting classes. But it could not be said that I was yet a communist. I was primarily preoccupied with formulating a strategy and gathering together the means to do away with the Batista regime. It was then that we organized our first plan, the attack on the Moncada Barracks in 1953, in order to seize a strong point and from there to gain control of a province and summon the people to overthrow the regime.

Castro went on to describe the Moncada abortive coup and his defense speech after his capture. He added that he had deliberately eschewed legal counsel and defended himself in order better to advertise his revolutionary program, and this was gradually disseminated around the country by his supporters. And when he was a prisoner on the Isle of Pines, he used to write secret messages in lemon juice on the paper of innocuous pen-and-ink letters and he included some of his famous Moncada speech ("History Will Absolve Me") in these letters. They were put together and distributed in pamphlets by the underground. Castro continued:

But even then, I could not be called a communist although, at the trial, I had spoken out clearly against the essence of the capitalistic system.

During my years in prison I evoked my concepts more profoundly and elaborated a new plan of attack. I developed a plan of guerrilla warfare and three years later we began this in Oriente after training in Mexico for the Granma landing. But I was not yet a communist although we had come back to Cuba determined to carry out a social revolution. We could not yet say how far that revolution would go but we were already working with the peasants and the workers not only against the regime but against the social structure.

I was still too idealist to be a Marxist-Leninist. I thought it was enough for things to be just and that if they were just everyone would understand us. By then I had read Lenin on imperialism but I had not yet come to realize in full just what the problem was.

I thought the United States would respect this attitude and would respect us. At that time, perhaps because our actual war, or military operations, was the immediate task, I did not clearly see that a social revolution would collide directly with the United States and that the antagonism arising from this would produce the concrete events of later years.

But we were determined to carry out the revolution at any cost. If I had then understood the meaning of international problems and the imperialism phenomenon, then I would truly have become a Marxist-Leninist. But to reach that point I had to have two years of armed conflict during which I saw United States planes and U.S. bombs being used to attack the defense-less population, doing enormous damage and causing measureless suffering, before my final enormous damage and causing measureless suffering, before my final evolution. A year of revolutionary government would have to pass before we reached the real experience which would make of us genuine revolutionaries and Marxist-Leninists in the full sense.

At this point I pinned Castro down and asked him precisely what was the date when in that full sense he became a Marxist-Leninist. He said he thought it was fair to call it the winter of 1960–1961.

"We announced the socialist nature of our revolution," he continued, "after the attacks by CIA planes bearing Cuban markings—on the eve of the Bay of Pigs [April 1961]. We contributed to the formation of a revolutionary movement and we opened new revolutionary roads on which all the revolutionary forces in Cuba joined together. This is more or less the way it came about. But already, as early as my university days, the communists and the persecutions they suffered called to my mind the first Christians and their persecution."

Castro explained that as a young man he initially found it "very difficult to register in any opposition party. I was sent to a Catholic school. I went to mass every day. I did everything the others did."

I asked him what he was today—a lapsed Catholic, an agnostic, or an atheist. He said: "In a religious way I reject all the explanations I was originally taught about nature and the development of life. I am convinced that science is the only way to understand things and science excludes divinity. It is interesting to see how science today explains many things that were not understood in the past. I am an atheist but I respect any man's religious belief. And I can see how men don't understand many things that science has not yet been able to answer. And therefore they believe in God."

I was much struck by his unusually disorganized personal schedule and asked why he had no office or permanent home which he was accustomed to use. He said:

In the first place, I am very opposed to bureaucratic forms of work and I am absolutely convinced that bureaucracy is one of the most pernicious aspects in any ideological system. I do not underestimate the importance of organization and the need for office and officials. But I fight tenaciously against the spread of bureaucracy and I recognize that this will be one of the most difficult battles for me to win. This and the agricultural problem are my main battles.

When I became prime minister I found that the office was costing a million pesos a year [one peso equals one dollar] and was fulfilling no useful function so I decided to suppress it. I reduced the prime minister's office to a very small bureau where we receive and answer mail with a few secretaries. The state has plenty of offices I can use when I need them. When I have military problems to discuss, I discuss them in the armed forces ministry. When I have educational problems, I discuss them in the ministry of education. When I have agricultural problems, I discuss them in the ministry of agriculture.

I have discovered several things since we took power. At the start I tried to work in the prime minister's office just like any other prime minister and I received everyone there. But I rapidly learned that I had no interest in seeing ninety percent of the people who were interested in seeing me. And I saved an enormous amount of time on matters of pure courtesy and protocol so I decided to adopt a method enabling me to see those people it was necessary to see or interesting to see without being bothered by the others.

As I see it, the prime minister's job here is not administrative but political. Perhaps thanks to this conception I have been able to establish a very wide contact with the people and with the countryside because I am incessantly visiting different places and talking with different people. To sum up, I am a determined enemy of organized bureaucracy.

I then said I understood Castro's closest family attachment was to his son and asked where the boy was and whether he often saw him. He said: "My boy is here in Cuba and I visit him frequently." He did not elucidate.

I was struck by the fact that Cuba had turned Hemingway's former house into a national museum, although Hemingway was an American and an anticommunist. Castro said: "Shakespeare was not a communist. Nor was Cervantes. Nor was Michelangelo. They were all admired for their genius. Hemingway wrote certain works which influenced me, like *For Whom the Bell Tolls*. This opened my eyes to many possibilities of guerrilla warfare. And then there was his story about a Cuban fisherman [*The Old Man and the Sea*] which is an extremely moving human story. I knew Hemingway and I liked him. He was a legendary figure. He was not a communist but he was far from being an imperialist or a reactionary."

I asked him how well he knew Hemingway. He said: "I talked with him first at the time of the fishing derby where he gave a prize which I won with a marlin. That was in 1959 and he personally awarded me the prize. I felt great sympathy for him."

I said Castro must forgive a question that might seem embarrassing and impertinent but nevertheless I considered it important. Why did his sister, Juana, leave Cuba and openly start to fight him? He hunched over in his chair, made a gesture as if washing his face with both hands, mumbled, and then began a long answer in fits and starts. He became very emotional during the course of this. At one point he was clearly on the verge of tears. This is what he said:

> Whatever I say on this might seem to be based on rancor. Juanita acted by her own lights as a member of the social class to which she belongs and which she defends. It is difficult to judge the actions of individuals and I prefer to judge symptoms. And the CIA played a role in all this which shows

the brutal and horrible lack of scruples of the CIA. [Here Castro became patently furious.] We know that the CIA played a role. A CIA official in Mexico and she had an interview with one of our Cubans and tried to urge him to defect. It is disgusting for the CIA to do things of that sort.

My brother Raúl and I could only have avoided this problem with our sister by being derelict in our duties and by practicing nepotism. This sister of ours is a girl who lacks a cultural foundation. She didn't even finish high school and has no political qualities. The differences between us arose precisely because she wanted to use the influence of her connection with us for business deals. Also, our revolutionary laws affected the possessions of our family. My father was a prosperous man and our family had about 12,000 hectares of land, but the agricultural reform reduced this property to 400 hectares.

When our mother died I firmly opposed the family distribution of her property for both moral and legal reasons. Morally, I and my brothers were the only boys of that region who were well clothed and fed, while there were hundreds of youngsters of our age who were never able to go to school. If I was privileged to study it was because my parents could pay for my education, and they could pay for it thanks to the fact that there were hundreds of poor workers employed on our farm. I had received a great privilege and in this sense all my brothers and sisters had the same privilege. None of them needed the property my mother left because they had jobs which paid them incomes. My sister Juana had a relatively high salary. Yet, only a few hours after my mother's death—and this hurt me a great deal—the discussion started on how to divide the inheritance.

I didn't want to act in arbitrary fashion. My mother had left some money in the bank and 180 hectares of land. Raúl and I agreed when the problem arose with Juanita, because she wanted the land, on how we should behave. Juanita went to the property and she wanted to sell the cattle and everything else without consulting anyone. So then the problem arose and we agreed to divide the estate, excluding myself and Raúl, letting the land itself become state property.

Castro was fumbling for words but pushed on.

And there was a legal argument. My father died after acquiring a large debt to a sugar enterprise to which he sold cane; he had been unsuccessful in business during his last seven years. When the sugar enterprise was nationalized, the state became the creditor. My father's farm was mortgaged and no one had a right to it. My decision on this was based on legal grounds. And anyway, I am strongly opposed to inheritance. It always foments unnatural family quarrels. There are many young people who just wait to inherit from their elders.

Communists are often accused of not having family ties but this is nonsense and we feel very close to each other. Nevertheless, in this case our enemies could not have given a greater demonstration of lack of scruples, for purely political reasons, than by trying to use one member of a family against the others. I don't like to speak of this; it is very distasteful to me; but you raised the subject and I must answer.

I asked Castro if he considered *Fidelismo* a symbol or a movement. He sniffed: "It is just a word. It is used to synthesize an idea. It is an expression of confidence—but I don't feel that it exists."

I asked him if he was really dogmatic enough to be a Communist, as he called himself, or if he was not in fact just pragmatic. I told him that Nasser called himself a pragmatist, not a dogmatist. Castro replied: "I am neither pragmatic nor dogmatic; I am dialectical. Dialecticism is the negation of dogmatism. Nothing is permanent but everything changes. As Heraclitus said, nobody bathes twice in the same river."

I turned to more precise subjects. I asked Castro why he gave up nonalignment as a policy by becoming a Communist. I pointed out that Ben Bella in Algeria maintained relations with both ideological blocs and that Nasser in Egypt had expressed to me an admiration for Tito, who had shown him how to get help from both sides without joining either. Castro said:

> Each country must develop its own policy on the basis of its own problems. I respect anyone else's position and I feel that Nasser is an intelligent, capable man. But it is not fair to say that he is nonaligned. He is aligned against imperialism and colonialism and in that sense we too are aligned.
>
> But we now receive aid from only one side for the simple reason that there is only one side to help us. It is practically impossible that the U.S.A. should help us because the U.S.A. would demand ideological concessions and we will never be prepared to make concessions of that sort.

I asked if, despite such pretended nonalignment, Cuba desired to strengthen its formal ties with Moscow by a military alliance on a bilateral basis or by membership in the Warsaw Pact. He said: "We desire to strengthen our ties with Russia and, if circumstances require it for our security, the possibility of an alliance would not be excluded."

I asked him how he interpreted the fall of Khrushchev, both ideologically and in terms of world communism. This was his answer: "In my opinion the political change in the Soviet Union creates the opportunity to make a serious effort to overcome the difficulties between Russia and China. It is already apparent that both parties have lately been demonstrating symptoms which favor that possibility. The leaders of both will surely take advantage of this in a responsible and intelligent manner, and other communist parties in other lands should work for this goal in order to strengthen the socialist camp. That would increase the security of smaller socialist countries like our own."

How and where was Cuba helping revolutionary movements in Latin America? He said:

> We help by our example but the greatest assistance revolutionary movements there receive is from the United States itself. U.S. commercial policies are accelerating revolution because of your low prices for raw material imports and your high charge for manufactured U.S. exports. The United

States extracts more money from Latin America than the amount it sends in through the Alliance for Progress. And the United States supports right-wing governments, oligarchies, and *coups d'état.*

Why, the United States won dozens of medals at the Olympic Games and Latin America won none. That shows the difference in the level of development [a rather strange observation]. The Alliance for Progress is an alliance between one millionaire and many beggars. There is only one country in the Organization of American States that has a stable political and economic system and that is Mexico—because Mexico had a revolution.

I then moved the conversation directly to relations between Havana and Washington. I started off by observing that although Ben Bella had been at war with France he had made up with the French; why didn't Castro make up with the United States with which he had not been at war? He said:

French policy is more intelligent than that of the U.S.A. France offered economic cooperation to Algeria but the United States only offered a blockade to Cuba. European countries are more experienced than you are, although I must admit that we share in the blame for the deterioration of relations with you. Nevertheless, it is mostly your fault.

I think it will require many years before diplomatic relations are restored. I don't think conditions exist in the United States that permit positive steps. I believe an improvement of relations must be regarded as a long-term affair. After all, one must be realistic.

We want relations to improve among all the countries of the world. The relations between Cuba and the United States can improve only when the relations of all socialist countries with the United States improve. [Obviously the innuendo here is addressed to China.] We are much more interested in the unity of the socialist camp than in improving relations with the United States for our own sake. We would not want to improve relationships with the United States while your intervention continues in Vietnam. We wouldn't want peace for ourselves alone. This question depends on the relations of the United States with *all* socialist countries and we are not interested in improving relationships for ourselves alone.

I said he seemed to have given contradictory statements about who initiated the Soviet military deal. Who proposed it first and when, who took the initiative? Castro said: "Cuba took the responsibility for the presence of the missiles here. It is not easy to clarify the details for security reasons, but both Russia and Cuba participated. We aspired to get an effective guarantee to warn off the possibility of a U.S. attack on Cuba and to make it evident that any such attack would provoke a nuclear world war and Russia had its own position. Each country had its own position."

Was it true that Khrushchev had urged Castro not to use the surface-to-air missiles, provided by the USSR, to shoot down American U-2s? Castro answered: "We are absolutely opposed to U-2 flights. We have never felt that we could tolerate such flights. But for a long time the SAMs were not under our control. We did not have the personnel trained to use them."

I asked if the crews at SAM sites were entirely Cuban, and when Cuba took control. He dodged this. I then inquired how many Soviet military personnel were left in Cuba and what they were doing, whether any were combat troops. He said: "There are a number of technicians left and we shall certainly continue their presence as long as the U.S.A. continues an aggressive policy toward us."

I repeated the inquiry as to whether these were combat troops. He said: "They are certainly not military tourists. All military technicians have a military capability and would fight in case of an aggression. The function of the Russians here is as technical advisors, but if Cuba were attacked they would serve as combat forces. When I say 'if Cuba were attacked' I don't mean something like the Bay of Pigs. I mean an actual invasion by the United States or by some such other country instigated by the United States or by the armed forces of the United States."

I inquired how many Russian military men had been here at the peak. He said: "That figure is still secret but I can tell you it was much larger than the figures published." (The figures published said 22,000.)

I asked if Cuba had held a veto power over Russia's right to fire the Soviet missiles stationed in Cuba. He said:

That is a theoretical question because circumstances would have made it impossible to have a disagreement. There would have had to be a general war in which Cuba was naturally involved.

Such missiles could not have been used independently of the use of Soviet nuclear missiles on a global basis. Had a conflict arisen elsewhere, as in Berlin, somewhere outside of Cuba, naturally there would have been a general war and these missiles would have been used.

The presence here of both tactical and strategic weapons was conceived in terms of a possible aggression against Cuba. The agreement under which the missiles came here was tied to the possibility of an act of aggression against Cuba.

Nothing was said about the use of the missiles if a conflict arose elsewhere in the world in which case their use would have been determined by specific circumstances.

But it is obvious they would have come into play in any general war. The accord with Moscow on the MRBMs in Cuba contained the understanding that they would be used in defense of Cuban territory in the event of aggression against Cuba and through agreement between the two contracting parties.

But in total war all strategic arms would obviously be used by both sides independently of where they were located.

I said Castro kept complaining about our U-2 flights. Nevertheless, I inquired how the United States could be assured beyond any doubt that all missiles and nuclear warheads had been removed from Cuban territory and that none had since been sent back. He became quite agitated and squatted down on his legs among the cigar ashes he had scattered on the carpet around him.

He said: "The first element of security for you is obviously that Cuba cannot produce such weapons. Secondly, you could be reassured if the United States removed any cause for the presence here of such arms by ceasing its aggressive policy. Cuba has no obligation to give the United States a guarantee that the missiles and warheads are out, are gone. We do not accept the right of the United States to inspect or control what arms Cuba has."

I remarked that this was a rather arrogant and short-sighted attitude. He resented our U-2 flights but refused to arrange for any other guarantee. The United States had every right, in its own security interests, to be positive on this point. It seemed necessary to me to arrange some formula that could reassure us if, indeed, there was ever to be a thought of ending the U-2 flights. Otherwise a situation might develop that could lead to an unintentional and undesired war by accident or, at the very least, a repetition of the October 1962 crisis.

By now it was 4:30 A.M. Vallejo and del Rio were somnolently balanced on the ends of their twin beds, but Castro was full of vigor. He came over beside me and squatted on the floor. He borrowed a pad to sketch out the bureaucratic organization he was seeking to diminish. He said he hoped to freeze the existing limits of bureaucracy and then gradually put useless bureaucrats to other work.

I remarked to Castro that on September 5, 1961, months after Castro's formal conversion to communism, Khrushchev had said to me he didn't think Castro was a Communist.

(A later check of the full notes on my Khrushchev conversation shows that he said: "As far as we know Castro is not a member of the Communist party. He is just a revolutionary and a patriot of his country. If he were to join the Communist party I should welcome him; he would make a fine addition to the ranks of the communists. But this is for him to decide.")

I thought he was too undisciplined and romantic to be an orthodox Communist, and I had known many. He seemed to be more of an anarchist, closer to Bakunin than to Lenin.

This produced an inchoate discussion. Castro insisted the aim of communism was to have less and less government until there was finally none. I said this confirmed my suspicions of his innate anarchism, because communism the world around had proven that it produced more and more government—more bureaucracy—rather than the reverse.

At this point, as our discussion was revolving like a squirrel in a cage, Castro proposed we go down and have some coffee and take a tour around sleeping Havana. We filed down to the elevator and, circled by Castro's guard, downstairs.

The porter led us through the bowels of the hotel to the kitchen, where a cook gave us tiny cups of sweet thick Cuban coffee. Then we piled into several cars. Castro got into the front seat of a modest Oldsmobile, and

Juan and I got in back. The driver was a soldier. The other cars followed us, and we drove around the port while Castro pointed out the sights and jabbered about his ideas.

I said that in a sense he was lucky to have his historical importance at this time when the really great powers like the United States and Russia were so strong that they became weak. Their possibilities of action were almost paralyzed by the terrible potential of their weapons, and this allowed more freedom of action to smaller countries. Cuba would have had a much more difficult time in an earlier period. Castro agreed. He also agreed that the impact of Woodrow Wilson in terms of encouraging the idea of self-determination, an idea which had spread to many continents although originally conceived for Europe alone, had produced perhaps a greater force than Leninism.

I said to Castro: "You are now thirty-eight. Twenty years ago, when you were only eighteen, what was your ambition, what did you want to be?" With great delight he swiveled round in the front seat and said: "I wanted to be doing exactly what I am doing now."

He told me that his father, who had been born in Spain, was a big farmer who had only a general and vague interest in politics. His father had come to Cuba as a soldier in the Spanish army during the independence war and then had returned after being demobilized.

We drove round by the fishing port of Havana, where a dry dock towed from the Soviet Union has been placed in position. It can repair vessels of a size up to 3,000 tons. Castro told me that the Russians will make this a base for part of their fishing fleet.

By 5:45 A.M. I was a bit nervous about catching my plane, so we drove back to the hotel—incidentally always at a reasonable speed. Apparently Castro is very opposed to reckless driving for fear of reducing Cuba's limited supply of automobiles. At the entrance of the hotel, at 6:00 A.M., we all got out, and Castro bade me a warm farewell. He did not look in the least bit tired. He asked when I would come back and promised to take me fishing.

I said I really couldn't tell but that I would like to see him again. Nevertheless, I reminded him, it had taken me over two years to get my present visa. With evident satisfaction he commented: "It's easier to see me than to get here."

20

PARIS, *November 9, 1964*

TALKED WITH PRIME MINISTER POMPIDOU THIS AFTERNOON. HE claims de Gaulle is the most European of Europe's leaders and despite his distaste for international organizations, he wants to establish a Europe that is politically, economically and militarily viable. He outlines the following hypothesis.

An East German invasion of West Germany begins, backed by Russia. NATO quite probably probes their intentions with an armored division. We find it is really serious, and we have to use nuclear weapons. With that we destroy Poland, Czechoslovakia and maybe Hungary. In the process Germany is destroyed and possibly even France. But Russia and the United States are untouched and finally decide to make a peace. What good would even a fine peace do to all the European dead?

PARIS, *November 16, 1964*

PLAYED poker last night at Chip Bohlen's. The game was arranged in honor of "Tommy" (Ambassador Llewellyn E.) Thompson, who won. Dean Rusk played with us for about three hours. I am glad to report that he (Rusk) is a shrewd, bland poker player.

PARIS, *November 18, 1964*

AN hour's talk with Couve de Murville at the Foreign Ministry. I asked if France was now making a real effort to draw closer to the Arab world and whether this was not having a repercussion in cooling off the previously warm relations and virtual alliance with Israel. Couve said: "We are normalizing relations with the Arabs and therefore we are obviously normalizing relations with Israel." I asked if he meant by this that France was less allied to Israel and he nodded affirmatively.

PARIS, *November 19, 1964*

LUNCHED with Y. Y. knew all about the Strauss and Chaban-Delmas incident and says I was slightly wrong in my facts. He says that Strauss and Chaban-Delmas discussed this in December 1957—at the initiative of Chaban. (The Félix Gaillard government, in which Chaban-Delmas was Minister of Defense, came to office on November 6, 1957, and left office on April 16, 1958.) No documents were signed. Chaban merely asked Strauss for German support on the French nuclear force in exchange for access to weapons, and Strauss agreed.

Y. continued that in July 1958, shortly after de Gaulle had come back to power, Strauss raised the matter with de Gaulle's first Defense Minister, Pierre Guillaumat, not later on with Messmer, as I had written. Guillaumat, according to Y., was fully *au courant* and turned the idea down bluntly, rather offending Strauss. A French mission went to see Strauss in November 1958 to explain to him in more delicate terms why France could not embark on a secret and bilateral nuclear project with Germany, and that this would only infuriate the United States and poison German relations with Washington as well as those of France.

PARIS, *November 23, 1964*

I SPENT yesterday with Couve de Murville playing golf and then lunching. Couve says he was not in the least surprised when Pope Paul VI refused to yield any power to the Ecumenical Council, causing a crisis this week. He says the Catholic church must remain an autocracy or disappear. It was ridiculous to think of Pope Paul as a liberal. He also said that it was silly to think the church was well informed on world affairs; it is very badly informed.

PARIS, *December 15, 1964*

THIS afternoon I went over to see Dr. Martin Luther King on his way back to New York from Oslo, where he received the Nobel Peace Prize. He is short and a warm brown, not black, with a moustache and a calm, resonant voice. He was in shirt sleeves, most informal and cordial as we sat and chatted.

I asked King if he didn't think the American Negro community should contribute more to Africa financially, technically, culturally, and by personal volunteer service. I pointed out that the Irish-American, Italo-American, and Jewish-American communities had all in one or another way contributed as separate American communities to help Ireland, Italy, and Israel at various periods. It seemed to me that it was thus in accordance with the traditions of America's mixed society and mixed origins for the Negro community to play a more useful role in helping the new nations of Africa.

King replied that he certainly agreed. He said:

> The American Negro has not contributed enough of his resources to Africa in the effort to aid Africa in its struggle for a better and higher life. But there is more conscious support in their field than ever before. There is an awareness on our part of the paucity of our support to date.
>
> There has been a slowness to act along these lines for two reasons. The first is that for so many years the Negro in America was so ashamed of his heritage that he didn't want to identify himself with Africa. He wanted to forget anything that reminded him of his past. His thinking was negative and misinformed both on Africa and on its history. The second reason is that we have been so involved in our own struggle for racial justice and dignity in the U.S.A. that we have tended to forget our brothers and sisters in Africa.

PARIS, *December 21, 1964*

I SPENT an hour with de Gaulle this afternoon. He was in a marvelous mood: brisk, chipper, funny, sarcastic. I started by asking him what he foresaw for 1969 when the North Atlantic Treaty expires. Did he foresee a new kind of treaty organization? Or a renewed general alliance?

Obviously he loved this subject. It was terribly hard for me to ever get him off it. He said: "Another organization, of course. There is an alliance and that should be conserved. The alliance is necessary. Obviously a certain number of states, such as the U.S.A. and France, should commit themselves to help each other in case of war. But the organization that has been based upon the North Atlantic Treaty, NATO, will not be maintained. The organization ends in 1969 and before then we must decide on another kind of organization to replace it or there will be none. France will not agree to keep NATO."

Throughout our conversation I found de Gaulle harping upon the German menace and insisting that German unity was completely *hors de question*.

I asked if it were true that relations between France and the United States were easier now. He said:

> Until now U.S. policy toward Europe has been one of integration, of domination—naturally *à la manière démocratique*. I recognize that since World War II this was a natural development, because of the immense power of the U.S.A. after the war and because of the direct menace of Russia to Europe. I recognize the effort you put into such projects as the Marshall Plan. It was natural that the U.S.A. should wish to exercise a hegemony over Europe.
>
> But it is no longer natural that this should continue. Now such hegemony

is becoming artificial. The Soviet menace is now much less. And the European countries have resumed, have restored, a stability—not power but stability. Above all this is economic. Germany and France have an economic stability.

Now the American protectorate is less justified. Nevertheless, the possibility of a war remains. This is inescapable. Therefore we must preserve an alliance between Europe and the U.S.A., above all between France and the U.S.A. But we want an alliance, not a protectorate.

The U.S.A. will recognize the changed circumstances and will change its attitude, above all vis-à-vis France. It will accept France as independent. But independence does not prevent friendship, or alliance. This is what the U.S.A. will realize. If France wants to make nuclear weapons it *will*.

We must not exaggerate things. At this time France is only starting its atomic force. It is just starting. It is still almost nothing. It will only be relatively important in four or five years.

But at that time, if the U.S.A. and France are still allied—which I hope— and allied in a normal way, then the two general staffs, or better yet the two governments, will work together and will draw up arrangements so that they can help each other in case of any war *in which they are both involved,* and will decide how to divide up possible targets.

This is the normal method among allies. But it is not integration. France will not accept integration. It is a question of the coordination of two policies—if the two governments want to work it out together.

Certainly the alliance as an alliance and not as an organization must continue for years. It is very useful. But do not forget the East is changing. [By the East he means the USSR and its satellites.] Externally it is changing toward peace and *détente* and internally it is changing toward liberty. It is good to encourage contacts and peaceful arrangements and it is possible to imagine some distant day when an alliance may no longer be necessary. But that day cannot be imagined soon.

Such nuclear strength as you have in Europe now is only here because you have U.S. divisions here. But one day these divisions will go and then your nuclear weapons will go. We must look ahead to the future.

Would France accept financial or technical aid from any other European country—such as Germany—to help build its nuclear force? "No," he replied categorically. "We will give our bombs to no one and we will accept aid from no one."

I asked if France envisaged the possibility of German reunification so long as Moscow retains any form of satellite control over Eastern Europe. Again quite categorically he said,

No, that would mean war. Germany can only be reunified in the foreseeable future by war. Neither Russia nor its satellites, the Poles, the Czechs, or the Rumanians, will ever accept German unification under anything resembling present conditions. That would lead to the abyss.

Europe remembers all too well the danger of Germany. This memory remains in the popular mind. And people are stronger than regimes. If the tsars still ruled in Russia they would oppose German reunification just as the communists do. The same is true of Poland. This fear of Germany and German reunification holds the Eastern countries together. And we French also suffered enormously from the Germans. We will not accept any terms for German unification that are not also acceptable to the East. German unification can only come some day when a European equilibrium is assured and built around it. There is no question of this now. Perhaps some day. But who can foresee the future?

I asked de Gaulle if he still considered valid his earlier phrase about a Europe from the Atlantic to the Urals. He said he did and that as the "Eastern regimes change and liberalize their internal policy while applying an external policy of peace such a development would gradually permit an East-West arrangement covering all Europe."

I asked de Gaulle if France had offered its good offices to the United States to settle the Vietnam crisis. He said,

> Yes, of course. We proposed what we could. We proposed to organize a conference that would discuss all the problems involved. This would seek to neutralize all of southeast Asia. But we have made no other proposal since.
>
> We told the Americans—you cannot succeed in Indochina. The ground is rotten [*le terrain est pourri*]. It is impossible. We in France know. We failed and you will fail.
>
> Naturally, you can continue the present system. A strong rich power can stay in by one or another way, using one or another general as your leader in South Vietnam; but that doesn't help. Things continue to get worse and worse.
>
> Or you can make war. You can make war on North Vietnam. Or you can make war on China. You can even start a world war. But is it worth it? Is it even worth it just in North Vietnam alone? Why would it be worth it? To continue the system that now exists in South Vietnam? That would not be a good policy.
>
> The best thing would be to have a conference as we suggested, a conference including China. This at least could neutralize Laos, Cambodia, and Vietnam—and then we could see what would happen next.

I told de Gaulle I had recently seen Castro, and he asked me a few questions about him. He said Castro wasn't really a Communist and that the United States should show more calm and reserve about Cuba. "Don't get all excited," he said.

ROME, *January 10, 1965*

LAST night Luigi Barzini gave us a dinner party at his farm outside Rome. Luigi started things off by saying the Christian Democratic Party is like a dead whale washed up on the beach and stinking up the atmosphere. The Christian Democrats *can't* reconstruct the state—they can't even make it function.

BONN, *February 5, 1965*

EXCELLENT and very friendly talk with former Chancellor Adenauer in the office that is provided him as a courtesy in the Bundesrat Building. Adenauer is now eighty-nine.

I asked what he thought of the policy of President Johnson. He said:

One interesting aspect of your political system is that the president is elected by the people but is not answerable to them. He is both chief of state and chief of government. Your press is therefore called upon to play a more important role than in other democratic countries. The president often deals with matters through the press, whereas a prime minister in another country would answer questions in parliament.

Thinking over the past few years it occurs to me how relatively short a time there has been to have so many changes in the personality of your president. You have had Eisenhower, Kennedy, and Johnson—all inside of twelve years. I feel that sometimes this change in personalities is reflected in U.S. policy. After all, these three men—Eisenhower, Kennedy, and Johnson —are all completely different in type. Let me explain why I now have a mistrust for U.S. policy.

The United States administration doesn't seem to be aware that the greatest danger to the United States remains in Western Europe, not elsewhere. Washington pays far too little attention to this fact. You are the biggest and most powerful country. You should take the lead in fixing up NATO and in making certain of the defenses of the West. But nothing happens. Of course there is an unpleasant situation in South Vietnam and, unfortunately, I am sure it will get worse. But this is an area of secondary importance to you.

My policy has always been based upon the two following ideas. The relationship between Russia and China would develop in such a way that Russia would be pleased to have no enemies in the West and would therefore feel free to turn its attention increasingly toward the East. Secondly I felt it was quite obvious that the Soviet Union was having increasing economic difficulties. I thought it would be folly to help Russia solve these economic difficulties unless the Russians made concessions on their side.

Unfortunately the democracies have not taken advantage of the latter situation. First the British Conservative government sent supplies to the Russians. Then the Americans sent their wheat, asking for no counter-concessions. This was a capital folly on the part of the British and the Americans.

Don't make any mistake. I don't want the Russians to starve. But I see no reason to send them factories unless they make concessions to us in exchange.

He continued: "Why have the Russians kept their hold so obstinately on the East Zone [of Germany]? It is for no reason except as bait to attract the Federal Republic. If France were to go communist, to fall to a popular front, and West Germany were between France and Russia, what should we do if the Russians offered some kind of false terms for unification with that East Zone bait?"

Adenauer went on: "When a nation is forced to fight a very distant war, as you are doing in Vietnam, there are certain psychological limits easily reached. People get fed up. And if you people get fed up because of your Vietnam war that will mean a return to isolationism."

PARIS, *March 1, 1965*

PLAYED golf yesterday and lunched with Couve de Murville and Bohlen. Couve said what France really wants in terms of fiscal reform is to double the price of gold. But France doesn't dare to say this openly because it would have an unsettling effect. Nevertheless, if gold were revalued to $70 an ounce, the United States would automatically end the problem of its leading reserves. England would be in much better financial shape. There would be enough gold available to finance international commercial exchanges.

SAIGON, *March 11, 1965*

TALKED for an hour and a quarter this afternoon with General Max Taylor, our Ambassador here. He feels Johnson lags behind Kennedy on "counter-insurgency" in general and Vietnam in particular.

He indicated it had been discussed as long ago as 1961 whether North Vietnam should be bombed. He (Taylor) had only come around to the decision a year ago: Since then (until February) the delay was Johnson's. The bombing would be slowly and selectively stepped up and moved northward to frighten Ho Chi Minh into calling off his dogs.

I asked if he thought the "falling dominoes" theory still tenable. He said: "No, I suppose not. There is nothing inevitable in this area. It is perhaps a 'tilting domino.' We could establish a Mekong barrier. We could hold Thailand and Malaysia. The pressure might also shift elsewhere. But things would certainly be much more bleak if we lost South Vietnam."

Taylor said that undoubtedly the end of [Ngo Dinh] Diem was a "great disaster." No alternative solid regime has developed.

I remarked that bringing in the 3,500 U.S. marines implied that we wished to release Vietnamese forces to do other jobs, and wondered if their presence didn't encourage Communist antiwhite racist propaganda— talking of "white" Americans and trying to unite all "Asians" against them.

Taylor said the marines helped ease the shortage. Government military strength, all told, was about 600,000, while the Vietcong had 34,000 hard-core regulars plus another 70,000 to 80,000 "local guerrillas." All recent successful counter-insurgency operations had shown that, even when there are no foreign sanctuaries for the guerrillas, you need from ten to twenty to one manpower superiority.

"We are trying to get tension to rise," he said. "Neither Peking nor

Moscow wants to get into this thing directly. Therefore we are most interested in Ho's reaction. He worked hard to build up, during ten years, such an industrialization program as he has been able to establish. Will he be willing to sacrifice this for an uncertain South Vietnam and/or the possibility of Chinese occupation? And don't forget, the Soviets are showing signs of unhappiness."

Taylor admitted that in the summer of 1963, when Diem was still in power, he and McNamara had both forecast that within two years (from then) the war here could be turned into a police action. It has gone way downhill since.

SAIGON, *March 15, 1965*

AN exceedingly interesting day yesterday, flying up to Hué with General William E. De Puy and then afterwards to Danang.

Until very recently the United States made the assumption that the Vietnamese could win this war by themselves. But events have proved this wrong. We have now resolved that we now need a much bigger ARVN and an overwhelming U.S. air force and basic involvement.

I asked how long the United States was willing to stay on here. He said as long as two political conditions were met: that the American public supports the commitments; that the Vietnamese government does not put in a neutralist government through a coup d'état or a "peace" government through Communist-front movements.

I met three university students: frail young men, all twenty-five years old but looking about sixteen. Two came from Hanoi and one was born in Hué. One said he was a Confucian, one said that he was a Deist, and the third said he was a Catholic.

One said: "Many people think the Americans are fighting here for their own interest only. The common people think the United States manipulate events. We appreciate your help. But you should help us to help ourselves without intervening in our domestic affairs. We think the Americans want a strong man in power. But we need a strong government, not a strong man."

None of them had done their military service yet, and although they talk like vivid patriots they don't seem eager to join the army.

The first said: "If you don't improve the situation here soon, morale will become very bad. The Vietcong continues to infiltrate everywhere."

They approved of U.S. air raids in the north; but at this point the second student, the one from Hué, changed his mind and said: "No. Most of the North Vietnamese people are true Vietnamese and not communists. We don't want to see the Americans kill them."

At the officers' mess, a timid but pleasant American captain sat at our table. He is district adviser a bit north of Hué, near the North Vietnamese border, the only American in a very unsteady area. The Vietcong was more or less in control of every hamlet. The captain gave 200 piastres (about $2 at the black market rate) reward for every Vietcong killed. He pays this out of his own pocket. De Puy complained he should know there are intelligence funds available for use in buying information. The captain said: "What's the use? You can't buy loyalty."

NEW DELHI, *March 31, 1965*

YESTERDAY evening I saw Prime Minister Shastri in his office. Shastri is unusually small—about four feet, eleven inches. He has a pleasant, square, tan face. He was wearing a white cap and the traditional brown homespun coat.

I asked if it was not frustrating to suddenly be called upon to fill the shoes of a very big man. He said: "It is a difficult task indeed—especially coming after Mr. Nehru who dominated the scene for fourteen years as prime minister and before that also as a great freedom fighter and liberator. We are a young country. Since independence, there has been a new urge toward different languages and different cultures. These sometimes create difficulties. But by and large there is a sense of unity and whenever there is any emergency people do work shoulder to shoulder and stand for the country as a whole."

PARIS, *April 9, 1965*

DINED last night at Alain de Rothschild's. Bertrand Goldschmidt said: "India will most certainly have manufactured an atomic bomb within three years at the latest." Bertrand, who is one of the top dogs in the French nuclear program, says it is perfectly apparent the Indians are working on this from the questions he is asked whenever he sees Dr. Homi Bhabha, their best physicist. Bertrand believes the Indians won't test their bomb; they will merely announce when they have one. Eight years ago Bhabha told Bertrand he asked Nehru whether to go ahead and make a bomb. Nehru did not answer him; he merely said, "Tell me when you have one."

PARIS, *April 14, 1965*

LUNCHED today with Etienne Manac'h, head of the Asia desk at the Quai d'Orsay. He told me there are now 125 Russian technicians in North Vietnam. The Chinese had been telling all neutralists and socialists that Russia was not serious in offering to help North Vietnam. The Russians were so enraged that they passed the word around to everyone, including the French Communist Party, that China was blocking Soviet attempts to send help to Hanoi.

Moscow is trying both to strengthen Ho Chi Minh's regime and the

Soviet position in North Vietnam. China, on the other hand, is trying to build up the Vietcong and its political expression, the FLN. Russia is working on a government-to-government basis, and China is working on a people-to-people basis.

The Chinese fear that if Russia is able to send modern weapons which require trained experts to handle them to North Vietnam, they will end up by bringing so many people to Hanoi that they can assert a political control and enter into a direct negotiation with the United States on North Vietnam, just the way they did on Cuba in 1962—paying no more attention to Ho Chi Minh's desires than they paid to Castro's.

WASHINGTON, *May 5, 1965*

GOOD talk with Secretary of State Rusk. We have evidence that Vietcong morale is continuing to slip. Defections are increasing. Prisoners tell us of shortages of food and medicine. Also they are complaining about having to move around all the time because of our bombardments.

The United States has plainly conveyed to North Vietnam that our bombing of the north will stop if they on their part stop other things. We have left it open—as far as the "other things" are concerned.

WASHINGTON, *May 6, 1965*

I WAS taking a bath when I received a call telling me to get over to the White House right away to see the President.

Johnson had quite a sunburn, which I imagine he gets from a sun lamp, but he didn't look well. He is too heavy. He was tired and yawned several times. His eyes twitched occasionally. He fiddled with a pencil and kept tapping his fingers.

He said France was the only problem in Western Europe and it was better to leave things as they are. He added, with reference to de Gaulle: "I see no point in feuding with an old man. He has his pride and his nationalism and I am glad that France now has some of that. It is a lot better than when they used to have elections every two weeks. And I will never forget when he came right in with us on Cuba. In seventeen months he hasn't bothered me. If he throws his fast ball, I just step aside and go on with my business. I am prepared to smile and turn the other cheek."

Johnson was anxious to ease tension with Russia,

but Vietnam has made them tense. I told [Ambassador Anatoli] Dobrynin I wanted him to come down to Texas for a few days. I see their problem on Vietnam and their necessity to denounce us. But we will have to learn how to live together, and the quicker the better.

My relations with Russia have been all right. I have said that I want to see the Russians here and that I am ready to go there. The more they see of our country, the better. Khrushchev was never the same after he visited an Iowa farm. Now the Russians should see some of our laboratories and then they will learn they can't catch us for another hundred years.

We can work together with the Russians. We have been working together on desalinizing water, on space and other things. The more we work together, the less likely we are to fight together.

PARIS, *June 8, 1965*

EXCELLENT talk with Couve de Murville. He said: "No nation has ever had such a power for destruction as the power you hold today. You want to be the gendarmes of the world. You don't admit it but this is a fact. And, while you can destroy the world, you cannot conquer it. For example you could destroy China, or a large part of it, but you cannot conquer China. We think this is the real question, the real issue today. And we also think this poses a deep-seated problem in your country."

PARIS, *June 21, 1965*

LUNCHED with (retired) General Pierre Gallois. Gallois says in 1963 McNamara promised that things were going so well American troops would be out of Vietnam by Christmas. And only two months ago Rusk assured the country that eventually our troops would pull out.

This kind of talk totally undermines our position with the South Vietnamese, who are scared, who know they couldn't last two hours without us, and who therefore make their own private accommodation. At the same time, by our bombing program we encourage the Vietcong to stick only to guerrilla operations, and that is the one kind of operation the United States cannot defeat.

The United States has shown the world that Asian alliances are meaningless. Hanoi and Peking are bound by both military and doctrinal alliances, but there has been no real reaction to Washington's policy from Peking—despite the fact that the Eastern world is united by its race complex and supposed to be more coherent than the Western world.

PARIS, *July 1, 1965*

THIS afternoon I saw de Gaulle. In view of the new Saigon government's decision to break relations with Paris, did he intend to recognize North Vietnam? He said: "French policy does not depend on Saigon. That is not a government. It simply does not exist. Now, as for Hanoi, that *is* a government. It is not a satisfactory government but it governs. Nevertheless we have not recognized it although it is not impossible that we will do so one day. But the question is not current now."

De Gaulle went on to say that quite obviously, the Chinese and the North Vietnamese are opposed to the thought of negotiations at this time.

There was a distinct possibility that a big war could break out in the Far East and

every day this becomes more likely.

Nor does this disturb the Chinese. Of course they would lose a great deal in such a war and if the United States were to use nuclear weapons it would bring vast destructions. But the Chinese don't care. On the contrary I wonder if they would not like to have the United States become involved in a large war.

I remember a very characteristic phrase of Chou En-lai. Someone had asked him if he did not think everything must be done to avoid the suffering caused by war. He replied that on the contrary, it was by war that big things were achieved. He said China had become what it is today as a result of invasion, destruction, and suffering. This philosophical attitude is very impressive and I am afraid it remains a factor in Chinese policy.

I said that I had always been puzzled by his reference to a Europe "from the Atlantic to the Urals." I recognized that the Urals were the conventional geographical boundary between Europe and Asia, but what did he mean politically, since this concept partitioned Russia? He replied:

I recognize that this phrase irritates the Russians but that is their affair, not mine. The real Russia stops at the Urals. All the rest—Turkistan, Siberia, parts of Mongolia—these are all colonies. Colonies colonized by the Russians.

And probably, almost surely, in the future they will become a part of China. China has 700 million people. It is not a great power today. But in twenty years it will be a great power and in fifty years it will be an enormous power. The Russians know this well—and so do the Chinese. This is the inner basis of their quarrel. Of course, being communists, they always put everything on an ideological basis. But the truth is the opposition between Russia and China has national origins.

I wanted to ask a philosophical question. Stalin had said the principal force motivating men was fear. Others cited religion, nationality, family. What did he think was the primary force governing men in their actions? Without a moment of hesitation he answered: "One must draw a distinction between the individual and the collective masses. For the individual it is ambition and a taste for adventure. I think the real motivation, the primordial motivating force for the individual is ambition, but for the masses it is fear. There Stalin was right. And this applies to masses of all countries."

I also wished to pose an indiscreet question which was a bit philosophical. He had attended Churchill's funeral and had seen what a tremendous historical spectacle it was. Because of his own sense of history he must have been impressed by such a spectacle and by the fact that Churchill had planned it. Had this incited him to make similar plans for himself because of his own well-known interest in history and his own role therein? I admitted the question was lugubrious and perhaps impertinent.

"No," de Gaulle answered. "It is indeed important and I have thought about it a good deal. But my funeral will be the opposite of Churchill's. There will be no spectacle. There will be no spectacle for de Gaulle."

BUDAPEST, *July 8, 1965*

THIS morning I was received by Janos Kadar, Hungary's boss. Kadar is moderately short, slender but strongly built, with a good strong face, a firm, cleft chin, brown hair, pale skin, and rather kindly blue eyes. He has large, strong hands with perfectly formed fingernails, belying the report they were torn out when he was tortured by Rákosi's police. The only sign of nervous strain left over from torture was an occasional but marked twitch of the right eye.

He said of peaceful coexistence:

Countries can proceed in the field of bilateral relations along the line of peaceful coexistence. It is more difficult to find spheres of cooperation between groups of countries: at least experience has tended to show this up to the present time.

[Palmiro] Togliatti, who was a deeply educated Marxist thinker and very conscious of what he was saying, enunciated something which was sensible. However, the way it is being interpreted in the West, and what Togliatti meant by polycentrism is quite another matter.

We, for instance, have very good relations with the Soviet Communist party as well as with the Italian Communist party. The reason is that these three parties, in matters of decisive importance and mutual interest, have an identical attitude. But this agreement does not extend to the hundreds of problems encountered by any of these three parties day by day, problems to which each has to respond. So the agreement between them does not mean an identity of views right down to the most minute problems.

If there is no imminent war conflict between the camps, then they coexist peacefully—and, if that is so, there are continuous sets of contracts. I see the future of peaceful coexistence in the form which it has assumed in these days. If events take a trend toward lasting peace, sooner or later a situation must arise where the Warsaw pact and NATO agree about something, and later still these groupings would be simultaneously wound up (in sense of winding up their operations). At that juncture, bilateral relations will continue to be decisive.

I think what you call Titoism came about in actual practice when a conflict, a particular situation arose—without any theory to it. The theory was elaborated later, and on both sides. Titoism—may I be permitted to say so—was elaborated by us. When the conflict arose over certain problems, and in a certain logical sequence, we had—based on fictional and assumptive grounds—laid a whole theory at the doors of the Jugoslavs which in reality —looking back at it now—had never existed. I think the Jugoslavs themselves in that given situation became isolated . . . they had to exist some way or another and so elaborated some practical rules and even set up a theory. This is the way I see it.

A long time ago—now almost 120 years—when Marx and Engels were still active in word and writing (they were both colleagues of yours, as in a certain period of their lives they worked as professional journalists), they too carried on discussions about this subject. They said, very satirically and bitingly, that anyone who mistook "a public lavatory free of charge" for socialism would be very wrong, because the two are entirely unconnected—even if the public lavatory is not privately owned. Of course, in a capitalist society there are—very consciously run—communal sewage systems and other public utilities run by cities, etc.—but that does not constitute socialism. I don't want to say that it is indifferent to a working man in a given capitalist country whether there is a system of social insurance or not. It is not an indifferent matter. It is better if there is such a system, but still such matters have nothing to do with socialism.

BUDAPEST, *July 9, 1965*

LONG talk with Elim O'Shaughnessy, U.S. chargé d'affaires. Our conversation was difficult because of a constant hammering. Workers have been sent over here by the state department to repair the legation and insure its security. Hidden microphones have been found in the walls.

It was odd thinking that as I talked with Elim, in the office next to his secretary lived Cardinal Mindszenty. He has been here since 1956. He has one huge room and then a little tiny bedroom with a cot in it and a bathroom across from a pantry where he has an icebox. This would have been the suite of the chief of mission.

Mindszenty has it furnished in usual routine U.S. Embassy furniture—a big round table, two leather sofas, two leather chairs, a large standard desk. He occasionally sees his sister; and a confessor, a Hungarian priest, comes in once a month. Every day Mindszenty says mass on a little altar he has set up on a table with white cloth.

The American legation staff takes turns in escorting him on walks around the courtyard around 6:00 P.M., after the office hours so that nobody will see him. He walks around as long as he wishes. He is now almost seventy-four but very spry although he wears glasses. Some of the legation staff attend his Sunday masses. Nobody except Foreign Service officers or code clerks are allowed to go in to see Mindszenty or take him on his walks.

He primarily speaks about his hatred of communism, his dislike of Kadar, and the Rumanian treatment of the Hungarian minority in Transylvania. He seems to live in a past world.

The state department is so rigid about the terms of his asylum that even President Kennedy's sisters, when they were here, could not talk with him although were allowed to attend mass.

Mindszenty is fed through the legation cafeteria (which is really a snack bar). His meals are brought up to the third floor by an ordinary servant and then taken in to him on a tray by the duty officer. Occasionally he has beer or wine.

VIENNA, *July 16, 1965*

LUNCH with Bruno Kreisky, the red-headed socialist who has been Foreign Minister of Austria for more than six years. Kreisky came from a very wealthy family but became a socialist before the war and was imprisoned by the conservatives during the civil war here. He is a Jew, the first Jewish Foreign Minister in a Germanic state since Rathenau in Germany.

Kreisky said the Rumanians are not halfway between Paris and Moscow, as some people think, but halfway between Moscow and Peking.

KASTRI, GREECE, *July 27, 1965*

I DROVE out to this little suburb about ten miles from Athens on this hot morning to spend an hour and a half with former Prime Minister George Papandreou.

Papandreou said: "There is one big difference between dictatorship and democracy. Dictatorship has an entrance but no exit. The exit from democracy is elections. The present crisis results only from the king's intervention. He can only create a fictitious government of the moment based on a lack of any real material support. We need elections as soon as possible. That is imperative."

ATHENS, *July 28, 1965*

INTERESTING lunch with Andreas Papandreou. Andreas told me he had started out at Harvard in 1940 although he did not have a degree from Athens University. He got an M.A. and a Ph.D. Then he was an instructor at Harvard until he was offered a post as associate professor at the University of Minnesota. He was made full professor and head of the economics department at the University of California.

He has considerable charm and talks well but has a shady look about him because his eyes are too close together. He glanced around furtively (we were sitting at a corner table) and then said: "I do not see any traitors."

KYP (the Greek Central Intelligence Service) is enormously tied to American CIA. He said they have the common job of counter-espionage in the area to the north of Greece. CIA gave KYP 10 million drachmas annually. Andreas says this should be paid directly to the Greek government and not directly to KYP.

Andreas said there had been a fundamental issue since the first day of the Papandreou government. The palace considered the army its personal property. After Paul died, King Constantine sent an envoy to George

Papandreou saying that he was sure they could get on very well together so long as Papandreou left the army alone.

Andreas says Constantine is young, intelligent, and a stronger personality than his father. But, he added: "He has no Western culture. He grew up in a small circle in Greece. And he believes he is the head of the Orthodox church just in the same way that a Byzantine emperor was. He believes the army is his own and he won't yield control. And he sees the Communist party as a gang, not a political movement. He feels this very strongly. This is at the root of the problem. We had an army problem and we partly won the elections on the slogan 'Take politics out of the army.' My father from the very start sensed a palace resistance to any thought of change in the armed forces."

Andreas told me: "I would like to be a prime minister, but I won't violate my principles to be one. There have been various offers by businessmen to buy me off. I have been offered up to $200,000 for one deal. But I won't do it. I have insisted on standing by our promises on social justice, economic and foreign policy. My father loves me as a son but my unbending tendencies have caused him trouble. I am a tough nut. I have a very wide popular base today. After George Papandreou, I have the widest popular base in Greece. I do not need George Papandreou [his father]."

ATHENS, *July 29, 1965*

LAST night I had a long talk and drinks with young King Constantine. I had the feeling he was a very grown-up young man; he is now twenty-five. He is tough, bright, and self-confident; perhaps even over-confident. He said he liked his job and felt prepared for it. I stayed with him, talking and drinking highballs, until 10:00 P.M.

The King speaks rapidly and extremely fluently although with a slight accent. A favorite phrase he uses both in conversation and telephone talk is "tic-tic-tic." He will say, for example, "and then so-and-so said tic-tic-tic and. . . ."

He began by reminding me that this was a very secret meeting. He said: "Maybe this is a sign of how well our democracy works. I am not *allowed* to be quoted."

Constantine said:

You know, I got on well enough with the old boy, Papandreou, until this crisis broke. I told him from the start that he was first-class on giving confidence to the armed forces and that I much appreciated this. But when the Cyprus thing began to get more peaceful and there was less of an atmosphere of danger, a period began when he started to look around. His policy commenced to shift and he started to ask for changes in the armed forces.

Then the old boy let me know his plan to fire his defense minister over the telephone and through a third person. He sent me a message and I told him that I would be glad to see him. But it was clear that he was planning a showdown.

Papandreou admitted to me that it had been a mistake of him not to talk the matter over with me first before firing the minister. When I mentioned the attacks on me in his press, Papandreou said: "But I am attacked by my own press also. I do not control it." I replied to him: "But you can talk back to your press, I cannot. I am constitutionally forbidden."

Then the old boy said to me: "You know, Your Majesty, I am the breakwater against the Communist party. I can bring its vote down in any election to ten percent." I said: "Yes, they will all vote for you."

Papandreou then said he wanted to take over the defense ministry himself. I recommended very strongly against this. I said a very delicate question was posed concerning the conspiracy his son was alleged to be involved with. [What the King obviously meant was the Aspida conspiracy of which one now hears so much.] I said I did not know about these charges but I thought it was better to leave the question of his taking the ministry until this issue had been investigated and settled.

He replied that he could not go down in history as the prime minister who was forbidden to take over the portfolio of defense minister. I replied that he could take it over—one month later.

At this point he said to me that he would have to resign if I was adamant on the issue. He said he had a right to demand national elections—but he would not ask for them. He would leave that until later. I was aghast when he even mentioned the subject because I knew he knew his deputies would not stand with him in an election coming from such an issue.

He then continued by saying that he would resign the next day. All this went tic-tic-tic. It was fast, just like that. I knew what he was up to. I figured that if I let him go until tomorrow he would get a hold of the radio and get his crowds out into the street.

So I said to him: "I will accept your resignation as of now. Now I am free to make my choice."

He said: "Your Majesty, I understand."

Our army had to be slowly brought back into a position of real capacity after the defeat in the war against the Axis and after the communist war. My father brought it back into a normal position after a long struggle. The army is loyal to me, myself, but it is also loyal to the crown as a continuity. The king's job is to keep the army and the crown out of any political party squabbles and out of any possible civil wars. But the fact of the matter is that they—the old boy and his people—want to grab control of the army and some day to make a dictatorship.

When the old boy left me the last time, I had to find out who could get the most votes inside his party. I wanted to keep his party intact but I had to get a new prime minister. Now I have a government of twenty-one ministers who are doing a splendid job. I am going to get this country out of this mess. We must fight it out in parliament. Not in the streets. This is a political argument that belongs in parliament, and not with the mob. That is the way I am going to play this game.

My father gave me a damned good piece of advice. He told me never to play any dirty tricks. I am going to play this straight down the line. My policy is a clear-cut policy.

I asked if he liked his job. Rather enthusiastically, young Constantine looked me squarely in the eye and said: "Yes. I was born into this job. It has terrible responsibilities, but I am ready to accept them. But I must admit that every now and then I feel terribly alone. Nevertheless, I have a feeling that it is my duty to steer my country into history."

The King walked to the door with me and said: "Do not tell anyone about this. I am ready to continue this conversation whenever you want."

ATHENS, *August 9, 1965*

THIS morning I spent another hour with the King, again going through the back door. Constantine seemed astonishingly optimistic about the chances that Stefanos Stefanopoulos, Papandreou's former Deputy Prime Minister and now splitting off from the old man, would be able to form a government. I was surprised and said that it seemed like trying to build the Parthenon out of wet macaroni. He had received Papandreou again yesterday.

He told him: "You tell me you do not want communist backing in order to form a government. That means of course that you have to have an election if I give you the mandate. But I have told you why I think it is a bad idea to have elections."

According to Constantine, Papandreou then said: "I see that my requests have been refused. I hope that God will enlighten you and help you to find a solution."

Constantine answered: "I also hope so. And I hope that you will help me."

Papandreou answered: "I cannot."

According to the King, he told Papandreou:

You have been speaking to the people and telling them untruths. You have been telling them that this is a question as to whether the king or the people should rule. The proof that democracy exists in Greece is that you are able to go and freely tell such tales. You talk to the press, the Greek press, and the foreign press. But I cannot. You spurred on Andreas and Margaret [his wife] and she wrote letters urging that the United States should intervene on your behalf. I have read those letters which urge Americans to protect democracy in Greece because it is supposed to be in danger. She wrote there was going to be a clash between you and me, even before it happened. How did she know?

ATHENS, *October 4, 1965*

LONG talk with King Constantine. I have just returned to Athens, having finished my holiday. He seemed rather relieved that the whole damned crisis is over—at any rate, as he said, "I hope it is over but it all depends on how this government does."

I asked him what this crisis had taught him concerning the role of a king in contemporary times. He said: "To be quite frank, this has increased my belief that politicians are damned shocking liars. That is what exhausted me—lies, lies, lies. I have now found out how complicated a thing this is. If you do nothing, you're dumb. If you do something, someone will get hurt and begin to scream. And I have no right under the law to explain and justify myself to the public. I can't talk about politics although I would love to. I would love to but I cannot and I think this is wrong. That is the biggest drawback to being a head of state."

SOFIA, *October 11, 1965*

THIS afternoon I spent an hour and a half with Todor Zhivkov, present boss of Bulgaria; Prime Minister and First Secretary of the Communist Party. Zhivkov is shortish, squat, fat, almost bald. He has a long nose, large ears, mobile mouth, cunning brown eyes. He was very friendly, indeed ingratiating, but gave the impression of being unsure of himself.

I asked if Zhivkov had any claims on Jugoslav Macedonia or considered there was a Bulgarian minority in that province. He said, rather idiotically:

> We're Marxists. [I didn't remind him of Marx's writings on the South Slavs as 'Balkan trash.'] The most important question is whether there is collectivism or not. We feel the life of anyone, regardless of origin, is all right if it is in a socialist republic. [This is kind of silly since Greece and Turkey, with Bulgarian minorities, aren't "socialist," and most of Jugoslavia's land is not collectivized.] We only are concerned with whether or not they are building revolution.
>
> The Macedonian problem doesn't exist now except in the minds of historians and extreme nationalists. We are developing the friendliest relations with Yugoslavia and with neighboring countries and socialist countries.

Why were VOA (Voice of America) broadcasts still jammed here? He said with a self-satisfied and cunning smile: "We'll jam until the U.S.A. stops discriminating." I asked if, putting it bluntly, what he meant was simply a flat deal—Bulgaria becomes a "most-favored nation" and simultaneously stops jamming. "Precisely," he said, delighted. "That's just what I mean. We can stop our jamming very fast."

He complained: "The United States considers Bulgaria the most intimate satellite of the Soviet Union. China also says the same thing." Then, rather to my surprise, he naively continued: "Of course, we are Russia's most confident ally so in a way perhaps this is true. The question is on how you define what a satellite is."

SPENT the day with Couve de Murville playing golf, lunching, and riding to and from Paris. Couve is not impressed by the improvement of our military situation in Vietnam. He says this can continue for as long as the United States is willing to spend the money and make the military effort. But the minute we cease, the guerrillas will filter back and whatever flimsy regime exists in Saigon will promptly collapse. Since this is a military conflict which cannot be "won" by either side, it must eventually be solved by a political negotiation.

Couve complains it is impossible to talk confidentially with either the Americans or the British. They immediately leak the substance of every talk to all the other allied capitals. A few months ago Couve had a long and very confidential talk with Bohlen, and two days later it was published in the press. If the French request that special care be kept to safeguard secrecy, reports of such conversations are merely labeled "top secret" instead of "secret" when they are circulated to the allies. This makes it hard to deal with the "Anglo-Saxons," and France feels it must talk seriously with the United States in early 1966 about NATO; yet it doesn't know how to do this because of this total indiscretion.

He is appalled by the indiscreet memoirs published in the United States by people associated with Kennedy; of course this comes about because of the enormous price offered by publishing houses. Such indiscretions would be for the most part banned in France, and what was not legally banned would be considered improper.

(PRIME Minister Georges) Pompidou invited me for lunch—en tête-à-tête. He said it was perfectly evident that de Gaulle had made up his mind to run again. At various times during our conversation he referred to aspects of this decision, but there was never even one-hundredth of one percent of doubt. De Gaulle had had a medical checkup some time since August and everything was fixed. But he also said quite frankly that de Gaulle clearly had no thought of remaining in office for the next seven years.

Rather to my surprise Pompidou himself brought up the subject of a possible incapacity of de Gaulle during his second term, and he mentioned first of all the possibility that de Gaulle might become insane (*devient fou*) rather than die or suffer a stroke. I asked what would happen in such a case.

He said everything had been arranged for a governmental decision when the president would be declared no longer able to fulfill his duties. Under the present law this would mean that the president of the senate would succeed him temporarily and then a new president would be elected. But

Pompidou made it very clear that one of the first things that would be done during de Gaulle's second term would be to change that law and provide for a new succession.

We talked about politics awhile. I asked him what he thought of (François) Mitterand. He looked at me quizzically and then he said: "Well, strictly between us, I think he is cold and ambitious. I mistrust him."

PARIS, *November 11, 1965*

LUNCHED with Baron Adolph "Dolf" Bentinck, the Dutch Ambassador. He saw de Gaulle October 18 and had quite an interesting conversation.

Dolf said to him: "You told my friend Cy Sulzberger that you believed Russia was bounded on the East by the Urals and that Soviet territory, in Asia, would someday return to China." I asked if de Gaulle had shown irritation to this reference to what he had told me. He said that on the contrary, de Gaulle had seemed very pleased and merrily talked on, confirming everything I had written.

Bentinck was specially interested because, during the summer, he had asked Soviet Ambassador Zorin for his reactions on my column concerning this point, and the Soviet Ambassador had scoffed at it, saying: "This is merely part of Sulzberger's typical wishful thinking."

PARIS, *December 15, 1965*

LAST night I spent more than two hours talking and drinking with Dean Rusk. Rusk said anybody working for the State Department had to sign a statement on leaving, pledging themselves not to take away or make use of official papers—classified or unclassified. He admitted that Secretary of State Byrnes violated this, but he could think of no one else in the postwar period. Generally State Department papers are locked up for twenty-two or twenty-three years before they are made available to the public. But some papers are locked up forever. This can be a Presidential decision. CIA or FBI papers are permanently out of the public domain.

We had a long discussion about de Gaulle. Rusk revealed an alarming tendency to oversimplify his analysis of the general. "Let's talk really off the record," Rusk said. "Do you think de Gaulle is the Cross of Lorraine or Pétain?"

I said I didn't have a clue as to what he meant. I gathered from the subsequent conversation that Rusk wished to know whether I thought de Gaulle would lead France to war beside the United States if we became involved in a conflict—in other words, whether France would fight or "collaborate."

I said I thought de Gaulle was an honorable man and he would fight. Rusk was more than sceptical. He also asked if I thought de Gaulle really understood the implication of nuclear weapons. I said I certainly thought he did and that we were the ones who didn't understand what de Gaulle was after.

I said de Gaulle had obviously built the *force de frappe* as a political weapon against his allies, and not as a military weapon against his enemies. For this reason he had decided on a cheap, high-level version of the Mirage IV instead of a much more expensive low-level version, because de Gaulle had no intention of using it as a weapon. This was an important distinction the United States failed to make.

PARIS, *February 8, 1966*

THE CIA is increasingly concerned about a scandalous problem which it is now investigating: the black market in South Vietnam. Chinese merchants from Cholon (the Chinese quarter of Saigon) traditionally bank in France. They are now transferring to France considerably more than 100 million dollars a year on profits from the black market on U.S. goods. This provides France with an enormous dollar surplus—far larger than any surplus in foreign trade—with which to buy gold from the United States. Thus, as a result of the American black market in Saigon, France is given a weapon with which to deliberately weaken the U.S. dollar.

PARIS, *February 17, 1966*

I SPENT an hour this morning at the Quai d'Orsay with Maurice Couve de Murville, the Foreign Minister.

Couve said: "One of the basic differences between the United States and France is that you believe there is a government in South Vietnam and the trouble is caused by foreign intervention: that you are fighting communism. We believe this is not the case. We believe you are fighting the population of South Vietnam helped by others—particularly by North Vietnam. The people of South Vietnam are fighting you. That is the basis of the present situation. Someday the United States must accept the idea that you are fighting the Vietnamese people."

2 1

JOHNSON IS OBSESSED WITH OPINION POLLS AND POLITICAL STATISTICS. He is shrewd but he doesn't impress me as being nice, wise, or possibly even strong—massive as he is physically and competitive as he is by nature. If Johnson succeeds in Vietnam he will almost certainly be regarded as a very great president. If he fails he may go down in history on a par with Andrew Johnson.

He began talking about the efforts of Senator Morse today to repeal the 1964 Congressional resolution endorsing any actions he might wish to take after the Gulf of Tonkin incident. He said:

> Anyone who wants to handicap the president should vote with Morse on this. Our policy is to support SEATO and to respond to an armed attack as carried out by the present aggressors. Those members of Congress who believe this should vote with me and the rest should vote with Morse. I want this thoroughly clear and I will not have the Gulf of Tonkin resolution diluted. That resolution, which was approved on October 10, 1964, specifically stated that it would not expire until the president determined that peace and security of the area affected had been reasonably assured or until the resolution was specifically terminated by Congress.

He said that last year we had had more than three hundred contacts of a diplomatic sort seeking to explore the chances of a negotiation and two pauses in bombing during which we suggested to everybody interested that the Vietnamese question could be settled by negotiation. But nothing had come of this.

> Nevertheless, there have been decided gains as a result of our effort. One hundred and fifteen nations genuinely responded to the American offer. Everyone except Hanoi and Peking. We hunkered down for thirty-seven days and didn't do any bombing and we suffered the consequences, and this

was obviously pleasing to many people—those in the Eastern European camp like Poland, Hungary, and Russia, and also the countries of Latin America, as well as Canada and Britain. But the other fellows just weren't interested.

Anyway that certainly put an end to propaganda talk that this is a colonialist war. That taint was erased. The world reaction was good. Why, the Pope's reaction was very generous. De Gaulle had doubts about the efficacy of the bombing pause—as I did. But I tried to go the last mile. I didn't think this would do the trick, but I thought it was necessary to satisfy all those who doubt us. Now we can see that it doesn't work.

Look at all we have done. Think back to when we assassinated Diem [I was startled to have him use that phrase], when we removed General [Paul D.] Harkins because he was supposed to be too warlike, when we moved Ambassador [Frederick] Nolting because he was supposed to be too close to Diem. None of those things did the trick. But people now know in their hearts that we would negotiate if we could and that we are strong enough and determined enough to be unafraid of negotiations.

Some people think that if you have one bombing pause and then another bombing pause it hurts. But it doesn't really change opinion substantially. I have looked at all the polls. Before the pause and the televised Senate hearings the poll takers said that ten percent of the people were doves. After the bombing pause and the TV hearings there were still ten percent.

You can get enormous support when you get tough, but I don't like that kind of inflation. After the bombing pause and the TV hearings those who supported me declined from sixty-three to forty-nine percent. But the shift didn't go to the doves. It went to the hawks. That's what worries me and that's what people should know. The figure for the doves stays unchanged.

I remarked that while it was perfectly clear to Americans that we weren't engaged in any kind of colonial war, this was far less clear overseas. Many people suspected us of fighting another imperialist war with racist overtones—the white man against the Asian. I thought it was necessary to make more of an effort to eliminate this impression.

Johnson:

The best way to refute that charge of colonialism is two hundred years of history. All our experiences have shown that this isn't true. Look at the case of the Philippines. I have said time and time again we are not fighting for any territory and we don't intend to hold any bases in that area. We would pull out tomorrow if the other fellow would just get behind his parallel.

Of course there are some people in this country, those Fulbrights, who only want a Fortress America, maybe supporting a Little White Europe. Those Fulbrights say about Asia—they are not our kind of people. Well, I don't share that view. I am preserving the brown man, not warring on him. Somebody has got to protect the 2½ billion people in Asia. I am interested in those people and their education and their food and their health, and that's what I am always saying. Why, I tell Ho Chi Minh—if you will just lay down your pistol I'll help you. I am ready to let them join in all our efforts to build up southeast Asia—if they will only make peace.

Of course there are people who think the Asians are not worth saving—
not as worth saving as the Europeans. Well, I am not one of those people
who went to Oxford and thinks that way. I think they are worth saving
whatever color they are.

Do you know, Cy, I find there is a little racial overtone in those who
oppose us. Don't you forget—Fulbright was against civil rights and he's
always been against civil rights. Well I'm for civil rights and for TVA and
for wages and hours. But he just wants a sweatshop and racism.

I asked him why we had never declared war in Vietnam, apart from the
obvious problem that it would be hard to decide against whom we should
declare war. He answered:

Why should we? I think we would stand to lose a lot. For example we
don't know what treaties Hanoi has got with Peking or the others. We don't
know what kind of a SEATO they have in their part of the world—in secret.
They may even have a secret deal with de Gaulle. If we declared war on
them we might spring all the agreements they have.

The SEATO treaty says we are going to prevent anybody from coming
into our area if they ask for help—as South Vietnam did—and we don't
need any declaration of war. Everything is clear on this for the members of
SEATO and the protocol states. We are simply defending ourselves. And just
look: we are not bombing Hanoi or Haiphong. We are not bombing Peking
or landing paratroopers up there. We are just standing where we are. We
don't want this war. We would rather show Hanoi how to grow better rice
and how to let its people learn how to read and get happy and they can do
all that the day they stop fighting. We are not declaring war; we are declaring
peace.

Johnson continued:

It was Dulles who decided that we should serve notice in Asia of where
we stood—Asia, where two and a half billion people live. We had never
really seen the importance of Asia. I was out in Asia during World War II. I
was there. And I saw how our armed forces in the Asian theater of war were
regarded as second-class citizens.

Dulles took the decision that we must say—this is the wall and don't tread
on me. Anyone who tries to swallow up southeast Asia now knows that any
country there can call on eight friends in that SEATO alliance and we are all
obliged to respond with all our power. Dulles hoped that making this plain
might prevent aggression. But if that didn't work at least it gave us the force
to act. And the Senate ratified that SEATO treaty eighty-two to one.

From 1954 to 1960 the communists didn't do much out there. Why they
didn't even form that National Liberation Front until December 1960. But
then they saw that we were getting weak. They looked around and saw what
Castro did and they saw that young man sit in here in the White House. And
when Khrushchev talked like war to Kennedy in Vienna we just didn't do
very much. We called up the reserves but that didn't scare Khrushchev. He
put his missiles in Cuba and all that young fellow here did was to say to
Khrushchev: "Please, sir, take your missiles out and we won't trouble you

any more. Yes, you can go ahead and propagate communism in Cuba and we won't touch you if you will just take those missiles out."

China and Hanoi concluded we were soft and that there wasn't going to be any massive retaliation no matter what they did. They figured they would have a little repeat performance of their own. Their propaganda began to stress that Diem was corrupt and no good. They said we will just talk those Americans into assassinating Diem and we will get them to remove Nolting and Harkins and we will call them colonialists and racists. And that's what happened.

The other fellow is paying very heavily now. Because we are there to stay. I don't know what [General] Westmoreland wants but whatever he wants he is going to get it. There are probably forty or fifty thousand more men going out to support him now and if he needs more he can have it. I am going ahead in a measured, moderate way. I am not going to spit in China's face. China knows what she would get if she spit in our face. And what I am doing is a prudent, moderate thing, and even the Chinese know that.

Then Johnson went on: "No small nation anywhere would be safe if we got out of Vietnam."

At this point I left. I chatted a while with Moyers and then, as I was walking to the room where I had left my hat and coat, who should appear but Lyndon B. Johnson. When he spotted me he grabbed me in his overpowering way and took me into the little one-room barber shop with him, asking if I didn't want to chat. I had no intention of missing the chance. The whole room is about eight by eight feet with one barber chair in the center. The President took off his jacket and sat in the chair, putting out his hand to a jaded elderly manicurist while the barber started to trim the sides of his skull.

Johnson never stopped talking. I was a bit horrified by the feeling that he was being indiscreet and that possibly the manicurist and barber were not the best audience for his confidences. He seemed to enjoy these peculiar circumstances. Here are some of the things Johnson said:

According to a White House study there have been 162 interventions of a military sort by the United States President, acting as Commander in Chief, without any declaration of war or Congressional assent. Thus, in 1798 a three-year naval war against France was begun in this way. Johnson said the conception of Congressional resolutions endorsing military acts by the President as the Commander in Chief became part of our constitutional process as a consequence of political conditions after World War II. Johnson said:

Now you look at the kind of thing we are in now. There was Kennedy in Vienna. Khrushchev scared the poor little fellow dead. Kennedy called out the reserves. He got a resolution. He said he was going to get Congress in on the take-offs as well as the landings and that's why he wanted that resolution.

We tried to push for social reforms in Vietnam in 1964. That is when I came in. My ambassadors—first I brought in Lodge and then he wanted to run for the presidency and I brought in [Maxwell] Taylor—worked hard on that. Taylor was a good man and he was a general, but he didn't seem as bellicose as the other generals so he was useful. Also he was Bobby's [Robert F. Kennedy's] selection—and President Kennedy's.

My ambassadors and my generals, they said to me that unless we were willing to stop this aggression in Vietnam and to extend a fly-line to the north so they couldn't bring their stuff in, all the king's horses and all the king's men couldn't save South Vietnam. So we started bombing the north. And we started to give them all the equipment and manpower they needed. Why they increased their forces up to 790,000.

But to avoid being driven into the sea we needed our own manpower. By last July I had agreed to send in 125,000 and we're going to send in everything that's necessary. But before I did this I reminded those people in Congress, I said to Congress—I don't need you to approve this. I am the commander-in-chief. Nevertheless, if you are going to be in on the landings I want you in on the take-offs.

Now when the going gets tough this pays off. I see these stories that the war over there is going to last three to seven years, although I don't know where these stories come from. I don't know where these stories come from but there are some pretty horrible things going on like the way those communists kill the teachers. So I am glad that Congress came into this act and they passed my resolution five hundred and four to two.

Dulles wanted SEATO to build a line and to give advice to everybody that any aggression against this line was at the other fellow's risk and they shouldn't be blind to the consequences. I don't know what the president will have to use to stop this aggression—whether it will be a kid's slingshot or an A-bomb—but we're gonna do the job.

Johnson got exercised about Presidential authority as Commander in Chief and the fact that he doesn't have to depend on Congressional approval. He said: "I did it in the Dominican Republic. There wasn't any resolution there. I did it in Guantanamo—when Castro cut off the water and I warned him what was going to happen. I ordered my general in Panama to do so—to shoot—and he did."

He then digressed about the (General James M.) Gavin theory that in Vietnam we should lock ourselves up in enclaves. He said: "We can't just hunker down like a jackass in a hailstorm. We must seek the enemy out and deter him. I don't think there is much sense to that Gavin theory but at any rate there *is* a *Gavin* theory. Morse doesn't even have a theory. He just wants to pull out. And then there are the folks who simply want to take out the primary China targets by bombing."

He got into a long session of worrying about India. He was deeply concerned about the food problem. He said, "Cy, did you know that we are sending more food to India this year than the U.S.A. consumes in a year. Yet more people are going to die in India than there are alive in Vietnam."

HONOLULU, *March 7, 1966*

THIS afternoon I went to Pacific Command Headquarters above Pearl Harbor, and first had a briefing on Vietnam, then a talk with Admiral U.S. Grant Sharp, the commander in chief of this combined headquarters.

Pacific Command covers everything from Japan down. Its mission is to defend the United States against an attack through the Pacific and to maintain "a forward strategy on the periphery of the Sino-Soviet bloc in the western Pacific." Also to check Communist subversion. I am interested to note the continued use of NATO's term "forward strategy," the outmoded phrase "Sino-Soviet bloc," and the "holy war" reference to Communist subversion.

PAPEETE, TAHITI, *March 9, 1966*

STROLLED through Papeete, a sordid port town of jerrybuilt shacks, filled with hot dust, stirred by cars, Vespas, and the trucks that are unloading ships bringing in material to be used in constructing the French nuclear test installations. Shops offer tawdry goods at steep prices. A cafe called Vaima is the main afternoon center—overpriced bad goods, customers idling in the heat. At night they gather at Quinn's, where drunks play slot machines, get roaring, and dance to disks.

In 1880 a Tahitian king gave the protected islands to France. There is no monarchist movement remaining. French is taught in the schools but Tahitian at home, and there are Tahitian hours on the radio. Tahitian (a Maori language) differs widely from one island to the next.

AUCKLAND, *March 15, 1966*

STAYING at New Zealand's government house where (Brigadier Sir) Bernard Fergusson is now Governor General (as were his father and two grandfathers).

The protocol is exactly the same as in Buckingham Palace, Bernard being here as a viceroy. He enters and leaves a room first, then his wife, then the various guests. He is served first. He is attended by various aides, in and out of uniform, and she by a lady-in-waiting.

CANBERRA, *March 20, 1966*

LUNCHED at Lord Casey's, now Governor General. He made cutting remarks about Senator Fulbright, who admitted to a press conference here that he didn't know Australia had any soldiers in Vietnam.

SINGAPORE, *March 27, 1966*

TALK with Prime Minister Lee Kuan Yew. Since last August Singapore has been an independent state, having been expelled from the Federation of Malaysia. Lee is an extremely bright man who did very well at Cambridge University and used to be a left-wing socialist. Despite his Marxist background, however, he has done a remarkable job of keeping the Communists from gaining influence in Singapore. He said: "The problem is basically one of finding a balance in this area after an interregnum of two hundred years of European empires. Changes and conflicts were going on among the peoples of this part of the world when it was taken over. Thus, for example, the French arrested the conflicts between Cambodia, the Thais, and the Viets and replaced them by a conflict of those people with France. Now the old problems must resume their place—with very different bits of furniture."

BANGKOK, *March 30, 1966*

WENT to see Graham Martin, the American Ambassador. It is perfectly evident from talking to Martin that Thailand is a military base of great importance for use in any war against China if such a war would come. Incidentally he says that 90 percent of the bombs dropped upon North Vietnam come from here.

DJAKARTA, *April 3, 1966*

WENT to see Adam Malik, new Foreign Minister. Malik is a member of the triumvirate that runs the country. The triumvirate: Malik, Sultan of Djogjakarta, General Suharto. Suharto is the most powerful. Malik said: "We want an independent Vietnam and if the United States can solve that problem by creating a strong South Vietnam, and then go, that is the best solution. The best result would be to have South Vietnam defeat the Vietcong and then be independent." After Malik's went to dine at Ambassador Marshall Green's. He said: Had the United States given up on Vietnam it would have had a bad effect here. If we gave up there now, the Communists would again become bolder here.

The old nightmare of a Chinese-Indonesian nutcracker in Southeast Asia is gone. China wanted Indonesia to be an honorary member of its socialist camp and to develop a Peking-Djakarta axis. The main Chinese weapon is the argument that "We are the wave of the future, the east wind will prevail."

The greatest massacres occurred in October. The probable total of people killed since October 1 is 300,000. This has been mainly done by Moslem youth organizations in east and central Java, Sumatra, Bali, the Celebes, and South Borneo, usually with knives; it was done for a combination of reasons; vengeance on the PKI (Indonesian Communist Party) for bullying; Moslem fanaticism in a rural setting and local mysticism. Indonesians don't like communism, but mainly they don't like Chinese— and identified communism with them.

The abortive coup changed all. People were enraged by the particularly brutal killing of six generals (tortured and mutilated; the army later distributed awful photographs). The gentle Indonesians were shocked when they learned the details and blamed communism. It was a near thing. Had either Nasution or Suharto been killed with the other generals, the Communist leader D. N. Aidit might now be boss instead of dead.

SAIGON, *April 15, 1966*

DRINKS with Major General Edward Lansdale (retired), former CIA chief here and now heading a special pacification team brought out by Lodge.

He says one fundamental problem is the disintegrating effect of U.S. society on this simpler social structure. No Vietnamese thinks we will stay on forever or try to be colonialists. They see that our temporary presence, with its complex way of life, is a phenomenon that will pass.

The values of the social structure have changed. The old cultural hierarchy, the university graduate and government worker, are slipping. Unschooled barmen, taxi operators, prostitutes move up the scale as newly rich. They outbid the wives of the old hierarchs in butcher shops, etc.

Also, inflation has hurt—especially the lower-paid like civil servants and NCO's, some officers. This breeds anti-U.S. feeling, which the VC soup up. The Vietnamese have a tremendous latent xenophobia, but VC propaganda has been heavy-handed and hasn't increased this much.

The VC follows Mao's line: first the mountains, then the countryside, then the cities. It doesn't surface in towns except in Hué—where it will pay for it. There is probably a good VC organization here in Saigon. These people don't commit themselves prematurely. They keep on just enough terror to maintain their own side's morale; collect taxes; keep food out.

SAIGON, *April 20, 1966*

FASCINATING day roaming about the countryside by airplane and helicopter with General William C. Westmoreland, commander of American forces here. Our first destination was Song Be, eighteen miles from Cambodia in an area mostly inhabited by primitive Montagnard tribes. Half-naked, barebreasted, ugly little brown Montagnard women stroll by the air strip. Helicopters laze overhead.

Later: fly on toward the Special Forces camp of Duc Co, near the Cambodian border, over miles of forested jungle occasionally punctuated by white puffs of phosphorous shell.

At Duc Co, the Special Forces unit has organized Montagnard tribesmen into what are called CIDG (Civilian Indigenous Defense Group) units. Tough, tiny tribesmen in leopard-spotted jump suits with blue kerchiefs at their necks, a few Vietnamese among their brown faces, line up in two double lines for review, their weapons at the ready.

The VC has been shooting from Cambodian territory. Captain Conway, commander of the Special Forces unit, was killed near the border and his body dragged toward it. There are four outposts across the border manned by Cambodians; these support the VC.

The tribes here are the Jarai and the Bahnar. An officer gives me a small crossbow and a quiver of arrows such as those the briefers use as pointers. Looks like a toy but is deadly for small game and birds up to thirty-five or forty yards. Larger bows for larger game—including humans.

On to Dak To, another Special Forces camp. The intelligence officer says the VC is "using Cambodia all over the place—right across from us. There is a very extensive VC build-up in Cambodia and Laos."

From here we take a helicopter-gunship, a machine-gunner leaning out of each open portal, Westmoreland, a Special Forces lieutenant-colonel, and I wedged between, strapped to the bench-seat, the wind blowing through. The crews have helmet emblems such as fire-belching dragons, painted above their names—like old-fashioned knights.

Fly on to Dak Pek, Special Forces outpost near the border. W. tells me this is perhaps the most isolated position we hold. We fly by chopper at a pretty high altitude to keep from the hilltops and VC fire. A series of lovely mountains and valleys, with the heights of Laos to the left, fly over a Montagnard village from which last week four hundred women and children were evacuated. Not one woman was pregnant; their men had all been abducted as forced labor by the VC.

We come in amid swirling dust and are greeted by the Special Forces commander, six feet two, two hundred-pound, red-headed Captain Sanford, who leads us once again through two lines of little Montagnards in camouflaged uniforms. He has some 746 of them on his roster. A battery of six 105-mm. howitzers is firing away as we drive a jeep up to his central command post. The 105s were flown in by Chinook helicopters and are supporting a clean-up operation of infantry.

The tribes are the Jeh, Sedang, and Hlang. They have 1,525 Montagnard dependents in camp with them. Around here there are numerous Montagnard hamlets of fifty or more families, which are each controlled by three or four VCs who make them cultivate mountain rice.

We rejoin our U-8 plane and take off for Binh Thuan province, far to the southeast on the sea, where we are to go to Phan Thiet, a fishing town which serves as the headquarters for the 101st Airborne Brigade.

We lose an engine and our radio over VC territory. There is a sputter-sputter-sputter and we begin to lose altitude. Our pilot finally brings us in over the mountains to Pleiku.

SAIGON, *April 22, 1966*

THIS morning Brigadier General J. A. McChristian, chief of intelligence, gave me a briefing on Cambodia.

We are convinced the Cambodian government is providing support to the Vietcong and North Vietnam. Large quantities of Chinese arms, ammunition and aircraft have been furnished to Cambodia. Sihanouk seems convinced the Vietcong will win in South Vietnam, that China will dominate Southeast Asia and is setting his sails accordingly. We have plenty of evidence of Cambodian support of the Vietcong. At least one hundred North Vietnamese prisoners taken in the area have admitted they were previously in Cambodia.

SAIGON, *April 24, 1966*

TALK with Air Vice-Marshal Ky, Prime Minister of South Vietnam, now threatened by a movement to oust him led by a Buddhist political activist. I saw Ky in the Prime Ministerial palace. This large ugly building is separated from the city by barbed wire and guards. A helicopter was standing in the courtyard ready for immediate takeoff. Guards wearing red berets and armed with tommy guns peeped from the corridors.

Ky said he was quite optimistic about the political situation and that he thought the Buddhist agitation had calmed down. He added: "They have no reason to continue their fight. The government and the generals' directorate have signed the electoral decree which satisfies the aspirations not only of the Buddhists but of the majority of the people. Why should they continue to fight? If they do they will only put themselves in a weak and wrong position."

MACAO, *May 2, 1966*

MACAO is a funny little enclave and now exists largely by exporting firecrackers and joss sticks, manufactured on a Portuguese island which also contains a leper colony and poor house.

It is a tiny peninsula (five square miles) with green fields on both sides of the narrow inlet which separates the neck leading to China (and Canton seventy-two miles away). There is a sleepy Portuguese police station and, one hundred yards down the dirt road, a yellow gate through a wall—and then China.

In the green field beyond the shallow inlet, across which Chinese refugees flee on rainy, dark nights, one of a series of rather tall, old-fashioned pillboxes in which China stations sentries. There used to be one in each pillbox; now two. Too often before a replacement would come to his pillbox, find his predecessor's rifle and uniform, the predecessor having skipped across to Macao.

TOKYO, *May 6, 1966*

THIS afternoon I had a talk with Prime Minister Eisaku Sato in his official residence.

He was comforted by the fact that 70 percent of the American people stuck behind Johnson on his Vietnam policy. He professed himself at a loss to understand why the Japanese were largely hostile to the United States over Vietnam. "I can't run this down," he said. "But certainly the government and the leaders of industry are not against our policy."

Sato believed the "domino theory" in Southeast Asia was logically correct and "there is a danger that Chinese influence would extend down to Singapore. We must be alive to the danger of communist expansion." Many Japanese leaders were aware of the threat to Japan of a Chinese grip on the Malacca Straits through which most of Japan's oil comes (from the Middle East).

WASHINGTON, *June 1, 1966*

APPOINTMENT with President Johnson. I went into his office, and Secretary of Defense McNamara was standing there.

The President said: "Why don't you come on in and have lunch with me?" So we trooped down to the small dining room. A table was set with cover and seven places. I told Johnson I only wanted a cup of coffee, and McNamara asked for the same.

The President then, waving me to his right hand, said: "I asked Bob McNamara here to stay on so he could answer any questions you want. Don't hesitate to throw them at him." Soon afterwards Rostow joined us; then eventually Moyers. The President ate little and kept thumbing through a folder of papers.

McNamara, to my surprise, denied that there were some ten thousand North Vietnamese troops in Cambodia. He said the defense intelligence agency had no "confirmed" evidence of the presence of any units inside Cambodia. It was true, as I had reported, that some had been there (near the Chu Phon massif) and some might be basing themselves from there, but there were none there now. I told him of what I'd seen and heard. McNamara said things had apparently "changed" since. I doubt it.

Johnson by then began to talk, warily at first, and then suddenly, as usual, in great torrents. He said:

> I want you to know I'm spending most of my time on Europe these days. We are trying to be constructive there and to establish a calm atmosphere. We have no desire to hurt the French people or to insult de Gaulle. But we look forward to the steady evolution of NATO. We would like it very much, were that possible, to have this occur with France. But we are prepared to do without that if necessary—although I hope not for always.

I don't agree with the French that NATO is no longer important. Our policy is one of dignified acceptance of de Gaulle's invitation to leave. We will leave in a gentlemanly, efficient, and effective way—in due time, and ahead of schedule. Now I want you to protect me on that. I don't want to seem to be threatening so be careful how you use this. We feel that maybe we and the French might want to come back together some time. But we'll leave in a dignified way—ahead of time. Just the way I expect you'd do if I had invited you here to the White House and then one day I said: "Cy, you have to get out of here by June 30." I expect you'd be dignified but you wouldn't wait 'til the last minute.

At this point Johnson went off on another long ramble. He discussed the way too many people thought he spent all his time on Vietnam and thought of nothing else. Thus, that very morning, he had arranged for reporters to come in and ask questions of those in his Cabinet most concerned with Medicare. But then (imitating a whining baby and with exaggerated mimicry): "All they did was keep whining Veetnam, Veetnam, Veetnam."

"This nation, if it's worthy of its leadership, mustn't concentrate only on Vietnam but on freedom all over the world. But don't you forget that now 18 million people [those who benefit under Medicare] have now had the yoke taken off their backs and they don't just have to keep worrying about which of their children is going to help them out. That's what I call progress."

Johnson asked when I was going back and I told him next week. He said: "We love France and look on her with sorrow rather than with anger. We hope the French people will not always feel about us the way they do right now—or maybe they don't. General de Gaulle may even find that there are some things he can work out with us. But right now it would be hypocritical if we thanked or complimented him."

WASHINGTON, *June 3, 1966*

LONG talk with Dean Acheson, who has been put in charge of preparing the U.S. position on the NATO crisis precipitated by de Gaulle.

I started by asking what Dean thought of the report that de Gaulle in Moscow might offer to pull back his two divisions from West Germany if Russia withdrew two divisions from East Germany. Acheson said he had heard such reports but they were pure speculation. "France is now like Russia under Stalin. There is no real source of information prior to the event."

It will be very difficult to negotiate a new agreement on NATO overflights across France. He says: "We can't make a deal. De Gaulle won't yield. However, if he says there can be no over-flights that will end any pose of France remaining an ally. Therefore he will probably continue permitting over-flights on a monthly basis. He will restrict things enough to embarrass us but not to wreck us."

Acheson scoffs at those who say that NATO will be stronger because de Gaulle has prodded it into necessary action. He quotes General Lemnitzer as saying "one more benefit of this sort and we will be out of business."

WASHINGTON, *June 4, 1966*

THIS morning saw Vice-President Humphrey. Rather to my surprise he said: "The odds are against my ever being president. I reckon the chance is only one in twenty. The way I see my future I shall probably go back to the Senate. But I like my job and it is a satisfying feeling to know that you can help to make things good."

Humphrey agreed that the political rot in the United States occasioned by Vietnam had become a great deal worse. He added that this "will take a heavy political toll." But he said his own position on Vietnam was not just a Lyndon Johnson position. He had drawn up a paper in August 1964, before he had been elected Vice-President, in which he recommended a policy on Vietnam very similar to that we are now following.

PARIS, *June 23, 1966*

LUNCHED with Martial de la Fournière, right hand of (future Prime Minister) Pierre Messmer. He was sent to Indochina in 1946. (Admiral Thierry) d'Argenlieu, the imperialist-minded French governor, wanted bloodshed to reconquer Indochina for France. And Ho Chi Minh and Giap wanted bloodshed to expel the French.

F. once gave a dinner for Giap, and among the guests was an Armenian Frenchman who had taught Giap as a youngster. Giap sat rudely, saying nothing, until the Armenian recalled the days when he had taught the general, and said: "Surely you must have something in common with the French." For the first time Giap opened his mouth. "Yes," he said, "they killed my father. They killed my brother. They imprisoned my mother. I have much in common with them."

BONN, *August 2, 1966*

AGREEABLE talk with old Dr. Adenauer (the ex-Chancellor) today in his office in the Bundesrat. I had been told he tires easily nowadays (at the age of ninety-one). But I was with him from noon until 1:20 P.M.; and it was I who broke off the conversation. He seemed prepared to go on indefinitely. His hearing and eyesight are excellent; no glasses. It is a remarkable physical triumph.

I asked if he thought Europe was actually entering a new epoch. He said:

Look at the map. Look at the size of the Soviet Union. In Europe alone it is enormous and yet more than half of it is in Asia. The rest of Europe is small compared with Russia.

Europe must not only stay together but there can be no united Europe without the United States. We need the United States by all means. If you are not with us, Europe will ultimately, in the long run, come under Russia's sway.

I am convinced the basic political line of Russia is this: if Russia can attract France and Germany into its sphere it will then be stronger even than the United States, both economically and militarily. And this would also enhance Russia's position in its confrontation with China. I have no doubt that this is the object of Russian policy, to gain control of France and Germany.

I put the following to Adenauer: "If by some magic you were suddenly made president of the United States, what would you do about Vietnam?" He looked at me sadly for a moment, then with a twinkle he said:

First of all, if I were president of the United States I wouldn't compare Wilson with Churchill (as Johnson just did last week). Anyone who can say that doesn't know much about Churchill.

As for Vietnam, it wasn't Johnson who started it you know, it was Kennedy. Johnson inherited it. Johnson has to eat the soup that Kennedy cooked.

But you must realize there is nothing humiliating or dishonest if a great nation discovers that a certain course of action is much more difficult than it had expected and therefore, in all sincerity, it tries to get out of it. And you must get out of Vietnam, get out of the problem. That is the only way.

Of course I don't think in terms of sudden, total, dishonest withdrawal in Vietnam. But is growing escalation the answer? Where will it lead? And won't there be a very bad effect on the American people as they begin to realize the extent of their own losses?

President Kennedy once told me that the most significant and dangerous area for the United States was Latin America, that this was of greatest importance to you, and that if communism came there he simply didn't know what would follow. So you can see the difference in outlooks: that was the same President Kennedy who started everything in Vietnam, who didn't heed de Gaulle's warnings not to get embroiled.

And Johnson's way out is certainly not by getting more and more strongly in. If I take a road and I find that I am going in the wrong direction, certainly I see no purpose in continuing along it. Instead, I seek a new road.

I'm greatly, gravely worried about the whole world. The United States is so seized by the Vietnam problem that there is a danger it, the greatest world power, will overlook other problems it must face. Europe, after all, is still the most important area for the United States, especially in political terms.

ATHENS, *October 1, 1966*

YESTERDAY evening I talked for an hour and three-quarters with young King Constantine at his palace at Tatoi. I asked what he thought would be the result of an Andreas Papandreou government if Andreas ever managed to get himself elected Prime Minister. He said: "Judging from his press statements and from his past history that would probably be just the push that Greece needs to go off the cliff. He would certainly, I suspect, swing the country toward the East and neutralism. We always go to the edge of the cliff and then, from the very edge, turn back. But I think with him at the helm we would go right over. Not his father. His father has some good men around him and I rather like the old man. But Andreas would get us over the cliff."

Constantine said he was convinced that the army is quite reliable now and that there is absolutely no danger of political infiltration or a coup.

I said to the King that I was going to ask a very indiscreet question: namely, would he bypass the Constitution or install a dictatorship under any circumstances, for example to prevent Greece from "going over the cliff" under Andreas? I recalled how his father had called me in, in 1949, to ask my advice on putting in a dictatorship under (Field Marshal Alexander) Papagos and how I had warned him against it. He answered:

> The best way to answer you is this. I will do my best to see that this country gets back to a peaceful, quiet, prosperous life. But you can be quite sure that if it depends on me to save this country from disaster, I will be ready to bypass one or two paragraphs of the constitution if necessary—that is to say if it is necessary in my opinion I will do it to protect Greece.
>
> I want to go down in history as willing to save Greece from what I regard as evil, and I know I am not evil myself. The question of the form is difficult. Will one have to act through a political party? Through generals? Through civilians? Would it have to be a real dictatorship or just the suspension of one or two paragraphs of the constitution on a temporary basis? I do not know and I hope it will never come to that, but if necessary I would surely act.

BUCHAREST, *October 9, 1966*

I DROVE to Transylvania in a rather shaky Soviet Volga with a little government interpreter named Bec. He speaks fluent but only fair English, is a party member, and has a touching innocence in all the wondrous accomplishments of "planification." He thought it was sheer propaganda when I told him America had invented basketball and self-service groceries, both of which he assumed were Russian.

We rattled on through the flat Transylvania plateau past vineyards, duck ponds, occasional dovecotes, to Alba Iulia. From before Alba Iulia it is evident big preparations have been made for Nicolae Ceausescu's visit: banners (party and national), peanuts, arches of evergreen, a few slogans: the best blankets and rugs laid out on windowsills along the main streets. Here and there officers in boots and Soviet-type uniforms.

Ceausescu, boss of the Communist Party, reads his speech from small pages of manuscript, has a good, resonant voice in the microphone. He is short, with dark curly hair, slightly florid complexion, fattish, black eyes, cleft chin, wearing a four-button, homespun squire's suit with high button-down breast pockets.

Afterward I was taken to C.'s open American car, over the red carpet (embroidered rug) leading to the dais, by a member of the party "protocol" and an "activist" of the Central Committee who told me Ceausescu would see me. Bec kept saying: "But he has never seen a noncommunist journalist before."

Suddenly C., diminutive and almost invisible, emerged from the throng, shook my hand, looked up with a poker face. I started asking questions right away, making B. translate, and C. looked puzzled but answered.

C: We expressed our position on European security at the Warsaw pact conference that was held in Bucharest this summer. Everyone is familiar with our position. Essentially, it is that the European countries should be allowed to solve their own problems without any interference by non-Europeans.

CLS: I assume by that you mean the U.S.A. Do you?

C: Yes, the U.S.A. is not European.

CLS: Russia?

C: Russia is European. How would you feel if Europe demanded a right to decide on America's future? What right have you here?

CLS: Well, we came over twice to save Europe, including Rumania, to liberate it. I think this gives us some right. And Germany, the biggest problem bequeathed by World War II, remains to be settled. There is no peace there. Many American men were killed to defeat the Nazis, after all.

C (truculently): America lost fewer soldiers in World War II than Rumania.

CLS: Mr. Ceausescu, you must remember that we fought on only one side. (Nudge to Bec.) Be sure and translate that. (Scarcely disguised smiles in entourage, which recalled that until autumn 1944 Rumania was with Nazis.)

BELGRADE, *October 13, 1966*

THIS morning saw Burke Elbrick, U.S. Ambassador. He says the Jugoslav motto should be: "We don't know where we're going but we're on our way."

PARIS, *December 2, 1966*

YESTERDAY evening Don Juan, the Spanish pretender to the throne, dropped in for a drink together with Count Motrico, former Spanish Ambassador here. Don Juan is a big bruiser. He looked rugged and healthy, with a beaked face like a ship's figurehead.

Don Juan said: "Franco is trying to perpetuate a period of legitimacy for his own kind of legitimacy." He claims Franco is deliberately avoiding any indication as to which royal candidate he favors for the eventual succession. He said that he and his supporters would have to move very quickly the minute Franco died in order to avoid being out-maneuvered.

Don Juan said Franco has not made any arrangements with Juan Carlos, Don Juan's son. His son "feels the pressure and is concerned but has not made a deal with Franco." But he seemed a little bit skittish on this, and I asked him point-blank whether his son would support him or oppose him. "I don't think you can say my son has a feeling against *me* but there are some who may think that he would be more convenient in terms of arranging a Franco-like solution after Franco."

I asked if Sophia, Juan Carlos' Greek wife, was exerting any political influence. He said that her mother, Queen Frederika, "quite obviously wants her daughter to be a queen just as soon as possible and she is pushing my son. She is not a Greek, she is a Prussian." (Frederika is the Kaiser's granddaughter.) "It got so bad that I had to tell her not to meddle in our affairs."

PARIS, *December 5, 1966*

LUNCHED for two and a quarter hours with André Malraux, a memorable experience. Emerging from a concentrated conversation with Malraux must be like emerging from a Bessemer steel furnace and discovering that one is still intact. He is an incredible man. He has been one of the great novelists of the twentieth century; he is one of the great experts on painting and sculpture; he was a soldier-adventurer of success and courage, having commanded a fighter unit on the Republican side in the Spanish Civil War and, having commanded a large Maqui unit in occupied France, holding the equivalent rank of brigadier general. He has been a Cabinet minister for years. Now he says: "It will not be a bad monument if, when I die, I shall have left one hundred new museums in France behind me."

Malraux thought the most important recent event was the naming of Madam Mao Tse-tung (Chiang Ching) as cultural consultant to the general political department of the Chinese army. It was immensely significant that she had been named to this new post, and it showed Mao's determination to take over control of the army and to put an end to the insolence of the Red Guard youth. Mao was very worried about the youth. He had confessed to Malraux during Malraux's visit to Peking in July and August

1965 that he knew the youth of China was against him. They did not seem to have the messianic qualities required.

He said Mao hasn't the remotest idea of what the United States is like and what the power of an industrialized state amounts to. He is building up an extraordinary torrent of hatred for the United States among the young Chinese; but it is a wasted emotion that can lead to nothing. Mao doesn't want to have a war with the United States, and it is perfectly obvious that the United States is never going to invade China. The Vietnam situation is impossible, and nobody can do anything with a man like Ky. But if there is an embroilment between the United States and China, all the United States has to do is destroy ten Chinese cities and it will set back Mao's revolution by fifty years. He cannot afford this.

Mao said one thing of tremendous interest. Malraux quoted him: "We, people like de Gaulle and myself, have no successors." It was perfectly evident that Mao thinks whatever has to be done will have to be done by himself. Malraux told this to de Gaulle when he came back to Paris, and de Gaulle was fascinated.

Malraux said Kennedy's role in history had been assured by the fact of his assassination and that even lesser men were ennobled by political murder.

I told him that once when I dined at the White House, Kennedy had said: "I don't understand Malraux. He is Jackie's friend." Malraux said this was correct, and he added that he had an enormous admiration for Jackie, that she had a great wisdom about what she could do and what she could not do, where she could interfere with her husband and where she could not interfere. He said she would be a first-class President, a woman of real talent. I suggested that she would also be an excellent ambassador, and maybe she could restore the electric current between France and the United States to which I had referred earlier.

He agreed—but he added: "It all depends for whom you are ambassador. I don't think she would do very well under Johnson." He didn't smile.

Malraux knew both General Pechkov, the French Foreign Legion officer and diplomat who has just died, and his stepfather, Maxim Gorki. He said Gorki always showed traces of his impoverished youth, and that he remembers vividly Gorki with an enormous mound of ice cream and being delighted to let the waiter pay for it.

He said Picasso is a very peculiar man who lives in his own private world where he is the absolute emperor. At various times it has included Françoise Gilot, his former mistress, Marie-Laure de Noailles, and Malraux himself. But Picasso doesn't like to come out of his world and, for example, was very frightened when he heard that de Gaulle was going to see his exhibition in Paris.

EXCELLENT talk with de Gaulle. I asked whether he thought England could come into the Common Market and whether it could really qualify as a "European" country. He said:

> Certainly up until now, until this moment, I frankly don't think that England could qualify for admission. It doesn't resemble the continental countries economically. Britain still thinks of itself as a world country and not a continental country. Its economic function is based on transit of goods, on banking and shipping. This is not the same thing as exists in Europe, which has another kind of industrial basis.
>
> Perhaps the British can change but the British are not great changers and I do not foresee that they will make any fundamental alterations. And yet their present role as a world power is far too much for them. They are more and more impoverished. Their burden has become too great. They cannot carry the load any more.

I asked if he foresaw an eventual reunification of Germany or simply a confederation of two German states under separate governments. He replied:

> I don't know. It is hard to foresee this. There is, of course, the basic fact that there is only one German people, not several. There is the same German people on one side and on the other side of the Berlin wall, for example, but this fact alone is not enough to make for a single German state.
>
> You should remember that this has always been the history of Germany. It is very hard to make German unity. Wilhelm I and Wilhelm II managed to do it. And it was reestablished under Hitler. But don't forget, German unity is never necessary. [And there he stressed the word *necessary*.] For a long, long time Germany has consisted of a single people but several states, and this fact remains today. It is an inescapable fact that there is one people but it is divided between the federal government and a communist government in the Eastern zone. This doesn't prevent the existence of one people; but it also does not prevent the existence of two states.
>
> Anything else must develop gradually as the over-all European situation develops, and the Russians must accept whatever changes come about. This will take a considerable amount of time. So, that is our policy on this. There must first be détente in Europe—and then let the German people find themselves within it.

I asked him whether he considered France to be anti-American. "Certainly not," he said.

> We are not anti-American. But you must remember that you are a big people, a colossal power. You have a huge industry, a gigantic economy and military force which give you enormous political power, the greatest in the world. Inevitably a country like France, wanting its own independence, doesn't want to be dominated, led by or integrated into your system. But this

does not make us hostile to you, not at all. We are simply taking precautions to avoid being absorbed because you are so especially powerful.

Perforce [*forcement*] a country like France must be on the alert to preserve its own personality. But the same thing is true vis-à-vis the Soviets. Without the United States—or with a less powerful United States—we would have to be very much on the alert against the Soviets. Indeed, we are on the alert vis-à-vis the Soviets and we do not wish to be absorbed by them. We are for an equilibrium. We are obliged to be for an equilibrium by the simple geographical and political facts. We oppose any hegemony, either American or Russian. But this does not prevent friendship. There is no instinctive ill will [*malveillance*] against the United States here in France.

I asked if he contemplated any political accord with Russia. He said: "Certainly there is cooperation in the sense of a concerted viewpoint on big political questions such as Germany and Vietnam. There are no major differences at this moment between us on these big issues. But I don't foresee any kind of a treaty or pact with them. Why? To do what?"

I asked whether he thought China would be a superpower in the future. Again without any hesitation he said: "Certainly. But in thirty years. And when this happens China will make claims against everybody, against the whole world, but above all against Russia. China will make claims against India. It will insist on expelling United States influence from Formosa, from South Korea, and it will even insist on removing your protectorate from Japan. But Russia, the Soviets, will feel tremendous pressure."

Was he worried about the chances of a world war exploding out of Vietnam? He said: "There will be no world war because of Vietnam. Nevertheless, without producing a world war, Vietnam prevents a true world détente and continued tension can lead anywhere, but I do not think it will lead to war."

I asked him which personage living or dead had most influenced him. He replied—*tout court*—

My father. My father was a great influence on my formation. He was a modest professor but a very eminent man, very cultivated and a gentleman, very balanced and reasonable, very, very patriotic. His influence on my formation was capital.

Then, also, there was Pétain. Pétain also had a great influence on my formation when I knew him as a young officer. I learned much from his method and manner of command when I was a lieutenant and he was my colonel. His influence was great but when he ceased to be the same man it ended, of course. Events separated us and turned us against each other. But he ended by moving toward me. Did you know that he sent someone to me, Admiral [Paul] Auphan, when I came to Paris in 1944? Auphan brought me a message from Pétain saying, "You must take over, you must lead France," but, of course, that was too late, alas, and you know how things ended.

PARIS, *January 12, 1967*

LUNCHED with Étienne Burin des Roziers, Secretary General of the Elysée. Étienne suggested that I should be the vis-à-vis interviewing de Gaulle on French television during the campaign performance prior to the March elections this year. I explained this would be quite out of the question; I could not possibly mix into the politics of a foreign country.

PARIS, *January 24, 1967*

LUNCHED with Étienne Manac'h. He said that last August (1966) the Cultural Revolution began in China. Even before that, Hanoi had started to show signs of increasing independence of Peking. The North Vietnamese are fearful that if the Chinese troubles continue there may be serious repercussions on their supply lines. And in recent months there has been a steady growth of Soviet influence in Hanoi.

The last congress of the Chinese Communist Party was in 1956, Manac'h points out. That was a "peace congress" and sponsored the famous "hundred flowers" line. It can be likened to Khrushchev's twentieth congress in Russia, where de-Stalinization began. There was no split with Russia, and the congress was followed by a deliberate effort by the Chinese to woo support in Asia and Africa. But since then, Mao's policy has swerved dramatically away from that peaceful line and has become increasingly hostile to both the United States and Russia.

The *heart* of the problem in China now is symbolized by the wall posters everyone reads instead of the press. Because of his quarrel with the apparatus of the party, Mao has had to create parallel institutions and irregular channels. After all, the party hierarchy still controls the regular apparatus. So there is an irregular kind of guerrilla parallel hierarchy being created by Mao. He is, as it were, using the techniques of revolutionary warfare against the revolution itself.

For the first time in history, says Manac'h, a Communist country is employing mechanisms outside the Communist Party for political purposes. This is the reason for the Red Guard made up of students. Normally in Communist countries, crises are regulated inside the party, which supervises, purges, arrests, tries, confesses, etc. The party is the only channel. Even in Russia, when the secret police took over from the normal party apparatus, they were controlled by Stalin as Secretary General of the party. But in China, Mao has chosen a nonparty device—the students and the Red Guard.

Without going into detail on the names of the factional leaders, Manac'h says that the Maoists are led by Mao himself and Lin Piao and the opposition is led by Liu Shao Chi, president of the republic (he succeeded Mao in that post) and Teng Shiao Ping, Secretary General of the Communist Party and therefore boss of the party hierarchy.

Chou En-lai falls in between these two groups, but he is a very important man. As Prime Minister he represents the state and tries to keep the state functioning.

The Russians, says Manac'h, now openly support Liu and the Chinese Communist Party hierarchy against Mao and Lin. Just this month Brezhnev told this to the Poles. What we now have is really a war of succession between Lin Piao and Liu Shao Chi.

PARIS, *February 21, 1967*

THIS afternoon I had a talk with Mai Van Bo, head of the North Vietnamese delegation here in Paris and Hanoi's most important diplomat in Europe.

Mai said there could be no conversations until there was first a definite and unconditional end to American bombing in the north. I asked what effect the Sino-Soviet dispute was having on the war, and he said it was "only speculating" to discern any effect. He added: "We are more determined than ever to follow our own independent policy. World events do not influence us. We run our own affairs."

I then said I wanted to go to Hanoi and showed him my passport with its State Department authority to visit North Vietnam. He said, "Your name is well known. Of course, there are many applications for visas at this time but I think that yours requires very special attention."

(I never got it.)

LONDON, *March 7, 1967*

DINED tonight with Dick Nixon. His gestures are strange (the way he continually moves his hands), and his heavy jaw is puffy. As a man I like him, but I simply don't know how he would be as a national leader—in charge.

He talked a lot about himself. His great hero is Churchill, and no one else of our time has similarly affected him. He has great respect and affection for the British. Saw Macmillan today and admires him. Thinks Harold Wilson has shown courage and ability although he overplayed his hand on Vietnam indicating things were nearer a settlement (with Kosygin) than was true. Nixon thinks we must keep the British going east of Suez even if we have to finance them, because we need their expertise on China.

He thinks Bobby Kennedy will make his play in 1968, either for President or Vice-President. Nineteen seventy-two is too far away. People will have forgotten the magic of his name and he will have suffered from too much exposure then. Johnson hates him (and vice versa), but they still might join on a ticket. Bobby knows there's no point in having a Republican elected in 1968. Nixon strongly disapproves of Bobby's Vietnam attitude and "playing politics" at the country's expense.

Obviously Dick is going to make one more big run for the Presidency next year and is going to make foreign policy a big issue. He says Vietnam would be an almost impossible GOP issue; hopes (politically as well as other reasons) the war is over. Thinks we are ignoring Europe too much.

He says the two men who most influenced him are his Whittier College football coach, an Indian former All-American named Chief Newman, and his history professor, named Smith. Dick never made the team after four years of trying, but Newman inculcated in him a competitive spirit, the need to keep trying against all odds. Smith taught him to love history. Had he not gone into a political career, he wanted to teach English history. Still loves to read history and biography most. He says writing comes very hard to him, and slow; he likes to outline and compose his thoughts.

BONN, *March 16, 1967*

THIS morning I met Kurt Georg Kiesinger, the new Chancellor of West Germany. He said de Gaulle "really favors German unification." I expressed great doubt on this, and Kiesinger looked surprised. He said de Gaulle had reassured him on this point.

Kiesinger was convinced the Russians wanted to feel free of worries on Europe in order to face their problem of China. He had discussed this with Khrushchev in Moscow in 1955. Khrushchev pointed out the danger of all those Chinese soldiers who could survive if each day they had a handful of rice. He told Kiesinger he wanted to bring 2 million Russian troops back to work on farms and factories in Siberia. "I said he should invite in the Chinese," said Kiesinger.

BRUSSELS, *April 12, 1967*

PLEASANT lunch and chat with Paul-Henri Spaak. He says NATO lacks leadership from the United States now. We are too involved in Asia. Look at what Vietnam is doing to NATO. All the alliance's main strains have been occasioned by issues outside the Atlantic area—Korea, Suez, Cuba, Vietnam.

If the United States got out of Vietnam, Europe would allow itself a sigh of relief—because Europe doesn't understand the problem. It would be like Europe's sigh of relief after Munich. "A policy of sighs is no good. And I say that although I am a man of peace and I abhor war."

CASTEAU, BELGIUM, *April 13, 1967*

THIS afternoon I went out to the new SHAPE headquarters for the first time, driving down from Brussels. I had a long talk with Lemnitzer. I asked if, in reality, he considered France as still an ally, even if it wasn't in the NATO organization. He said no. "France is no longer in the alliance."

22

E ARLY THIS MORNING THERE WAS A COUP D'ÉTAT IN GREECE. COMmunications have been cut off. Shortly before noon I talked to (Constantine) Caramanlis (former Prime Minister, now a voluntary exile here) on the telephone. He thinks this is a dead-end street and on the road to disaster.

ARMED sailors and soldiers with helmets are in front of some ministries, and armored personnel carriers with machine guns trained on the surrounding streets are parked outside Parliament. I saw a police car go by containing a young man shackled between two gendarmes.

Began my peregrinations with Brigadier General Stylianos Pattakos, one of the three prime movers of the military coup d'état and a former tank commander.

I asked when the plot had started, how and by whom. He said this information was "classified," and the leaders were "the Greek army." I asked him what the code name of the operation was, and he said "Plan Prometheus."

Pattakos said the preelection campaign for the scheduled May elections had been slated to start last weekend (April 22–23). According to the plotters' information the Communists had planned to use the occasion to provoke bloodshed. Pattakos continued: "We wanted to avoid harming innocent people."

Did Pattakos call this regime "a dictatorship"? He said no. I asked him then to please define what it could be called. "Freedom under law," was the curious reply. The junta hoped to establish a system somewhere between that of the United States and Gaullist France.

I asked if both George and Andreas Papandreou would be tried and on what charges. He said Andreas would be tried for treason but that his father, George, would not be tried and was being kept "for his own sake" in a hospital—"the best army hospital in the Athens area."

I asked whether he had read any political philosophers. He quite solemnly said: "Abraham Lincoln." If it were not also frightening, it would be funny.

I then called on Colonel George Papadopoulos, minister to the Prime Minister's office. Papadopoulos is even shorter than Pattakos but has a considerably more intelligent appearance: flat face with shrewd eyes and high forehead.

I asked which of the three—Pattakos, Papadopoulos, and Colonel Nikolaos Makarezos, Minister of Coordination, was boss. He said: "The chief of the general staff is the boss." He then conceded that Spandidakis had not been kept informed about the conspiracy until it actually broke out—although he joined it promptly. My own assumption is that Papadopoulos is *primus inter pares*."

Papadopoulos said: "We enjoy the confidence of the entire officers' corps and we merely initiated what they wanted." He said that when they were ready to strike, "the chief of staff was briefed and he accepted." The briefing had been done by "Makarezos, Pattakos, and me."

A limited number of officers—about fifteen—had been brought into the picture one day before the actual outbreak on April 21. The rest were only brought in fourteen hours before the plot exploded. In other words they came in at noon on Thursday, April 20 and the coup took place at 2:00 A.M. on Friday, April 21.

I asked who was the political philosopher of this revolution. He answered: "Aristotle, basically. [An odd mixture with Abraham Lincoln.] Part of Aristotle's theory is that the state intervenes in the regulation of the individual and different public bodies. I would describe our ideology as 'directed liberalism.' No, perhaps 'guided liberalism' is the philosophy we are seeking to bring about. At least, that is as I see it. I would feel at ease under the American system. I would like all Greeks to feel much as American citizens do."

I asked why the King had initially opposed the coup. He answered: "The king did not oppose it. He was simply displeased because we acted without his knowledge. And the king as head of a constitutional government would naturally oppose our movement."

I then went down to see the Prime Minister, Constantine Kollias, previously chief prosecutor of the supreme court. Kollias is sixty-six, a short, plump, little man with black hair, rather pink cheeks, moustache. He said "seven or eight" articles of the Constitution had been suspended. Kollias hoped that "even if the U.S.A. changes its policy we Greeks will never alter our friendship for the Americans."

I concluded my morning with Defense Minister and Vice-Premier (General G.) Spandidakis.

I asked Spandidakis how he could be sure the armed forces supported the coup. I pointed out that, after all, only forty-eight hours before the coup took place he did not know anything about it. So how could he be confident there is no plot brewing against him right now?

Today, he thought, the army was "completely dedicated to its military duties. But many political leaders in the past were corrupt and the nation's youth was abandoned and without guidance. There was a general feeling in the army of the necessity to intervene. I can say that the coup really represented the initiative of the entire army."

He said the coup had succeeded in three hours. It was done in order to prevent the possibility of a Communist coup. The army had drawn up a plan against a Communist coup—"the kind of plan any defense staff has in any country. I only had to implement this plan." The particular plan used had been drawn up about eighteen months ago.

I asked if the coup plot as well as the long-range plan which enabled the coup to work so well had also been named "Prometheus"—in other words was that the code name for the coup itself as well as for the blueprint on which it functioned? He said yes.

ATHENS, *April 29, 1967*

THIS is the second dictatorship I have seen in Greece. The first, under Metaxas, was also in the King's name. Oddly enough many old liberal opponents of dictatorship *one* are now in favor of dictatorship *two*. Perhaps the reason is an emphasis on the adjective "old" as compared with "liberal."

This morning I went to see Colonel Nikolaos Makarezos, Minister of Economic Coordination and third of the triumvirate responsible for the coup. Makarezos said: "Our positive aim was to achieve the goals that had been frustrated by the political bankruptcy of the past. Greece belongs to the Western world and to NATO, and we had to make sure that this would continue. Our primary aim was to develop closer ties with the United States because our government sees the United States as the leader of the free world."

When I was through with Makarezos I got one of his aides to take me downstairs, put me in a taxi, and instruct the driver to take me to the Hotel Pikermi, in Pikermi, where Andreas Papandreou is held. As we drove by the Greek general headquarters, which they rather proudly call "the Pentagon," I noticed three tanks dispersed at the entrance with one armored personnel carrier behind them.

It was a bright, warm, spring day with everything from the olive trees to the late April grass glowing. Even the Pikermi Hotel, despite its present dour assignment, looked merry. The taxi driver had no idea what was going on; but both gates of the hotel were locked, and he had to stop. There were helmeted guards with bayoneted rifles all over the place, plus two armored cars and another American armored personnel carrier.

An extremely fat regular-army captain strode down the driveway. The gate was opened, he read my permit, ordered the taxi driver to park outside and waved me in. He offered me a Nescafé, and then an unusually tall lieutenant—a handsome fellow about six foot three inches—came down the stairs and joined us. His English was excellent.

The captain asked if I wanted to see any other people incarcerated in the hotel. I said no, only Andreas. They took me upstairs and down a small, narrow hall. Outside each door stood a soldier wearing a helmet and carrying a bayoneted rifle. The captain opened one door, and I squeezed by his pot belly to see Andreas stretched out on a bed and another man sitting in an armchair. Greek hotel rooms are small, and this was on the small side for a Greek hotel room. There were two narrow twin beds; I eventually sat down on the corner of one of them. The captain and the lieutenant stood in the doorway.

Andreas got up off his bed and greeted me with unusual cordiality and warmth as I entered the room. He was wearing a blue Brooks Brothers shirt (with no necktie), trousers and socks. He looked extremely well. He made a great effort to be casual, but underneath it I could see he was quite nervous.

He shook hands with a solid grip, grinned widely and said: "You and I have exchanged some pretty hard words in the past and they have been in public. Well, it is all over. Let's forget it. I am glad to see you." Then he introduced me to his roommate, a fat, oily, dark character named Alevras, a Center Union deputy.

Andreas stretched out on the bed, and I squatted on the next bed explaining meanwhile: "Andreas, as I understand the ground rules I am not supposed to ask you anything dealing with politics. But you can tell me anything you feel like and before you start I want to tell you that I saw your father this morning and although he did not feel like talking he looked pretty well physically."

He admitted the coup had been a total surprise. He had had not the slightest advance suspicion. After a late dinner at the Hilton Hotel, he had come home and had been asleep about an hour when the army arrived for him at the door. He was sleeping heavily when the bell rang, and I gather that they busted in when there was not a swift answer.

Andreas had a few detective stories in English beside his bed and told me he would like to get a few more plus at least one serious book. He asked me to call his wife and request her to send some. He gave me the telephone number and told me to tell his wife "you and I have made up." Poor fellow, I guess we have in a way but I have not changed my mind about him.

ATHENS, *May 2, 1967*

I TOOK a taxi to Kifissia, where Panayotis Canellopoulos (former Prime Minister) is staying in the house of his wife's nephew, a comfortable old-fashioned place surrounded by a large wall and with shady trees in the garden.

The coup had come as a total surprise. He was arrested at 2:55 A.M. A group of officers and men burst into his apartment armed with tommy guns. He did not know if they were really army, or disguised Communists. He had a revolver but they grabbed it. Canellopoulos explained: "We have to have a revolver here with communism such a threat." He said King Constantine tried to call him, but the telephone was cut. At last he was "obliged" to follow. Outside, where there were more tommy gunners, he told the captain: "Give me back my revolver or you can kill me here."

Many people heard him say this, and the captain returned the revolver. He did this because he was still Prime Minister of Greece and could not permit any officers to take his gun; also because he calculated that if they were Communists they would not return the weapon to him. He wanted the revolver so that if anyone tried to force him to sign a paper against his will, he could kill himself.

Saturday, Pattakos and General Spandidakis told Canellopoulos he could go home under house arrest, and he requested the same privilege for all other Cabinet ministers. It was granted. He is still under house arrest.

ATHENS, *May 3, 1967*

I SPENT two hours this morning with King Constantine. He gave me a warm handclasp when I came into his study, and we sat down, beside the fireplace. He told me he wanted me to know the facts. Then he started talking a mile a minute. He said:

I was out at Tatoi [his country place] and the very first I heard about the coup was around 2:15 Friday morning. I had been reading late and just dozed off when the telephone rang. I had told the telephone center not to disturb me. But it rang again and I picked it up. It was my secretary, Arnaoutis. He is a trusted friend of mine. He shouted into the phone: "They are smashing my door in with guns." "Who?" I asked. "I don't know," he shouted.

I told him: "Hold on. I am coming to help you."

Arnaoutis said, "For God's sake don't come, call the police. Have they announced anything to you? What's the army doing? I am trying to get reinforcements sent up to Tatoi."

Constantine summoned his aide-de-camp immediately and told him to double the guards and to alert everybody on the royal property. He continued:

I grabbed my revolver. My ADC came and the guards took up their positions. Then I rang up another officer, a friend of mine, and told him to help Arnaoutis. Soon after that he reported to me he couldn't help because there were ten soldiers with machine guns outside Arnaoutis's house.

I called my mother at her house. The telephones hadn't been cut yet. So I asked her to get my sister and her children (who are visiting from Spain) all into the same part of the house and I told her I was trying to send reinforcements. Then the phones were cut.

My mother told me later that after that two tanks arrived at her house; she was delighted, assuming these were the reinforcements I had promised her. Only too late she realized they were working for the coup. One officer in the group that surrounded her put a machine gun right on top of her house, and when she demanded that they let her come and see me, they refused.

It is hard for me to remember all this in consecutive order. [The King rubbed his hands over his face and knuckled his eyes.] I think it was about this time that [Dimitri S.] Bitsios called me up. You know, my counselor. I told him to get hold of the prime minister and tell him to do something.

Bitsios rang up Canellopoulos who was then standing in his apartment with a bunch of coup officers around him, one of them holding a tommy gun in his tummy so Canellopoulos couldn't do anything.

Then I alerted the air force. I told them to send some men right away to Arnaoutis's house but it was too late. The air force did send some men over to Tatoi, but by the time they got here the tanks of the coup were starting to roll up and they turned back the air force, so I instructed my guards that they should only shoot if they were shot at.

Arnaoutis has one of those old-fashioned houses in Psychiko with great big iron grille doors and the coup people couldn't get in. They kept beating on the door and shooting through it and his poor wife fainted dead away. But Arnaoutis kept his head. They kept shouting to him demanding that he open the door but he kept ringing up various people trying to get help.

They started machine-gunning the house right into the hall, but he had gone into the basement and had come up again the back way so he was actually sitting quietly in a room off the hall when they finally burst in and started looking for him in the cellar. But the poor fellow couldn't escape. They caught him and manhandled him. They hit him and cursed him. They finally took him to the "Pentagon" and locked him up.

Suddenly [George] Rallis [the Minister of Justice] got through to me on the telephone. By God, that was good news. He has an enormously low deep voice, you know. He said to me: "I managed to get away. Right now I am in Maroussi police station." [Maroussi is a village between Athens and Tatoi.]

I interrupted the King and said I couldn't understand how he had kept going on the telephone all this time, but he explained that his phones had not been cut for more than an hour after the coup started at 2:00 A.M. Friday, April 21.

He continued:

I told Rallis to mobilize the troops in the north and tell them to come down and take over Athens. A few minutes later Rallis called back as soon

as he had finished drafting an order. The order said that the Greek government had been arrested and the only free minister of the government, Rallis,
under the direct orders of the king, was commanding all troops in the north
to proceed south immediately and to act on behalf of the king.

By now the tanks had taken up their positions outside my house. It was
still dark. I sent word to the commander of the coupist tanks ordering him to
report to me. He didn't show up.

At that time I didn't know who was running the coup. I didn't know who
they were, Left or Right, or what the hell was going on.

The air force commander at the little Tatoi airfield rang up and told me he
had received an order that no planes were to be allowed to take off. I asked
him who signed the order. He didn't know. I said: "You bloody fool, you
read an order and don't even look to see who signed it!" My ADC checked
and we found that it was Pattakos. It was only then that I knew that the
coup was a right-wing coup.

I kept telling my wife to calm down. You know she is expecting a baby in
three weeks. She was pretty nervous and we were all isolated and there is no
doctor on the place. I couldn't go out and I didn't know where to go if I
could get out.

Just before 8:00 in the morning I was informed that three officers were
coming to see me. It turned out to be Pattakos, Papadopoulos, and
Makarezos. I had been listening to the radio, which was my only source of
news after the telephone was cut, and I knew they had made an announcement suspending the constitution and signing it "The prime minister and the
members of his government" without giving any names.

When the three officers showed up they informed me that they had saved
Greece for my sake. They had a letter from General Spandidakis [Chief of
Staff at the time of the coup] which said the coup had been done in my
name in order to save the country. When I saw this I blew my top.

I stormed at them. I raged at them. I asked them: "How could you do a
thing like that?" They tried to stand their ground, and Pattakos said the chief
of staff would be ready to receive me later. This made me even angrier.
"Where is my prime minister?" I shouted. "Where is my government?"

Pattakos then answered: "You have none. We have arrested them all."

Constantine continued: "I told the three officers I would refuse to see
anyone—Spandidakis or anyone else—until Arnaoutis was released. They
stood at attention like cadets in front of me. I told them the letter from
Spandidakis was not good enough. Pattakos said the king should know
they supported him and he pledged this on his honor as an officer. 'What
honor?' I demanded. 'You go back and tell Spandidakis to come here. I
want to talk to him.' They left. Just as they got outside the house I stuck
my head out and yelled to Pattakos as he was walking to his car, 'I give
you exactly two hours to come back here with Arnaoutis. It is an absolute
disgrace'."

I asked the King: "Did they?" "No," he said.

He continued his account:

Around 10:00 Spandidakis finally came. I told him what I thought of him. Spandidakis said he had heard about the coup at the last minute and that he only took command in order to prevent junior officers from taking over and plunging the country into chaos.

I told Spandidakis to remove the tanks from my mother's house and they did. After Spandidakis left, I chased through Athens looking for Bitsios but I couldn't find him. They had grabbed him. I passed by my mother's house and she was all right so I asked her to go out to Tatoi and wait.

Then I went to our "Pentagon" around noon. There was a real atmosphere of revolution there. There were tanks all over the place and officers wandering around inside shouting at each other. They were all jabbering. But they put together a kind of guard of honor for me and I went through the main room to the office of the chief of the defense staff. I found him but he didn't know what in hell was going on because he had been arrested and so had the chief of the air force and the chief of the navy.

When I saw the three officers who made the coup I gave them a direct order to release Arnaoutis at once, now, and to get all the generals to the "Pentagon" and gather them into one room so I could talk to them, and also to bring my prime minister, Canellopoulos, immediately.

When Arnaoutis finally showed up he told me they had come for him with tommy guns and pistols. The officer who arrested him when they broke in shifted his pistol from his right hand to his left hand so he could shake hands because he said, "We are on the same side." Arnaoutis refused. Then one of the men hit him. Arnaoutis looked him in the eye and said, "I can see you never fought for your country. No soldier who was ever in combat would hit an unarmed man." And Arnaoutis said to me: "Be careful. This is a revolution. Be very careful how you handle them."

Then Canellopoulos came in. He was in desperate condition. He was absolutely livid and shaking. Well, I told him my story and he told me his. Then I asked him what he recommended. He suggested there were two possible solutions. I could call the generals together and ask the generals on my side to stand up and then order them to arrest the coup-makers. I told Canellopoulos that the mere fact that the coup-makers had moved without my knowledge and arrested him showed that they meant business. They would shoot all the generals—and everyone else. Canellopoulos agreed. The other solution he suggested was some form of acceptance. I suggested that it might be best to put some civilians into the government to gain time and I thought of Kollias who is a conservative trusted by the army. Canellopoulos said he would stand by me.

Then I went to the room where all the generals were and I said to them that I was convinced that what the army had done, it had done to save the country, that what had happened had happened. I then said: "I want to know if you are still with me. My father taught me discipline, the discipline of an officer. I want to know which officers are on my side. Will those on my side please stand up?" They all did. But I realized that this was a gesture that meant nothing. They had no power, all those generals. They didn't even have a pistol among them.

And the chief of staff kept charging in. He kept saying: "Stop seeing generals and make a government!"

So I saw the three leaders of the coup again and I told them: "You have done all this without my knowledge. But the mere fact that you succeeded was because you used my name. Without the name of the king you would be nowhere. Now, take my orders!"

I screamed at them. They were slouching. I said: "The first thing a Greek officer learns is to stand at attention. Now, stand at attention!" They all stood up like ramrods.

Then I called in the service chiefs. At this moment Arnaoutis stuck his head in and hollered: "They are going to arrest me again." I tried to intervene. I told the chief of staff: "If you don't release him now I will never agree to anything you want."

But it was complete anarchy. You can't even imagine what an atmosphere of anarchy there was. Why, I saw a captain roughly pushing a general to one side.

I had a two-hour struggle to force a civilian government on the three. They wanted Spandidakis as prime minister. I said: "You must be completely mad. It is bad enough with a military coup, and now you want a military man to head the government." They said the army must run the show. They said the Americans were on their side.

I told them: "Obviously you are mad. Certainly the Americans are not on your side. Remember the case of Argentina? When the army took over there, the United States withdrew its ambassador. The way you are going you are bound to fail and you will isolate Greece from its friends. I tell you you need a respectable judge as a head of government, not a soldier."

There were loads of young officers downstairs screaming when they heard the news I was asking for Kollias, shouting, "We won't take him, we won't take him." But I had convinced the three. Pattakos went down to the young officers and said: "We will appoint Kollias or I will shoot myself right here." They accepted.

The three named themselves as ministers which I thought was very foolish. I told them they would be wiser to stay out of the light. I refused their first two choices for minister of foreign affairs. And I insisted that the other ministers should also be civilians.

When I had finally finished these discussions, I was informed I could leave when I wished but that Arnaoutis was staying. I told Spandidakis: "If I go, Arnaoutis goes. Otherwise you can all go to hell." They realized I meant business. Then I ordered that a guard of honor be prepared. I wasn't sure whether to shake hands with its commander but at the last minute I decided to, and they all roared approval.

Just as I was about to get into my car, Kollias arrived. "What's going on?" he asked. I told him. I said: "I haven't got time for details. I have just appointed you as prime minister. If you don't accept, there will be chaos. Goodbye." I slammed the door of my car. When I came back to the palace —this house, not Tatoi—it was completely surrounded by tanks.

At this point, Constantine said, he had tried to mobilize the navy from Tatoi in the early morning and ordered all ships to shoot if anyone attempted to board them. But only one destroyer apparently got off to sea.

He then went on: "Later in the day I swore in the government. I told

Pattakos, the new minister of the interior: 'I hold you personally responsible that no drop of blood shall be shed and no politician shall be harmed'."

We then got to the tricky point of whether the King had ever signed the first declaration to the people issued in his name. He said when he was in the "Pentagon," Papadopoulos gave him a paper which he was supposed to broadcast to the nation, but he did not do this; nor has he done so since.

When the three came to Tatoi, they asked him to sign the document legalizing the coup and he told them to go to hell. "I never signed," he said to me. "But they broadcast the declaration." I told him I had heard they forged his signature, but Papadopoulos furiously denied this to me. Constantine said: "I doubt if they forged the signature but they used my name. Then next evening they sent me the document. I have still got it. I never signed it and I never will but that is a tremendous secret. If they knew I had told you there would be awful trouble. But I don't want to go down in history as the king who is known for suspending the constitution."

I asked him what he knew about the conspiracy itself. He said he had known of the defense plan (he didn't remember the code name "Prometheus"): He had first heard of it when he became an officer. And the three coup-makers had been in key staff positions. "They knew all the right code words. They moved fast. And they used my name. That is what did it. Pattakos told me: 'If we hadn't used your name we would never have succeeded'."

Constantine told me that (Phillips) Talbot, the American Ambassador, "behaved beautifully—he couldn't have been better." I asked what he thought the United States could do to help. He said:

> What the United States can do depends on what I do. Nobody doubts my disapproval of the coup and everybody realizes that I knew nothing about it, so now I really believe my duty is to make this new government succeed.
>
> If I denounce them or fail to take a part in events, what happens? Many of the army units would become bitter and try to move against the coup. Even if only some units move it will be a ghastly first-class civil war. To have a nationalist army fight itself would be terrible. The best thing I can do is to influence people and to bring my country back to a parliamentary democracy as soon as I possibly can.
>
> Those who have criticized me in the past now depend upon me. I can serve my country better by staying and helping. I told Pattakos and Papadopoulos: "No executions. Remember you can't execute politicians." Pattakos replied: "Turks we shall never become!" I told them bloodshed would ruin all their efforts.

I told Constantine that Pattakos had informed me Andreas Papandreou would be tried for treason in a special military court, that there was no appeal, and that the maximum sentence possible was death. Constantine was furious. He said: "There is always appeal to the king, and if they sentence anyone to death and he appeals to me I won't confirm the sentence. If I have any power left I will stop it."

PARIS, *May 23, 1967*

I SPENT an hour with Prime Minister Georges Pompidou. While I was sitting in the antechamber Couve came out looking tired and grey. Obviously Couve had been briefing the Prime Minister on the Middle East crisis.

Pompidou said France's policy would be decided tomorrow at a Cabinet meeting. In other words, there have not yet been any definitive decisions. He thought France still considered the 1950 U.S.-British-French guarantee valid; this was a pledge that the three Western powers would act forcibly if need be to preserve the territorial status quo in the Middle East (in other words, safeguard Israel). (But, I may recall, the 1950 pledge was violated —against Egypt—in 1956 by Britain and France.) I asked P. flatly: "Does it still hold for you?" He thought a moment. "Yes," he said, "I think so."

I asked if France had any kind of alliance with Israel. He said not. Furthermore, since 1956 France had drawn much further away from Israel. It still had friendly relations; but that was all.

I asked if France would participate in any joint operation with the United States to keep the peace if necessary. Again he hesitated a long time. Then he finally said he thought so, but I wouldn't really know until tomorrow; the matter would be discussed at the Cabinet meeting. He assured me again, however, that France strongly supported the status quo in the Middle East. But he was deeply worried by Moscow's failure to give any indication, public or diplomatic, that it wanted to cool the flames. He thought U Thant had behaved very foolishly in yielding UN's trumps by caving in right away to Nasser's demands.

PARIS, *May 24, 1967*

POMPIDOU was wrong. Today there was a Cabinet meeting, and obviously de Gaulle decided that France would not stick with the United States and Britain and does not think the 1950 tripartite declaration applies any more. Also, France is neutral—which means less pro-Israel, more pro-Egypt—in the present argument. Clearly these were the general's own decisions.

WASHINGTON, *June 17, 1967*

LONG talk this morning with Dick Helms, head of CIA. He wondered if Soviet intelligence appraisals could be so wrong about the Middle East, how bad are they when they assess the United States, or the Vietnam war? Do they have a mechanism capable of producing objective appraisals?

The Soviet bloc has resumed extensive arming of the Arabs, above all Egypt. Possibly the aim is to help Nasser keep office. Moscow has always been interested in supporting the "radical Arabs."

WASHINGTON, *June 18, 1967*

TOMMY (Llewellyn) Thompson, Ambassador to Russia, who is staying with us at the Wisners', says that this month, during the Palestine war, was the first use of the Washington-Moscow "hot line" teletype—on both the Israeli attack on our ship the *Liberty* (when we sent off planes) and on the Israeli march toward Damascus, which we sought to prevent.

WASHINGTON, *June 19, 1967*

GOOD talk with Secretary Dean Rusk. I said it was saddening to see how isolated we were becoming in the world. "Where have *you* been?" he asked. I said he knew perfectly well, and repeated the observation. He claimed we are not getting isolated. Rusk said the Egyptians were in bad trouble in Yemen. They had been using a poison gas there which was so deadly that a single drop killed.

WASHINGTON, *June 21, 1967*

LUNCHED with Bill Bundy, Assistant Secretary of State for Far East, Mac's older brother, and Dean Acheson's son-in-law. Our conversation was wholly about Vietnam.

The last approach to negotiations for peace started late last year through the Poles, who initiated things through Janusz Lewandowski, their man on the international control commission in Vietnam. On December 1, 1966, he told Lodge (in Saigon) that Hanoi was ready to talk to Washington if the United States accepted as a basis ten points drawn up by Lewandowski and previously submitted by him to Hanoi.

When Lodge reported this to Washington, Washington authorized U.S. Ambassador (John A.) Gronouski in Warsaw to go to Foreign Minister (Adam) Rapacki and say we would be happy to meet and discuss the "interpretation" of the ten points "during" talks. Rapacki stalled and, after we had bombed Hanoi December 2 and 4, sharply criticized these attacks around the capital.

Then we put a ten-mile circle around Hanoi unconditionally exempting the area inside it from bombing. On that basis—although there had been no *quid pro quo* conditions—we asked the North Vietnamese in Moscow if they wanted to meet us. A series of meetings occurred between John

Guthrie of the U.S. Embassy and the North Vietnamese chargé d'affaires.

The climax to this phase came in President Johnson's February 8 letter to Ho Chi Minh in which we proposed there would be no future bombing if they simultaneously ceased reinforcing the south. The letter specified that the cut on infiltration should coincide with the halt in bombing.

WASHINGTON, *June 22, 1967*

EXTRAORDINARY evening. It started with a chat with President Johnson in the little "think tank" off his office, moved on to his armored Cadillac down to the Presidential yacht, *Honey Fitz*, continued over drinks and then dinner on a slow cruise down the Potomac, and endured until midnight, when the President sent me home in that same monster, bulletproof Cadillac.

He is a strange man, but I cannot say I either like or admire him. I wish I did because he has always been exceptionally nice to me. But there is something that puts me off. He is almost pathetic in his efforts to please and to build himself up in the visitor's (and his own) mind as a tremendous and fine figure. He is hospitable, generous, incredibly energetic. But he always seems to be aggressively on the defensive.

On the boat trip was a distinguished assemblage of about two dozen people including the executive committee that has been put together on the Middle East crisis and which had just met that late afternoon: Mac Bundy (executive secretary), Clark Clifford (special intelligence adviser), General Earle G. Wheeler (Chairman of the Joint Chiefs of Staff), Secretary of Defense McNamara, Dick Helms (head of CIA), and Walt Rostow. Also a few others had been rounded up including Mesdames Wheeler and Rostow, Kay Graham (owner of the *Washington Post* and *Newsweek*), etc. They didn't really look as if they enjoyed the undoubtedly great privilege. Some seemed to be unnecessarily toady-like (for example, McNamara), while others sat with a certain quiet, glum dignity.

At the wharf, we boarded the *Honey Fitz* (named for Kennedy's grandfather by Kennedy) as the crew saluted, and went up on the top deck. It is a modest little yacht about the scale of that of a low-rank Greek ship owner, certainly no more, except that it has a marvelous set of communications: antennae sticking out in all directions. From time to time a light blue telephone was brought to the President and plugged in so he could accept calls from his wife. He would sit there, a satisfied grin on his face, saying "Lady Bird" this or "Bird" that.

As we swung slowly downstream, followed about forty yards behind by two little protective navy boats, Johnson sat in an olive green leather-covered armchair at the stern, in the center, waved Kay beside him and me beside her.

There were drinks for all. Then, to my surprise, the crew brought little tray-tables placed in front of everyone, set them and produced a supper of rice, curried shrimp, meat, vegetables, etc., ice water, rolls, and vanilla ice cream.

Finally, after coffee, the President said: "How about a little movie?" He sat back while the screen was swiftly set up and the projector produced. Successively we had incredibly boring films (three of them) of the President and how government runs; a long, long series of shorts advertising U.S. savings bonds; and finally a film on the awarding of a Medal of Honor (by the President) to a marine sergeant from Vietnam.

The yacht drifted slowly downstream under a haze-obscured full red moon, then turned and slid slowly back upstream and was pulled beside the wharf a good fifteen minutes before the final reel concluded and we rose, filed off, were driven back to the White House. Everyone seemed to have a car. "Have you got a car?" Johnson asked. I said no and he said: "Take mine." So I gave Kay a hitch home and then was driven in the armored Cadillac up the narrow Georgetown street to the Wisners' house where I'm staying.

So much for the ambience. I shall now try to recapitulate some of the things Johnson said. By all odds the most important thing was on the subject of Russia and the "hot line."

Apparently we had used the hot line during the incident when Israel attacked the U.S. communications ship *Liberty* and we sent off planes, but Moscow initiated its use later during the last phase of the war—between Israel and Syria—and most ominously.

As the story emerged, Israeli troops were driving into Syria and toward Damascus when a Soviet warning came rattling over the teletype (which is what the hot line is) warning that if we didn't make the Israelis stop, Russia would take action "including military action." Johnson promptly ordered a formation of ships from the Sixth Fleet, including carriers, to turn eastward and head for Israel.

This being done, he started to answer Moscow, but in paragraphs considerably spaced apart in time, so that by the time the second paragraph was on the wire, Soviet vessels and planes in the Mediterranean would be fully aware of the direction our ships were heading. He said in his message that the United States was trying to curb Israel but explained this was difficult. Then he asked what Moscow was doing to curb Syria, remarking that no indications had been reported to him on any such actions. Of course, the crisis simmered down and the Israelis never got to Damascus, as they had intended, to oust the regime, which is one of Moscow's favorites.

Johnson went on at length to talk about Russia, about (Russian Premier Aleksei) Kosygin's difficulties both at home and in China, and about Russia's serious miscalculation in the Middle East. He admitted we are disturbed about the implications that Moscow can make so large an error; where else would it miscalculate?

He expressed much admiration for Israel's army. He said (Ambassador) Arthur Goldberg had called up from UN when the war started and was deeply worried. Johnson said General Wheeler had given him an estimate that Israel could easily and quickly handle all its enemies.

Johnson said he had sought to get a naval force into the Aqaba straits, including us, the British, Scandinavians, etc., and had warned Israel not to move, that "they'd be alone if they go alone." He had told this to Abba Eban, whom he admires. However, Israel did in the end move. And it did go alone, successfully.

He said that day the State Department had begged him—and he'd yielded—to halt the ban on U.S. visitors to Israel and several Arab states. "And who do you think was the first person to take advantage of this? Richard M. Nixon." (Nixon flew briefly to Israel.) "I mentioned this at EXCOM this afternoon and Bundy said: 'I suggest we proceed to the next item of business—rapidly'."

Talking about his decision to send the ships toward Israel and call Russia (it wasn't a bluff, he said, because Israel did stop) he admitted it was "the most open-ended, filled-with-dire-consequences decision" he had had to make (like Kennedy and Cuba) because it might have started World War III, but there was no alternative.

The Russia-Syria decision was easy because a man couldn't be bullied. Johnson was opposed to "cowardice" in any form (he pronounces it "ice," not "iss"). He had learned this as a little boy; if you gave way to bullies, they bullied you even more. It was an easy decision. After all, every President did his best, and he had done his best. Kennedy, Eisenhower, why even Herbert Hoover had tried to do their best.

Johnson said another very, very tough decision he had had to make was on Cyprus. During the height of the crisis there a Turkish invasion fleet had actually taken off for a military intervention, and he had to order them back, warning otherwise of U.S. armed opposition.

WASHINGTON, *June 23, 1967*

LONG talk with Vice-President Humphrey. I had the impression that Nixon, who is an expert politician, was being very clever by traveling all around the world these days and making himself genuinely familiar with foreign policy issues because he recognized that this is issue number one in the next election. Humphrey agreed emphatically. He said:

Nixon is pushing this. You are quite right. Don't underestimate him—even as a candidate. I wouldn't have a chance to get identified with foreign policy as vice president because all vice presidents are overwhelmed by their president. Don't forget that Jack Kennedy had the solid Catholic vote, the solid Jewish vote, and a lot of other solid strength, and yet Nixon ran so close behind him that a shift of only a county or two would have changed the outcome. He is still very much there. And he has been very responsible in his foreign policy statements.

As a Republican candidate—and I think he will probably be nominated—he will run against an incumbent of his own age and not against a young nonincumbent as he did in 1960. He will run against an incumbent with scars, just the way he himself has scars, and not against an unscarred young nonincumbent. Nixon will be a very strong contender. He is no fool. And he knows that foreign policy is the issue for our day—more than ever.

The big issue in 1968 will be Vietnam. This produces grave new pressures because it is a new moral and ethical question and you may recall that Aristotle said that ethics and politics are inseparable.

NEW YORK, *July 11, 1967*

FASCINATING day yesterday. I had an appointment with Eisenhower down in Gettysburg so, having bummed *The New York Times* company plane, I took my son David along. When we arrived at the little airstrip, there was a car from Eisenhower's establishment which drove us to his office on the campus of Gettysburg College.

Considering what I had heard about his health and that he is now more than seventy-six, Ike looked pretty well. When I said so he grinned rather sadly and said: "Well, you know, there are three ages of man. Youth. Middle age. And 'How well you look'."

He said the trouble with policy-making today was that there were too many "intellectuals" involved who thought they knew the answers to everything but who had never been up against the "hard knocks" of reality. He specifically mentioned Kenneth Galbraith, Mac Bundy, and Walt Rostow.

I recalled that before he had made up his mind to run for the Presidency he often used to say that what he really preferred was to look forward to a period of retirement when, as a kind of elder statesman on a nonparty basis, he would be at the service of his country. Such being the case, what would be his advice concerning the Middle East today. This is the essence of what he said.

The United States should take the lead in facing the real issues of the Arab-Jewish problem, which were the shortage of water and the question of the Arab refugees. It required an imaginative plan, especially because diplomacy had shown itself ineffective in recent UN discussions.

Two or three large nuclear plants should be built to desalt water and generate between 750 million and a billion gallons a day of sweet water. There should be really enormous plants, because "the bigger the plant, the more economic the operation. This water would cost more than the price of New York City water but it is cheap for a country that doesn't have water at all. And Syria, Jordan, Israel, and Egypt would all profit so much from such a plan that the people couldn't permit their governments to refuse participation."

The plan he envisioned would meet both requirements in the Middle East because it would not only provide work for the refugees in building and manning the plants. Once they were in production they would recover enormous areas of barren ground in Syria, Jordan, the Israeli Negev, and Sinai.

I expressed great interest in this idea and he then said it originated with (Admiral) Lewis Strauss, (formerly Eisenhower's chief of the Atomic Energy Commission). Eisenhower stressed that something new enough and big enough had to be done to end the present stalemate, because now all that was happening was a name-calling contest among the Arabs and the Jews against each other and against the United States.

But he thought the idea had such obvious material value to both sides that it must be of major interest to them. The idea would be to create a worldwide corporation like the International Atomic Energy Agency established in Vienna as the sole concrete outcome of Ike's own 1953 "atoms for peace" proposal. In this the U.S. government would take up 51 percent of the stock and private investors and traders would take up the rest. Maybe the cost of the program could never be completely amortized, but it would certainly produce some income—just the way the cost of the Panama Canal and its operation was never completely amortized, but some income was produced.

Ike continued: "Lewis Strauss and I have been great advocates of atomic power and what can be done with it." He recalled that he had tried to get the Arabs and Jews together when he was President by sending Eric Johnston to the Middle East to work up a Jordan River water-sharing program, but this never took. However, the scale of the present scheme was so enormous that one would think it had to attract support. One plant alone would produce as much as the entire water flow of the Jordan and all its tributaries, simply by transforming sea water into fresh water.

He said that if I wanted to go into this more thoroughly I should talk to Strauss. I asked him if he could call up Lewis, and he did, reaching him at his farm in Brandy Station, Virginia. I told him to tell Lewis I had a plane and could I come down and have lunch with him together with my son? Ike transmitted the message and the answer was yes.

Ike then settled back in his swivel chair, and we resumed our conversation. I asked if he had to play over again the 1956 policy of the United States and the Suez crisis if he would do it the same way. He chuckled ruefully and said:

Of course, hindsight is more accurate than foresight. But foresight is more valuable. I suppose, looking back on it, I would have made a greater effort in advance to win over Israel, France, and Britain to my viewpoint. The Suez Canal was owned by a private company. Nasser had every right to nationalize. And the British were damn fools. They claimed it was impossible for the Egyptians to operate the canal, but within weeks of taking over Nasser was getting through more tonnage than ever before.

I talked to Anthony [Eden] time after time, and then the damn fools, when they decided in spite of us to act as they did, they did it very badly. Their operation was a mess. I like Anthony and I still write to him. We have always been friendly. The British attitude then was understandable in terms of their resentment. But they did it all wrong. And I can tell you in confidence that I sent a hell of a message to Ben-Gurion also.

I moved the conversation out of the past and into the present, asking Ike what he thought of the 1967 Middle East war. He scratched his chin and said:

Well, I was certainly surprised by the speed of the victory. Naturally, when I saw the first claims of Israel I said right away this looks like an Israeli surprise attack. But I don't know what they could have done except that, with all those Arab armies on their borders and Nasser talking of a total war to drive Israel into the sea. Try and make an analogy for this country. Supposing I had been president and some combination of enemies, much bigger than us, had been gathered on the seas and in Canada and Mexico promising our extinction. If I hadn't attacked first while I had the chance I would have been tried for treason.

I will tell you that as a professional military man I was amazed that the Egyptians could be caught that way after bragging so much about what they were going to do. I was surprised that they could be caught tactically like that with their planes parked all together on airfields and not even any revetments. But that sure was some harvest the Israelis got. I never had a harvest like that in World War II—340 planes in one night.

Ike reminisced a moment about the German surrender. He said all he had told Jodl was: "Do you understand every word of this document and what it signifies?" When Jodl said yes, he dismissed him. "I wasn't one of those fellows in favor of hobnobbing with the Nazis after we licked them," said Ike sternly.

Ike said, "I don't want to hurry you but if you are going to get down to Strauss I think you had better be moving," so he gave me a pretty good handshake for an old man, and off we went. Strauss met us at a small Virginia airport. He said he had sent Eisenhower a memorandum on a Middle East water plan. It was obvious from the UN debate that the resources of diplomacy were exhausted and we could not expect peace negotiations in a decent climate. Therefore, he saw the need for something dramatic to change that climate. The two basic issues that had exacerbated the Middle East are water and displaced populations. A single bold stroke by the United States could solve these both.

Strauss wanted to build three very large nuclear plants, two on the Mediterranean coast of Israel and one at the head of the Gulf of Aqaba, probably in Israeli territory. These would be dual-purpose plants, to provide electric energy and fresh water. For energy it was necessary for a plant to operate at one temperature and another for water. But the basic objective of the plants would be to produce water with energy as an incidental.

The nuclear material to fuel these plants had already been allocated by President Eisenhower in 1956 to the IAEA (International Atomic Energy Agency) in his offer to encourage plants for peaceful purposes. All principal belligerents in the Middle East were members of IAEA so they have both a forum and the material with which to get going on this project. The IAEA would be responsible to account for the fuel and to see to it that there were no diversions which could be used for atomic weapons.

This vast scheme required thousands of unskilled workers, and the Arab refugees were ideal for this. First they could work and then they could be settled on irrigated lands with plenty of electricity available. The method of desalting water originated at the U.S. laboratory at Oak Ridge, Tennessee. The idea sprang from the need to do something with waste material produced by weapons.

WASHINGTON, *September 14, 1967*

THIS evening I had an appointment with the President, and I arrived a little before 6:00 P.M., which was the time of our date. Walt Rostow came down and sat with me in one of the consultation rooms.

He told me he had heard Johnson say at his ranch in Texas: "This is the tree I expect to be buried under. And when my grandchildren see this tree I want them to think of me as the man who saved Asia and Vietnam and who did something for the Negroes in this country. Yet I have lost twenty popularity points on Vietnam and ten on the Negro question."

Suddenly [Presidential aide] Marvin Watson opened the door and told us the President was waiting. We went through a secretarial office and past the little "think tank" to the Oval Room, and Johnson came in from the other door: looking rather tired, not wearing glasses, appearing somewhat greyer in the hair. He seemed preoccupied.

He sat down in the Presidential rocking chair (a newer and more padded variety than that Kennedy once used) with Walt on his left and me on his right. He asked if we wanted a drink. Walt took a scotch on the rocks, I a scotch and soda. The President ordered a Fresca, mumbling apologetically: "I have to watch my weight these days."

He said I could use whatever I wanted concerning what he said and I could write anything I wished from the papers he was giving me. I should merely say, "I believe President Johnson feels, etc., etc." He then started to muse, not very brilliantly.

His Administration had substantially increased the U.S. aid program for Latin America and Africa. His Administration had virtually doubled Latin American aid as compared with the Kennedy Administration. He had sent Under Secretary (Nicholas deB.) Katzenbach to Africa—the highest

American official who had ever been there. He himself had gone to Punta del Este for the OAS conference, "and I met all of them there."

His approach to the Latin American leaders was always: "I am glad to meet with you fellows to discuss our common problems because this is helpful to all of us. We have a very big country but we must work in partnership and I think when we get together like this it emphasizes the fact of our partnership. I want to make you fellows into good junior partners." I don't think the President noticed a conversely jarring note in that adjective.

Patience and understanding were particularly required in Africa, where economic and political development simply had to be slow. Our commitment to Africa was to push for self-determination and the political conception of one man, one vote, just as we wished elsewhere in the world. We wanted to press for moderation and good sense in both black and white Africa.

He admitted there was a deep connection between our foreign policy in Africa and our internal policy on civil rights. He said: "We know Lincoln had his emancipation proclamation. But that was just a proclamation not a fact. And we are paying the price for this. Of course we are a more mature and sophisticated nation than the African countries. Our people have lost their jungle instincts, but we still have terrible national problems. You can't deny that. So obviously what happens here has its effect in Africa and the same thing is true in reverse."

When I went off with Rostow, he took me down to his office (although it was already twenty minutes past eight). I remarked that the only really interesting thing the President mentioned was the fact that he had sent a warning to Castro through the Russians. Walt then said:

> Around May 13, when the Russians were sending word to Cairo that Israel was mobilizing against Syria—an untrue maneuver which set off the Middle East War—the President sent a most remarkable message to Kosygin.
>
> In short he made it perfectly plain that we knew what was happening in the Middle East, that we knew the Cubans were expanding communist subversion in Latin America, and that we knew that Russia was not being helpful in Vietnam. But he wanted to point out that, powerful as our two countries were, Russia and the United States, we could not entirely control dangerous spots elsewhere. We were the older children in the family and if we stayed together we could influence the others, but if we did not stay together and exercise some kind of joint control, it was difficult to read the future.

WASHINGTON, *September 16, 1967*

THIS afternoon I drove out to see Bobby Kennedy at Hickory Hill, his pleasant house near McLean, Virginia. A colored maid showed me into a cozy sitting room where I was immediately besieged by children. (The

Kennedys now have ten of them.) Young Max, aged two, and Christopher, not quite four, crawled all over me, aided by a huge wet English sheepdog, while Carey, a pretty little girl of around ten, did startling handsprings on a slippery rug. Bobby was excellent with the children—checked up on their manners, quite firm and yet unusually gentle.

Bobby said there were quite a few differences between the Kennedy and Johnson Administrations on Latin American policy. There is a closer relationship now between the South American Establishment, and we are more identified with it, less identified with reform. Bobby was not really sure which would prove to be the right approach.

CARACAS, *September 25, 1967*

THIS afternoon I saw President Raúl Leoni at his new official residence, which used to be a great plantation in Spanish days. I asked why agitators among the youth were permitted to stay on year after year in the universities. He agreed this was bad, that there were adult agitators among the students. The government had ordered the end of this by executive order, but this had "provoked great opposition from the student body."

LA PAZ, *September 28, 1967*

STAYING with Ambassador Douglas (and Dorothy) Henderson, a nice Massachusetts couple who have served all around here. It is evident the CIA plays an important role, and the station chief is in personal touch with the president (semi-dictator), Barrientos. We have a sixteen-man Special Forces team at Santa Cruz which has trained a Bolivian battalion in counterinsurgency but which takes no part in the fighting.

Barrientos, an ex-air force general who took part in previous leftist revolutions, is optimistic about the guerrilla war and confident he has Ché Guevara bottled up. The Régis Debray incident is a nuisance. Henderson had to intervene to save Debray's life at the very start. This country has no death penalty but dissidents have been shot (or dropped from airplanes). It's a rough place. H. thinks Havana was making use of Debray, who was a contact with Mexico, a main center in the underground link.

LA PAZ, *September 29, 1967*

TALK with the president, General René Barrientos Ortuño. B. thought the Communists were focusing on Bolivia. Their strategy was to link guerrilla fighting with agitation in the cities. The guerrillas were doing badly, "and I am sure I will get Ché in a few days at most."

LA PAZ, *September 30, 1967*

HENDERSON told me something about Ché Guevara today. When he first left Cuba (1965?) Ché went to the Congo. He found the people there treacherous and lacking in revolutionary fervor, so he returned to Havana. He then sent out an agent with the *nom de guerre* Ricardo to scout Latin American prospects. Ricardo told Ché Bolivia offered possibilities but he must move swiftly. In autumn 1966 he decided to come here.

RIO DE JANEIRO, *October 17, 1967*

JOHN Mowinckel told me a telegram had been distributed among U.S. embassies from La Paz. In this our spooks described the end of Ché Guevara. He was executed by the Bolivians after being interrogated. He was asked: "What do you do to prisoners you capture in Cuba?" Ché replied boldly: "Shoot them." After his interrogation, he was shot by the Bolivians. He died bravely.

DAKAR, SENEGAL, *October 19, 1967*

ADMIRAL Édouard Rivière, French commander, told me he keeps a regiment of paratroopers assigned to intervene, if need be, anywhere in Francophone Africa where Paris has permissive accords. They went to Gabon for the crisis. It is necessary to move fast—a thirty-man commando can do the job in two hours; a company in twelve hours; three regiments in two days.

DAKAR, SENEGAL, *October 20, 1967*

AN hour this afternoon with Léopold Senghor, poet-president of Senegal. I started by inquiring whether there were any other poet-presidents nowadays. "Mao Tse-tung and Ho Chi Minh," he replied right away, adding that he didn't have many other things in common with them. He thought Mao a better poet, "less political."

He only wrote poetry during his holidays in Europe. "I have to have a certain distance in order to write. All my poems evoke Africa and when I am here I am too close, I have my nose in Africa. Abroad I develop a certain nostalgia that helps."

Senegal had inherited qualities and defects from France. The Anglophone states were better in practical and economic ways. But the French had "gone beyond prejudice. I am a Catholic but we represent not even ten percent of the Moslem population. And my wife is French; but that doesn't count here. In Anglophone countries tribalism is more developed. This human aspect is most important."

ACCRA, GHANA, *October 24, 1967*

PLEASANT talk at the University of Ghana, in Legon, a suburb, with the Vice-Chancellor, Professor A. A. Kwapong, actual head of the university; the Chancellor is the Chief of State. He got both an M.A. and a Ph.D. at Cambridge and spent a year at Princeton as a visiting professor.

He said it was a mistake to think American Negroes had any particular bond with Africans. In fact they often did not get on very well because the Americans came over with all their complexes, from a tragic past, and met the Africans who had large happy families, tribal ties, etc., and were therefore psychologically much more content.

ACCRA, GHANA, *October 27, 1967*

I WAS received in the castle by Lieutenant General J. A. Ankrah, chairman of the National Liberation Council and thus chief of state. I asked him to describe Ghana's current ideology. He said: "Before our revolution the communist ideology tried to prevail here with the help of Nkrumah. But nobody can analyze or even attempt to interpret Nkrumahism. Nkrumahism is no more and no one in Ghana wants anything to do with communism. We just want to be democratic people governed for ourselves and by ourselves. We follow no particular bloc of powers but we want to be just as democratic as we can be."

LAGOS, *October 30, 1967*

DROVE over to the residence of General Yakubu Gowon, the thirty-three-year-old chief of state, a pleasant young man of middle height, lean and athletic, with guardsman's moustache (he went to Sandhurst), dressed in green-tan bushjacket uniform with one ribbon and major general's tabs. He said:

"I'm not a believer in coups. My upbringing as a soldier teaches that my role is to support the government of the day irrespective of the political party in power. The great countries like the United States and Britain have able soldiers who don't dream of taking power. And they are the most stable governments in the world. That is my hope for this country in the future."

He said: "The general public here was fed up with the political situation in the country. There was a lot of corruption. The place was filled with ten-percenters. People were looking after their own ambitions and interests. The coming in of the military was to clean up that political mess."

Gowon said (Biafran President Odumegwu-) Ojukwu's civil war regime was effective in propaganda but it had brutally eliminated opposition, and people were afraid to ask questions. He said Ojukwu had sent an agent to Paris to negotiate with the Rothschilds and had offered them all the mineral concessions in Biafra ("in inverted commas," said Gowon) in exchange for six million pounds. "He's clever. He can fool the devil himself."

KINSHASA, CONGO, *November 3, 1967*

CALLED on President Mobutu this afternoon in his residence within the compound of the first paracommando barracks; a sort of pretorian guard: ugly men in red berets and tiger jump suits. Mobutu and his Foreign Minister, Justin Bomboko, were standing inside the large house. A record player was grinding out French jazz.

Mobutu is a big man, thirty-seven, with sullen expression, easy smile, large veins swelling on his temples. I suspect he could blow his top easily. Bomboko is fat, round, short, with a streak of white running through the center of his wooly hair.

Mobutu suggested we go out in the garden, where we strolled chatting until we sat down in a flower-surrounded nook near a bar, looking down on the roaring rapids of the Congo. Mobutu ordered beer and coffee.

Mobutu said: "My policy is to prove to the world that the Congo is right and is an innocent victim. My policy is to live on good neighborly terms with all countries. But Portugal is obviously in this affair. It is an aggressor. And we provoked no one."

He said about "250–300" mercenaries had come in from Angola, seized sixteen trucks, then a train, were now back in trucks heading for Kamina, in Katanga province.

Bomboko said the aim of the whole scheme was to take control of the entire Congo and reconquer the Union Minière properties.

KINSHASA, CONGO, *November 4, 1967*

YESTERDAY the Soviet Ambassador in Brazzaville came across the river to see Bomboko (there are no Soviet-Kinshasa relations). He offered Bomboko MIGs for use against the mercenaries. The Ambassador said Russia could provide fifteen Congolese pilots they had been training. Bomboko said: "But these are Gizenga men [leftists]. I'd be their first target."

LUANDA, ANGOLA, *November 8, 1967*

THE U.S. consul general confirms the presence here in Luanda of seven mercenaries (all Belgian) and estimates that 100 to 150 have been here during the past four months. They come from Lisbon. A small group definitely crossed into West Katanga.

LUANDA, ANGOLA, *November 9, 1967*

I CALLED on the Governor General, Lieutenant Colonel Camillo de Miranda Rebocho Vaz.

I asked how he explained the fact that Portugal was the last dinosaur, that while all other overseas empires had virtually vanished, this one was almost intact. He said: "Perhaps it is because we see no difference between black and white. This is the truth, it is emotional, not just legal. We have black doctors, black officials. Merit is the only measure for promotion. It is this different psychological feeling we have that is most important."

The greatest danger is "a revolution in the metropole. We can't foresee what influence that might have on us."

SALISBURY, RHODESIA, *November 13, 1967*

THIS morning I called on Sir Humphrey Gibbs, the last British Governor. The Rhodesians have appointed an acting chief of state and don't recognize Sir Humphrey—but the British do. He is a kind of unperson. He lives in a pleasant-looking Governor's palace, Cape Dutch architecture with nice grounds and lovely jacaranda trees.

Said he sadly: "We could be an example to the rest of Africa. The countries to the north could follow our example if we made a success of things. But the way the countries to the north of us are now going simply solidifies the people here behind Smith."

Ian Smith's propaganda apparatus had built him up so that "he now gets standing ovations everywhere no matter what he says and how often he contradicts himself."

PRETORIA, *November 16, 1967*

THIS morning I had a long talk with Prime Minister B. J. (John) Vorster. Vorster was a lawyer, and during the war he was a member of the pro-Nazi *Ossewabrandwag*. He was interned from 1942–1944. He has never been timid about this experience—nor ashamed. He said:

> Our basic philosophy of separate development is not based on the assumption that we think that we are better than the other man, richer or more learned. It is simply that we are different. We have lived together for generations and we know they are different. Segregation has always been the traditional policy of this country. The difference is that under previous governments it was horizontal segregation to a great extent. Previously the nonwhite could develop up to a ceiling, no more. That wasn't the intention but it was the fact. Now the sky is the limit.
>
> When we took over as realists we decided that the only moral and practical thing to do is to create universities for all the various racial groups and to enable students to be students in the full sense of the word; to give those

who could qualify an opportunity to become professors and everything else and thus to take over completely.

Likewise we are building up the black homelands. The Transkei is the Xhosa homeland; Zululand is the Zulu homeland; the Northern Transvaal is the Venda homeland; the Western Transvaal is the Tswana homeland. These are black nations which will be led to complete independence like that of Malawi.

I remarked to Vorster that it seemed to me the aims of his separate development policy and that of Black Power in the United States were strikingly parallel. He said:

The obvious difference is that these black nations have their own land and have always had it and it is not a question of expelling anyone as would seem to be the case with America's Black Power movement. You must remember our history. The Dutch settlers moved up as the Bantus moved down and each settled portions of the territory.

We have more whites than all the rest of Africa. We produce 70 percent of the free world's gold. We have more uranium than all Western countries but Canada. We furnish 20 percent of Africa's exports. We buy 18 percent of Africa's imports. We operate 50 percent of Africa's vehicles and have 50 percent of all its telephones. We honestly and sincerely are trying to find a solution to our problems. Disagree with us or condemn our approach—but give us the fair break of recognizing that we are honest and sincere in our attempts.

GABERONES, BOTSWANA, *November 17, 1967*

DROVE across this sprawling hamlet to the office of the president, Sir Seretse Khama. The president is fairly tall and is getting quite a belly, which he admits with a smile, is very brown, wears glasses, a moustache, speaks good English. Met his wife in England and was dethroned by the British for marrying her at a registry (the Church of England refused). He said: "Here we have a nonracial state and we believe that black and white can live together if an effort is made. As far as I am concerned, this experiment is succeeding. If it succeeds in Botswana, I see no reason why it cannot also succeed in South Africa and Rhodesia, provided good will exists racially on both sides."

23

PARIS, *December 13, 1967*

A NEW COUP D'ÉTAT IN GREECE! APPARENTLY THE KING HAS COM-
mitted himself to overthrow the junta by force. I called Caramanlis
immediately. He sounded nervous, complaining: "I don't know
what's going on. I have tried to get word to the King but I have no answer."

ROME, *January 13, 1968*

I FLEW down to see King Constantine. I must have spent at least six
hours with him in a little unadorned study in the Greek Ambassador's
residence, where he is staying.

The King indicated that the real blocks to his return at the present are
two of his conditions: committee to investigate political prisoners, and free
press. He speculated: "Maybe the top boys want me back—but not the
juniors. They hate my guts." I asked him why, and he said he thought their
feeling was "to hell with the old officers and everything that went before."

I asked why he had chosen December 13 to attempt his coup. Was it
because he knew that many of the monarchist senior officers were about to
be retired and this might be his last chance? He said: "That was one of the
main reasons. But there was another."

One general—Peridis—made a terrible miscalculation. I had been in
touch with him for some time. During the Cyprus crisis he had moved all his
troops to the Turkish border from Salonika. He said we should move before
the Cyprus crisis eased too much and while his forces were at their greatest
strength. I wanted to wait. I argued it was essential to get Salonika and it
would be much easier if his forces were back there in strength. But he
assured me we would have Salonika by 11:00 A.M. on the day we struck. He
was wrong. I wanted to wait—but he is one of the best generals we have.

Of course, if we had taken Salonika, there would have been no discussion.
Everything would have been finished. There would have been absolutely no

further discussion. Did you know that in Larissa people were coming out with Easter eggs to celebrate? I would have had a mass rally. I would have spoken on the Salonika radio and I would have called the ambassadors up there to be with me. And all the generals who were hesitating would have stuck with me.

The King said he was disappointed in the lack of support abroad. He added: "Here you've got all these big politicians in all these big countries talking about democracy. But only one of them, Harold Wilson, a socialist, had the courage to get up in the House and say, 'I pay tribute to a brave man.' What happened to President Johnson? What happened to Fulbright?"

PARIS, *January 22, 1968*

GOOD talk with de Gaulle. I asked if it was true that he considered the United States had become too powerful in the scale of world power balances and that he considered this was dangerous and was trying to offset this fact by his policy.

He said: "Certainly your country is very, very strong. Maybe it is not too strong but it is extremely strong. This is not the first time in history that one nation has been so formidably strong in relation to others but at any rate now it is evidently the turn of the United States. This makes your policy and your wisdom a matter of especial interest to the whole world. It is inevitable that other countries, especially mine, must adjust to this appearance on the world scene of such a formidable power. Of course we must do everything to seek an equilibrium, to restore a balance. Such is the eternal history of the world." De Gaulle said:

> If the United States and England had accepted the arrangement I suggested to coordinate among the three of us a closer policy and a global strategy, certainly this would have been a strategy of *"tous azimuts."* It would have been capable of being applied in Asia or in Africa or anywhere. But this wasn't done. My proposal was not accepted.
>
> For France, therefore, we have had to take into consideration our own position. We are now making our own atomic arms. Naturally, we must be concerned with all points of the compass—just like the United States whose strategy must aim in all directions. For example, its submarines can cover the entire world. Although we are not nearly so strong, we also must devise systems of atomic weapons that are able to act in all directions. Who knows what the world will be like in several years' time?

I asked point-blank whether he had decided if France should stay in the North Atlantic Alliance—pointing out that I did not mean the organization but the alliance—when it became legally possible to opt out. De Gaulle replied cagily: "Until now I have not decided whether or not to leave. When we left the NATO organization [March 1966] I wrote to President Johnson saying that France would stay in the alliance after

1970, when it becomes possible to denounce the alliance, if East-West relationships had not by then commenced to change very substantially. The decision will be announced in 1969 and we will have until then to judge whether there have been considerable changes in East-West relationships. Certainly until now there have not been sufficient changes in such relationships. If I had to take a decision this evening, France would not leave the alliance."

I asked if his deep interest in the fate of the French Canadians implied a similar interest in the French-speaking populations of Belgium and Switzerland. "No," he replied quite categorically. "There is no connection. The French-speaking people of Canada are French but the Swiss who speak French are Swiss. [I don't wholly follow this logic.] The people of Quebec are French living under foreign rule. England took Canada and the Canadian French when France was preoccupied with other parts of the world. The French people of Canada are under foreign domination. In the whole world this is the only people subjected to foreign domination with the possible exception of the Arabs in Palestine and the Tibetans in China."

I inquired if the special relationship between France and Israel was categorically at an end. "Yes," he said. "It is finished. They exaggerated and they continue to exaggerate. Israel must agree to evacuate all the territory it has taken by force although in some cases there might be negotiations adjusting certain frontiers. But they cannot keep what they have seized by force."

PARIS, *January 23, 1968*

LONG talk with Georges Pompidou, de Gaulle's Prime Minister and certainly, at the moment, heir apparent. He said: "What you must remember is that the General thinks that after the Vietnam war is over, there is bound to be an *entente* between Moscow and Washington, and it may come at Europe's expense. Peking *fears* such an *entente*. De Gaulle doesn't fear it but he foresees it. After all, American and Soviet interests coincide on two points: (1) the need to control Chinese dynamism, and (2) neither wants Europe to develop as a rival superpower capable of acting on a scale equal to their own."

Pompidou concluded by saying there were no profound differences except for ideology dividing Moscow and Washington, and ideology was losing its importance. "After all, when the Russians have automobiles, what will be the difference?"

PARIS, *March 5, 1968*

LUNCHED today with Étienne Manac'h who has been head of the Asian department of the Quai d'Orsay for eight years. Manac'h assured me categorically that if the United States announces a cease-bombing—or conveys such a guarantee to Hanoi secretly—the North promises *immediate* negotiations.

Unfortunately, the conflict has become "an American war aided by South Vietnam" instead of a "South Vietnamese war aided by the U.S.A." Washington finds it is unable to de-Americanize the war sufficiently to make Saigon assume enough responsibility and become strong.

The last thing Manac'h said as we parted was, "Be sure and tell your son to be prudent when he goes to Vietnam. You remember when the three of us lunched together and I told him to be prudent and then the Tet offensive came. Now tell him on my behalf to be even more prudent and tell him again."

CAIRO, *March 21, 1968*

THIS morning I dropped in on Mohamed Heikal. He took me to the immensely impressive new fourteen-story office *Al Ahram* has built and will move into this May.

He told me that this morning Israel invaded Jordan with armored columns and helicopters to punish terrorists' bases. (Later in the day this event canceled my scheduled 6:00 P.M. talk with Nasser.)

Heikal says U.S. and Western influence are declining; that in ten years there will be 4 million Israelis against 100 million Arabs who are developing also, as well as the Israelis. If necessary the Arabs were ready to join the Soviet bloc to win. The United States has a bad policy and hardly any influence left.

BELGRADE, *May 16, 1968*

THIS afternoon I spent an hour and a half with Tito. I asked if he didn't think present events in Czechoslovakia, like other events in Eastern Europe over recent years, were a direct consequence of what the world calls "Titoism." He answered: "I call this democratization, not Titoism. People in other countries are trying to democratize and liberalize situations that had previously been stagnant. It doesn't mean that they will follow the same path we have pursued in Yugoslavia. But practice in the past has shown that changes are necessary. We are dialecticians and we know that what is good today, or necessary today, becomes neither as good or necessary tomorrow."

I observed that Jugoslavia, in asserting its freedom to develop its own road to socialism twenty years ago, had made it easier for other Eastern European lands to do so. He said: "It was more difficult for us in 1948 than it has perhaps been for others since. Yet our desire was not to give an example to others but to act because it was a necessity. We have never said any particular aspect of Marxism is outdated. We still use Marxism as our main inspiration. Marxism remains a dogma, but we apply it to our own special needs and to the international situation as a whole—as it develops. We think the truth of Marxism is more than ever confirmed today." (I noted that Tito never once mentioned Leninism; in the past, he used to talk of Marxism-Leninism.)

"As soon as Trotsky's idea of the permanent revolution was defeated it became evident that there were different roads to socialism. Nowadays, only China wants one road to socialism."

With special reference to current events in Prague, Tito added elliptically: "I now do not expect exceptional events there. I am sure Czechoslovakia will find a peaceful way of achieving liberalization and democratization. It is a question of putting democracy into practice; there is no need to change theory, only practice. We here in Yugoslavia have often found the need to change practice. But it is more difficult for them to apply this change because they let their errors accumulate too long. As for Poland, the situation there is different and less known. I don't expect anything sensational. The influence of religion is very strong and there is more foreign influence." Plainly implying he meant the United States, he said: "You know what I mean."

I asked what area Tito envisioned as within Europe. Tito acknowledged that perhaps a fair definition of "Europe" was everything west of the Soviet border, including Britain and Ireland.

I turned to Vietnam and the Paris peace talks. Tito said: "I want military operations there to end. The bombing must end. The Vietnamese people must be given the possibility to decide on their own fate; and the sooner the better, for them and for the world. If this happens the Americans will rid themselves of a certain hatred abroad. I know the people of the United States want peace but there are some Americans who are responsible for this situation."

I asked him, as an atheist, what he considered death and the purpose of life was. Tito said: "Death depends on how one lives. If you have done something useful it will survive you. If someone has played a certain role in life, even then the world won't go downhill when he dies. What he has done for the good will remain. Much depends on what one has contributed to a country or a people. History is a long process. People never forget what was positive in the contribution of any leader. They will always remember what was good in his achievements. There is a proverb: 'Happy is the man who lives forever.' What this means is that he has done something good."

BELGRADE, *May 17, 1968*

FASCINATING day revisiting Milovan Djilas for hours. I hadn't seen Milovan in years. When I rang the doorbell to his apartment, he answered, shook

my hand warmly, and said: "But you have become smaller." "So have you,"
I answered. Both statements were true. He said:

> Prison refined and deepened my thinking, my ideas. Prison for a short
> period is good—from two to five years. You have the possibility of thinking
> about life, about destiny. But now I have been there too long; I do not need
> it again. During those years in prison I changed many of my thoughts on
> history, on policy. But I did not change my personal thoughts, my personal-
> ity. I became more and more courageous. I cannot explain this but it was a
> fact.
>
> The first time I was imprisoned under Tito I wasn't guilty, juridically
> speaking and from a Western viewpoint, but I had really been aggressive
> toward the party and the government in opposing their views. However, the
> second time [over *Conversations with Stalin*] I was absolutely innocent.
>
> The first time I was a rebel and a malcontent. The second time I was
> not. I was sure of my innocence then and that it would be legally proved. I
> was arrested the second time only because I didn't capitulate and also be-
> cause Russia was involved as a matter of state policy when *Conversations
> with Stalin* came out. They would have arrested me even without that
> book—just for seeing the foreign press.

I asked how he described his ideology today. He said:

> Today I don't know if I'm a Marxist. I'm surely a democratic-socialist,
> politically—not a regular social-democrat in the Western sense. I'm an athe-
> ist. I'm a materialist. But not in a Marxist sense. Marxism is outdated. It is
> old-fashioned. The human being and modern society are too complex to be
> adjusted to Hegelian dialectics.
>
> I am not a religious man but I know that a human being must have
> conscience and morality. I agree with religion that a man must believe in
> something; but not in God. All versions of communism are becoming deca-
> dent. They must inevitably change into a new democratic society. This is
> absolutely inevitable. Communism is a combative warrior's concept and
> organization, and society cannot bear to live indefinitely in such a tense
> atmosphere.
>
> Imprisonment involves moral elements that I could not at first understand.
> But I knew. I knew from the start that I could not be broken. Now there is
> much more tolerance. My picture has been removed from museums and
> records and there are still the restrictions but everything is less rigid.

Milovan said: "In East Europe, anywhere, there is no communism any
more. But what you and some people call Djilasism is synonymous with
democracy. Now I am even more convinced that communism must move
toward democracy than I ever was before. I have always been fundamentally socialist. Socialism and socialist ownership must be the main
force, but unfortunately this form of ownership is allowed to produce
bureaucracy and dictatorship."

He continued: "I still think Karl Marx is the greatest man of modern
history. He was a prophet, not a scientist. You cannot find in all human
history any idea that has taken hold of mankind like Marxism."

I remarked that Professor (Hugh) Trevor-Roper had compared events in China now with Stalin's purges in the thirties; what did he think? He said:

No. Only superficially. Mao, indeed, was treated as a godlike figure, like Stalin. But there were major differences. His methods are not the same as Stalin's. Stalin had cruel methods in the party. Mao has killed no party leaders, even if he disagrees with them. And Mao has understood that what has come about in Russia now is the development of a new privileged class. He is trying to prevent the same thing from happening in China; but he will succeed only during his own lifetime, as long as he lives.

After he dies, everything will change. Ultimately there must be an understanding between China and the United States. The United States is infinitely the greatest economic power, and the second greatest power is the United States in Europe, the American economic empire in Europe. There is a strange phenomenon today, the expansion of American technology, not of American military force. The only modern empire today is that of the United States. The Russian empire is old-fashioned, continental, not global, world-wide, and modern. America is a great military force, has a great military power, but it is not a military empire, only a technical empire.

I remarked that Tito now seemed to talk only of "Marxism," no more of "Marxism-Leninism." He said with a tired smile:

Now he is going back to Marx, to the young Marx. Now he is a Marxist theoretician. The young Marx wasn't a Marxist; he was half Hegelian. And you can't stop there. The thinking Marxists here now believe that Lenin and Stalin were wrong from a *Marxist* point of view. We are going back to Marx from Lenin the way the Protestants went back to the Bible from the Vatican.

Democratization will occur here in Jugoslavia without any revolution; it won't be quick or easy but it will happen without a civil war. After all, in 1956, the trouble in Hungary wasn't a revolution in the classical sense. It was just one single mass explosion. In several days it was finished. There was never really a civil war. Today in Czechoslovakia a peaceful revolution is going on.

At this point Djilas ventured into prophesy. He said: "The East and the West [meaning Russia and the United States] are going toward each other, together, not as societies but as countries: Russia has an old imperial idea but this will be changed and modified in the West as a great China develops and Moscow sees the old-fashioned danger of a yellow threat. You know, there are genuine elements of racism in Maoism."

PARIS, *May 29, 1968*

LUNCH today with Étienne Manac'h as the Fifth Republic began visibly to come apart. This morning de Gaulle suddenly called off a Cabinet meeting without even advising his ministers and took off for Colombey-les-deux-Églises.

Occasional trucks filled with people carrying the red flag rumbled through the Place de la Madeleine. At the end of our luncheon, Alex Allegrier, owner of the restaurant, came and joined us with a bottle of Marc de Chablis (*age inconnu*) from the private cellar of André Tardieu, who was Prime Minister of France from 1929–1930 and in 1932. He insisted we drink this, saying that he would never sell it and the situation was so uncertain he didn't want to see it wasted.

Manac'h told me the present "revolution" was reaching down to the very roots of the government. Alphand, as Secretary General of the Foreign Ministry, spent his entire consultation with the principal officials of the Quai d'Orsay discussing logistical problems. The Quai has commandeered emergency army signals corps services to help transmit diplomatic messages.

The government cannot get ballots printed for the proposed referendum because the French trade unions refuse to do the job. The government tried to get the ballots printed in Belgium, and the Belgian unions refused.

This is a really revolutionary atmosphere—not in terms of violence of rumbling tumbrels—but in terms of rotting garbage and intellectual ferment.

PARIS, *May 30, 1968*

YESTERDAY in the late afternoon I watched a CGT (pro-Communist labor federation) mass demonstration against de Gaulle. The demonstrators walked from the Bastille to the Gare St. Lazare demanding de Gaulle's departure and "popular government." Most of the shouts for *"gouvernment populaire"* and *"de Gaulle à l'hospice"* were with exactly the same rhythm as the mass screams of demonstrators ten years ago for *"Algérie française"* and *"de Gaulle au pouvoir."* Here and there were red curly revolutionary caps of 1789. I could not help but reflect on the cruelty of history. Ten years ago de Gaulle came in with the tanks when armored units were rumbling across the Pont de la Concorde. Now they want to push him out with the garbage festering in uncollected cans.

De Gaulle disappeared from the Élysée yesterday and did not show up in Colombey-les-deux-Églises for seven hours. Nobody knows where he was. It is my guess that he must have been conferring with General (Jacques) Massu and other commanders of the French forces in Germany along the Franco-German border.

PARIS, *May 31, 1968*

YESTERDAY de Gaulle came back from Colombey, held a Cabinet meeting, then went on the radio (television is blocked out by the strike) and announced he was going to fight to keep the Communists from taking over.

A demonstration supporting de Gaulle had already been organized on the Place de la Concorde and the Champs-Élysées. More than half a million people took part.

Right across the river parked along the quays as usual were the long lines of grey-green beetle-shaped trucks in which the CRS (armed gendarmerie) moves from threatened point to threatened point.

PARIS, *June 3, 1968*

WENT over to the Odéon, which has been taken over by students who use the theater as a kind of debating hall. The lobby is filled with scrawled posters, and there are others attached to the main curtain hanging above the stage. Dominating these is one huge sign saying: *"L'ex-Odéon est une tribune libre,"* and another says *"La Révolution n'est pas seulement celle des comités mais avant tout la vôtre."*

PARIS, *June 6, 1968*

LUNCHED with Harriman. The news just came that Bobby Kennedy had died. There is some strange hell taking place in the United States.

Bobby's assassination removes from the American political race the one man who could be regarded by Hanoi as a "dove." Harriman said Bobby wasn't really a dove and wanted a genuine compromise settlement without any surrender, but he admitted Hanoi might have misinterpreted it.

Averell described General Maxwell Taylor and Walt Rostow as bitter-end hawks who wanted a military victory. He thought Fulbright and McCarthy were extreme doves; Bobby came between them.

Poor Randolph Churchill died today—as always, a footnote.

PARIS, *July 8, 1968*

AN hour today with Georges Pompidou. He has just pulled de Gaulle's fat out of the fire, and now he is rewarded by having his throat cut.

The story is simple: de Gaulle is firing him as Prime Minister, and he is being succeeded by Couve de Murville. This is likely to be announced the day after tomorrow after the Cabinet meeting.

TEL AVIV, *July 24, 1968*

DROVE down to Sde Boker, the desert kibbutz, to see David Ben-Gurion, Israel's grand old man, former Prime Minister and (together with Chaim Weizmann) principal founder of the Zionist state.

His study was an incredible mess. Behind him in the center of one shelf was a bad plaster bust of Plato. Books and papers littered his desk and cluttered up most of the chairs and the other table. He has a messy filing system of his own, including all kinds of precious documents such as letters from de Gaulle and Kennedy, stashed in simple portfolios. In one bookcase is a set of four volumes, bound in leather, containing all the records, papers and conversations of the 1956 Suez war. He says there are only three sets, and they will not be published "until after Eden's death." He said:

> When I had lunch with de Gaulle in 1960, he asked me: "Are you satisfied with your present frontiers?" I replied: "In 1920, three years after the Balfour declaration, I sent a memorandum to the British Labor party outlining my ideas on this point. Our northern border should some day be," I said, "the river Litani in southern Lebanon. In the east the frontier should be a line running south of Damascus along the Awage river and then through the desert east of Jordan. And our southern border should be the Red Sea."
>
> These, I felt in 1920, should be the proper boundaries of an eventual state of Israel. But when the UN adopted the 1947 resolution which we accepted —even without Jerusalem—I was prepared to agree on this frontier—yes, even without Jerusalem. If the Arabs had accepted this we would have that border today.
>
> Had the Arabs agreed in 1947, the borders fixed then by UN in the partition plan would have been final. But the Arabs refused. War came and the entire situation was changed. The boundaries of Israel, after the 1948 war, included five thousand more square kilometers than the 1947 partition plan.
>
> Now I return to that conversation with de Gaulle. I told de Gaulle that if the Arabs had accepted the UN decision in 1947 we would have stuck to it. The area designated by UN in 1947 was big enough for all the Jews I could imagine coming to Israel, five, six, or seven million of them. They could have fitted in. After all, not all the Jews in the world intended to come.

I asked what he thought should be Israel's boundaries today, after three wars. He said:

> I am now a private citizen. I speak only for myself. But look: after the six-day war two groups came into being here. One wanted peace with the Arabs, peace on a reasonable basis. The other wanted the entire area of old Palestine, the area I described in my letter to the British Labor party. My private view, now, is that if the choice lies between peace and the boundaries we obtained as a result of our victory in the six-day war, peace and the boundaries that existed in early 1967, I prefer peace.
>
> But I don't just mean a signed document. The Arabs don't respect papers. They didn't keep the armistice agreement, after all. I mean a real peace. I mean cooperation between Israel and the Arabs, economic, political, cultural cooperation. For such a peace I would prefer to yield all the territory we took last year.

I asked: "Including East Jerusalem?" His reply was Delphic: "It would be very hard to give up East Jerusalem."

We talked about death. He said: "The purpose of life is to enjoy it, to make it pleasanter for every human being. We don't know of another world so we must concentrate on this one. People should be just and decent and loving. There is no mention in our Bible of an afterlife. Death is simply the end; there is no word of another world. This is what it seems to be. But I don't know. Nobody knows. Once I talked about this to Einstein and he said: 'The more we progress in science, the more we realize what we don't know. Our ignorance increases; the riddle grows.' I asked him: 'Is there life after death?' He said: 'I wish I knew.' But remember, in his will he left orders that his body should be burned. He didn't think he would come back again. Remember, there is no word in the Torah that concerns any other life."

NICOSIA, *July 26, 1968*

PLEASANT talk with Archbishop Makarios, still president of Cyprus. I inquired who, alive or dead, had most influenced his life. He said: "First of all the Stoic philosophers of ancient Greece." This was not unexpected since Zeno, the great Stoic, was a Cypriot, born at Citium (now Larnaca).

> But from our era, of those alive in my time, I have no doubt it was Gandhi. Especially during my stay in the Seychelles Islands [where he was exiled by the British during the wind-up of colonial days]. I had the time to read a good deal about him. He was the greatest moral personality of our time, a real prophet.
>
> You know, people admire two kinds of personalities—the hero and the saint. Most people prefer the hero type but I believe the saint is greater. For me, I will always be a man about whom people will disagree. Some people will say that I didn't care about bloodshed, people outside Cyprus. But people in Cyprus will say that I am too moderate, that I compromise too much. You cannot please everyone.

ATHENS, *August 17, 1968*

THIS morning I had a talk with Prime Minister George Papadopoulos. He recalled our last meeting just after the coup d'état—and made it quite clear that he did not recall it with favor.

He said: "We have no differences with America, but America does not realize what the situation here is—especially with reference to the Russian fleet in the Mediterranean. And this has its consequence on the sentimental ties of the Greek people vis-à-vis the American people. The Greek people do not understand this cool U.S. policy. And it affects the military preparedness of Greece. The Greek government does not request arms from the United States to impose its own political views, but only in order to be prepared to fulfill its obligations within the alliance."

ROME, *October 10, 1968*

DRINK and long talk with King Constantine. He looked pale and tired.

He asked what I thought he should do. I said get out of Rome, go either to London, a serious capital, or take a house in Zurich and go to the polytechnical institute. "I'm bad at mathematics," said he.

He thinks Papadopoulos is going to keep things as they are for years. It will be at least three years before there are elections. He arrests people of right and left without any excuse, just to keep them off balance. "It's like judo, political judo."

BUCHAREST, *October 30, 1968*

TALK with Nicolae Ceausescu, president of the state council (chief of state) and General Secretary of the Communist Party, total boss of Rumania. He had recently, in a speech, said Rumania sought the "broadest democracy" possible. Were the ultimate implications of this a free press and a permitted political opposition? Ceausescu said:

> To be quite frank, I did not have such things in mind. When I spoke of the "broadest democracy" I meant that all of the members of our society possess equal rights and participate directly in the discussion of all problems on both internal and external questions. They can speak their minds and openly criticize such errors and shortcomings as may appear, and which are bound to appear.
>
> I don't think, however, that in a socialist society where conditions for a permanent partnership of all groups have been created, there is any need for different political parties. Furthermore, I for one think our press enjoys the broadest freedom. [It is quite state-controlled.] Of course, if this means the freedom of anyone to write anything—we do not agree.

He said Rumania did not regard intervention in Czechoslovakia as justified from any point of view, "And with the passage of time our conviction has become even stronger."

I asked if he considered President Johnson's August 30 warning to the Russians on laying off Rumania had been helpful. "Yes, it was useful," he said. I asked for permission to quote him on that. "No," he replied, politely but firmly. "But next time you see the president please pass on my message."

When I had finished and was tucking my notebook in my pocket, Ceausescu looked at me a bit timidly and asked if he could now ask a question. Who did I think would win the American presidential election next week? I said it looked as if Nixon would win, but that in any case I did not think there would be any difference in the foreign policy of a Nixon or a Humphrey. As for Wallace, he was just a sad joke.

"I met Nixon," said Ceausescu. "That was about four years ago. Of course, he wasn't a president then. But neither was I." (Ceausescu became chief of state last December.) I asked what he thought of Nixon.

"We had a very good talk. He impressed me. He showed a real understanding of international problems and of our own situation. I found that we agreed very substantially on China. We both thought there could be no solid basis for world peace until China was brought into it. We also agreed on disarmament. He impressed me as being an experienced and knowledgeable man."

BUDAPEST, *November 6, 1968*

I WAS received by the boss, (Janos) Kadar, at Communist Party headquarters, the first Westerner of any sort Kadar has seen since August 21 (Czechoslovakia).

I asked if the cold war was now reviving because of Czechoslovakia. He was gloomy. He said: "The cold war has revived, first and foremost because of the Vietnamese conflict. To this trend the Czechoslovakian events and clashes have had an additional effect. In my opinion, there are many dangerously sensitive questions in the world—like the Middle East or Germany.

"The cold war trends are plain. First came the extension of the Vietnam war. Then there was the Middle East crisis and war. Then, this year, came the political debate on Czechoslovakia." ("Political debate" is not probably the way history will describe the events of August 21.)

Why, I asked, had Hungary felt it necessary to join in "physical action" against Czechoslovakia? He said: "Because in our judgment the situation there had developed to such a degree that it seriously endangered socialism and there was a real threat that they might end up in taking Czechoslovakia out of the Warsaw pact."

Did this imply, I inquired, that Czechoslovakia in 1968 was comparable to Hungary in 1956, Dubček to Nagy? "In the essence," said Kadar, "there were many similarities, although the form in which they expressed themselves was different."

PARIS, *November 18, 1968*

Y., of the Czech Embassy, called today and told me this riddle: Which is the most neutral country in the world today? Czechoslovakia—because its government doesn't even dare intervene in its own affairs.

MOSCOW, *November 22, 1968*

YURI Zhukov suggested I come on over. His views, summarized: The Czechoslovakian occupation demonstrated only that Russia was determined to maintain the status quo, not that it wished to change it. Any change in the status quo is dangerous.

If NATO says it wishes to avoid any alteration in its frontiers or what lies behind them, OK. But there can be no "grey area" as now suggested in the November Brussels communiqué of NATO which spoke of Austria, Jugoslavia, Finland, Albania, and without mentioning it, implied Rumania also.

I said Moscow's new "commonwealth doctrine" as expressed by Gromyko, implied a "right" to interfere in the affairs of any "socialist" state. What were they? Cuba? China? Mali? Egypt? Yuri said such states were "well known." It was sheer "romance" for (Leopold) Senghor, president of Senegal, to consider himself a "socialist."

Russia had no desire to send its forces into other lands. Czechoslovakia was a very special case. First of all it was necessary to "help the Czech people to defend themselves." And secondly, from a strategic viewpoint, it was necessary to keep the status quo.

MOSCOW, *November 23, 1968*

PLEASANT chat with (Ambassador Llewellyn) Tommy Thompson. Tommy said Khrushchev was not regarded here as just a chief of the opposition but as an enemy who would have his successors bumped off if he ever were able to scramble back to power. Nixon had made the great mistake of trying to see him on his last trip. This left a bad taste, and the regime still looks on Nixon with skepticism.

Tommy thinks the essence of Soviet foreign policy is now to keep the status quo—in order to concentrate on internal affairs. This was the real meaning of Czechoslovakia, whose occupation was a purely defensive move. Russia will probably try and scare Rumania into line, and its attitude toward Jugoslavia is unclear. But this is not the forerunner of further expansionist tendencies.

As for the Far East, Russia wants the United States to counterbalance Chinese influence. But there is no serious worry here about a war with China—either about having such a war or about losing it; Russia could clobber China.

MOSCOW, *November 28, 1968*

LUNCHEON in my honor given at the Prague Restaurant by Ambassador Leonid Zamyatin. He pointed out in a toast that he had deliberately chosen the Prague! Zamyatin said Russia was Public Enemy Number One in China (way ahead of us), but he thought the people who opposed Mao were pro-Soviet, that the United States had no friends. When change comes it will be pro-Moscow.

WARSAW, *December 4, 1968*

SAW Jozef Winiewicz, acting Foreign Minister. He hopes Czechoslovakia's role in the Warsaw Pact's northern tier grouping will be reestablished. Poland's special position in the Communist world ("let's not use the euphemism, socialist," he suggested) resulted largely from Gomulka's personality, as "personalities do play a role in politics."

PRAGUE, *December 10, 1968*

EXCELLENT talk this morning with P. of the economic institute, a large man with glasses, uninhibited and nice. A good Communist Party member, he thinks communism is going to hell. He is not going to take part in the Soviet-Czech economic talks due to start soon and is glad: "I would have to commit either murder or suicide; suicide is easier."

He is convinced Russia is doomed if there is no change in its economic system, therefore its society. Czechoslovakia's big mistake in the past was to think what was being done—"here, or in Russia, was socialism." In Russia it isn't even state capitalism. It is tsarist bureaucracy mixed with Byzantium. If this continues, at most Russia has two years before a bust.

PRAGUE, *December 11, 1968*

THEN I went to the Prime Minister's office to see Peter Colotka, Vice-Premier, a pleasant, well-built Slovak whose healthy appearance was belied by a very nervous eye twitch. He said "normalization" could only be considered as returned when all Soviet troops leave (which I forecast as decades hence). "Our neighbors must understand our problems."

PARIS, *December 25, 1968*

LUNCHED and played bridge yesterday with the Harrimans. Averell told me that he had congratulated Stalin at Potsdam for being in Berlin. Stalin's only reply was "Tsar Alexander got to Paris."

BELFAST, *January 21, 1969*

YESTERDAY I went to Stormont, the Parliament, where Prime Minister O'Neill gave me lunch. O'Neill (Captain Terence) comes from an old family of loyal aristocrats (taking over the ancient royal name from distant maternal relatives) and is thoroughly anglicized: Protestant, World War II, Eton, etc.

O'Neill said: "Partition bought peace for Ireland. It ended the war and murder that had continued to feature here since Norman times. The reformation had only made things worse by introducing the religious element—Catholic versus Protestant."

I then drove on a terrible, sleety day to Armagh, site of St. Patrick's best-known church and uniquely the see of both the Catholic primate and the Church of Ireland primate. I was shown into Cardinal William Conway's residence by a pleasant servant who turned on the electric fire, took my coat, and invited me into the cold, unattractive sitting room. A moment later he came in, a sturdy, tall, agreeable man with a clear, strong face and courteous manner.

He said that in Northern Ireland politics and religion were inextricably mixed. The Protestants were descended from English conquerors and Scottish colonists, from garrison soldiers and from postreformation settlers. "The presumption here is that if you know a man's religion you know his politics."

PARIS, *February 14, 1969*

THIS afternoon I saw de Gaulle. He said: "I think we can hope to further the rapprochement between Washington and Paris. And there is another aspect to the whole problem—namely relationships with Russia. Little by little, you are becoming more like us in your view of this problem. Like us, you don't want to have them submerge Europe. But you are beginning to see that it is useful to develop practical contacts such as those we started. You will follow the same path that we have been following because that is the practical approach."

I asked if his 1958 concept—the so-called *directoire* idea about which he wrote to President Eisenhower—was philosophically still valid. Categorically, he replied: "No, that is over. It is ended. It was possible in 1958 because there was a big Soviet danger at the time but there is no reason for it now. After all," said the general, "nobody thinks the Russians will move west any more, do they?" I did not mention the word "Czechoslovakia."

I observed that in the past he had told me no country in the long run could avoid being drawn into the orbit of influence of one or the other superpowers, Russia and America. Was he worried about this possibility now? He answered:

That is not quite precisely what I told you. Let me explain. Since always, we have favored the United States. Historically, we have always been friends. This has been for various reasons. World reasons, the nature of the country, ideology. Also, we have never been rivals before. Remember, in the past, you were never in Africa, in Asia, or even in Europe.

Also, you should remember that we have old reasons for being friends of Russia. For us, in Europe, this Russian friendship has always been necessary as a counterweight to Germany. Constantly in history, we have sought to be on good terms with Russia, with the tsars, with the Soviets, as a counterweight to Germany. We have been old friends with America and old allies of

Russia. And the Franco-Russian feeling is a natural event. Today we have no reason to renounce friendship with the United States. Neither, especially now that Germany reemerges, have we any reason to break off with Russia.

And another thing, something we should never forget, is that one must always remember what France was, historically, just after the war and what it is today. France is as it is and the French are as they are. If the French don't think of France, it disappears. But you cannot think of France if you lose a sense of independence. The friendship of the French for the United States requires no American hegemony. The same is true with Russia. It is for that reason that the communists have never succeeded here, for national reasons, not for social reasons.

Germany has been demolished, has been cut in two. And we must remember that Germany has only been one country for a relatively short period of time. Germany's history is not the same as that of France. The Germans are readier to accept a United States hegemony—and anyway [here de Gaulle flashed a malevolent quick smile] they can't avoid it. As for Britain, Britain has renounced its independence. It has sold it off for advantages of all sorts. And Italy counts for very little. It knows less than one century as a united, independent country.

I asked how long he thought American troops should remain stationed in Europe. He replied: "Until there is a real East-West *détente*, it is obviously normal to keep American troops in Germany. But if there is a *real* [and he stressed this] *détente*, there would be no more reason for such detachments except for symbolic units. But the fact that you have troops in Germany now doesn't irritate us; so have we."

I asked if France considered itself neutral as between Israelis and Arabs, in the sense that it would support either side if it were attacked by the other. He said, "Yes. In 1967 I told Israel not to attack. I also told the same to the Arabs. We told both sides that we would hold either one responsible if it attacked the other."

I observed that on the basis of what he had been saying concerning West Germany, I had a distinct impression the special friendship pact wasn't working well. Was this true? De Gaulle shrugged his shoulders very high. An expression that was half whimsical and half disagreeable came over his white face. "It is not a big thing now. I suppose that is the least one can say," he observed.

24

S PENT TWO HOURS WITH NASSER IN HIS RESIDENCE IN EASTERN CAIRO. Mohamed Heikal took me out. Nasser had just had a "throat treatment" from a Soviet doctor. Later in the conversation he said he had gained fourteen kilos last year, when he had been seriously ill, had lost them all, was now gaining them back. He has given up smoking, which is one reason, of course, and can't play tennis any more because he apparently has rheumatism in his left leg. He now walks before lunch and tries to cut down on his food. (Heikal says it's no trouble dieting around Nasser's house because he has an abominable cook.)

Nasser said: "We are ready to resume relations with the United States, but as long as the United States supports the Israeli occupation of our territory and as long as the United States supplies Israel with planes while it is occupying our territory, there will be difficulties."

I asked if he foresaw a fourth round of war. He said: "This is a very simple question. We are striving to end the occupation of Arab territory in Egypt, Jordan, and Syria by a political solution—by peaceful means. If we don't achieve it by peaceful means, what result? We must strive by other means to achieve it. One could not accept occupation of his country. One has to fight."

I then asked if there was danger of a nuclear explosion in the Middle East. He answered: "As long as the Israelis don't sign the nonproliferation treaty, there is danger. We have signed it, but if they begin there will be a race. If they tried to build nuclear weapons we would try to have our own. We have the capacity but what we need is the investment money required. I do not believe the Israelis have such weapons now."

He said there were no Soviet naval bases here, adding: "We don't have any base in our country for any foreign country. Of course the Soviets were visiting our ports before the aggression against our country and they visit our ports also now. We welcome visits because the Soviet Union helped us after the aggression, they supplied us with arms after we lost our arms."

I asked: "How many Soviet military training personnel and technicians are there today in the UAR?" He said: "Really, I don't know the figure, but I am asking for more technicians."

I observed: "It seems to me that you have an unusual talent for turning defeat into victory and for climbing out of pits. What is the secret?" He said: "You know, I believe that I am a lucky man in spite of the catastrophe we face now. On the other hand, I don't plan it. It is natural. After the defeat, I was willing to leave. But, you know, when I said that I was selfish. I was trying to escape, but I was not able to. I was really intending to leave. I was very tired and sick. But now it is over. I am not going to surrender. I believe in God. I am a fatalistic man. I believe in his will."

I asked what he dreamed Egypt will be in twenty-five years' time. He said: "My main dream is to develop this country. To have electricity in each village and have work for every man. I want to see this country without servants before my death. Now it is difficult for people to find servants. And this always-increasing problem about getting servants means an increasing standard of living. I have no personal dreams. I have no personal life. I have nothing personal. Many people may not believe that, but this is the truth."

RAWALPINDI, PAKISTAN, *March 3, 1969*

TROUBLE is obviously coming here. This time the power may leave the elite. The future is murky. Will the Constitution be changed? Will the East get autonomy?

NEW DELHI, *March 10, 1969*

THIS afternoon I spent an hour with Mrs. Indira Gandhi, the Prime Minister. As far as I am concerned, she has more charm than the legendary appeal of her father, Nehru.

She is a small woman with dark brown eyes, black, greying hair. She was seated behind a large desk, remained in her chair as she shook hands, but produced a pleasant smile. She was wearing a white blouse under a blue sari. I remarked that there must be both advantages and disadvantages to being a female chief of government. She said: "I don't think it really makes any difference. Obviously every person has some advantages and some disadvantages in a job like this. For India you can have pluses and minuses in terms of the region you come from or the caste to which your family belongs. Some people say that a woman hasn't as much stamina as a man. Of course, I can't tell, never having been a man. But I certainly have more physical stamina than anyone else around here."

I observed that, in any case, a woman Prime Minister might benefit because men were more polite to her. "Certainly not," said she with only half a smile. "They surely are no more polite. Don't think that."

I said her father's ideology had been described frequently as Fabian socialism, although I personally thought that a rather fuzzy label. How would she describe her own ideology? She answered:

I don't think I can be said to have any ideology at all in this vague sense. After all, I have to face specific problems and specific situations. You just have to find the best way of doing things as they arise. Sometimes you just have to compromise with what you would prefer. For example, we didn't want to import food. But we had to; it was a matter of life and death.

Our party wants to use the tool of socialism to raise living standards, but this obviously isn't necessarily the socialism of other countries. Our methods must be fitted to the minds and the backgrounds of our people. Essentially, there are no two ways open to us. Ours is such a large mass, so poor and so backward economically that you can't afford just to let things take their course. The people won't wait that long. The state must take things upon itself. It would just create more problems were we to leave everything to private enterprise. Private enterprise always seeks to make a profit and you can't have a profit in all the aspects of the problems facing us, above all with the enormous need for social justice and for welfare. We must be pragmatic.

It's hard to say just what our ideology is. We use the word socialism as the nearest thing. But there is no particular prophet of our socialism. We are really seeking a new and middle path. We believe in a mixed economy.

I observed that some people thought India—and her government—were over-dependent on Russia because it was so heavily the source of the country's military equipment nowadays. She said: "We want to stand on our own feet and we try our hardest to be self-sufficient. And remember this—just because we get equipment from a country doesn't mean we'll do what they want. We won't do what anyone wants simply because we get hardware there."

I asked if ideology represented any barrier between India and the United States. "Not for us," she said.

What does come up is this sort of thing. When we learned that the CIA was indirectly financing institutions that were helping us there was a wave of anger at getting any such help. That's upsetting. But we have no ideological divisions; I have none and I hope the majority of us don't.

Some people in the United States say that we are too close to Russia and that we vote too often on the Soviet side in UN. But this really isn't so; it is only true on such issues as those involving colonialism and racism, and here it is not a question of us following the Russians but a question of the Russians taking the stand that happens to agree with ours. The Russians have simply shown a greater understanding of the needs and mentality of newly-freed peoples.

I asked if she actually liked being Prime Minister. She smiled and said: "You know, I had a very strict training. My grandfather, who died when I was thirteen, brought us up in a most Spartan way. My grandfather told us: 'You can't ever do anything well unless you enjoy it. If you think a job is boring or a drudgery you will never succeed in it.' I guess that is your answer."

SAIGON, *March 25, 1969*

LONG talk with President Nguyen Van Thieu in the presidential palace, surrounded by a coil of barbed wire in which a gap is opened by guards for vehicles or pedestrians. Inside, I saw two helicopters poised in a state of readiness and several tanks and armored personnel carriers. On the roof I noticed two machine guns manned, presumably against a possible airborne attack.

Thieu is small, delicately made, and has an alert but hooded intelligent face. The president started off in English and handled it extremely well.

I asked if any kind of nonalignment for South Vietnam was possible in the eventual postwar situation. He replied: "No. That would clearly not be realistic. South Vietnam must belong to the free world. We should work within that framework. There can't be any form of neutralism that does not result in our being dominated by the communists. Any other interpretation is simply an illusion. I don't believe in all this talk about Ho Chi Minh as a kind of Tito. You can't compare Vietnam and Jugoslavia. We know perfectly well that the Chinese simply would not permit that kind of development, even if the communists tried it, because we know what the Chinese intend to do."

SAIGON, *March 26, 1969*

THIS afternoon I met General Creighton W. Abrams, commander of our forces here. He is a very tough-looking man of about five feet ten inches, stockily built with slightly reddish complexion, balding brown hair. He has a gentleness to him that sometimes very strong men have, a soft look in his blue eyes and a low, soft voice. I am told he is extremely fond of music. He was wearing fatigues and smoking a cigar when he received me.

I asked what was the strategic goal of the present Communist offensive? He answered: "It is too early to assess this with any high degree of confidence. Certainly I think one objective of this offensive is its effect on the American people. But then, don't forget the communists *do* want to overthrow this government and that is the number one objective—to get Thieu, Ky, and Huong out of there."

The enemy had "realistically sought to accomplish his objectives in the most effective way." But Abrams disagreed with his own staff, which argued that the Communists were trying to conserve manpower in their present tactics. "Look at those figures," said Abrams. "I say that's a hell of a way to conserve manpower. I think we got into his machinery more than we ever did before. And we need a good understanding of this before we can really understand what his strategy was—whether it was to weaken American public opinion, to change the situation at the Paris talks, or to knock down this government."

The general said our program of bombing the north had the tendency of pulling all the people there together, "because it gave them something real to fight against." He did not think that the complete bombing halt against the north had "adversely affected what we are doing here in South Vietnam."

I had a feeling that the greatest U.S. strategic success in our Vietnam commitment had been saving Indonesia from Chinese Communist control. He agreed and said: "That's the idea I came out here with." He thought the United States was now gaining time as a result of the continued war and the enemy was losing time; that, therefore, we were benefiting in a relative sense during the protracted peace talks.

SAIGON, *March 31, 1969*

YESTERDAY I flew up to see Dick Stilwell, now a lieutenant general in command of Twenty-fourth Corps at Phu Bai. A moment after my arrival Dick came in from a helicopter tour, and we sat down and chatted. As we talked I heard outgoing artillery rounds. The VC rocketed the headquarters a few days ago blowing up his officers' bar.

Dick says we have now reached the point where time is on our side, and the longer Hanoi refuses to make peace the more we gain. The Saigon government is improving, and the army is more and more capable each passing day.

We had a quick steak sandwich and raced off to his Huey helicopter, manned by a pilot and copilot and two gunners. Once strapped in, Stilwell handed me earphones and mouthpiece so that we could carry on our conversation despite the noise.

We put in at one fire base of a unit of the 101st Airborne Division where artillery trains in on the Laotian border area. A young major was briefing us when a Chinook came down with a load of ammunition and knocked down the briefing board as well as ourselves with its tremendous wind-blast.

The A Shau Valley is a key point for infiltration of material from Laos. Every now and then Dick pointed to slashes in the jungle where VC grow manioc in order to alleviate their food problem.

We landed at his headquarters so he could show me a VC hole he had had dug in the lawn right by the entrance and plugged by a regular plug taken from a real VC hole. Although everyone knew exactly where it was, it took two officers about four minutes to find the top, so skillfully was it camouflaged and set into the ground. When the plug was pulled up it disclosed an entrance into a cave about eight feet deep.

HONG KONG, *April 10, 1969*

THE "China-watching" section of the consulate general says a fascinating development is the new flirtation between Chiang Kai-shek and the Kremlin. Since 1927, when Chiang turned against the Communists and his own Soviet advisers, he has been violently anti-Soviet. But, now that he is an octogenarian, he says that he is willing either to forget ideology or to revert to the ideology of his youth. When Victor Louis, a Soviet literary agent, journalist, and undoubtedly a representative of the intelligence apparatus, applied for admission to Taiwan, the desire was referred up to Chiang and the visa was granted. Louis saw General Chiang Ching-kuo, son of the Generalissimo and heir apparent. The flirtation has proceeded since then.

TOKYO, *April 17, 1969*

SAW Prime Minister Eisaku Sato at his official residence, a singularly hideous building. He is reassured that the United States is exercising great caution and restraint in the present crisis brought about by the shooting down (two days ago) of a U.S. reconnaissance plane, far out at sea, by the North Koreans.

I observed that Japan still had no proper military force and asked whether Sato favored eventual constitutional amendment to allow this. Sato said: "The truth is we are tired of war."

SEOUL, *April 19, 1969*

STAYING with Ambassador Bill Porter. Porter says the United States was correct to restrain the South Koreans from warlike reactions to the Blue House raid of January 21, 1968, when thirty-one infiltrators came across the line and tried to assassinate President (Chung Hee) Park. (The alternate target was Porter.) Two days later the *Pueblo* incident came. There was a borderline question there as to whether it was in international waters or not, although now it seems certain that it was. But this plane incident is different. There was no violation of North Korean territory.

Bill, who was previously Deputy Ambassador in Saigon, admits he was a real hawk. He is convinced the United States could have moved fast to end the war by extensive bombing of the north (including the dikes) and mines, a naval blockade, and amphibious invasions far enough to the south so that China would not have been frightened.

SEOUL, *April 23, 1969*

LAST night Prime Minister Chung Il Kwon invited us to a *Kaesang* party ("us" being the males, including my son David). Porter brought us, and there we met George Ball, former U.S. Under Secretary of State, who had just come in on a mission for his banking firm. President, in addition to our host, were about ten of South Korea's big shots. Each of us was furnished with his private *Kaesang* girl, the Korean equivalent of Japanese geishas, dressed in the flowing, high-waisted silk dresses of the country. Mine was a lovely little dish named Hopeful Angel.

Chung is a rotund man with glasses, a forty-nine-year-old ex-general, who adores orchestras. He firmly gripped a wooden chopstick and stood up before our little jazz combo, leading it like some fervent Asian Toscanini. When Chung tired of orchestral antics, he danced a mean tango. Everyone was in stockinged feet.

SEOUL, *April 24, 1969*

LONG talk with Prime Minister Chung Il Kwon. He started off by asking, anent the crisis: "Why should we be patient? How should the U.S.A. and Korea prevent a major war here? If war does start, we will have to sacrifice many lives and much prosperity and the world will be miserable. Nevertheless, Kim Il Sung should not be allowed to miscalculate the strength and intentions of the U.S.A. and the Republic of Korea. We want no repetition of the situation caused when your secretary of state Acheson excluded Korea from the American defense perimeter in Asia and a few months later North Korea attacked us. Kim is getting over-confident again."

WASHINGTON, *May 16, 1969*

PLEASANT lunch with Dick Helms, head of the CIA. Dick says the Russians have now doubled their troop strength on the Chinese border. They are scared of the Chinese starting something simply because they regard them as crazy. The island (Damyansky) in the Ussuri over which they squabble is a worthless mud flat. Furthermore, the Chinese have a legal right to it because it's on their side of the river channel.

For the Middle East he is very gloomy. He foresees a fourth round of war unless there is first an arms freeze and an imposed settlement, and there is scant hope of that.

WASHINGTON, *May 19, 1969*

GOOD talk with President Nixon (the first as President) and then lunch (in latter's office) with Henry Kissinger, Nixon's special assistant for national security and foreign policy matters. Kissinger came out, shook hands and shoved me in ahead of him to the President's office. Nixon was sitting at his massive desk. Behind was a table stacked with folders of classified documents. There was scarcely anything on the desk save a copy of my latest book, *A Long Row of Candles.*

Nixon expressed himself well, never fumbling for a word. Kissinger told me later that he writes far more of his own speeches than any other political figure Kissinger has known. Nixon has slightly odd gestures as he talks, seeming to shape ideas or to embrace them with both rather small, unimpressive hands, in a slightly feminine gesture. But he exudes strength and self-confidence.

He recalled his visit to Paris last February and his talks with de Gaulle. De Gaulle had told him it was easier for the United States to leave Vietnam than it had been for France to leave Algeria. After all, there had been "two million Frenchmen" (the real figure is 1 million) in Algeria when the decision was taken. Had Nixon been in his place, "I would probably have done the same thing. He saw the way history was going and knew withdrawal was inevitable. He carried it out with vision and courage."

Nixon said de Gaulle had known all along he couldn't achieve certain things, such as the unification of Europe. There wasn't any chance of unifying Europe today, "and we all know that. Of course, I'll go on making the proper noises—but it isn't going to happen. Things are moving in another direction. Just as with NATO. It isn't possible any more to return to the military emphasis on NATO. The Left would simply object too much."

The present trend was one of disintegration rather than unity, and this was true all over the world, in Europe, in Asia, in the free world and in the Communist world. The stress was now on national states and national policies working for national interests. We had to look at reality and base our policy on it, not on inherited dreams. France was more nationalistic, and so was West Germany. And inside each country there was less unity, more fragmentation.

This, he said, was the particular problem of the United States. He agreed with what I had written of the need for unity here if we are to persist in Vietnam. And he meant everything he had said about our determination "not to fold" and to adhere resolutely to "our very modest objectives."

We can't fold. A great nation sometimes has to act in a great way. Otherwise it destroys its own moral fiber. The British knew that. There is more to this war than just prestige and I am not speaking only of the thousands of people who would be slaughtered if we just pulled out. I don't know what you think of the dominoes theory, but it is obvious that if we pulled out other countries would crumble.

And think of Europe. No matter what some of the politicians say about hoping the "dirty war" will end and that then America can pay more attention to Europe, they really know this wouldn't happen. They fear this would be the start of isolationism and a weakening, not a strengthening, of the American position there. We would be forced by isolationism to go home from there too.

A great power like ours sometimes has to meet challenges elsewhere in the world. The British knew that and there was something valid in the *Pax Brittanica*. It worked. Well, some people talk of a *Pax Americana*. But we have to stay with it.

And we would destroy ourselves if we pulled out in a way that really wasn't honorable. It might take our people a year or two to realize what had happened but they would know in the end. And the reaction would be terrible. I hate to think of it. It would be destructive to our own morale.

You know our objectives in this war are very limited. We only want to establish a real peace. The true objective of this war is peace. It is a war for peace.

He said the real moral crisis in this country was a "leadership crisis." He continued: "The trouble is that the leaders, not the country as a whole, are weak and divided. By the leaders I mean the leaders of industry, the bankers, the newspapers. They are irresolute and lack understanding. The people as a whole can be led back to some kind of consensus if only the leaders can take hold of themselves."

❧❦❧

LUNCH with Kissinger. Two waiters came in with trays, so he waved me over to a small, low table and we chatted. He said Johnson had been a patriotic man but he had simply not applied policy well in Vietnam. He had not told the people straight out what our aims were, and he had always increased the degree of our intervention too slowly and too late; this vitiated its effect.

At this point I observed that in Vietnam I felt the basic problem was to relate internal and external U.S. capabilities and policies more tidily. "Precisely," said Kissinger. He went on: "We've run out of the policy concepts of the thirties, the liberal theories that we had no inherent conflict with any people, that economic action can solve political problems. In this respect Kennedy wasn't the great innovator; he was the sunset on an era."

I said I thought the most disturbing thing that had struck me on returning was the moral decline of the United States; even distinguished Americans were declining official jobs offered to them by the President; the old idea of serving the nation was dead. Kissinger said:

This is our biggest challenge, the loss of moral fiber. This is why Nixon worries so much about what he calls the leadership problem. There is a real crisis of authority. The leadership class has lost its will. To restore it we need some sort of success—preferably on something they disagree with. I don't mean that we should look for an artificial field in which to achieve this.

I have been struck by the Harvard riots. You heard about the students who rifled university files and found a telegram from Harriman praising me for my peace efforts a few years ago. They stole this and published it without comment. But the mere fact that I had done something for my government was considered damning.

PARIS, *July 1, 1969*

LUNCHEON with André Malraux. Malraux indicated that de Gaulle intends to continue exercising a rather active "blackmail veto power" on the Pompidou government. Furthermore, he implied that if the opportunity presents itself—presumably a Communist threat—that the Gaullists might once again consider a coup d'état by force.

He made a very interesting point—namely that the only two positions of real power in terms of a coup d'état are held by the most ardent of the Gaullist *"fidèles."* The first is Michel Debré, now Minister of Defense; there are some fifty of the highest French officers corps who are 100 percent Gaullist and would back Debré in any test or showdown. "It is a matter of the tanks," said Malraux, "and Debré can rest assured that the tanks are with him, come what may." The other *"fidèle"* in power is Jacques Foccart, who has been restored to his official position as Secretary General for African and Malgache affairs which, of course, says Malraux, is unimportant; but it is "the police aspect that counts." He adds that he doesn't think "the police" would really matter much in any conceivable test, that would remain for the tanks. But he conceded there was no harm having a good intelligence apparatus loyal to the general. This whole concept stuns and horrifies me.

We then moved into an entirely different set of ideas. I remarked that in Carlos Baker's biography of Hemingway, Malraux is mentioned from time to time. Malraux said he had known Ernest quite well but there had never been any genuine intimacy. Although Hemingway was a writer of immense talent, he was not at all as "solid" a personality as the image he cared to cultivate; and he was devoured by jealousy. After the liberation of Paris, Malraux ran into Hemingway in the Ritz Hotel, but not at all in the manner described by Hemingway, although there is some similarity between the two stories. He said Hemingway was carousing when he (Malraux) came into the room. "He was disporting himself ridiculously while I stood before him dressed in a tank officer's uniform. I asked him how many men he had commanded and he said perhaps twenty. It was disgusting. I turned and left the room."

Malraux said that Picasso was not really a great "painter" although he was a fine artist. He was not like Goya or Vermeer, because he did not really have the genius of colors. A truly great painter knew exactly which blue he wished to put on the canvas and which grey to place beside it, and then did so. Picasso was simply unable to paint with that degree of perfection.

Categorically Malraux said, "There has been only one great painter in modern times—Braque. And then, but far, far below him, there is Poliakoff. That is all."

DROVE out to the gloomy Château de Verrières, where Louise de Vilmorin lives with André Malraux. It was a small dinner party. Malraux described Pompidou as a Louis-Philippe and said that his program was simply another version of *"enrichissez-vous."* He described the present government in France as "a triumph of mediocrity."

ARRIVED here at 4:45 A.M. aboard a special Boeing that *Paris-Match* had hired on a brilliantly organized promotional and goodwill trip. The passengers included Ambassador Sargent Shriver, Prince Jean of Luxembourg, Prime Minister Werner of Luxembourg, and a large assortment of top-level French businessmen.

Breakfasted in Melbourne, a village near Cape Kennedy, with Shriver, Wernher von Braun, the head of the rocket building program for space, and Jacqueline Auriol, the aviatrix. After breakfast we loaded into air-conditioned buses and inched our way through traffic jams to Cape Kennedy.

The countdown was announced on loudspeakers and then, at the precise scheduled second of 9:32 A.M., there was a huge ferocious orange blaze. For several seconds the rocket seemed to be hung in suspension, struggling to get away, then there was a thunderous noise like a great artillery barrage and slowly it moved upward, accelerating with enormous rapidity until its smoke cut a great scar into the sky.

FASCINATING briefing all morning at the "manned space center" run by NASA. Then we were flown in smaller planes from the NASA airport to Houston airport, where we climbed wearily aboard our chartered Boeing.

Visited a laboratory and medical section which will study moon samples when material is brought back by *Apollo* XI. The astronauts will live in this building, quarantined entirely for twenty-one days to prevent any chance of an epidemic starting from some strange moon germ.

In space itself, all waste material from the mission will either be sterilized before it is left on the moon or will be released to burn up in the sun's orbit. It was pointed out that *all* earth organisms die if they are left on the lunar surface—even if they are in a sealed tin can. They would have to be deposited below the surface to survive.

PARIS, *July 29, 1969*

TALK this afternoon with President Georges Pompidou. I observed that relationships between France and the United States had warmed up. He commented: "Two things have been fundamental. (1) The United States position on Vietnam has made a big difference, the manifestation of a desire to end the war, and (2) the visit of President Nixon to General de Gaulle, which showed a new U.S. conception of general strategy. This seems to demonstrate that the Nixon government admits the position of France as an ally—but an ally that is not integrated into NATO."

Was it safe to assume that France has no intention of denouncing the North Atlantic treaty for the next few years or the predictable future? He said this was a safe assumption. Certainly France would not denounce the treaty for the predictable future. France was perfectly prepared to discuss joint strategy planning with its allies. But it preferred to talk directly with the United States rather than with NATO, which was virtually the same thing since it was under an American military commander. Among the things France was prepared to discuss were joint targeting and a common understanding on the use of the French nuclear force.

JERUSALEM, *August 14, 1969*

THIS evening I had a long talk with Mrs. Golda Meir, the seventy-one-year-old grandmother who runs Israel as Prime Minister. She is a homely but pleasant-looking woman whose face contains a warmth that rarely appears in her photographs, humorous blue eyes, wrinkled brow, long nose and chin, a bun of greying hair. She was neatly dressed in an unpretentious dress. Whenever she talked of her grandchildren, a soft look crept over her features. She smoked several cigarettes and said she didn't dare ask me how I had stopped (since I last saw her) because she wouldn't be able to do so.

She admitted: "Security as it is now is an extreme burden for Israel. And if we have to do more the burden will increase. But there is no limit to what we can take. How do you know how much pain you can suffer before you die? This people won't commit suicide. We know we suffer and we have other dreams. But if this is our fate—war can be made by one side but peace must be made by two—we are prepared to endure. There is no alternative."

She continued: "I am convinced the only solution for this complicated problem is for us and our neighbors to make peace. But negotiations must be direct, not through mediators. When this will happen, I don't know. But in December 1967 and again last year we told Jarring (the UN mediator) we were ready to meet the Arabs any place."

She said Israel was even prepared to have secret negotiations at the start. It didn't wish to insist on negotiations as a means of blocking peace, but as the only sure way of getting it. However, "This time it must be the real thing." Israel wanted "agreed frontiers" which meant not "imposed." There are no preconditions, no maps outlining Israel's demands. But first there had to be someone to negotiate with. Now there were only armistice lines, not frontiers. And after each war the Arabs wanted the borders they had lost in the previous war.

She admitted that war was "unwinnable" here because Israel couldn't conquer and occupy the Arabs. "The only solution is peace. We didn't initiate the last war—but we won it. Yet we say, come and negotiate with no preconditions. We see that we must live together. Regional economic development would be so simple. We have everything to contribute."

AMMAN, *October 7, 1969*

TALK with King Hussein in the Basman palace. Just three days ago there had been an attempted coup against Hussein by right-wing Moslem fanatics. The air of anxiety has not yet fully subsided.

I started by asking Hussein whether he thought there would be a fourth round of the Palestinian war. He said: "If the situation continues in this area without any real progress brought about by the help of the big powers —on a basis of justice—another explosion is inevitable."

I asked, could not an Islamic "Vatican City" be established within the walls of Jerusalem under a religious ruler or committee which would at the same time have temporal authority the way the Pope does inside Rome? Its security, in a police sense, might be arranged by a Turkish guard hired in exactly the same way that the Vatican hires its Swiss guards.

Hussein had no interest in new thoughts. He said the Arab part of Jerusalem—both Moslem and Christian—must continue on the same political basis of administration as the last 1,300 years. He asked: "How far can we go to establish peace? Everything hinges on the 1967 Security Council resolution. Jerusalem is covered by the UN demands for an Israeli withdrawal. Our political and other rights must be recognized in the old city, the Arab city. Israel says the issue is security, not annexation. But Jerusalem has been annexed. We insist on freedom of access to the holy places of all who are concerned with their holiness; but politically our rights must be recognized."

MOKHTARA, LEBANON, *October 11, 1969*

LUNCHED today with Kamal Junblatt, the socialist yet feudal Druze chieftain, who is one of Lebanon's best-known politicians. Junblatt is cultivated and rather elegant, speaks excellent French, good English. His family came here 250 years ago from Dyarbekir in Turkey, was Kurdish and originated in the Caucasus. They were converted from Islam when they arrived. He said the Druze religion is "the religion of everyday life, not faith." It has no church, is not Islamic, believes in gnostic wisdom, and worships holy or wise men from Pythagoras to Vishnu. He said:

You Americans lack a comprehensive view of the problems of this part of the world—the Arab problem *and* the Israeli problem. We ask you only to study these problems objectively and make up your own views. But no American has dared to do this since Franklin Roosevelt. The Russians have an objective view. The Soviets like to help all nationalisms and cultures to succeed. They accept the principle of neutralism. Russia doesn't wish Israel wiped out. It accepts its presence. It simply wants to solve the Arab refugee problem, not to wipe out Israel. Your CIA is more powerful than your president. It always seeks to back strong men, meaning the military. It is not helping the people to create democratic conditions. It always goes with the military—even here in Lebanon.

The United States has lost all its influence in this area. People believe that you are governed by the Jews of New York, the CIA, and Caesarist imperial complexes. You regard the whole world as your satellites.

We don't want to be aligned. But the trend is going toward the Soviets. Even Nasser doesn't want to be aligned. But you are obliging the Arab world to be aligned. Our youngsters are all studying Mao and Guevara.

PARIS, *October 19, 1969*

WE dined last night at the Windsors. The Duke criticized King Constantine and said: "He never should have listened so much to his mother. When I made my big decision I told my brother, my mother, and even my prime minister not to come near me because I didn't want them involved in this. It was my decision. I made it and that's the way it should have been."

BONN, *October 25, 1969*

HAD a good talk with Willy Brandt, the new West German Chancellor. He said the philosophical importance of his regime was a major matter. He added: "I want, in a peaceful and understanding way, to make it clear that Hitler has been conquered not only by external military power but by his own people. I want to make the foundations of parliamentary democracy still safer."

STOCKHOLM, *November 24, 1969*

I SPENT two hours with Olaf Palme, the new Prime Minister of Sweden. He is forty-two, but looks twenty-eight. I asked Palme why relations between the United States and Sweden were so bad. He said: "On a per capita basis we are the largest customer of the United States. It is only on Vietnam that we haven't agreed."

Palme said Sweden began to take a sharper view on Vietnam after the U.S. bombings of the north began in February 1965. It was felt Sweden should speak up on the attitude to be taken toward small nations. There has been hardly anything said since the bombing stopped. But certain "issues" were developed since then.

The first was that of the deserters. "According to our laws and traditions we must accept them—as we took in French deserters from the Algerian war during the fifties."

The second issue was the recognition of Hanoi. But, he said: "This was done according to our principle of recognizing any regime which controls the territory it rules."

Palme said: "The wish of the United States was to go to Vietnam to promote democracy and social progress. But the fate of the United States has been to become a remnant of the old colonial system. That is the tragedy."

HELSINKI, *November 28, 1969*

PRESIDENT Urho Kaleva Kekkonen received me this afternoon out at his suburban residence on an arm of the Gulf of Finland. Kekkonen, who is in his third term, is sixty-nine, about six feet tall, strongly built, with bald (and totally shaven) head, and pink complexion. He wears thick glasses behind which gleam shrewd eyes.

I inquired if he thought it possible that the existing kind of relationship between Finland and Russia might some day extend southward into East Europe; that is to say close relationships but a non-Communist social system. He considered it difficult to imagine how the "East European socialist countries" could develop social and economic systems like Finland's, which was, after all, essentially Western.

He couldn't believe free enterprise could return to East Europe. Nevertheless, it was clear that if military blocs did disappear it would become less important for the Soviet Union to worry about the security of Czechoslovakia or East Germany, for example.

Kekkonen said: "It is possible to have communism and capitalism co-exist peacefully and effectively yet without either changing its system— along the same lines which developed over the centuries between Christianity and Islam."

PARIS, *December 6, 1969*

ON November 10, I wrote to President Truman because of my increasing concern with the revolt against President Nixon by Congress. I attach herewith quotes from his reply.

> The framers of the Constitution were clearly circumspect in being too definitive about the role of the President. In the critical and sensitive area of foreign policy the President had the responsibility. In the matter of national security he was designated as Commander-in-chief. The provision for advice

and consent, I believe, is concerned with keeping the Congress fully informed on all decisions and commitments of the Chief Executive.

Even under our carefully guarded system of power vested rather than imposed, as a practical matter, someone has to be in charge. Someone has to make decisions—and that someone is the President.

It goes without saying, that under our system the President must keep the people fully informed in all matters that touch on their lives, and he must schedule regular press conferences to give a continuing account of his stewardship—as well as to learn of what is troubling them by the questions put to him by the press.

A President who fails to communicate with the people forthrightly and courageously, runs the risk of fostering a public detachment or, what could be even worse, a loss of public confidence.

Presidents from the time of George Washington have been subjected to attacks and abuse. It is a way that a free and open society keeps its government institutions on the alert. It is a small price to pay for an aroused and active public opinion.

PARIS, *January 19, 1970*

LUNCH with General Pierre Gallois. He said the French recognized that despite the enormous superiority in the Mediterranean of the United States Sixth Fleet, American policy was unable to prevent Russian penetration, and the landlocked sea is now shared by Moscow and Washington. This is the basic consequence of the six-day war.

The more aggressive the Israelis are, the more frightened the Arabs become and the more they request weapons from Moscow. And the more weapons Moscow supplies, the more concessions it asks and the greater Soviet presence in the Mediterranean becomes. If they send out arms to the Arabs, the Russians also send out more and more training missions, technicians, and propagandists, therefore increasing their role in the Mediterranean littoral.

ROME, *February 2, 1970*

DINED last night with the Jozsef Szalls (Hungarian Ambassador). Jozsef is a disappointed revolutionist. He says Kadar is a decent but weak man. Things are going downhill, and the Russians are destroying all vestiges of liberalism. He sees his ultimate choice as prison or defection. I warned him strongly against defection, pointing out how *déraciné* all exiles get.

ROME, *February 3, 1970*

WENT out for drinks with King Constantine in his comfortable villa.

He is browned off with the United States and felt slighted by President Nixon when he was in Washington for Eisenhower's funeral. He is told by his friends in Greece that there is a growing conviction the United States no longer "supports democracy" and, when I objected, he said, "Well, I don't agree but even I have a mini-suspicion." He doesn't think the United States should embargo arms to Greece and has told us so twice. His view is that Greece merits heavy weapons as an ally for the defense of the West, but we should be careful, in sending them, not to imply approval of the regime and also not to send light weapons that might be used in civil action.

ROME, *February 4, 1970*

THIS morning I saw President Giuseppe Saragat in the Quirinale. Although almost seventy-two, Saragat is a big, healthy-looking Piedmontese. He is an agreeable man, with spectacles and informal manner, who converses easily in French.

He said there was no doubt that Italy continues to move gradually leftward, but the problem is to carry on with this trend while at the same time avoiding the danger of Communist bureaucratic dictatorship. The Communists, he said, represent about one-third of Italy's population. It is necessary to avoid the danger of being engulfed by their power, in order to keep national liberty. This has been the basic problem since the republic began after World War II.

For the present there is no alternative to the governing center-left coalition, if freedom is to be saved. Of course it is theoretically possible— although not probable—to envision an evolution by the Communists toward democracy, which would enable them to participate genuinely in a democratic government.

"However," said Saragat, "when I consider the Italian Communist party objectively, I do not think it is possible to foresee in it a democratic evolution. Maybe within a decade there could be a change; I don't know. I think the communists are too allied to Soviet bureaucracy."

PARIS, *February 10, 1970*

INTERESTING talk with President Pompidou. He said:

Anyone can see that France is seeking ways to reconcile the assertion that Israel has an absolute right to exist, to function freely, and to live in peace within safe, recognized borders, with our refusal to recognize Israel's rights of military conquest. France has not forgotten the Nazi martyrdom of European Jews, including French Jews, whose courage during the ordeal earned the admiration of all our people. However, France also intends to maintain and develop its ancient ties with most of the Moslem world and more particularly with the Arab countries.

In the Middle East crisis, France wants and seeks only peace—a peace which I believe is indispensable to everyone and first of all to Israel. This is why we have placed the embargo on the shipment of arms to all the countries in the field of battle. The fact that at first this affected Israel in particular is correct. But since then, all these countries have received increasingly powerful arms sometimes from one nation, sometimes from another, but never from France.

As far as the Libyan affair is concerned, we do not consider Libya directly involved in the conflict between Israel and a certain number of countries including Egypt. Naturally, Libya is Egypt's neighbor, and an Arab nation. The Libyan leaders have made declarations of solidarity with the other Arab countries. All this is true.

But France has treated this affair separately for two reasons: first, our ties with the countries of north Africa and the Maghreb, of which Libya is not an integral part but to which it is far from foreign. Because of French interests in the Maghreb, our economic, cultural, and intellectual position in that region, we cannot disassociate ourselves from Libya. As long as she was tied to the Anglo-Saxon countries under the regime of King Idriss, we never tried to make our presence particularly felt in Libya. But the day she offered and requested more cooperation, our north African policy obliged us to reply favorably.

It is France's duty to herself and also to all the western Mediterranean, to look after those interests common to European and Mediterranean countries. We are not going to seek Libyan oil; we buy oil from Libya, of course, but we are not seeking to extend our control of oil reserves in Libya in particular. It is a country whose strategic position is important.

PARIS, *February 18, 1970*

LAST night dinner with André Malraux. Malraux adduced a new theory for the incomprehensible defeat of the heavily armed French contingent at Agincourt which outnumbered the British by five to one. He claims the British had a "captainry" of cats who drove the rats toward the French camp where they promptly set about eating the bowstrings of France's archers so they were not in a position to shoot back at the English.

We talked about de Gaulle and his lunch with the general last autumn— the only time he has seen him since he left the *Élysée*. He said de Gaulle really hates the somber forest of Colombey-les-deux-Églises, although he never says so. It is a huge and all-embracing mass of trees, and the general's house, set in a clearing among them, is quite small. In a strange way this smallness is emphasized by the fact that at lunch they talked only about picayune and little things.

WASHINGTON, *February 23, 1970*

LUNCHED in his White House office with Henry Kissinger, President Nixon's national security adviser. We spent most of our time talking about the Middle East, a gloomy subject and much in the news because of Jewish protests against Pompidou's current visit—because of his sale of Mirage planes to Libya. Kissinger thinks protests are counter-productive, likely to stimulate anti-Semitism here rather than any anti-French feeling.

The Middle East crisis is very difficult. Apart from its political and sentimental interest in Israel, the United States cannot allow Soviet military support to win a victory there by triumphing over an American client. This would have grave worldwide repercussions. Right now the Russians keep trying to maneuver America into the position of initiating all peace offers in the Middle East and demanding of its client all concessions. But, after all, it was a Soviet client state that started the 1967 war.

The United States is fully aware that once Egypt possesses Sinai again, it will immediately resume working against American interests as hard as possible in the Persian Gulf. If Moscow is truly willing to impose some sacrifices on its clients we on our part can press Israel to be more reasonable. The problem is really dual: (1) there is the Arab-Israeli quarrel and (2) the Soviet-Western relationship.

The United States simply cannot permit Soviet domination in the Middle East. This would, among other things, make Western Europe depend on Russia for all its petroleum.

Someday the Arabs are bound to realize that the only power in a position to really deliver help is the United States. After all, we can force Israel to get out of Sinai; Russia can't.

Our long-range objective is to make the Russians gradually realize they risk losing more in the Middle East by not settling than by settling. And the Russians can't basically change things with anything less than a large intervention of Soviet manpower. If they just send in better planes or SAM-2 and -3 missiles the Egyptians can't run them. If they send in Soviet crews they run the risk that Israel's excellent air force will work over the missile sites as they put them in, preventing their effective use.

The Russians, however, are not entirely rational on Israel. There is a hysterical edge. They are basically anti-Semitic and hate being licked by Jews. When Kissinger was in Moscow in 1968 he found he could talk to the Russians rationally on all subjects, even including Vietnam—except for Israel.

WASHINGTON, *February 25, 1970*

LAST night we and the Bohlens, with whom we are staying, went to the White House, where President Nixon gave a state dinner for Pompidou.

After dinner we stood around in various rooms and halls drinking coffee and liqueurs, smoking cigars, when I felt a hand on my shoulder. Turned around, and it was Nixon. "Come over here, Cy," he said. "You know these people." The "people" were President and Mrs. Pompidou and Mrs. Nixon. I stood with the two Presidents for fifteen minutes (their wives moved a yard or so away). General Walters and Prince Andronikov, the two interpreters, rushed up, and an odd conversation ensued.

Nixon patted my back and said to Pompidou (Andronikov murmuring away like a machine gun) "You know, Cy is an old friend of mine. All the years I was out of office he kept in touch with me. Whenever I went to Paris or London we'd see each other. We used to golf together. You know, Mr. President, when a newspaperman keeps in touch with you when you are out of office it is a proof that he is both a good newspaperman and a good friend." Pompidou smiled and said, *"Monsieur le Président,* I know what you mean because Mr. Sulzberger also kept in touch with me when I was out of office."

WASHINGTON, *February 26, 1970*

STIMULATING lunch with Dick Helms, head of the CIA. Dick said the United States had been incredibly lucky during the postwar years because it depended for its power on an overwhelming military superiority and a constantly expanding economy. Now both of these special advantages were coming to an end. The Russians were carefully preparing for a military machine by around 1975 which would undoubtedly be ahead of us in virtually all respects and, given existing sentiments and political conditions, there was absolutely nothing we could do about this. Moreover, we ourselves were deliberately braking our own expanding economy. So the two primordial factors were coming to an almost simultaneous and predictable end.

On the Middle East, Helms said Israel still has a definite military advantage over the Arabs but this cannot endure forever. There is an attrition rate on plane losses, etc., and the only ultimate replacement source is the United States. The day must come when Israel—while it has its advantage—must somehow start or provoke round four in the Palestine war. Otherwise it will lose its edge. And the Israelis foolishly don't understand the mood in the United States and the deep distaste for any kind of foreign adventure.

There is no doubt the Israelis could blow up the High Aswan Dam if they become desperate, and no doubt that they have been experimenting with military devices at the Dimona reactor. Some six months ago they floated some mines down the Nile toward the old Aswan Dam; but they caught up on the sides of the river, and the project failed. Nevertheless, Egypt is in a sense even more vulnerable than Israel.

What would the United States do in a disaster? Probably, after fulminating, nothing. If Egypt were destroyed, we would be horrified but most unlikely to go to war. If Israel were destroyed, ditto.

As for the Sino-Soviet situation, there is equal confusion. The United States has cards but we don't know which way to play the hand. We know that the Peking talks have been going very badly since they started last autumn. The Chinese pulled troops back from frontier areas, but the Russians refused. There is no advance. The Russians have approximately the same kind of choice that on a mini-scale faces Israel. Today they could wipe China out. But in a certain amount of time the Chinese will have a missile arsenal as well as warheads, and the Russians will no longer have an overwhelming, knock-out, first-strike capacity. Should they hit now—or not?

I went over to the White House at 4:15 P.M. and sat in Kissinger's office where we chatted. Henry, who is a German Jew from near Munich, was deeply disturbed about the emotionalism of the American-Jewish community during this Pompidou visit.

He went on to describe the irrationality of the American Jews. Rockefeller, for whom Henry worked prior to Nixon's election, was enormously pro-Jewish, said Henry—"Genuinely and emotionally so, not intellectually or politically or as a disguised anti-Semite. And before the nominating convention he received a letter from Jewish organizations demanding his views on the sale to Israel of fifty American Phantom Jets. Rockefeller replied that he wanted to insure that Israel always had enough arms to defend itself but simply wasn't in a position personally to say about the Phantoms. The result was that Rockefeller received letters attacking him as unsympathetic and saying the Jews would oppose him."

Henry is worried about the repercussions in the United States of organized Jewish opinion. He foresees a wave of anti-Semitism—"and I speak as a Jew"—and a further rise in the extreme right. "And, furthermore, I very much wonder what the President's own repercussions and reactions will be."

At this point we got word to go in to the President. Nixon shook hands warmly and waved me to an armchair. Then we started chatting. He had been impressed by the fact that Pompidou was a sturdy country type, not the "Paris intellectual" he had been told about, and a tough, intelligent, solid man. They had talked openly and honestly, and it had been "most successful."

After about a quarter of an hour, Nixon rose and said: "Henry, you know the last time Cy was here he was in this room and he gave me his book. I think it might be fun to show him where I write, don't you? Let's take him over to my EOB [Executive Office Building] office across the way and have a coffee." He led the way and off we went.

We walked through the west gate where I had entered; it was very cold, well below freezing, and none of us had coats. We crossed the street and climbed the stairs where he opened the door and led the way to a two-room suite.

Nixon started talking about the way he organized his life. He had learned from Eisenhower that it was silly to read through and amend every single document presented to him for signature. He signed the unimportant ones and didn't worry about whether they were in good or bad English. He accepted, without pondering, all recommendations for appointments to judgeships or embassies except for a handful. He signed routine proclamations.

On the other hand, he made it a point to study important documents or contemplate important appointments. He carefully prepared his press conference statements in advance and worked hard on addresses like that on the State of the Nation. "Anything I have to say or write I want to be said or written by me," he added. It was in this comfortable room with its cheerful cream-colored walls that he did this: "Here is where I write."

He tried to assign Vice-President Agnew to as much ceremonial and political work as possible, and he also tried to delegate the organizational preparation of policy analyses to Kissinger.

He considered his job to be to take a look at the long-term implications of problems and also at the broad-scale geographical areas. He started talking about the need for a President to plan far ahead in a "conceptual" way, both for national and international policy. He wanted to lay the groundwork for a period long after he himself would be out of office. For example, he was now working hard on a genuine project for establishing a national minimum wage and eliminating poverty. He was working with a special committee against pollution. The birth control problem had to be faced squarely; it was idiotic to keep exporting millions of tons of grain to India to feed a growing population.

All our allies must be made to realize that the Russians were swiftly catching up to us in missile strength. All we wanted vis-à-vis Russia was "sufficiency." But we had to have that. It was evident that pressures were mounting to withdraw our troops (from Europe), and in the end, slowly, they would have to be responded to. But we couldn't knuckle under in weapons. The minute our allies realized we were a second-rate power militarily, the political effect would be enormous.

The President had to retain his options. "Right now," Nixon said, going over to the desk, "wherever I am, at this desk or in the Oval Room or at Camp David or in California, I am in direct contact. If the 'line' rings I can give the answer. I am not worried about this. I can sleep. It is part of the job. But it is a fact."

If the line rang right now, telling me that unknown missiles were on the way, I would have fifteen minutes to make up my mind. The only thing to do, if it appeared that unknown missiles were coming at us, would be to order a reply. That might kill seventy million people. What president is willing to kill seventy million people?

We can build a system at an annual rate of about $900 million that would be able to defend the North American continent against up to a hundred enemy missiles. In other words, they would have to make an advance decision to let go with everything. If there were a mistake, if there were a stray missile—and we mustn't ignore the fact that other, smaller countries are getting into a position where they can build them—a president could at least push an "alarm" for ABM defense. We could knock down the incoming missiles without millions of deaths—like the reply of ICBMs.

Of course this isn't total defense. It is only against a maximum of 100 ICBMs. It isn't a thick defense. But we know the Russians have got it, that they are moving in this direction. We can't afford to let them suddenly become the only protected power. And our allies know this. This thin defense—which would take time to install—might protect North America ten years, into the mid-eighties, against anything China might develop. And China's policy might evolve during that time. And also, it would force the Russians to make the decision that any attack had to be deliberate and all out. Finally, it would allow a U.S. president to avoid ordering that retaliatory ICBMs be fired but only put ABMs on "alarm."

Nixon wanted very much "to bring China back into the normal international community." But meanwhile it took time. He thought his job was primarily "conceptual" and long-range and that he had to think of our diplomatic as well as our strategic position. If our European or Asian allies suddenly realized we had become a second-class power instead of a power at least on parity with the other top powers, they would fall off immediately. We would no longer have options of war and peace. We wouldn't even have decent options on such things as the SALT negotiations. We could never afford to give our allies the feeling that they were hostages, that we were in so weak a position that we simply had to sacrifice them.

WASHINGTON, *February 27, 1970*

PLEASANT talk this afternoon with Secretary of State Rogers, a nice man, very decent, no Talleyrand. He said:

One reason I went to Africa was to familiarize myself with that continent because of the special relationship of race questions there and here in our country. Eleven percent of our population has a strong emotional attachment to black Africa. And this will become more apparent as they learn more about the continent from which they came. Their emigration was a forced emigration and this occasions a particular emotional feeling. I don't think the emotional involvement between American Negroes and the countries of black Africa has yet become fully apparent, but I think it has begun to increase. There is a black-white problem both here and in Africa and each relates to the other.

PARIS, *March 13, 1970*

JOZSEF Szall, Hungarian Ambassador in Rome and special representative to the Vatican, had sent word asking if he could see me in Paris. I invited him for lunch. With little ado he told me that he has decided in principle to defect.

He wants to do this in the quietest way possible and without publicity. He doesn't want to denounce his country publicly. He would like eventually to get some job at a college in America or some kind of foundation grant.

I told him I was inexperienced in these matters and in no position to give him any assurances that he could get a job. Furthermore, I warned him there is an economic recession in the United States. But if there was no future except ultimate prison, he had no choice.

LONDON, *March 16, 1970*

INTERESTING lunch with Denis Healey, Defense Minister. Denis thinks Henry Kissinger the best, most intelligent, and nicest of all the Presidential assistants he has known in Washington. Mac Bundy had a fine mind but was arrogant, a bit "too British—mixed with Boston Brahmin." Walt Rostow was not quite up to it.

President Johnson, he thought, was unfortunate. Had he been lucky he would have been assassinated in 1967—a year before he was forced to announce he wouldn't run again. Then history might have said that he had achieved everything in which Kennedy failed (his internal legislation). Denis personally was repelled by him. "He never listened, simply spoke all the time."

Nixon, on the other hand, had done amazingly well. Healey was surprised to find himself acknowledging this, as he had been strongly antipathetic. Nevertheless, on the things that concerned Denis, foreign policy and defense, Nixon hadn't made a single false step.

He said Harold Wilson was a brilliant politician and party leader but only did things in terms of what their political effect might be, not their value. Nevertheless, Wilson didn't know how to make decisions or to delegate authority to his Cabinet. He was a sloppy and ineffectual chief of government: nothing like Lincoln, who would say, "Very well, the majority decision is one to twelve; I am the one and we will do it."

THE HAGUE, *April 8, 1970*

CALLED on Joseph Luns, the veteran Dutch Foreign Minister, a charming man, about six foot five, lean, strong, and healthy looking. Most of our talk was about the Middle East. Luns has just returned from a tour of Lebanon, Jordan, and Egypt. He is deeply pessimistic. "The Israelis must look at history. In 1786 Prussia was unbeatable. Yet, twenty years later, its armies were smashed at Jena and Auerstadt." He has told this to the Israelis more than once. He also warned that even the Arabs might some day produce their own Napoleon.

MADRID, *May 8, 1970*

DINED last night with José María de Areilza, Count of Motrico, former Ambassador to Washington and Paris. Motrico was both brilliant and funny.

The Vice-Premier and right hand of Franco, Admiral Carrero Blanco, is reactionary and *dépassé*. M. calls him "our Spiro Agnew." He says he is "a great hollow tree, filled with bees." The "bees" are the industrious secret society, Opus Dei, which has filled the government and the economic structure with its members. M. says fourteen of the eighteen Cabinet ministers are in it. Opus Dei has immense power but no popularity, and its head, the Aragonese priest Escriva de Balaguer, lives in Rome. It has dominated the political scene since the political coalition of 1958–1968 fell apart, and it is detested by the Falange, conservative monarchists, and the Left.

MADRID, *May 9, 1970*

TODAY three young men from Madrid University came to my room and spent a couple of hours: all in their early twenties, of bourgeois antecedents, well-educated, and hoping to lead normal lives. They represented the committee of Madrid University which coordinates student movements. Only one said he was an avowed Marxist. What they wanted was a nonviolent take-over as soon as Franco dies, if not before. They spoke sadly and bitterly of U.S. policy.

One said: "In Vietnam and Cambodia you are not helping the people's needs, and you obey the dictates of the Pentagon, not your Congress. Another important thing that bothers us is that your executive ignores your legislature" (one of the complaints in Spain). "Our students are disturbed that your long democratic tradition is being overcome by fascist tendencies, a trend toward totalitarianism. And this is reflected by your relations with Spain."

MADRID, *May 11, 1970*

FASCINATING conversation with three members of the liberal clergy. Two, Father G. and Father C., were Jesuit priests. The third, P., had been a Jesuit but left the order to become a layman.

G. and many other liberal priests had "acknowledged" the regime until the second Vatican council (1962–1965), whose liberal deliberations echoed through Spain like a shock wave.

The younger clergy swiftly turned against Franco. No country in Europe had more priests in prison today.

C. interjected that another profound influence had been the public protest of 140 Catalan priests in the streets of Barcelona against the torture of a Communist student. "That," he said, "was the first time people could see with their own eyes how many priests opposed the regime." All agreed that the heaviest proportion of opposition came among priests under forty and that young men now leaving theological seminaries were more and more anti. Indeed, some actually quit the church and became "Maoist-extremists."

G. said the United States is regarded today as an unpopular right-wing country, especially because of the American bases here. The students and workers are especially anti-United States. Nor is there much American effort to offset this. Our radio programs here never mention Spain, while the Communist broadcasts do.

MADRID, *May 12, 1970*

THIS morning I drove out to Zarzuela Palace, a few miles from Madrid, to see Juan Carlos de Borbón, the thirty-two-year-old Prince of Asturias who has been designated as Franco's official heir and next King of Spain. Still unknown as a political figure and overshadowed by the bleak heritage of Francoism, he is widely called "Juan Carlos the Brief," because many people believe it will be impossible for him and a monarchy to survive very long. The old-fashioned conservative and liberal monarchists strongly preferred his father, Don Juan, Count of Barcelona. The present young generation is quite republican.

The Prince is about six feet two, slender but well set-up, with reddish fair hair. I had met him years before in Corfu, and he greeted me as an old friend. I sat on a sofa facing color snapshots of his three youngsters, on a mantlepiece, and he sat in an armchair beside me, smoking filtered cigarettes.

I started things off by asking if he automatically assumed power the moment Franco died. He said: "As I understand the law, within eight days there must be a special session of parliament and once I swear an oath there, it is done. Of course there will probably be some kind of *Te Deum* or religious ceremony. And as I understand it, General Franco can choose either to stay on or, if he wants, to resign. Moreover, I think that if he became physically incapacitated a crown council could decide if he was no longer competent to rule. But that is unlikely, I personally think it would be much easier for his family if he were to decide to retire."

I asked if he felt legally obligated to carry on the present ideology imposed by Franco? Wouldn't that place him in the position of the old Spaniards who rallied to battle behind the corpse of El Cid strapped to his horse?

He said: "I am not obliged to continue the ideology. The idea is continuity but not continuation. The basic theory will be carried on symbolically until a new generation takes over. We don't want to risk a big dramatic shift, a kind of revolution."

He acknowledged that he was lucky to be only thirty-two, because today more than half the country was thirty or less. This would help him to establish a bond with the nation. He thought a king in Spain, which was not only European but also Mediterranean, could never be only a symbol, as in Scandinavia or England. He had to rule through a government and Prime Minister, not to try and rule himself, but in a sense he had to influence events within the reigning formula. The best technique would be to show "that I am strong but not to use my strength except on very important occasions." It would be possible to do this, to exert pressure when need be, but tactfully and behind the scenes, more or less the way King Paul had done in Greece. "Not Constantine," he added, laughing. Constantine, his brother-in-law, is now an *émigré* in Rome as a result of an unsuccessful counter-coup attempt against the colonels.

I asked whether he thought there was much chance that he would run into immediate opposition and deliberately engineered trouble as soon as he took over. He suggested that things would be a great deal easier for him "if Franco opens the doors a bit first, while he is still in power."

Was there any way of insuring against a "colonels' conspiracy" here in Spain? He said the only thing to do was to keep a sharp eye on "the national requirements and interest" so that the army, among other elements, would feel reassured. Military people are nationalists, he added, and loyal to their duties and vows. "They want no break in either unity or command." I remarked that no one could say the Greek colonels had not been "nationalist," but they had certainly broken army unity and the chain of command.

I then inquired whether it was possible for him to have any serious contacts with anti-Franco elements so as to know the real mood of the nation. He assured me he did so, that anyone could come and see him, that he also could send for politicians and others he wished to see. He added: "Many think I don't see the variety of people I actually do see in fact, because this isn't reported in the press. The public doesn't know."

He wanted to be King of "all the Spaniards—that is to say, the Spaniards in Spain itself" (underscoring disinterest in Spanish-speaking areas abroad)—so I asked how he could guarantee that "all Spaniards" would be represented in a government under him. He said vaguely: "One has to create the value of existing institutions—the municipality, the family, the labor syndicates. And from this point one has to proceed very carefully, step by step. You must remember we are walking along the edge of a precipice and we must above all avoid the risk of falling over."

I asked how his relations were today with his father, Don Juan, and the latter's supporters who still refer to Don Juan as "the King" and think of Juan Carlos as almost a usurper who sold out to Franco. He replied:

> In a family sense our relations are very good. I speak to him often by telephone, but I do see him less than before because now I am in an official position. You know, he really did a wonderful thing in accepting this

change. Politically, he says nothing, even when he talks with me. He wants to wait and see how things go. No one, not even myself, knows for certain whether he "politically" accepts the change. But I think he does.

He obviously didn't like the situation created when Franco named me, but for the good of the family he accepted it, at least in the sense of doing nothing but watch and wait. And his old supporters are still loyal to him but they accept reality for the sake of Spain. Now I want to show them and everyone that I am above ideology, above personal friendships, that I am ready to hear all viewpoints and talk with anyone.

He wanted to know my opinion of Greece. He thought Constantine should go back to Athens under any circumstances. I remarked that he had set conditions and made himself a symbol of opposition to dictatorship. "People will forget easily," said Juan Carlos. "He should go home." A rather cynical approach!

MADRID, *May 13, 1970*

LAST night Motrico invited a group of opposition leaders and intellectuals (all middle-of-the-road or conservative) for drinks and a chat.

All agreed that the United States now had an unfortunate image here of authoritarian imperialism; that it was a mistake to renegotiate the base arrangement; that Rogers should listen to opposition views during his visit; that Hill, the present Ambassador, was a disaster and both he and his staff were outright regime supporters with whom these people could no longer maintain contact. They said Opus Dei controlled the government, that Franco was going slowly gaga, that Correro Blanco was a tough, fanatically loyal (to Franco) fool.

25

MOSCOW, *June 2, 1970*

EVERY NATION, I SUPPOSE, GETS THE TOURISTS IT DESERVES AND has its own way of treating them. The French clip them; the Italians pinch them; the British disdain them; the Japanese kowtow to them; and the Americans regard them as curiosities. Only the Russians wholeheartedly make them at home (Soviet style) by according them the treatment of Soviet citizens.

Within two hours of arriving, I had a tic in my writing hand from filling out papers and was automatically ready to join any queue of more than twenty people. I was prepared to acknowledge as impressive a traffic "jam" that would seem sparse on Sunday in Keokuk, Iowa, and to accept as beautiful a hotel room with a view of the brown, polluted Moskva River across from a power station with ten immense, grim chimneys and a sign recalling Lenin's slogan: "Communism is Soviet power plus electrification of the land."

The Hotel Russia is about the size of the Pentagon. It might have been built and staffed by Rameses II. It would certainly exceed the combined administrative talents of the best Swiss, Japanese, and French hotel schools—none of whose graduates are on its staff—and one can get lost for three hours en route to the dining room. Its operational system combines Parkinson's Law and the Peter Principle. Payment for everything is issued in the special scrip of Intourist, the only travel agency in the world's largest (acreage) country, and every piece of scrip even on the way from waitress to kitchen seems to require a countersignature.

It is probably a compliment to be accepted as one of them by this remarkably durable people, but one does feel like a sheep in sheep's clothing as one is pushed around by the lowest-scale functionaries who have no incentive to be helpful, efficient, or polite.

⌘

In the last few months Brezhnev has moved increasingly to the fore. Collective leadership remains, but he is *primus inter pares*. In 1964 he became First Secretary of the party. In 1966 this was changed to General Secretary. It is inevitable that power accrues to the man in that post; everything is geared to the party. Brezhnev couldn't move forward like this without army support, but the army is not "engaged" in politics.

ᵈᶠᵇᵉᵉ

The Greek military attaché drove to Tbilisi and Yerevan, and on the way he picked up a Georgian hitchhiker. The Georgian said he'd like to buy his car—black market. He explained: "There are wonderful places here to hide it." Seems they pay a huge ruble price, hide the car some weeks in a canyon, then remove the plates and sell it.

Moscow, *June 3, 1970*

Called on Leonid Zamyatin, head of TASS, former head of the Foreign Ministry press department. Zamyatin said the SALT talks were going very well. Said Mao had attacked Russia as heavily as the United States in his speech last week. China is trying to divert attention from internal problems by its external quarrels.

Sochi, USSR, *June 8, 1970*

Sochi, which was warm, sunny, and lovey today, is a perfect example of "where every prospect pleases and only man is vile." Magnificent trees and flowers, the Black Sea rolling up to pebbled beaches, banks of high mountains climbing behind. Even, one might add, splendid trains, huge hydrofoil sightseeing craft, helicopters whirling tourists into the hills. But heaven forbid that anyone should ever dream of advertising communism by its holiday set on the beaches. I say communism, not Russia, because during the day I walked several miles along the sea front and saw not only our little Intourist Hotel beach (crowded with Finns and East Germans) but many other Russians-only *plages*, all filled with great puddings and barrel-molds of women and men, hideously taking the sun or playing cards with rakish hats atilt and pieces of paper on their noses to fend off the burn.

Tbilisi, USSR, *June 11, 1970*

Judging from its benign aspect in Georgia, I know that while I would never make a revolution *for* communism I am not sure I would ever make a revolution *against* it. When I think of the poverty, beggars, and corruption to the south in Iran and Turkey—as well as the elegant intelligence on the tiny top layer and the glitter of their booming new bourgeoisies—I wonder if they are healthier as nations than this pleasantly sluggish haven of the Marxist malformation.

This system eliminates the top and brings everything and everyone down to the lowest common denominator in order to start upwards afresh. Of course, the bureaucrats, technocrats, and a few intellectuals rise like yeast from its depths. They are the most needed. However, half-baked capitalism to the south aspires to hoist the impoverished masses upwards, but it is too greedy to make a serious effort.

TBILISI, USSR, *June 13, 1970*

DROVE to Gori on the Liakhvi River in a broad valley with peaks to the west. This is Stalin's birthplace and the one city in the USSR where he is still openly admired with a Stalin museum, his original house, a Stalin square with a large bronze statue, and a Stalin avenue running into it.

YEREVAN, USSR, *June 16, 1970*

IN the afternoon we drive over the Hrazdan River toward Echmiadzin along a flat plain past vineyards, orchards, and mulberry trees (for silkworms). Echmiadzin was built in the second century A.D. and was capital for four centuries.

Visit the austere and beautiful St. Rhipsime Church. She was an early Christian proselytizer slain after spurning the King's offer of his hand. Then drive to the cathedral, originally built between 301 and 303 but substantially modified since. It is inside a large walled enclosure where the Catholicos (Patriarch) has theoretically sovereign powers.

LONDON, *July 2, 1970*

AGREEABLE chat with Sir Alec Douglas-Home, back as Foreign Secretary. With reference to UK-U.S. relationships, now that London's government has changed, he said: "One thing, of course, is that we understand power perhaps better than Labor. For a long, long time the Tory party has been involved in the power politics of the world. We understand the burden of the United States, both instinctively and sympathetically. We understand what your involvement in Vietnam and Cambodia is about. We know that there is a place in world stability for the discreet application of power. We sympathize with the United States in the difficult position you have assumed. It is a lonely business to have to do some of these things alone—as only your president can really know."

DUBLIN, *July 6, 1970*

CALLED on Eamon de Valera (Dev, as he is popularly known), grand old man of Ireland, eighty-seven, president of the republic and president of the first *Dail* (Parliament) in 1919. I saw him in his residence at Phoenix Park, where the English lord-lieutenants used to live, a splendid house in a magnificent setting of lawns, trees, ponds, which the poor man cannot see.

The greatest disappointment in his whole life, his greatest failure, had been "the treaty" that was negotiated between Irish representatives and the British in 1921. (This was the cause of the Irish civil war, when de Valera's backers fought those of Michael Collins.) De Valera said this treaty, which acknowledged the sovereignty of the English King, had been imposed by the British and did not regard Ireland as a sovereign state, although the independence war had just been won. Nor had Ireland's negotiators even reported a word of its contents to Dublin. The first he learned about it was from the afternoon newspapers reporting its text. He had been appalled and furious. He added, "I never recovered from that."

WASHINGTON, *September 16, 1970*

STARTED the day with an 8:00 breakfast at the White House with Henry Kissinger (trays in his office). His office has moved upstairs, acquiring the space once used for press rooms.

Nixon is visiting Tito. Kissinger said Tito had "very useful credentials with Nasser" and we did not; therefore Tito could be effective if he wished. I asked if Tito would also be asked to help in Hanoi. Kissinger answered: "We don't need him on Hanoi. We have our own direct contacts. But he can be useful on Nasser where we have very bad communications right now."

The Russians are quite "psychopathic" on the subject of China. (I doubt this. The Russians don't really get psychopathic. I have heard Henry use this word about Moscow on Israel before.) Henry says there is no evidence that the Soviet-Chinese crisis is easing. Soviet military strength on the Chinese border is increasing. There are today more Soviet divisions facing China than Europe. I asked if Henry was sure. "Positive," he said. "And they're smack on the border."

WASHINGTON, *September 17, 1970*

SPENT most of today with Dean Acheson at his farm in Sandy Spring, Maryland. It is a pleasant, comfortable building set in rolling corn country. I talked with Dean for an hour and a half in the little former print shop which he uses as his study. Then he and Alice drove me to the Olney Inn in a nearby village, where we lunched because today the Achesons' servants were off. I was amused to notice that Alice, who is both lovely and frisky as a septuagenarian, ordered a whisky sour before lunch.

I told Dean I had only one question to ask. Was there any way of substituting for the old "gunboat diplomacy," which has become too dangerous in the nuclear age, some other means of applying restrained threats of force for diplomatic purposes? He answered:

> We are in a big fix. The essential difference between our problems and those of Russia is that ours are almost entirely in the field of being constructive and theirs are in the field of letting things go to pot and then picking up the pieces.
>
> Russia wins by everyone else losing. The Russians don't give a damn about the Arabs or the Israelis. They only want to establish a suzerainty over the Middle East. Israel cannot win any more great victories and the Arabs are too weak. But the United States will be the big loser if the Russians move in and take over.
>
> Part of our problem is that you cannot make terrible mistakes without in the end paying for them. [Here he was referring to his opposition to the creation of the State of Israel and its support by the United States.] And the tremendous advances the Soviets have made in the military would make gunboat diplomacy too difficult and too dangerous.

He went on:

> Europe is the area where the lesson of power can be learned. One discovers about power that it is a subjective as well as an objective problem. Certain people can do more than others with physical force. Take the example of the Russians and ourselves. The Russians were smarter than we thought. They developed their own thermonuclear weapons. And all this was worsened when we made the mistake of joining the Russians in 1956 against Britain and France [Suez].
>
> Now there is stagnation. We can't even deal with Castro. When I was called back during the Cuban crisis in 1962 I found the Kennedy brothers in a terrible flap. If Khrushchev hadn't been crazy he could have won. What would President Kennedy have done if Khrushchev had just paid no attention? We announced a blockade in order to get Soviet missiles out. But you don't blockade things in when you want them out.
>
> When I talked with Adenauer at the time, after Kennedy had sent me abroad to explain our position, Adenauer said he couldn't understand our policy and asked me to explain it. I only told the chancellor: "Faith moves mountains."

Acheson continued:

> What is the answer when one side has a positive program and the other side has a negative program? We are now in a period where there are mediocre men everywhere. People have opinions but no knowledge, and leaders are made in the image of the masses. Democracy is only tolerable because no other governmental system is.
>
> There is no substitute for gunboat diplomacy. I think it was Elihu Root

who said that when governments were run by tyrants the danger of war came from deliberate purposes. But when governments are run by democracies the dangers of war come from faulty premises. Of course both tyrants and democracies can suffer from both weaknesses. It is often possible in this world to have fools and rascals together.

Dean told me Nixon had called him in once for his advice and he had told the President that the only way to end the Indochina war was to start removing our troops. We had in Vietnam too small a force to crush the opposition and too large a force to be accepted by the patience of the American people.

WASHINGTON, *September 18, 1970*

LUNCH with Dick Helms. We are now investigating reports that Russia is building a submarine base at Cienfuegos, on the southern coast of Cuba. This, in a sense, is like putting missiles in there, although, of course, Soviet submarines could launch a surprise attack from the high seas. It is said the base is designed to shelter Y-class Russian subs, their equivalent of our Polaris-launchers. This is *not* yet confirmed.

WASHINGTON, *September 20, 1970*

WENT out to McLean, Virginia, for a drink with Senator Edward (Teddy) Kennedy at his lovely house on a bluff above the Potomac. I asked what kind of Secretary of State he would choose if he were ever elected President. He hemmed and hawed and said that of course this was not a subject he could give serious consideration to, but when I pressed he continued: "Frank Church [Democratic Senator from Idaho] would certainly be a good man. He is extraordinarily perceptive and realistic. He might today be very qualified for that job. Of course, in connection with the question you pose, I think of younger people I know well. Don Fraser [Democrat-Farm-Labor, Minnesota] in the House of Representatives is the kind of man I mean. Or John Culver [Democrat, Iowa] of the House foreign relations committee. I think of men whose performance I know. And with whom I have had to deal."

CAIRO, *October 16, 1970*

I SPENT the day in the Suez Canal area, at Port Suez and Port Taufiq, at the extreme eastern entry of the canal.

When I asked the general who was my host at lunch if I could visit a SAM missile site, he said: "What sites? We have never admitted there are any." "But," I protested, "your foreign minister says you won't withdraw a single missile from the zone. If you won't withdraw, it means you are there." He said nothing.

I then asked if I could at least visit an artillery position. He said it was forbidden for any civilian, even an Egyptian, to do so; not even Russian journalists were permitted. Then I asked to be taken to Soviet troops. "In my area there are none," he said.

Port Taufiq, a small town, used to be the eastern headquarters of the canal company and was also a prosperous resort filled with middle-class seaside villas. It is now badly chewed up, although the only total damage is right up by the canal.

We climbed a rampart of sandbags and there, just below us, ran the canal. Two Egyptian soldiers, one with binoculars, were in a foxhole in front. Then the water, less than 500 yards wide, and then the Israelis, three or four of them staring at us out of their wired, mined positions.

CAIRO, *October 20, 1970*

YESTERDAY, just after 7:00 P.M., I went to Al Tahira palace with Mohamed Heikal to see President Anwar el Sadat, Nasser's successor. El Sadat is not used to interviews (this was the first he has given since becoming president) and is not good at grabbing abstract thoughts or playing with ideas. I had a feeling his mind is pragmatic and certainly conspiratorial. We talked for about an hour and a half, and although the substance was pretty tough, the means of expression couldn't have been chummier. The more interesting part was that dealing with his personality and ideas, as he is a virtually unknown man.

His ambition had always been to be an officer. He had educated himself substantially after graduating from military academy in 1938. He sent out to a "library" for books and got a collection of miscellany, largely history, which he most enjoys. From 1942 to 1948 he spent four years in concentration camp and two in prison (solitary confinement) for plotting against the British-dominated regime (with the Germans, during the war). He had "ample time" there and studied German, read "lots of books of every type." He was most influenced by Lloyd Douglas, the American writer, and on an official visit to the United States in 1966, he bought a complete secondhand collection of his works.

A year after he graduated from officers' academy, he met Nasser (1939) and began political action. He hopes some day to retire, but "first comes the battle, the liberation of our territory. After that, when I have put everything in shape, I would like to retire and live my own life in my village at the mouth of the Delta, Mit Abu El Kon."

While in prison he kept a notebook of quotations that appealed to him in his reading. He also wrote a novel, a political novel on the subject of revolution versus reform. It was called *The Prince of the Island*. It was never published. (Heikal has the manuscript and says it is more of a tract than a novel.) He was once a journalist, an editor of *Goumouriya*, and wrote daily articles during the 1956 Suez campaign, bitterly attacking Dulles. He still dreams of writing. He says: "It is nonsense to think that you can make a nation like ours succumb to Israel, especially a nation that is 7,000 years old and that gave civilization to the whole world. Attempts to force a settlement by terror and blackmail do not work with us. The United States is a big power. Why should the United States as a big power take sides in a problem where the issues are quite clear? Why should it help Israel occupy our territories and give money and aid to the country whose forces do the occupying?"

AMMAN, *October 22, 1970*

TALK with King Hussein. He was wearing a khaki uniform with his pilot's wings and a bank of ribbon decorations. I started by asking him how the pact with the *Fedayeen* was working. It gave me the impression of formally recognizing the existence of two governments in Jordan—his and the *Fedayeen's*. He answered: "The pact, as far as it goes, appears to be working. I have every confidence that the end result will be the establishment of law and order in Jordan. We have always supported the right of the Palestinians to oppose the occupation of their territory by *any* means they choose. We are still searching for a means of achieving unity."

I asked him what kind of role Russia and China had played in Jordan's tragic troubles last month when an undeclared civil war was fought. He said Russia had behaved correctly. I must say they played the game. The Chinese might have had a different attitude. It looks as if they are trying to get a foothold in the Arab world.

I asked him if he excluded the idea that a third state might be formed of the Palestinian area, pointing out that the former mandated territory was now shared by Israel and Jordan (although Jordan has lost most of what it held). Some Palestinian Arabs were talking about creating a separate Palestine based in the West Bank area of Jordan. He said: "I do not *exclude* anything. The people can choose what they want. But I do not think there is any strong desire among the people of the West Bank to leave Jordan."

THAT afternoon, drove off with Abu Omar, a member of the central committee of Al Fatah, to Arafat's command post, a shabby building outside which guerrillas were striding about covered with hand grenades and carelessly brandishing Kalashnikov tommy guns.

I followed Abu Omar into a bare, cube-shaped room lit by one naked bulb hanging from the ceiling and furnished with a wooden desk and four plain wooden chairs. A moment later Arafat came in. He is a decidedly unimpressive-looking man: rather short, much too fat, sensuous, heavy

features, glittering eyes, and a somewhat evil face. He was wearing a black
and white *kafiyya*, khaki pants, khaki sweater, and had a three-day growth
of beard. He was carrying a Kalashnikov automatic rifle and also had a
pistol and clip of bullets strapped to his side.

He was most friendly but wholly useless to talk to since he refuses to
answer any question in a straight, factual way, and is enormously pleased
with his orotund, meaningless responses. I asked him about his experience
in guerrilla warfare. He said: "Our aim is to liberate our homeland, Palestine, from the river [Jordan] to the sea [Mediterranean] and to create
there a democratic society with no discrimination in race or creed. We are
Palestinians. We believe in the unity of our people on both sides of the
Jordan. We want to create a Palestinian democratic state for whoever
desires to live there.

PARIS, *October 30, 1970*

DAVID Bruce is now head of our negotiating mission at the Vietnam peace
talks. It is David's guess that Hanoi is going to continue to stall here until
it takes one more military crack at the structure in South Vietnam in the
hope that it can force a decision elsewhere which only needs to be ratified
at the Paris peace conference.

Point two is the crux. We are *not* going to try to oust a government in
Saigon and impose a new government. We have tried that before (Diem),
and it didn't work. We now know this is impossible. Furthermore, we don't
intend to do the dirty work for Hanoi.

PARIS, *November 1, 1970*

I PLAYED golf and lunched with Couve de Murville, who had returned two
days previously from a trip to China. Couve said someday the United
States would make a deal with China against Russia. He was convinced of
this and "that will be a policy. You don't have a policy now." The fate of
Taiwan was increasingly a matter of Japanese rather than American decision, as they were beginning to realize in Peking.

PARIS, *November 10, 1970*

GENERAL de Gaulle's death was announced this morning. Actually, he
died yesterday evening while playing a solitary game of patience in his
somber home at Colombey-les-deux-Églises. I am glad for the old man's
sake that death was swift. He had a horror of the gradual decline which
struck so many people before they succumbed. "Old age is a shipwreck,"
he said.

PARIS, *November 12, 1970*

DE Gaulle was buried with maximum solemnity, and French newspapers boasted that on this day Colombey-les-deux-Églises was the capital of France while Paris was the capital of the world. It is interesting to think that this great man who had so rigidly prescribed that his own interment should be marked by no honors and no great visitors but only by simple obsequies at his own village, should, in fact, have benefited simultaneously from both more panoply and also more simplicity than anyone in French history. On the one hand the stark and simple village ceremony was held and he was finally laid to rest beside his retarded daughter Anne in a cheap wooden coffin; on the other hand, a commemorative service was also held in the Cathedral of Notre Dame in Paris.

ROME, *November 18, 1970*

A SAD evening (yesterday). I had invited poor little Jozsef and Trudi Szall for dinner. They have skipped from Hungary, as political refugees, and are here with their ten-year-old son, near the end of the tether. They keep talking of suicide.

Jozsef is the senior Hungarian diplomat. Although only forty-nine, he has been in the career service of the People's Republic longer than any other.

Jozsef went to see U.S. Ambassador Graham Martin. Martin advised him to talk with the Hungarians and also to ask asylum from the Italians. Budapest sent a vice-minister and wife to meet the Szalls. They were afraid to meet anywhere but in St. Peter's, in Vatican City.

They argued three and one-half hours with the vice-minister and his wife, but they saw people all around them—Hungarian, Russian, Italian, and American security agents, they thought. The American Ambassador had given Jozsef a small tape recorder to tape the conversation and offers made by the Hungarians (who undoubtedly had their own recorder).

Both he and Trudi kept clamoring they "must" go to America. Italy was unsafe.

PARIS, *December 1, 1970*

GOOD talk with President Pompidou. He is confident Russia is now territorially satisfied with its domain. It is not expansionist. Therefore, it wants to see the status quo established everywhere. It wants Germany to sign agreements delimiting its border in the east and it hopes China will accept the frontiers in Asia.

But basically, China does not recognize the Soviet border. Germany does recognize the Oder-Neisse line: only because of the prevailing balance of forces. Were Germany ever to become great and powerful, it would

again move east. To sum up, Russia now wants a status quo and consequently favors both coexistence and *détente*.

There is another aspect, however. Russia is aware of its strength, and it
knows it has become a world power. This is a relatively new experience. It
is just like the United States, which was never a world power before World
War I. He added:

> As Russia expands in terms of world power—above all through its fleet
> and air force, it penetrates everywhere. As a result, this penetration creates
> frictions. Nevertheless, I am profoundly convinced that despite such fric-
> tions, Russia will halt such penetrations whenever they cause trouble because
> it definitely wants peace.
>
> Moscow realizes that China is a problem for tomorrow; but the United
> States is still, for Moscow, a problem for today. The Russians want a kind of
> equality with America, a partition of power. But at the same time, they are
> not prepared to retreat or withdraw in any sense on the ideological front.

LONDON, *December 8, 1970*

HAD a drink with Prime Minister Ted Heath at 10 Downing Street. He
didn't think there was any reason to change NATO's strategy from "flexible response." Change to what?" he asked.

Heath is worried about the Mediterranean situation, where Russian
strength continues to increase. Only a few days ago Mrs. Meir, the Israeli
Prime Minister, had assured him there was no chance of a military confrontation between Russia and America. "I told her I was more worried,"
he said, "that the Soviet Union might get its way without a confrontation."

PARIS, *December 19, 1970*

DINED last night with Prince Paul and Princess Olga: a quiet dinner *en
famille*. Both talked at length about their luncheon with Hitler in early
1941. Hitler had made an effort to be quite charming, but it was a curious
meal. The protocol problem was solved by having the three of them (there
were no other guests) served simultaneously by butlers who sprang out at
the same instant as if in a ballet. Since no plates were passed, in order to
avoid the problem of precedence, they were each served a huge salmon—
although Hitler, a vegetarian, didn't eat his. Behind each chair stood a
grim officer in the SS, looking like an assassin.

They were convinced Hitler was a homosexual. He talked of the tragedy
of seeing beautiful young English and German boys lying dead beside each
other on the battlefield. Olga said she rushed to tell this to Princess Bonaparte, Freud's most distinguished pupil, who said Freud would have been
fascinated.

Hitler assured Prince Paul that his [Hitler's] speeches were the only immortal prose being produced in Germany and would live as long as Luther's *Theses*.

They were also entertained by [Hermann] Goering, who gave a luncheon at his Prussian hunting lodge. Said Paul: "He was dressed like Wilhelm Tell with a dagger in his belt and jewels hanging around his neck. He was clearly mad—but also very intelligent."

Paul said Goering had told him: "Of course, I know I am greedy. That is why I'm so fat. Every night I have a tray with cheese and cold cuts placed on the table by my bedside so if I wake up I can turn over and eat it and go to sleep again."

The main part of the conversation had to do with poor King Peter II, who replaced Prince Paul in 1941 at the age of seventeen and who died in the United States last November 3. Paul gave me copies of Peter's will and death certificate. He died after a liver transplant operation in Denver, Colorado, and the causes are listed as "cardio-respiratory arrest (ten minutes), chronic brain injury (three months), chronic liver cirrhosis (six months)."

Paul says Peter had become a hopeless drunk and fell into the hands of a woman who was close to a splinter faction of the Serbian Orthodox Church headed by two monks. Apparently they cooked up a will—and got him to sign it—in which he left a quarter of his estate to "Liberty Eastern Serbian Orthodox Monastery, Liberty, Illinois" and added, "Notwithstanding any other desires of my family, it is my desire that I be buried in the United States of America at Liberty Eastern Serbian Orthodox Monastery, Liberty, Illinois."

BONN, *January 19, 1971*

LUNCH with Chancellor Willy Brandt in his Schaumburg Palais office. He said:

I am very much interested in cooperation with East Germany. But I do not believe in a mishmash, in just mixing. This is impossible. Yet I still think since it is one nation in the feeling of the people, since there are all these family links, since there is only one language and many other aspects of common culture, there could be instead of the situation we have now, that the distance between West Germany and East Germany is greater than the distance between West Germany and Japan (it is easier for me to go to Japan or Kenya or I don't know where than to East Germany)—I think it should be possible to move in the direction based upon common history, common language, common culture, and an economy that also originally belonged together. A good deal of cooperation could be worked out.

I would not call it a confederation. I cannot see how a confederation could work between a state economy on the one side and a market economy on the other side. What we do not like to recognize is the split of Germany. We have to live with it, but one should not expect that we make this part of our own position. Now we are aiming at good relations with East Germany, because we know these two states exist. We hope one day they will not exist in the same way. They either will be closer together or perhaps even under one roof.

PARIS, *February 8, 1971*

TALK with Georges Marchais, French Communist Party boss. He says it is wrong to consider the French party more "national" than in the past. It has always been "national." However, in previous years it had taken pains to be very precise about its socialistic program. Since the war the party had rejected Stalin's thesis of the "unique party" and was now working as strongly as ever for unity and an electoral alliance with other left-wing parties.

BRUSSELS, *February 10, 1971*

TALKED for an hour and a half with King Baudouin. He said he had been delighted by the way Alan Shepard had hit two golf balls during his moon voyage. He was impressed by the entire U.S. moon program and the astonishing coordination of all its elements. It should help the U.S. image abroad, but unfortunately people were getting blasé. It was silly to say men should not go to the moon because it costs so much money which might otherwise be spent on the poor. There was no relationship. One had to do both.

Baudouin is hopeful about European federation and Britain's ultimate entry into the Common Market. He thinks de Gaulle's European policy actually helped the Market because it prevented it from moving too rapidly too far. Now it was progressing at the correct pace.

He asked if I thought Russia would permit the establishment of liberty in Eastern Europe before some profound change inside the Soviet Union. I said if we thought so we were kidding ourselves. The King asked if we had to accept the extinction of freedom in East Europe. I said regrettably that although it was immoral there was nothing else we could do. There had been less of an international ruckus over Czechoslovakia '68 than Hungary '56, and the biggest problem was still to come. "You mean Jugoslavia after Tito's death?" Baudouin inquired intelligently. "Precisely," I said.

ALGIERS, *February 23, 1971*

AN hour and forty-five minutes with Houari Boumedienne, president of Algeria, in his residence-office. The doorway is watched over by two members of the presidential guard in grey cloaks, white turbans, and carrying scimitars.

Boumedienne is a thin man with heavy, reddish-brown moustache, very dark brown hair, pale white skin, unusually bright small eyes, a somewhat stern expression. He was wearing a black *djellaba* over a grey business suit and let the robe fall to his hips after sitting himself on a sofa beside my armchair. He was smoking a long, thick cigar. A servant brought tea, coffee, and fruit juice.

Did Algeria consider itself both neutral and nonaligned? "Exactly," he said.

> We are nonaligned. But I must explain. We are very jealous of our own national independence. And we sincerely think the only sound policy for Algeria, given its history and the terrible price we paid for our freedom, given its geographical position, is to insist on nonalignment, avoiding entanglement with the power blocs. We will defend this position with all our force. We need continuity and stability and must avoid being entangled in the quarrels of others.
>
> We don't want our future to depend on any foreign country—France or the Soviet Union or the United States. We must depend upon ourselves. Of course, this does not mean that we are neutral as between just and unjust causes. We are independent and we support all just causes.
>
> We stick to the requirements imposed by reality. It is not a question of great ideologies and the ideas elaborated in other lands. This is a different kind of world today. Ideas are evolving at a dizzying pace. Communications are instantaneous and they carry ideas all over.
>
> The real purpose of our socialism is to achieve happiness for our nation, our national entity. The means of production are all controlled by the state. We have liquidated the last vestiges of colonial dependence. The great masses of Algeria have been freed. But it takes time to alter the disparity between different regions and different groups of society.
>
> We are not at all dogmatic. We are pragmatic. The world goes too fast for theories. We can't take the risk of tying ourselves to theories that will be bypassed soon by events. This is no longer 1917 [the year of the Soviet revolution]. This is a time when men are going to other planets. . . .
>
> Our official ideology is that we wish to build a socialist society, adjusted to realities and suitable to our own traditions. Thus, for example, it cannot be an atheist ideology because we are religious Moslems. And we will not impose socialism by force. Our peasants must voluntarily desire it. They must participate.

NEW YORK, *March 4, 1971*

DELIGHTFUL evening with George and Ruth Ball. George, sixty-one and head of Lehman Brothers, the investment banking firm, was for several years Under Secretary of State. Although he disagreed strongly with President Johnson over his Vietnam policy, he is still loyal to him and thinks he was a good President with that exception. He thinks McNamara was an intellectually efficient but heartless machine, that he changed his mind drastically on Vietnam in a way that really was illogical.

After dinner, George said, "I have something to show you." He brought down an official state department "briefing book" with the Department of

State seal on it and marked "Vietnam Papers" and "Master Copy." He told me to take it home and write what I wanted from it.

Among other things that struck me were the following.

October 5, 1964 (Memo to Secretary Rusk, Secretary McNamara, McGeorge Bundy)

In spite of the strategic importance of the real estate involved, our primary motive in supporting the government of South Vietnam is unquestionably political. It is to make clear to the whole free world that we will assist any nation that asks us our help in defending itself against communist aggression. . . .

It is the nature of escalation that each move passes the option to the other side, while at the same time the party which seems to be losing will be tempted to keep raising the ante. . . . Once on the tiger's back we cannot be sure of picking the place to dismount. . . .

April 21, 1965 (Memo to the President)

We cannot continue to bomb the north and use napalm against South Vietnam villages without a progressive erosion of our world position. This erosion will be limited if we appear to be moving toward some kind of political solution. But that will take more than words.

June 18, 1965 (Memo to the President)

Before we commit an endless flow of forces to South Vietnam we must have more evidence than we now have that our troops will not bog down in the jungles and rice paddies—while we slowly blow the country to pieces.

February 12, 1966 (Memo to Secretaries of State and Defense)

There is no assurance that we can achieve our objectives by substantially expanding American forces in South Vietnam and committing them to direct combat. On the contrary, we would run grave risks of bogging down an indeterminate number of American troops in a protracted and bloody conflict of uncertain outcome. . . . Politically, South Vietnam is a lost cause.

We cannot ignore the fact that the war is vastly unpopular and that our role in it is perceptibly eroding the respect and confidence with which other nations regard us.

WASHINGTON, *March 8, 1971*

AGREEABLE lunch in the White House with Henry Kissinger. We were served in his office, now a nice sunny room upstairs in the area that used to be occupied by the White House press. Henry, no slouch in the art of flattery, assured me that both he and the President thought my column was the best being written. I suspect that similar words have been spoken to others, but it rings pleasantly in the ear.

The White House has not yet made up its mind about Salvador Allende in Chile, but he is an extremely shrewd man and has yet to make a false step. Nevertheless Henry indicated deep suspicion, saying that a man who had been in politics for so long, and who had gone out of his way to receive all of Ché Guevara's colleagues when they were released from Bolivian prison, was fundamentally against us.

Henry was worried about the degree of anti-Semitism in this country. He was astonished at how many people in the Establishment told him of their own feelings, which were evidently although unconsciously anti-Semitic. Because of his high White House position they seem to forget that he is Jewish.

At the end of our conversation Henry asked me if I would please write him a personal letter as soon as I left Chile giving my forthright opinions of the situation there. He wants this letter for the President.

≈§§≈

THIS afternoon I had an interview with President Nixon. He agreed to let me take notes with the express purpose of quoting our conversation, the first such interview he has granted. I saw him in the President's suite in the executive office building. He summoned a photographer, who took several pictures. "You might want one of these," said Nixon with a friendly grin, "just in case you are planning to write another book."

He said I could quote him directly. I didn't have to send him any text. He had absolute faith in me. "After all, if I felt I had to edit what you wrote, I wouldn't have agreed to see you in the first place. I know you are a good reporter and will write the truth."

At the end he asked where I was bound and I told him Chile. "You lucky fellow," he commented. "I wish I could go there." I told him Kissinger had asked me to write him a letter after my trip—to show the President. "Yes, I wish you would help me by doing that," he said. "Tell me straight what you think."

To start his summation, the President said:

I would strongly commend to you my second foreign policy report. I have noticed in some quarters a tendency to discuss this rather condescendingly, saying there is nothing new in it. But that isn't so. It sets forth new policy directions and outlines the goals we hope to achieve—the goals not only for this administration but for subsequent administrations. This is a long-range effort. It doesn't get into a country-by-country analysis except in connection with the Soviet Union.

The irony today, for those who look at the Washington scene, is that the great internationalists of the post-World War II period have become the neo-isolationists of the Vietnam War period and especially of the period accompanying the ending of that war. And it is ending.

Why have many former internationalists developed neo-isolationist tendencies, at least in some degree? Part of the answer is simply that Americans, like all idealists, are very impatient people. They feel that if a good thing is going to happen it should happen immediately.

And a great many of these people are very disillusioned with the United

Nations. I am not, personally, because I never expected it could settle all problems involving major powers but could nevertheless play a useful role in development and in peace-keeping in areas where the superpowers were not directly involved.

I know that some national leaders and some countries want to expand by conquest and are committed to expansion and this obviously creates the danger of war. Moreover, some peoples have hated each other for years and years.

With this in mind, I am deeply devoted to a desire that the United States should make the greatest possible contribution it can make to developing such a peaceful world. It is not enough just to be for peace. The point is, what can we do about it?

We got caught up in a vicious crossfire and it became increasingly difficult to make people understand. I must say that without television it might have been difficult for me to get people to understand a thing. The crossfire I referred to was this. The superdoves opposed our commitment in Vietnam and all world responsibilities—Korea, the Philippines, the Middle East, Europe. This was the kind of isolationism of those who felt the United States shouldn't have played any role at all in southeast Asia from the very start. For these people, Vietnam was a distant, small, foreign country in just the terms Chamberlain mentioned concerning Czechoslovakia at the time of Munich [1938]. These were the superdoves.

But on the other side, the opposite crossfire came from the superhawks. This group stood by their commander-in-chief, the president, but became fed up with the war for their own reasons. They felt that if the United States can't handle a stinking little war, why then let's just pull out and build up our strength at home. Their logic also favored isolationism but from another angle. And they want to develop a fortress America at home and cram it full of missiles, while the superdoves want us to pull out of the world also, but reducing our strength at home.

In between there are those of us who stand in the middle of the crossfire. The superhawk feels it is his duty to support the president even if that same superhawk isn't sure he wants to see us do what we are doing. The superdove has a different attitude. He is a good-hearted fellow, but, when he looks around and sees the problems of the poor, the blacks, the Indians, the poor whites, the pot-smoking kids, crime in the cities, urban slums, the environment, he says: "We must get out of the war right away and concern ourselves only with problems at home."

The fact is, however, that there has never been so great a challenge to U.S. leadership. This war is ending. In fact, I seriously doubt we will ever have another war. This is probably the very last one.

Our idea is to create a situation in which those lands to which we have obligations or in which we have interests, if they are ready to fight a fire, should be able to count on us to furnish the hose and water. Meanwhile, in Europe, we can't cut down our forces until there is a mutual agreement with the other side. We must stand with our European friends if they will only do a bit more themselves in NATO—as they have indicated they will do. And we cannot foolishly fall behind in the arms competition.

The Soviets are a great land power opposite China as well as having far-reaching interests elsewhere. We are a great sea power and we must keep our strength. I am a strong navy man myself.

I want the American people to be able to be led by me, or by my successor, along a course that allows us to do what is needed to help keep the peace in this world.

Let us look at the world today. There are two great powers facing us, Russia and China. They are great powers and great people. Certainly neither of them wants war. But both are motivated by a philosophy which announces itself as expansionist in character. And only the United States has sufficient strength to be able to help maintain a balance in Europe and other areas that might otherwise be affected.

What I am saying is not a cold-war philosophy. I hope that we can further develop our negotiations with the Soviet Union. For, although we recognize that their ideology is expansionist, they know what it means if the genie comes out of the bottle and that their interest in survival requires that they avoid a conflict with the United States. This means that we must find a way of cooperating.

In past times, the Number One nation was always in that position because of military conquests. But the mantle of leadership fell on American shoulders not by our desire and not for the purposes of conquest. We have that position today and how we handle ourselves will determine the chances of world peace.

When I asked the President if he could give any precise indication as to how many American troops he expected would be in South Vietnam by mid-1972, he grinned and replied: "Well, you know I can't disclose the withdrawal figures. But let me say this: those who think Vietnam is going to be a good political issue next year are making a grave miscalculation. Those who are counting on Vietnam as a political issue in this country next year are going to have the rug jerked from under them."

26

THIS MORNING TO THE PRESIDENTIAL PALACE (ALSO KNOWN AS *Casa de Bolívar* after the liberator, who lived there). The entrance is romantic. One walks by the window, above a narrow street, from which Bolívar escaped while his mistress talked off would-be assassins at the doorway of their bedroom above.

President Misael Pastrana Borrero is a youthful (forty-eight), elegent man with intelligent face and courteous manner. I asked what he thought was wrong with our Latin American policy. He said: "Even though the Alliance for Progress didn't have the quantitative effects expected, it did create a new atmosphere in inter-American relationships. In fact, although the framework has not been substantially modified, there is now a new feeling that the United States priority interest in solving social problems has faded."

Pastrana observed: "About 150 years ago, Bolívar said Chile would be the last country in Latin America that would cease to be a republic. I wonder if he was right."

Bogotá, *March 20, 1971*

THE gold museum, with its pre-Colombian collection of artifacts that helped give rise to the legend of El Dorado, the Golden Man, who walked into a lake regularly, covered in gold dust and wearing a golden headdress, is impressive. One can understand how greedy conquerors were stirred by these endless necklaces, pendants, head pieces, bracelets, idols, etc., gleaming among feathers from the lowland Indians or recovered from the funerary urns of mummies.

544

SANTIAGO, *March 23, 1971*

Two and a half hours this evening with President Salvador Allende in his office, called La Moneda. Allende, who is sixty-two, is a small, stocky, quick-moving man with grey moustache, ruddy face, and wavy brown hair, untouched by white. He wears thick, heavily rimmed spectacles. He has a determined, obstinate face with small cleft chin. He preferred to walk up and down, gesticulating as we talked. He resembles a slightly overweight, agitated fox.

I asked about his coalition. He said,

Essentially there are different types of popular front. There were three popular front governments in the world during the 1930s: those of Spain, France, and Chile. In France the experiment disappeared into limbo because Léon Blum, the premier, was a good intellectual but a bad politician. The Spanish popular front government disappeared in the civil war.

But the Chilean popular front lasted from 1938 into 1941 when World War II came to this hemisphere. The popular front of that period for the first time brought the middle class and workers' parties into active collaboration. I was minister of health and I was just as much of a socialist then as I am today.

The popular front government succeeded in creating, thanks to state initiative, Chile's oil, electrical, and steel industries. It started Chile's initial industrialization. Trade unions participated in all these decisions. It also saw the beginning of our social legislation. It was, in fact, a government of great significance.

That popular front regime was on the left of the capitalistic system. But the Popular Unity government now wants to transform the capitalistic system entirely. Today, in our Popular Unity government, the socialists, communists and other left-wing groups hold equal roles.

The Chilean communists are a very serious party, known for its political honesty, which has taken an engagement to fulfill our announced governmental program. And the Chilean Communist party is sufficiently realistic to know any policy that might subject Chilean interests to those of another country would have disastrous effects here. Don't forget, I am the president, and I run things, a socialist. I have no need to import strength from outside.

The socialists don't want to be changed and the radicals, who in Chile have had a party for 110 years, surely won't commit suicide. Don't forget that Karl Marx foresaw a time when there would be no governments at all. But when? It hasn't come yet. The strategy of socialism must depend on the realities of any country where it is attempted. To be a socialist is obviously not the same thing as being a communist.

There are different roads to socialism. Jugoslavia is a socialist country. So is Rumania. So are China, Cuba, the Soviet Union, and many others. But all of them have followed different paths. I think capital must be placed at the service of man. I think that man must come before everything and anything else. I hope, for the time being, to utilize the existing constitution and our present laws in order to achieve the reforms we urgently need. But as a second step—some time later on—I envisage proposing an entirely new constitution.

Allende said: "My word is formally engaged to respect all the fundamental rights of man. No matter how extensive our economic and social reform will be, we will not only respect human rights but actually increase them. So far they exist only for a minority. Human rights are not merely political; they are also social and economic. Freedom alone is just a fiction for the poor. Not the slightest violation of freedom of the press exists."

I asked: "Do you foresee the possibility of any violent confrontation in Chile as a consequence of opposition to your program?"

He said: "Sadly, very sadly, I admit this possibility exists. That is the lesson of history. There is no doubt at all on this point. It would come from the Right. I know it would come from the Right because it has already done something that never before occurred in Chilean history— namely assassinated the army commander, General Schneider. What they really wanted to do was to kill me. There have already been two attempts on my life."

Allende said: "Certain groups in the United States, groups including the copper mine owners who have always been influential in your policy, are trying to upset my government, to interfere with our program. What I mean is that there are local plots, inside Chile, supported or encouraged by certain interests in the United States. Obviously I do not think that the United States government would lend itself to such efforts, to a policy that would clearly violate the principle of self-determination."

He promised to give financial compensation to foreign companies with interests in Chile that are being nationalized, adding: "This is not a process of confiscation. We fully accept the principle of compensation."

He said Chile intends to stand by its existing international commitments.

> We want respect for our policy and understanding of our aims which seek to make of Chile a country progressing along the paths opened up by science and technology.
>
> The United States should recognize and accept that the dignity of man is not in any sense related to his per capita annual production rate. In this world small countries should be respected quite as much as big countries.
>
> There is a strange and paradoxical relationship between imperialism and underdevelopment. Underdevelopment is primarily due to imperialism which prevented the full use by a subjected land of its potential wealth and abilities. Imperialism in fact exists as a phenomenon in some countries because of underdevelopment in others.
>
> But the paradox is that the underdeveloped countries are traditionally forced, despite their relative poverty, to sell their products at a cheap price and to buy abroad the products they need at an expensive price. This paradox is one of the things we are trying to solve.
>
> The United States should recognize that our democracy here is authentic democracy and that we will never do anything against the United States or

contribute to injuring its sovereignty. For example, we will never provide a military base that might be used against the United States. Chile will never permit its territory to be used for a military base by any foreign power, by anybody.

BUENOS AIRES, *March 30, 1971*

LAST week Argentina had another military coup d'état. General Roberto Levingston, then president, was chucked out, and the army commander, General (Alejandro Agustin) Lanusse, took over.

Today I had a long talk with Lanusse. It was his second day in office. I was enjoined to the strictest secrecy, not even to tell our Ambassador.

The president took part in the abortive 1951 coup against Perón and was sent south to a military prison. He is a tough-looking man with white hair, sallow color, youthful hands, kindly brown eyes, but a tough, thin mouth and resolute jaw.

I asked why he thought Argentina had had recourse to military government so many times during the century since its last war in 1870. He said: "The army has always played an important role in building an Argentine nation. This is a particular Argentinian characteristic. Looking back on our history, at crucial moments military men appeared on the scene to solve the most difficult crises."

I asked what he considered the necessary preconditions for a return to normal civilian rule and when. He said, "My view is that we must do all that is necessary to revitalize obsolete institutions as a first step toward democratic government. After all, why was our revolution [the coup] made? To make democracy possible."

I wondered if it would be possible to recreate representative political parties without their being drowned by the Peronistas and neo-Peronistas. It became evident he is ready to make a deal with them, even with Perón himself.

"It would be unwise and foolish," Lanusse said, "to try and ignore that section of the population which follows the ideas represented by Perón from 1944 to 1955."

I spent four years in prison for my opposition to Perón. But I share the concepts of social improvement and the principles of reform being sought. The theories underlined in the plans of Perón don't contradict my own thoughts—neither then nor now. But I have been in the past and still am ready to oppose his procedures—

We don't have much time and none of it should be wasted by looking backward. When I am in a true position to know how the Argentinian people want to solve their problems I am ready to talk with the Peronistas and even with Perón himself to hear his ideas, if he approaches problems in a constructive way. The only precondition is that whoever comes to talk with me as president of the republic must come in order to construct the future.

RIO DE JANEIRO, *April 2, 1971*

LUNCHED with former President Juscelino Kubitschek de Oliveira at his office. He is now president of an investment bank. Kubitschek was president from 1956–61, a modernizer, and one of Brazil's great men. By building Brasilia, he thrust the country's dynamism inland.

I asked why there were leftist governments to the west of the Andes and rightist governments to the east. He said this came from misery and underdevelopment in the west (like Bolivia and Peru) and a high percentage of Indians who are badly prepared for democracy. "There are three Americas: North, South—and Brazil, which is very different and special. Bolívar's genius was unable to maintain unity in Spanish America, but Brazil remained united with its mass internal market growing every day." He said there was a tendency of the noncommunist world to move right, and the word "Christian" has lost its meaning in Christian democracy. The church had lived by serving those in power.

In Latin America a popular reaction to this had begun. Bishops and priests in Brazil had been arrested. The church, as an organization, had been serving the Establishment and lost influence with the people. Now the majority of more than 200 bishops were in revolt against oppression.

"When I was president," he said, "I invited Cardinal Montini [now Pope Paul] to visit Brazil. At that time Archbishop Helder [the principal leftist priest] was auxiliary archbishop of Rio and I attached him as an aide to Montini. During a period of five days the three of us met several times and we found much common ground in support of liberalization. When Paul was elected Pope, he invited me to Rome and I noticed his first speech followed the same lines. It was clear Helder's influence was continuing."

He thought Allende and his movement in Chile "represent a real danger that Chile is going communist. I believe Allende is trying to bring about democratic socialism, but the pressure of his political allies and of communism abroad is tremendous. If Chile goes communist there will be a threatening situation in Latin America. No one else in Latin America will return from right-wing systems to democracy. We would lose all hope of liberty."

He said military governments in Latin America were composed of officers trained in the United States to fight Communist efforts to take power. Their tendency, when in power, is toward nationalism, as in Peru or Bolivia. As it seeks to develop an internal market and industry this nationalism tends toward socialism. But the military, like the church, is changing and finds it can move to the left. It is a small step from socialist nationalism (or vice versa) to communism. The great danger to Latin America is the move from military governments to nationalism to leftist totalitarianism to communism.

MASERU, LESOTHO, *April 9, 1971*

DROVE to the residence of Chief Leabua Jonathan, the Prime Minister—
a round structure guarded by a policeman in battledress. Chief Jonathan's
office is wood-paneled. On the walls were a picture of an ancestor in an
antiquated top hat, a picture of himself in a Panama hat, several decorations in a glass cabinet, two shelves of books, and a wooden plaque with
the motto: "Lesotho. The impossible we shall do right away. Only mira-
cles will take a little longer." He said: "I favor a nonracial society with
equal opportunity for all, regardless of color. A guarantee of this was
written into our constitution which was recently suspended, but the new
constitution, which is now being drafted, will contain exactly the same
guarantee."

I asked if he thought South Africa's racial policy could work. "No," he
replied. "It cannot possibly work. I am certain it will fail, both for moral
reasons and for practical reasons."

CAPETOWN, *April 15, 1971*

TODAY B. J. (John) Vorster, the Prime Minister, received me in his
simple, long office hung with pictures of the republic's presidents and
Prime Ministers and those of the Transvaal and Orange Free States, stern,
forbidding men like Vorster himself.

Vorster said his doctrine was to "fight terrorism, not only in our own
country, but also in any other country in Africa where the government
requests us to do so." Although he had offered nonaggression pacts to all
African states, none had taken up the offer.

I inquired whether the logical aim of apartheid, or "separate development," as he calls it, wasn't extensive partition and creation of more and
larger black states, so that it was possible to envision a day for a smaller
South Africa with a white majority. He said:

That is our aim and objective.

Now you have workers in South Africa from all the different black homelands, their number running into millions; plus the Swazis, Lesothos,
Botswanas, and Malawians. For generations the chief export of these black
states will be labor because they are not industrialized and can't use their
own labor, can't employ their own people. This is a problem of all Africa.

But as they industrialize they will naturally employ more of their own
people and that will decrease the export of labor. Their policy is to develop
and it is also our policy to develop people who are not yet independent. But
this can't happen in too much of a hurry.

And as elements of our African population become independent, the time
might eventually come when the whites are actually a majority here. That is
the ideal. We have stated on the issue of one-man-one-vote that we subscribe
to it fully, but each in his own country.

I asked if he thought Russia was trying to cut across Africa and split it ideologically. "I'm more concerned about China," he replied. "Tanzania can rightly today be called a vassal state of red China. I am terribly worried that they will ultimately take over Tanzania and Zambia. Those countries are playing with fire. Thousands of Chinese are being sent to help build the Tan-Zam railway. If they remain, they can take over."

There was ample evidence that the Russians and Chinese were helping guerrilla movements aimed at South Africa. Their weapons were all of Communist origin. They were trained in China, Russia, or East Europe.

CAPETOWN, *April 19, 1971*

I CAN'T help feeling that while the Afrikaners produce the most bigoted and reactionary people in South Africa, they also produce the best. They are neither *fin du race* nor third-rate remittance men or petty bourgeois snobs like the English-speakers; even the worst of them have quality, and I often wonder if the British hadn't turned New Amsterdam into New York what the United States might have become under Dutch Puritan rather than English Puritan sponsorship.

LE MORNE, MAURITIUS, *April 25, 1971*

GAETAN Duval, the Foreign Minister, invited me to dinner at a little restaurant. Duval is a handsome mulatto with unrefined but not Negroid features, tan skin, rings of long curly hair. He was wearing a flowered open shirt, velvet trousers, and patent leather boots of calf length. He fancies himself as a kind of hippie and has been told he looks like the young Dumas (which is probably true; Dumas was a quadroon).

The government is a coalition, and Duval says his is the largest of the parties in it but is strongly anticommunist, whereas the Prime Minister's Labor Party is more neutral. Duval said he had made it a rule never to receive or speak to any Soviet diplomat which, if true, is a singular position for a Foreign Minister.

He added: "I'm not white, I'm black. But I know we will have to find a way through South Africa's race policy because this is absolutely essential to the Indian Ocean."

TANANARIVE, MADAGASCAR, *April 28, 1971*

THIS is a lovely, romantic town with indigenous, terraced, gabled buildings, to which the architecture of a small French provincial capital is added. It is set on a series of hills atop the inland plateau, 4,500 feet above sea level. The climate is superb.

Local customs are quaint, including the removal (every July) from their tombs of ancestors' bodies or bones, which are dressed up, driven around to see the sights, presented to friends and family, honored with drinks, and then returned to their cemeteries.

Jack Hasey of the embassy told me China (Peking) is the big problem. He said: "Official figures show a colony of 9,000 Chinese but actually there are from 20,000 to 25,000, mostly Cantonese. They frequently go back to communist China and also send remittances. Many of them have married Malgaches and remain on here as 'sleepers' for long-range penetration. Their main effort seems to be to try and neutralize the Soviets."

TANANARIVE, MADAGASCAR, *April 30, 1971*

CALLED on President Philibert Tsiranana. He is said to be in his late sixties; an official stamp was printed last year honoring his "sixtieth" birthday. He was wearing a straw hat shaped like an army overseas cap, colored tan, red, yellow, and blue; also a grey suit and bedroom slippers. He opened his coat to display an assortment of objects chained to his belt, including key rings and two German miniature cameras. He proceeded at one point to haul one of these out and gravely take our pictures. He speaks French but is hard to understand because he has had a stroke which partly affected his tongue.

The president said that this week a South African general came here to confer with a Malgache general on means of stopping communism. The two were in the same "promotion" at the French *École Supérieure de Guerre*. He said the Chinese had big ambitions here, "but they won't succeed."

MORONI, GRANDE COMORE, *May 8, 1971*

A LARGE island with several small, seeping, semiactive volcanoes, whose chocolate-colored lava has worked itself slowly down over the jungles to the sea, where it forms steep escarpments. The dusk comes down like thunder, and we saw huge fruit bats with wings more than two and a half feet in span and bodies as large as rabbits, wheeling in the sky and then coming in to hang upside down from branches by their claws. Little bright red birds, maroon-headed birds, and mynah birds flitted among the dense shrubs: thick-leaved vanilla leaves, manioc plants, numberless bananas, and coconut palms.

NAIROBI, *May 10, 1971*

LAST night the (U.S. Ambassador Bob and Alice) McIlvaines, with whom I'm staying, gave a small dinner. Joe Murumbi and his white wife were there; both charming. Murumbi was Foreign Minister. (Marina had to fly on to our sick grandson in London.)

Murumbi says: "We have learned democracy well enough to know how to get people into power but not well enough to curtail them once they are there."

TALK with Kenya's Foreign Minister Njoroge Mungai, a medical doctor, graduated from Stanford and then Columbia Medical School. He said the East African federation was essential despite political differences among its members, Kenya, Uganda and Tanzania. Nevertheless, right now there was a problem. General Idi Amin had staged a coup in Uganda ousting Milton Obote as president. Tanzania refused to recognize Amin, and Obote was Julius Nyerere's guest (Tanzania's president) in Dar es Salaam.

There had already been twenty-seven coups d'état in Africa. Kenya therefore made it a practice to recognize each government that accepted its country's existing international obligations and demonstrated that it was in effective control.

THERE has been a big crisis, placing under various forms of arrest Vice-President Aly Sabry, Interior Minister (and police boss) Gomaa, Minister of the Presidency Sami Sharaf. Mohamed Heikal told me the story of the coup. It should have succeeded because the Minister of the Interior (police), the head of intelligence, the main official of the Arab Socialist Union (only party), and the Minister of War were all in it.

Security police in the telephone tapping setup were under the direct supervision of Interior Minister Gomaa. He had his own private archive of tapped tapes, distinct from the regular storage library, and was so suspicious that he was even tapping the lines of fellow-conspirators.

A police major was given some special tapes to be put in Gomaa's library. But the note labeling one tape was unclear, and he didn't know in which archive it should be stored. So he played it and found it was a conversation between two of the principal leaders and very hostile to el Sadat.

He decided to inform the president. The guards called el Sadat's principal secretary. He agreed to give the secretary two tapes for el Sadat to play right away. At 3:00 A.M. Wednesday, May 12, el Sadat woke up and sent for a recorder. When he listened he really woke up.

He heard one leader describe how the broadcasting station could be sealed off so el Sadat would be unable to make a radio speech. Then he heard his own voice in a taped telephone conversation. He summoned the major, who told him all he knew. Then the major said he had to take the tapes back to his office before 6:00 A.M. or he would be fired. El Sadat said: "As president I order you to leave these tapes with me."

The plotters planned to oust him Thursday, May 20. A handful would seize el Sadat, because about half of the presidential guard was already won over. El Sadat decided to play it cool. He had a scheduled appointment to speak to commanding officers of the Second Army May 12. At 11:00 A.M. he carried on and spoke with the War Minister beside him on the platform. He told Second Army commanders that centers of antiregime conspiracy existed in the country but that he was determined not to accept a police state. General Mohammed Fawzi, the War Minister, sat unhappily behind him.

When el Sadat got back to his office he alerted the presidential guard and dismissed Interior Minister Gomaa, secretly ordering the Governor of Alexandria to take over and seize the rooms in which tapped recordings were stored. El Sadat told Sami Sharaf, Minister of the Presidency (and one of the plotters) that he was dismissing Gomaa but permitting him to let it appear in public as a "resignation."

At that moment the main conspirators were meeting in the Minister of War's office. When they heard the news on Gomaa they decided to resign together in order to create panic and confusion. They thought this would precipitate chaos; if people were shot at by the police, General Fawzi could use the army "to maintain order."

The Minister of Information promptly broadcast this mass resignation, and they waited for el Sadat to collapse and quit. El Sadat called Heikal, who rushed over to the president's house. At this time the War Minister was asking the air, navy, and army commanders to join in the plot, but all three refused. The Chief of Staff heard about them meeting, entered, and told General Fawzi: "You have resigned. Therefore you have no right to be here now. We do not tolerate political meetings in the Ministry."

When Heikal rushed over to el Sadat, he was sitting on a balcony over the Nile in pajamas and dressing gown. He said: "Thank God they've done it." He had instructed the new Minister of Interior: "Arrest those people."

Then the Chief of Staff called for orders. El Sadat said: "I have decided to name you minister of war." The chief, a general, replied: "The army has no interest in politics. We only await orders in one battle [Israel]. Everything is secure."

TEL AVIV, *May 23, 1971*

SPENT an hour and a half with Major General Aharon Yariv, chief of intelligence. Yariv said el Sadat is moving on internal Egyptian affairs. To stay in the saddle he must either deliver a concrete diplomatic settlement or resort to war. Therefore he depends more on the army now than when he first succeeded Nasser. He found he couldn't rely on the police, the ASU Party or intelligence.

He won the allegiance of the army on the thesis that there *is* a chance for a peaceful settlement and this chance must be exploited, but if it fails, he will fight. The army agrees. El Sadat's freedom of internal maneuver is restrained by that same army, which won't agree to any settlement that hurts its own prestige.

Yariv said the Soviet military buildup in Egypt stressed an expensive air defense but included a heavy buildup in fighter strength that could be used offensively, above all the advanced MIG-21 strike aircraft. There was a perceptible offensive buildup in equipment, especially in amphibious and bridge-building materiel.

PARIS, *June 5, 1971*

IN this morning's mail I received a letter from President Nixon. He referred to a paper I prepared for him with recommendations on policy toward Chile. The President says the approach being followed conforms with my recommendations. My memorandum said in part:

> Every country has the right to reform or revolutionize its social system if this is the desire of its citizens. There can be no valid U.S. objection if the Chilean people wish to revise their economy and society without bloodshed and by electoral means.
>
> But the United States has a legitimate right to see that such changes are not produced at our expense. We have a fair claim to compensation for property sufficient to cover insurance commitments otherwise chargeable to the U.S. taxpayer. And we must try and safeguard against the spread across South America of an obviously anti-U.S. movement deliberately encroaching on our legitimate interests—especially if (as in Cuba) hostile military installations are permitted. We cannot tolerate a Monroe Doctrine in reverse. . . .
>
> Allende is bound to face serious economic and political problems. There will be inflation, declining production in key sectors, sizeable unemployment. Although the anti-Allende parties have displayed timidity and an inability to unite, those leaders who don't flee the country are destined to coalesce in an opposition to the right of the President. . . . I would recommend:
>
> (1) That Washington should never allow any development to precipitate a break in relations with Santiago, thus sacrificing the ultimate potential of being able, some day, to influence developments from within. The error of Cuba should not be repeated in Chile, even if humble pie features the menu.
>
> (2) That a single individual, directly responsible to the President's staff, be assigned to coordinate all Chilean affairs (diplomatic, economic, propagandistic, military, financial, commercial, and intelligence—including the private sector). Thereby, policy can be directed effectively from the top on both a long-range basis and, should such be needed, an immediate *ad hoc* basis.
>
> (3) That the U.S. ambassador and his entire staff be rigidly enjoined to assume an unruffled, infallibly courteous, low-profile posture, regardless of what develops.

PARIS, *July 10, 1971*

LATE yesterday afternoon Régis Debray dropped in for a beer. Debray told me that at the age of twenty he first became interested in Latin America as a consequence of an interest in Spanish revolutionary thought which he had acquired from his reading on the Spanish Civil War and above all through Alejo Carpentier, the Cuban writer.

He spent a great deal of time in Cuba and became an intimate of Castro and Ché Guevara. Later he joined Guevara's dead-end guerrilla uprising in Bolivia and was captured by the Bolivian authorities, tried, and sentenced to prison. He was released last year. He said de Gaulle had saved his life by sending a cable to President Barrientos of Bolivia just a day or two after Debray was picked up, urging Barrientos to give him full legal protection.

Debray described Guevara as perhaps romantic in his strategic vision and the broadness of his scope, but added that he was a cold, hard man in his tactical actions.

Several times Debray referred to the fact that we were on "opposite sides of the barricade." I said of course this was true, but it shouldn't preclude human contact. He agreed.

ROME, *July 16, 1971*

TWO hours this afternoon in the unattractive Quirinale palace with President Giuseppe Saragat. At one point Saragat remarked it was a hot day and we should have something cool to drink. He ordered champagne, which came in promptly.

We talked about Italy. Saragat smiled when he recalled the column of mine called "Spaghetti with Chile Sauce." He said the drift toward an increasing Communist importance had ended. He continued: "In order to understand what is going on here you must recognize that a very swift industrial revolution has taken place in which ten million people, about one-fifth of the population, have been transferred from the country to the city, mostly moving up from the south. This includes some four million peasants and their families. An enormous change has occurred in a few years' time, accomplishing in Italy what it required one century for England to do."

REYKJAVIK, *August 3, 1971*

U.S. AMBASSADOR Replogle yesterday gave me a large dinner. Among those there was Halldor Laxness, Iceland's Nobel prize novelist.

Laxness is a charming man with a bluff, hearty manner and open face. He holds contemporary writers everywhere in low esteem. It was easy for the great nineteenth-century authors to produce huge books quickly; the need now is to condense much into short space; for this he values journalism.

 REYKJAVIK, *August 5, 1971*

I AM impressed by the way 200,000 people here can maintain a civilization with two airlines, ships, telephones, road building, etc. But in the end, I don't think they'll have enough people to keep it up. The only place they could go to join or seek sponsorship would be England, not Scandinavia. They are nearer Glasgow than Oslo or Copenhagen, and English is the first language in schools, even if they still must learn Danish, which is very foreign now. The kids like English—language of the movies and TV.

ANKARA, *August 16, 1971*

TALK for about an hour and a half with Foreign Minister Osman Olcay, a career diplomat and highly intelligent. I asked him what had gone sour in U.S.-Turkish relations? He said the process had begun in 1964 when President Johnson wrote his harsh letter warning the Turks not to go to war on Cyprus. But the unnecessarily high profile of the American presence in Turkey was the real reason for the decline in friendship.

ISTANBUL, *August 19, 1971*

FLEW here to see President Sunay at his summer residence at Floriya, on the beach of the Sea of Marmora. His face is brutal and strong; he is quite humorless and almost without emotion, wearing thick-lensed spectacles. Behind his desk was a large picture of Ataturk.

He said:

> Turkey has a special case, both historically and philosophically. During the war of independence the country was in a shambles. The Ottoman empire lay in ruins after World War I and the only force in the nation that stood up to correct the lamentable situation was the army.
>
> Only Ataturk and the officers serving under him unleashed the necessary struggle against the great powers and many odds. Therefore, the army regards the republic as its own creation and is as solicitous about its health as a mother is about her child's.
>
> After Ataturk's death, it was natural for the army to continue the fight against religious reaction and against communism and to prevent either from gaining an upper hand in an attempt to upset the republic. This was the spirit of the army's intervention this year; it was in no sense a search for political power.

PARIS, *November 1, 1971*

TODAY I had one of the most interesting lunches of my life. André Malraux and Régis Debray and his wife came to our house together with Clem and Jessie Wood. Jessie is the daughter of Louise de Vilmorin, and Malraux regards her as a member of his own family.

It was a moving occasion. Malraux is seventy, still illuminating a feverish and brilliant mind. He is extremely hard to understand, but his mind races along. On the other hand, Debray is a handsome young man with blond hair and drooping moustache, small, composed. He has a calm soft voice and a cold, ideological, unromantic Cartesian mind.

I felt that I was introducing to each other—across a gap of two generations (forty years)—two French literary revolutionists. And for their own part, they were both clearly aware that such was the case. I knew from Jessie's cousin, who acts as Malraux's secretary, that he had written in his diary *"déjeuner très important."*

Régis was prepared for an "occasion" and very well-dressed, like a true member of the Parisian *haute-bourgeoisie* to which he belongs by birth. So was his wife, a Venezuelan girl (and fanatical Communist) with glowing eyes of black and the little sharp beak nose of a parrot.

Malraux arrived early. I detected a slight note of nervousness. I have a feeling that he was afraid to meet the ghost of his own youth. I offered him the choice between a Bloody Mary and a whisky and soda.

"Whisky," he said. *"Il ne faut pas changer."*

As soon as Debray came in, Malraux shot at him, "What were your objectives in Bolivia?"

"The establishment of revolutionary centers as a base for all Latin America," Debray replied. But he was not able to enlarge; Malraux immediately interrupted, bringing up Bengal.

Malraux, when questioned by Debray on his reasons for choosing Bangladesh as his special cause, answered in difficult fashion. The gist was that he had been asked to adopt Bangladesh. His aim, he said, was to become a kind of center or rallying point for volunteers. "If I succeed," he added, "then so much for the cause of national freedom. If I fail, what better way to die." "Their cause is desperate," he said. And he added, "No cause can survive without a leader with a name. They need a de Gaulle. *Il leur faut un de Gaulle. Il faut un de Gaulle à tout le monde."*

When asked whether a class conflict would not develop in Bengal, Malraux bristled. His view is that class is *"antérieur"*; it comes after national liberation. And national freedom, he insisted, is always the strongest force of all, a force which unites all. Over and over he repeated, "One thing at a time: one problem at a time."

Debray wanted to know about the international brigade's role in Spain. Malraux told him it had indeed saved Madrid, but that—above all else—it had answered the dream element of republican Spain. "If they are on our side, then we know we are not so pathetic," he said.

The conversation moved on to other topics. The resistance was brought up. Malraux commented: "One day I may write the book about *la résistance Française*," and then he went on to tell a resistance story. A group of maquis were ordered to capture a convoy of trucks transporting German sugar. The group attacked, failing to see that machine guns flanked the convoy. All the group's members were killed.

In the Corrèze, the group's region, all the women put on black clothing when going to their respective family tombs. The following day the Germans threw the dead bodies into a collective grave while every woman of the Corrèze stood by, dressed in black. The next day a cross was found on the collective tomb. And what is more, in a town which had nothing, every day a kilo of sugar was hung from the tomb's cross.

Malraux later talked about the right and the left. "The Right no longer exists, and today everybody is on the Left, which means the Left no longer exists."

Debray asked him whom—or what—he considered to be the primordial enemy. Again Malraux bristled. "There is no enemy, there is no single enemy. There are just many, and these are all symbolic."

When the subject of capitalism came up, Malraux said, "The matter is no longer important. One asks oneself if one is good or bad, charitable or egoist, brave or cowardly—but not: am I a capitalist?"

He asked Debray if treason had not played a larger part in his failure in Bolivia with Ché Guevara than had the lack of arms. Debray half-agreed. Debray pointed out that Tania was in no way the "movie star" that Malraux had made her out to be. Debray also explained that Tania's parents had been German Communists, and that she had lived a while in East Germany.

Malraux courteously acceded that he might well have been misinformed about Tania. "I had not been minister for eleven years without knowing that one can be misinformed by the *'services spéciaux'*," he admitted. Then he said that the facts were not so important, and he dwelled at length on the importance of *"la légende."* "What is important in legend is that legendary aspect. One must never overlook the 'Jeanne d'Arc' side of things."

Malraux gave a long monologue on the "mysterious relationship between great men, simple men, and women." During it, he presented his differentiation between great and not-great men. Alexander and Napoleon were great, the Maréchal de Saxe (who never lost a battle) and Turenne were not. In heaven, Saxe could say "You lost a battle," but Napoleon would answer, *"Vous n'avez jamais fait rêver les femmes."*

On his way out, Malraux shook Debray's hand. He wished him good luck. Debray was obviously impressed. He said he felt rather uncomfortable with his polemic writings on Malraux's work, after having met the man. "He is more human than the heroes in his novels," he avowed.

Debray was rather bemused by the list of great men adduced by Malraux—ranging from Alexander to Napoleon. "Why doesn't he include himself?" he asked. "Maybe he is the greatest."

PARIS, *November 1, 1971*

JESSIE (Wood) called this evening to tell me her cousin said Malraux liked Debray. Nevertheless he added: "But that young man has a lot to learn."

I told Jessie: "So did Malraux when he was the same age."

VIENNA, *November 9, 1971*

THIS morning I had a long talk with Chancellor Bruno Kreisky in the famous Chancellery on the Ballhausplatz, where Dollfuss was murdered. Kreisky, a cultivated, civilized man, is the first Jew to head the government of a German-speaking state.

What happened in 1968 in Czechoslovakia "totally convinced" him that "there is only a little room for political development in the communist world" of East Europe. There was always "some chance" of more "national identification," as in Hungary and Poland. But there would never be more real freedom in those countries than in the Soviet Union.

LONDON, *November 16, 1971*

TEA with Prime Minister Heath—at 10 Downing Street.

He said that after the 1959–1961 troubles, he had shared the view of Eire's then Prime Minister, Sean Lemass, that when both Irelands and the United Kingdom were in the Common Market, a settlement between the two states (Irelands) could be worked out in a European framework. But the 1959–1961 troubles were less serious than today's.

I said I felt the traditional intimacy of relationships between Washington and London was doomed to fade, now that Britain was joining Europe, and, indeed, had already faded as a result of Nixon's abrupt announcement of his Peking trip and equally abrupt monetary moves.

Heath said: "My relations with Nixon have been and remain perfectly all right. It is not so much a question of Britain as of U.S.-world relationships. Once Nixon had announced his intention to go to Peking, many countries felt they must make their own immediate policy adjustments. People thought the U.S.A. would adjust to the new China reality but most thought the adjustment would be gradual. Nobody thought that in one jump you would go from pingpong to major league baseball."

CAIRO, *December 9, 1971*

SAW President Anwar el Sadat at noon. I drove to el Sadat's house with Mohammed Heikal. El Sadat said:

I think the United States, as a big power, should be keen for peace in the area, if there are diplomatic relations or not. We have severed our diplomatic relations with the U.S. because of its complete alignment with Israel, before the aggression in 1967 and after the aggression. But I told [Secretary of State] Rogers when he was here we are ready, if the first-phase withdrawal of Israeli troops is completed, to restore diplomatic relations and create a new atmosphere in the whole area.

I am dead sure something was cooked up between Johnson's administration and Israel, and we shall know about it in years to come. The U.S. has come to the same starting point taken by the American administration under Johnson: that Israel must impose whatever she wants. I mean using the occupation of our land, the Arab land, as an instrument for this.

But as the man to take the decision here I must say this, I am in a fix now. The U.S. gives Israel everything to put pressure on me, and to impose its conditions on me. We shall do whatever is possible to avoid this situation and to prove to the U.S. and to the whole world that we shall not accept what they want. I don't want the U.S. to be on my side. I don't ask this. I just want the U.S. to be like a big power—responsible for world peace, to be just neutral, to see the facts as they are. I would like to make your administration remember that I have lost a battle but I did not lose a war. I am quite ready for a peaceful solution, an honorable one—that will last. But not at the cost of my dignity nor at the cost of my land.

Yet, as I told you, we have played hide-and-seek for eight months. I have always felt the Americans were playing this game—until they showed quite clearly that they can't put pressure on Israel. Israel would not survive without the help of the United States.

I told the Americans that we are speaking of peace and when we speak of peace let us not speak of the strategic values of Sinai, Sinai is my land. On Israeli withdrawal, they say that a withdrawal from the Bar Lev line would cause strategic inequalities and would put Israel in a bad position. I told them when we are speaking of peace let us drop all these strategic problems. The Bar Lev line is in my land. I am dead sure something was cooked up during the Johnson administration between Israel and the U.S. Nixon, it appears, cannot get himself loose from it.

I asked if he meant something like a treaty, some kind of written alliance? He said: "Written alliance, secret agreement."

PARIS, *December 17, 1971*

I LIMPED goutily over to the Élysée—for an appointment with President Pompidou. I was sitting in the waiting room outside his office when Maurice Schumann, the Foreign Minister, came briskly out. He strode over for a warm handshake and said: "I just finished your book. An excellent book. I can hardly wait for the next volume." Pompidou looked well and energetic, although he is slowly losing the battle of the waistline.

I asked whether the agreement reached with Nixon at the Azores could provide the beginning of a new monetary balance that might endure a quarter of a century as the Bretton Woods accord had. He answered: "I hope so. Nevertheless, the accord we made was only to thaw out the situation. The French attitude has led the United States to reconsider its policy. But it wasn't my intention to [*rouler Nixon dans la farine*] take Nixon for a ride. He came with his ideas and I came with mine. But soon we found that we were really quite close together. It was a realistic talk."

PARIS, *December 23, 1971*

INTERESTING lunch with Michel Jobert, Secretary General of the Élysée and Pompidou's right-hand man. Jobert is a short, very thin man of fifty. He is intensely intelligent, sensitive, and has a good sense of humor.

Jobert says Brezhnev is a rough, strong man and you can see in his behavior to his Soviet associates and their reactions that he is rather a tsar. They are scared of him. Jobert had the good fortune of riding with Brezhnev to and from Versailles when he talked with Pompidou. He had about two and one-half hours of direct conversation with him. Brezhnev posed lots of problems of a protocol nature. He kept wanting to see "Gay Paree." Jobert said he would be glad to take him around in his own car incognito, shaking the security forces in charge; that was the only way and it violated all protocol. It never happened. Brezhnev's indiscretions were astonishing. He would point out that Russian to Pompidou and say, "His wife didn't come with him but he wears horns." He would say this in the presence of these unfortunate men who just looked downcast.

When [Valerian] Zorin, the Soviet Ambassador who recently departed, said farewell to him, Jobert remarked: "You know, Mr. Ambassador, your position in Indochina is like ours. Neither Peking nor Washington is going to listen to either of us. But unlike France, Russia is going to have to pay."

27

T HIS MORNING I TALKED FOR TWO HOURS WITH MRS. GOLDA MEIR, the seventy-five-year-old Prime Minister. She looks like a simple grandmother, dressed in white shirtwaist and skirt, amiably puffing cigarettes and wrinkling her homely features into a smile. But she is obdurate and hard as nails. She obviously isn't going to budge from her position that, if there is to be a formal peace, it must see adjustment in Israel's favor of the frontiers of Egypt, Jordan, and Syria plus permanent retention of Jerusalem with no administrative concessions to Islam except for supervision of the holy places. The failure of the UN to do anything but talk during the recent India-Pakistan war and the failure of Pakistan to get help from any of its allies merely confirmed her in her belief that Israel must rely on itself alone to survive.

Israel, she points out, has never known peace or had recognized frontiers. It can't imagine that a UN force, now perhaps including the mutually hostile but anti-Israeli Russians and Chinese, could help out. But she seems convinced—or pretends to be—that her hard line will, in the end, cause the Arabs (starting with Egypt) to yield and accept the need for reason (as she sees it).

> One basic article in Israel's policy is that the borders of the fourth of June 1967 cannot be reestablished in the peace agreement. There must be changes in the border. We want changes on all our borders, for security's sake. So our policy is, we want to negotiate peace treaties with our neighbors on secure, agreed, and recognized borders.
>
> New frontiers must have two elements: one, as a deterrent for further wars and further attacks, and, two, if they are not deterrent enough and some day some Arab leader will want to try it again, we should be able to defend our borders with as few casualties as possible. This is our policy in a nutshell. We want to be strong enough to defend ourselves and we want to negotiate. One is not dependent upon the other.

Anybody in Israel who ever had any doubts as to the value of international guarantees and to put the security of our country and our people in the hands of international guarantees, whatever that may be, I think was convinced by this tragic incident of the India–Pakistan War. To see the security council, while a war was going on, people were dying, people were being killed, and it took how much?—a week—for them to agree to a ceasefire resolution.

We have to have borders and we have to have sufficient military strength so that we can, how do you say it in the United States, do it yourself, that we can do it ourselves, as we did in 1967. If we hadn't been able to do it by ourselves, where would we have been by this time?

Israel has taken a definite position that Jerusalem will not be divided again and is a part of Israel and is the capital of Israel. On the twenty-ninth of November 1947, the UN decided partition of Palestine and the internationalization of Jerusalem. How did Jerusalem become divided? How did the Old City of Jerusalem become Jordanian? How was the Old City acquired by Abdullah? By serenading? It wasn't by force? And the entire Christian world was not disturbed when, for nineteen years, no Jew was allowed to come into the Old City; our synagogues were destroyed.

Now, people say that this is a city of three big religions. What happened between 1949 and 1967? There were not three religions, but in the Old City there were only two religions and the third one was excluded and everybody slept well.

I asked: "Could you tell me a little bit about both the advantages and the disadvantages, if there are any of either, of a woman being chief of government?"

She answered: "How do I know how a man feels to be chief of government? I have a lot of sympathy with all the men who were prime ministers of Israel. They were all my friends and I knew them very well. I don't think they adopted positions because I was a woman and they didn't give up their opinions because I was a woman. I was treated as equal with them, for good or for bad."

TEL AVIV, *January 30, 1972*

I VISITED Moshe Dayan, the Defense Minister, this afternoon in his office at the Ministry here. Another general and a civilian sat with us and took notes.

He said a great difference in weapons systems had come about. But Israel was aware that it was impossible to achieve a decisive victory over the Arabs in one or two or even three strikes because, after all, to conquer them one would have to take Cairo and Damascus. It was easy to capture these cities, but nothing would be gained if they were held. With conventional weapons, it was impossible for either Israel or the Arabs to win a definitive war because this meant conquering the other.

He made the point that Israel has the qualified personnel to man these modern U.S. weapons. "We don't want Americans here in any form— soldiers or technicians. This is basic. We have the necessarily qualified people ourselves. But the Egyptians don't."

He said that because Israel is now on the Suez Canal, it can win any battle started by Egypt because the Egyptians would have to use ground troops; they can't do it with MIGs. "And we are not faced with this problem. Our problem is only to meet them when and if they try to cross over."

Egypt and Israel were therefore planning for two different things. "We can plan our way of fighting by being there, on the canal, and not to aim at taking Cairo. They have to plan to push us back with ground forces and, if they are to dream of succeeding, an immense air force."

SHIRAZ, *February 3, 1972*

WE flew here before breakfast and visited Persepolis this morning. Persepolis is a great tableland palace of tan granite, carved out of the forbidding plateau below a low range of hills, built by Darius in memory of his grandfather, Cyrus II, who started the first Persian empire in the sixth century B.C.

The bas-reliefs show processions of imperial infantrymen with spears and swords: Medes; Persians; Susians with hooked, Semitic noses. There are horses and wheeled chariots, bullocks led by tribute bearers, Bactrian camels, Ethiopians with giraffes and ivory tusks, Scyths with pointed hats, bearded Armenians, horned rams, Phoenicians carrying jewels, Babylonians in tasseled caps, Arabs with cloths muffling their faces.

We then saw the tent city the Shah had erected to entertain visiting chiefs of state last October for the official twenty-five hundredth anniversary of Cyrus, and which will be kept as a kind of supermotel.

RAWALPINDI, PAKISTAN, *February 7, 1972*

SAW President Zulfikar Ali Bhutto at his residence, a pink-washed building in a pleasant park by the golf club. We drank tea and coffee, talked.

He kept sneering at Yahya Khan, the general he replaced as president last December. He said the 1971 war was "a result of the follies of an Ivan the Terrible, a drunken, irresponsible man; but the country shouldn't be dismembered because of him and a handful of his followers."

Incidentally, I asked Bhutto for help in getting to China, and he asked me to send him a letter "right away, before I leave town this afternoon, so I can get it off to them." He added:

China stood by us as a friend and neighbor in two wars: 1965 and 1971. We want a profound dialogue with them just as we want one with the United States. And in Peking I found encouragement on this. The Chinese understood our viewpoint and liked it.

You and China are two great powers on the same ocean, the Pacific, and you have had a long association in the past. This Nixon Peking trip is a welcome development. Nothing sensational will come of the talks but that is good. Nobody wants an earthquake. Let the stream flow gently and build relations gradually on the basis of mutual confidence. Nixon showed admirable statesmanship in moving for this meeting.

NEW DELHI, *February 11, 1972*

GOOD talk with Mrs. Gandhi, the Prime Minister. She said: "India has always been conscious of its destiny. This was true long before the recent war and our victory. There certainly was a dynamism before these events because, after all, without it, it would have been impossible to fight a war. Nevertheless it is true that the last months have given a greater sense of self-confidence to our people."

I asked if India feels obligated to demonstrate gratitude to Russia for its help in any tangible way. She replied with a smile: "Well, one of our faults is that we are unable to display gratitude in any tangible sense for anything. I think you know that. And I might add that it would be a very different kind of aid if it were based on the expectation of gratitude. Countries help one another because they need one another. Obviously countries are not disinterested when they help one another. But I don't think the record shows an inclination to display tangible gratitude here."

She continued: "I suppose your attitude toward India changed when your policy to China changed. I think the United States always has had difficulty in understanding India. Western nations have a habit of regarding the West as the world's center. But obviously we can't see always through the same eye."

DACCA, BANGLADESH, *February 14, 1972*

LONG talk with Prime Minister Sheikh Mujibur Rahman, popularly known as Sheikh Mujib. Sheikh, here, means a sign of social status, like "esquire." He is the son of a middle-class landowner. He received me in his office, an unpretentious, rambling, informal place set amid a large lawn with huge trees. There were armed guards at the gate but they seemed little-interested in protecting him from his legions of admirers. Even when we talked, a few wandered in and out, as we sat side by side on a sofa and chatted.

Nice as he is, Mujib doesn't make much impression intellectually. He seems to have very hazy ideas of what the art of government entails: administration, economics, finance, diplomacy, defense. It is odd to think of this land of some 75 million heading so uncertainly into the future.

He said no guerrilla bands (*Mukhti Bahini*) were operating "as such" any more but there were some local "hooligans" who had been armed by the Pakistanis for *dacoity* (armed violence). But, he insisted, "the entire country is under the control of my government." Throughout his conversation the "Is" rushed by like telephone poles.

I asked if Bangladesh would welcome help from America. "From the American people," he said. "I know the American people want to help, and I welcome their help. But I don't want anything from the U.S. government. You saw how Nixon supported the Pakistanis when they were murdering us, how he sent them arms instead of protests."

SAIGON, *February 18, 1972*

SAW General Creighton Abrams at U.S. headquarters. I asked if the South Vietnamese armed forces could hold together if there was a governmental change. He said: "I guess that would depend a lot on what kind of change you are talking of. The present senior leadership in the armed forces really never wants to see again the kind of period [of successive coups] they went through from 1963 to 1966. They want stability."

I then asked about drugs in our forces. He said:

> In terms of the numbers of men here who have used heroin, it's really not a great number. It used to be a kind of mod thing to try it. But now there's some resentment against it. When a fellow gets really hooked on drugs, this means someone else has got to do his work. And that fellow resents it. I can't dependably say if the drug habit is being brought here by civilians from the United States who came in the armed forces or if they acquired it here.
>
> Morale right now is in excellent shape. We still have fragging incidents, unfortunately. Also shooting incidents. And these are by no means confined to officers. But all this has declined.
>
> Racial problems of course are also a subject, like drugs, that every commander has got every day. But the situation here, at the present time, is that we're just not having any significant violence between the races. The potential is there. But race problems are like drug problems in that the men don't learn it here, they bring it with them.

SAIGON, *February 20, 1972*

LUNCHED at Ambassador Ellsworth Bunker's today, just Marina and myself. He is a charming, vigorous old man, about seventy-seven or seventy-eight. Bunker told me that in 1967 he had recommended we cut the Ho Chi Minh trail by an operation across southern Laos; but this was vetoed by the White House.

Both the Chinese and the Russians have to support Hanoi as a Communist capital; they would be reproached by others if they didn't do so. The Russians are very active in Asia. They have now increased their aid to Hanoi to the degree where it runs 40 percent over last year.

He says Hanoi is basically rather pro-Moscow, partly because of Vietnam's traditional apprehensiveness of China. The Soviets give Hanoi fine weapons: the MIG 21- and 130-millimeter guns, longer-range than anything we have here except cumbersome 175s. Russia wants to extend an arc around to the south of China. Peking wants to counter Soviet influence. The question is, can either succeed in this?

SAIGON, *February 23, 1972*

HOUR's talk with President Nguyen Van Thieu. I asked if he thought the Communists were prepared for a negotiated settlement under any conditions. He answered:

What the communists really want is to defeat Nixon. They know it will be very hard to impose their viewpoint if he is reelected. Therefore they want to smash his Vietnamization program and they must also have a victory on the battlefield first if they are to get any great concessions.

There is no doubt Moscow pushed Hanoi to try an offensive now while Nixon was in Peking. Moscow wanted to demonstrate that it is impossible to negotiate over the head of Hanoi. Moscow wanted to show Nixon the only way he could negotiate a settlement in Vietnam was with the Russians, not the Chinese.

Peking is in a difficult position. It cannot abandon North Vietnam and yet it is tied up by its own rivalry with Moscow. Nevertheless, both Washington and Peking can see that it is in the interests of the world not to have Soviet influence predominating in this region.

We must never lose sight of the Russian desire to expel the United States and to drive the Seventh Fleet from these seas. If the United States ever does leave, Russia wants to replace her. China cannot. It is not strong enough. It has no navy and its army is not powerful enough. But the Russians would like to complete a circle through here and around China that goes all the way from India to Vladivostok.

HONG KONG, *February 26, 1972*

DAVID Osborn, U.S. consul general in Hong Kong, said that if Nixon's trip only arranged a "hot line" with Peking it could be regarded as a failure. If there was an agreement on a "hot line" plus an exchange of roving ambassadors, that would be a modest success. If there was an arrangement to establish a U.S. "interests" section that would be a "fair success." If there was to be an exchange of "trade and cultural affairs" officers, that would be a "good success." If there was intention to exchange missions to formalize relations that would be a "howling success."

Basically speaking, one must look on the Peking talks from the standpoint of defusing the Taiwan question. This will be done if it contains an assurance that the United States will recognize that Taiwan is a province of China. Both Peking and Taiwan say as much.

If the people of Taiwan were offered only a choice between immediate Communist Chinese control or independence, they would prefer independence. However, if they were offered the choice between independence, or Chinese autonomy, and autonomous relationship with Mainland China, the latter would win.

TOKYO, *March 2, 1972*

THIS morning I was received by Emperor Hirohito, a rare experience, I am told. Ambassador Armin Meyer accompanied me. We drove to the modern new palace of steel and glass externally but inside traditional, with the illusion of lengthy paper walls.

Ambassador Shigenobu Shima, grand master of the ceremony, met us at the entrance. He led us upstairs, where we bowed when the door opened, then went in and shook hands with the Emperor. He sat between Takeshi Usami, grand steward of the imperial household agency, and real controller of the Emperor's contacts, movements, security, etc., and Ambassador Hideki Masaki of the Foreign Office, who is used as his English-language interpreter. Facing them sat Shima, Meyer, and myself.

Hirohito, who is seventy, looks frail, although not exceptionally old. His hair is largely black and his moustache even blacker. He is small but not vigorous-looking, speaks with a slight stutter, has a tiny tic of the head, moves his hands nervously while he talks. He speaks no English.

He wore rimless glasses of an old-fashioned sort, a black suit and shoes and, at first, seemed ill at ease. However, soon he began to talk away and several times he chuckled, or even grinned, exposing large teeth. Apparently he relishes contact with the outside world now more than he did prior to his precedent-breaking 1971 trip to Europe, the first abroad by a reigning Emperor. But, although protocol was relatively relaxed, I noticed Masaki almost fell through his chair in mortification when he started saying something, thinking the emperor had finished, and Hirohito continued to speak.

I started by asking how the Emperor envisaged the profession of emperorship in this evolving era of the Space Age. He said it had shown an ability to keep up with changes, and one of its main functions was to continue to modernize itself.

I asked if because of evolving requirements he thought it desirable to educate an Emperor differently today than when he himself was young, for example, stressing physics and other sciences.

The Emperor acknowledged this was desirable and that science was very important. But he emphasized the need for moral qualities. The most important aspect was the link between the Emperor and his people. This must be kept alive as social changes came about.

Was it true that he considered his most momentous experience the decision to bring World War II to an end? This was correct, but he added that an equally critical occasion was the February 26, 1936, incident when a military coup sought to take over the government.

Concerning World War II, he pointed out that the Cabinet had been unable to come to a unanimous decision on ending the war, and the matter had been referred to him. Therefore, he took one of his very rare initiatives and ordered an end to fighting. In 1936 it had not been known where the Prime Minister was when he had to make his decision.

I asked if any man or woman—alive or dead—had particularly influenced his own life and development. He said there were "countless" people who had influenced him, and he couldn't possibly recapitulate. But, as I wanted to know a single person, it was a historian, Genpachi Mitsukuri, who lived in the late nineteenth and early twentieth centuries (1862–1919, studied zoology in Germany, and became an authority on Occidental history on his return to Japan).

I said I had a feeling that the imperial rescript stating that sovereign power rests on the will of the people had been a most significant event. The Emperor responded that there has always been a great love of the Emperor for his people and this, in his judgment, was fundamental. Beyond that, going back to the Meiji era, there had been the "five articles" (Go-Ka-Jo Go-Seimon), which presaged the status of the Emperor reflected in the rescript.

In this connection, he again referred to Professor Mitsukuri and his importance in interpreting democracy as he had observed it from outside Japan, notably history of the West. This had contributed to the changed status of the Emperor in his rescript after the war.

Ambassador Shima smilingly suggested that perhaps the Emperor himself would like to pose some questions. He started by asking if I had any observations to make about President Nixon's journey last week to Peking. I said I thought it was a very good thing to reestablish contact with the world's largest country, and I personally felt this was long overdue. I also said that personally—I made this plain because Ambassador Meyer was sitting beside me—I hoped that one outcome of this reestablished contact would be discovery of a means for ending the Vietnam War.

The Emperor said it would be a good thing to end all wars and nobody liked the thought of hostilities in Vietnam. Did I think the Peking visit alone could achieve such a settlement in Vietnam?

I replied that it might help to create a proper atmosphere for ending the war, but I recalled that "our mutual friends," the Russians, were sending by far the greatest proportion of military equipment to North Vietnam, not the Chinese.

We bowed and shook hands and then were conducted outside by Ambassadors Shima and Masaki. Usami stayed behind. Shima told us a bit more about Mitsukuri. He was a great specialist in European history and had more or less introduced Western historical thought to Japan during the latter part of the nineteenth century.

He also explained about the 1936 incident which, like the conclusion of the war, impelled the Emperor to assume responsibility which normally is handled by the government; the Emperor, in other words, was a last resort when the normal governmental machinery broke down. In 1936, Shima noted, the Prime Minister (Keisuke Okada) was in hiding although the public thought he had been assassinated. It was, therefore, incumbent upon the Emperor to preside over the Cabinet in a meeting during the crisis.

At the end of the war, the Cabinet, which was headed by Prime Minister Kantaro Suzuki, was unwilling to assume responsibility and asked the Emperor to make the decision about stopping hostilities.

TOKYO, *March 8, 1972*

LONG talk with Prime Minister Eisako Sato in the Prime Ministerial residence, which includes his offices.

Sato is seventy-one but looks much younger. I remarked on this and he said: "I have had to give up three things, that is to say, the doctors told me to give up three things: smoking, drinking, and women. To tell you the truth, I didn't have to 'give up' women. That was already finished."

Sato said of Nixon's China trip: "It must be seen as a great and significant event in history that the chiefs of two powers who have not even yet recognized each other should have met and sat down and talked together. I think the Chinese communist regime itself will now voluntarily limit its support of the Vietnamese Communists."

HONOLULU, *March 13, 1972*

BRIEFING from Admiral John S. McCain, Jr., U.S. Commander of the Pacific and Indian Ocean areas. He said U.S. strategy here had to change as a result of the Nixon Peking trip. "Hell, I'm not even allowed to say Red China any more; just China." The United States has now worked up a new and different strategy which is under review right now. He talked of Russia's new Strategic Island Concept. The Russians now anchor ships overnight, even off Hawaii, and have started to plant anchored mooring buoys for their ships. Strategic islands can be centers on land as well as sea from which power can be projected. Russia was moving everywhere, and its naval strength and missiles steadily grew.

McCain thought chances of a Sino–Soviet war slim, but Russia would try to turn China's flank from the south as it had turned NATO's. China now had the third largest submarine fleet (forty-seven) and 4,400 aircraft, 179 divisions in its army (as of 1971). By 1976, it will have ten to twenty ICBMs.

He said: "The Soviets are rapidly forging ahead of the United States in naval and missile power and I notice this strikingly in the Indian Ocean area. We won't be saved by oceans now. They've shrunk."

UNITED NATIONS, NEW YORK, *March 23, 1972*

I HAD my first talk today with Kurt Waldheim, the former Austrian diplomat who is the new Secretary General of the UN. I asked if the expulsion of Taiwan and admission of Peking does not set a precedent against admitting both halves of partitioned states like Germany and Korea. He said no precedent had been set.

The point was only who would assume the seat of China, which everybody admitted existed. Peking was not admitted as a new member. The General Assembly simply decided that Peking was the only government of China.

WASHINGTON, *March 27, 1972*

LUNCH with Dick Helms (director of the CIA). I asked what was the real story about the arrival of the nuclear aircraft carrier *Enterprise* in the Bay of Bengal during the India-Pakistan war. Dick said the real reason was to back up Nixon's warning to the Russians not to let India go too far. Nixon had been in direct touch with Moscow two or three times warning them to cool India off and prevent an attack on Kashmir and West Pakistan. The *Enterprise* was a tangible signal to the Kremlin that he meant what he said. We know the Russians told India to cool it.

I asked why a Communist offensive had not developed against South Vietnam in February (at the time of Nixon's Peking trip). He said: "We are absolutely positive it was intended. And everything is still there, whenever they want to go. But we anticipated it and our bombing has been very intensive."

Helms is worried about Yugoslavia. We know, Dick says, that the Russians want to bring the Yugoslavs back inside their orbit. But they can't succeed by threatening or enticing Tito while he's alive. Therefore they're waiting until he goes. Meanwhile all possible pressure points have been worked up and inflamed by Moscow. They have curried the favor of all anti-Tito elements and are now biding their time.

Dick says Nixon came to the White House with the full intention of running foreign policy himself, and he picked Rogers as a trusted friend to carry out his wishes. He didn't know Kissinger at the time, but Rockefeller did; on this reputation, the President set Kissinger up as his main helper.

Nixon soon discovered he could do nothing in the foreign field without having it leak to the press. Therefore, he came increasingly to lean on the people directly around him. Nixon soon saw how intelligent and hardworking Kissinger was. Moreover, he was good at dealing with the press and keeping Nixon's name clean. Rogers remained loyal, but he showed himself to be very lazy while Kissinger worked like a Trojan. Gradually Nixon found he could do his work assisted by Kissinger, and Rogers simply faded away.

Nixon dealt directly with Kissinger on intricate problems and sent him off on surreptitious trips to Paris, then Peking. Rogers didn't even know that Kissinger was going to China until he was actually in Peking. Rogers wasn't even permitted to see Mao Tse-tung with Nixon and Kissinger.

Helms said that Kissinger is, in fact, eager to get into the Middle East situation, although he pretends not. He says: "They keep me out of this because of my religion [Jewish] but I could get the Israelis to move." Henry has become fascinated by power and will move in wherever he can. He is never satisfied until he is on top of everything.

WASHINGTON, *March 28, 1972*

I CALLED on Senator J. William Fulbright, chairman of the Senate Foreign Relations Committee. He admitted he was tired, old and defeatist. Sadly he observed: "I guess I'm coming to the end of my road." He said: "As a member of the Senate Foreign Relations Committee I object to the shift of responsibility from the secretary of state to the National Security Council [Kissinger]. This insulates the makers of our foreign policy from consultation with and information to the committee. We are excluded and we also feel strongly the secretary of state is no longer regarded as a primary policy-making instrument."

Fulbright complained that Kissinger doesn't qualify for executive privilege, which should apply only to information, not to the person. If Kissinger came before his committee he wouldn't be forced to divulge confidential exchanges. But he wouldn't come.

I asked why Fulbright didn't test this by summoning Kissinger by subpoena and then prosecuting him for contempt of Congress if he failed to show up. Fulbright kept complaining "the Constitution isn't self-executing." I remarked it was worth getting a Supreme Court opinion on this issue. It seemed to me certain that Kissinger himself would be happy to cooperate. Fulbright should subpoena; Kissinger, advised ahead, should refuse; then the matter could go to the courts. It would take years to decide, and all the individuals now involved would no longer be in authority, but the idea was worth clarifying. Fulbright said the Senate wouldn't back him up with a majority in a vote on contempt—"not even the members of my own committee."

WASHINGTON, *March 29, 1972*

THIS morning with Senator Mike Mansfield, the Montana Democrat who is Senate majority leader. He remarked that we often disagreed on things but he didn't hold it against me.

Mansfield was not at all worried about the way our foreign policy-making system was working nowadays. Credit should go to Nixon, as well as Kissinger and Rogers. He added: "We must learn a lesson from China —to be patient and not to be impetuous, shooting from the hip. You must have time to think things through."

Mansfield promised to do his best with Chou En-lai to get me a visa.

WASHINGTON, *March 31, 1972*

THIS morning I went to the Soviet Embassy for a talk with Ambassador Anatoli Dobrynin. He admitted Nixon's project of a Peking trip initially excited suspicion in Moscow; but this has vanished, and Moscow knows there has been no secret U.S.–Chinese alliance. Furthermore, Moscow knows that Russia is more important to this Administration than China. Russia and the United States remain *the* superpowers, and there is no escaping this. They can destroy each other, and no one else can destroy them.

He thought China's future would probably depend largely on generals, because this had always been the case through China's history. Military men moved to the top. But, although they liked to watch big parades and make big speeches, they usually were a moderating element.

WASHINGTON, *April 3, 1972*

THIS morning I went over to the State Department to see Secretary Bill Rogers. I then asked if we were going to deliberately try and use our power and prestige to influence the outcome of this year's Italian elections. Rogers said: "I can tell you Ambassador Martin has been given full authority to do whatever he deems necessary—and he knows what to do. We are not going to do anything open or obvious but Martin is a very wise man."

WASHINGTON, *April 3, 1972*

LUNCHED with Henry Kissinger in the White House. I asked if he could help me unofficially to approach the Chinese about a visa.

While the trays were being brought in Henry smilingly said he understood I had suggested to Fulbright he should subpoena Kissinger and force him to testify before the Senate Foreign Relations Committee. I replied this was essentially correct but I am sure Fulbright hadn't given it the proper innuendo.

From here on, the conversation assumed a more Kissinger-like form. I asked if he was optimistic about the Moscow summit starting May 22. He was. But it would be a different kind of meeting from the President's Peking visit. The China trip marked a bifurcation in the road. It was a historic event and could lead to major changes by Peking. But it left much for the future and one could not yet judge what it had accomplished. The Moscow summit seeks agreements which will be justifying in themselves. It will be a major political event but not a historic landmark. It should manage to achieve either an agreement on the SALT disarmament agreement or a breakthrough leading to agreement.

It was obvious the Middle East would have to be discussed, but he doesn't expect any kind of agreement there. Neither Moscow nor Washington is prepared to dump its clients. At this point Henry said the Israelis had shown absolutely no sense diplomatically since their 1967 victory in the Six-Day War. He recalled that while he himself is Jewish and liked to stay out of Middle East affairs for this reason, he had been in Israel in December 1967 and had suggested to the Israelis that they make a peace offering yielding at least half of the Sinai region taken from Egypt. Nothing was done. Now the situation was a stalemate.

I then asked him—as I have been asking people for weeks now—why the nuclear aircraft carrier *Enterprise* had been sent to the Bay of Bengal during the India–Pakistan war. Henry said U.S. strategy was approximately as follows: The White House had been convinced for months that war was coming because India wanted to settle the balance of power once and for all.

As we saw it, an India armed by Russia, backed in UN by a Soviet veto, and Soviet threats against countries that might intervene against India, would—if unchallenged—change Moscow's assessment of the United States and its world role. The United States had to react in a demonstrably tough way to show Moscow we weren't collapsing everywhere.

Second, Sadat in Egypt had promised a war with Israel by December 31, 1971. We felt that by a show of force in the Indian Ocean we could discourage Sadat from running wild.

Thirdly, Nixon's Chinese trip was already scheduled. While we did not think events on the subcontinent might conceivably cancel the trip if we failed to back China's friend Pakistan, we did feel that China looked upon the Indian subcontinent with a view to its own position. If the United States did not react to Russian moves, the Chinese could fear this might be a dress rehearsal for what Russia might attempt against China. Therefore we felt we had to show the Chinese that we also were tough.

What was his impression of Mao? Kissinger said the chairman was grossly overweight but had a remarkable capacity to dominate things around him. Physically he exuded willpower. De Gaulle had dominated any room in which he stood because of his sheer character. Adenauer dominated by his serenity. But Mao equally dominated by this feeling of will.

Henry found Chou En-lai enormously impressive, but Mao even more so. They talked only for a little over an hour, and Kissinger has no way of knowing if Mao has more than an hour or two of effective mental force during a day. But he did convey this impressive atmosphere of tremendous power. Henry added: "Very recently I reviewed the transcript of our conversation and I found it like the overture of a Wagnerian opera. Every single thing we discussed in the subsequent conversations with Chou En-lai was previously mentioned in that single talk with Mao."

I asked what we were going to do if the Russians try and disintegrate Yugoslavia after Tito dies, because I was sure this would happen. He answered: "I agree entirely. Certainly it is going to happen. But I can't get our bureaucracy to do anything about planning on this. All the bureaucracy does is give me a lot of triple talk." He thought one of his major functions in foreign policy-making was "to drive the bureaucracy against its inclinations." By "bureaucracy" he meant the State Department, of course.

PARIS, *April 21, 1972*

THANK God I have one good ear, but it is nearly beyond its capacity when in conversation with André Malraux. Today I was startled when toward the end of a long and agreeable conversation he suddenly said to me: "You know, the first part of your book was absolutely Shakespearian. The section about the Balkans was a *préface Shakespearienne.*" A Long Row of Candles, published in English in 1969, came out here as *Dans le Tourbillon de l'Histoire.* I told him I was astonished he had found time to read the book. He said: "But of course. We are accomplices. We are accomplices before history."

We talked about Nixon. Malraux had never known Nixon well because he had always seen him in the presence of de Gaulle, and "the General naturally dominated the scene." During his recent trip to Washington, he never heard the word Pompidou mentioned. It was as if de Gaulle still represented France.

He thinks Nixon is a strong, serious, tough man who learned a great deal from adversity after his defeat in 1960. He has a more profound sense of history than Kennedy. "Kennedy was like a young boxer," said Malraux. "He was nothing but reflexes—jabs and reactions. But Nixon thinks along deliberate patterns."

We talked at length about Vietnam. He said rather wearily: "Objectively you Americans can never lose there. Even if the Saigon army crumbles, you can fall back to a sure place and hold it. Giap knows that. He can win, but you can't lose." He added, "But the North has leadership and motivation. It's as if the North were led by de Gaulle and the South by Mitterand."

Malraux made the interesting observation that only a physically courageous man can command volunteer troops. Personal courage is by no means necessary when commanding conscripts. Then you just put your orders into the machine—colonel to major to captain to lieutenant to sergeant, etc. Malraux said that he certainly does not "like war," but "it has been around me all my life." He added that combat was less of a strain in a sense nowadays, for soldiers did not usually see the men they were killing. The era of the bayonet charge ended fifty years ago.

PARIS, *April 22, 1972*

MARINA and I lunched quietly with Prince Paul and Princess Olga of Jugoslavia at their modest house in Rue Scheffer. The only other person present was young Prince Alexander, pretender to the nonexistent Jugoslav throne.

Paul showed me a seventeenth-century folio of original letters sent by Peter the Great (Olga's ancestor) to his Minister in Paris, requesting him to state officially that the Czarevich, Alexei, had died of apoplexy before the eyes of several leading Russians. (In fact, he was beaten to death by Peter.)

ROME, *April 27, 1972*

LUNCHED with Ambassador Graham Martin. He told me his only instruction from Nixon had been to keep Italy from going Communist. He has full authority to play details his way. He claims that despite the prevalent theory that modern communications have made ambassadors unnecessary, no envoy at any time has ever had a freer hand. That is all he needs.

ROME, *April 28, 1972*

TWO hours with King Constantine. He had run into Vice-President Agnew in Persepolis last summer when the Shah invited dignitaries and royalty to attend a ceremony celebrating the twenty-five hundredth anniversary of Persia. Agnew asked the King if he could call on him. So he came to Constantine's tent next morning as arranged.

"You know, he spoke to me as if I was one of those liberal pinkos he is always talking about," Constantine said. "He had the nerve to tell me that this was the best government Greece had ever had because it kept out the communists, that in the past Greece was changing its government every year. I blew up. I said: 'Mr. Vice President, you don't know what you are talking about. From 1953 to 1963 we had only two prime ministers. We fought a bloody civil war against the communists and we had new parliamentary elections right afterward'."

Agnew seemed surprised by all this and said that after all Tom Pappas (a Greek-American) and other businessmen seemed to like the colonels. Constantine replied: "Mr. Vice President, they are businessmen and it is their business to like any government that is in power."

The King was gloomy about his prospects. He does not think the United States is the least interested in helping him. He does not foresee any chance of a personal contact with Nixon or Kissinger. They think of Greece only in terms of its strategic position in the Mediterranean. This is a terrible mistake, because it is bringing an increasing amount of anti-Americanism among disappointed Greeks and changing the basic opinion of the traditionally most pro-American country in the Mediterranean.

ROME, *April 30, 1972*

DINED last night with Luigi and Paola Barzini and Gino Tomajuoli (our old mutual friend). Very moving; not the least was the song of a nightingale cleaving the moonlit night. Their two sons, Andrea and Luigi, are far-out leftist revolutionaries in a "groupuscule" called "Potere Operaio" (Workers' Power). Young Luigi is in a Sicilian jail for distributing incendiary propaganda.

Luigi's stepson by his first marriage, Giangiacomo Feltrinelli, a brilliantly successful and enormously wealthy Milan publisher (he scooped the world on *Dr. Zhivago* and published *Il Gattapardo*), was killed this spring, apparently while preparing to blow up power pylons outside Milan. He was a leftist terrorist, and Luigi wrote a deeply emotional piece after his death, clearly thinking of young Luigi and Andrea. He wrote in part:

> He embraced his new faith [communism] with the same blind fanaticism as his previous [fascism]. He was that kind of man, who is common in Italy and who is able to go from an extremist movement to the opposite provided it be illiberal and mythological, without stopping at the stage of the ideas (perhaps boring and too serious as they don't promise any miracles but only toil) of the bourgeois revolution, of freedom laboriously conquered and defended every day, allowing the facing and gradual solution of problems, tolerating—or rather extracting and using—what is valid in dissident and heretical movements. . . . It was difficult for me, a man who believed in reasoning, to follow him, who was confident in romantic apocalypses. . . .
>
> That he would have abandoned the party as soon as he would have felt its discipline, its control, its constraints, and as soon as he would have noticed that it was not an organization of terrorists and dynamiters spreading corpses of foes in the streets at night, but a vast, cautious, and erudite movement treasuring fifty years of defeat in every country and determined to win while avoiding a catastrophic civil war (for Italy's and for its own sake) was clear to anyone who knew him. . . . It was useless to put some order into his ideas. . . .
>
> Perhaps he was like Pisacane, also a rich man, with the feudal title of duke of Santospirito. Pisacane [a hero of the early *risorgimento*] also met his death with courage and levity, under the illusion he could provoke an immediate revolution that would not be stopped.

LONDON, *May 2, 1972*

CHAT this afternoon with Sir Alec Douglas-Home, Foreign Secretary and former Prime Minister. He said:

The Russians are doing much too well. They're moving down to the Persian Gulf, pushing into Iraq and Syria and pressing on Iran. They're active in Somalia. They've established themselves well on the subcontinent through their Indian treaty. And they have a huge naval building program. Any weakening of U.S. influence in Europe now would be a very bad thing.

It would certainly pay to see a return to a reasonable U.S. policy in India. That should be very high on the list. And this will become easier as you Americans, who are very generous, display generosity toward the impoverished people of Bangladesh. The Russians have been penetrating there much too fast and the Indians are uncomfortable.

We see a poor picture everywhere. Moscow is building a submarine base in Somalia. It is really penetrating Mauritius. The picture has deteriorated in the Indian Ocean. And now, in southeast Asia, if Vietnam falls, the pressure on Thailand will be enormously stepped up. We all want to see a nonaligned bloc in southeast Asia with a Chinese guarantee of its security. But the Russians don't really want nonalignment—except as a system they can penetrate.

PARIS, *May 6, 1972*

GENERAL of the Army Pierre Elie Jacquot called me yesterday, and I invited him for lunch. He now is retired after a long and successful military career. During the war he served under Malraux in the Vosges resistance network although already a regular colonel. Subsequently, he was French Commander in Chief in Indochina—in 1955.

Jacquot said he was in correspondence with Marshal Grechko, Soviet Defense Minister and very intelligent. Once when Jacquot was discussing East and West Germany with him, Grechko said: "We have an advantage over you—we know the East Germans will be disloyal and what to do about it."

He said: Malraux would have made a great medieval mercenary or an adventurer in America's Wild West. He was a true romantic and he was dominated by an extraordinary passion for tanks.

PARIS, *May 13, 1972*

KOČA Popović, a colonel general and Tito's Chief of Staff before he became Foreign Minister of Jugoslavia—a job from which he has now retired—came for lunch.

There is a perceptible generation gap in Jugoslavia today. The youngsters are far to the left of their parents, and Ché Guevara is their great hero. Popović knew Ché and thought he was "almost crazy," though intelligent. The Bolivian episode in which he was killed was idiotic.

Popović said the Nixon trip to Jugoslavia was a great success. Nixon had made a clever and correct move in ordering the blockade of North Vietnam, but nobody believed he could achieve a real military victory.

BRUSSELS, *June 13, 1972*

SPENT an hour with Joseph Luns (NATO Secretary General). Two years ago a Czechoslovakian general defected to the West and spilled the basic Moscow war plan. This was to take the whole Atlantic coast of Europe in two weeks, spend two more weeks mopping up, and then face up to the United States. The United States couldn't atomize occupied West Europe and kill all its friends. And Russia would thereby gain an area surpassing in economic and technical output all the USSR and its satellites—plus an entry to all the world's seas. It could blackmail the United States into recognizing the legitimate preponderance of the USSR in Europe, achieving this continent's "Finlandization."

AMSTERDAM, *June 16, 1972*

LUNCHED with Ernst van der Beugel, the exceptionally intelligent Dutch foreign affairs expert. He has close connections with the United States and is an old friend of Kissinger's.

He says Adenauer had great admiration for Kissinger, who used to be sent to Bonn by Kennedy (when Henry was still with JFK) at times of strain between Washington and Bonn. One time Henry was dispatched by Kennedy, who said: "I want you to find out what's gone wrong with our German policy." "That will be easier," Henry said, "if you'll tell me one small thing: What is our German policy?"

Van der Beugel asked Kissinger a few months ago: "How's your ego?" "Not too obsessive," said Henry, "thanks to Lyndon Johnson." One of his jobs is to brief former President Johnson on foreign policy about every three months. Last time, after a lengthy session, LBJ said: "Thank you. That's very interesting, Doctor Schlesinger."

BAARN, THE NETHERLANDS, *June 16, 1972*

I HAD drinks and two hours of talk today with Queen Juliana of The Netherlands and her husband, Prince Bernhard, at Soestdijk Palace. I drove out from Amsterdam to the palace, a pleasant gray and tan building with two semicircular Palladian wings facing out across a densely green lawn.

Bernhard was standing inside, wearing well-cut tweeds, thin as a rail, smiling and healthy. He is now sixty-one but looks forty-five. He shook hands, asked what I wanted to drink and led me in, saying he wanted to chat a bit before his wife came in as he had to fly off shortly to dine in Germany with Foreign Minister [Walter] Scheel.

In a moment she arrived, dressed in a pink and blue dress with pink jade earrings, glasses, a plump, gray-haired woman, but much prettier than her photographs lead one to suspect. She is very feminine, with light blue eyes, a pink complexion, and womanly gestures. She sat down a bit uneasily and waved me to the next armchair. A servant brought her a long drink—either Campari or grenadine. Then she got up and drew back the light cloth curtains so we could look directly through the picture window at the quiet pond in the lawn, covered with lily pads.

We talked about her family, now eight grandchildren from the three girls who are married (a fourth, unwell, isn't). All the kids are boys "which is very strange in my family; I'm afraid the first girl baby is now going to be spoiled."

She said there was a visible generation gap problem in Holland, but, "after all, that's always true, isn't it? What generation has been the same as that of its parents? Come to think of it, I was horrified at the way my mother told me she had been brought up. And our generation [she is about sixty-three] thought we had new ideas and we were confident there would never be another war. We did such things as marathon dances. We couldn't imagine another disaster was coming. It was hard to believe when it happened. And it is just as hard to believe, looking back, that it did happen."

She expressed abhorrence for any form of dictatorship. I said that anyway, dictatorships rarely exceeded the political life of one tyrant. "That's much too long," she commented.

She thought it difficult to analyse how children should be brought up nowadays for the limited profession of kingship. Certainly her children had been educated differently from herself and she from her mother. But she expected the generation gap (and education gap) was not very different from those in other families.

She talked about Hirohito's visit. There had been some very ugly and hostile demonstrations. She could understand how people felt—"he was the same man who led them in the war, after all"—but it would have been more dignified for people to simply stay at home.

She then asked if I had seen the film *Tora, Tora, Tora.* I said yes. "They never got to Washington as their navy said they would," she observed with a twinkle.

She couldn't understand why but, fortunately, conquerors were almost always insane and overreached themselves and thus were destroyed. For her, the important thing was that they conquered at all—not that they didn't hold on to their gains a few generations.

PARIS, *June 20, 1972*

BILL Porter (Ambassador to the Vietnam peace talks) took me to lunch. According to Bill it was agreed during the Moscow talks that [Nikolai] Podgorny would go to Hanoi and try to work for a solution. The Russians really impressed Nixon as desiring to deescalate the war. They are fed up with Giap's strategy. Moreover, they are furious with Giap because he never told them how he planned to use Soviet-supplied weapons. This year he told Moscow: "You do your socialist duty of helping us and we will fight the war."

BELFAST, *July 4, 1972*

THIS capital of Northern Ireland is even more dreary than usual, a cold, desperately wet summer day and politics worse than ever. Drive in past new steel-bar-and-cement barricades put in by the Protestants' Ulster Defense Association (UDA) just now, in defiance of the British, to create isolated Protestant "No Go" areas. Here and there is the Ulster flag, red and white, quite properly bearing the national symbol—a red hand. Outside the hotel is a barrier where cars must stop and all visitors are searched, both person and baggage. The IRA has twice bombed it. Drove around in the rain. Signs smeared on walls: FOR GOD AND ULSTER . . . NO SURRENDER . . . IRA BASTARDS . . . UDA RULES . . . THIS IS PROTESTANT BELFAST.

Up to Stormont to see William Whitelaw, Britain's Minister of State for Northern Ireland and benevolent dictator here. He sees his job as: "Try and stop the shooting in order that a new future can be opened up under new conditions. Three years of violence have left behind all kinds of pressures and a feeling of bitterness and desire for revenge among the militants. The more the minority is pleased, the more the majority is angry. As a result, Britain is permanently caught in a cleft stick. Eighty-five percent of this population is happy to live together; fifteen percent is not. And the fifteen percent includes extremists on both sides. The situation is totally illogical."

LISBURN, *July 6, 1972*

DROVE out to this small market town to see the British Lieutenant General Sir Harry Tuzo, general officer commanding, Northern Ireland. He said:

How can you combat uncivilized methods with civilized methods? You really can't do it. While you operate that way you can hold your head high in world opinion, but if you lapse once, the world condemns you. Sometimes you must logically use harsh and sharp means to get speedy information and save lives. We might have won this campaign at the cost of considerable casualties and short-term bitterness if we had been more ruthless.

The West cannot win a campaign like this within the rules of ordinary civilized common law. No military victory is possible—wiping out the guerrillas and their weapons. All you can do is create a climate in which it is possible for the politicians to make a settlement.

ARMAGH, *July 6, 1972*

COFFEE with Cardinal Conway, Catholic primate of all Ireland (both North and South). Armagh is an ancient Irish seat where Saint Patrick preached and King Brian Boru is buried. Conway, a massive man with charming manner, lives in a cold and sparsely furnished residence behind his cathedral. He turned up the electric heater and talked easily.

Stoking his briar pipe, he sat back, puffing, and said: "Article forty-four of the constitution of the republic says the state recognizes the special position of the Catholic Church. It confers no legal privilege on the church. It is a simple statement of social fact. I would not shed a single tear if that article were repealed tomorrow. In a united Ireland, I think the constitution would have to be acceptable to all the people of the republic. There would have to be provision for divorce. Of course, this is a personal opinion. Obviously each religious community would continue to follow its own customs."

When I asked if he approved of IRA violence, he said: "Who in his senses wants to bomb a million Protestants into a united Ireland?"

DUBLIN, *July 10, 1972*

DAVY O'CONNELL, adjutant general of the IRA (provisionals), came to see me. I can't help being confused by the fact that the IRA is officially banned and membership is a criminal act; some few members are in jail, but the leaders circulate without trouble.

O'Connell is tall, thirty-four, with pale skin, dark hair, light blue eyes. O'Connell told me he did not think the problem could be settled by force. "Eventually there will have to be a negotiation" before his goal of a united Ireland is achieved.

RABAT, *July 15, 1972*

YESTERDAY afternoon I had a talk with King Hassan II, starting at the white Palais des Hôtes. Hassan was wearing a light blue *djellaba*, white pointed Moroccan slippers, a conventional red fez, dark sunglasses, and a blue-striped shirt with no necktie. He suggested I ride out with him to his summer palace at Skhirat (about eighteen miles). We strolled down to the largest Mercedes I have ever seen. Behind us, a formation of military and police cars scooted to follow. There is plenty of security now since the murderous military coup at Skhirat just a year ago (July 10, 1971), when dozens of royal guests were mowed down at Hassan's birthday reception (and ten generals were executed afterward).

We began discussing the old idea of a Mediterranean pact, for a time one of de Gaulle's favorite theories. Hassan said:

When thinking of the Mediterranean, we must acknowledge that in our time it is both too big and too little for the countries which border on it. It is too small because the smallest tempest on it involves us all, and it is too big because the political and economic distances between different Mediterranean lands are too wide. Both factors produce contradictions.

De Gaulle knew France could not play a really great power role as against the United States or the Soviet Union. But he hoped to demonstrate that France could be a great power with respect to Africa. And, of course, any eventual project that would neutralize the Mediterranean by excluding both the American and Russian fleets would leave the French navy supreme.

The concept is still alive in Algeria and above all in Tunisia and, despite de Gaulle's death, it is still kept in mind in France. Jugoslavia is especially interested, for obvious reasons, in creating a nonaligned Mediterranean. But that is very, very hard to do. Just suppose the Mediterranean nations wanted this and asked the Russians and Americans to pull out their ships. Do you imagine they would agree?

I said the generation gap was clearly a major problem here, where half the population is twenty-one or younger. He observed: "There will always be a generation gap. The young want space and the old want time."

I asked, as a closing question, who had most influenced him and whom he most admired, apart from his father. He said: "Leon Blum and Pierre Mendès-France, but above all, Blum. He was a great follower, practitioner, and teacher of the law, a fine jurist. He spoke for the public responsibility to the law and the relationship of the law to the public." It is striking to have a direct descendant of Mohammed admire two French Jews.

ALGIERS, *July 25, 1972*

AT noon I saw President (Houari) Boumedienne in his office. He said socialism had essentially been realized here now. The basis had been established. But Algeria's socialism was not dogmatic, and "we stick to the requirements imposed by reality. It is not a question of great ideologies and the ideas elaborated in other lands. This is a different kind of world today. Events are moving too fast for old-fashioned ideologies. Ideas are evolving at a dizzying pace. Communications are instantaneous and they carry ideas all over."

I asked what he thought of the Nixon visits to Peking and Moscow. He said: "Certainly the Nixon visits were a positive factor. They helped *détente* by reducing tension."

He predicted a world energy crisis in the 1980s and said the Middle East and North Africa would then become a vital key in world development. Israel had nothing even remotely comparable to offer the great powers.

LUNCH and excellent talk with Milovan Djilas. We started talking about Sadat's expulsion of the Russians from Egypt. He said: "This is very important. It was a courageous act of Sadat. It recognizes the importance of Egyptian nationalism. At last the Egyptians have understood that the Russians did not intend to help them win their war. The Russians always think in a classically imperialist way, in terms of territory, of an army, of control. They are backward and do not consider things in terms of finance, economics, technology the way the United States does."

Djilas continued that despite recent reforms and changes "the atmosphere here is bad. Nothing fundamental has changed. It is impossible to renew a Marxist–Leninist ideology here. You can't renew the party ideology. The younger generation doesn't believe in these things at all. And even the older ones are demoralized. They just want to live better; even old partisan leaders like Koča Popović. No intelligent man believes any more in the future of the Leninist or Stalinist form of party. Everyone wants freer forms. They don't want to feel confined or persecuted.

"There is no doubt that a great crisis is inevitable when Tito dies. It will not only be a crisis because of the nationalities question, but also for political reasons. Each nationalistic faction is politically splintered within itself. Even the Jugoslav idea is splintered. It may eventually be renewed, but right now it doesn't even exist. The Croats are very nationalistic-minded. They have a vigorous old tradition. And the newest Tito formula for a collective leadership with a rotating president cannot work here. That can work only in Switzerland."

He thought Nixon's trip to Peking and Moscow had been "very impressive, a historical event as important as a war. This showed that Nixon understood what communism is. President Johnson played on the conflict between the Russians and the Chinese. But Nixon saw that it would be better to have good relations with both of them—while at the same time remaining strong. He knows that you can't afford to be weak; but this has nothing to do with the Russian-Chinese question."

He said: "Ideologies are dead and religion is in a crisis. Ideology is only a pseudo-religion. It is only good for a fighting sect in time of war or revolution, not for people as a whole. And ideology must be totalitarian to carry conviction whereas religion can never be totalitarian. Ideology as such was really invented by Marx. Then his successors and others, like fascists and various kinds of socialists, evolved different ideologies. Ideology even has to pretend to describe religious events in modern terminology. Ideals, of course, continue. Mankind cannot live without ideals." He added:

> It is wrong to think communism can evolve toward democracy; it can't. It will only split up, as it is now doing. It will not transform itself into a Western form of democracy.

Jugoslavia is developing into a nonideological police regime which will *speak* only in the name of ideology. There will be some more freedom of press and thought. But remember, the only kind of unification between Europe and Russia can be economic. There are bound to be political and social differences for centuries more. Communism is dying. Old-fashioned capitalism is dying. But American society is not in a crisis. It is changing but not dying and here the New Left is wrong.

Ideology is excellent in a country—for a period, a revolutionary period or, for example, when you tried to develop ideology during the cold war. Dulles succeeded in this respect because he was narrow-minded and that is useful during a cold war period. Ideology is only vitally important in times of war or revolution.

But humanity cannot live without religion—including philosophy as a form of religion. I am not a religious man but that itself is a form of religion. I don't believe in God. But I believe in conscious human improvement. I believe we are a part of this great cosmos in which we are living.

BELGRADE, *August 5, 1972*

DINED last night at the Djilas'. Milovan said, "War today is only logically possible as a nuclear war. Conventional war is simply too expensive. Look at Vietnam. Not even the richest nation, the United States, can afford it. Imagine a conventional war between Russia and America! How expensive it would be! It would be crazy. Only a nuclear war is relatively cheap today. And yet a nuclear war means absolute and total destruction." Djilas said:

> The United States won the cold war because of the internal disintegration of communism; because you remained strong you were able to accelerate this inevitable process. Nixon's Peking and Moscow trips were a result of this cold war victory. But the United States should neither overestimate nor underestimate that victory. You won because you are nonideological and thus were able to avoid a stalemate like that which prevailed between Christianity and Islam after their wars, a victory for neither side.
>
> The so-called crisis in American society is largely imaginary. Of course racist and class and generation gaps exist. But there is no fundamental crisis. The crises you do have are an aspect of the difficulty of adjusting to the electronic and technological revolutions of our time.

I asked how, despite all this, the United States had gained a cold war "victory" vis-à-vis Russia. He said: "Simply because the communist world divided into fractions. At the same time the United States succeeded in enlarging some of the basic democratic ideas—like individual human rights—thus helping to erode the communist system. And economically you succeeded in pressing the communist world into collaboration with you. You proved the truth of your theory that no economic system can develop isolated from others. You showed how crazy Stalin's belief was that there were two world markets, capitalist and socialist. In fact there was always only one market and another, Stalin's, artificially conceived. That is now ending."

I then asked him what prison does to a man. He said:

> Prison is good, but not for a long time. It is good if one is both a fighter and a thinking man. Isolation helps a man to analyze and correct his opinions. You have a chance to truly see what you are in the world and in society. Prison is a unique place in which a man can discover his own capabilities. Of course I speak of a strong, healthy man able to resist.
>
> On the whole, prison made me more courageous; I don't know why. I feel that now that my existence in the world is completely mine, more than when I was a committed communist. As a communist I was a good fighter but I felt that I was not completely exercising my own personality. Now I am a more integral man. Now I live in my own world and I am happier than I ever was before, even when I was in power.
>
> Prison purified me. I am now a more sincere and open man. I may sin occasionally now but if I do I recognize and acknowledge that fact, the fact that I am sinful and not perfect. But twenty years ago I would have sinned and not admitted it even to myself.

ISTANBUL, *August 13, 1972*

LUNCHED with Foreign Minister Haluk Bayülken. He thought a basic change was occurring in Russia's political, economic, and social outlook. They wanted to keep Europe quiet and face toward China. But at home, ethnic groups were pressing the regime for more freedom. And it is impossible to keep the Russian "box" sealed; Western ideas infiltrate.

NICOSIA, *August 17, 1972*

PLEASANT talk with the president, Archbishop Makarios. I knew he liked King Constantine and wondered if, since his title was king of the Hellenes, he regarded him as king of the Cypriot Greeks who were, after all, Hellenes. He said: "I consider him king of the Hellenes all over the world and that includes the more than 500,000 here. But it is not in any political sense, only symbolic. Yet it is symbolically somewhat more than, for example, the queen of England's relationship to Canadians. We feel that Constantine is closer to our Greeks than the queen is to members of her commonwealth."

I said Cyprus was one of the rare states with no national feeling, only Greek or Turkish. He replied: "Cyprus is a new state but not a new nation. All Cypriots will always feel Greek or Turkish. But this shouldn't prevent them from living together as both are geographically Cypriot. But I don't think they can become politically Cypriot the way Swiss French or Germans are Swiss."

28

PARIS, *October 13, 1972*

Lunched today with Jean Sainteny, French delegate general to North Vietnam from 1954 to 1958. Henry Kissinger is his personal friend. After Nixon became President, Washington became disturbed to find that official negotiations taking place in Paris were getting nowhere. Kissinger wondered if Sainteny would act as a kind of broker to Hanoi. This was in early 1969. Sainteny made a discreet inquiry to Xuan Thuy, head of the North Vietnamese delegation to the peace negotiations. Finally, on August 4, 1969, he was able to arrange a secret meeting at his own house between Kissinger and Thuy. The only people present were Kissinger and General Vernon Walters (at that time American military attaché in Paris and a remarkably expert interpreter in French) and Xuan Thuy.

The meeting was not attended by Sainteny. He merely stayed home to introduce the two parties when they arrived, to show them where the whisky was and then to say goodbye and leave them alone.

This first meeting—the only one held in Sainteny's house—resulted from Kissinger's request for a contact in Hanoi. Earlier that year Sainteny had served as "postman" to get a letter from Nixon to Ho Chi Minh via Xuan Thuy in Paris. Sainteny did not go to Hanoi himself to deliver it.

He had told Nixon and Kissinger the big mistake of United States strategy was to imagine it was possible to win a war by smashing the North Vietnamese army. The war was absolutely and undoubtedly against the entire 18 million people of North Vietnam, and they were totally united in this endeavor. Furthermore, they were just tougher than the South Vietnamese.

He said that Ho Chi Minh was in no sense a remarkable personality in terms of intellectuality or dynamism. He was simply an extraordinarily hard worker devoted to one cause—his country. Sainteny knew Ho and

587

liked him. He said that the last request he ever had had from Ho Chi Minh was for a set of phonograph records of the songs of Maurice Chevalier.

PARIS, *October 18, 1972*

LUNCHED with Michel Jobert, the hard-working, quiet and charming Secretary General of the Élysée and Pompidou's "Kissinger." He told me he handled all logistics for the secret Kissinger meetings going on for the last three years in Paris. Kissinger stays at the home of one of the American diplomats stationed here. Everything was kept secret until Henry made the mistake last year of appearing on television. Within no time the cook at the American family let it be known that the "colonel" who had often been a guest was the man whose face she had seen on the TV screen. Likewise, Jobert had been handling Kissinger's most secret travel by direct conversation between himself and the pilot of Henry's plane. The pilot, a Frenchman, was astonished to find out from TV who he had been conveying around.

PARIS, *October 20, 1972*

LONG talk with Piotr Abrassimov, the Soviet Ambassador. He asked me if I ever went to East Germany (where Abrassimov was stationed in the past). I said yes. He asked me whom I had seen. I told him I had talked at length with Ulbricht, who was a terrible bore. Abrassimov grinned and agreed. He said I should go and see Honecker, the present boss, and offered to arrange an appointment.

BONN, *November 15, 1972*

COFFEE and a long talk with Franz-Josef Strauss, burly head of the Christian Socialist Party (the Bavarian faction of the Catholic-Conservative Christian Democrats) and king-maker of the right. He assured me that Chinese diplomats were telling everyone within range that Peking wished to cooperate with a unified West Europe and hoped it could shape up as soon as possible. Moscow, he added, says a unified West Europe means more cold war and Chinese influence here.

ABOARD BRANDT'S CAMPAIGN TRAIN, *November 16, 1972*

EARLY this morning I joined Willy Brandt's campaign train. At Frankenthal, on a grim, sleety evening, he received me in the little dining room of his personal car. We sat drinking red wine while he puffed a cigarillo, a bit hoarse and obviously tired.

I inquired whether the ultimate goal of his *Ostpolitik* was the reunification of Germany. He replied: "Yes, but not as an isolated thing or in the traditional sense of going back to the kind of state that existed before Hitler. I envisage a new kind of relationship between Eastern and Western Europe which would produce closer relations of the two Germanies inside it. And we must leave such a broad development to historical processes. There is no possible isolated solution of the German problem."

WEST BERLIN, *November 21, 1972*

INTERESTING day in East Germany, visiting the famous Dresden art gallery. Rolf Muth, press officer of the East German Foreign Ministry, called for me in West Berlin. A chauffeured car drove us through Checkpoint Charlie, on Friedrichstrasse, to the travel bureau in East Berlin, where another car with driver picked us up.

We whizzed along the autobahn through fir and birch forests on the flat Brandenburg plain. Just outside Dresden I noticed two separate walled-in camps which must have been prisons; both were surrounded by wire-topped walls and had guard towers at the corners. A helicopter flew over one of them.

The gallery is superb, one of the finest in the world, richly endowed. You name it; they've got it. The Saxon electors (later kings) apparently put their faith in their advisers and bought well. And thanks to the Meissen pottery, silver and copper mines, they had lots to spend.

I noticed in the catalogue a statement by the director general: "More than 35,000 people suffered a futile death in the blizzard of bombs of the barbaric Anglo-American air raid of Feb. 13, 1945, meaningless to the assailants." The raid was aimed at busting up Hitler's defenses—to help the Soviet advance.

EAST BERLIN, *November 22, 1972*

LONG conversation with Erich Honecker, First Secretary of the Central Committee of the Socialist Unity Party of Germany, in other words, the Big Boss of East Germany, who has taken over from Walter Ulbricht. Ulbricht has the purely honorary job of chief of state.

Honecker is youthful-looking for sixty, with strong hands; a white, clear skin; graying hair, rather shortly cut; gray eyes, and glasses. He seems strong and vigorous, despite the years he suffered in a Hitler concentration camp (he was a Saarland Communist). He said with a smile: "In German we have a saying: prison is good for your health—if it doesn't kill you."

I asked if he saw any possibility of ideological convergence between West German social democracy and East German socialism (which is what we call communism). He replied categorically:

I can see no such possibility because, ideologically speaking, we base our systems on totally different fundamental principles. I see great possibilities of cooperating and working together at both governmental and party levels in order to build peace both in Germany and in Europe. Cooperation on the issues that exist will be useful not only to us Germans but to *détente* in all the world. After all, two world wars were launched in the past from German soil.

We strive for the power of the workers and peasants and the development of a truly socialist society. On this issue the West took a totally opposite view—and this will continue. To be candid, these two ideologies mutually exclude each other. There never can be convergence ideologically. The difference must continue as it did for so long in history between Islam and Christianity.

I asked what preconditions were necessary for pulling down the Berlin Wall. He said: "The Wall—and the frontier—is an existing reality. Maybe just how high or how low the Wall is might be said to depend on our relations with the Federal Republic. [Here he was obviously talking in a figurative sense.] But it is hard to speak about this. We are just at the beginning of our peaceful neighborliness with the West. I assume that more and more people will use the border crossing points. But the frontier and the Wall remain. It is a fact that stabilized borders constitute an aid to peace."

I asked if he thought that ultimately, some day, all Germany could be unified again. He answered negatively:

The GDR will continue to develop on a socialist [Communist] basis as an inseparable part of the socialist community. On the other hand, not only the present government but the opposition in the Federal Republic [Bonn] stress the need for basing their relations on the Western alliance. On this issue history has already made the decision. And we think this is an advantage to the world—to see two independent sovereign states in German soil.

The German Democratic Republic has been existing as an independent and sovereign state for twenty-three years. And it is a good thing for the world that the German Democratic Republic exists.

PARIS, *December 6, 1972*

ANDRÉ Malraux invited me for lunch today. He was charming, infinitely courteous, friendly. He told me he would give me a personal letter to Chou En-lai urging him to see me and also urging him to recommend that I be received by Mao Tse-tung. He said he would send this to me within a week.

Malraux offered to drive me back to my office. On the way he asked me about Djilas, and I told him not only that I had seen Djilas at length in August but that we were very close friends. Nevertheless, when Djilas was Number Two to Tito in 1946, he had announced on the Jugoslav national radio that he would have me hanged if I dared come to the country. "You know," said Malraux, "we ought to compile a list of all our friends who once wanted to hang us."

He said communism was doomed by the political thought of Marx plus the technique of Lenin. But communism in France was a different thing, and here the people who voted Communist were in reality only expressing an opposition vote.

Democracy again was different. Democracy was most effectively expressed in the United States. It is based on the old conceptions of human rights and is not a method of government. It is difficult to describe an ideology for democracy. Of course during the period leading up to World War II democracy could oppose fascism, but democracy does not have an avowed form of government itself.

What is particularly important to it—and especially in the United States —is its sense of civism (the virtues and sentiments of a good citizen). This led to the fact that the private sector was much more important in its positive contributions than was true in other countries. For example, in France, if the state didn't intervene, very little happened. One could cite the status of universities as an example.

I asked if Malraux thought there was any possibility of a convergence in ideology between the loose capitalistic bloc and the differing Communist countries. He said that depends on how much time you allow for the process. There was no question of this over a fifteen-year period. But he thought it would come about in fifty years.

The proportionate position of the proletariat was shrinking everywhere. In the Western world there had already been an enormous change, and the combined roster of peasants and workers was no longer a majority of the population. The proletariat was continuing to diminish in the West, and the same would eventually happen in Russia and China. At that time, when this occurred, convergence or symbiosis would become probable.

Certainly the Russians would have to change their agricultural system. It was a complete failure, and the methods employed were absurd. Kosygin knows this. Stalin destroyed the peasant economic system, and the Russians don't want to return to that method; but Malraux was certain they would not continue to keep the system they were using, and they say so themselves.

Malraux thought it would be at least a year before there were diplomatic relations between the United States and China. He also added a curious comment on Chou. He said: "Chou En-lai lies all the time—but he lies well. You can be sure that when you talk to him he will tell you what he thinks will be helpful for China but only that. There will be no hostility but he will lie to suit his own conception of his own purposes."

PARIS, *December 14, 1972*

AN hour and a quarter at the Elysée Palace. Pompidou has grown enormously fat; he must have gained at least thirty pounds during the past year.

He claimed he looked better than he felt, and his mind really wasn't working very well.

He said: "The future of southeast Asia will depend on the solution of the Vietnam talks. Certainly there will be a kind of neutralization of the area which will avoid its falling under the sway of any great power. And the great powers themselves want to keep each other from obtaining a dominant influence. Therefore the consensus is to let the region become neutralized; and you know it is most interesting to think that in various ways the United States, Soviet Russia, China, and even France and Britain have given aid in that area. But to whom do you think the most important role will eventually fall?"

"To Japan," I said. "Precisely," he agreed. "Japanese commerce will move in."

He then speculated: "There is always the possibility of a U.S.–Soviet accord to neutralize Europe. We cannot, of course, accept this. The United States and Russia both deny that this is their intention. I am not skeptical of their intentions. But the road to developing such a neutrality seems to be opening up *de facto*. That would be a very dangerous development and a major error by the United States because it would represent a huge gain for the Soviet Union."

PARIS, *January 9, 1973*

YESTERDAY afternoon the telephone rang, and when I picked it up I heard a deep and gloomy voice say, "This is Henry Kissinger." Poor Henry has been spending a lot of time in Paris this autumn and winter trying unsuccessfully to negotiate a settlement of the Indochinese war, but to date he has had very poor luck. He sounded abysmal and said "it is hard to talk about this thing without feeling racist." I said I was glad to hear his voice and would be glad to see him.

"That is what I am calling about," he said. "When can you do it?" He suggested I come around at 8:30 that evening for a drink.

Henry was obviously in no euphoric mood. What he had to say was just as gloomy as the sound of his voice. I asked him what on earth he meant by "racism" in our telephone chat. He said he had become so frustrated in his dealings with Hanoi's representatives that—and this was said with bitter humor—he really felt he was becoming almost racist on the subject of the Vietnamese—"all of them."

I asked him how he had ever been such an idiot as to give that strange interview to Oriana Fallaci of the Italian magazine *L'Europeo* on November 4, 1972. He said: "That was the dumbest thing I have ever done in my life. I still don't know why I did it. What happened was that Egidio Ortona, the Italian Ambassador in Washington, called me up and told me, 'I have this very important journalist on my hands and she wants to interview you. Can you help?' I agreed to see her and it really was a stupid thing to do."

He said she had taken it down on a recorder but he was convinced she had changed his wording. Henry insisted: "She had me saying things I know I could not have said. For example, she had me comparing myself to a lone cowboy on the American plains. How on earth could I have said that? I have never even been on a horse in my whole life."

I asked Henry if the interview had harmed him. He said sadly: "Well, the president didn't like it much." He also conceded that it hadn't helped him with his enemies in Washington or in Saigon. But he added that he retained the full confidence of Nixon: "I simply wouldn't stay in this job if I felt I was losing his confidence. To work as I do with the president I need one hundred percent of his confidence. A secretary of state can function with only eighty percent confidence—but not a man in my special position."

Henry insisted that despite widespread international criticism of the United States touched off by the Hanoi–Haiphong bombings, Moscow and Peking had been surprisingly soft in their reaction. They were "even softer" in their private reactions to Washington than in their public statements.

Henry said: "The North has lost the war. But this hasn't helped us. The trouble is that if we could continue to hit them for two months more as we hit them in December, we could end the whole thing. But as things are—in the condition they are in today, even if they have been badly hit—they can endure. If it were not for our prisoners of war in the North we could get out. We could withdraw. But the paradoxical thing is that Hanoi wants *us* in the show in order to help them force a political settlement on Saigon."

He talked at great length about the hostility of the press—above all the American press—to anything Nixon sought to do. He said: "The American press is wholly anti-Nixon now. It is convinced the American government is lying on everything." Poor Kissinger continued:

And there is a terrible worrisome phenomenon at home. People ask why did Nixon do this bombing before the inauguration. Can you tell me why it is that so many people easily accept him as a kind of murdering maniac? Why can't people believe the truth—which is that Hanoi has goaded us beyond endurance.

Nixon has shown himself a strong leader. I had no predisposition in his favor. I opposed him in three elections. I worked for Kennedy and then I worked for Rockefeller—who was against him. There is no doubt at all that it was difficult for him to ask me to take the job I hold. But I respect him as a man of courage. He has been standing alone against the entire U.S. Establishment, the intellectuals, and the press. He could sell out seventeen million Vietnamese tomorrow and be considered a national hero. But he is not going to do this.

We know for a fact—and the record will prove it—that the North Vietnamese were not serious with us in the negotiations in October or those resumed in November. They were playing with us. It is now too early—on the basis of our first session today of this January series of talks—to tell if they are going to be serious now or not. All the previous negotiations have begun in precisely the same way as those today. We cannot draw any deductions.

LONDON, *January 10, 1973*

DRINKS with Prime Minister Ted Heath. He said:

Obviously the war in Vietnam has not worked out the way Henry Kissinger was hoping it would. I know that Nixon is genuinely concerned about establishing a good working relationship between the United States and the European Community. Nevertheless, it is obvious he will be preoccupied with Vietnam as long as the war goes on.

From the European Community's side it is not impossible to work on a new relationship even if the war hasn't ended. But there are difficulties posed. There is the problem with public opinion over the bombing. Naturally if this brings a success at the negotiating table that will certainly diminish the impact. After all, I can't forget that people were saying the bombing of Hanoi and Haiphong would start World War III—and it didn't.

So this phase of the war is not a major impediment for the working out of trade balances and a monetary policy. But I can see how the United States might resent recent criticisms among members of the European Community and take the line "Why should we help out Europe if they hit us so hard on Asia?"

I remarked that obviously China endorsed the community as a way of pressing Russia from the West. Heath grinned. He said: "The Chinese have even invoked divine aid for the community. They regard it as a major bulwark for Chinese freedom. Chou En-lai reads all my speeches. I find that very flattering."

NEW YORK, *January 23, 1973*

THIS morning I went to see Chou-nan, First Secretary to the permanent mission of the People's Republic of China (to the UN). His Ambassador, Huang Hua, is back in Peking.

I went for the purpose of leaving a letter sent to me by French Ambassador to China Etienne Manac'h. Manac'h had written the letter specifically with the idea that I would leave it with Huang Hua in order to facilitate getting visas for Marina and myself to visit China during our forthcoming Pacific trip. Whether or not it will work is another question.

WASHINGTON, *February 9, 1973*

HAD tea this afternoon in his home at Fort Myer with Dick (Lieutenant General Vernon G.) Walters, deputy director of the CIA. His last post was as military attaché in Paris. Before he left Paris he dined with the Chinese Ambassador, a general and a member of the Communist Central Committee, who wished him good luck on his new job. "You know what it is?" Dick asked (meaning the CIA position). "Of course," said the Chinese. "And I hope you keep a close eye on those awful Russians."

WASHINGTON, *February 13, 1973*

THIS afternoon I spent an hour with Elliot Richardson, the new Secretary of Defense, at the Pentagon. He is a handsome, well set up, youthful-looking man with brown hair, glasses, firm jaw, intelligent, well dressed.

He thought it obvious that Nixon, Chou En-lai and Brezhnev had a common approach to their respective national needs and how to adjust them in negotiations. They all wanted to be better off in certain respects after a deal therefore acknowledging each had to yield in some respects. And they each were happy that "realistic people" were at the helm in the other's country. (For my part I think the last observation is excessive; Brezhnev and Chou, for example, would like nothing better than to see each other or each other's country torn apart.)

MEXICO CITY, *February 22, 1973*

THIS afternoon I was received by President Luis Echeverria. He is a compulsive talker. He said Mexico's great problem was population growth. This required expanded agriculture, industry, education and a family planning program. Oddly enough, demographers have discovered poor countries with the least proteins in their diet grow fastest.

The president thought that now that America and Russia no longer dominated a bipolar world, the Third World could look after itself better. Even the superpowers were having their problems finding food and energy. He wants Third Country development and higher prices for raw materials, less for industrial imports.

YANUCA ISLAND, FIJI, *March 1, 1973*

THE Fijians are tall, well-built, very black Melanesians. Until the late nineteenth century they had regular wars with the Tongans (a few hundred miles away), fighting with spears and large warclubs and the victors eating the losers. They have a fine sense of music, dance and sing well.

When the Indians came the British imported mynah birds to pick the lice off the Indian zebu cattle and mongooses to kill the snakes. Now there are no landsnakes left. Flocks of merry, hopping mynah birds gurgle to each other among the coconut palms.

SYDNEY, *March 5, 1973*

THIS morning I had a talk with Gough Whitlam, who became Prime Minister last December, heading the first Labor government since 1949. A huge, handsome man with a mop of shaggy gray hair.

I inquired what difference there was between his government's foreign and defense policies and those of his predecessors. He said:

> We are more overtly nationalistic. In the past we persevered too long in historically understandable traditions, always waiting for first the British, and then during the last twenty years, the Americans, to pursue their own interests. We would follow along. But we now think we should make our own assessments in terms of our own interests and express our own policies on such a basis.
>
> Australia obviously has a greater interest in Indonesia than in Malaysia and Singapore. There isn't any point continuing to give precedence to historical policies derived from British interests in Malaysia. Likewise we have been caught up in the U.S. obsession on Vietnam. Your country might have gone less astray on this issue if Australia had expressed its own opinion based on its own assessment instead of echoing that of the United States.

DENPASAR, BALI, INDONESIA, *March 10, 1973*

IT is hard to think that these gentle, courteous people, survivors of Hindu kingdoms who fled here from the Moslem invaders of Java, were murdering Communists and Chinese with knives seven years ago, giving parties before dragging out their victims, playing football with their decapitated heads.

DJAKARTA, *March 13, 1973*

TALK with President Soeharto of Indonesia. I asked what he thought could now be judged as the results of the Vietnam War. He replied: "If we go back to the definition of war—as Clausewitz defined it, the continuation of policy by other means—it was a complete failure. No belligerent achieved anything."

DJAKARTA, *March 14, 1973*

LAST night Ambassador Frank Galbraith and his bright wife, Martha, gave a dinner for us. Among those present were Ambassador and Mrs. Nugroho, former Indonesian envoy to Hanoi.

Mrs. Nugroho told me that in West Irian the Stone Age tribes use a certain bark of a tree as a birth control "pill," and it keeps the rate way down. I said this was a more valuable national asset than oil and might solve the Vatican's birth control problem, since it is a natural product.

Today Jack Bresnan, Ford Foundation expert on Indonesia, said they are carefully studying this method of birth control. They haven't yet identified the bark or how it is treated by tribal sorcerers, but there seems no doubt that it does work.

TOKYO, *March 21, 1973*

TODAY, the first day of spring, is a national holiday in Japan. I went out to the private residence of Prime Minister Kakuei Tanaka and talked with him for an hour and a half.

I asked if Japan still based its defense on the U.S. nuclear deterrent plus the U.S. Seventh Fleet. He said that was correct. I continued: "Such being the case," I persisted, "shouldn't Japan which is now so prosperous pay a visible share of the cost of this protection?" Tanaka said that if Japan tried to pay a fee to help finance American military protection in the Pacific, that would merely strengthen the argument of those who wished to abrogate the Security Treaty. He added: "We are not Germany. We have no Berlin Wall staring us in the face. Japan is not going to become a big military power like the United States nor does it have any intention of doing so. We were the first nation to suffer from a nuclear holocaust. And don't forget that 1945 was our first defeat in a foreign war. Unlike the nations of Europe we are not used to the game of sometimes winning and sometimes losing wars. This was a tremendous and significant experience and there is great resentment among the Japanese people at the very idea of becoming a military power."

I said the Chinese had told Nixon when he visited Peking that they had no intention of becoming a superpower. Did he believe that? He replied:

> I certainly believe it. They told me that also when I was in Peking. And remember that in their five-thousand-year history the Chinese have never been so greatly esteemed as they are today. But they have a long frontier with Russia and India and one-third of that frontier is restless and uneasy. It has not yet been precisely defined by international agreement.
>
> Also China must raise its gross national product. They say their population is increasing 1.5 percent each year but I suggest it is closer to 2 percent. Yet their gnp is only one-half of Japan's. It will take them twenty to thirty years to reach our present gnp. And unless their gnp grows they will have increasing problems and difficulty. Therefore China must concentrate on its internal development.

HONG KONG, *March 24, 1973*

DINED with David Osborn, U.S. consul general, and his wife. I asked if he thought the function of the U.S. consulate general as a China-watching establishment was doomed because of the liaison mission headed by Ambassador David Bruce which will be going to Peking. Osborn said the China-watching role here was unlikely to lose importance rapidly. The United States depends heavily on its extensive China files here and the much broader pool of experts, both American and foreign, who were available to exchange impressions in Hong Kong. Also there is a considerable passage of visitors to China in and out of Hong Kong. The new U.S. mission to Peking is at present limited in size to thirty members. The consulate general in Hong Kong is more than ten times larger.

Chou En-lai told a group of American teachers last autumn that Hong Kong had the best intelligence on China, with Tokyo second and Moscow by far the worst.

MANILA, *March 27, 1973*

ARRIVED early this evening from Hong Kong and were met by young Imelda Marcos, seventeen-year-old daughter of the president, and various functionaries who drove us off in a huge black air-conditioned Mercedes. We are staying as guests at Malacañan Palace, the presidential residence, where we have an immense suite (bedroom with a bed which is at least twice the width of the largest double bed I've ever seen), a private dining room, sitting room, enormous bath, and a study for me fitted with a stuffed tiger lurking at my elbow. We have a staff of private servants and liaison officers.

Mrs. Imelda Marcos, the lovely-looking wife of our host, received us in the hall. She led us in to the president, who was sitting at his desk. He is a short, slender, smiling, soft-spoken man who certainly doesn't look old enough to have been a guerrilla hero in World War II, which he was.

Marcos said his own guerrillas fought beside the Communists in World War II, but he was amazed when the Communists turned against their allies and sought to seize power. The Americans had no formal liaison officers with his outfit. He and his men had helped some Americans to escape from the Bataan death march to the mountains. The U.S. Navy sent arms in by submarine. John McCain, later admiral and CINCPAC, a tough little bantam cock, brought in the first arms by submarine. He asked what Marcos needed most. "Ice cream," said Marcos, to McCain's astonishment.

MANILA, *March 28, 1973*

I HAD the unusual experience of being invited by President Marcos to join him in a full Cabinet meeting where he, his ministers, and his generals gave me a long briefing on the situation.

There is a serious Moslem insurrection in the South, and Maoists support it. There are 16,900 rebels led by Nur Misuari, a thirty-year-old

Maoist professor. He is chairman of MNLF (Moslem National Liberation Front), which with MIM (Moslem Independence Movement) are the main branches under a Supreme Revolutionary Council. MIM is secessionist; MNLF is Maoist. The MRG (Moslem Revolutionary Forces) link them. The government troops had bad reverses and losses in Mindanao. But the rebels suffered large casualties, and hundreds applied for amnesty. Marcos claims Christians and Moslems fight side by side in both government and rebel forces. Nevertheless, he says Libya is sending financial aid to the rebels.

MANILA, *March 29, 1973*

LAST night the Marcoses gave an enormous state dinner for us (about five hundred people) and U.S. Ambassador Hank Byroade. Marina sat on the president's right, and I was next to Mrs. Marcos. The food and drink were excellent, and afterward there was a splendid entertainment, culminating in Filipino dances by a troupe selected from Igarotes from the north of Luzon and Moros (Moslems) from the south.

The president is clearly a remarkable man. (He told me his golf handicap is 4, which is exceptional for a fifty-six-year-old of small, frail stature.) He won more decorations in World War II than any other Filipino and was put up by MacArthur for the Congressional Medal of Honor. He was an expert shot as a youngster, and because he once said "I'll kill that man" about a family adversary, was arrested when the man was later found drilled through the heart. Marcos was only sixteen. After a year in prison and a long trial he was sentenced to the electric chair on the same day he was admitted to the bar, having finished his law studies in prison. His family had gone broke defending his case, so he acted as his own lawyer and won acquittal at the court of appeals.

❧

THIS morning, I went over to the embassy to see Byroade. He said democracy is not dead here, despite martial law. There is lively participation at the local level all over the country. But Filipino society was sick. The president's reputation has fallen way down, and this led to speculation whether he could accomplish the job he's set himself. His program is good, but it probably seeks more than the national administrative talents available can manage.

The situation in the rebellious South is bad. Arms and money are going to the insurgents from abroad. Rebels go to Sabah (in Malaysian Borneo), where they are trained and sent back. There is enough material on hand to keep the insurrection going a long time. The guerrillas have the initiative.

This problem goes back four hundred years. The Moslems don't "want" Christians in and resent their legal takeover of land titles. The area is probably rich in oil to boot.

MANILA, *March 30, 1973*

WE arose at five, leaving the palace just before six, and to our astonishment the president and Mrs. Marcos were up to say farewell. She rode to the airport with us. A whole group of generals and palace functionaries handled our passports and baggage and induced Pan American (without our knowledge) to give us first-class seats on our economy tickets. We climbed aboard; but one engine went dead. A general came in and said Mrs. Marcos was still there and wished to invite us for breakfast. The plane would be held until our return.

She told us about the attempt on her life last December, when a madman rushed at her with a bolo knife and almost sliced her hand off before he was shot dead. He turned out to be a psychotic who had been engaged twice and each time the girl turned him down in the end for fear he was crazy. The second girl came from Leyte, Mrs. M.'s district, and bore an astonishing physical resemblance to the First Lady.

She said her husband had escaped from the Bataan death march during the war and joined the guerrillas. He was recaptured by the Japanese, who tortured him. But he escaped again, killing his guards. His father was bayonetted and hanged in an effort to make Marcos give up; he didn't.

SAIGON, *March 30, 1973*

WHEN we finally got to Saigon, an embassy man met us and told us Ambassador Bunker (who is putting us up) was already in his plane ready to take off to Washington as President Thieu leaves for there on an official visit. But when we got to Bunker's house a message came that he had delayed his departure. A moment later he turned up—elegant, courteous as ever. He is almost seventy-nine and has been here six years.

This is a stalemate. He said Saigon lost more troops last year than at any other time. And Hanoi even more. Now there is neither war nor peace; but that's better than war. The big lesson of Vietnam was that if the United States goes to war it must be ready to win quickly. We got sucked in more and more, and the enemy could always retreat to sanctuaries when he was weakened.

SAIGON, *April 1, 1973*

WENT over to see Ambassador Michel Gauvin, head of the Canadian delegation to the four-power ICCS (International Commission of Control and Supervision) for the cease-fire. Normally he is Canada's Ambassador to Athens. He was wearing khaki trousers and bush jacket with no insignia.

He said Canada had come here on the assumption of good faith. Usually a war ends with one side exhausted and ready to make concessions. Here the situation was unusual. The powerful United States quit. It found its tremendous effort had grown beyond the conflict's worth. It went too far and not far enough.

Its intentions were good—to prevent a country from succumbing to aggression—but the United States appears to be the loser. It wouldn't lose if South Vietnam's freedom could be assured. But it's difficult. Hanoi underestimated Nixon in October when it wanted him to leave and also lose face: a peace without honor. It linked the release of U.S. prisoners to Saigon's release of political prisoners. But Nixon decided to bomb again. This brought Hanoi to the real negotiating table.

Nixon got his peace with honor. So he won't come back into this mess. But does Hanoi believe the United States won't use its air force on Hanoi and Haiphong? Hanoi figures the chances of the PRG (Vietcong) are small. It is not very popular in the south. And the Third Force isn't well organized. It is anti-Thieu but prefers him to Hanoi. There are two ways for the north to take over: a campaign of sabotage and assassination and destruction of the economy; or another offensive. The Communists are preparing for both.

Hanoi's position today is that of a victor in a long and costly war. It is convinced of its righteous cause. The sole powers capable of restraining it are Russia and China. But neither is prepared to risk losing influence in North Vietnam. It is more likely both will continue to compete for Hanoi's favor.

As a result the behavior of Moscow's satellites (Hungary and Poland) in the ICCS is the same as would be the behavior of Peking's satellites (Albania and North Korea) if they were on the commission. The very composition of the ICCS (Canada and Indonesia, Hungary and Poland) prevents its impartiality. In no way does it reflect the East–West *détente* in Europe. Because of the China rivalry, Russia won't let Indochina go.

The Communists say Nixon's statements on infiltration are a "fabrication of the American imperialists" (although I've seen dozens of photos of tanks, trucks, and guns being hauled down). They have the crust to deny that there are *any* North Vietnamese troops in South Vietnam.

We cannot count on either Moscow or Peking pressing for conciliation here. In an emergency we can only count on United States bombing of Hanoi and Haiphong—and that is very difficult to contemplate.

The Poles and Hungarians on the ICCS have established their own independent communications network throughout South Vietnam. The Poles handle the northern network and report directly to Hanoi. The Hungarians handle the southern network and report to COSVN (Vietcong headquarters) for Hanoi.

NEW DELHI, *April 4, 1973*

LUNCHED with Ambassador (Daniel Patrick) Moynihan, just the two of us and wives. He seems to be starting off tactfully and slowly, after six weeks on the job. The big problem is the huge supply of rupee counterpart funds amassed by the United States as the result of PL 480 aid loans. We now own about 8 percent of India's entire rupee supply. A settlement must be worked out canceling this impossible debt.

NEW DELHI, *April 5, 1973*

GOOD talk with Prime Minister Indira Gandhi. I asked if she thought Washington had "used" India in 1971–1972 as a kind of stepping stone toward its own new relations with China? "I wouldn't go so far," she said. "They didn't 'use' India. They ignored us. Pakistan was more useful as a bridge to China. We have always believed in friendship with all nations and especially with the United States. We would be glad for any move that would improve relations with you."

She added that between India and the United States "there is no ideological gap, as such. There are many rumors that we are giving up our policy of nonalignment [because of the closer tie with Moscow] but this is simply not true."

Was the report accurate that she was contemplating nationalizing the press. "No. Never. On the contrary, we have no intention at all of doing this. People just make up their minds, without the slightest basis, that we are going to do things—and then they spread the rumor."

I had read that her heroine was Joan of Arc. She said: "It is so. That is correct. I admire her for seeing the necessity to do something regardless of whether it was appreciated or not. And as for how it was appreciated— you know her end. She knew she was right and she pursued her goal all out, even when no one was with her at the start. Unless one tackles problems with that determination, regardless of sacrifice, nothing can be done."

NEW DELHI, *April 6, 1973*

LAST night Ambassador Pat Moynihan and his wife gave a dinner party for us. A big, merry-looking man, he entered politics in the Harriman-for-Governor New York State campaign (1954) and remains on excellent terms with him despite Averell's Nixonophobia. Moynihan also worked for President John F. Kennedy.

He is now plainly loyal to Nixon and thinks his foreign policy excellent, that the row about the Watergate affair is exaggerated and will blow over.

SRINAGAR, KASHMIR, *April 9, 1973*

FLEW up here through thick clouds two days ago so we couldn's see either the famous Karakorum range or the Hindu Kush. Came down over the Vale of Kashmir above lovely green and yellow terraced fields of rice and mustard, pocked with little villages, high houses with sharply angled, thatched roofs. The shades were the pastels of spring, framed by tall, lacelike poplars. The whole vale is marked by valleys where rushing streams have cut through the rich loam.

Through the cold rain one suddenly felt that here, a mile higher than the Delhi plain, one was back in central Asia—Afghanistan or Turkestan. Men mostly wear *karakul* hats or little white skull caps about which turbans used to be wrapped. (Only a few old men still wear turbans.) They wander the cold, wet streets in bare feet or sandals (they are that poor!), carrying fire baskets (straw baskets containing an earthenware pot filled with hot ashes) and blankets.

TEHERAN, *April 12, 1973*

CALLED on Dick Helms, recently named U.S. Ambassador to Iran. When Dick was named, Prime Minister (Amir Abbas) Hoveida was told at a party by the Soviet Ambassador, dean of the diplomatic corps here, "I see you are getting America's Number One spy as ambassador." The bright, tough Hoveida replied: "Yes, why not? You are only Number Ten on the Russian list." When Helms paid his call on the Soviet envoy, the latter said: "I am dean of the corps and as such it is I who am Number One. Furthermore, I expect to remain here several years more—until well after you have gone."

Russia is really hung up on China. It will *not* allow China to get into a position—ever—when it could at some future time jump on the Soviet Union.

We talked a bit about Dick's departure from his old job and the implications of the White House staff leadership. He said the White House bosses were quite insensitive to human beings and were virtually ideological in their blind loyalty to what they considered Nixon's interests. This led them to such incredible blunders as the whole sordid Watergate affair.

TEHERAN, *April 14, 1973*

SPENT an hour and a half this morning with the Shah. He is about five foot ten and basically slender, with a long head and face, long nose and solemn expression. He has a veneer of strength and self-confidence, but one can conjecture it is not marrow-deep.

One thing that disturbed me profoundly is the way he kept solemnly referring to his "mystical" belief and the "mystical" forces that were leading him on to the right destiny for his nation. I had the impression I was talking to a man who had been listening only to himself for so long that he had finally begun to believe what he heard. It is obvious that no man, even one with good intentions, like Mohammad Reza, can go through life never hearing anything but praise.

He said: "I don't want this generation to go threadbare in order to pay for the future benefits of succeeding generations. We want the present generation to be happy too. As for oil, we are in a position to express our desires and to see them come true. People contact us, not vice versa. People recognize our stability and that we can carry out our promises. But we won't have a problem of a surplus of funds for years."

The Shah recalled that he had continually insisted on heavy investment to build up Iran's own armed forces "against the better judgment of our good American friends who thought that with two airborne divisions the United States could police the world." Nowadays Iran invested over $2 billion a year in defense. "Our armed forces are becoming very sophisticated. Our officers and nco's have to have more and more technical knowledge and therefore we have to keep increasing pay levels in order to meet the competition of private industry."

I reminded him that some years ago he had remarked to me that Russia's aim was "unchanging"; that by one or another means, by subversion, threats, or votes, Moscow intended to impose a Communist regime here. Did he still believe this? He said: "No. This had to change as our regime became both more powerful and more representative of what the people wished. There was no longer any room left to try subversion. We have had vast programs of land reform and of social reform for the workers. In most fields, everybody participates in the benefits. In many respects we are more advanced than some of the so-called socialist societies in Europe. But we don't adhere to any particular 'ism' of our own. We take from everyone what we need, what suits us. This is true in industry. It is true in the huge mechanized farms we now have started to operate."

I asked whether he considered that the bilateral pact between Iran and the United States, established during Eisenhower's Presidency, still applied today. He answered: "Officially it still exists. It hasn't been denounced. But I don't really believe in pacts. I prefer to believe in crude reality and in the paramountcy of the national interests of countries. But the fact remains that our relations are the same now as in the days when the pact was formulated because, with or without a pact, the United States cannot afford to see anything happen to Iran."

I asked if he thought Iran was now in a position to defend itself in any nonnuclear war. He replied: "That is my ultimate aim. Some people laughed when I started off with such a program. But now I estimate we are only about five years away from our goal. We can't rely entirely on any foreign intervention to help us against an aggression."

He spoke of the special role of monarchy in Iran, and added: "There is a special, mystical relationship between the sovereign and the people of Iran. You shouldn't be surprised by my own mystical belief. I feel dedicated to goals that were decided already by something I call God. Any step that I take is weighed in advance by this something, weighed in terms of the advantage for a strong and happy nation."

This was very peculiar stuff to hear, and even stranger, I am persuaded that this Swiss-educated sovereign of the latter twentieth century really believed it.

He predicted that in ten years Iran will have attained a "European" level of living standards, the only Asian country to do this save for Japan. He thought China would try its hardest to achieve this level but wouldn't succeed. Already Iran had a $600 average annual income on a per capita basis, and this figure was expected to double within five years.

These goals depended largely on the speed of agricultural development and the amount of foreign investment that would enter Iran. He recalled that the United States had invested billions in Western Europe, and added: "Now we will soon see the United States, Europe, and Japan investing large amounts of capital here."

I turned to foreign problems. What would Iran do if Pakistan disintegrated? "We must see to it that Pakistan doesn't fall to pieces. It is in the interests of everyone in this region. And we are the same people, after all. I am not in the least bit racist but we are all Indo-Europeans, Aryans: the Iranians, Afghans, Pakistanis, and the Indians. If there were a disintegration of Pakistan it would produce a terrible mess in this part of the world."

I asked who, in his life, he had most admired. He said there were "many," but "I can repeat one thing, something I said earlier: There is a mystical power I feel behind me urging me on."

TEHERAN, *April 15, 1973*

DRINKS this evening with Sir Peter Ramsbotham, British Ambassador, and his wife. Peter thinks the Shah has a sense of doom and that he is going to be killed. There have been three assassination attempts already. Peter also is struck by the Shah's belief in a "mystical" guiding force. He says it is tragic that nobody ever talks straight to him. Hussain Ala, the Court Minister (a childhood friend of the fifty-three-year-old Shah) could do this; also Hoveida, the Prime Minister. But they don't.

PARIS, *May 18, 1973*

LUNCHED with Jean Monnet, now eighty-five, still looking like a solemn, sturdy little *poilu*. I said it seemed to me the entire capitalistic world—but especially Western Europe—depended for industrial growth on a kind of indentured labor force of cheap unskilled workers from foreign countries.

Monnet acknowledged that foreign labor plays an important role. But there would unquestionably be a serious economic crisis without such foreign workers, because this would cut industrial growth. Europe needs the cheap foreign labor that voluntarily makes itself available.

I asked if he thought diminishment of Nixon's authority because of the Watergate scandal would delay or frustrate negotiations between the

United States and Europe. He said that everything could be affected unless Nixon wins his battle. It would be catastrophic if he were stripped of his power, but Monnet didn't think this would happen.

PARIS, *May 21, 1973*

AN hour today with Michel Jobert, the first time I have seen him since Pompidou named him Foreign Minister. He told me he dislikes the job and didn't want it but took it as a favor to Pompidou. He told Pompidou he couldn't envisage himself as becoming an expert on the European community and such matters and he didn't like giving up the nonforeign policy questions he dealt with in the *Elysée*. But Pompidou told him he knew Jobert would never be corrupted by power, and that's why he wanted him as Foreign Minister.

I asked about the change of U.S. policy. We had decided this spring to advise Britain and France that the United States was changing its attitude on the European nuclear project and henceforth did not object if Britain wished to make available to France nuclear weapons secrets that the United States had previously made available to Britain. Jobert sees this as a major change. But if Paris and London join in taking some initiative for a European nuclear force, that raises the matter of Bonn's participation. And this in turn would raise the matter of Soviet reaction.

PARIS, *May 23, 1973*

BREAKFAST with Henry Kissinger in the library of his suite at the American Embassy residence. He was clearly deeply alarmed and nervous about the ever-spreading Watergate scandal engulfing the White House. I asked about the effect of Watergate on U.S. foreign policy. He said: "So far it isn't important. We are able still to continue running on momentum. For example, practically all the decisions that will be announced after Brezhnev's summit with Nixon [next month] have already been made. You know, I spent four days with Brezhnev talking all the time. The things that have been started off, that already are under way and have their own momentum, are going ahead. But the effect of Watergate—if it hasn't ended soon—is bound to be felt in autumn."

Kissinger admitted his own negotiating position here (he is talking on Indochina again with Le Duc Tho) has been weakened. Above all, the restriction imposed by Congress on bombing Cambodia makes things very tough.

Henry then went off on a tangent. He said he had only agreed that the telephones of four of his own staff members should be bugged because those people were accused of being security risks. And the bugging endured only a few months. After all, this way of insuring security was not new. Kennedy had had eighty people bugged. Johnson had also done this. But Nixon had only thirteen bugged, and this was stopped after nine months. I frankly thought this beside the point and confusing the issue. I also felt Henry was extraordinarily tender on this point.

I asked if he would like to be Secretary of State and run policy from that post. He thought the moral authority of the State Department had perhaps been too far eroded—a curious remark, since he helped so much to erode it. He said the naming of his former right-hand, General Alexander Haig, as chief of Nixon's White House staff to replace Haldeman, had "symbolically improved my position. Everybody knows Haldeman was my enemy."

Kissinger said the next "two or three weeks" would be critical. "As things are right now, we can continue along this course. But that will depend on how long this period of national masochism [over Watergate] lasts. It will depend on a change in the existing mood. Certainly these Vietnam negotiations right now have been made more difficult because of this."

He then went into an aside about the insanity of much that has been uncovered. It was "crazy" to steal the files on Ellsberg from the latter's psychiatrist. What on earth would anyone want with them? It was equally crazy, after a decision had been made to burn some papers, to give them to the acting head of the FBI to burn. "Why are people burning papers all the time? Why didn't they just tear them up and throw them in the wastebasket? That would have been better."

He was pretty gloomy about Cambodia (in his current talks with Le Duc Tho). There was no project by us to seek a "Sihanouk solution" (returning Norodom Sihanouk to power). "But we have to adapt to realities. There is no escape."

He said that with Le Duc Tho he had reached substantial agreement on "methods to improve the implementation" of the January agreement on an Indochinese cease-fire. On the whole this represented "a net gain" for the United States—"except for Cambodia." What an exception! Henry admitted that the United States had far fewer cards in its hands now than in earlier negotiations.

He said a few final words on Watergate: "Our foreign policy has been painfully built up so that now all the pieces are in place. We are at last in a position to reap the fruits. Now everything may be wrecked. There is a masochistic effort to dismantle the executive power and this is being led by those very same liberals who used to wish to strengthen it under other presidents. This runs counter to the tide of current history and it will hurt our policy and world position more than Watergate."

PARIS, *June 4, 1973*

LUNCHED with Malraux. He visited India in April and early May and was touched by the experience. He likes Mrs. Gandhi a great deal. He observed that she had been very heavily influenced by Joan of Arc—something I noted earlier. He told me Sophie de Vilmorin had accompanied him on his trip. The Vilmorins are one of the two French families descended from Joan of Arc's family. They were ennobled by Charles VII. All this was of great interest when Mrs. Gandhi met Sophie.

He was enormously moved by Sheikh Mujibur Rahman, the Bangladesh Prime Minister. Malraux says the P.M. is most impractical as a political leader, but he has great courage and "intelligence of the heart."

PARIS, *June 7, 1973*

LAST night we gave a dinner party for Henry Kissinger and Caramanlis. Costa swore to me he knew nothing of the recent plot against the colonels in Greece prior to the event, and that his call for a return to democracy under the King was not connected with it. He begged me to tell Luns in Brussels that Greek officers are being brutally tortured, and NATO should do something about it since they are part of an alliance force.

The most interesting person was undoubtedly Kissinger. He is showing signs of strain from the Watergate scandal. He drank little but talked somewhat indiscreetly in front of our French guests, who are bound to repeat much of what he said.

After dinner I put Caramanlis and Kissinger together. Henry said to Costa: "What do you want us to do?" Costa of course wants us to intervene. He claims Andreas Papandreou is finished and that is why Andreas just issued a statement endorsing the ouster of the King and in effect backing the colonels on this key issue.

Henry talked at the table in front of everyone about Watergate. He said the people now being exposed (like Haldeman, Ehrlichman, Dean, etc.) were small-town, middle-class politicians who were used to fixing municipal elections and thought they could do the same thing in the White House. He failed to mention that Nixon had, after all, brought them in and let them run wild. He also said it was all right to lie for "a great cause" but not for a small one.

He is enormously seduced by the Chinese. He says that Chou En-lai is a great charmer and "his word is as good as a formal agreement." I reminded him that General Marshall and Walter Robertson (Dulles' Assistant Secretary for Asia) had once believed this too. Also, he said, Gromyko is a wise and excellent man, whereas Brezhnev is unimaginative.

He fears that Brandt's adviser (and now Cabinet minister) Egon Bahr wants to get out of NATO and neutralize Germany. Bahr said: "If the French won't go along with us, they must realize that we can make our own deal with Russia."

Kissinger expresses confidence that Nixon will survive the Watergate scandal but says it will leave him "wounded." He says there is a "bitter, suicidal" instinct in America today.

PARIS, *June 11, 1973*

LUNCHED with Caramanlis. I strongly urged Costa to stop waiting for the United States to throw out the colonels and put in Constantine plus Caramanlis. I then recalled that only one Greek had been killed in the April 1967 coup d'état by which the colonels took power—and this was the result of an accidental ricochet bullet. Not a single Greek lost his life on either side when King Constantine, Chief of Staff and commander of all the armed forces, summoned an uprising against the colonels in December of the same year—which ended when the King fled to Rome.

PARIS, *June 16, 1973*

WE gave a lunch today for André Malraux and Sophie de Vilmorin. André de Staercke, Belgian envoy to NATO, was there, as well as Manes Sperber and his wife. Manes is an old friend of Malraux, a student of Freud and Adler, a former Communist who once was underground courier between secret Jugoslav Communist headquarters in Vienna and the underground party in Jugoslavia before the war.

Malraux, who knew him well, says Picasso was fascinated by the fact that he did not know why he painted as he did. He did, however, know he was a genius. He expected to be misunderstood and could never understand how it was that some people could understand what he himself did not comprehend in his own works. Malraux said Picasso had the same kind of genius as the sculptors of African masks.

Malraux considers Titian the greatest man of his time. He invented the method of painting women like goddesses. There is no equivalent in poetry to an equally great writer spanning Titian's period.

BELFAST, *June 18, 1973*

THE number of bombings has declined, but a nastier phenomenon has started: automobile bombings. A car is loaded with explosives and parked by a target. It makes a big bang and shows up well on TV. Before a car goes up, the television crews in Belfast are usually notified and told where and when to be—just like the Buddhist burnings in Saigon around 1963.

LONDONDERRY, *June 19, 1973*

I DROVE up to Londonderry through rolling, wooded country and rich green fields full of sheep. The clouds hung low and occasional trout streams rippled past. Crows, pigeons and magpies flew overhead.

Derry dates from foundation of the monastery there by St. Columcille (Columba) in A.D. 546. He called it "Derry, my own oak grove, Little cell, my home, my love." James I granted 20,000 acres, including the borough, to the citizens of London and a large colony of Protestants was imported. Walls fortifying the town were completed in 1618.

The famous siege took place in 1689. Protestants in Derry plus refugees held out 105 days, urged to resist by the Apprentice Boys, until an English convoy forced a boom across the Foyle River and relieved the city. On the walls, now running through the town, are some old cannon, including "Roaring Meg," made famous in the siege.

Occasional British armored cars rumbled by. There are great cement blocks in front of shops to prevent cars (with possible bombs) from being parked there. Traffic is checked at the bridge entering town for weapons and contraband. Nets attached to floats on the Foyle prevent the bridge from being blown up by floating mines. Papers are checked by soldiers in berets and bulletproof vests, armed to the teeth. Plenty of buildings have been bombed out near the old wall and in the marketing center. Coils of barbed wire lie among the wall. There are few people around, and trade seems paralyzed.

Lead on this evening's Belfast paper: "Five Protestant funerals, including that of an eighty-three-year-old blind woman, to Belfast's city cemetery had to be cancelled today after grave-diggers were threatened that they would be shot if they stayed at work. Corporation workmen at the Falls Road cemetery said they stopped work after their foreman was warned by phone this morning: 'If you dig those graves you will be dead'."

DUBLIN, *June 20, 1973*

THIS afternoon I saw Garret Fitzgerald, Foreign Minister in the new government. Fitzgerald said that Senator Teddy Kennedy's speeches on Ireland had produced great irritation in the South as well as the North. Kennedy's speeches show an insensitivity to the reality of the situation. It isn't, as he seems to think, polarized into Ireland against England. Dublin in no sense wants to see the British army withdraw from Ulster. Kennedy seems more interested in the Irish-American vote than in Ireland.

DUBLIN, *June 21, 1973*

PLEASANT talk with President Erskine Childers, new chief of state for the Irish republic. He is a small, trim man who was wearing a bright green suit. He is a Protestant but comes from a well-known nationalist family. His father, also Erskine, was shot during the civil war. "If the election of a Protestant as president can demonstrate to the world at large and especially to the Unionists of Northern Ireland that we live in an ecumenical state, why then I am very glad. Maybe my election can help to dispel the vestigial impressions of some people that we live in a sectarian state."

ROME, *July 2, 1973*

LONG talk with King Constantine of Greece at his very comfortable house. I said that as I understood it, when Britain and the United States announced they did not think the change in regime in Greece required any new act of recognition, it appeared to me that Washington and London were simultaneously recognizing both the King and the Papadopoulos republic. Constantine chuckled grimly and said this was exactly the case. He added that not only were Britain and the United States stuck on the horns of this dilemma, but also both the armed forces and the civil service of Greece.

He continued: "Anyone joining as of June 1, when the republic was declared, must now swear allegiance to that republic. But all those who had taken an oath previously—before June 1, 1973—swore allegiance to the king. That means all the officers of the armed forces today are still by oath sworn to serve the monarchy."

I asked Constantine about his present financial status. He answered: "That one's easy. My financial status is nonexistent. As of July 1, yesterday, I have no income. And such income as I may have, as may be allotted to me, won't be let out of the country. Under the extraordinary law that has been decreed, after the July 29 plebiscite all my movable and my nonmovable property will be expropriated."

PARIS, *July 6, 1973*

HAVING heard nothing by yesterday, one month since my last China visa talk with Kissinger, I called the White House and was immediately switched to San Clemente, California (President Nixon's western residence). The time of my call was 7:25 A.M. California time (3:25 P.M. Paris time), and poor old Henry was already up and at 'em. When I asked what news there was on the visa situation, he said, "I haven't had any." He said he hoped to know more this week and added "I will be in touch with you next week."

I am much consoled by a confidential letter from David Bruce four days ago, written in his own handwriting, from Peking. David is now chief of the liaison mission there with the personal rank of Ambassador. The burden was that David had made a very special intervention on my behalf, although this transcends his apparent terms of reference as chief of the liaison mission.

PARIS, *July 9, 1973*

TSAO Kuei-sheng, the man at the Chinese Embassy with whom I have been dealing for so many months about my visa, called up my secretary and asked if I could come and see him at 4:00 P.M.

He had more than the usual green tea waiting for me in the salon where I am customarily received: tea, biscuits, some kind of candied fruit and dried lichee nuts, which Tsao carefully peeled for me.

Finally Tsao could no longer restrain himself, and said: "I wish to announce good news to you. You know I have always told you that I was optimistic and now I wish to tell you that your visa has been granted."

My visa would be activated for a trip starting September 20 or somewhat later and would be good for a one-month visit. He said he would request Peking to issue instructions to have the visas granted in the United States in September.

PARIS, *July 10, 1973*

AN hour's talk with President Pompidou at the *Elysée*. He is definitely overweight.

I asked how he saw relationships among the United States, Russia, and China as a result of Nixon's trip to Peking and Brezhnev's trip to Washington. It was evident that Nixon (with Kissinger's help) had achieved some spectacular acts, first involving Moscow (the Brezhnev talks last month) and immediately following this up with the spreading of a red carpet for the Chinese envoy (the liaison ambassador who was received by Nixon).

Pompidou admitted that for "Europe" there had been no direct part played in these affairs. The triangle excluded "Europe," which had not been sufficiently unified and developed to be considered as a great power.

I then asked if he thought the Watergate scandal had weakened President Nixon's authority as a factor in foreign policy and world affairs. He answered:

I don't believe it. Naturally I abstain from speaking publicly on this at all. Nevertheless, I am convinced that the U.S. national destiny is so strong that neither Democrats nor Republicans wish to destroy the president's power and his function. Clearly, after it has worked so well for two hundred years, you cannot foolishly tear your system apart. I think Nixon will stay. I don't think he is even tempted to leave. Therefore, vis-à-vis the world at large, the authority and importance of the United States remains unchanged.

Naturally Nixon has his troubles with Congress. We know about this because it is traditional in France to have such troubles; also in other European countries like Italy. But I can tell you that France has been more irritated by the U.S. embargo on soya beans than frightened by the Watergate affair.

I think that Watergate is a plot. What I mean is that at a certain moment a group of people were trying to get at Nixon and pull him down but now they are retreating from that phase. It was a plot to get the American president and the presidency.

PARIS, *July 12, 1973*

LUNCHED with Nijaz Dizdarević, Jugoslav Ambassador. He claims while Western Europe talks of its fears of being "Finlandized" in terms of being subjected to more Soviet influence, Eastern Europe thinks of being "Finlandized" in terms of reducing its dependence on the Soviet Union and becoming as close to real independence as Finland is in most respects today.

NEW YORK, *September 4, 1973*

WHILE in Aspen, Colorado, on holiday I arranged with the Chinese liaison mission in Washington to come down September 5 (tomorrow) and pick up the visas as well as to see the chargé d'affaires. Everything seemed fine. Therefore I was thunderstruck when told my visa had been canceled. I was informed it was merely "a postponement," and I should come next year.

I called Henry Kissinger, who has just been named Secretary of State and is awaiting confirmation, and asked if he could help. He promised to do something.

To my surprise and delight the telephone rang this afternoon and it was David Bruce. He had just flown to Washington from San Clemente, where he had consulted with Nixon and Kissinger. He had told Kissinger how pleased he was Marina and I were coming and how he had asked us to stay. David said I should not give up the ship but should keep trying. He is going to see Kissinger before flying back to Peking, and he will again discuss the subject with Henry and ask him to help.

NEW YORK, *September 11, 1973*

THIS morning General Brent Scowcroft, who has replaced Haig as Kissinger's right-hand man in the White House, telephoned from Washington. He confirmed that the White House had called the Chinese [mission] on my behalf.

NEW YORK, *September 14, 1973*

EVERYTHING broke at last on China. Both the Chinese mission in Washington and Scowcroft called to say Peking had reversed its ban and was now ready to let Marina and myself in.

I telephoned Chi Li-teh, the counselor of the Chinese liaison mission, at the Mayflower Hotel. He asked if I would be able to get to China on September 27. I said yes. I would fly to Washington Monday (this was late Friday) and discuss details with him. He said we could stay in the People's Republic until October 27.

WASHINGTON, *September 17, 1973*

I FLEW to Washington on a very brief visit to call upon Chi Li-teh. I was interested, when I arrived on the fifth floor of the Mayflower Hotel where the Chinese mission has its offices and residences, to find the section they inhabit blocked off by two enormous Americans, presumably FBI or Secret Service.

Chi received me in the usual hotel sitting room together with another member of the mission who also spoke good English and took notes. One was wearing a gray Mao-type suit and the other a navy blue Mao-type suit. We were served unsweetened Chinese tea, while I filled out visa forms.

One of the questions on the visa form was: Had I ever been in China before? I said it was difficult to answer this because I had visited Taiwan several times, but after all it was not part of the People's Republic. Chi smiled and said the question was unimportant. Another question was the religion of the applicant. I wrote down "atheist." He seemed surprised. I said I was a vigorous atheist and had even written a book on the subject.

I pointed out that our passports were marked invalid for travel to "Mainland China" and asked whether this would pose any difficulty. I said I could easily have the restriction removed in Hong Kong. He smiled and said it was quite unnecessary, that he knew the Secretary of State was interested in our trip and that we would be staying with the American liaison chief.

HONOLULU, *September 22, 1973*

AT a Pearl Harbor briefing, I was told that along the Sino–Soviet border the Chinese posture is one of defense in depth. They have made no big movement in the direction of the border since the immediate aftermath of the Ussuri clash (and others farther west) in 1969. There are about one million Chinese military in the area, excluding paramilitary units. This amounts to approximately fifty infantry divisions concentrated in the north and northeast. That does not refer to the immediate frontier area but behind it; most units are about sixty miles back.

There are extensive Chinese fortifications in both the Peking and Shenyang regions. But they do not indicate either an offensive threat or rationale on the part of the Chinese. The major Chinese reinforcements were sent to these areas about three years ago; not since.

From the Soviet side, there seem to be heavy fortifications in the Maritime Province and East Siberia. But there are not one million Russian troops there as Chou En-lai likes to say. What they really have is about forty-four divisions of about five hundred thousand men, including everything sent in since 1969. Their basic deployment is near the main communications lines. In terms of unit strength, this indicates an increase of twenty-five divisions on the Soviet side since 1969—although many are below strength. They are backed by awesome Soviet air and missile forces.

For their part, the Chinese could punish cities like Vladivostok and the Trans-Siberian Railway with their medium jet bombers but it is a relatively modest force. The Chinese position is definitely defensive, whereas the Soviet potential is offensive. But there have been no major changes on the Soviet side during the past year or more.

The most important reflection to the United States stemming from the crisis is that for the next ten years or so the Chinese "threat" to our interests, as we once conceived it in Asia, has been defused. We must, of course, hedge against possible changes in Chinese policy, but it is obvious that now, at this juncture, the Chinese are most worried about the Brezhnev Doctrine, about the Soviet Union moving into areas of influence we abandon in Asia, and they wish to restrain the Russians from seeking ascendancy in places where the Americans were previously top dog.

Oddly enough, the only people who want us out of Indochina entirely are the Americans, the Russians, and the North Vietnamese (and Vietcong). The Chinese want us to reduce our presence in Southeast Asia— but not to erase it. They want no precipitous withdrawal.

HONG KONG, *September 26, 1973*

THIS afternoon I had a good talk with David Osborn, U.S. consul general. He said the theory of Peking is that the conflict between Moscow and Washington is absolute, and such collusion as may be implied by Brezhnev's visit to the United States is temporary. Peking believes American power is waning. In the end China firmly hopes to see us weakened, but on the other hand it does not want us to go down the drain too fast.

The Lin Piao crisis did not derive from arguments over foreign policy, although these may have played their role. He was after power, and he sought to block Chou En-lai.

Even Liu Shao-chi was not Moscow's stooge. He probably admired Soviet methods and industrialization, and there are certainly other Chinese pragmatists still around. They are not Soviet agents in any sense, but they sympathize with Soviet methods. Moscow knows this but clearly is not going to try and mess around in Chinese politics until after Mao's death.

29

W E CAME HERE YESTERDAY FROM HONG KONG. AROSE EARLY in the luxury of the Mandarin Hotel and were driven to the Kowloon railway station, where we were taken in hand by the efficient China Travel Service. After a long wait with a mixture of New Zealand and U.S. Communist delegations, a Mexican soccer team, and various Japanese leftist and businessmen's groups, we were taken aboard a slow, old-fashioned train that rattled through the leased territories to the border.

On the border, we were herded through a long station on the Hong Kong side, where our documents were checked, and into an even larger Chinese station, where each group was led into a different waiting room, we with the New Zealanders. A China Travel Service agent named Wu joined us and got us through baggage, passport and money-changing formalities.

From Canton comfortable flight on huge Ilyushin 62 jet (Soviet-made) copy of British VC-10. Smiling stewardesses in pigtails, white jackets, and baggy pants served ice cream, dinner, tea.

David Bruce, U.S. Ambassador who heads our liaison office (no full relations yet), with whom we are staying, was at the airport with Brunson McKinley, of his mission, a tall young man who speaks fluent Chinese, and his wife. David says his mission is expert and good on facts, background, and language.

We sat around and had drinks and supper. David's residence is a peculiar place. He brought little with him except for his flat silver because he had been warned it is so difficult to take things out at the end. Anything you buy must have a specially stamped receipt on purchase to enable its export. No genuine antique may be bought or sold.

All servants work from 8:00 to 5:00, six days a week, then go home.

They ride back and forth on bikes, the Number One, Mr. Chiang, going an hour and a half each way. They are entitled to a siesta period and stretch out all over the place and sleep. Bruce's driver quits at 5:00 and there is always cold supper left on the table because there is neither cook nor waiter at home.

But despite all this he and Vangie (who has gone home to Virginia to look after problems for a few weeks) adore China, are fascinated, find it filled with surprises and laughs, and don't mind the austere life. David is full of beans, fascinated with China, an experiment on a scale never before attempted in history.

He is filled with interesting comments. For example, the people are so frugal and honest that he couldn't even throw away an old pair of pajamas with a split in the back; every time he cast them in the waste basket, the pajamas came back darned and ironed. Finally he explained carefully, and one of the maids made pillow covers from them.

David says the old imperial Forbidden City, where the top bosses now live and which is heavily guarded and surrounded by barbed wire, is banned to foreigners. It is linked with key points by underground tunnels, part of the intricate air raid shelter system. He believes Chou sees Mao every day, probably often going through one of these tunnels.

PEKING, *September 29, 1973*

WE dined last night with Etienne Manac'h, French Ambassador. Only his wife and two bright young aides were present. They leave tomorrow for a holiday in France, so I was happy to get a glimpse of him. He said it is obvious that Pompidou (who was here this month) is unwell.

Manac'h thought there were certainly internal policy reasons as well as external reasons behind Lin Piao's fall. The army had been given great power during and after the cultural revolution, but the basic slogan is that the party dictates to the guns. Therefore the army had to be trimmed in authority. But Lin had the entire army with him. It is possible (and Mao and Chou feared) he wished to maintain an army so strong that it could help him take power himself. Furthermore, Lin Piao probably opposed the opening to the West policy, which featured friendship with America.

But Chou and Mao wanted the latter because they felt China could not afford to face two vast enemies at the same time. They picked the United States as their choice for friend because they felt American strength was waning while Soviet strength was waxing. Therefore it was easier and less dangerous to accommodate with the former. Moreover, the Indochina problem was being solved, and America was no threat there, now realizing that China had no desire to communize the area, merely to neutralize it, while Brezhnev wanted to move in and use Hanoi as his tool.

Finally, Manac'h speculated that Lin Piao might have retained secret contacts with Moscow since the period just before World War II, when he went to the Soviet Union for over a year to be cured of tuberculosis. This is the kind of thing no one will ever know.

The split between China and Russia, said Manac'h, really began in 1927 at the time Borodin was Chiang Kai-shek's adviser and the Canton coup occurred. That was the period when Mao strongly argued that communism here must be based on peasant support, not workers, because China had no proletariat.

Manac'h felt China is obsessed by the "unequal" treaties existing with Russia. Late one night in the spring of 1970 he had been talking with Chou En-lai and said: "I know you do not like to be pinned down by yes or no answers but allow me to make some statements analyzing your policy and then you merely say yes or no to indicate whether my analyses are correct or incorrect." Chou agreed. Manac'h then said:

China doesn't want any kind of treaty or accord with Russia for the present because you consider yourselves too weak, which is correct. You are militarily inferior, have no navy, few missiles, and your economy is weaker. Therefore you consider it would be pointless to try and negotiate a treaty now and to try and alter the present frontiers. You will agree only to minor arrangements such as an accord to withdraw troops some distance from the border on each side and to permit seasonal workers to cross back and forth when needed.

But there will be no big deal on frontiers. Anyway you believe that treaties are really meaningless. You have noted how three wars were started with no advance declarations: Germany's invasion of Russia, the Japanese attack on America, the Soviet occupation of Czechoslovakia [1968].

Furthermore, you are very preoccupied with the time aspect of this period. You fear that Russia might attack you while you are gradually growing stronger. The Russians know that although you cannot acquire a military strength equal to theirs, once you have the missile force able to destroy several Soviet cities, war becomes impossible for them. Therefore you fear they may attack before you achieve enough strength to negotiate a new treaty on a basis of equality.

Chou, according to Manac'h, smiled, slapped him on the back, and turned to some Chinese colleagues with them, saying: "He knows exactly what we think."

Manac'h said that although it is convenient for the leaders to stress the Russian danger and thus keep people here united and on edge, they were not distorting the picture for political purposes. They sincerely feared Moscow. Otherwise it would be lunatic to spend such vast sums on a useless and enormous air raid shelter program. But they reckoned that even if there was only a 10 percent chance of conflict, they must be ready. They had seen how France was under the illusion it was prepared for war in 1939 and wasn't strong enough either to fight or to negotiate.

When we got back to the Bruces', David was supping with our new co-guest, Lady John Manners, a vivacious, lovely Englishwoman. David made these points: There are 1,700,000 bicycles in Peking alone. There is no single private automobile in China except the few belonging to diplomats. There is no venereal disease. During the reforestation program of the last few years, 50 million new trees have been planted. There are no beggars and no thieves, very little violence (in between revolutionary ruckuses). There is no brothel but also little entertainment and no real theaters. There is full employment, but productivity of workers is low in order to get everyone a job.

In the morning I had gone over to the Foreign Ministry for an appointment with Ma Yü-chen, deputy director of information. Ma received me very amiably together with Yü Chung-ch'ing, who appears to be the case officer assigned to me, and Wu Shih-liang, who is to be my interpreter. All speak English well. Mrs. Wu, who is warm and charming, is the wife of a playwright. She is staying at a hotel here and has been coopted from cultural affairs to help the information department with me.

Over cups of tea Ma asked whom I wished to see and where I wanted to go. He solemnly wrote down all my answers and then gave me documents to fill out in order to get press credentials. He said it was okay to stay until October 27 and asked why we didn't wish to remain even longer. (David Bruce said he'd never heard either of a full month's visa or a suggestion from them that a visitor stay on further.)

We spent the day outside Peking, being driven by Ma, Yü, Mrs. Wu, and a colleague in two cars to the Great Wall and then to the Ming tombs, where we lunched. Ma explained that the wall was started in the fourth century B.C. In the third century the Chin dynasty linked these sections into the Great 10,000 Li Wall, which is 6,000 kilometers long and goes from the sea in the east almost to Sinkiang in the west. Since then it has continually been repaired. In the fourteenth and fifteenth centuries the Ming dynasty rebuilt and reinforced it.

We walked along about a kilometer of wall, climbing to a high tower. On the way back, on the wall path, we were introduced by other guides to Mrs. Edgar Snow, widow of the reporter-writer, who has come here with her family bearing some of her husband's ashes to bury in China.

Then we drove back toward the Ming tombs, twenty-five miles from the capital. The Ming were of Han nationality (pre-Manchu). The first Emperor founded the dynasty in Nanking, but his second son moved it to Peking. The first was buried at Nanking; the other thirteen here, north of Peking.

The Ming (1368–1644) graveyard is called the Thirteen Emperor Tombs and includes forty square kilometers, each huge tomb far from the next and covering a large underground palace of the dead. In some respects, both for grandeur of scope and gloominess, it reminded me of pharaonic Egypt.

We visited the tomb of the tenth Ming Emperor, Chu Li-chun, who ruled from 1573 to 1620. Placards stated his court had a huge, costly bureaucracy numbering 100,000 eunuchs alone. There were paintings of imperial oppression and of peasant uprisings (numerous in the last Ming years). Statistics showed the Emperor spent a fortune on food while the people ate grass and bark and wore patchwork rags.

Signs proclaimed that the tomb cost 8 million ounces of silver, enough to feed one million people for six and a half years, the equivalent of two years of the empire's total revenue.

On the way back Ma told me there was now a strong movement in the press against Confucius, which puzzled me. He said the May 4, 1919, movement started the opposition to Confucius by declaring him a reactionary, which agreed with current educational philosophy. The May 4, 1919, movement derived from resentment of the Treaty of Versailles, which awarded Germany's Shantung concession to Japan despite the fact that China had backed the Allies (although it sent no soldiers). Mao was in the May 4 movement, a political phenomenon that preceded by two years the founding of the Chinese Communist Party in 1921 at Shanghai.

PEKING, *September 30, 1973*

LAST night Peng Hua, director of the information department in the Foreign Ministry, gave us a dinner in the Peking Duck, one of the capital's best-known restaurants. David Bruce was giving a dinner in our honor in another restaurant (it is hard to entertain at home in the evening because servants usually leave early). However, David told us the cardinal rule was to accept every invitation, do everything suggested. It would mean loss of face to the Chinese who proposed something if we declined.

Peng Hua's dinner included the people we had spent the day with at the wall and tombs plus himself and an elderly lady, Mrs. Rang Chen, his deputy. She wore glasses, smoked incessantly, seemed very bright. Peng Hua spoke only a few words of English so Mrs. Wu, Ma, and Yü shared in the interpreting. But Peng gave me the impression of being a thoughtful, wise, nice man. As usual, of course, all wore the "Mao uniform." Apparently every Chinese has two suits of these, thus simplifying the clothing problem and also establishing a kind of instant egalitarianism. Only the big shots seem to have theirs cut by a better tailor.

The meal was lubricated with constant toasts of mao-tai, a strong drink made of sorghum. I have developed the practice, advocated by David, of using beer as a chaser. Chinese beer, derived from German brewers in their former concession of Shantung and Tsingtao, is excellent.

As soon as we had finished with the formalities Peng got down to the main theme I have encountered so far on this trip: What are the prospects of West Europe and the United States getting together now, will Nixon go to Europe, will U.S. troops stay there? China obviously wants a strong NATO on Russia's west.

I am astonished by the vigor and consistency of their attacks on Russia and Brezhnev. They have huge posters of Marx, Engels, Lenin, and Stalin around town for the October 1 national holiday. But they say a "period of transition" set in with Malenkov; then came the devils Khrushchev and Brezhnev. The latter are socialist-imperialists and aggressors. This explains all. Stalin was a great guy, although Peng acknowledged ruefully that his "last years" were perhaps not so hot.

Incidentally, an apt quote from Mao is the main feature of the vast entrance to the restaurant: "Serve the People." And they did.

Mrs. Wu called for us this morning and en route to an agricultural commune she read a rough translation of a long article in the September 28 *People's Daily* on the subject of the current topic A: that Confucius was a reactionary like Liu Shao-chi and Lin Piao. The essence was as follows.

The first Chin dynasty Emperor was a great man who unified the country and established a uniform language and system of weights and measures. Without him China might have become "another India," with divers languages and peoples.

The Emperor was a despot, and on occasion he burned some books and buried certain scholars alive. Undoubtedly he was a reactionary, but it can be argued that for his time he was progressive. That was a transitional period. The slave system was declining and the feudal system was rising. Historically, feudalism represented progress vis-à-vis what preceded it. Moreover, it was necessary for China of 221 B.C. to have a strong central power to avoid the danger of disintegration. The Emperor abolished rival kingdoms and dukedoms and divided the new China into thirty-six districts. He did away with the power of slave owners.

This was opposed by the latter class, and they were backed by some contemporary scholars and learned men. But the Emperor's ministers supported him and passed a strict law insisting that the people should burn some of Confucius' books and cease attacking the regime through his teachings. Disobedience of this decree was made punishable by death. The Emperor buried 460 rebellious scholars and burned their books.

Today the current regime says this was not vandalism but an attempt to unify the new China of its day. The only books burned dealt with ideology and politics. Confucius is represented as typifying the period of slavery, whereas the feudal landlords who carried out social reforms were an advance over the corrupt slave system. Confucius and his disciple Mencius reflected the dying effort of the slave-owning nobility, who tried to restore slavery and failed.

Therefore, the Emperor's burning of books and burying of scholars was not reactionary. Bringing the lesson home to contemporaries, the *People's Daily* said Lin Piao had attacked the Chin Emperor, and this attack was in fact aimed at Chairman Mao and the party. Lin had sought to reverse history and restore capitalism like the reactionary scholars of the Chin Emperor, who were smashed by the tide of history.

This is all, of course, in the Aesopian language familiar to communism everywhere. It seems odd to Western minds but is quite understandable here—although no one really knows where this new anti-Confucian line will finally strike. Are any earlier books of this regime to be banned (or burned)? Are the intellectuals—always preferred game—to be smacked again?

We arrived at the Shuang Chiao People's Commune after a pleasant drive along the flat tableland that surrounds Peking. We were greeted by the handsome, smiling deputy chairman of the commune's revolutionary committee, a man of about sixty named Chuang Ho-shan. He knew a few words of English, and I was surprised to learn from him that English lessons are given by Peking Radio and English as well as Japanese from Shanghai.

A commune is a vast establishment, much larger than the Soviet collective farm and somewhat nearer to the still-born Soviet concept of an *agrogorod* (agricultural city). Chuang took us to his office, adorned with pictures of Marx, Engels, Lenin and Stalin, and explained: "Our commune has thirty-nine thousand people. Its total area is more than ninety square kilometers. It is divided into six production brigades which are subdivided into fifty-nine production teams which work eighteen commune-run enterprises."

"We started from scratch," Chuang Ho-shan said, smiling all the time. "We are still imperfect and backward in many ways. We have insufficient mechanization and are really just starting scientific agriculture. But we have a great potential. We must work harder on the line of self-reliance."

PEKING, *October 1, 1973*

LAST night we went to dinner for about two thousand people in the Great Hall of the People, honoring the eve of October 1, twenty-fourth anniversary of the revolution. Chou En-lai was at the main table, which included Chiang Ching, wife of Chairman Mao; Wang Hung-wen, the thirty-eight-year-old Shanghai leader who now seems to be Number Three in the pecking order; Prince Sihanouk of Cambodia (who heads an *émigré* government here); etc. The main table was long and straight, all guests there sitting on one side looking at the rest of us, who were at numerous small round tables.

The Great Hall is immense and was constructed in less than a year, rather ugly but impressive Stalinist-style architecture on Peking's main square near the principal gate to the Forbidden City.

We were at a table with David Bruce, a young member of his staff named Nick Platt who speaks good Chinese, a representative of the protocol department, and the usual Ma, Mrs. Wu, and one other information official. The food was astonishingly good for a dinner on that scale.

PEKING, *October 3, 1973*

IN the late afternoon I went out in the drizzle for a walk in the nearby park. I must say, this really is a nation clad in dungarees and mounted on bicycles. When I returned, we tasted a new drink, even stronger than mao-tai, which Marina and Mary Manners had acquired in the day's shopping expedition. It is called fen-jo, and tastes like a mixture of kümmel, cod liver oil, and dynamite.

David then took us to the International Club for dinner, along with Clare Hollingworth of the London *Daily Telegraph*. Very pleasant and excellent food. David emphasized that while the Chinese are exceptionally polite, they remain basically antiforeign. It is idiotic to assume they "love" us.

I hadn't realized until last night that I am the only American journalist in all of China today, which is probably an advantage should anything of interest happen.

This morning I went to Mrs. Wu's room at the Hsin Chiao Hotel to telephone two more columns to New York. Thanks to her help I again got through quite fast, and even when I was cut off, contact was soon reestablished. The line was clear and good.

There are various foreigners living in Peking who are rarely seen by visitors and who are ardent Maoists. These include the American, Dr. George Hatem of Buffalo, who came to Shanghai in 1933 and helped the Communist guerrillas set up a hospital and after they took power, opened the Institute of Venereology and Skin Diseases. Another American is Sydney Rittenberg, arrested for being too pro-Red Guard during the cultural revolution. Also arrested but later released were Israel Epstein (American) and his British wife, Elsie Fairfax-Cholmondely.

It is astonishing how absent security precautions seem to be. There are two little soldiers outside the U.S. liaison office compound, but the gate and front door are always left unlocked. We have five marine guards who double as guardians and telephone centrals, wear mufti, live in a one-room dormitory.

Obviously China, with some skill, is continuing its age-old policy of trying to play the barbarians—and all foreigners are barbarians—off against each other. They have not even allowed the Westerners to collaborate (as the embassies do in Moscow) on an instant translating service and bulletin of the daily Chinese press and weekly magazines. The fundament of policy is that permanent rivalry between Moscow and Washington "provides favorable conditions for the victory of the revolutionary people"—meaning China and her friends.

PEKING, *October 4, 1973*

LONG talk with Chen Chung, described as "head of a bureau in the ministry of agriculture and forestry." Chen is a middle-aged man, stocky, with an intelligent face. He was accompanied by a girl named Chu Chen Hsuan from "the foreign affairs bureau" of his Ministry, who spoke some English.

Poor Mrs. Wu, who interpreted, had a hard time with technical matters, describing wheat as "keeling" when she meant "a key crop." The only point really worth recounting was the following. Mrs. Wu had descended to search for my driver, and I was making laborious simple conversation with Mr. Chen through Miss Chu. I inquired whether he had met any American farmers or agricultural experts. "Mr. Joe Alsop," he replied with a happy grin. I grinned too.

This afternoon Mrs. Wu and Ma accompanied me to a meeting with three representatives of the Institute of Economics of the Chinese Academy of Science. Li Cheng-rei (who did almost all the talking) and Hsu Li-chang are research fellows. Cheng-li (a woman) is a member of the institute staff.

Miss Cheng, wearing glasses, is aging and somber. It was her assignment to take notes along with Mrs. Wu.

I asked how China was able to avoid worldwide inflation and keep its money and prices stable. Li said:

> Our money is not like the West's, based on gold or the gold exchange standard. Of course we have some gold. But we mostly rely on commodities produced by our own national industry; and all our enterprises belong to the state.
>
> Therefore the prices of commodities are all controlled by the state. Quantity, supply, and transportation are planned by the state. The amount of money in circulation and the amount of commodities produced are balanced. We produce just the right amount of commodities to balance off the wages paid each month.
>
> Foreign trade is a state monopoly. The Chinese Export Company buys our home products at the domestic price—regardless of the world price—and then sells them, usually at a profit, which goes to the state. Thus you could theoretically buy a pack of cigarettes for half a yuan and sell it for a yuan. You could also buy a tea cup at the Chinese price and sell it for a thirty percent loss, if the state wished, and the state would absorb the loss. We buy at our own prices and can keep these prices steady while ignoring world prices.
>
> Once the goal of a communist society is achieved, there will be no need for the existence of money. In a communist society everyone will receive according to his needs. Perhaps there will be a form of coupon instead of currency.

Li said: "We think money appeared on the basis of commodity production. In a communist society it would lose its significance." Hereupon Hsu added in English: "The value of a commodity depends on the work that went into its manufacture."

The GNP figure is not published, but Li insists the average annual growth of the GNP since 1949 has been 15 percent! Li said the population is "above 700,000,000," and its annual increase is "around 2 percent."

PEKING, *October 5, 1973*

LAST night I had a long talk with Prince Norodom Sihanouk, former King of Cambodia, then chief of state after he voluntarily abdicated, since 1970 head of an exile government here. He is a close friend of Chou En-lai and lives in great style in the former French Embassy compound. Sihanouk had complained about some of my columns in the past and we have exchanged many cables. But he was friendly and charming and at the end said: "There are journalists and journalists. On the whole I think the Americans are the most objective. I know you have made mistakes but I respect you as an honorable man who tries to ascertain the truth and it was a pleasure to meet you."

I started by asking if Sihanouk would receive Kissinger, should the Secretary request it, when he comes here. He replied no.

He declined my offer to see him here twice and President Nixon declined once, in 1972. Chou En-lai told Nixon I was ready to meet him but Nixon replied that it would be difficult. Then I told Kissinger via Chou that I would be happy to talk with him about Cambodia and about our dispute with the United States. Kissinger said he didn't have Nixon's authority for such a meeting.

So now it is impossible for me to see him. Why should I accept a meeting with him? I received a message from our revolutionary leaders [Khmer Rouge] several months ago telling me that our honor should not again be involved or our dignity engaged. Anyway, there is very little chance of our two governments reaching an understanding. If I were to see Kissinger it would be viewed as a loss of face for me.

The Khmer Rouge are not stooges of North Vietnam. At the start Hanoi helped us a lot; but they never led us, commanded us. It was just the way you helped de Gaulle and the French resistance to fight the Nazis; you were an ally, not a master.

Furthermore, I can assure you that since June 1972 North Vietnamese have not been fighting beside us. They have evacuated their troops. By January 1973, when the Paris peace pact was signed on Vietnam, the North Vietnamese were all out of Cambodia, moving into Vietcong zones of South Vietnam. They left only elements crossing the Ho Chi Minh Trail, that section in Cambodia the United States calls the Sihanouk Trail south of Laos. I don't try to hide from you that they still use that portion of the trail. Apart from that, there are only a few liaison, ordnance, and economic units and military advisers, not combat troops. China sends us arms and these liaison units transport them. Also their economic units buy rice and cigarettes from us. We produce lots of food and tobacco in the liberated zone. And they pay well, often in U.S. currency. We receive ten million dollars a year from Peking and Hanoi also gets dollars.

At present North Vietnam doesn't give us many arms. That would disturb their plan to get dollar aid from the United States for reconstruction. Secondly, Hanoi has received a warning from Washington not to change the prevailing situation in Cambodia too much. Let the Cambodians fight it out, is the idea. Don't intervene. Otherwise the U.S. air force will intervene again in Cambodia and North Vietnam.

And we can't win without support from North Vietnam. I asked the Khmer Rouge to take Kampong Som [Sihanoukville] during the Algiers Conference of nonaligned nations which I attended last month. We occupied it but we had to leave because of the lack of ammunition. North Vietnam stops the flow of supplies whenever we assault an important town. We have learned not to rely on them. It would disturb their plan if we won.

Therefore we must look forward to a long period of fighting. We tell the Khmer Rouge it won't end before the end of 1976 when Nixon's term finishes. Then maybe a Democrat will be elected president. We hope the next president will be a Democrat and that he will accept our proposal: Let Lon Nol fall; and he can't exist without U.S. aid. Then we are ready to renew friendly diplomatic relations with the United States, which wouldn't lose face by such an arrangement.

As a secondary condition, if the United States drops Lon Nol I am ready to let him and ten or twelve other leading traitor collaborators out together with their families. The main war criminals can be flown out in an American plane. They have plenty of money to support them stowed away abroad. Then the lesser traitors, those we call "the sheep of Panurge," will be granted amnesty. We promise a general amnesty. We are reasonable but Nixon doesn't want to accept. Therefore we must fight until Nixon goes at the end of 1976.

However, Sihanouk said that once there is a settlement and peace comes, he will cease playing any role. He added: "I won't stay as chief of state when we regain our independence. The Khmer Rouge will rule and Sihanouk will retire. I am very tired and not so young any more. And I'm disgusted with politics. I have decided to pass the rest of my life in China. My mother, who is very old, is now extremely ill in Phnompenh. If she dies without my seeing her, which is her last wish, I shall never return to my country. Lon Nol prevents my seeing her. I can never pardon that," he added, a mist of tears in his eyes. "I will stay here for the rest of my life. Until the final victory I shall support the Khmer Rouge. But I am demoralized and discouraged."

I asked if he favored neutralizing Southeast Asia. He answered:

It is hard to prophesy. There is a miscellany of countries differing from each other. You can't foresee the future. Nixon believes in the domino theory; so do the prime ministers of Singapore, Malaysia, Thailand, and South Vietnam.

Therefore Nixon won't abandon Lon Nol. But I don't believe the Indochina revolution will change all Southeast Asia just like that. There are too many contradictions. For example, Singapore, Malaysia, Thailand, Japan, and Indonesia are strongly pro-U.S.A. Pham Van Dong, premier of North Vietnam, told me the Communist party in Thailand is very badly organized and won't ever be able to win. In Cambodia, the Khmer Rouge fights for Cambodia, not to export revolution.

Anyway, what is neutrality? India isn't neutral; it's virtually an ally of Russia. Burma's neutrality is very special; you might call it neutralized neutrality. And Laos can never be neutral. The Pathet Lao are pro-Russian while Souvanna Phouma is a man of the Right and pro-U.S.A., whatever they call him. All over there are fundamental contradictions between the Reds and what I call the Blues, the conservatives. After the war I know I won't be able to get on with the Khmer Rouge myself. I'm not a Marxist and you can't mix with communism, they mix like oil and water with noncommunists. I am by inclination a democrat in the French sense, a man like Mendès-France. Surely you can't imagine Mendès-France married to Georges Marchais [French communist boss].

It is better to renounce the idea of neutralization of Southeast Asia. The only solution is peaceful coexistence, like de Gaulle's idea of independence for both big and little countries and noninterference in any nation's internal affairs. After all, you don't need the same kind of political system.

Sihanouk thought Moscow was seeking to encircle China. He added: "The principal means is through the Soviet pact with India. They gave massive aid to India during its 1971 war with Pakistan. And the Soviet fleet is getting stronger and stronger in the Indian Ocean. Russia is slowly penetrating Malaysia. Moscow is very interested in our port of Kampong Som [Sihanoukville]. The Soviets also have bases in Mongolia and nuclear arms there."

Sihanouk said he was most influenced in his life by Buddha and de Gaulle. He added:

I am a Buddhist so Buddha above all influenced me. But I followed de Gaulle's struggle from the day France was occupied. You know, I came to the throne in 1941 at the age of eighteen and a half.

In 1946 when I went to France just after de Gaulle had resigned the first time, I visited him at Colombey. His conception of independence and of nationality greatly influenced me.

Buddha, long before Marx, found truth in the equality of men and the value of honesty. He renounced his great wealth, his lovely wife, richness, and abandoned everything for moral values. That is better than communism. Communism is not always disinterested; it has its disagreeable aspects. Many of its theories applied to nineteenth-century Europe but not to modern times. But Buddha's moral conceptions and spiritual life are always applicable.

In the liberated zone of our country there is no Buddhism; that is real Marxist communism. And everything is so tragic. All I have done for my country has been destroyed—factories, bridges, schools, hospitals.

He concluded: "Nevertheless, between the Khmer Rouge and Khmer Bleu [blue], I respect the Khmer Rouge even if communism is not admirable. My own hope in Buddhist socialism has proven a total failure. I prefer communism to reaction. One must say things as they are. Everything is relative. What a world. When the United States chooses to be friends with the two greatest communist powers, Russia and China, why not Cambodia?"

This afternoon we were taken by Mrs. Wu to the Peking factory for construction materials in order to inspect their underground air raid shelter and tunnel system, which is linked with the entire burrow of tunnels that run under all the city.

We were met by Chiao Chang-yu, of the factory's revolutionary committee, wearing the universal cotton dungarees and visored cap. He told us the tunnel was begun at the start of 1970. We were taken into the courtyard entrance, down a stairs beneath a heavy, sliding panel of steel. It was explained the system is "not quite finished" yet.

Then we began an endless tour past brick, or concrete walls deep in the earth, with occasional hortatory slogans or direction signs. The narrow tunnel, low enough to make a six-foot man stoop, is electrically lit. Here and there are steel antiblast doors with heavy bolts. There is an electrically operated fan-ventilation system, pump wells if the water supply fails, first aid station, operating room, pharmacy, beds for infirmary, and stretchers. The shelter network didn't cost much (!) because it was built with voluntary labor and largely made of state-supplied materials or the factory's industrial waste. It followed the principle of Mao's new slogan: "Dig tunnel deep. Store grain everywhere. Never seek hegemony."

On the whole it was depressing: an enormous waste of funds and energy, useless in a nuclear war, which is all that Russia is likely to attempt. Blast and fall-out would render it worthless, I think.

Spent late afternoon with Chu Mu-chi, head of the New China News Agency (Hsinhua) and a member of the central committee. First we talked at length with him and six top colleagues; then we all dined at the Feng Tse-yuan Restaurant, where we were introduced to slimy sea slugs, one of the prize delicacies. Marina did not relish this.

Chu is about sixty with a smiling face and thinning hair. He told me he had become a journalist when he went to Nanking during the Japanese war and it was easy to get a job since most of the staffs of newspapers had fled because of the bombing. It was at that time that he became a Communist (underground). He has not been a journalist ever since, only off and on. "I have had various other jobs," he said.

I asked what the role of journalism was. They replied that the chief points had been explained in a 1948 article by Chairman Mao based on a talk he had had with the staff of a daily paper. This is published in his collected works. Put simply, he says that the press and other media enable the party to keep close touch with the people.

The party's policies, line, and principles are thus conveyed to the masses "as swiftly as possible." And the press "reflects the experiences and working methods of the people. In short, our aim is that the press shall play a useful role in the construction of the country and the building of the revolution. We want to serve the people and Chairman Mao."

I was told there is no internal censorship (but everything reflects the party line) and no regulation that articles transmitted abroad should be censored before sending. To sum up: "We are all under the unified leadership of the party and state. But a journalist writing his own comments consults experts first. This is not a regulation, but what is practiced."

Circulation of the Peking *People's Daily* is 3,500,000 for all China, not large considering the immense population. Each province has its own local newspaper. Communications are limited and it takes the *People's Daily* two and one-half days to reach some areas. But eleven cities besides Peking print the *People's Daily* simultaneously from mats sent by air or from facsimile, these editions averaging about a half day late. The *People's Daily* circulation is broken up into 1,400,000 in Peking and 2,100,000 national.

Were there any wartime emergency preparations for a press if China was besieged, like the food storage and shelter systems? Answer: "Chairman Mao instructs us to dig tunnels deep."

There is no competitive journalism—"except in the efficiency" of individual newspapers. Editors decide on what subjects editorials shall be written. The *People's Daily*, as the party newspaper, has "close relations" with "other departments."

I asked how it was decided when delicate news, such as Lin Piao's defection, should be held up and when released (which happens despite "no censorship"). The central committee decides. And such a system "is not a handicap to our work. On the contrary it is useful."

How was crime reported? "Generally we don't report crimes because they are not in the mainstream of life. We let the people know about these things by other methods. In our country if there is a serious criminal case it is not just a police matter. The masses take part in investigating the case. Then it becomes known to many people. And a court, when making a judgment, explains its views to the people and they explain their views. We don't have a jury system. In case there is an offense in Peking, for example, we discuss it at Hsinhua and the staff of our agency recommends its judgment. All the population of Peking eventually takes part. And in major cases, the public puts out public notices."

I asked what crimes were punishable by death. He answered: treason, murder, "serious arson," or "serious rape. Our principle is to kill as little as possible. But we cannot yet do away with capital punishment. Generally, execution is by shooting. But there are two kinds of treatment. One is immediate execution because the people are disgusted at a crime. The other is sentencing to death but postponement of execution for one or two years. If the criminal performs well and reforms, sentence is remitted."

I inquired about the "private" bulletin of Hsinhua, which is widely circulated but not published. Chu said this is called *Reference News* and is not printed in papers.

> It is an objective presentation of foreign news and distributed by us without comment. Its readers become more knowledgeable about world opinion and ideas and therefore can be better judges of events. Some of the articles circulated back our views, some oppose them. Some are correct, some are not. This is different from Western journalism which pretends to be objective but isn't. Our foreign correspondents send selected editorials and news and they are translated here.
>
> We admit openly that our papers serve our policy. But we don't think Western papers are objective. The *Reference News* is sent to our leaders and to ordinary working officials, students, factories, commune brigades. Nearly seven million are distributed—and perhaps as many as ten persons read each copy.

I asked if my columns were cited. "Yes, you are in the *Reference News*."

YENAN, *October 6, 1973*

WE drove to Peking Airport at 6:50 A.M. Lots of people were riding to work on bikes, others pushing wheelbarrows or riding in donkey or ox carts, sometimes drawn by both.

In the airport is one of Mao's slogans, which starts, appropriately: "Go all out and aim high." The plane was a twin-engined Soviet-built Antonov, the first prop plane I've been in for a long time. Signs and announcements aboard were in Chinese and English, the latter not very comprehensible but admirable in the effort.

We flew over low broken clouds across endless terraced hills and muddy rivers and a gray and brown autumnal landscape. Came down at Taiyuan, capital of Shansi Province, where we laid over forty-five minutes. It is set among eroded, well-farmed, red-brown hills. The city's population is one million.

We took off again for Yenan, flying through clouds and over craggy mountains, tan and dull green, and then across the muddy Yellow River into barren country that seemed as isolated as another planet. But even here the valleys were well farmed and, where possible, some mountains were terraced. Finally we landed on a small airport composed of flagstones and concrete blocks, rimmed by loess cliffs.

Yenan is 3,300 feet high. It has fifty thousand people. On the airfield were two large single-engine biplanes that looked like leftovers from the 1920s. The roads, of dirt, were filled with bicycles and donkey carts. We drove across the Yen River, a tributary of the Yellow, to the Yenan Hotel, where we were given a fine two-room and bath suite with a double bed, radio, thermos bottle, tea, and mugs.

Then we were briefed by the officials in charge of our visit. In substance: after a twenty-five thousand *li* (six thousand miles) Long March, Mao Tse-tung and his central committee arrived in north Shansi in October 1935. In January 1937 they came to Yenan. In March 1947 (ten years later) they withdrew to avoid a Kuomintang attack. In March 1948 they left Shansi for the east. Mao was in north Shansi for thirteen years, from October 1935 to March 1948.

One thing I reaffirmed today was that people waste an unconscionable amount of time here. Despite all the slogans, I sense great inefficiency and cheerful laziness. After our "briefing" it was suggested we lunch and then start sightseeing at 3:00. (It was then 12 noon.) The siesta is a well-established habit, although they go to bed early. And on our sightseeing trip everyone ambled along, and we saw in an afternoon what could easily have been covered in an hour.

We started at the Phoenix Mountain. They call Mao's house a "cave house," which it isn't at all. It is a three-room stone house with tiled roof and nowhere near a cave. His office included a bedroom on a raised platform with a real bed (he prefers this, coming from the south, to the usual hard mat). His office had a kerosene lamp, brass ink box, and desktable. He wrote his famous "Protracted War" here. The windows are paned with paper and covered with wooden lattice work. Next to the bedstand were two large square tin boxes in which documents were carried on the Long March and which he used as a desk. The bed was covered by a quilt in cold weather. A second bedroom contained one of the northern-type stove-heated beds with a straw mat spread on a hard surface. He used this as a library. The house was destroyed by Chiang Kai-shek troops in 1947 but later restored.

Whenever the Chinese talk of Mao they call him "Chairman Mao." His picture is everywhere, and his slogans are on all public walls. It is a cult of the personality at least equal to Stalin's, whatever they say about "modesty."

We then drove to Yang Chia Ling, and on the way you could see the true poverty of China. Many men wore white turbans. They say this is a local peasant habit, but old books talk of "Turkish invaders" in this area, and the guide said there had been some "Moslems." This town is cut off from Sian and Peking except by plane or an arduous bus trip.

We first visited party headquarters, built in 1942, and saw the hall where the Seventh Party Congress met in 1945, sitting on simple unvarnished benches. All around were quotations from Mao on red placards, red banners, a huge picture of Mao and small ones of Engels, Marx, Lenin, Stalin. We were taken to a rest room where Mao used to play Ping-Pong and chess with Congress delegates.

Then we went to the real "cave house" where he lived from fall 1938 to early 1943. There is a one-room "office" with a desk, brass ink box, kerosene lamp, and two single semideck chairs. The windows are paper and lattice. The floor is hard clay. There was a towel and basin, a teapot and four simple mugs. At the back was a narrow door leading into a tunnel air raid shelter and connecting with other tunnels, an absolute fetish of Maoist strategy.

Next door is a simple bedroom with bed and mosquito net of homespun material. That was a difficult period when Mao ate mainly millet with the rest and wore rough homespuns, heavily patched. Our sweet little girl guide sang a song of the "spinning wheels" they used, in a clear, fine voice.

I was told the Yenan area people have lived in cave houses carved out of the loess cliffs for many generations; it is not just a wartime thing. It was in his house at Yang Chia Ling that Mao said all reactionaries are paper tigers and the atom bomb is a paper tiger. This attitude, I was told, "defeated the Chiang Kai-shek reactionaries armed with the planes and tanks of U.S. imperialists." He taught everyone to be tough like pine trees, flexible like willow trees.

YENAN, *October 7, 1973*

LAST night we went to a movie made in December 1965 called *Tunnel Warfare*. It was explained that *Tunnel Warfare* is an aspect of people's war that can be won only by organizing the masses. The incidents described were said to have occurred in 1942 in Hopei Province during the people's war against the Japanese occupation forces: A series of complex tunnels are built in a village which enfilade and surround the Japanese where they come in, have blocking and damming devices to prevent suffocating by poison gas or drowning when water is pumped in. Eventually the guerrillas are joined by the Eighth Route Army and win.

This morning we were driven off in our (Soviet) ZIM limousine to a series of stations of the Maoist cross, starting with the Revolutionary Museum. We drove under cloudy skies past fields of millet, sorghum, corn and vegetables.

Then we went to Mao's third residence here, driving past men and women peasants gathering sweet potatoes with mattocks, donkey-drawn barrel-carts of fertilizer (surely "night-soil"), an ox-drawn harvester. I noticed many rather Tartar-like faces and lots of white turbans, although I am earnestly told they are not "minority peoples" but Han peasants with "weatherbeaten faces."

This third residence is called the Date Garden, but the "date" trees are deciduous (not palms) and bear a small round red fruit. Mao moved here in 1943 when his former house became too noisy as they built the party hall. He remained until 1945.

We were taken to a table where Mao's eldest son reported to him after he graduated from Moscow University in 1946. Mao told him he must now go to "life's" university and sent him to work on a farm. The boy was killed at twenty-eight in Korea (1950).

After lunch a pair of student "volunteers" from Peking was produced. As I talked with them, through two interpreters, the local Communist Party official and the local interpreter took meticulous notes. The pair consisted of a girl, Ho Huei-ju, twenty-one, pretty, with pigtails, pink cheeks, a friendly smile, wearing gray jacket and darker trousers; and a boy, Su Yi-shuan, twenty-three, with glasses, wearing faded cotton dungarees. Both were carrying khaki musette bags. Both were graduated from secondary school in Peking, she at sixteen, he at eighteen. Both were working in a commune of four thousand people some seven miles away. They said they'd come here "voluntarily" in response to Chairman Mao's call in 1968 asking the educated youth to go to the country.

Su said they had been warmly welcomed when they arrived almost five years ago in the snow. "We had difficult city habits but we learned fast." He said in the cities people marry between twenty-six and thirty. In northern Shensi it was generally in the early twenties. Late marriage and family planning are now strongly encouraged.

YENAN, *October 8, 1973*

A gloomy, foggy day. Last night entertained by Tu Chin-chang, vice-chairman of the revolutionary committee of the Yenan region, at a banquet. Marina was in bed with a bad cold, so I did the family honors.

He gave a picture of an almost perfect society: no drug problem, few cases of gambling and theft, rare murders. Finally he said: "There are some thieves." He claimed that crime is dealt with by thirty men of the public security bureau.

I asked how crime was punished. He said a thief was released "after criticism" and education. He admitted there was a local jail for "class enemies or those who refuse to recant, or murderers."

Courts are run by judges "elected by the people. We have a jury system which comes from the people." The jury is made up of "three or four ordinary people." It decides on guilt or innocence and the judge sentences. Murderers are shot—by the army. Before execution there is a public meeting. The guilty person is bound and listens to denunciations. Then he is taken to "a distant place" for execution. How many men comprise a firing squad? "It only takes one man with a gun to kill," said Tu.

SIAN, *October 8, 1973*

SIAN is the capital of Shensi Province, a big city (1,400,000) whose old part is surrounded by a thick, moated wall. The Emperor used to defend the town with Tartar troops. The airport is good-sized but had very few planes, only two of which were twin-engined and none of which were jets. Sian was China's official capital from the eleventh century B.C. to A.D. 786. Most of the newer buildings are outside the wall, but we are established in a ridiculously immense "people's hotel," a complex of three large buildings. The streets are broad and paved. The slight traffic is bicycles with tricycle trucklets, trucks, buses and a few pedicabs.

SIAN, *October 9, 1973*

LAST night Lu Man, "leading member of the administrative office of the provincial [Shensi] revolutionary committee," gave us a banquet.

He is a competent, tough-looking, heavyset man in his late fifties. He wore his hair *en brosse* but longish. He was born in Nanking and was in the Red Army for years, rising to quite high rank. I asked if he commanded one thousand men, and he laughed and said "quite a lot more." When I asked if he missed the army now he said: "We serve the people. It is not a matter of personal interest. We do what the state wants."

He introduced me to the strong drink of Shensi, called *xi fen jo*. He said it is 68 percent alcohol (136 proof). Like mao-tai, it is of sorghum. He also served beer, wine and Shensi rice wine—hot, milky and only 3 percent alcohol. He himself is abstemious and took orange pop.

He told me religion is free, but "people are disinterested." He said there were some Buddhists and Taoists and "a few Christians" here. I asked if Nagel's guidebook was correct in saying there were fourteen mosques functioning. He hemmed and hawed, said yes, then changed his mind and left it hanging. I gathered that only 1 percent of the population was Moslem—that would make fourteen thousand people. He also said the Great Mosque could not be visited because it was closed for repairs. It was founded under the Tang in A.D. 742, not much more than a century after Mohammed's hegira. (When I visited the mosque today, after much pushing, I was told I was the first foreigner allowed in years and that the Moslem population of Sian is thirty-three thousand.)

❧

TODAY we rose early for an extensive sightseeing tour including a ninety-mile auto trip to the tomb of the Empress Wu. At the tombs, the first we visit is that of Princess Yung Tai.

The Princess was Wu's seventh granddaughter, and she married her cousin, Wu Yen-ji, grandnephew of the Emperor. It is said she and her husband indiscreetly gossiped about Wu and therefore were executed at a very young age. In any case, both were buried first at Lo Yang in Honan Province and, after the Empress Wu died in 706, were reburied in Chien County (therefore Chien Ling), Wu's chosen family cemetery.

Yung Tai married in 700 at the age of sixteen. Her husband died that winter and she in 701. Her father was Wu's third son and became Emperor Chung Tsung, following Wu. She was his seventh daughter. Five years after her death her body was brought here from Honan, and her father promoted her from the highest nobility to the rank of Princess.

Then we drove on a few miles to the Empress Wu's tomb, one of a group of sixteen (none of them yet excavated) on a mountainside just beyond a village where we saw several old men in old-fashioned black pajamas smoking long thin pipes. Wu's tomb on a windy hill is behind lines of stone statues of officials, generals and courtiers. She and her husband are buried deep beneath the large mound topping a small mountain.

The most interesting external feature is a cluster of about forty stone statues of envoys from abroad honoring the funeral, including one from Afghanistan and one from a small Turkestan kingdom. All stand with hands clasped in awe, and all have had their heads knocked off in past centuries. There were sixty-one ambassadors at Wu's funeral, and China then had relations with three hundred countries, our archeologist guide told us.

We then drove back to Sian and the Great Mosque near the West Gate. It is being repaired but proved quite accessible, only one building was shut (and the Moslem caretaker took us in). It looks very like a Buddhist temple, and the Hui minority people, who use it, speak Chinese to each other, said the caretaker, although they use Arabic in services. There are many Arabic inscriptions. It was built by the Tangs in 742, but the present edifices (there are several) date mainly from the end of the fourteenth century, restored in the seventeenth and eighteenth.

There is a Chinese-style minaret (unrecognizable as such) and a prayer hall (under repair) with a coffered ceiling decorated in Arabic, wooden pillars, an old altar, and a pulpit deep inside a carved, dark wooden room. Right now, during reparations, prayers are said in another building off the courtyard, and I saw some shoes left by worshippers. The caretaker was vague on whether prayers were said five times a day (I doubt it), but said there were thirty-three thousand Moslems. He described Hui (Hwei) as meaning both "Moslem" and one of the eleven minority peoples of Sinkiang, such as the Khazakhs.

SIAN, *October 10, 1973*

YESTERDAY evening we went to the big new People's Theater to see a display of acrobatics, juggling, and magicians' tricks. It was excellent.

Entered through the main lobby over which a large picture of Chairman Mao gazed benevolently. The crowd was clearly made up of workers and peasants, mostly dreary-looking, tough men, a few children. An official got up and announced "no smoking" but until the performance started people sat blithely in their chairs puffing out clouds of foul-smelling cigarette smoke.

The performance began with the lion dance, a famous old comic demonstration in which one man is dressed as the tamer and two pairs of men act the part of happy lions, inside costumes with grinning faces and orange sides. They did a marvelous balancing act on a huge rubber ball, with the two men in each lion costume coordinating perfectly.

Then came a series of acrobatics and juggling against a screen-drop background quote from Chairman Mao: "Promote physical exercise to develop the health of the people."

30

WE FLEW HERE YESTERDAY FROM SIAN, TAKING ALMOST ALL day in the process because bad weather kept delaying the plane at its various stops. First landed at the city of Cheng Chow, coming over a mountain range on to a well-farmed, windy plateau.

I was interested to note on the airfield (which is both civil and military) some fifty-five MIG-19 fighters, a few with hatches off the engines, and ground crews and pilots squatting near them, ready to fly at an instant's notice. I wonder (now that I know there's a new war in the Middle East) whether this is an early stage of emergency alert.

We took off again for Nanking, a smiling little stewardess hunting a few flies (not supposed to exist at all in modern China) with a tiny swatter. We flew across Kiangsu Province and came in at Nanking, the "southern capital" and frequently China's capital. It has a population of 1,400,000, and the site has been inhabited since 4,000 B.C. Sun Yat-sen's 1911 regime set up its base here in January 1912. Earlier it had been the seat of the Taiping rebellion. Sun Yat-sen's tomb is here.

Finally came in to Shanghai in a bad rainstorm and low clouds and were met by the usual group from the revolutionary committee and driven to the excellent, old fashioned Ching Chiang Hotel. We had a splendid two-room suite and bath and sat there with our greeters to map out a program. Then the two of us and Mrs. Wu went off to a nice "typical" small Shanghai-type restaurant to dine.

David Bruce (in bed with the flu). Mary Manners (who stayed to look after him) and Brunson and Nancy McKinley of our liaison office are here until tomorrow. The McKinleys ate at our restaurant, so we joined forces. He has been listening to VOA regularly and for the first time told us there is a bad war on in the Middle East. Egypt and Syria attacked Israel five days ago and are doing quite well, having driven across Suez through the

Bar Lev line and also through the Golan Heights, knocking down lots of planes. What a hell of a remote, cut-off place to be at a time like this!

This morning I visited Clifford Leslie, local representative of the Chartered Bank of London. He is one of two English residents of Shanghai. The other is the local representative of the Hong Kong and Shanghai Bank.

Leslie admires the present China, which has become truly self-sufficient, is "a giver, not a taker, like India and other countries. They have pride."

I started by asking what is the basis of money here, how it is connected with other world currencies. He said he didn't really know, but his bank suspected some link with Comecon money levels. The rates of exchange do alter from time to time. The sterling rate has changed 20 percent in nineteen months and a pound is now worth only 4.63 yuan, whereas it was previously worth well over 5.5 yuan. There is some formula—which he doesn't know—to keep the yuan in line with currencies abroad. Nor does he have any idea of how much money there is in circulation, or what foreign currency or gold reserves are. He said the interest paid on savings accounts is between 2.5 percent and 3 percent. The figures I had been given were really 1.9 percent and 2.7 percent.

There are two Chinese banks—the People's Bank and the Bank of China. The People's Bank has branches all over the country and is for savings accounts. Shops are grouped in blocs and have accounts with the People's Bank. They can have two kinds of checking account, cash or transfers. The Bank of China concerns itself only with internal trade and exports and imports. It has branches in Hong Kong, London, had one in Singapore, is opening one in Beirut. It has offices in big Chinese cities. It finances all trade.

Foreign banks are confined to China's export trade. If China wants to export something to the United States a foreign bank can get involved. Supposing, after the Canton trade fair, an American firm arranges a major contract. It would open a letter of credit with the Chartered Bank or the Hong Kong and Shanghai, and then the local offices here would work their way through the bureaucracy and finally produce necessary documents to conclude the deal.

No American bank is allowed by Peking to do business in this country yet. The Bank of China authorized eight other foreign banks to operate; Pakistani, Swiss, and others of this group work through offices in New York. When David Rockefeller came here he tried to get Chase National a permit to do business in China, but there has not yet been full agreement on this.

SHANGHAI, *October 12, 1973*

TOOK a three-hour boat trip down the Huang Po River to its confluence with the Yangtse and then back up to the Bund, where we had embarked.

It was a gusty, wet day with the dun-colored river choppy. The Bund, with its prewar massive gray British buildings (from the British concession), gives one a feeling that it is a preview of the future Hong Kong. The great former banks and mercantile establishments are hung with red placards of Chairman Mao's sayings, and the old hotels and clubs have been turned to new uses—as will undoubtedly be true in superdeveloped Hong Kong when the lease ends on its land territories. Incidentally, our newspaper ideologist, who accompanies us on all tours, says there is a Polish consulate in Shanghai; there used to be a Soviet one but it's closed.

Our captain joined us, a pleasant, efficient, intelligent fellow who started out as a seaman in tugs. He said Shanghai can take at its docksides ships up to 60,000 tons. In 1972 a Norwegian freighter of that size was here. Each day thirty ships move in and out. Today, he said, was average. It was very busy. There have been *no* U.S. ships here since 1949, said the captain, nor were there any today. However, Shanghai trades with 130 countries.

This afternoon I was taken off to a shipyard while Marina went to see workers' homes, including a children's home in the former house of a Baghdad-Jewish millionaire. Most impressed. The kids were taught all kinds of things. A seven-year-old learned that she was very happy because her grandparents, at her age, were either starving or begging. (Correct, I'm sure!)

SHANGHAI, *October 13, 1973*

MARINA went to a concert with Mrs. Wu and the local officials assigned to us, while I worked. Here is her report.

Song and Dance Performance

Philharmonic: music called "The Happiness of the Tenth Party Congress" spreads everywhere. Chinese traditional music. Dance. Weaving the nets to catch fish for the people. Music. Solo on so-na a kind of trumpet.

Dance: The red guards on the railway. A young guard on the railway. A maintenance man comes along, and gives him his own coat, as it is snowing. A bad guy sneaks in and tries to sabotage the lines, but the young guard overpowers him and at the risk of his own life saves the train.

Solo tenor: "I love the great beautiful landscape of the motherland." Praise of Peking.

Orchestra: In praise of the Red Banner. Dance. The Tai-Ping rebellion bow and arrow dance. Soprano solo. "Brightness of Tenth Party Congress shines in all our hearts."

THIS morning [October 13] I had a very interesting meeting with the editors of Shanghai's leading newspaper, who attempted to explain the reasons for the current campaign of criticism against Confucius. The people I met at *Wen Huei Bao*, with the largest circulation of the two journals in Shanghai, including: Shen Kuo-hsiang, vice-director (and apparently actual editor); a tallish man in a gray Mao suit, with solemn face and hair *en brosse*, about fifty or more; Chou Bing-chuan, in charge of stringers (whose functions will be explained); Chang Chi-cheng, in charge of theory and ideology; Chang Li-kang, in charge of literature and education; and our friend Hsia Shu-tsai, assistant to Chang Chi-cheng and our escort in Shanghai.

Shen then began his briefing on Confucius, which I had requested. From time to time he was joined or aided by Chang Chi-cheng, a bright young man. According to Shen, Confucius lived from 551 to 479 B.C. in the state of Lu, during the "period of the spring and autumn annals," and was a second son, which is why he was named Kung Chiu (Kung, apparently being "second"). Shen then said:

> Confucius was a spokesman for the declining slave-owning system at a time when the new landlord class had just emerged. The landlord class represented an advance and sought to overthrow the slave-owning class. The landlord class was a progressive force at that time. But Confucius tried his best to oppose them. He spent his entire life propagating reactionary views.
>
> He ran a private school where he trained students to serve his reactionary purposes. Even then, in his own time, many people opposed him. Hsao Cheng-mao opposed him, and Confucius, who was then minister of justice for Lu, had him executed. The people who opposed the confucianists were called "legalists."
>
> The struggle against his reactionary thoughts started during his very lifetime and there has always been criticism of Confucius since then, for twenty-five centuries. Whenever a reactionary ruler tried to consolidate his position he would cite Confucius as an example but those who favored a new social system opposed confucianism. Confucianists always opposed reform, were conservative, and wished to restore the old regime.
>
> The May 4 movement begun in 1919, which started out with attacks on Confucius, led to the Chinese Communist party that was started in Shanghai in 1921. The May 4 movement had two slogans: anti-imperialism and anti-feudalism, down with confucianism.
>
> Chairman Mao repudiated Confucius from his early years, and in 1927 he specifically denounced confucianism's four bonds: that of god over man, that of prince over subject, that of father over son, that of husband over wife. In 1939, Chairman Mao, in an article on the orientation of youth, again repudiated Confucius; and still again in 1940 in an article printed in *New Democracy*. After the 1949 liberation he continued this line, stating that those who wanted to restore the old order cited Confucius. But Confucius supported a reactionary hierarchical system.
>
> Liu Shao-chi, our greatest capitalist-roader, continually used confucianism as an excuse and propagated his thoughts. He was a real believer in Confucius. He actually wrote a book frequently quoting Confucius. Liu always

used Confucius as his reason for endorsing any reactionary line. Therefore, when we criticize Liu, we must criticize Confucius.

The same is true of Lin Piao. He also cited Confucius often in his speeches although he didn't write a book. Therefore if we criticize Lin, we must also criticize Confucius. Lin's thought is confucianism—reactionary conclusions based on subjective theory rather than on objective experience.

You must realize that socialism is a long, protracted historical stage, and therefore the ideological struggle must be long and protracted; so will the criticism of Confucius.

We are aware that future revisionists and bourgeois agents in our party will also make use of Confucius. This is a matter of political philosophy, not religion. Confucius believed in God, but confucianism is not a religion, it is a form of political philosophy.

We believe that bourgeois agents within our party will use confucianism against our ideology and therefore we will go on criticizing him. In this way we root out the remnants of the exploiting classes in an ideological sense. The struggle against Liu and Lin has ended organizationally; but it has not ended ideologically. Although their two bourgeois centers inside the party have been destroyed, their ideas still poison the minds of some people.

But you must remember that in our party criticism of Confucius was not just recently revived. It began as a revival even before the cultural revolution started in 1966.

Shen then said that the Soviet Union is now boosting Confucius a great deal "and making him into a saint. The 1965 edition of the Great Soviet Encyclopedia praised him, and in the March and June issues of *Questions of History* this year, Confucius was highly praised. Moscow is advocating a reactionary ideology and uses Confucius as the theoretical basis to oppose our government and policy.

"Confucianism is a theoretical base for support of Liu and Lin. The Russians would like to see the restoration of old order people like Liu and Lin who represent the bourgeoisie. Ideologically, Liu and Lin are linked."

I said everyone knew Lin was dead but asked where Liu was. All insisted they didn't know. Odd!

HANGCHOW, *October 14, 1973*

WE took a train to here from Shanghai last evening; about three hours. The train absolutely packed in the "hard" class, with people standing up and bundles all over the place. There was a huge group of Japanese tourists (some sort of mission), but they were easily absorbed together with us in the large "soft" cars, which are sleepers with four bunks, where we sat and were continually served tea.

Having had no supper, I got Mrs. Wu to write out "mineral water and a sandwich" and went to the diner. This proved to be filled with simple tables covered with blue oilcloth; there were lots of folding metal chairs.

Each table bore a pot of growing flowers (not cut), two bottles of Tsing-tao beer and two bottles of Chinese rosé grape wine (as distinguished from rice wine), never corked but capped just like the beer. They had no mineral water but gave me hot tea. The sandwich was a jam omelet between two thick pieces of bread.

The train was very, very slow with poor springs. There were long stops at many stations. Marina and Mrs. Wu showed each other various games of solitaire. Chinese cards are precisely like ours. Mrs. Wu said Chinese play both ordinary bridge and their own version as well as other games including poker—so long as they don't gamble, which is forbidden.

Today is Sunday, the usual day off for most people (although rest days are staggered in communes and factories), and the numerous parks were filled. I saw young people and children sitting on the green lawns beneath weeping willows, a few with transistor radios blaring Chinese music.

We went to Three Towers Reflecting the Moon Island, which contains its own little lake covered with lotus leaves, across which arch stone bridges with tiled roofs. In the walls of pavilions are cut little windows in which are carvings of terra-cotta birds: cranes, eagles, swans, crows. Some water lilies were still in bloom beside the lotus leaves. There were also (nonflowering) iris plants. We were taken to a modern teahouse in the old style set beside ancient pavilions. Inside it were hanging several bird cages with parrots from Szechuan, canaries, lovebirds, and a fat mynah bird.

Hangchow is the capital of the province of Chekiang. The southern Sung dynasty made its court here. It is covered with canals and ponds which are used for fish-raising.

Hangchow probably has a population of 750,000 now but gives a sleepy appearance, as if it were far smaller. In A.D. 1270 it had 900,000 as a Sung capital and was so crowded that many tall houses, up to five or even ten stories, were built. Marco Polo described it as "the greatest city which may be found in the world, where so many pleasures may be found that one fancies himself to be in Paradise." Even in his day the Western Lake was famous for its fleet of pleasure boats.

The Mongols captured it in 1276 and assimilated it into their Yuan (dynasty) empire. Odoric da Pordenone came here in the fourteenth century and called the city "greater than any in the world."

In the afternoon we drove to the Ling Yin Temple, built in the fourth century by an Indian Buddhist monk, from which Buddhism spread rapidly in this area. The temple has been repaired so often that I wonder if any of the original remains; the present specimen is certainly twentieth century, although along olden lines. On the way we passed a rock hill, covered with shrubbery, called Peak-Flying-from-Afar because it supposedly reminded the monk of a hill in his native country. It is filled with carvings of more than two hundred Buddhas, cut out during the Sung and Ming dynasties.

From there we drove through lovely parks and a botanical garden to the

Jade Fountain. We entered this group of buildings through a courtyard and a miniature rock garden filled with tiny pine trees. On the walls were calligraphies of some of Mao Tse-tung's poems. In an artificial walled pool swam large goldfish and the hugest carp I have ever seen, many over four feet long and surely weighing more than seventy pounds. Everyone crowded around to feed these hundreds of fish chopped-up bits of pumpkin. They lazily gobbled these off the surface, clambering over each other, looking for all the world like lost souls in Hell. I was told that originally this pool had been started within the temple to release fish that had been caught, as a token of kindness and humanity.

HANGCHOW, *October 15, 1973*

THIS morning we drove to the Liu-he Pagoda on a hill facing the Chien Tang River. It was built in the Sung dynasty and was more than one thousand years old but has often been restored. It is of brick and wood, octagonal in shape, and looks like thirteen stories from the outside but is actually only seven stories high inside. It served as a lighthouse for ships, and, according to superstition, it calmed the tides.

We took tea in a pavilion. The water there is so filled with minerals that careful pouring can make it rise above the surface of a cup without spilling and light coins will float on its surface (as a smiling waitress showed us). While we were doing this, the counselor of the Soviet Embassy in Peking came by with two Chinese guides. I spotted him as a Russian, talked to him in my pidgin, introducing myself, and he said: "I hope you won't write any nonsense like Mister X [referring, I suppose to X's constant predictions that Russia is going to launch a blitz against China]."

Our guides said the best thing imaginable was to drink Dragon Well tea made with Tiger Spring water as we were doing.

PEKING, *October 15, 1973*

WE took off on the return flight to Peking in a large Ilyushin-62 jet. The Russian diplomat we had met at the pavilion was aboard the plane. As we walked past him to our seats he boasted: "Now you are on a Soviet plane."

Later he came and sat beside me. He introduced himself as Mikhail Ivanov, sixty-one, born and bred in Moscow, a career diplomat. I had a feeling he was a spook: a burly, big, snub-nosed man with ready smile and graying hair. He told me he had been in Peking four years and was leaving soon. He couldn't wait. His wife has already returned to Moscow to look after their nineteen-year-old daughter, who is studying to be a pianist. He also has a married thirty-year-old son, an aircraft engineer.

He hates it here, feels cut off and is almost stir-crazy. He says the Chinese are all "dogmatic and that when Mao says something is white they all say it's white, no matter what color it is." I was tempted to remind him of his own country. He said Mao disliked Stalin while he was alive but once he was dead found it convenient to make him a hero. He added that he personally had liked Khrushchev (now disliked in Russia and hated here) "because he was human and he did a lot for us."

When we arrived in Peking Mr. Yü was at the airport to meet us. Another Boeing 707 (the second brought to Peking of the ten the Chinese have bought) was being towed past our IL-62. "Thank God we've got your Boeings," said Yü. I remonstrated and said the IL-62 was a copy of the British VC-10 and a fine plane. "It's tail-heavy," he told me. "Every time they take off we have to pump six tons of water into the nose first to balance it." I had noticed that all the rear rows of seats were empty and the tops turned forward to keep them so. David also said he had heard the same thing.

HUHEHOT, INNER MONGOLIA, *October 16, 1973*

WE flew up here this morning on a lovely, bright, cold autumn day. Huhehot (Hu-he-hao-te, in Chinese) is the capital of the Autonomous Region of Inner Mongolia, a northernmost part of China, bordering the Outer Mongolian People's Republic, a Soviet satellite. (Manchuria goes much farther north but is well east of here.) The airport was decorated with Mongolian letters, which are phonetic but certainly look to me like ideograms, although they aren't.

We were met by a committee of three, including two Han Chinese and one Mongolian named Dergöl, vice-director for foreign affairs of the regional revolutionary committee, a quiet, pleasant man, quite solidly built, who is a Mongol but came from Manchuria. Mrs. Wu said he speaks Han Chinese with a good accent.

We passed horses grazing on the plain under the Great Blue Mountains. The name of the city is Hu-Ho ("blue") Hao-te ("city"), and it was first settled about four hundred years ago. They have found a few relics of Han Chinese, but before the Yuan dynasty there was no Mongolian nationality, said Dergöl (a statement later contradicted at the university we visited). The houses are of clay brick for the most part. In the grasslands people live in felt tents called *yurts*. The main livestock is sheep, horses, some camels (Bactrian).

On the way Dergöl said *kumyss* the Mongol nomad's drink (fermented mare's milk), is never bottled, therefore it can be found only in summer when the mares have foaled and are in milk; it is homebrewed. We passed little Mongolian ponies from which sheep are herded. The coldest part of the year is at minus thirty degrees centigrade; the hottest is thirty-two degrees centigrade. The average altitude of the plateau is one thousand meters.

Dergöl told me the total population of Inner Mongolia was 8 million, with only 420,000 Mongols, 80,000 Huei, and 20,000 Manchu plus a handful of other minorities.

This area was famous for its Tibetan-style monasteries, the Sino-Tibetan style (like the Da jao, Huhehot's five-pagoda monastery), and Chinese style. Of old buildings recommended by Nagel's, Dergöl said all but one no longer existed. Gone with the wind—or rather the revolution—apparently during the last decade at most. The only one left, according to Dergöl, is Wu ta si, a monastery famous for its pagoda.

Dergöl claims the Mongol population of the region has increased from only 180,000 in 1947. (He doesn't "know" what the region's total population was then.) The second lack of information implies Peking is stuffing the place with Han Chinese.

The Mongolian language and Han Chinese are both official. One-twentieth of the population, according to Dergöl, is Mongolian, but it has equality of language. A special theatrical group called the Red Artistic Cavalry rides around the villages and *yurts* in trucks to entertain the people with music and dancing.

Dergöl said there used to be many diseases, above all plague and syphilis. Both have been wiped out. "That's why the Mongolian population has increased so much." He said that here the "barefoot doctors" of the regular Chinese communes are called "horseback doctors" and actually do ride horses; there are thirteen thousand of them.

After lunch we went to the University of Inner Mongolia, quite a large group of buildings but dreadfully bare and drab and cold. Dergöl went with us, and we were introduced to Yang Wang-fu, vice-chairman of the university's revolutionary committee; Shi Yun, director of research on Mongolian history; Chingertai, director of the Mongolian Language Department; (Mrs.) Liu Hsu-ching, of the administrative staff; and Sun Chao-wen, also of the administrative staff. Chingertai was the only Mongolian of the five.

The university staff told me there was "a feeling of brotherhood" between the people of the two Mongolias. Dergöl said that historically Outer Mongolia used to be part of China. It didn't get its independence until 1921, and China recognized this in 1945 (the Chiang Kai-shek regime). I asked if there was a desire for unity. Chingertai said: "If one day there were another revolution in Outer Mongolia or the world became communist, the present situation would be different."

They grudgingly admitted that Genghis Khan was esteemed highly by many Mongolians, sometimes as a hero, even a deity. Chingertai said: "Our professors regard Genghis Khan in two ways. Before him this was a divided country, split by wars. He unified it and created a Mongolian nationality. And he created a written Mongolian language. But he had class defects. He was a nobleman with selfish class interests and waged aggressive wars." He added there were various estimates as to the total number of Mongols in Genghis' time—from 500,000 to 1 million.

I asked what kind of propaganda was beamed here from Outer Mongolia. The answer: "There was a period after liberation when relations were very friendly. Then the Outer Mongolian government followed the Soviet revisionists and this caused difficult relations. They attack us now in their press and radio. But our people are still ready for friendly relations."

We saw students sitting in class, the few Mongols in their own costume standing out against the drab Han Chinese. The Mongol girls wore splendid blue and pink silk robes, the boys wore black with gold embroidery and high collars. I noticed that signs on all room doors were in two languages.

When we drove away from the university we passed many small, thickset Mongolian ponies. Dergöl said they grew heavy coats in winter. Some carts were hauled by twin-humped Bactrian camels, one pulling, another tethered behind, in each case. They were driven by peasants in sheepskin-lined coats. Others drove carts pulled by three horses, two ahead, then another just behind them. We went through the old part of town (not very old) built of low, dried clay houses, and visited a carpet factory.

Dergöl gave us dinner: fine Mongolian food with lots of fat mutton. He talked about his days as a youth in Manchuria, his birthplace, where the Japanese occupying forces practiced a policy of "three alls": kill all, burn all, destroy all.

The wine we had was called Princess Shao Jün, in honor of a Han princess who married a Hun chieftain two thousand years ago. She is now hailed as a symbol of unity.

Dergöl told us of an August sporting season when the grasslands people hold a competition called *Nadamu*, which includes horse racing, archery, wrestling, and riflery. He said that apart from *kumyss* (from the Russian word for yoghurt), they drink *arekh*, a wine made of cow's milk or horse's milk. They also have a sorghum drink stronger than mao-tai called erkuoto. (Later I bought two bottles of another Mongolian sorghum booze for David Bruce, called *harerh*—"black wine.")

Dergöl said Mongolian silk (for robes) and tea (in bricks) comes from southern China. The Chinese buy Mongolian mutton and fabricated goods here. The favorite Mongolian sport is horse racing. Next come archery or riflery, then wrestling. Dergöl said the grasslands people are sturdier than city folk. The average calorie intake is two thousand a day.

HUHEHOT, *October 17, 1973*

BEFORE starting off on the day's tour, checked Stuart Schram's *Mao Tsetung* and find Mao mentioned Genghis Khan twice in his writing, once in a poem and another time in 1935 when he appealed to the Inner Mongolians, saying: "We are persuaded that it is only by fighting together with us that the people of Inner Mongolia can preserve the glory of the epoch of Genghis Khan, prevent the extermination of their nation."

(A large poster again shows Chinese soldiers fighting the Russians on the Ussuri River.)

We then drove to the Wu ta si Pagoda, which used to be part of a monastery. Apart from the five-tower pagoda, the monastery like all others here, has disappeared.

On the way Dergöl described to us how in the grasslands area horses are rounded up with a special Mongolian lasso—a five-meter-long wooden pole at the end of which is a three-meter rope, ending in a noose.

Wu ta si is quite small, a Buddhist temple. We entered through a schoolyard, where hundreds of children were doing setting-up exercises to music. The pagoda seems only about twenty meters high, has five towers. Wu ta si means "five pagados" in both Han and Mongolian, I was told. The style was described as Indian, but the writing on the walls is Mongolian and Tibetan.

Dergöl told us Mongolian lamas used to study in Tibet. Lamas from Tibet first introduced Buddhism here during the Yuan dynasty, but it wasn't popular. Then the Ming dynasty popularized it so "each family could keep only one son at home, the rest becoming lamas and not marrying." A large proportion of the population became lamas and lived off the people.

We drove out to the tomb of Shao Jün at a place called Baishihu, passing some old crones with tiny bound feet. As we drove Dergöl said he had checked and the 1947 population of Inner Mongolia was 3,160,000 (showing they imported many Han Chinese since). He acknowledged many Han "workers" had been brought in.

Finally we arrived along the plateau at a round high tumulus with a modern pavilion on top. This is the tomb of Princess Shao Jün, who married the Hun King ruling this part of Mongolia. Hops were growing on vines before the tumulus. The commune at this place is called Peach Blossom. It was here that the Hun King had his nomadic capital, a city of yurts, and Shao Jün was brought here from Sian, then the Han Chinese capital, about 33 B.C.

Dergöl said the Huns were great fighters "but the people suffered heavily and demanded peace." The Han Emperor decided on a policy of intermarriage. He gave a court lady-in-waiting the title of princess and married her off to Hohansheh, the Hun King. The Hans and Huns stopped fighting then, and 33 B.C. was declared by the Emperor as the "First Year of the Frontier Peace."

The Huns started moving westward. The east Han Emperor defeated the Huns and shattered them in the first century A.D. They disappeared from Chinese history. Their remnants were either assimilated by Hans, Tartars (a Mongol branch), and Mongols, or they rode westward.

Shao Jün was born in Hopei Province. The Han Emperor sent a portrait painter around to paint the beauties he saw. The families of these girls usually paid him bribes so as to gain prestige through their daughters, but

Shao Jün didn't pay up as she came from a poor family. He painted her very ugly instead, so the Emperor didn't make her a concubine. She was simply made a lady-in-waiting. When the Prime Minister suggested the Emperor send a daughter to marry the Hun King, Hohansheh, who had his capital some kilometers from Baishihu (Bashiga in Mongolian), the Emperor balked. He hated losing a daughter so, at random, selected Shao Jün and promoted her from lady-in-waiting to princess.

However, before she left he received her to say farewell. When he saw her loveliness he was appalled that such a great beauty had not been brought to his attention. Reluctantly he let her go—and had the painter executed. Shao Jün is one of the four great beauties in Chinese history. Her marriage promoted peace and intermarriages among the border peoples. She had several children. Her tomb is called the Green Tomb because the tumulus rose green against the desert, not too far from the Hun capital.

After lunch we were taken to the race course to see an exhibition of riding. The leader of an "equestrian team," a heavyset Mongol from the grasslands, with low black boots, met us and took us up to a reviewing stand, where we were given the inevitable tea and then a pair of Zeiss (Jena) binoculars. First we witnessed performances of sabering targets at a gallop, beginning with one saber, then riders with sabers in each hand, leaving the reins loose. The horses are close-coupled, strong, with long manes and tails. Men and girls rode, all wearing Mongol robes, the girls with long pants underneath and pigtails. They wore low black boots.

Next came hurdle-jumping, jumping through a flaming hoop, trick riding: standing in one stirrup, then balancing on the hands, body above and parallel to the horse's back, lying athwart the horse, both feet and one arm in the air, standing up in the saddle, hands raised, balanced on one hand, one foot, then standing on one foot, holding one hand up, the other clutching a short rope tied to a saddle ring. Horses galloped by with the riders hidden on the far side of them; then the riders stood on their heads at a gallop, swung from side to side, touching the ground, at a gallop. They are marvelous horsemen here and play polo quite a lot, the equestrian team leader said. Dergöl added: "They are small but very strong and brave." How true.

Then we were taken to the projection room of a film unit and saw two movies, the first made in 1973, the second in 1972. The first was called *Conquering the Desert and Building the Grasslands;* the second, *Nadamu Festival in August.*

I noticed in the film that in the grasslands everyone wears silk robes, fur-lined in cold weather, with sashes, trousers, and the men usually in caps, sometimes men and/or women in turbans. The desert is very windy and barren. It was impressive to see how they developed it, harnessing the dunes with hardy plants, fencing off the herds of sheep and goats, horses and camels. The horsemen rode about with their pole-lassos and broke wild horses bareback. The *yurts* looked quite warm and comfortable, erected on scaffolding of zigzag poles. Many of the saddles were cavalry-type, with high cantle and pommel.

At the end of the film we saw militia guarding the northern frontier against Soviet threats while harvesters worked and herds of camels, sheep, horses and cattle grazed.

TATUNG, *October 18, 1973*

WE arrived last midnight by train from Mongolia and were met by the usual friendly delegation from the local revolutionary committee, who took us to an immense hotel. In the morning we went off with our delegation. We first drove through the broad avenues by the Stalinist buildings of modern Tatung, and then past the low one-story houses of the older quarter. This was the capital of the northern Wei dynasty (A.D. 420–589), when China was partitioned in two.

First we visited the famous Nine Dragon Screen built during the Ming dynasty (1368–1644), which is more than five hundred years old (although restored). It was designed to protect the palace of the royal governor from the public gaze. The dragons symbolize imperial rule.

Tatung was strategically important against the Mongols, and the first Ming Emperor, who had ousted the Mongol Yuan dynasty, kept his ablest son here because he was worried about the traditional enemy. The Great Wall is only forty kilometers north; there is a section of wall also one hundred kilometers south, built as additional protection for Shansi and Hopei Provinces. This is the only section of the Great Wall with a double length of fortification.

Tatung is an ancient city. It was once occupied by the Huns, the scourge of north China. It often changed hands and was sacked, despite the Great Wall. For two hundred years it was the western capital and second city in the empire.

After lunch we went to the Yun Kang grotto, west of Tatung in a valley of sandstone cliffs with huge carvings that reminded me greatly of the Egyptian Valley of the Kings at Luxor. These carvings were begun by the northern Wei dynasty in A.D. 460 on an escarpment of the Wu Jo Mountains. The entire set of caves is one kilometer long from east to west, includes fifty-three caves and 51,000 statues. The grotto is one of the three most famous cave groups in China. All the Buddhas in all the caves have the long ears and wide shoulders described in scripture. In some, coal seams showed through the sandstone where paint had faded.

To my horror I was told the Japanese army (here from 1937 to 1945) used this grotto as stables.

TATUNG, *October 19, 1973*

JUST before we started off on a grim morning we were told that we are the first Americans to come here. There have been very few foreigners, also, except for the visit last month of President Pompidou's party.

We visited what is called the "Ten Thousand Man Pit," where I had assumed ten thousand corpses had been chucked in by the Japanese. Only later, after seeing two such pits and hearing there were over twenty in the country around Shansi and Manchurian mines, did I remember that "ten thousand" is figurative for "many."

Under the Japanese the miners and their families were housed in isolated compounds surrounded by barbed wire. They were beaten, ill-fed, and often died of diseases like cholera. Some rebelled and were thrown alive into pits, like those we saw. We were shown photos of skeletons indicating they had had their hands and feet severed before death. The exact number of bodies has never been counted because there were many small pits, and lots of corpses were just left in the barren hills; others were incinerated.

In the entrance to a former mine shaft under glass and lit by electricity, were masses of skeletons, but, all told, I don't think there were more than a hundred or so. They were in all positions of death and pretty dreadful-looking, dust-tan bones against dust-tan earth. I was told miners during the Japanese occupation often died after two or three months' work.

The Japanese murdered more than sixty thousand men in the mines of the Tatung area alone between 1937 and 1945. There were pitiful paper flower wreaths at the entrance to the second pit, sent by various Chinese groups.

PEKING, *October 21, 1973*

I GATHER from David that the United States is in a pretty deep freeze here because of our support of Israel in the current Mideast war. China is in the odd position of backing the same Arab clients as Russia, while hammering away at Moscow.

Although Kissinger supposedly arrives in five days, none of the details has yet been arranged.

PEKING, *October 22, 1973*

DAVID Bruce gave a most agreeable dinner party last night, and then Nick Platt, one of the exceptionally bright and agreeable members of his Chinese-speaking batch of diplomats, sang and played the guitar. At dinner his wife told me their youngest son goes to a Pakistani school here run for English-speaking students. No Chinese children are allowed in the

large apartment house compound where the Platts and other foreign diplomats live. In fact, no Chinese without a special pass can get in.

She told me that when people are executed here (by shooting) their
bodies are almost always reviled, with the masses enthusiastically pissing
and spitting on them. Appalling.

David made the interesting remark that China captures the Third World
by banquets—giving vast entertainments to all the Third World leaders
coming here, even those from the weakest, tiniest states.

PEKING, *October 23, 1973*

YESTERDAY afternoon Ma invited me for tea—with Yü and Mrs. Wu, as
usual, in attendance. Ma was very friendly, and it soon became clear that
he wished to know what I wanted to ask Prime Minister Chou En-lai in
case the latter receives me. I am beginning to get a feeling that at long last,
just before I go, I will be admitted to the presence.

This afternoon we went to the Summer Palace built by the last Empress
Dowager late in the nineteenth century after Lord Elgin had had the old
one burned down. It was a clear, cold, sunny autumn day with a high
wind. We went in the dark red main gate past a pair of bronze lions, past a
large rock of the sort ancient Chinese and modern American arts-and-
crafters admire, past a Chinese two-horned unicorn, to the red-walled
throne room. The throne is a big yellow, padded armchair, surrounded by
twelve gray cloisonné cranes and two green phoenixes as well as four large
gilt incense burners. The ceiling is in the classical style of brightly painted
panels.

Finally we saw the famous Marble Boat which the Empress had built in
the water with misappropriated navy funds, a squat monstrosity, with
stone paddle wheels on the side, a tiled main deck.

PEKING, *October 24, 1973*

VISITED the headquarters of the 196th Infantry Division today, just outside Tientsin, off the Yellow Sea, North China's largest port.

Along the road we were met by a car bearing a divisional officer who
spoke quite fluent but terribly accented French, and he led the way, his
white military license plates flashing in front of us.

The divisional deputy commander, Geng Yü-chi, took charge of us
(Marina, Mrs. Wu and myself). He is a youthful-looking, stocky man with
an air of competence. I later found out he is forty-three, his rank approxi-
mates that of brigadier general, and he has been in the army twenty-eight
years.

We were taken first to the 578th Battalion barracks and club, where a
continuous briefing began. The 196th Infantry Division was formed in

had had no effect on discipline. All officers and men saluted each other on the basis that the first to see the other saluted.

A normal division is "more than ten thousand men," and is composed of five regiments, three of infantry, one of artillery, one armored. There are three battalions in each regiment and five companies in a battalion: There are eighty tanks in a full-strength division's armored regiment and forty artillery pieces in its artillery regiment, of which the heaviest are 120 millimeter. The division is flexible, and its punch can be reinforced by corps or army tanks and guns.

An ordinary soldier enlists as a volunteer for three years' service. He can reenlist, or be kept on by order. The requirements for admission are: (1) a man must be politically orthodox; (2) he must volunteer to serve; (3) he must be approved by his local revolutionary committee.

There is no need for conscription here. The population is so enormous that the government can easily choose from the best of those who volunteer. The divisional staff is organized basically like that of a Western division, with a chief of staff, intelligence, operations, logistics, etc., except there are political commissars at every level from divisional commander down.

I asked if there was any special "alert" nowadays because of Soviet fulminations. (I didn't notice any, myself.) I was told: "The division must always maintain a high vigilance. The tenth party congress called upon the armed forces to be prepared. We are always on the alert and highly vigilant. We are calm but we are only on the defensive. We build tunnels but the Russians talk about our 'threat'."

Geng admitted that nowadays "our political education courses stress Russia—both in our class struggle education courses and our situation education courses."

After lunch we were taken to a reviewing stand, where we watched a series of exercises with live ammunition: firing semiautomatic rifles, machine guns, bazookas (at a moving target), mortars and dummy bayonet fighting. They are tough, trim-looking soldiers. Everything was done efficiently, and those participating trotted to and from each operation.

PEKING, *October 25, 1973*

DAVID told me today of the difficulty of doing business here. Nixon sent him a message with a letter for Chou which Bruce was supposed to deliver in person. He tried, couldn't get an appointment, after a time began to get queries from Washington: What was the response? At last, in desperation, he gave it to his friend Chiao, the Deputy Foreign Minister. Delivery to Chou was subsequently acknowledged but no precise answer ever given.

Had a talk with an expert of our mission. He told me there are now about 2,800,000 people in the Chinese armed forces—not including the

1937 out of Red Army guerrilla veterans in the Shansi–Hopei border area. By 1945 it had been fleshed out to a full division.

The mission was described as follows: "We have to fight for the liberation of the classes and the freedom of the nation. Chairman Mao is our commander as supreme commander of the armed forces."

The 196th fought eight years against the Japanese around Shansi and Hopei; then it fought against the Kuomintang for three years during the Civil War of Liberation. In 1950 the division was sent to Korea as one of the first units of the Chinese "volunteer army" and fought the Americans. All told, in its history, the division has killed 38,000 adversaries, captured more than 370 guns and more than 16,000 machine guns and small arms.

During peacetime it follows Mao's instructions of being at the same time a fighting force, a work team, and a production team. It is a school for training the masses. One of the briefing officers said: "We study political, military, and cultural subjects, but primarily we are a fighting force. As a working force we organize propaganda teams that travel around and we also help the people with industrial and agricultural production. We send out cadres to help build up the militia forces with training. And above all we try to be self-sufficient. We produce some of our own food and we furnish other materials to the state in order to be less of a burden. We follow Chairman Mao's principles: (1) to integrate officers and men; (2) to integrate army and people; (3) to disintegrate the enemy."

There is allegedly no difference in the status of officers and men, none of whom wear any rank insignia (the officers have four pockets, the men only two). Men are encouraged to criticize officers. I was told: "Military democracy means that only ability counts, both in training and in fighting." The food for officers and men is the same. Men don't have their wives around, however, whereas officers apparently have theirs working in the various work-shop projects of the division.

The army is especially on the alert to ward off the influence of antiparty cliques like those of Chen Du-shiu (party Secretary around 1926–1927, purged as a rightist); Wang Ming (both a "left" and a "right" opportunist in the early thirties); Peng Te-huai (Minister of Defense from 1953 to 1959, who "wanted to minimize party control of the army"); Liu Shao-chi and Lin Piao.

To stress this ideological purity, I was assured: "By struggling against deviationists we can guarantee that our army won't change colors and become like the Soviet army which served the revisionist party of Khrushchev."

At lunch, Geng told me that between 1955 and 1965 the Chinese army had ranks and insignia like other armies, but "we found it didn't correspond to our traditions. It had a bad effect on the relations of officers and men." He said the return to a system without grades of officer (only titles like division commander or deputy battalion commander) or insignia militia and paramilitary units. He thinks there are about 140 to 150 infantry and artillery divisions and another 20 engineering and support divisions. The ground forces are organized in thirty-six field armies of which each includes approximately three divisions. Extra divisions go to corps and armies.

He estimated the Russians now have from 600,000 to 700,000 men in the China military region. Incidentally, he said China has two kinds of extra divisions—old-fashioned horse cavalry and special divisions trained for being carried by aircraft, which means that they are lighter divisions than the by-now usual parachute and airborne variety.

ABOARD PLANE FROM PEKING TO PARIS, *October 27, 1973*

YESTERDAY we invited our trio of official nursemaids, Ma, Yü, and Mrs. Wu, to lunch at David Bruce's. The lunch was pleasant, but a certain pall was cast over the affair by the fact that, although I arrived in Peking September 27, a month ago, and it was known I wished to see Premier Chou En-lai, we hadn't had an answer; neither yes nor no.

At 7:40 P.M. the phone rang. It was Yü saying the appointment was on—for Marina as well as me—and would we please be at Mrs. Wu's hotel room at 8:20 P.M. in order to wait there for a signal from Ma, which would alert us to go straight to the Great Hall of the People, where the meeting would occur. My hired car would be at the U.S. liaison office, where we live, at 8:05. We arrived in Mrs. Wu's room at the scheduled moment.

We stayed there only a few minutes before the phone rang and we were instructed to proceed to the Great Hall. We actually arrived there and were talking to Chou less than an hour after our first alert. All told, we were with him for about two hours and a quarter. In addition to Chou, Marina, and myself, there was an interpreter; Ma; Mrs. Wu (poor Yü, who had done so much for us, wasn't invited); Chu Mu-chi, head of the Hsinhua news agency; Mrs. Wang Chen, deputy director of the Foreign Ministry information department; and two other Chinese officials who took notes (as did Ma, Mrs. Wu, Chu, and Wang).

As it turned out, this was convenient for everyone, because the poor interpreter stank. It wasn't the famous American-born Nancy Tang (who is a member of the central committee and speaks flawless English), but a young woman who stammered, faltered, spoke bad and badly accented English, seemed to have trouble translating my questions, was frequently corrected and badgered by Chou.

Later both Mrs. Wu and Ma corrected many of her mistakes (even including mistranslated dates!). Indeed, Chou assigned Ma to ride out to the airport with me at 6:30 this morning to go over the entire record and correct the interpreter's errors, a tedious but necessary process.

When Chou received us in an antechamber of the room in which we had our conversation, he was smiling and friendly and shook hands warmly. He is smaller, frailer, and looked older and more tired than I had expected from what I'd heard (although he's seventy-five) and from his photographs.

He is a tough little man in fact, not as handsome as reputed. He has very thick eyebrows and heavier whiskers than most Chinese. His hair is black but stranded with gray. His complexion is pale and marked heavily by what we used to call "liver spots." His hands have a youthful skin and small veins, for a man of seventy-five, but I noticed his knuckles were swollen as if he were gouty. His fingernails were long and exceptionally well tended, polished and rather pointed. He wore a quite well-tailored very dark gray Mao suit, with cuffs in his trousers, and a Mao button on his left breast.

I had been warned by Ma that Chou preferred to have a give-and-take conversation and wanted to ask questions himself. I said to Ma that my readers were far more interested in Chou's words than in mine and, as soon as I saw the opportunity, I dove in and kept boring ahead with questions.

Chou guided us into a reception room with a semicircle of ugly, comfortable, red-upholstered chairs with small tables between them on which the usual lid-covered mugs of tea were placed and an ugly white cuspidor on the floor between Chou and me. He offered cigarettes. When I declined but Marina accepted (and he also failed to smoke), he observed that the world had indeed changed when women smoked and men didn't. (Incidentally, all over China I have noted that almost everyone is a heavy cigarette smoker—and I am told Chairman Mao heads the list, that he can't stop although the doctors tell him to.)

Chou was extremely polite, although he looked careworn and fatigued. Ma later told me he is very tired because Chiao, the Deputy Foreign Minister and China's chief for its present UN delegation, is twelve hours behind in time at New York and they have to keep conferring by phone. This hits during normal sleeping hours. (Chou is known to work very late habitually and to sleep late in the morning.) Hot towels were passed around by a silent servant girl five or six times during our talk. I noticed that each time he took one and rubbed his face and hands with relief. I think he must have been sweating with fatigue.

I asked whether the "Watergate scandal" had had any effect on Sino-American relations. He said it had had no effect. He added: "We never use the word 'scandal' in discussing this. Since it is entirely your own internal affair, we have never published anything about it in our press. It doesn't affect the over-all situation." Looking at Chu, he added: "Only our Reference News Service [the unpublished report put out by Hsinhua] mentions it and issues American commentaries."

He continued: "We think it perhaps reflects your political life and social system. It is of interest to your own political life and you have had such things occur in your society and undoubtedly will again. There are many social aspects interwoven into it and it is better not to discuss this issue. I hope your president will be able to overcome these difficulties. Do you think he will?"

I expressed the opinion that in the end I thought he would manage to do so, but I had not been in a position to read U.S. newspapers recently. I had a feeling, incidentally, that Chou was very well briefed on this as well as many other American questions. Indeed, he had been astonishingly well briefed on me, on my efforts to come here since 1956, on my comments on Chiang Kai-shek, etc. He even quoted me once.

I asked when formal exchanges of full recognition would occur between China and America, adding that—as he knew—we were staying with Ambassador Bruce, head of our liaison office. He replied: "That depends on the U.S. side as well as the Chinese side. On the U.S. side, you should sever diplomatic relations with Taiwan and recognize the People's Republic as the sole legal government of China, just as Japan did. And the United States is clearly prepared to do so as can be seen from the Shanghai communiqué following President Nixon's visit to us last year. From the Chinese side, we must unify our country by liberating Taiwan as can also be seen from reading the Shanghai communiqué. The question that remains is one of timing."

I inquired whether this meant that a solution would occur once Chiang Kai-shek (now in his mid-eighties) dies. He said: "It shouldn't be put in such a specific way. The continuation of the Chiang Kai-shek regime is one element, of course; but not the only one."

I then switched to Russia. What did Chou think of the two Brezhnev "doctrines," one asserting Russia's right to interfere in internal affairs of any "socialist" land and the other seeking to create a pro-Soviet bloc throughout Asia, starting in India. (Incidentally, I noticed that on this, as other subjects, he was always very circumspect with regard to India). He said:

There is only one Brezhnev Doctrine. That is the doctrine of expansionism in Soviet foreign policy, the doctrine of social imperialism. In Europe if Russia wishes to expand, it is not only in East Europe but also in West Europe, to dominate everywhere it can. And this is also true with respect to China and elsewhere in Asia. It is furthermore true in the Middle East and South Asia, the Subcontinent. The Russians want to expand on the oceans and in the air. Their fleet is growing in the Atlantic, the Pacific, the Mediterranean, and the Indian oceans, and has even gone to the Arctic and Antarctic. They are therefore expanding on land, at sea, and in the air. That is their international aim.

And domestically their privileged class controls everything. They suppress the masses and dissenters by means of fascist rule. That is why they are particularly dissatisfied with us for describing the Brezhnev clique as a new czarist regime. We started to use this term when they invaded Czechoslovakia in 1968. And now in the UN other people use this same term. [Here he was evidently referring to Pakistani Prime Minister Bhutto.] They are certainly very displeased with that term of description.

But that is why we don't recognize Russia as a socialist country. From Khrushchev through Brezhnev the ruling clique of the Soviet Union has changed its nature. It is taking a capitalist road; it is no longer a socialist country led by a Communist party. It is following a policy of foreign expansionism and domestic fascism. They use the term "socialism" just to mask their real aims. [Here I assume Chou was referring to Brezhnev's claim of the right to interfere in "socialist" lands.]

I asked if it was true that China felt the United States had failed to implement some of its accords with Peking reached during the Nixon visit. Here his answer was that of an artful dodger. He said:

It is more than a year and a half since the Shanghai communiqué was published at the close of your president's trip. That communiqué comprised two sections. Each side stated its own positions and disagreements. Each acknowledged the other's right to criticize the other's position. On the other hand, both the United States and China have sought to normalize their relations and to seek a common ground.

President Nixon and Mr. Kissinger opened up a new channel and the joint Shanghai communiqué shows that there are common grounds as well as differences. In this respect the past year and a half have shown certain useful developments. There has been a great development in the exchange of individual visits to our citizens and this constitutes a breakthrough. Both the Chinese and American peoples want to be friendly. In 1955, at the Bandung Conference [of underdeveloped nations], I predicted this to American journalists. Didn't you try to come here after that meeting and weren't you prevented by Secretary of State Dulles? [He looked at me with a slight smile.]

I replied that had it been Dulles alone I would have come. It was only a question of not wishing to offend or embarrass my uncle, then publisher of the *Times*, who had foolishly promised Dulles no *Times* man would go to China without the Secretary's permission.

"Ah," said Chou. "You have the pioneering spirit still." I replied it really was a matter of not hurting someone in my own family. Alas, I had had to wait a long time to get here as a result. Chou smiled. He continued: "The development of exchanges of visits helps to promote friendly relations between our two peoples. And there are many other fields in which this is occurring: culture, arts, sports, science, technology, and trade."

I noted that China had not voted in the Security Council debate on the recent Middle East war and asked what he thought could be done to produce a final settlement and peace. He replied: "It is difficult to have peace there. In that region there are many seeds of conflict; it contains many seeds of conflict. Only today I read the speech of the Saudi Arabian ambassador to the United Nations [Jamil M. Baroody]. He very clearly stated the historical background. And he is an experienced, veteran diplomat. He even took part in the Lake Success meeting where the United Nations was finally organized."

I asked whether, if India or Afghanistan were to attack Pakistan, with Soviet aid, China would help the Pakistanis. He said: "The Soviets will claim they aren't instigating the Afghans to attack Pakistan, just as they say they would never attack China. [He did *not* mention India, I noted, again giving me the impression he is trying to improve relations.] Afghanistan is a country friendly to China. But, as far as recent events are concerned they clearly have their external course." (I checked this word with Ma afterward and he said it was an exact translation. I suspect "course" means "impact" or "implication.") I asked if Chou meant the recent coup d'état of Prince Daud, who ousted the King and declared a republic with himself as president. He nodded and said "the Soviets were behind that." He continued:

> Those big powers with ambitions to expand invariably put pressure on or bully other countries. China will always be on guard against this. Furthermore, we will never be a superpower or seek hegemony ourselves. But if other countries are the victims of aggression, so far as we are able we will help them to oppose such aggression from the viewpoint of upholding justice.
>
> Now if you speak of the subcontinent, if the East Bengalis [he didn't say Bangladesh] and the Indians and Pakistanis can coexist in a friendly way and peacefully, we hope that can happen, we favor it. In such a case the superpowers will not be able to reap a profit. You know, we have an old Chinese saying: "When a clam and a snipe are locked in a struggle, only the fisherman profits." By the same token we hope that the Pakistanis and the Afghans will develop friendship and friendly relations.

I asked what territory now possessed by Russia was claimed by China. He was very interesting, moderate, and also bitter on this. He said:

> With respect to the Sino–Soviet boundary, we never said China wished to recover all the territories lost under the unequal treaties. That is a rumor spread by the Soviet Union.
>
> My statement can be borne out by referring to the official document issued on October 7, 1969, after the verbal agreement by the two prime ministers [Chou and Kosygin] following their meeting at Peking Airport, September 11, 1969 [in the wake of the bloody fighting on the Ussuri River].
>
> In that document it was made very clear that although the nineteenth-century Sino–Russian treaties were unequal and although they had been abolished by Lenin, we were willing to accept them *as a basis* for holding negotiations. The alignment of boundaries that had been fixed hadn't even been properly surveyed so that the map actually didn't accord with reality. Some places were claimed by both parties and these are the "disputed areas."
>
> Therefore we said that, after settling those questions in a rational way we could conclude a new frontier treaty. By settling the question in a rational way we mean by mutual accommodations and understanding. Some of the

areas concerned were formerly ours but are now inhabited by Soviet citizens. Some are marked as Soviet territory on the map but have been inhabited by Chinese citizens for a long time. But the whole problem can be settled if the principle of mutual understanding and accommodation is followed—just as we have settled boundary questions with Afghanistan, Pakistan, Burma, and Outer Mongolia. [Again I noticed the absence of any reference to India, where two border wars have been fought by China.] Why is it not possible to settle questions involving Sino–Soviet borders accordingly?

Yet in March 1969 the Soviet Union committed armed aggression against islands in the Ussuri River belonging to China and we, of course, counter-attacked. Since then they have massed great numbers of troops on our borders. It is impossible to carry on negotiations under an armed threat. We must dispel that first. That is why, on September 11, 1969, during the talks between the two prime ministers, we reached a provisional agreement providing:

(1) There should first be a written provisional accord which would be followed by specific talks on the boundary questions; and the status quo should be kept for that period.

(2) All armed clashes should be avoided and both sides should withdraw their military forces from the border regions.

(3) Then we could discuss a new realignment of the boundary, which we think would not be a difficult matter to settle.

At that time the Soviet prime minister agreed to this in principle and a written draft was prepared. But nothing has come out of this in more than four years that have elapsed since. The Russians haven't even recognized objective facts like the existence of "disputed areas."

In truth, using the phrase that you yourself made famous in your column, their policy has been: "What's mine is mine, what's yours is negotiable." That accurately expresses the substance of the matter.

Just recently Brezhnev spoke in Tashkent and more or less repeated what the Russians first said a year ago and then said a second time last June: that they had proposed to China that both countries should sign a nonaggression pact but that China had turned a deaf ear to this proposal.

But there was no point in this contention. What was suggested had already been included in my agreement with Kosygin. The definition of avoiding armed clashes [Point Two of the provisional accord] naturally includes avoiding the threat of force or the use of armed forces including nuclear weapons.

Since the Russians didn't agree on that, what would be the point of concluding a separate nonaggression pact? In the past four years they haven't even agreed to accept our original provisional understanding. They wouldn't even recognize the objective fact that "disputed areas" exist. In these circumstances, how can other points be discussed?

A simpler way to describe this situation, paraphrasing your own words, the Soviet attitude is: "What's mine is mine; what's yours is mine." Your original phrase implies there is a point to be discussed, to be negotiated. But that hasn't proven to be the case. They say: "What's yours is really mine; it is *not* negotiable."

The only purpose of the bilateral negotiations they suggest for a non-aggression pact is to drag the matter on and on without a settlement, while waiting for other opportunities.

(I took this to be a clear hint that Moscow was waiting for its secret supporters in China to stir internal trouble—like the Lin Piao plot, which Peking blames on Russian sympathizers.)

I inquired what his reaction was to U.S. policy toward Russia, which Kissinger had just visited again because of the Middle East war. He said:

We both understand your policy—and sometimes don't. We understand that the two superpowers have many disputes to settle and such disputes demonstrate that each side wants to surpass the other in their power competition. Since there are such contradictions, they are difficult to settle. When one problem is composed, another one crops up. Why?

After World War II the United States considered itself a conquering hero. At that time it opposed the Soviet Union but in fact it was primarily contending for influence in the intermediate zones. In your own president's words, wherever money was needed you would give money generously, and wherever there were incidents you would send troops. In our words, you overextended yourselves. And President Nixon at Kansas City on July 6, 1971, when he spoke to journalists, said that at the end of World War II the United States never dreamed that its prestige would sink so far during a quarter of a century. I think it was honest of him to say this.

At that time your president had already contemplated withdrawing from some places; but this was not isolationism. The two things, withdrawal from some places and isolationism, must be clearly distinguished.

Just because of this, these withdrawals, another superpower wishes to fill any vacuum left by U.S. withdrawals. Whenever the United States pulls out, they [the Russians] want to move in. If there are any places the United States cannot take care of, they'll try and penetrate—just as on the [Indian] subcontinent two years ago.

As we see it, this shows that the two superpowers are contending for hegemony. This is an objective fact, quite independent of any subjective thinking. The Middle East is a case in point. The superpowers wanted talks there to avoid trouble. But it is impossible to have talks in order to avoid trouble there.

Our own viewpoint is different. We think there is no power vacuum. It is true that when a foreign force leaves a place another force moves in. But in the last analysis the people themselves in such an area will rise and fill the vacuum.

Take the example of China. According to the secret Yalta agreements, the United States and the Soviet Union intended to divide up spheres of influence and settle the China question accordingly. The United States got the biggest share [meaning through its support of Chiang Kai-shek's regime]. Russia got a smaller share—the Northeast [Manchuria], Northwest China [Sinkiang], and an "independent" Outer Mongolia.

As a result Chiang Kai-shek unleashed a civil war. In August 1945, right after World War II, he signed a treaty with Russia accepting the Yalta accords and agreeing to a Sino–Soviet friendship and alliance pact. Chiang thought that since he was backed by the United States and had a treaty with the Soviet Union his position would be assured. Why, even a friend of Britain said at that time, sadly: "Britain will no longer be able to take care of China; there is no room for the British."

Did you know that the British foreign secretary, in order to keep Hong Kong, agreed to sacrifice certain East European countries? You didn't know that? It was kept a secret for a long time in the British archives. The deal was very strange on two accounts: first of all, a Conservative government much later published these secret documents which had been agreed to by a previous head of the Conservative party; second, the Soviet Union didn't ever deny it, although it concerned its former leader, Stalin. (Obviously this concerns deals between Churchill—not his Foreign Secretary, Eden—and Stalin during World War II.)

Chiang Kai-shek was delighted with his situation and he unleashed a civil war. We thought we would have to fight for at least five or ten years but unexpectedly victory came in only four years. The Chinese people rose and took control of China. Thus, there was no vacuum in China; and there were no longer any areas of Soviet control [meaning Manchuria and Sinkiang and some former treaty ports].

At this point I said I had been struck by his speech to the Tenth Party Congress last summer in which he indicated that Russia was still plotting with agents inside China—against the Peking regime. What evidence of this was there? He said:

From Khrushchev's time right through Brezhnev's, in their dealings with any country—especially those friendly to the Soviet Union—the Russians never ceased sending in agents, spies, and subversives. Some countries submissively accepted this and therefore became Moscow's victims. Others resisted. And China is among those which would never accept such stuff because China, under the leadership of Chairman Mao Tse-tung, would never submit. It is precisely because of this that the Russians have never resigned themselves to defeat here and that they are always trying to do something. That is why you have seen certain things happen, our struggle against the two lines represented by Liu Shao-chi and Lin Piao.

To my amazement, Chou reminded me that I had said the Soviet Union was a "laboratory" from which China could learn lessons. (Ma later recalled to me that I had used this phrase when we all dined together with Chu Mu-chi. Obviously either Chu or Ma included this in the very extensive briefing on me given to Chou just before our arrival last night.) Chou said:

In fact our cultural revolution used the Soviet Union as a mirror. One might say that after looking in the mirror we could see our own weak points and that it was necessary for us to accomplish improvements in our society. We can best see our weaknesses by looking in a mirror.

There is an old Chinese saying that only when something rots does it start producing worms. You are right to discern the reason for the continuous revolution advocated by Chairman Mao [as I had described it in a column from Peking called "The Permanent Revolution"]. A revolution is just like a human being; it can be regenerated by continuous changes in metabolism. Otherwise one just degenerates.

The conversation was wandering now. Chou had glanced at his watch and, long ago, Marina had whispered that he looked tired. I stubbornly kept on, however, because I had waited so long for this occasion. Nevertheless, I didn't raise any more of my long list of specific questions, merely let him carry the ball. He said:

As for U.S.–Soviet relations, perhaps the United States wishes to relax its relationships with the Soviet Union but objective developments are simply not like that. You can relax on one point; but then another will arise. That's why last year, when the Soviet–American agreement on arms was published, there was an accord on strategic weapons. Some limitations were placed on the competition in nuclear arms.

But right afterward your secretary of defense, Laird, said straightforwardly that the United States must increase its military budget to finance the variety and quality of your arms. And this year an agreement was reached between the United States and Russia on the prevention of nuclear war. The defense ministry again asked for an increase in its budget, not a cut. Does this show objective developments, independent of subjective desire? [I did not understand this one—then or now.] The United States has made its position public, as is the tradition in your country. But no one knows the Soviet figure for its defense budget. That is why Gromyko's recent draft resolution is so ridiculous. [Gromyko proposed a 10 percent across-the-board cut in arms expenditures.]

Although your new secretary of state [Kissinger] didn't criticize the Soviet Union on this, as a gesture of détente, another foreign secretary, Sir Alec Douglas-Home, said publicly that the Gromyko draft resolution was ridiculous. He also said that Britain's expenditures on foreign aid exceeded the total in that field provided by the Soviet Union.

For this reason the comments at the United Nations on this subject by Mister Chiao, the head of our delegation, have been very incisive.

To sum up in one word, we will speak the truth. On this point your president and your secretary of state know our position. But still the Soviet Union tries to abuse us. There will be no tranquility with regard to the Chinese problem or elsewhere or other world questions because of this Soviet attitude.

There is no point in Americans—as some of them do—worrying about a recurrence of isolationism in your country because it is simply impossible to produce this. When Senator Mansfield and Senator Scott, the Democratic and Republican Senate leaders, came here we didn't discuss this matter. But later, a congressional delegation came and I told them then it was impossible for you to become isolationists again, that America couldn't return to isolationism. They were very glad to hear me say that. And if Mansfield comes here again, as I believe he will, I shall discuss this with him.

Moreover, even if the Democrats elect the next president they won't be isolationist either. President Nixon put it frankly when he openly expressed his opposition to isolationism. It is odd that in the past it was the Republicans who favored isolationism and now it seems to be the Democrats. But neither will achieve it. Among other things, the idea is opposed by the Pentagon, the State Department, and the CIA. Of course, it is especially opposed by the big monopoly groups who have influence with the Pentagon.

I asked if he favored keeping NATO and Western Europe strong. He said:

In the past we opposed NATO but now the Warsaw Pact has changed its nature. It is no longer a defensive alliance. It has become dominated by a single country [Russia]. Therefore, in this respect, NATO has assumed a partly defensive character. And we think Western Europe is right to maintain its vigilance and avoid Finlandization.

But NATO also has partly an aggressive aspect. It helps Portuguese aggression in Africa, which is wrong. We oppose NATO on this. It would be good if both NATO and the Warsaw Pact could maintain the principle of safeguarding the independence and integrity of all nations as equal and sovereign. But they have been unable to do so. And what shall we do in this situation?

As long as NATO and the Warsaw Pact are still there, while they exist, they seek only to strengthen themselves, respectively. And much public opinion in Western Europe has the illusion that peace prevails. We remind them that they should not have such illusions.

For us, ourselves, the most important thing is to handle China's affairs well. For a country like China, with so large a population, it will take us several decades to develop our economy. That won't be done during the twentieth century. We will need millions of trained successors to carry on this program.

We had now just about reached the end of our talk. Chou was tired. My neck was stiff from straining toward the interpreter, who sat on Chou's left; I was on his right. My wrist was almost broken from scribbling.

Chou said courteously: "I am sorry I asked you so late to come and see me. Our views may not be identical. But with regard to the new China you wrote long ago that Chiang Kai-shek was outdated. As I recall, you wrote that Chiang was an Oriental Napoleon on his Corsica. He shouldn't be compared with Napoleon. In his early years Napoleon was active in the French revolution. It was only later that he betrayed these views."

I explained what I had really written about Chiang—and stressed it was Elba, not Corsica that I referred to. He then said Chiang spent much of his time reading about Napoleon. I hadn't known this. We then strolled slowly out, followed by the others. The photographer got active again, snapping the two of us standing and shaking hands; then with Marina. He looked old as we said farewell, and I don't feel he'll be active much longer.

Ma called up after midnight to say he was coming around to review everything because of the poor interpretation. Chou wanted me to get everything straight—and also to limit myself in quoting directly, not to overdo it. I agreed; although the instructions are pretty vague.

At the airport we had a foul-up over a ticket. But at last we got aboard, and I've spent almost five hours typing this.

PARIS, *November 5, 1973*

TODAY the American Embassy here received a personal message for me from Secretary Kissinger: "Your notes on your Chou En-lai conversation were a most welcome addition to the briefing book for my forthcoming Peking visit. Many thanks for your generosity in sharing another Sulzberger journalistic coup. Warm regards, Henry."

Last Wednesday (five days ago) I got a message from New York saying the State Department would like very much to see the full account of my talk with Chou En-lai. I gave it to the American Embassy here to transmit by cable. Kissinger's message was in answer to that.

Index